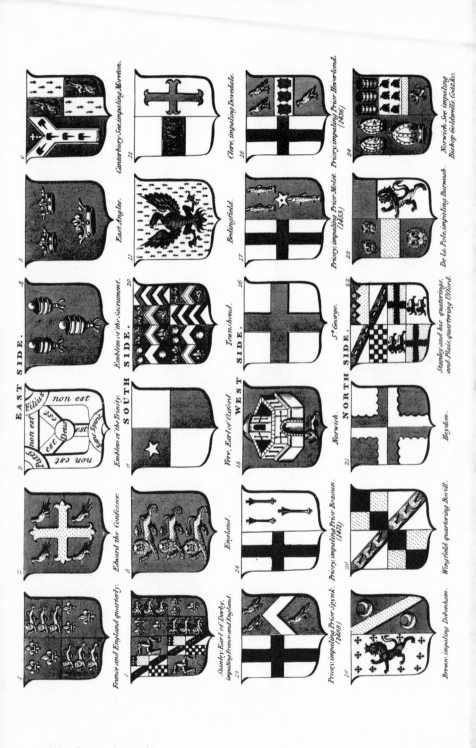

EAST SIDE.

1. France and England quarterly.
2. Edward the Confessor.
3. Emblem of the Trinity.
4. Emblem of the Sacrament.
5. East Anglas.
6. Canterbury See impaling Morton.

SOUTH SIDE.

7. Stanley Earl of Derby, impaling France and England.
8. England.
9. Emblem of the Trinity.
10. Emblem of the Sacrament.
11. East Anglas.
12. Canterbury See impaling Morton.

WEST SIDE.

13. Priory impaling Prior Spynk. (1488)
14. England.
15. Vere, Earl of Oxford.
16. Townshend.
17. Bedingfield.
18. Clare, impaling Prior Dovedale.

NORTH SIDE.

19. Brewse, impaling Debenham.
20. Priory impaling Prior Bozoun. (1471)
21. Norwich.
22. St. George.
23. Priory impaling Prior Molet. (1453)
24. Priory impaling Prior Heverland. (1436)

25. Wingfield quartering Bovill.
26. Heydon.
27. Stanley and his quarterings, and Plais quartering Ufford.
28. De la Pole impaling Burwash.
29. Norwich See impaling Bishop Goldwell's Goldus.

SIR THOMAS BROWNE'S WORKS

INCLUDING HIS LIFE AND CORRESPONDENCE

EDITED BY SIMON WILKIN F.L.S.

VOLUME IV

LONDON

WILLIAM PICKERING

JOSIAH FLETCHER NORWICH

1835

AMS PRESS
NEW YORK

First AMS EDITION published 1968
Manufactured in the United States of America

Library of Congress Catalogue Card Number: 68-57225

AMS PRESS, INC.
New York, N.Y. 10003

CONTENTS TO VOLUME FOURTH.

———◆———

PREFACE TO THE FOURTH VOLUME.

In completing this volume, I wish to offer some observations, partly in addition to the brief notices which precede several of the pieces it contains, and partly with reference to those which are now first printed from the original MSS. of the author.

I omitted to remark, respecting the *Posthumous Works*, and the *Christian Morals*, that copies are in existence with *reprint titles*—that contemptible form of lying under which publishers have endeavoured to persuade the public of the rapidity of their sales. This was especially the case with the former work, which was first published in 1712.[1] In the

---

[1] With this title:—*Posthumous Works of the learned Sir Thomas Browne, Knt. M.D. late of Norwich, printed from his Original Manuscripts, viz.* 1. *Repertorium; or, the Antiquities of the Cathedral Church of Norwich.* II. *An Account of some Urnes, &c. found at Brampton in Norfolk, Anno.* 1667. III. *Letters between Sir William Dugdale and Sir Thomas Browne.* IV. *Miscellanies. To which is prefixed his Life. There is also added Antiquitates Capellæ D. Johannis Evangelistæ ; hodie Scholæ Regiæ Norwicensis. Authore Johanne Burton, A.M. ejusdem Ludimagistro. Illustrated with Prospects, Portraitures, Draughts of Tombs, Monuments, &c. London, printed for E. Curll, at the Dial and Bible ; and R. Gosling, at the Mitre in Fleetstreet.* 1712. *Price 6s.*

In a copy which belonged to Mr. John Ives, (the author of *Garianonum*, &c.) occurs, in his hand writing, the following list of plates, which a perfect copy ought to contain. It is remarkable, however, that he has not mentioned the portrait by Vander Gucht, published with the volume, but wanting in his copy, which has instead of it a copy of White's portrait, engraved for the folio of 1686.

" Plates in this volume, originally belonging to the book ;—

libraries of the Royal Institution, and of E. H. Barker, Esq. are copies (the former on large paper) having a reprint title with this imprint :—*Printed for W. Mears, at the Lamb without Temple Bar, and I. Hooke, at the Flower-de-Luce against St. Dunstan's Church, in Fleetstreet.* MDCCXXIII. *(Price six shillings.)* Others are mentioned of the dates 1715, 1721, and 1722 :—the latter said to be "edited by Owen Brigstock, Esq." An assertion which was probably occasioned by a passage in Curll's preface.[2]

We are informed that the *Posthumous Works* was a *speculation* of Curll's, by the following passage in a letter from Dr. (afterwards Bp.) Tanner, to Dr. Charlet, the master of University College, Oxford, Oct. 20, 1712. "Curll, the bookseller, has bought, of Dr. Browne's executors, some papers of Sir Thomas Browne, one of which is some account of the Cathedral, which he is printing under the title of the *Antiquities of Norwich.* If I had perfectly liked the thing, I should not have been backward to have given a cut; but it was hurried by him into the press, without advising with any body here, or with Mr. Le Neve, who has great collections that way. However, out of regard to Mr. Hase, the herald, the Dean has suffered them to reprint his catalogue of Bishops, Deans, and Prebendaries, and, I think, to send a list of the Chancellours and Archdeacons." *Ballard's MS. Letters in the Bodleian Library*, vol. iv, p. 58.

Besides these Mr. Ives inserted in his copy a number of other engravings, and I apprehend that the enumeration of plates given in Mr. Upcott's *Topography*, as belonging to this volume, may have been taken from a similarly illustrated copy, or perhaps collected from several.

[2] *a passage in Curll's preface.*] "The public is here presented with those other remains of the learned Sir Thomas Browne, so long since promised, (and for which we are obliged to Owen Brigstock, Esq. grandson by marriage to the author.)"

It may be presumed, that the *Repertorium* was too slight a sketch to satisfy " perfectly " the antiquarian taste and knowledge of Tanner. May we not, however, fairly urge in extenuation, a similar plea to that which has been offered by D'Israeli, in defence of Dugdale, Sir Thomas's learned friend and correspondent?—" He hurried on his itinerant labours of taking draughts and transcribing inscriptions, as he says, to preserve them for future and better times. Posterity owes to the prescient spirit of Dugdale, the ancient monuments of England, which bear the marks of the haste, as well as the zeal, which have perpetuated them." *Curiosities, &c. Second Series, Chapter on Prediction.* Kippis says (on what authority does not appear) that the work was printed in Norwich.

Of the *Christian Morals* I have a copy which belonged to Archdeacon Wrangham, with reprint title, dated 1761 ;[3] and I believe there are such copies dated 1765.

I will take this opportunity to correct an error in my preface to the *Christian Morals,* at p. 55. It was not *Dodsley,* as I have there inadvertently said, but *Payne,* who published the second edition of that work, and for whom Dr. Johnson wrote his biographical sketch. In the first volume, p. 141, of *The Literary Magazine, or Universal Review,* (not *Register,* as stated by Mr. Croker in his edition of *Boswell's Life of Johnson,*) I have recently met with the Doctor's review of the work ;—if that can be called a *review,* which comprises in the following few words all that is offered by way of stricture or opinion on the work reviewed :—" This little volume consists of short essays, written with great vigour of sentiment, variety of learning, and vehemence of style." A quotation of two pages from the Life, closes this article. In 1773 Davies republished the Life, with those of Blake, the King of Prussia, and others, in his *Fugitive and Miscellaneous Pieces,* 3 vols. 8vo. vol. ii, p. 254.

In the half title to *Miscellany Tracts and Miscellanies,* I

---

[3] The half title is, *True Christian Morals : by Sir Thomas Browne, M.D.* Title, *True Christian Morals : by Sir Thomas Browne, M.D. Author of Religio Medici, &c. with his Life written by the celebrated Author of the Rambler ; and explanatory Notes. The Third Edition.* There is an engraved vignette of a lamb browsing in a hedge, and this imprint below :—*London : printed for, and sold by Z. Stuart, at the Lamb in Paternoster Row.* MDCCLXI.

have omitted to number the present as the *third* edition of the former and *second* of the latter. I have also erroneously assigned to the former 1684 as the date of its first appearance. I have a copy of it bearing the date 1683, which belonged to John Evelyn, and contains several important, though brief, MS. notes by himself, with his autograph and motto, " *Catalogo J. Evelyni inscriptus ;—Meliora Retinete,*" inscribed above the portrait; which is by Vander Banc, and was, without doubt, published with the volume. I am inclined, however, to think, that only a few early copies were thus dated, and that 1684 was the date of the impression. I have already remarked Browne's habit of multiplying transcripts of his compositions in MS. On the fly leaf of one of his volumes (MS. Sloan. No. 1827, folio,) I find two small square parchment labels, probably cut from the original cover, giving (in autograph) brief titles to the vol. with this addition, "*Also in 4to.*"[4] As No. 1827 contains copies, more or less complete, of a greater number of the pieces published under the title of *Miscellany Tracts,* than are to be found in any other of his MSS. now remaining, it may be supposed that the copy "*also in 4to.*" is not in existence, having been that from which the vol. was printed. Of several, however, there still remain in MS. two or three copies, each differing from the other. I have collated these with some care, and have inserted the most remarkable variations; but two sheets of copy containing some of these collations were mislaid, so that they could not be inserted in their place. I shall therefore give them at the close of this preface.

Respecting the hitherto unpublished portion of the present volume, I shall say but little. Whether it was judicious to publish so much, and of a character so miscellaneous, must be left to the reader to determine. I readily admit, that the greater part was not intended by its author to meet the public eye;

---

[4] *two small square, &c.*] The one thus:
     Of Oracles
     De Re Accipitra, &c.
     Also in 4to.

The other label runs thus:
     Amico Ardua Med.
     &c.
     Ys in 4to. also.

and none perhaps were *prepared* for that purpose (unless we except the Harveian Oration, which was intended for his son's use.) But on the other hand, it must be allowed, that the papers on Natural History, the fragments on Dreams, and on Mummies, with some others, are fully as characteristick, and as interesting as several of those printed by Abp. Tenison. But the especial object which I have had in view in my selection, is to exhibit, as far as possible, the literary and scientific character, pursuits, and habits of my author: in natural science, his unwearied love of experiment and observation ;— in literature, his laborious reading, and his constant habit of accumulating treasure for future use ;—in every thing, that intellectual life and activity which never flagged, that play of fancy and imagination which was ever on the wing. Now all these, it seems to me, will be as strikingly displayed by his commonplace books, and occasional sketches, as by his more digested or systematic productions,—if not much more so.

With these observations and explanations, I leave my work to the judgment of those who may care to read it.

ADDITIONAL NOTES TO TRACTS.

TRACT ix. p. 215, line 8. *England.*] The following paragraphs occur here in *MS. Sloan.* 1827. fol. 41.

"And whereas these are observed in the fen lands, it is not impossible that some hereof may be the monuments of the noblest of the *Girvii*, or fen inhabitants; for that there were princes and mighty men among them, you cannot doubt, from historical records, and while you read of Tombert, prince of the Southern *Girvii*, or fen men, whose daughter Audrie was married to the Northumbrian King, and whose name is yet observable in these and other parts.

However probable it is that this part of the land hath been the seat of many notable exploits, not only since the Normans, but in the time of Saxons, Danes, and also of the Romans in their conquest of the Britons, and their own civil dissentions; this being a fast and retiring place in all ages.

Nor wholly improbable that the dust of Boadicea, the famous queen of the Iceni, may lye about these quarters, whither after her overthrow by the Romans she might best retreat, and where not long after, the surviving Britons might honorably inter her, although not after this hilly and submontaneous sepulture; for according to the account of ...? the historian, before the battle she told the Britons that if they went against them, they would retire into the fens where the enemy should neither take nor find them; and that they should be able to swim over those rivers and waters which the Romans could hardly pass with boats."

p. 215, line 23. *Danes.*] *MS. Sloan.* 1827, ends with the following continuation of the present passage: "and therefore, though some might conceive that these hills might be raised in this low drowned country, as a retiring place unto men and cattle, upon great floods and inundations, yet, in regard of the former customs of the fore-mentioned nations, we rather entertain them in the acception of sepulchral and funereal mountains."

p. 217, line 12. *and Grotius.*] Grotius and Vadianus. *MS. Sloan.* 1827.

p. 217, line 17. *and this, &c.*] Instead of this sentence, the following occurs in *MS. Sloan.* 1827 :—

"And even in some scripture relations, as that of the going of St. Paul from Mysia unto Troas, as Vadianus acknowledgeth, some region may be understood. And even in our texts alledged this sense may seem sufficient to salve the intention of the description when he came to or went from Troas, and may also seem strange unto many, how St. Paul should be said to go from that city, which all writers had laid in ashes about a thousand years ago."

p. 218, line 13. *Strabo.*] 'and the tables of Ptolemy.' *MS. Sloan.* 1827.

p. 218, line 26. *which from Antigonus, &c.*] *MS. Sloan.* 1827, reads instead ; "set down by Ptolemy under the name of Alexandria-Troas, together with Lectum and Assum. It was also called, &c.

TRACT x, p. 221, line 13.] The preceding part of these remarks on the Dead sea resembles the copies in the *MSS. Sloan.* very nearly; but these are so much more copious, and they differ so considerably from the printed copy, that I give them at length.

"It is also probable, that the cities were built on some rising and eminent parts of the valley; because it was watered like Egypt, where we find they contrive their habitations on such parts.

Whether any of the cities should be set in or near the bottom of the lake, some question may be made ; for Jordan and other rivers running always into the valley, without any manifest effluxion or discharge, and Jordan also yearly overflowing, it is not improbable the waters gathered into a lake, or great water, towards the bottom or lower part, and was thereabout absorbed and drunk up by the subterraneous receptacles : but, where distinctly to place this absorption, there is no authentic decision ; yet the most probable place may be the southward and lower part, after the rivers from the eastern and western shores have met with Jordan in the valley : somewhat agreeable unto the account which Brocardus received from Saracens living near the lake. *Jordanem ingredi mare mortuum et rursum egredi, sed post exiguum intervallum a terra absorberi.* And from about these parts the learned Kircherus hath drawn his conjectured subterraneous channel unto Eltor, unto the Arabian side of the Red Sea, where this bituminous lake is conceived to discharge and vent at least some part of itself.

Though the destruction of the cities and valley, with all living things, be only mentioned in this text, Gen. xix, yet the superinduction of the lake is also considerable in this story. The destruction of the cities and all things in the plain, and even the plain itself burnt and covered with ashes, was performed by the showers of brimstone and fire sent down by the hand of God, according to the singular expression of the text. " The Lord rained upon Sodom and Gomorrah brimstone and fire from the Lord out of heaven ; and he overthrew those cities, and all the plain, and all the inhabitants of the cities, and that which grew upon the ground.

The continuation and consummation of his judgment was performed by the lake, without which if the cities and plain had been only burnt and destroyed by these fiery showers, time might have restored the place to a tolerable habitation again ; for, besides the rains which would have fallen upon it, the rivers and brooks which run into it, and Jordan which yearly overflowed it, might, in process of time, have made a new mould upon it, and so have restored it to some fertility and habitable uses again.

And therefore, to leave a lasting monument of his wrath, and that it might never become the seat of man and living things again, God let loose the salt and bituminous treasures below it, which, in a small and competent measure, shewed themselves before, and might have lain quiet unto all time ; continued still by salt and bituminous supplies, which are not like to fail ; which, whether he opened by these fiery showers setting the slime-pits on fire, and by the holes and channels where the river went down, only splitting and opening the earth by these piercing storms of fire, by earthquake, or otherwise, is not yet determined."

Repertorium:

OR SOME ACCOUNT
OF THE TOMBS AND MONUMENTS IN THE CATHEDRAL CHURCH OF NORWICH.

SECOND EDITION.

WITH NOTES

BY MR. SAMUEL WOODWARD,

HONORARY MEMBER OF THE YORKSHIRE PHILOSOPHICAL SOCIETY.

ORIGINALLY PUBLISHED IN

1712.

EDITOR'S PREFACE.

————◆————

THE REPERTORIUM was one of the very last of Sir Thomas's productions; his especial object in drawing it up, was, to preserve from oblivion, as far as possible, the monuments in the Cathedral of Norwich, many of which had been defaced during the civil wars. It pretends not to the character of a history of the antiquities of the church, and therefore neither deserves the sneer bestowed by Bagford, (in his MS. collections in the British Museum, No. 8858,) that "it rather feared than deserved publication;" nor justified the anxiety of the author's friends to prevent its publication, on the ground alleged by Archbishop Tenison, *(Preface to Miscellany Tracts,)* that "matter equal to the skill of the antiquary was not afforded." The volume containing it has afforded a favourite subject of illustration for topographers: the list of monuments was continued to the date of publication by the editor, (said[1] to have been John Hase, Esq., Richmond Herald,) and very many copies exist with numerous manuscript additional continuations and notes, some of which I have availed myself of. The most valuable is that of the late Mr. John Kirkpatrick,[2] now in the hands of Dr. Sutton, to

---

[1] On the authority of a MS. note in a copy which had belonged to Thomas Rawlinson, Esq. and was presented, by his brother, Dr. Richard Rawlinson, to the Bodleian Library.

[2] This gentleman, who was a merchant of Norwich, was indefatigable in his exertions in collecting materials, and making drawings of public buildings, to form a History of Norwich; which, had he lived to digest it properly, would have been most complete and invaluable. He died the 20th of August, 1728, aged 42. (See *Blomefield's Norwich*, part 2nd, p. 379, Edit. of 1806.) In his Will, dated 17th of July, 1727, (preserved in the Bishop's Office,) he says, "*I give to my brother, Thomas Kirkpatrick, all my MSS. books and papers (which I have with no small pains and expense collected and purchased) relating to the History of Norwich, to*

whom I beg to offer my thanks for his kindness in affording me the use of it. My object, however, has been to give that only which proceeded from the pen of Sir Thomas himself; and I have, therefore, not re-printed either the continuation or Burton's History of the Free School, &c.

I have great pleasure in acknowledging the kind assistance of my friend, Mr. S. Woodward,[3] in preparing explanatory and corrective notes throughout, and in giving a very interesting graphic and descriptive illustration of the notice at page 32, of the green yard, in which the combination sermons were of old preached.

On the recommendation of Mr. Woodward, I have not re-engraved all the plates which *adorned* the Posthumous Works, but a selection only; with the addition of his plan of the green yard.

enjoy the same during his natural life, and after his death I give them all to the mayor, sheriffs, citizens, and commonalty, of the said city, to be kept in the City Treasury, in the Guild Hall there, as well for their use and service on occasions, as that some citizen hereafter, *being a skilful antiquary, may from the same have an opportunity of completing and publishing the said History, or such part of it as my said brother shall not publish.*" We are not aware that Mr. Thomas Kirkpatrick ever published any of these interesting collections, except the large North-east view of the city, which has been so frequently copied. The MSS. referred to were some years ago in the possession of the corporation, as were also Mr. K.'s fine collection of "Medals and Ancient Coins of Silver and Brass;" but we fear the original intention of the donor has been lost sight of, and that these valuable MSS. are for ever lost to the lover of local antiquities. Mr. Kirkpatrick's father was a native of Closeburn, near Dumfries, and we believe Col. Harvey, of Thorpe Lodge, is a descendant in the female line.

[3] Who has paid considerable attention to the local antiquities of his native city, and made several interesting communications to the Society of Antiquaries; some of which are published in the *Archæologia.* He has also published " *A Synoptical Table of British Organic Remains.*"

Repertorium.

---·---

IN the time of the late civil wars, there were about an hundred brass inscriptions stolen and taken away from grave-stones and tombs, in the cathedral church of Norwich; as I was informed by John Wright, one of the clerks, above eighty years old, and Mr. John Sandlin, one of the choir, who lived eighty-nine years; and, as I remember, told me that he was a chorister in the reign of Queen Elizabeth.

Hereby the distinct places of the burials of many noble and considerable persons become unknown; and, lest they should be quite buried in oblivion, I shall, of so many, set down only these following that are most noted to passengers, with some that have been erected since those unhappy times.

First,[1] in the body of the church, between the pillars of the south aisle, stands a tomb, covered with a kind of touch-stone; which is the monument of Miles Spencer, LL.D. and Chancellor of Norwich, who lived unto ninety years. The top stone was entire, but now quite broken, split, and depressed by blows. There was more special notice taken of this stone, because men used to try their money upon it; and that the chapter demanded certain rents to be paid on it. He was lord of the manor of Bowthorp and Colney, which came unto the Yaxleys from him; also owner of Chapel in the Field.

The next monument is that of Bishop Richard Nicks, *alias* Nix, or the Blind Bishop, being quite dark many years be-

---
[1] *First.*] Beginning from the west end.—*Kirkpatrick.*

fore he died.   He sat in this see thirty-six years, in the reigns
of King Henry VII. and Henry VIII.   The arches are
beautified above and beside it, where are to be seen the arms
of the see of Norwich, impaling his own, viz., a chevron between three leopards' heads.   The same coat of arms is on
the roof of the north and south cross aisle ; which roofs he
either rebuilt, or repaired.   The tomb is low, and broad,[2]
and 'tis said there was an altar at the bottom of the eastern
pillar.   The iron-work, whereon the bell hung, is yet visible
on the side of the western pillar.

Then the tomb of Bishop John Parkhurst, with a legible
inscription on the pillar, set up by Dean Gardiner, running
thus :

> Johannes Parkhurst, Theol.Professor, Guilfordiæ natus,
> Oxoniæ educatus, temporibus Mariæ Reginæ pro
> Nitida conscientia tuenda Tigurinæ vixit exul
> Voluntarius: Postea presul factus, sanctissime
> Hanc rexit Ecclesiam per 16 an.   Obiit secundo die
> Febr. 1574.

A person he was of great esteem and veneration in the reign
of Queen Elizabeth.   His coat of arms is on the pillars,
visible at the going out of the bishop's hall.[3]

Between the two uppermost pillars, on the same side, stood
a handsome monument of Bishop Edmund Scamler, thus :

> Natus apud Gressingham, in Com. Lanc. SS. Theol. Prof.
> apud Cantabrigienses.   Obiit Ætat. 85. an. 1594 nonis Maii.

He was household chaplain to the Archbishop of Canterbury,
and died 1594.   The monument was above a yard and a half
high, with his effigies in alabaster, and all enclosed with a

---

[2] *broad.*]   It fills up all the space between the two pillars, and on the two
sides there was a rail of iron, the going
up (on the platform of the monument,)
was at the west end of the south side.—
Kirkp.

[3] *bishop's hall.*]   Bishop Parkhurst
"having lived much at his palace, at
Norwich, which he beautified and repaired, placing arms on the pillars going
out of the hall, which lately were visible
there, he died February 2, 1574, and

was buried in the nave of the cathedral,
on the south side, between the eighth
and ninth pillars.   Against the west
part of the latter is a monument erected
to his memory, engraved by Hulsberg,
in Browne's posthumous works ; but his
figure in a gown and square cap, with
his hands in a praying posture, and the
following inscription (that in the text)
was taken away in the civil war."—
Gents. Mag. 1807, vol. 77, p. 510.

high iron grate.   In the late times the grate was taken away, the statue broken, and the free-stone pulled down as far as the inward brick-work; which being unsightly, was after-wards taken away, and the space between the pillars left void, as it now remaineth.

In the south side of this aisle, according as the inscription denoteth, was buried George Gardiner, sometime Dean.

Georgius Gardiner Barvici natus, Cantabrigiæ educatus,
Primo minor Canonicus, secundo Præbendarius, tertio Archbidiaconus
Nordovici, et demum 28 Nov. an. 1573, factus est Sacellanus
Dominæ Reginæ, et Decanus hujus Ecclesiæ, in quo loco per 16
Annos rexit.

Somewhat higher is a monument for Dr. Edmund Porter, a learned prebendary sometime of this church.

Between two pillars of the north aisle in the body of the church, stands the monument of Sir James Hobart, Attor-ney-General to King Henry VII. and VIII.   He built Lod-don church, St. Olave's bridge, and made the causeway ad-joining upon the south side.   On the upper part is the achievement of the Hobarts, and below are their arms; as also of the Nantons, (viz., three marlets) his second lady being of that family.   It is a close monument, made up of handsome stone work: and this enclosure might have been employed as an oratory.[4]   Some of the family of the Hobarts have been buried near this monument; as Mr. James Hobart of Holt.   On the south side, two young sons and a daughter of Dean Herbert Astley, who married Barbara, daughter of John, only son of Sir John Hobart, of Hales.

In the middle aisle, under a very large stone, almost over which a branch for lights hangeth,[5] was buried Sir Francis

---

[4] *oratory.*] The enclosure to this mo-nument was of stone work, in the form of windows, having an entrance on the north side, the south side was sur-mounted by the arms which are now placed against the inside the pillar op-posite the monument; the tomb was also visible on this side, having an arch or canopy over, the upright wall of which was covered with stars, on the top the arms of Hobart, *sab.* a star of eight points, *or* between two flaunches *erm.*, in the star a crescent for difference, and on the dexter side of the shield a bull (the crest of Hobart,) as one supporter, and on the sinister, a martlet from the Nanton's coat as the other supporter.

[5] *hangeth.*] This branch must have hung opposite Bishop Nix's monument, and directly in front of the ancient stone pulpit, the remains of which are still visible against the pillar, at the east end of the said monument.

Southwell, descended from those of great name and estate in Norfolk, who formerly possessed Woodrising.

Under a fair stone, by Bishop Parkhurst's tomb, was buried Dr. Masters, Chancellor.

> Gul. Maister, LL. Doctor Curiæ Cons. Epatus Norwicen.
> Officialis principalis.   Obiit 2 Feb. 1589.

At the upper end of the middle aisle, under a large stone, was buried Bishop Walter de Hart, *alias* le Hart,[6] or Lyg-hard. He was bishop twenty-six years, in the times of Henry VI. and Edward IV. He built the transverse stone partition or rood loft, on which the great crucifix was placed, beautified the roof of the body of the church, and paved it. Towards the north side of the partition wall are his arms, the bull, and towards the south side, a hart in water, as a rebus of his name, Walter Hart. Upon the door, under the rood loft, was a plate of brass, containing these verses:

> Hic jacet absconsus sub marmore presul honestus.
> Anno milleno C quater cum septuageno
> Annexis binis instabat ei prope finis.
> Septima cum decima lux Maij sit numerata
> Ipsius est anima de corpore tunc separata.

Between this partition[7] and the choir on the north side, is the monument of Dame Elizabeth Calthorpe, wife of Sir Francis Calthorpe, and afterwards wife of John Colepepper,[8] Esq.

In the same partition, behind the dean's stall, was buried John Crofts, lately dean, son of Sir Henry Crofts, of Suffolk, and brother to the Lord William Crofts. He was sometime fellow of All-Souls college, in Oxford, and the first dean after the restoration of His Majesty King Charles II., whose predecessor, Dr. John Hassal, who was dean many years, was not buried in this church, but in that of Creek. He was of New college, in Oxford, and chaplain to the Lady Eliza-beth, Queen of Bohemia, who obtained this deanery for him.

---

[6] *le Hart.*] Spelt Hert, or de Hert, in MS. Sloan. 1885.

[7] *partition.*] This partition was taken away in 1806, (when the interior of the church was repaired,) and the monu- ment removed to the north aisle of the choir near the confessional.

[8] *Colepepper.*] Cullpeper on the mo- nument.

On the south side of the choir, between two pillars, stands the monument of Bishop James Goldwell, Dean of Salisbury, and secretary to King Edward IV., who sat in this see twenty-five years. His effigies is in stone, with a lion at his feet, which was his arms, as appears on his coat above the tomb, on the choir side. His arms are also to be seen in the sixth escutcheon, in the west side over the choir; as also in St. Andrew's church, at the deanery, in a window; at Trowse, Newton Hall, and at Charta-magna, in Kent, the place of his nativity; where he also built or repaired the chapel. He is said to have much repaired the east end of this church; did many good works, lived in great esteem, and died Ann. 1498 or 1499.

Next above Bishop Goldwell, where the iron grates yet stand, Bishop John Wakering is said to have been buried. He was bishop in the reign of King Henry V. and was sent to the council of Constance: he is said also to have built the cloister in the bishop's palace, which led into it from the church door, which was covered with a handsome roof, before the late civil war. Also reported to have built the chapter-house, which being ruinous is now demolished, and the decayed parts above and about it handsomely repaired, or new built. The arms of the see impaling his own coat, the three *Fleur des Lys*, are yet visible upon the wall by the door.[9] He lived in great reputation, and died 1426, and is said to have been buried before St. George's altar.

On the north side of the choir, between the two arches, next to Queen Elizabeth's seat, were buried[1] Sir Thomas Erpingham, and his wives the Lady Joan, &c. whose pictures were in the painted glass windows, next unto this place, with the arms of the Erpinghams. The insides of both the pillars were painted in red colours, with divers figures and inscriptions, from the top almost to the bottom, which are now

[9] *The arms, &c.*] By him within the rayles under two great marble stones, lye two of the family of the Bulleyns, of which family Queen Elizabeth was.— *MS. note in Bodleian copy.*

[1] *were buried.*] In removing the pavement of the North aisle (near this place) to make a vault for the remains of Dr. Goodall, in 1781, a tombstone, thought to be that of Sir Thomas Erpingham, was found, with its face downward; it is of purbeck marble, ridge formed, and having a Calvary cross on the ridge; the rivets of a brass inscription on the edge of the stone are still visible: it remains near the place where it was found.

washed out by the late whiting of the pillars. He was a Knight of the Garter in the time of Henry IV. and some part of Henry V., and I find his name in the list of the Lord Wardens of the Cinque-Ports. He is said to have built the Black Friars church, or steeple, or both, now called New-Hall steeple. His arms are often on the steeple, which· are an escutcheon within an *Orle of Martlets,* and also upon the out-side of the gate,[2] next the school-house. There was a long brass inscription about the tomb-stone, which was torn away in the late times, and the name of Erpingham only remaining, *Johannes Dominus de Erpingham, Miles,* was buried in the parish church of Erpingham, as the inscription still declareth.

In the north aisle, near to the door, leading towards Jesus' chapel, was buried Sir William Denny, recorder of Norwich, and one of the counsellors at law to King Charles I.

In Jesus' chapel stands a large tomb (which is said to have been translated from our Lady's chapel, when that grew ruinous, and was taken down), whereof the brass inscription about it is taken away; but old Mr. Spendlow, who was a prebendary 50 years, and Mr. Sandlin, used to say, that it was the tombstone of the Windhams; and, in all probability, might have belonged to Sir Thomas Windham, one of King Henry VIII.'s counsellors, of his guard, and vice admiral; for I find that there hath been such an inscription upon the tomb of a Windham in this church.[3]

> Orate pro anima Thome Windham, militis, Elianore, et Domine Elizabethe, uxorum ejus, &c. qui quidem Thomas fuit unus consiliariorum Regis Henrici VIII. et unus militum pro corpore, ejusdem Domini, nec non Vice Admirallus.

And according to the number of the three persons in the inscription,[4] there are three figures upon the tomb.

---

[2] *gate.*] In a nich of the wall above the gates is an armed knight on his knees.—*MS. note in a copy in Bib. Bodl.*

[3] *In Jesus' chapel, &c.*] "That Sir Thomas Windham, Knight, by his will, dated 22 Oct. 13 H. 8. 1521, willed that his body be buried in the middle of the chapel of the blessed virgin, within the scite of the monastery of the holy Trinity of the city of Norwich; where he would have a tomb for him, with his arms and badges, and his two wives, if his wife Elizabeth will be there buried, &c. *See his will among my papers of Felbryge.*"—*MS. Note in Bodl. Copy.*

[4] *inscription.*] Weever saith that this (in his time maimed) inscription was upon a goodly tomb in the Chapter-house.—*Kirkp. MS.*

On the north wall of Jesus' chapel there is a legible brass inscription in latin verses; and at the last line *Pater Noster*.[5] This was the monument of *Randulfus Pulvertoft, custos caronelle.* Above the inscription was his coat of arms, viz. six ears of wheat with a border of cinque-foils; but now washed out, since the wall was whitened.

At the entrance of St. Luke's chapel, on the left hand, is an arched monument, said to belong to one of the family of the Bosvile's or Boswill, sometime prior of the convent. At the east end of the monument are the arms of the church (the cross) and on the west end another (three bolt arrows), which is supposed to be his paternal coat. The same coat is to be seen in the sixth escutcheon of the south side, under the belfry. Some inscriptions upon this monument were washed out when the church was lately whitened; as among the rest, *O morieris! O morieris! O morieris!* The three bolts are the known arms of the Bosomes,[6] an ancient family in Norfolk; but whether of the Bosviles, or no, I am uncertain.

Next unto it is the monument of Richard Brome, Esq. whose arms thereon are ermines; and for the crest, a bunch or branch of broom with golden flowers. This might be Richard Brome, Esq. whose daughter married the heir of the Yaxleys of Yaxley, in the time of Henry VII. And one of the same name founded a chapel in the field in Norwich.

There are also in St. Luke's chapel, amongst the seats on the south side, two substantial marble and crossed tombs, very ancient, said to be two priors of this convent.[7]

At the entrance into the cloister, by the upper door on the right hand, next the stairs, was a handsome monument on the wall, which was pulled down in the late times, and a void place still remaineth. Upon this stone were the figures of

---

[5] *brass inscription.*] Inserted from Burton's Account of the Freeschool, p. 22.

En morior, prodest michi quid prius hoc quod habebam,
Preterit omne quod est, eo nudus, sic veniebam,
Sola michi requies manet, hic non sunt mea plura,
Antea nulla quies, modo pro nichilo michi cura,
Sed fleo, dum fueram modicum vel nil bene gessi,

Crimina multa feram fuerant mea quando recessi,
Pulvertoft Radulphus eram Custos Caronelle,
Christe Deus pro me passus mea crimina pelle,
Sic exoro petas qui mea scripta legas, Pater noster.

[6] *Bosomes.*] Bozouns.—*MS. note in Bodl. copy.*

[7] *There are also, &c.*] Taken away about 1738 to make room for seats.—*MS. note in Bodl. copy.*

two persons in a praying posture, on their knees. I was told by Mr. Sandlin, that it was said to be the monument for one of the Bigots, who built or beautified that arch by it, which leadeth into the church.

In the choir towards the high altar, and below the ascents, there is an old tomb, which hath been generally said to have been the monument of Bishop William Herbert, founder of the church, and commonly known by the name of the founder's tomb. This was above an ell high; but when the pulpit, in the late confusion, was placed at the pillar, where Bishop Overall's monument now is, and the aldermen's seats were at the east end, and the mayor's seat in the middle at the high altar, the height of the tomb being a hindrance unto the people, it was taken down to such a lowness as it now remains in.[8] He was born at Oxford,[9] in good favour with King William Rufus, and King Henry I. removed the episcopal see from Thetford to Norwich, built the priory for 60 monks, the cathedral church, the bishop's palace, the church of St. Leonard, whose ruins still remain upon the brow of Mousehold hill; the church of St. Nicholas at Yarmouth, of St. Margaret at Lynn, of St. Mary at Elmham, and instituted the Cluniack monks at Thetford. Malmsbury saith he was *vir pecuniosus*, which his great works declare, and had always this good saying of St. Hierom in his mouth, *erravimus juvenes, emendemus senes.*

Many bishops of old might be buried about, or not far from the founder, as William Turbus, a Norman, the third bishop of Norwich, and John of Oxford the fourth, accounted among the learned men of his time, who built Trinity church in Ipswich, and died in the reign of King John; and it is delivered, that these two bishops were buried near to Bishop Herbert, the founder.

In the same row, not far off, was buried Bishop Henry le Spencer, as lost brass inscriptions have declared. And Mr.

[8] *as it now remains in.*] . The present tomb was built by the dean and prebendaries in 1682, and the latin inscription thereon is said to have been composed by the learned Dr. Prideaux, who was at that time one of the prebendaries.—See *Blomefield's History of Norwich*, part 1, p. 471.

[9] *Oxford.*] The present inscription says, "qui *Oximi* in *Normania* natus;" this is understood to allude to Hiems near Caen.

Sandlin told me, that he had seen an inscription on a grave-stone thereabouts, with the name of Henricus de, or le Spen-cer:[1] he came young unto the see, and sat longer in it than any before or after him: but his time might have been shorter, if he had not escaped in the fray at Lennam[2] (a town of which he was lord), where forcing the magistrate's tipstaff to be car-ried before him, the people with staves, stones, and arrows, wounded, and put his servants to flight.   He was also wound-ed, and left alone, as John Fox hath set it down out of the chronicle of St. Albans.

In the same row, of late times, was buried Bishop Richard Montague, as the inscription, *Depostum Montacutii Episcopi*, doth declare.

For his eminent knowledge in the Greek language, he was much countenanced by Sir Henry Savile, provost of Eaton college, and settled in a fellowship thereof: afterwards made Bishop of Chichester; thence translated unto Norwich, where he lived about three years. He came unto Norwich with the evil effects of a quartan ague, which he had about a year before, and which accompanied him to his grave; yet he studied and wrote very much, had an excellent library of books, and heaps of papers, fairly written with his own hand, concerning the ecclesiastical history. His books were sent to London; and, as it was said, his papers against Baronius and others transmitted to Rome; from whence they were never returned.

On the other side was buried Bishop John Overall, fellow of Trinity college in Cambridge, master of Catherine Hall, regius professor, and dean of St. Paul's: and had the honour to be nominated one of the first governors of Sutton hospi-tal, by the founder himself, a person highly reverenced and beloved; who being buried without any inscription, had a

---

[1] *Spencer.*] The stoute and warlike Henry Spencer, Bishop of Norwich, who supprest by his courriage and valour, that dangerous rebellion; and about North Walsham, overthrew Litster the captaine, hath (as it is to be seene upon his monu-ment in the body of the quire of Christ-church, in Norwich) over his proper coate of Spencer, upon an helmet, his episcopall miter, and upon that Michael, the archangell, with a drawn sword.— *Peachem's Compleat Gent.* p. 164. *Ed.* 1634.

[2] *Lennam.*] Lynn. See *Blomefield's Norwich*, part 1, p. 516.

monument lately erected for him by Dr. Cosin, Lord Bishop of Durham, upon the next pillar.

Under the large sandy-coloured stone was buried Bishop Richard Corbet, a person of singular wit, and an eloquent preacher, who lived bishop of this see but three years, being before Dean of Christ-church, then Bishop of Oxford. The inscription is as follows :

> Richardus Corbet Theologiæ Doctor,
> Ecclesiæ Cathedralis Christi Oxoniensis
> Primum alumnus, inde Decanus, exinde
> Episcopus, illinc huc translatus, et
> Hinc in cœlum, Jul. 28, Ann. 1635.

The arms on it, are the see of Norwich, impaling, or. a raven sab. Corbet.

Towards the upper end of the choir, and on the south side, under a fair large stone, was interred Sir William Boleyn, or Bullen, great grandfather to Queen Elizabeth. The inscription hath been long lost, which was this :

> Hic jacet corpus Willelmi Boleyn, militis,
> Qui obiit x Octobris, Ann. Dom. MCCCCCV.

And I find in a good manuscript of the ancient gentry of Norfolk and Suffolk these words. Sir William Boleyn, heir unto Sir Thomas Boleyn, who married Margaret, daughter and heir of Thomas Butler, Earl of Ormond, died in the year 1505, and was buried on the south side of the chancel of Christ-church in Norwich. And surely the arms of few families have been more often found in any church, than those of the Boleyns, on the walls, and in the windows of the east part of this church. Many others of this noble family were buried in Blickling church.

Many other bishops might be buried in this church, as we find it so asserted by some historical accounts; but no history or tradition remaining of the place of their interment, in vain we endeavour to design and point out the same.

As of Bishop Johannes de Gray, who, as it is delivered, was interred in this church, was a favourite of King John, and sent by him to the pope: he was also Lord Deputy of Ireland, and a person of great reputation, and built Gaywood Hall, by Lynn.

As also of Bishop Roger Skerewyng [or de Skerning], in whose time happened that bloody contention between the monks and citizens, begun at a fair kept [3] before the gate; when the church was fired : to compose which, King Henry III. came to Norwich, and William de Brunham, prior, was much to blame.—See *Holingshed, &c.*

Or of Bishop William Middleton, who succeeded him, and was buried in this church; in whose time the church that was burnt while Skerewyng sat was repaired and consecrated, in the presence of King Edward I.

Or of Bishop John Salmon, sometime Lord Chancellor of England, who died 1325, and was here interred; his works were noble. He built the great hall in the bishop's palace; the bishop's long chapel on the east side of the palace, which was no ordinary fabric; and a strong handsome chapel at the west end of the church,[4] and appointed four priests for the daily service therein. Unto which great works he was the better enabled by obtaining a grant of the first fruits from Pope Clement.

Or of Bishop Thomas Percy, brother to the Earl of Northumberland, in the reign of Richard II., who gave unto a chantry the lands about Carlton, Kimberly, and Wicklewood; in whose time the steeple and belfry were blown down, and rebuilt by him and a contribution from the clergy.

Or of Bishop Anthony de Beck, a person of an unquiet spirit, very much hated, and poisoned by his servants.

Or likewise of Bishop Thomas Browne, who, being bishop of Rochester, was chosen bishop of Norwich, while he was at the council of Basil, in the reign of King Henry VI., was a strenuous assertor of the rights of the church against the citizens.

Or of Bishop William Rugge,[5] in whose last year happened Kett's rebellion, in the reign of Edward VI. I find his name Guil. Norwicensis among the bishops, who subscribed

---

[3] *fair kept.*] This occurred on the 9th August, 1272.—See *Blomefield's Norwich*, part 1, p. 53.

[4] *a strong handsome chapel at the west end of the church.*] St. John's Chapel, now the Freeschool.

[5] *Rugge.*] He lies in the midst of the choir.—*MS. in Bodl. copy.*

unto a declaration against the pope's supremacy, in the time of Henry VIII.

Or of Bishop John Hopton, who was bishop in the time of Queen Mary, and died the same year with her. He is mentioned, together with his Chancellor, Dunning, by John Fox, in his *Martyrology*.

Or lastly, of Bishop William Redman, of Trinity College, in Cambridge, who was archdeacon of Canterbury. His arms are upon a board on the north side of the choir, near to the pulpit.

Of the four bishops in Queen Elizabeth's reign, Parkhurst, Freake, Scamler, and Redman, Sir John Harrington, in his *History of the Bishops in her Time,* writeth thus :—For the four bishops in the queen's days, they liv'd as bishops should do, and were not warriours, like Bishop Spencer, their predecessor.

Some bishops were buried neither in the body of the church nor in the choir, but in our Lady's chapel, at the east end of the church, built by Bishop Walter de Suthfield,[6] (in the reign of Henry III.) wherein he was buried, and miracles said to be wrought at his tomb, he being a person of great charity and piety.

Wherein also was buried Bishop Simeon de Wanton, vel Walton, and Bishop Alexander, who had been prior of the convent; and also, as some think, Bishop Roger Skerewyng, and probably other bishops and persons of quality, whose tombs and monuments we now in vain enquire after in the church.

This was a handsome chapel; and there was a fair entrance into it out of the church, of a considerable height also, as may be seen by the outside, where it adjoined unto the wall of the church. But, being ruinous, it was, as I have heard, demolished in the time of Dean Gardiner; but what became of the tombs, monuments, and grave-stones, we have no account. In this chapel the bishop's consistory, or court, might be kept in old time: for we find in Fox's *Martyrology*, that divers persons accused of heresy were examined by the bishop, or

---

[6] *Suthfield,*] or Suffield.—*S. Wd.* He built the hospital of St. Giles in   Norwich. P. L. N.—*MS. note by Le Neve, in Bodl. Copy.*

his chancellor, in St. Mary's chapel. This famous bishop, Walter de Suthfeild, who built this chapel, is also said to have built the hospital [7] not far off.

Again, divers bishops sat in this see, who left not their bones in this church; for some died not here, but at distant places; some were translated to other bishopricks; and some, though they lived and died here, were not buried in this church.

Some died at distant places, as Bishop Richard Courtney, Chancellor of Oxford, and in great favour with King Henry V. by whom he was sent unto the king of France, to challenge his right unto that crown; but he dying in France, his body was brought into England, and interred in Westminster-abbey, among the kings.

Bishop William Bateman, LL.D., born in Norwich, who founded Trinity-hall, in Cambridge, and persuaded Gonvil to build Gonvil-college, died at Avignon, in France, being sent by the king to Rome, [8] and was buried in that city.

Bishop William Ayermin died near London.

Bishop Thomas Thirlby, doctor of law, died in Archbishop Matthew Parker's house, and was buried at Lambeth, with this inscription:—Hic jacet Thomas Thirlby, olim Episcopus Eliensis, qui obiit 26 die Augusti, Anno Domini 1570.

Bishop Thomas Jann, who was Prior of Ely, died at Folkston-abbey, near Dover, in Kent. [9]

Some were translated unto other bishopricks; as Bishop William Ralegh was removed unto Winchester, by King Henry III.

Bishop Ralph de Walpole was translated to Ely, in the time of Edward I.; he is said to have begun the building of the cloister, which is esteemed the fairest in England.

Bishop William Alnwick built the church gates at the west end of the church, and the great window, and was translated to Lincoln, in the reign of Henry VI.

---

[7] *hospital.*] Saint Giles's Hospital, Bishopsgate Street.

[8] *to Rome.*] Kirkpatrick, in his copy, has struck out these words, and substituted " thither," adding the following explanatory observation, " viz. to Pope Clement VI., who lived at Avignon."

[9] *Kent.*] In Blomefield's Norwich (part I, p. 543) it is stated, that what is here said of his having been prior of Ely, and in Le Neve's Fasti of his dying at Folkston-abbey, is a mistake.

And of later time, Bishop Edmund Freake, who succeeded Bishop Parkhurst, was removed unto Worcester, and there lieth entombed.

Bishop Samuel Harsnet, master of Pembroke-hall, in Cambridge, and bishop of Chichester, was thence translated to York.

Bishop Francis White, almoner unto the king, formerly bishop of Carlisle, translated unto Ely.

Bishop Matthew Wren, dean of the chapel, translated also to Ely, and was not buried here.

Bishop John Jegon, who died 1617, was buried at Aylsham, near Norwich. He was master of Bennet-college, and dean of Norwich, whose arms, two chevrons with an eagle on a canton, are yet to be seen on the west side of the bishop's throne.

My honoured friend, Bishop Joseph Hall, dean of Worcester, and bishop of Exon, translated to Norwich, was buried at Heigham, near Norwich, where he hath a monument. When the revenues of the church were alienated, he retired unto that suburban parish, and there ended his days, being above 80 years of age. A person of singular humility, patience, and piety: his own works are the best monument and character of himself, which was also very lively drawn in his excellent funeral sermon, preached by my learned and faithful old friend, John Whitefoot, rector of Heigham, a very deserving clerk of the convocation of Norfolk. His arms, in the Register Office of Norwich, are sable three talbots' heads erased argent.

My honoured friend also, Bishop Edward Reynolds, was not buried in the church, but in the bishop's chapel; which was built by himself. He was born at Southampton, brought up at Merton-college, in Oxford, and the first bishop of Norwich after the king's restoration: a person much of the temper of his predecessor, Dr. Joseph Hall, of singular affability, meekness, and humility; of great learning; a frequent preacher, and constant resident. He sat in this see about 17 years; and, though buried in his private chapel, yet his funeral sermon was preached in the cathedral, by Mr. Benedict Rively, now minister of St. Andrews. He was succeeded by Dr. Anthony Sparrow, our worthy and honoured diocesan.

It is thought that some bishops were buried in the old bishop's chapel, said to be built by Bishop John Salmon, [demolished in the time of the late war,] for therein were many grave-stones, and some plain monuments. This old chapel was higher, broader, and much larger than the said new chapel built by Bishop Reynolds; but being covered with lead, the lead was sold, and taken away in the late rebellious times; and, the fabric growing ruinous and useless, it was taken down, and some of the stones made use of in the building of the new chapel.

Now, whereas, there have been so many noble and ancient families in these parts, yet we find not more of them to have been buried in this, the mother church. It may be considered, that no small numbers of them were interred in the churches and chapels of the monasteries and religious houses of this city, especially in three thereof; the Austin-friars, the Black-friars, the Carmelite, or White-friars; for therein were buried many persons of both sexes, of great and good families, whereof there are few or no memorials in the cathedral. And in the best preserved registers of such interments of old, from monuments and inscriptions, we find the names of men and women of many ancient families; as of Ufford, Hastings, Radcliffe, Morley, Windham, Geney, Clifton, Pigot, Hengrave, Garney, Howell, Ferris, Bacon, Boys, Wichingham, Soterley; of Falstolph, Ingham, Felbrigge, Talbot, Harsick, Pagrave, Berney, Woodhouse, Howldich; of Argenton, Somerton, Gros, Benhall, Banyard, Paston, Crunthorpe, Withe, Colet, Gerbrigge, Berry, Calthorpe, Everard, Hetherset, Wachesham. All lords, knights, and esquires, with divers others. Beside the great and noble families of the Bigots, Mowbrays, Howards, were the most part interred at Thetford, in the religious houses of which they were founders or benefactors. The Mortimers were buried at Attleburgh; the Aubeneys at Wymondham, in the priory or abbey founded by them. And Camden says, that a great part of the nobility and gentry of those parts were buried at Pentney abbey. Many others were buried dispersedly in churches or religious houses, founded or endowed by themselves; and, therefore, it is the less to be wondered at, that so many great and considerable persons of this country were not interred in this church.

There are twenty-four escutcheons,[1] viz., six on a side on the inside of the steeple over the choir, with several coats of arms, most whereof are memorials of things, persons, and families, well-wishers, patrons, benefactors, or such as were in special veneration, honour, and respect, from the church. As particularly the arms of England, of Edward the Confessor; an hieroglyphical escutcheon of the Trinity, unto which this church was dedicated. Three cups within a wreath of thorns, the arms of Ely, the arms of the see of Canterbury impaling the coat of the famous and magnified John Morton, archbishop of Canterbury, who was bishop of Ely before; of bishop James Goldwell, that honoured bishop of Norwich. The three lions of England, St. George's cross, the arms of the church impaled with Prior Bosviles' coat, the arms of the church impaled with the private coats of three priors, the arms of the city of Norwich.

There are here likewise the coats of some great and worthy families; as of Vere, Stanley, De la Pole, Wingfield, Heydon, Townshend, Bedingfield, Bruce, Clere; which being little taken notice of, and time being still like to obscure, and make them past knowledge, I would not omit to have a draught thereof set down, which I keep by me.

[1] *escutcheons.*] These are now covered by the painted ceiling. In Blomfield's Norwich the author complains that these escutcheons are "misplaced, and wrong described;" the arrangement on the annexed plate, and in the following description, has consequently been adopted:—

EAST SIDE.
1. France and England quarterly.
2. Edward the Confessor.
3. Emblem of the Trinity.
4. Emblem of the Sacrament.
5. East Angles.
6. Canterbury See impaling Moreton.

SOUTH SIDE.
7. Stanley, Earl of Derby, and his quarterings; impaling France and England quarterly.
8. England.
9. Vere, Earl of Oxford.
10. Townshend.
11. Bedingfield.
12. Clere impaling Dovedale.

WEST SIDE.
13. Priory impaling Prior Spynk (1488).
14. Priory impaling Prior Bozoun(1471).
15. Norwich.
16. St. George.
17. Priory impaling Prior Molet (1453).
18. Priory impaling Prior Heverlond (1436).

NORTH SIDE.
19. Brewse impaling Debenham.
20. Wingfield quartering Bovill.
21. Heydon.
22. Stanley and his quarterings, and Plais quartering Ufford.
23. De la Pole impaling Burwash.
24. Norwich See impaling Bishop Goldwell's coat and devices.

There are also many coats of arms on the walls, and in the windows of the east end of the church; but none so often as those of the Boleyns, viz. in a field Arg. a Chev. Gul. between three bulls heads' couped sab. armed or; whereof some are quartered with the arms of noble families. As also about the church, the arms of Hastings, De la Pole, Heydon, Stapleton, Windham, Wichingham, Clifton, Heveningham, Bokenham, Inglos.

In the north window of Jesus' chapel are the arms of Radcliff and Cecil; and in the east window of the same chapel the coats of Branch and of Beale.

There are several escutcheon boards fastened to the upper seats of the choir: upon the three lowest on the south side are the arms of Bishop Jegon, of the Pastons, and of the Hobarts; and in one above the arms of the Howards. On the board on the north side are the arms of Bishop Redmayn; and of the Howards.

Upon the outside of the gate, next to the school, are the escutcheons and arms of Erpingham, who built the gates. [Also the coats of Clopton and Walton,] being an orle of martlets; or such families who married with the Erpinghams. The word *pœna*[2] often upon the gates, shews it to have been built upon penance.

At the west end of the church are chiefly observable the figure of King William Rufus, or King Henry I., and a bishop on his knees receiving the charter from him: or else of King Henry VI., in whose reign this gate and fair window were built. Also the maimed statues of bishops, whose copes are garnished and charged with a cross moline: and at their feet, escutcheons, with the arms of the church; and also escutcheons with crosses molines. That these, or some of them, were the statues of Bishop William Alnwick, seems more than probable; for he built the three gates, and the great window[3] at the west end of the church; and where the

---

[2] *pœna.*] This word is not Pœna but **penk** the old way of writing *think*, (this was first suggested by the late Dr. Sayers,) it appears to have been intended for his motto; as was also the word **Bewar** on a brass label at the corner of his tombstone.—See *Blomefield's Norwich*, part II, p. 39, and *Britton's Norwich Cathedral.*

[3] *the great window.*] The great west window has been found on a late survey to have been put in like a frame into the

arms of the see are in a roundele, are these words,————
Orate pro anima Domini Willelmi Alnwyk.————Also in
another escutcheon, charged with a cross moline, there is the
same motto round about it.

Upon the wooden door on the outside, there are also the
three mitres, which are the arms of the see upon one leaf,
and a cross moline on the other.

Upon the outside of the end of the north cross aisle, there
is a statue of an old person; which, being formerly covered
and obscured by plaster and mortar over it, was discovered
upon the late reparation or whitening of that end of the aisle.
This may probably be the statue of Bishop Richard Nicks,[4] or
the Blind Bishop; for he built the aisle, or that part thereof,
and also the roof, where his arms are to be seen, a chevron
between three leopards' heads gules.

The roof of the church is noble and adorned with figures.
In the roof of the body of the church there are no coats of
arms, but representations from scripture story, as the story
of Pharaoh; of Sampson towards the east end; figures of
the last supper, and of our Saviour on the cross, towards the
west end;[5] besides others of foliage and the like ornamental
figures.

The north wall of the cloister was handsomely beautified,
with the arms of some of the nobility in their proper colours,
with their crests, mantlings, supporters, and the whole
achievement quartered with the several coats of their matches,
drawn very large from the upper part of the wall, and took up
about half of the wall. They are eleven in number, particularly these. 1. An empty escutcheon. 2. The achievement of Howard, Duke of Norfolk. 3. Of Clinton. 4.
Russel. 5. Cheyney. 6. The Queen's achievement. 7.
Hastings. 8. Dudley. 9. Cecil. 10. Carey. 11. Hatton.

---

west front, and being ready to fall out
was fastened with irons; Dean Bullock,
about 1748, chipt off all the outer ornament of the west front and new cased
it.—*MS. note probably by Ives.*

[4] *Nicks.*] Bishop Nix only re-built
the roof, the effigy is of Herbert, the
founder, it being exactly in the same
manner as that on his seal.—*Blome-*

field's History of Norwich, part I, p.
546.

[5] *end.*] This part was done in the
time of, if not by Bishop Lyhert, as appears by his arms and his rebus alter-
nately upon the pillars on each side,
where the foundations of the vaulted
roof begin upon the old work.—*Kirkpatrick's MS. notes.*

They were made soon after Queen Elizabeth came to Norwich, *ann.* 1578, where she remained a week, and lodged at the bishop's palace, in the time of Bishop Freake, attended by many of the nobility, and particularly by those whose arms are here set down.

They made a very handsome show, especially at that time, when the cloister windows were painted unto the cross bars. The figures of those coats, in their distinguishable and discernable colours, are not beyond my remembrance. But in the late times, when the lead was faulty and the stone work decayed, the rain falling upon the wall washed them away.

The pavement also of the cloister on the same side was broken and the stones taken away, a floor of dust remaining: but that side is now handsomely paved by the beneficence of my worthy friend William Burleigh, Esq.

At the stone cistern[6] in the cloister, there is yet perceivable a lion rampant, argent, in a field sable, which coat is now quartered in the arms of the Howards.

In the painted glass in the cloister, which hath been above the cross bars, there are several coats. And I find by an account taken thereof and set down in their proper colours, that here were these following, viz. the arms of Morley, Shelton, Scales, Erpingham, Gournay, Mowbray, Savage now Rivers, three coats of Thorpe's and one of a lion rampant, gules in a field or, not well known to what family it belongeth.

Between the lately demolished chapter-house and St. Luke's chapel, there is an handsome chapel, wherein the consistory or bishop's court is kept, with a noble gilded roof. This goeth under no name, but may well be called Beauchampe's chapel or the chapel of our Lady and All Saints, as being built by William Beauchampe, according to this inscription[7]—*In honore Beate Marie Virginis, et omnium*

---

[6] *cistern.*] The lavatories at the south-west angle.

[7] *inscription.*] Kirkpatrick, in his MS. notes to his copy of the Posthumous Works, (now in the possession of Dr. Sutton,) says, "that it was certainly William Bauchun who was the founder of this chapel and gaue lands to it, in the latter end of King Edward the Second's time, as out of the records of the church may be collected. The said William Bauchun being often mentioned therein, but Beauchamp never." It also appears from Kirkpatrick's sketch of the inscription, that there was not sufficient space on the stone for more than " Bauchun."

sanctorum Willelmus Beauchampe *capellam hanc ordinavit, et ex propriis sumptibus construxit.* This incription is in old letters on the outside of the wall, at the south side of the chapel, and almost obliterated. He was buried under an arch in the wall which was richly gilded; and some part of the gilding is yet to be perceived, though obscured and blinded by the bench on the inside. I have heard there is a vault below gilded like the roof of the chapel. The founder of this chapel, William Beauchampe or de Bello Campo, might be one of the Beauchampes, who were Lords of Abergavenny; for William Lord Abergavenny had lands and manors in this country. And in the register of institutions it is to be seen, that William Beauchampe, Lord of Abergavenny, was lord patron of Berg cum Apton, five miles distant from Norwich, and presented clerks to that living, 1406, and afterward: so that if he lived a few years after, he might be buried in the latter end of Henry IV., or in the reign of Henry V., or in the beginning of Henry VI. Where to find Heydon's chapel[8] is more obscure, if not altogether unknown; for such a place there was, and known by the name of Heydon's chapel, as I find in a manuscript concerning some ancient families of Norfolk, in these words;—*John Heydon of Baconsthorpe, Esq. died in the reign of Edward IV., ann. 1479. He built a chapel on the south side of the cathedral church of Norwich, where he was buried. He was in great favour with King Henry VI., and took part with the house of Lancaster against that of York.*

Henry Heydon, Knight, his heir, built the church of Salthouse, and made the causey between Thursford and Walsingham, at his own charge. He died in the time of Henry VII., and was buried in Heydon's chapel, joining to the cathedral aforesaid. The arms of the Heydons are argent, and gules a cross engrailed counter-changed, make the third escutcheon in the north-row over the choir, and are in several places in the glass windows, especially on the south side, and once in the deanery.

---

[8] *Heydon's chapel.*] This chapel is placed on the west side of Beauchampe's or Bachun's chapel; see plan in Blomefield's Norwich.

There was a chapel[9] to the south side of the gaol or prison, into which there is one door out of the entry of the cloister ; and there was another out of the cloister itself, which is now made up of brick work: the stone work which remaineth on the inside is strong and handsome. This seems to have been a much frequented chapel of the priory by the wearing of the steppings unto it, which are on the cloister side.

Many other chapels there were within the walls and circuit of the priory, as of St. Mary of the Marsh, of St. Ethelbert, and others.[1] But a strong and handsome fabric of one is still remaining, which is the chapel of St. John the Evangelist, said to have been founded by Bishop John Salmon, who died ann. 1325, and four priests were entertained for the daily service therein: that which was properly the chapel, is now the free school: the adjoining buildings made up the refectory, chambers, and offices of the society.

Under the chapel, there was a charnel-house, which was a remarkable one in former times, and the name is still retained. In an old manuscript of a sacrist of the church, communicated to me by my worthy friend, Mr. John Burton, the learned and very deserving master of the free school, I find that the priests had a provisional allowance from the rectory of Westhall, in Suffolk. And of the charnel-house it is delivered, that with the leave of the sacrist, the bones of such as were buried in Norwich, might be brought into it. *In carnario subtus dictam capellam sancti Johannis constituto, ossa humana in civitate* Norwici *humata, de licentia sacristæ, qui dicti carnarii clavem et custodiam habebit specialem ut usque ad resurrectionem generalem honeste conserventur a carnibus integre denudata reponi volumus et obsignari.* Probably the bones were piled in good order, the skulls, arms, and

[9] *There was, &c.*] There can be little doubt but that this was the original chapter-house ; its octangular east end and its situation corresponding with those of the cathedrals of Durham, Hereford, Worcester, Gloucester, Lincoln, &c.

[1] *and others.*] The chapel of St. Edmund has been placed by Blomefield on the site of the chapter-house. In the late repairs, part of the old gaol has been appropriated to the dean's vestry,

in the centre of which, in the intersecting groins is a *boss*, containing the representation of the head of a king, which I think can be no other than that of St. Edmund, and that we may with propriety consider this place as the chapel dedicated to St. Edmund. Adjoining this, north, was another chapel, with a semicircular east end ; corresponding with that on the east side of the north transept. This was probably the Priors' Chapel.

leg bones, in their distinct rows and courses, as in many char-
nel-houses. How these bones were afterwards disposed of
we have no account; or whether they had not the like removal with those in the charnel-house of St. Paul, kept
under a chapel, on the north side of St. Paul's church-yard:
for when the chapel was demolished, the bones which lay in
the vault, amounting to more than a thousand cart loads,
were conveyed into Finsbury Fields, and there laid in a
moorish place, with so much soil to cover them as raised the
ground for three windmills to stand on, which have since
been built there, according as John Stow hath delivered in
his survey of London.

There was formerly a fair and large but plain organ in the
church, and in the same place with this at present. (It was
agreed in a chapter by the dean and prebends, that a new
organ be made, and timber fitted to make a loft for it, June
6, ann. 1607, repaired 1626, and £10. which Abel Colls
gave to the church, was bestowed upon it.) That in the late
tumultuous time was pulled down, broken, sold, and made
away. But since his Majesty's restoration, another fair, well-
tuned, plain organ, was set up by Dean Crofts and the chapter,[2] and afterwards painted, and beautifully adorned, by the
care and cost of my honoured friend Dr. Herbert Astley, the
present worthy dean. There were also five or six copes belonging to the church; which, though they looked somewhat
old, were richly embroidered. These were formerly carried
into the market-place;[3] some blowing the organ pipes before

---

[2] *another organ, &c.*] Finished in
1664.—*MS. Kirkp.*

[3] *Market place.*] This occurred on
the 9th March, 1644; of which the following curious account is given in Bishop
Hall's *Hàrd Measure*, p. 63.

"It is tragical to relate the furious
sacrilege committed under the authority
of Linsey, Tofts the sheriff, and Green-
wood; what clattering of glasses, what
beating down of walls, what tearing
down of monuments, what pulling down
of seats, and wresting out of irons and
brass from the windows and graves;
what defacing of arms, what demolishing
of curious stone-work, that had not any
representation in the world, but of the
cost of the founder and skill of the ma-
son; what piping on the destroyed organ
pipes; vestments, both copes and sur-
plices, together with the leaden cross,
which had been newly sawed down from
over the greenyard pulpit, and the sing-
ing books and service books were carried
to the fire in the public market-place; a
lewd wretch walking before the train in
his cope trailing in the dirt, with a service book in his hand, imitating, in an
impious scorn, the tune, and usurping
the words of the litany, the ordnance
being discharged on the Guild day, the
cathedral was filled with musketeers,
drinking and tobacconing as freely as if
it had turned alehouse."

them, and were cast into a fire provided for that purpose, with shouting and rejoicing : so that, at present, there is but one cope belonging to the church, which was presented thereunto by Philip Harbord, Esq. the present high sheriff of Norfolk, my honoured friend.

Before the late times, the combination[4] sermons were preached in the summer time at the cross in the green-yard,[5] where there was a good accommodation for the auditors. The mayor, aldermen, with their wives and officers, had a well-contrived place built against the wall of the bishop's palace, covered with lead ; so that they were not offended by rain. Upon the North-side of the church,[6] places were built gallery-wise, one above another ; where the dean, prebends, and their wives, gentlemen, and the better sort, very well heard the sermon : the rest either stood, or sat in the green, upon long forms provided for them, paying a penny, or halfpenny apiece, as they did at St. Paul's cross in London. The bishop and chancellor heard the sermons at the windows of the bishop's palace : the pulpit had a large covering of lead over it, and a cross upon it ; and there were eight or ten stairs of stone about it, upon which the hospital boys and others stood. The preacher had his face to the South, and there was a painted board, of a foot and a half broad, and about a yard and a half long, hanging over his head

[4] *combination.*] Dr. Littleton thus defines the word ; " A combination, or circle of preachers in a cathedral or university church."—Vide *Lat. Dict.*

The combination preachers were appointed by the bishops from the clergy of the diocése ; to come and preach a sermon in the cathedral, or its preaching yard, at their own charges : the Suffolk preachers in the summer half-year, and the Norfolk in the winter ; which is still continued.

[5] *green-yard.*] See the annexed plan.
A. North aisle of the cathedral.
B. Entrance to the green-yard.
C. Gallery of the dean and prebendaries.
D. Ditto of the mayor and aldermen.
E. Presumed site of the pulpit.
F. Remains of the palace built by Bishop Herbert, A.D. 1100.

G. Part built by Bishop Salmon, A.D. 1320.
H. Ditto by Bishop Reynolds, A.D. 1660.
[6] *church.*] See the elevation accompanying the plan shewing the extent of galleries.
I. Entrance to the green-yard.
K. Joist holes of the first floor.
L. Ditto of the second floor.
M. Presumed height of the roof.
N. Series of holes, 4 inches by 3.

The galleries appear to have extended nearly across the three compartments : the masonry of the centre compartment has been very much altered and disturbed ; the double billet string-course is obliterated on each side of the window ; two of the columns directly above the centre of the window are removed, apparently to form a passage from the church into the upper gallery.

before, upon which were painted the arms of the benefactors[7] towards the combination sermon, which he particularly commemorated in his prayer, and they were these; Sir John Suckling, Sir John Pettus, Edward Nuttel, Henry Fasset, John Myngay.   But when the church was sequestered, and the service put down, this pulpit was taken down, and placed in New Hall green, which had been the artillery-yard, and the public sermon was there preached.   But the heirs of the benefactors denying to pay the wonted beneficence for any sermon out of Christ-church, (the cathedral being now commonly so called) some other ways were found to provide a minister, at a yearly salary, to preach every Sunday, either in that pulpit in the summer, or elsewhere in the winter.

I must not omit to say something of the shaft or spire of this church, commonly called the pinnacle, as being a handsome and well-proportioned fabric, and one of the highest in England, higher than the noted spires of Lichfield, Chichester, or Grantham, but lower than that at Salisbury, (at a general chapter, holden June 4, 1633, it was agreed that the steeple should be mended [8]) for that spire being raised upon a very high tower, becomes higher from the ground; but this spire, considered by itself, seems, at least, to equal that.   It is an hundred and five yards and two feet from the top of the pinnacle unto the pavement of the choir under it.   The spire is very strongly built, though the inside be of brick. The upper aperture, or window, is the highest ascent inwardly; out of which, sometimes a long streamer hath been hanged, upon the guild, or mayor's day.   But at his Majesty's restoration, when the top was to be mended, and a new gilded weathercock was to be placed upon it, there were stayings made at the upper window, and divers persons went up to the top of the pinnacle.   They first went up into the belfry, and then by eight ladders, on the inside of the spire, till they came to the upper hole, or window; then went out

---

[7] *benefactors.*] These gentlemen, in consideration of the expense necessarily incurred by the preachers in coming to Norwich, devised certain estates, &c. to the corporation in trust, out of which each preacher is paid one guinea towards his expences.

[8] *at a general chapter, &c.*] Christ-church pinnacle was re-edified 1636.— *MS. Starling. Kirkp.*

unto the outside, where a staying was set, and so ascended up unto the top stone, on which the weathercock standeth.

The cock is three quarters of a yard high, and one yard and two inches long; as is also the cross bar, and top stone of the spire, which is not flat, but consists of a half globe and channel about it; and from thence are eight leaves of stone spreading outward, under which begin the eight rows of crockets, which go down the spire at five feet distance.

From the top there is a prospect all about the country. Mousehold hill seems low, and flat ground. The Castle hill, and high buildings, do very much diminish. The river looks like a ditch. The city, with the streets, make a pleasant show, like a garden with several walks in it.[9]

Though this church for its spire, may compare, in a manner, with any in England, yet in its tombs and monuments it is exceeded by many.

No kings have honoured the same with their ashes, and but few with their presence.[1] And it is not without some wonder, that Norwich having been for a long time so considerable a place, so few kings have visited it; of which number, among so many monarchs since the conquest, we find but four, viz. King Henry III. Edward I. Queen Elizabeth, and our gracious Sovereign now reigning, King Charles II. of which I had particular reason to take notice.[2]

---

[9] *walks in it.*] The sea is also to be seen from the North-west towards Wells, to the South-east off the Suffolk coast; and with the aid of a telescope, vessels are to be seen sailing along the coast between Happisburgh and Lowestoft.

[1] *presence.*] This is certainly an error :—

Henry I. spent his Christmas at Norwich.—*Sax. Chron.* 1122.

Richard I. visited Norwich.—*Kirkpatrick's MS. notes.*

King John was at his castle in Norwich on the 12th and 13th October, 1205. —*Archæologia*, vol. 22, p. 142.

Henry III. visited Norwich, 1256 and 1272.—See *Blomefield*.

Edward I. kept his Easter at Norwich, 1277.—*Stowe*.

Edward II. was at Norwich in January, 1327.—*Blomefield*.

Edward III. held a tournament at Nor-

wich 1341, and was there again in 1342 and 1344.

Richard II. visited Norwich in 1383, according to *Holingshed*.

Henry IV. visited the city in 1406 as appears by the Norwich Assembly Book.—*Blomefield*.

Henry V. visited Norwich. —*Kirkpatrick's MS. notes.*

Henry VI. visited Norwich in 1448 and 1449.—*Blomefield*.

Edward IV. was in Norwich in 1469.— *Ibid.*

Richard III. was in Norwich in 1483. —*Ibid.*

Henry VII. kept his Christmas at Norwich in 1486.—*Ibid.*

Elizabeth came on her progress to Norwich in 1578.—*Ibid.*

Charles II. visited Norwich in 1671, and is the last sovereign who visited that city.

[2] Sir Thomas being then knighted.

The castle was taken by the forces of King William the Conqueror; but we find not that he was here. King Henry VII. by the way of Cambridge, made a pilgrimage unto Walsingham; but records tell us not that he was at Norwich.[3] King James I. came sometimes to Thetford for his hunting recreation, but never vouchsafed to advance twenty miles farther.

Not long after the writing of these papers, Dean Herbert Astley died, a civil, generous, and public-minded person, who had travelled in France, Italy, and Turkey, and was interred near the monument of Sir James Hobart: unto whom succeeded my honoured friend Dr. John Sharpe, a prebend of this church, and rector of St. Giles's in the fields, London; a person of singular worth, and deserved estimation, the honour and love of all men; in the first year of whose deanery, 1681, the prebends were these:

Mr. Joseph Loveland,	Dr. William Smith,
Dr. Hezekiah Burton,	Mr. Nathaniel Hodges,
Dr. William Hawkins,	Mr. Humphrey Prideaux.

(But Dr. Burton dying in that year, Mr. Richard Kidder succeeded,) worthy persons, learned men, and very good preachers.

[3] *but records, &c.*] From the authorities cited by Blomefield (*Norwich*, part I, p. 174) there can be no doubt but that this sovereign visited Norwich in his way to Walsingham.

ADDENDA.

I have by me the picture of Chancellor Spencer,[4] drawn when he was ninety years old, as the inscription doth declare, which was sent unto me from Colney.

Though Bishop Nix sat long in the see of Norwich, yet is not there much delivered of him: Fox in his Martyrology hath said something of him in the story of Thomas Bilney, who was burnt in Lollard's pit, without Bishopsgate, in his time.

Bishop Spencer lived in the reign of Richard II. and Henry IV., sat in the see of Norwich 37 years: of a soldier made a bishop, and sometimes exercising the life of a soldier in his episcopacy; for he led an army into Flanders on the behalf of Pope Urban VI. in opposition to Clement the Anti-pope; and also overcame the rebellious forces of Litster, the dyer, in Norfolk, by North Walsham, in the reign of King Richard II.

Those that would know the names of the citizens who were chief actors in the tumult in Bishop Skerewyng's time, may find them set down in the bull of Pope Gregory X.

Some bishops, though they lived and died here, might not be buried in this church, as some bishops probably of old, more certainly of later time.

Here concludes Sir Thomas Browne's MS.[5]

---

[4] *the picture of Chancellor Spencer.*] P. L. Neve saw this picture in 1715, at the house of Mr. Statham.—*MS. note in his copy in the Bodleian.* In Kirkpatrick's copy occurs this note: "This or another such picture is at the Duke of Norfolk's house in Norwich, A.D. 1715."

[5] *Here concludes, &c.*] This is the editor's memorandum in the Posthumous Works. His continuations are omitted in the present edition.

Letter to a Friend,

UPON OCCASION OF THE DEATH OF HIS INTIMATE FRIEND.

THIRD EDITION.

———————

ORIGINALLY PUBLISHED IN

1690.

EDITOR'S PREFACE.

THE LETTER TO A FRIEND was printed, after the author's death, by his son, as a folio pamphlet, in 1690. The only copy I ever saw is in the library of the British Museum. It was re-printed, in the Posthumous Works, in 1712; and the latter portion of it (from page 48, *Posthumous Works,*) was included in the Christian Morals, and for that reason is not here re-printed.

From a collation with a MS. copy in the British Museum, (MS. Sloan. 1862,) several additional passages are given.

Letter to a Friend.

───◆───

GIVE me leave to wonder that news of this nature should
have such heavy wings that you should hear so little concerning your dearest friend, and that I must make that unwilling repetition to tell you, *ad portam rigidos calces ex-
tendit*, that he is dead and buried, and by this time no puny
among the mighty nations of the dead; for though he left
this world not very many days past, yet every hour you know
largely addeth unto that dark society; and considering the
incessant mortality of mankind, you cannot conceive there
dieth in the whole earth so few as a thousand an hour.

Although at this distance you had no early account or particular of his death, yet your affection may cease to wonder
that you had not some secret sense or intimation thereof by
dreams, thoughtful whisperings, mercurisms, airy nuncios or
sympathetical insinuations, which many seem to have had at
the death of their dearest friends: for since we find in that
famous story, that spirits themselves were fain to tell their
fellows at a distance that the great Antonio was dead, we
have a sufficient excuse for our ignorance in such particulars,
and must rest content with the common road, and Appian
way of knowledge by information. Though the uncertainty
of the end of this world hath confounded all human predictions; yet they who shall live to see the sun and moon
darkened and the stars to fall from heaven, will hardly be deceived in the advent of the last day; and therefore strange
it is, that the common fallacy of consumptive persons, who

feel not themselves dying, and therefore still hope to live,
should also reach their friends in perfect health and judgment;—that you should be so little acquainted with Plautus's
sick complexion, or that almost an Hippocratical face should
not alarum you to higher fears, or rather despair, of his continuation in such an emaciated state, wherein medical predictions fail not, as sometimes in acute diseases, and wherein 'tis
as dangerous to be sentenced by a physician as a judge.

Upon my first visit I was bold to tell them who had not let
fall all hopes of his recovery, that in my sad opinion he was
not like to behold a grasshopper, much less to pluck another
fig; and in no long time after seemed to discover that odd
mortal symptom in him not mentioned by Hippocrates, that
is, to lose his own face, and look like some of his near relations; for he maintained not his proper countenance, but
looked like his uncle, the lines of whose face lay deep and
invisible in his healthful visage before: for as from our beginning we run through variety of looks, before we come to
consistent and settled faces; so before our end, by sick and
languishing alterations, we put on new visages: and in our
retreat to earth, may fall upon such looks which from community of seminal originals were before latent in us.

He was fruitlessly put in hope of advantage by change of
air, and imbibing the pure aerial nitre of these parts; and
therefore, being so far spent, he quickly found Sardinia in
Tivoli,[1] and the most healthful air of little effect, where
death had set his broad arrow;[2] for he lived not unto the
middle of May, and confirmed the observation of Hippocrates[3] of that mortal time of the year when the leaves of the
fig-tree resemble a daw's claw. He is happily seated who
lives in places whose air, earth, and water, promote not the
infirmities of his weaker parts, or is early removed into
regions that correct them. He that is tabidly inclined, were
unwise to pass his days in Portugal: cholical persons will find
little comfort in Austria or Vienna: he that is weak-legged
must not be in love with Rome, nor an infirm head with

---

[1] *Tivoli.*]   Cum mors venerit, in
medio Tibure Sardinia est.

[2] *where death, &c.*]   In the king's forests they set the figure of a broad arrow
upon trees that are to be cut down.

[3] *observation of, &c.*] See *Hip. Epidem.*

LETTER TO A FRIEND. 39

Venice or Paris. Death hath not only particular stars in
heaven, but malevolent places on earth, which single out our
infirmities, and strike at our weaker parts; in which concern,
passager and migrant birds have the great advantages; who
are naturally constituted for distant habitations, whom no seas
nor places limit, but in their appointed seasons will visit us
from Greenland and Mount Atlas, and as some think, even
from the Antipodes.[4]

Though we could not have his life, yet we missed not our
desires in his soft departure, which was scarce an expiration;
and his end not unlike his beginning, when the salient point
scarce affords a sensible motion, and his departure so like
unto sheep, that he scarce needed the civil ceremony of
closing his eyes; contrary unto the common way, wherein
death draws up, sheep let fall their eye-lids. With what
strife and pains we came into the world we know not; but 'tis
commonly no easy matter to get out of it: yet if it could be
made out, that such who have easy nativities have commonly
hard deaths, and contrarily; his departure was so easy, that
we might justly suspect his birth was of another nature, and
that some Juno sat cross-legged at his nativity.

Besides his soft death, the incurable state of his disease
might somewhat extenuate your sorrow, who know that
monsters but seldom happen, miracles more rarely in physic.[5]
Angelus Victorius gives a serious account of a consumptive,
hectical, phthisical woman, who was suddenly cured by the
intercession of Ignatius.[6] We read not of any in scripture
who in this case applied unto our Saviour, though some may
be contained in that large expression, that he went about
Galilee healing all manner of sickness and all manner of diseases.[7] Amulets, spells, sigils, and incantations, practised in
other diseases, are seldom pretended in this; and we find no
sigil in the Archidoxis of Paracelsus to cure an extreme consumption or marasmus, which, if other diseases fail, will put
a period unto long livers, and at last makes dust of all. And

[4] *Antipodes.*] *Bellonius de Avibus.*
[5] *who know that monsters but seldom happen, miracles, &c.*] Monstra contingunt in medicina. *Hippoc.* — "Strange and rare escapes there happen sometimes
in physic."
[6] *Angeli Victorii Consultationes.*
[7] Matt. iv, 25.

therefore the stoics could not but think that the fiery principle would wear out all the rest, and at last make an end of the world, which notwithstanding without such a lingering period the Creator may effect at his pleasure: and to make an end of all things on earth, and our planetical system of the world, he need but put out the sun.

I was not so curious to entitle the stars unto any concern of his death, yet could not but take notice that he died when the moon was in motion from the meridian; at which time an old Italian long ago would persuade me that the greatest part of men died: but herein I confess I could never satisfy my curiosity; although from the time of tides in places upon or near the sea, there may be considerable deductions; and Pliny[8] hath an odd and remarkable passage concerning the death of men and animals upon the recess or ebb of the sea. However, certain it is, he died in the dead and deep part of the night, when Nox might be most apprehensibly said to be the daughter of Chaos, the mother of sleep and death, according to old genealogy; and so went out of this world about that hour when our blessed Saviour entered it, and about what time many conceive he will return again unto it. Cardan hath a peculiar and no hard observation from a man's hand to know whether he was born in the day or night, which I confess holdeth in my own. And Scaliger to that purpose hath another from the tip of the ear:[9] most men are begotten in the night, animals in the day; but whether more persons have been born in the night or the day, were a curiosity undecidable, though more have perished by violent deaths in the day; yet in natural dissolutions both times may hold an indifferency, at least but contingent inequality. The whole course of time runs out in the nativity and death of things; which whether they happen by succession or coincidence, are best computed by the natural not artificial day.

That Charles the Fifth was crowned upon the day of his nativity, it being in his own power so to order it, makes no

---

[8] *Pliny.*] Aristoteles nullum animal nisi æstu recedente expirare affirmat: observatum id multum in Gallico Oceano et duntaxat in homine compertum, lib. 2, cap. 101.

[9] *Scaliger, &c.*] Auris pars pendula lobus dicitur, non omnibus ea pars est auribus; non enim iis qui noctu nati sunt, sed qui interdiu, maxima ex parte.— *Com. in Aristot. de Animal.* lib. 1.

singular animadversion; but that he should also take King
Francis prisoner upon that day, was an unexpected coincidence, which made the same remarkable. Antipater who
had an anniversary feast every year upon his birth-day,
needéd no astrological revolution to know what day he should
die on. When the fixed stars have made a revolution unto
the points from whence they first set out, some of the ancients thought the world would have an end; which was a kind
of dying upon the day of its nativity. Now the disease pre-
vailing and swiftly advancing about the time of his nativity,
some were of opinion that he would leave the world on the
day he entered into it: but this being a lingering disease, and
creeping softly on, nothing critical was found or expected,
and he died not before fifteen days after. Nothing is more
common with infants than to die on the day of their nativity,
to behold the worldly hours, and but the fractions thereof;
and even to perish before their nativity in the hidden world of
the womb, and before their good angel is conceived to undertake them. But in persons who out-live many years, and
when there are no less than three hundred and sixty-five days
to determine their lives in every year; that the first day
should make the last, that the tail of the snake should return
into its mouth precisely at that time, and they should wind up
upon the day of their nativity,[1] is indeed a remarkable coincidence, which, though astrology hath taken witty pains to
salve, yet hath it been very wary in making predictions of it.

In this consumptive condition and remarkable extenuation,
he came to be almost half himself, and left a great part behind him, which he carried not to the grave. And though
that story of Duke John Ernestus Mansfield [2] be not so easily swallowed, that at his death his heart was found not to
be so big as a nut; yet if the bones of a good skeleton weigh
little more than twenty pounds, his inwards and flesh remaining could make no bouffage,[3] but a light bit for the grave. I
never more lively beheld the starved characters of Dante [4] in
any living face; an *aruspex* might have read a lecture upon

---

[1] *nativity.*] According to the Egyptian hieroglyphic.

[2] *John Ernestus Mansfield.*] Turkish
history.

[3] *bouffage.*] Probably from *bouffée,*
inflation.

[4] *Dante.*] In the poet Dante's description.

him without exenteration, his flesh being so consumed, that
he might, in a manner, have discerned his bowels without
opening of him: so that to be carried, *sextâ cervice*,[5] to the
grave, was but a civil unnecessity; and the complements of
the coffin might outweigh the subject of it.

Omnibonus Ferrarius[6] in mortal dysenteries of children
looks for a spot behind the ear; in consumptive diseases some
eye the complexion of moles; Cardan eagerly views the nails,
some the lines of the hand, the thenar or muscle of the thumb;
some are so curious as to observe the depth of the throat-pit,
how the proportion varieth of the small of the legs unto the
calf, or the compass of the neck unto the circumference of the
head: but all these, with many more, were so drowned in a
mortal visage, and last face of Hippocrates, that a weak
physiognomist might say at first eye, this was a face of earth,
and that *Morta*[7] had set her hard seal upon his temples,
easily perceiving what *caricatura*[8] draughts death makes
upon pined faces, and unto what an unknown degree a man
may live backward.

Though the beard be only made a distinction of sex, and
sign of masculine heat by *Ulmus*,[9] yet the precocity and early
growth thereof in him, was not to be liked in reference unto
long life. Lewis, that virtuous but unfortunate King of
Hungary, who lost his life at the battle of Mohacz, was said
to be born without a skin, to have bearded at fifteen, and to
have shewn some grey hairs about twenty; from whence the
diviners conjectured that he would be spoiled of his kingdom,
and have but a short life: but hairs make fallible predictions,
and many temples early grey have out-lived the psalmist's
period.[1] Hairs which have most amused me have not been
in the face or head, but on the back, and not in men but
children, as I long ago observed in that endemial distemper
of little children in Languedoc, called the *morgellons*,[2]

---

[5] *sextâ cervice.*] i. e. "by six persons."

[6] *Omnibonus Ferrarius.*] *De Morbis Puerorum.*

[7] *Morta.*] Morta, the deity of death or fate.

[8] *caricatura.*] When men's faces are drawn with resemblance to some other animals, the Italians call it, to be drawn *in caricatura.*

[9] *Ulmus.*] *Ulmus de usu barbæ humanæ.*

[1] *period.*] The life of a man is three-score and ten.

[2] *morgellons.*] See *Picotus de Rheumatismo.*

wherein they critically break out with harsh hairs on their backs, which takes off the unquiet symptoms of the disease, and delivers them from coughs and convulsions.[3]

The Egyptian mummies that I have seen, have had their mouths open, and somewhat gaping, which affordeth a good opportunity to view and observe their teeth, wherein 'tis not easy to find any wanting or decayed; and therefore in Egypt, where one man practised but one operation, or the diseases but of single parts, it must needs be a barren profession to confine unto that of drawing of teeth, and little better than to have been tooth-drawer unto King Pyrrhus,[4] who had but two in his head. How the banyans of India maintain the integrity of those parts, I find not particularly observed; who notwithstanding have an advantage of their preservation by abstaining from all flesh, and employing their teeth in such food unto which they may seem at first framed, from their figure and conformation: but sharp and corroding rheums had so early mouldered those rocks and hardest parts of his fabric, that a man might well conceive that his years were never like to double or twice tell over his teeth.[5] Corruption had dealt more severely with them than sepulchral fires and smart flames with those of burnt bodies of old; for in the burnt fragments of urns which I have enquired into, although I seem to find few incisors or shearers, yet the dog teeth and grinders do notably resist those fires.[6]

---

[3] convulsions.] The following occurs in *MS. Sloan*, 1862:—'Though hairs afford but fallible conjectures, yet we cannot but take notice of them. They grow not equally on bodies after death: women's skulls afford moss as well as men's, and the best I have seen was upon a woman's skull, taken up and laid in a room after twenty-five years' burial. Though the skin be made the place of hairs, yet sometimes they are found on the heart and inward parts. The plica or gluey locks happen unto both sexes, and being cut off will come again: but they are wary of cutting off the same, for fear of headache and other diseases.'—*MS. Sloan*. 1862.

[4] *King Pyrrhus.*] His upper and lower jaw being solid, and without distinct rows of teeth.

[5] *teeth.*] Twice tell over his teeth, never live to threescore years.

[6] *fires.*] In the *MS. Sloan*. 1862, occurs the following paragraph:—

'Affection had so blinded some of his nearest relations, as to retain some hope of a postliminious life, and that he might come to life again, and therefore would not have him coffined before the third day. Some such virbiasses, [so in MS.] I confess, we find in story, and one or two I remember myself, but they lived not long after. Some contingent re-animations are to be hoped in diseases wherein the lamp of life is but puffed out and seemingly choaked, and not where the oil is quite spent and exhausted. Though Nonnus will have it a fever, yet of what disease Lazarus first died, is uncertain from the text, as his second death from

In the years of his childhood he had languished under the disease of his country, the rickets; after which, notwithstanding, many have become strong and active men; but whether any have attained unto very great years, the disease is scarce so old as to afford good observation. Whether the children of the English plantations be subject unto the same infirmity, may be worth the observing. Whether lameness and halting do still increase among the inhabitants of Rovigno in Istria, I know not; yet scarce twenty years ago Monsieur du Loyr observed that a third part of that people halted : but too certain it is, that the rickets encreaseth among us; the small-pox grows more pernicious than the great: the king's purse knows that the king's evil grows more common. Quartan agues are become no strangers in Ireland ; more common and mortal in England: and though the ancients gave that disease [7] very good words, yet now that bell makes no strange sound which rings out for the effects thereof.[8]

Some think there were few consumptions in the old world, when men lived much upon milk ; and that the ancient inhabitants of this island were less troubled with coughs when they went naked and slept in caves and woods, than men now

good authentic history ; but since some persons conceived to be dead do sometimes return again unto evidence of life, that miracle was wisely managed by our Saviour; for had he not been dead four days and under corruption, there had not wanted enough who would have cavilled [at] the same, which the scripture now puts out of doubt: and tradition also confirmeth, that he lived thirty years after, and being pursued by the Jews, came by sea into Provence, by Marseilles, with Mary Magdalen, Maximinus, and others: where remarkable places carry their names unto this day. But to arise from the grave to return again into it, is but an uncomfortable reviction. Few men would be content to cradle it once again : except a man can lead his second life better than the first, a man may be doubly condemned for living evilly twice, which were but to make the second death in scripture the third, and to accumulate in the punishment of two bad livers at the last day. To have performed the duty of corruption in the grave, to live again as far from sin as death, and arise like our Saviour for ever, are the only satisfactions of well-weighed expectations.'

[7] *disease.*] ᾿Ασφαλέστατος καὶ ῥήϊστος, securissima et facillima.—*Hippoc.*

[8] *that bell, &c.*] Pro febre quartana raro sonat campana. The following paragraph occurs here in *MS. Sloan.* 1862 :—

' Some I observed to wonder how, in his consumptive state, his hair held on so well, without that considerable defluvium which is one of the last symptoms in such diseases; but they took not notice of a mark in his face, which if he had lived was a probable security against baldness (if the observation of Aristotle will hold, that persons are less apt to be bald who are double-chinned), nor of the various and knotted veins in his legs, which they that have, in the same author's assertions, are less disposed to baldness. (According as Theodorus Gaza renders it: though Scaliger renders the text otherwise.)'

in chambers and featherbeds. Plato will tell us, that there
was no such disease as a catarrh in Homer's time, and that
it was but new in Greece in his age. Polydore Virgil delivereth that pleurisies were rare in England, who lived but in the
days of Henry the Eighth. Some will allow no diseases to
be new, others think that many old ones are ceased: and that
such which are esteemed new, will have but their time: however, the mercy of God hath scattered the great heap of
diseases, and not loaded any one country with all: some may
be new in one country which have been old in another. New
discoveries of the earth discover new diseases: for besides the
common swarm, there are endemial and local infirmities proper unto certain regions, which in the whole earth make no
small number: and if Asia, Africa, and America should bring
in their list, Pandora's box would swell, and there must be a
strange pathology.

Most men expected to find a consumed kell,[9] empty and
bladder-like guts, livid and marbled lungs, and a withered
pericardium in this exsuccous corpse: but some seemed too
much to wonder that two lobes of his lungs adhered unto his
side; for the like I have often found in bodies of no suspected
consumptions or difficulty of respiration. And the same more
often happeneth in men than other animals; and some think
in women than in men; but the most remarkable I have met
with, was in a man, after a cough of almost fifty years, in
whom all the lobes adhered unto the pleura,[1] and each lobe
unto another; who having also been much troubled with the
gout, brake the rule of Cardan,[2] and died of the stone in the
bladder. Aristotle makes a query, why some animals cough,
as man; some not, as oxen. If coughing be taken as it consisteth of a natural and voluntary motion, including expecto-
ration and spitting out, it may be as proper unto man as
bleeding at the nose; otherwise we find that Vegetius and
rural writers have not left so many medicines in vain against
the coughs of cattle; and men who perish by coughs die the

---

[9] kell.] The caul, or omentum.
[1] pleura.] So A. F.
[2] Cardan.] Cardan in his Encomium
Podagræ reckoneth this among the Dona
Podagræ, that they are delivered thereby from the phthisis and stone in the
bladder.

death of sheep, cats, and lions : and though birds have no mid-
riff, yet we meet with divers remedies in Arrianus against the
coughs of hawks.   And though it might be thought that all
animals who have lungs do cough ; yet in cetaceous fishes, who
have large and strong lungs, the same is not observed ; nor
yet in oviparous quadrupeds : and in the greatest thereof, the
crocodile, although we read much of their tears, we find nothing of that motion.

From the thoughts of sleep, when the soul was conceived
nearest unto divinity, the ancients erected an art of divination,
wherein while they too widely expatiated in loose and incon-
sequent conjectures, Hippocrates [3] wisely considered dreams
as they presaged alterations in the body, and so afforded
hints toward the preservation of health, and prevention of
diseases ; and therein was so serious as to advise alteration of
diet, exercise, sweating, bathing, and vomiting ; and also so
religious as to order prayers and supplications unto respective
deities, in good dreams unto Sol, Jupiter cœlestis, Jupiter
opulentus, Minerva, Mercurius, and Apollo ; in bad unto
Tellus and the heroes.

And therefore I could not but take notice how his female
friends were irrationally curious so strictly to examine his
dreams, and in this low state to hope for the phantasms of
health.   He was now past the healthful dreams of the sun,
moon, and stars, in their clarity and proper courses.   'Twas
too late to dream of flying, of limpid fountains, smooth waters,
white vestments, and fruitful green trees, which are the visions
of healthful sleeps, and at good distance from the grave.

And they were also too deeply dejected that he should
dream of his dead friends, inconsequently divining, that he
would not be long from them ; for strange it was not that he
should sometimes dream of the dead, whose thoughts run
always upon death ; beside, to dream of the dead, so they
appear not in dark habits, and take nothing away from us, in
Hippocrates' sense was of good signification : for we live by
the dead, and every thing is or must be so before it becomes
our nourishment.   And Cardan, who dreamed that he discoursed with his dead father in the moon, made thereof no

---

[3] *Hippocrates.*]   Hippoc. *de Insomniis.*

mortal interpretation: and even to dream that we are dead, was no condemnable phantasm in old oneirocriticism, as having a signification of liberty, vacuity from cares, exemption and freedom from troubles unknown unto the dead.

Some dreams I confess may admit of easy and feminine exposition; he who dreamed that he could not see his right shoulder, might easily fear to lose the sight of his right eye; he that before a journey dreamed that his feet were cut off, had a plain warning not to undertake his intended journey. But why to dream of lettuce should presage some ensuing disease, why to eat figs should signify foolish talk, why to eat eggs great trouble, and to dream of blindness should be so highly commended, according to the oneirocritical verses of Astrampsychus and Nicephorus, I shall leave unto your divination.

He was willing to quit the world alone and altogether, leaving no earnest behind him for corruption or after-grave, having small content in that common satisfaction to survive or live in another, but amply satisfied that his disease should die with himself, nor revive in a posterity to puzzle physic, and make sad mementos of their parent hereditary. Leprosy awakes not sometimes before forty, the gout and stone often later; but consumptive and tabid[4] roots sprout more early, and at the fairest make seventeen years of our life doubtful before that age. They that enter the world with original dieases as well as sin, have not only common mortality but sick traductions to destroy them, make commonly short courses, and live not at length but in figures; so that a sound Cæsarean nativity[5] may out-last a natural birth, and a knife may sometimes make way for a more lasting fruit than a midwife; which makes so few infants now able to endure the old test of the river,[6] and many to have feeble children who could scarce have been married at Sparta, and those provident states who studied strong and healthful generations; which happen but contingently in mere pecuniary matches or marriages made by the candle, wherein notwithstanding there is little redress to

---

[4] *tabid.*] Tabes maxime contingunt ab anno decimo octavo ad trigesimum quintum.—*Hippoc.*

[5] *a sound Cæsarean nativity.*] A sound child cut out of the body of the mother.

[6] *river.*] Natos ad flumina primum deferimus sævoque gelu duramus et undis.

Not to be content with life is the unsatisfactory state of those who destroy themselves;[1] who being afraid to live, run blindly upon their own death, which no man fears by experience : and the stoics had a notable doctrine to take away the fear thereof; that is, in such extremities, to desire that which is not to be avoided, and wish what might be feared ; and so made evils voluntary, and to suit with their own desires, which took off the terror of them.

But the ancient martyrs were not encouraged by such fallacies ; who, though they feared not death, were afraid to be their own executioners; and therefore thought it more wisdom to crucify their lusts than their bodies, to circumcise than stab their hearts, and to mortify than kill themselves.

His willingness to leave this world about that age, when most men think they may best enjoy it, though paradoxical unto worldly ears, was not strange unto mine, who have so often observed, that many, though old, oft stick fast unto the world, and seem to be drawn like Cacus's oxen, backward, with great struggling and reluctancy unto the grave. The long habit of living makes mere men more hardly to part with life, and all to be nothing, but what is to come. To live at the rate of the old world, when some could scarce remember themselves young, may afford no better digested death than a more moderate period. Many would have thought it an happiness to have had their lot of life in some notable conjunctures of ages past; but the uncertainty of future times hath tempted few to make a part in ages to come. And surely, he that hath taken the true altitude of things, and rightly calculated the degenerate state of this age, is not like to envy those that shall live in the next, much less three or four hundred years hence, when no man can comfortably imagine what face this world will carry : and therefore since every age makes a step unto the end of all things, and the scripture affords so hard a character of the last times; quiet minds will be content with their generations, and rather bless ages past, than be ambitious of those to come.

---

[1] *themselves.*] In the speech of Vulteius in Lucan, animating his soldiers in a great struggle to kill one another.—'Decernite lethum, et metus omnis abest, cupias quodcunque necesse est.' ' All fear is over, do but resolve to die, and make your desires meet necessity.'

Though age had set no seal upon his face, yet a dim eye might clearly discover fifty in his actions; and therefore, since wisdom is the grey hair, and an unspotted life old age; although his years came short, he might have been said to have held up with longer livers, and to have been Solomon's[2] old man. And surely if we deduct all those days of our life which we might wish unlived, and which abate the comfort of those we now live; if we reckon up only those days which God hath accepted of our lives, a life of good years will hardly be a span long: the son in this sense may out-live the father, and none be climacterically old. He that early arriveth unto the parts and prudence of age, is happily old without the uncomfortable attendants of it; and 'tis superfluous to live unto grey hairs, when in a precocious temper we anticipate the virtues of them. In brief, he cannot be accounted young who out-liveth the old man. He that hath early arrived unto the measure of a perfect stature in Christ, hath already fulfilled the prime and longest intention of his being: and one day lived after the perfect rule of piety, is to be preferred before sinning immortality.

Although he attained not unto the years of his predecessors, yet he wanted not those preserving virtues which confirm the thread of weaker constitutions. *Cautelous* chastity and *crafty* sobriety were far from him; those jewels were *paragon*, without flaw, hair, ice, or cloud in him: which affords me a hint to proceed in these good wishes, and few mementos unto you.

[2] *Solomon's.*] Wisdom, cap. iv.

⁎ The rest of this letter served as the basis for his larger work, the *Christian Morals*, in which having, with some few alterations, been included, it is here omitted.

Christian Morals.

PUBLISHED FROM THE ORIGINAL AND CORRECT MANUSCRIPT OF THE AUTHOR,

BY JOHN JEFFERY, D.D.

ARCHDEACON OF NORWICH.

WITH NOTES, ADDED TO THE SECOND EDITION,

BY DR. JOHNSON.

THIRD EDITION.

ORIGINALLY PUBLISHED IN

1716.

EDITOR'S PREFACE.

———◆———

The original edition of the CHRISTIAN MORALS, by Arch-deacon Jeffery, was printed at Cambridge, in 1716; and is one of the rarer of Sir Thomas's detached works. Dodsley, in 1756, brought out a new edition, with additional notes, and a life by Dr. Johnson. It has been said that Dr. Johnson inserted in the *Literary Magazine* a review of the work, but I have not been able to find it. The sixth volume of *Memoirs of Literature* contains a meagre account of the Posthumous Works, but no notice of the Christian Morals.

The latter portion of the Letter to a Friend is incorporated in various parts of the Christian Morals; except some passages, which are given in notes to the present edition; together with some various readings from MSS. in the British Museum.

THE PREFACE.

———◆———

If any one, after he has read Religio Medici, and the ensuing discourse, can make doubt whether the same person was the author of them both, he may be assured, by the testimony of Mrs. Littleton, Sir Thomas Browne's daughter, who lived with her father when it was composed by him; and who, at the time, read it written by his own hand: and also by the testimony of others (of whom I am one) who read the manuscript of the author, immediately after his death, and who have since read the same; from which it hath been faithfully and exactly transcribed for the press. The reason why it was not printed sooner is, because it was unhappily lost, by being mislaid among other manuscripts, for which search was lately made in the presence of the Lord Archbishop of Canterbury, of which his Grace, by letter, informed Mrs. Littleton, when he sent the manuscript to her. There is nothing printed in the discourse, or in the short notes, but what is found in the original manuscript of the author, except only where an oversight had made the addition or transposition of some words necessary.

JOHN JEFFERY,
Archdeacon of Norwich.

Christian Morals.

PART THE FIRST.

Tread softly and circumspectly in this funambulatory track [1] and narrow path of goodness : pursue virtue virtuously : [2] leaven not good actions, nor render virtue disputable. Stain not fair acts with foul intentions : maim not uprightness by halting concomitances, nor circumstantially deprave substantial goodness.

Consider [3] whereabout thou art in Cebes's [4] table, or that old philosophical pinax [5] of the life of man : whether thou art yet in the road of uncertainties ; whether thou hast yet entered the narrow gate, got up the hill and asperous way, which leadeth unto the house of sanity ; or taken that purifying potion from the hand of sincere erudition, which may send thee clear and pure away unto a virtuous and happy life.

In this virtuous voyage of thy life hull not about like the ark, without the use of rudder, mast, or sail, and bound for

---

[1] *funambulatory track.*] Narrow, like the walk of a rope-dancer.—*Dr. J.*

[2] *Tread, &c.*] This sentence begins the closing reflections to the *Letter to a Friend*, which were afterwards amplified into the *Christian Morals*, and, therefore, have been omitted as duplicate in the present edition.

[3] *Consider, &c.*] The remainder of this section comprises the 2nd and 3rd paragraphs of the closing reflections to the *Letter to a Friend.*

[4] *Cebes's table.*] The table or picture of Cebes, an allegorical representation of the characters and conditions of mankind ; which is translated by Mr. Collier, and added to the *Meditations of Antoninus.*—*Dr. J.*

[5] *pinax.*] Picture.—*Dr. J.*

no port. Let not disappointment cause despondency, nor difficulty despair. Think not that you are sailing from Lima to Manilla,[6] when you may fasten up the rudder, and sleep before the wind; but expect rough seas, flaws,[7] and contrary blasts: and 'tis well, if by many cross tacks and veerings, you arrive at the port; for we sleep in lions' skins[8] in our progress unto virtue, and we slide not but climb unto it.

Sit not down in the popular forms and common level of virtues. Offer not only peace-offerings but holocausts unto God: where all is due make no reserve, and cut not a cummin-seed with the Almighty: to serve Him singly to serve ourselves, were too partial a piece of piety, not like[9] to place us in the illustrious mansions of glory.

SECT. II.[1]—Rest not in an ovation* but a triumph over thy passions. Let anger walk hanging down the head; let malice go manacled, and envy fettered after thee. Behold within thee the long train of thy trophies, not without thee. Make the quarrelling Lapithytes sleep, and Centaurs within lie quiet.[2] Chain up the unruly legion of thy breast. Lead thine own captivity captive, and be Cæsar within thyself.[3]

* Ovation, a petty and minor kind of triumph.

[6] *Lima to Manilla.*] Over the Pacific Ocean, in the course of the ship which now sails from Acapulco to Manilla, perhaps formerly from Lima, or more properly from Callao, Lima not being a sea-port.—*Dr. J.*

[7] *flaws.*] Sudden gusts or violent attacks of bad weather.—*Dr. J.*

[8] *lions' skins, &c.*] That is, in armour, in a state of military vigilance. One of the Grecian chiefs used to represent open force by the lions' skin, and policy by the fox's tail.—*Dr. J.*

[9] *like.*] Likely.

[1] SECT. II.] The first and last two sentences compose par. 17th of closing reflections to the *Letter to a Friend.* The succeeding par. (18) is given here, having been omitted in the *Christian Morals:* —'Give no quarter unto those vices which are of thine inward family, and, having a root in thy temper, plead a right and property in thee. Examine well thy complexional inclinations. Raise

early batteries against those strong holds built upon the rock of nature, and make this a great part of the militia of thy life. The politic nature of vice must be opposed by policy, and therefore wiser honesties project and plot against sin; wherein notwithstanding we are not to rest in generals, or the trite stratagems of art: that may succeed with one temper which may prove successless with another. There is no community or commonwealth of virtue; every man must study his own economy, and erect these rules unto the figure of himself.'

[2] *Make the quarrelling, &c.*] That is, thy turbulent and irascible passions. For the Lapithytes and Centaurs, see Ovid. —*Dr. J.*

[3] *thyself.*] In *MS. Sloan.* 1848, I met with the following passage, which may be fitly introduced as a continuation to this section :—'To restrain the rise of extravagances, and timely to ostracise the most overgrowing enormities makes

SECT. III.[4]—He that is chaste and continent not to impair his strength, or honest for fear of contagion, will hardly be heroically virtuous. Adjourn not this virtue until that temper, when Cato[5] could lend out his wife, and impotent satyrs write satires upon lust; but be chaste in thy flaming days, when Alexander dared not trust his eyes upon the fair sisters of Darius, and when so many think there is no other way but Origen's. *

SECT. IV.[6]—Show thy art in honesty, and lose not thy virtue by the bad managery of it. Be temperate and sober; not to preserve your body in an ability for wanton ends; not to avoid the infamy of common transgressors that way, and thereby to hope to expiate or palliate obscure and closer vices; not to spare your purse, nor simply to enjoy health; but, in one word, that thereby you may truly serve God, which every sickness will tell you you cannot well do without health. The sick man's sacrifice is but a lame oblation. Pious treasures, laid up in healthful days, plead for sick non-performances: without which we must needs look back with anxiety upon the lost opportunities of health; and may have cause rather to envy than pity the ends of penitent public sufferers, who go with healthful prayers unto the last scene of their lives, and in the integrity of their faculties[7] return their spirit unto God that gave it.

SECT. V.—Be charitable before wealth make thee covetous, and lose not the glory of the mite. If riches increase, let

* Who is said to have castrated himself.

a calm and quiet state in the dominion of ourselves, for vices have their ambitions, and will be above one another; but though many may possess us, yet is there commonly one that hath the dominion over us; one that lordeth over all, and the rest remain slaves unto the humour of it. Such towering vices are not to be temporally exostracised, but perpetually exiled, or rather to be served like the rank puppies in Tarquin's garden, and made shorter by the head; for the sharpest arrows are to be let fly against all such imperious vices, which, neither enduring priority or equality, Cæsarean or Pompeian primity, must be absolute over all; for these opprobiously denomi-nate us here, and chiefly condemn us hereafter, and will stand in capital letters over our heads as the titles of our sufferings.'

[4] SECT. III.] The 4th paragraph of closing reflections to the *Letter to a Friend*.

[5] *Cato.*] The censor, who is frequently confounded, and by Pope, amongst others, with Cato of Utica.—*Dr. J.*

[6] SECT. IV.] Except the first sentence, this section concludes the first paragraph of the concluding reflections of *Letter to a Friend*.

[7] *and in the integrity, &c.*] With their faculties unimpaired.—*Dr. J.*

thy mind hold pace with them; and think it not enough to be liberal, but munificent. Though a cup of cold water from some hand may not be without its reward, yet stick not thou for wine and oil for the wounds of the distressed; and treat the poor, as our Saviour did the multitude, to the reliques of some baskets.[8] Diffuse thy beneficence early, and while thy treasures call thee master; there may be an atropos[9] of thy fortunes before that of thy life, and thy wealth cut off before that hour, when all men shall be poor; for the justice of death looks equally upon the dead, and Charon expects no more from Alexander than from Irus.

SECT. VI.—Give not only unto seven, but also unto eight, that is unto more than many.* Though to give unto every one that asketh may seem severe advice,† yet give thou also before asking; that is, where want is silently clamorous, and men's necessities not their tongues do loudly call for thy mercies. For though sometimes necessitousness be dumb, or misery speak not out, yet true charity is sagacious, and will find out hints for beneficence. Acquaint thyself with the physiognomy of want, and let the dead colours and first lines of necessity suffice to tell thee there is an object for thy bounty. Spare not where thou canst not easily be prodigal, and fear not to be undone by mercy; for since he who hath pity on the poor lendeth unto the Almighty rewarder, who observes no ides[1] but every day for his payments, charity becomes pious usury, christian liberality the most thriving industry; and what we adventure in a cockboat may return in a carrack unto us. He who thus casts his bread upon the water shall surely find it again; for though it falleth to the bottom, it sinks but like the axe of the prophet, to rise again unto him.

---

* Ecclesiasticus.   † Luke.

---

[8] *Be charitable, &c.*] The preceding part of this section constitutes the 5th paragraph of the closing reflections of *Letter to a Friend.*

[9] *atropos.*] Atropos is the lady of destiny that cuts the thread of life.— *Dr. J.*

[1] *ides, &c.*] The ides was the time when money lent out at interest was commonly repaid.
——Fœnerator Alphius
Suam relegit Idibus pecuniam,
Quærit calendis ponere.
HOR.—*Dr. J.*

SECT. VII.[2]—If avarice be thy vice, yet make it not thy punishment. Miserable men commiserate not themselves, bowelless unto others, and merciless unto their own bowels. Let the fruition of things bless the possession of them, and think it more satisfaction to live richly than die rich. For since thy good works, not thy goods, will follow thee; since wealth is an appurtenance of life, and no dead man is rich; to famish in plenty, and live poorly to die rich, were a multiplying improvement in madness, and use upon use in folly.

SECT. VIII.[3]—Trust not to the omnipotency of gold, and say not unto it, thou art my confidence. Kiss not thy hand to that terrestrial sun, nor bore thy ear unto its servitude. A slave unto mammon makes no servant unto God. Covetousness cracks the sinews of faith; numbs the apprehension of any thing above sense; and, only affected with the certainty of things present, makes a peradventure of things to come; lives but unto one world, nor hopes but fears another; makes their own death sweet unto others, bitter unto themselves; brings formal sadness, scenical mourning, and no wet eyes at the grave.

SECT. IX.[4]—Persons lightly dipt, not grained in generous honesty,[5] are but pale in goodness, and faint hued in integrity. But be thou what thou virtuously art, and let not the ocean wash away thy tincture. Stand magnetically upon that axis,[6] when prudent simplicity hath fixt there; and let no attraction invert the poles of thy honesty. That vice may be uneasy and even monstrous unto thee, let iterated good acts and long confirmed habits make virtue almost natural, or a second nature in thee. Since virtuous superstructions have commonly generous foundations, dive into thy inclinations, and early discover what nature bids thee to be or tells thee thou mayest be. They who thus timely descend into themselves, and cultivate the good seeds which nature hath set in them,

---

[2] SECT. VII.] Paragraph 7th of closing reflections of *Letter to a Friend.*

[3] SECT. VIII.] Par. 6th of closing reflections to the *Letter to a Friend.*

[4] SECT. IX.] Par. 8th of closing reflections to the *Letter to a Friend.*

[5] *not grained in generous, &c.*] Not

deeply tinged, not dyed in grain.—*Dr. J.*

[6] *that axis.*] That is, " with a position as immutable as that of the magnetical axis," which is popularly supposed to be invariably parallel to the meridian, or to stand exactly north and south.—*Dr. J.*

prove not shrubs but cedars in their generation. And to be in the form of the best of the bad* or the worst of the good, will be no satisfaction unto them.

SECT. x.[7]—Make not the consequence of virtue the ends thereof. Be not beneficent for a name or cymbal of applause ; nor exact and just in commerce for the advantages of trust and credit, which attend the reputation of true and punctual dealing : for these rewards, though unsought for, plain virtue will bring with her. To have other by-ends in good actions sours laudable performances, which must have deeper roots, motives, and instigations, to give them the stamp of virtues.[8]

SECT. XI.[9]—Let not the law of thy country be the non ultra of thy honesty; nor think that always good enough which the law will make good. Narrow not the law of charity, equity, mercy. Join gospel righteousness with legal right. Be not a mere Gamaliel in the faith, but let the sermon in the mount be thy targum unto the law of Sinai.[1]

SECT. XII.—Live by old ethicks and the classical rules of honesty. Put no new names or notions upon authentic virtues and vices.[2] Think not, that morality is ambulatory; that vices in one age are not vices in another; or that virtues, which are under the everlasting seal of right reason, may be stamped by opinion. And therefore, though vicious times invert the opinions of things, and set up new ethicks against virtue, yet hold thou unto old morality; and rather than fol-

---

* Optimi malorum pessimi bonorum.

[7] SECT. x.] Par. 10th of closing reflections to the *Letter to a Friend.*

[8] *virtues.*] The following (11th par. of closing reflections to the *Letter, &c.)* seems to have been omitted in the *Christian Morals:*—'Though human infirmity may betray thy heedless days into the popular ways of extravagancy, yet let not thine own depravity, or the torrent of vicious times, carry thee into desperate enormities in opinions, manners, or actions : if thou hast dipped thy foot in the river, yet venture not over *Rubicon ;* run not into extremities from whence there is no regression, nor be ever so closely shut up within the holds of vice and iniquity, as not to find some escape by a postern of recipiscency.'

[9] SECT. XI.] Par. 9th of closing reflections to the *Letter to a Friend.*

[1] *targum, &c.*] A paraphrase or amplification.

[2] *vices.*] From *MS. Sloan.* 1847, the following clause is added :—' Think not modesty will never gild its like ; fortitude will not be degraded into audacity and foolhardiness ; liberality will not be put off with the name of prodigality, nor frugality exchange its name with avarice and solid parsimony, and so our vices be exalted into virtues.'

low a multitude to do evil, stand like Pompey's pillar conspicuous by thyself, and single in integrity. And since the worst
of times afford imitable examples of virtue; since no deluge
of vice is like to be so general but more than eight will escape;[3]
eye well those heroes who have held their heads above water,
who have touched pitch and not been defiled, and in the
common contagion have remained uncorrupted.

SECT. XIII.[4]—Let age, not envy, draw wrinkles on thy
cheeks; be content to be envied, but envy not. Emulation
may be plausible and indignation allowable, but admit no
treaty with that passion which no circumstance can make
good. A displacency at the good of others because they enjoy it, though not unworthy of it, is an absurd depravity,
sticking fast unto corrupted nature, and often too hard for
humility and charity, the great suppressors of envy. This
surely is a lion not to be strangled but by Hercules himself,
or the highest stress of our minds, and an atom of that power
which subdueth all things unto itself.

SECT. XIV.[5]—Owe not thy humility unto humiliation from
adversity, but look humbly down in that state when others
look upwards upon thee. Think not thy own shadow longer
than that of others, nor delight to take the altitude of thyself. Be patient in the age of pride, when men live by short
intervals of reason under the dominion of humour and passion, when it's in the power of every one to transform thee
out of thyself, and run thee into the short madness. If you
cannot imitate Job, yet come not short of Socrates,[6] and
those patient Pagans who tired the tongues of their enemies,
while they perceived they spit their malice at brazen walls and
statues.

SECT. XV.[7]—Let not the sun in Capricorn * go down upon
thy wrath, but write thy wrongs in ashes. Draw the curtain

* Even when the days are shortest.

[3] *eight will escape*.] Alluding to the
flood of Noah.
[4] SECT. XIII.] Par. 13th of closing
reflections to the *Letter to a Friend*.
[5] SECT. XIV.] Par. 12th of closing
reflections to the *Letter to a Friend*.
[6] *Socrates*.]
..... Dulcique senex vicinus Hymetto,

Qui partem acceptæ sæva inter vincla cicutæ
Accusatori nollet dare.—JUV.
Not so mild Thales, nor Chrysippus thought;
Nor the good man who drank the pois'nous
draught
With mind serene, and could not wish to see
His vile accuser drink as deep as he:
Exalted Socrates!——CREECH.—*Dr. J.*

[7] SECT. XV.] Par. 15th of closing
reflections to the *Letter to a Friend*.

of night upon injuries, shut them up in the tower of oblivion,* and let them be as though they had not been. To forgive our enemies, yet hope that God will punish them, is not to forgive enough. To forgive them ourselves, and not to pray God to forgive them, is a partial piece of charity. Forgive thine enemies totally, and without any reserve that however God will revenge thee.

SECT. XVI.[8]—While thou so hotly disclaimest the devil, be not guilty of diabolism. Fall not into one name with that unclean spirit, nor act his nature whom thou so much abhorrest; that is, to accuse, calumniate, backbite, whisper, detract, or sinistrously interpret others. Degenerous depravities, and narrow-minded vices! not only below St. Paul's noble Christian but Aristotle's true gentleman.† Trust not with some that the epistle of St. James is apocryphal, and so read with less fear that stabbing truth, that in company with this vice "thy religion is in vain." Moses broke the tables without breaking of the law; but where charity is broke, the law itself is shattered, which cannot be whole without love, which is "the fulfilling of it." Look humbly upon thy virtues; and though thou art rich in some, yet think thyself poor and naked without that crowning grace, which "thinketh no evil, which envieth not, which beareth, hopeth, believeth, endureth all things." With these sure graces, while busy tongues are crying out for a drop of cold water, mutes may be in happiness, and sing the *trisagion* ‡ in heaven.

SECT. XVII.—However thy understanding may waver in the theories of true and false, yet fasten the rudder of thy will, steer straight unto good and fall not foul on evil. Imagination is apt to rove, and conjecture to keep no bounds. Some have run out so far, as to fancy the stars might be but the light of the crystalline heaven shot through perforations on the bodies of the orbs. Others more ingeniously doubt whether there hath not been a vast tract of land in the

---

* Alluding unto the tower of oblivion mentioned by Procopius, which was the name of a tower of imprisonment among the Persians: whoever was put therein was as it were buried alive, and it was death for any but to name him.

† See Aristotle's Ethics, chapter of Magnanimity. ‡ Holy, holy, holy.

[8] SECT. XVI.] Par. 14th of closing reflections to the *Letter to a Friend.*

Atlantic ocean, which earthquakes and violent causes have long ago devoured.[9] Speculative misapprehensions may be innocuous, but immorality pernicious; theoretical mistakes and physical deviations may condemn our judgments, not lead us into judgment. But perversity of will, immoral and sinful enormities walk with Adraste and Nemesis[1] at their backs, pursue us unto judgment, and leave us viciously miserable.

SECT. XVIII.—Bid early defiance unto those vices which are of thine inward family, and having a root in thy temper plead a right and propriety in thee. Raise timely batteries against those strong holds built upon the rock of nature, and make this a great part of the militia of thy life. Delude not thyself into iniquities from participation or community, which abate the sense but not the obliquity of them. To conceive sins less or less of sins, because others also transgress, were morally to commit that natural fallacy of man, to take comfort from society, and think adversities less because others also suffer them. The politic nature of vice must be opposed by policy; and, therefore, wiser honesties project and plot against it: wherein, notwithstanding, we are not to rest in generals, or the trite stratagems of art. That may succeed with one, which may prove successless with another: there is no community or commonweal of virtue: every man must study his own economy, and adapt such rules unto the figure of himself.

SECT. XIX.[2]—Be substantially great in thyself, and more than thou appearest unto others; and let the world be deceived in thee, as they are in the lights of heaven. Hang early plummets upon the heels of pride, and let ambition have but an epicycle[3] and narrow circuit in thee. Measure not thyself by thy morning shadow, but by the extent of thy grave; and reckon thyself above the earth, by the line thou

---

[9] *devoured.*] Add from *MS.* CIX *Rawl.* "Whether there hath not been a passage from the Mediterranean into the Red Sea, and whether the ocean at first had a passage into the Mediterranean by the straits of Hercules."

[1] *Adraste and Nemesis.*] The powers of vengeance.—*Dr. J.*

[2] SECT. XIX.] Paragraph 16th of clos-ing reflections to the *Letter to a Friend.*

[3] *epicycle.*] An epicycle is a small revolution made by one planet in the wider orbit of another planet. The meaning is, "Let not ambition form thy circle of action, but move upon other principles; and let ambition only operate as something extrinsic and adventitious."—*Dr. J.*

must be contented with under it. Spread not into boundless expansions either of designs or desires. Think not that mankind liveth but for a few; and that the rest are born but to serve those ambitions, which make but flies of men and wildernesses of whole nations. Swell not into vehement actions which imbroil and confound the earth; but be one of those violent ones which force the kingdom of heaven.* If thou must needs rule, be Zeno's king,[4] and enjoy that empire which every man gives himself. He who is thus his own monarch contentedly sways the sceptre of himself, not envying the glory of crowned heads and *elohims* of the earth. Could the world unite in the practice of that despised train of virtues, which the divine ethics of our Saviour hath so inculcated upon us, the furious face of things must disappear; Eden would be yet to be found, and the angels might look down, not with pity, but joy upon us.

SECT. XX.[5]—Though the quickness of thine ear were able to reach the noise of the moon, which some think it maketh in its rapid revolution; though the number of thy ears should equal Argus's eyes; yet stop them all with the wise man's wax,[6] and be deaf unto the suggestions of tale-bearers, calumniators, pickthank or malevolent delators, who, while quiet men sleep, sowing the tares of discord and division, distract the tranquillity of charity and all friendly society. These are the tongues that set the world on fire, cankers of reputation, and like that of Jonas's gourd, wither a good name in a night. Evil spirits may sit still, while these spirits walk about and perform the business of hell. To speak more strictly, our corrupted hearts are the factories of the devil, which may be at work without his presence; for when that circumventing spirit hath drawn malice, envy, and all unrighteousness

* Matthew xi.

[4] *Zeno's king.*] That is, "the king of the stoics," whose founder was Zeno, and who held, that the wise man alone had power and royalty.—*Dr. J.*

[5] SECT. XX.] The first part of this Section, varying slightly, is preserved in MSS. in the Rawlinson collection at Oxford, NO. CIX. It is immediately followed, without break, by the whole of the 17th Section, with slight variations, and with the addition which is now added to that Section, in a note at p. 67.

[6] *wise man's wax.*] Alluding to the story of Ulysses, who stopped the ears of his companions with wax when they passed by the Sirens.—*Dr. J.*

unto well rooted habits in his disciples, iniquity then goes on upon its own legs; and if the gate of hell were shut up for a time, vice would still be fertile and produce the fruits of hell. Thus when God forsakes us, Satan also leaves us : for such offenders he looks upon as sure and sealed up, and his temptations then needless unto them.

SECT. XXI.—Annihilate not the mercies of God by the oblivion of ingratitude; for oblivion is a kind of annihilation; and for things to be as though they had not been, is like unto never being. Make not thy head a grave, but a repository of God's mercies. Though thou hadst the memory of Seneca, or Simonides, and conscience the punctual memorist within us, yet trust not to thy remembrance in things which need phylacteries. [7] Register not only strange, but merciful occurrences. Let Ephemerides not Olympiads [8] give thee account of his mercies: let thy diaries stand thick with dutiful mementos and asterisks of acknowledgment. And to be complete and forget nothing, date not his mercy from thy nativity; look beyond the world, and before the æra of Adam.

SECT. XXII.—Paint not the sepulchre of thyself, and strive not to beautify thy corruption. Be not an advocate for thy vices, nor call for many hour-glasses [9] to justify thy imperfections. Think not that always good which thou thinkest thou canst always make good, nor that concealed which the sun doth not behold: that which the sun doth not now see, will be visible when the sun is out, and the stars are fallen from heaven. Meanwhile there is no darkness unto conscience; which can see without light, and in the deepest obscurity give a clear draught of things, which the cloud of dissimulation hath concealed from all eyes. There is a natural standing court within us, examining, acquitting, and condemning at the tribunal of ourselves; wherein iniquities have their natural

---

[7] *phylacteries.*] A phylactery is a writing bound upon the forehead, containing something to be kept constantly in mind. This was practised by the Jewish doctors with regard to the Mosaic law. —*Dr. J.*

[8] *Olympiads. &c.*] Particular journals of every day, not abstracts comprehend-ing several years under one notation. An Ephemeris is a diary, an Olympiad is the space of four years.—*Dr. J.*

[9] *hour-glasses, &c.*] That is, "do not speak much or long in justification of thy faults." The ancient pleaders talked by a clepsydra, or measurer of time.—*Dr. J.*

thetas [1] and no nocent [2] is absolved by the verdict of himself. And therefore although our transgressions shall be tried at the last bar, the process need not be long: for the judge of all knoweth all, and every man will nakedly know himself; and when so few are like to plead not guilty, the assize must soon have an end.

SECT. XXIII.—Comply with some humours, bear with others, but serve none.   Civil complacency consists with decent honesty: flattery is a juggler, and no kin unto sincerity.   But while thou maintainest the plain path, and scornest to flatter others, fall not into self-adulation, and become not thine own parasite.   Be deaf unto thyself, and be not betrayed at home. Self-credulity, pride, and levity lead unto self-idolatry.   There is no Damocles [3] like unto self-opinion, nor any Syren to our own fawning conceptions.   To magnify our minor things, or hug ourselves in our apparitions; [4] to afford a credulous ear unto the clawing suggestions [5] of fancy; to pass our days in painted mistakes of ourselves; and though we behold our own blood, [6] to think ourselves the sons of Jupiter; * are blandishments of self-love, worse than outward delusion.   By this imposture, wise men sometimes are mistaken in their elevation, and look above themselves.   And fools, which are antipodes [7] unto the wise, conceive themselves to be but their periœci, [8] and in the same parallel with them.

SECT. XXIV.—Be not a Hercules furens abroad, and a poltroon within thyself.   To chase our enemies out of the field, and be led captive by our vices; to beat down our foes, and fall down to our concupiscences; are solecisms in moral schools, and no laurel attends them.   To well manage our

* As Alexander the Great did.

[1] *thetas.*]   Θ a theta inscribed upon the judge's tessera or ballot was a mark for death or capital condemnation. — *Dr. J.*

[2] *nocent.*] ..... Se Judice nemo nocens absolvitur.
                   Juv.—*Dr. J.*

[3] *Damocles.*] Damocles was a flatterer of Dionysius.—*Dr. J.*

[4] *apparitions.*] Appearances without realities.—*Dr. J.*

[5] *clawing suggestions, &c.*] Tickling,

flattering.   A clawback is an old word for a flatterer.   Jewel calls some writers for popery " the pope's clawbacks." —*Dr. J.*

[6] *our own blood.*]   That is, "though we bleed when we are wounded, though we find in ourselves the imperfections of humanity."—*Dr. J.*

[7] *antipodes.*]   Opposites.—*Dr. J.*

[8] *periœci.*]   Only placed at a distance in the same line.—*Dr. J.*

affections, and wild horses of Plato, are the highest *circenses:* [9] and the noblest digladiation [1] is in the theatre of ourselves; for therein our inward antagonists, not only like common gladiators, with ordinary weapons and down-right blows make at us, but also, like retiary and laqueary [2] combatants, with nets, frauds, and entanglements fall upon us. Weapons for such combats, are not to be forged at Lipara: [3] Vulcan's art doth nothing in this internal militia; wherein not the armour of Achilles, but the armature of St. Paul, gives the glorious day, and triumphs not leading up into capitols, but up into the highest heavens. And, therefore, while so many think it the only valour to command and master others, study thou the dominion of thyself, and quiet thine own commotions. Let right reason be thy Lycurgus, [4] and lift up thy hand unto the law of it: move by the intelligences of the superior faculties, not by the rapt of passion, nor merely by that of temper and constitution. They who are merely carried on by the wheel of such inclinations, without the hand and guidance of sovereign reason, are but the automatous [5] part of mankind, rather lived than living, or at least underliving themselves.

SECT. XXV.—Let not fortune, which hath no name in scripture, have any in thy divinity. Let providence, not chance, have the honour of thy acknowledgments, and be thy Œdipus in contingencies. Mark well the paths and winding ways thereof; but be not too wise in the construction, or sudden in the application. The hand of providence writes often by abbreviatures, hieroglyphics or short characters, which, like the laconism on the wall, [6] are not to be made out but by a hint or key from that spirit which indicted them. Leave future occurrences to their uncertainties, think that which is

---

[9] *circenses.*] Circenses were Roman horse races.—*Dr. J.*

[1] *digladiation.*] Fencing match.—*Dr. J.*

[2] *retiary and laqueary.*] The *retiarius* or *laquearius* was a prize-fighter, who entangled his opponent in a net, which by some dexterous management he threw upon him.—*Dr. J.*

[3] *Lipara.*] The Liparæan islands, near Italy, being volcanoes, were fabled to contain the forges of the Cyclops.—*Dr. J.*

[4] *Lycurgus.*] Thy lawgiver.

[5] *automatous.*] Moved not by choice, but by some mechanical impulse.—*Dr. J.*

[6] *laconism on the wall.*] The short sentence written on the wall of Belshazzar. See *Daniel.*—*Dr. J.*

present thy own; and, since 'tis easier to foretell an eclipse than a foul day at some distance, look for little regular below. Attend with patience the uncertainty of things, and what lieth yet unexerted in the chaos of futurity. The uncertainty and ignorance of things to come, makes the world new unto us by unexpected emergencies; whereby we pass not our days in the trite road of affairs affording no novity ; for the novelizing spirit of man lives by variety, and the new faces of things.

SECT. XXVI.—Though a contented mind enlargeth the dimension of little things ; and unto some it is wealth enough not to be poor; and others are well content, if they be but rich enough to be honest, and to give every man his due : yet fall not into that obsolete affectation of bravery, to throw away thy money, and to reject all honours or honourable stations in this courtly and splendid world. Old generosity is superannuated, and such contempt of the world out of date. No man is now like to refuse the favour of great ones, or be content to say unto princes, ' stand out of my sun.' [7] And if any there be of such antiquated resolutions, they are not like to be tempted out of them by great ones; and 'tis fair if they escape the name of hypocondriacks from the genius of latter times, unto whom contempt of the world is the most contemptible opinion; and to be able, like Bias, to carry all they have about them were to be the eighth wise man.   However, the old tetrick [8] philosophers looked always with indignation upon such a face of things ; and observing the unnatural current of riches, power, and honour in the world, and withal the imperfection and demerit of persons often advanced unto them, were tempted unto angry opinions, that affairs were ordered more by stars than reason, and that things went on rather by lottery than election.

SECT. XXVII.—If thy vessel be but small in the ocean of this world, if meanness of possessions be thy allotment upon earth, forget not those virtues which the great disposer of all bids thee to entertain from thy quality and condition; that is,

---

[7] *stand out of my sun.*] The answer made by Diogenes to Alexander, who ask- ed him what he had to request.—*Dr. J.*

[8] *tetrick.*] Sour, morose.—*Dr. J.*

submission, humility, content of mind, and industry. Content
may dwell in all stations. To be low, but above contempt,
may be high enough to be happy. But many of low degree
may be higher than computed, and some cubits above the
common commensuration; for in all states virtue gives quali-
fications and allowances, which make out defects. Rough
diamonds are sometimes mistaken for pebbles; and meanness
may be rich in accomplishments, which riches in vain desire.
If our merits be above our stations, if our intrinsical value be
greater than what we go for, or our value than our valuation,
and if we stand higher in God's, than in the censor's book;[9]
it may make some equitable balance in the inequalities of this
world, and there may be no such vast chasm or gulph between
disparities as common measures determine. The divine eye
looks upon high and low differently from that of man. They
who seem to stand upon Olympus, and high mounted unto
our eyes, may be but in the valleys, and low ground unto his;
for he looks upon those as highest who nearest approach his
divinity, and upon those as lowest who are farthest from it.

SECT. XXVIII.—When thou lookest upon the imperfections
of others, allow one eye for what is laudable in them, and the
balance they have from some excellency, which may render
them considerable. While we look with fear or hatred upon
the teeth of the viper, we may behold his eye with love. In
venemous natures something may be amiable: poisons afford
antipoisons: nothing is totally, or altogether uselessly bad.
Notable virtues are sometimes dashed with notorious vices,
and in some vicious tempers have been found illustrious acts
of virtue; which makes such observable worth in some actions
of king Demetrius, Antonius, and Ahab, as are not to be
found in the same kind in Aristides, Numa, or David. Constancy, generosity, clemency, and liberality have been highly
conspicuous in some persons not marked out in other concerns for example or imitation. But since goodness is exemplary in all, if others have not our virtues, let us not be
wanting in theirs; nor scorning them for their vices whereof

---

[9] *censor's book.*] The book in which   estate was registered among the Romans.
the census, or account of every man's   —*Dr. J.*

we are free, be condemned by their virtues wherein we are deficient. There is dross, alloy, and embasement in all human tempers; and he flieth without wings, who thinks to find ophir or pure metal in any. For perfection is not, like light, centered in any one body; but, like the dispersed seminalities of vegetables at the creation, scattered through the whole mass of the earth, no place producing all and almost all some. So that 'tis well, if a perfect man can be made out of many men, and, to the perfect eye of God, even out of mankind. Time, which perfects some things, imperfects also others. Could we intimately apprehend the ideated man, and as he stood in the intellect of God upon the first exertion by creation, we might more narrowly comprehend our present degeneration, and how widely we are fallen from the pure exemplar and idea of our nature: for after this corruptive elongation from a primitive and pure creation, we are almost lost in degeneration; and Adam hath not only fallen from his Creator, but we ourselves from Adam, our tycho [1] and primary generator. [2]

SECT. XXIX.—Quarrel not rashly with adversities not yet understood; and overlook not the mercies often bound up in them: for we consider not sufficiently the good of evils, nor fairly compute the mercies of providence in things afflictive at first hand. The famous Andreas Doria being invited to a feast by Aloysio Fieschi, with design to kill him, just the night before fell mercifully into a fit of the gout, and so escaped that mischief. When Cato intended to kill himself, from a

---

[1] *tycho.*] ʼΟ τύχων qui facit, ʼΟ τύχὼν qui adeptus est: he that makes, or he that posseses; as Adam might be said to contain within him the race of mankind.—*Dr. J.*

[2] *generator.*] Add from *MS. Sloan.* 1885, the following passage:—"But at this distance and elongation we dearly know that depravity hath overspread us, corruption entered like oil into our bones. Imperfections upbraid us on all hands, and ignorance stands pointing at us in every corner in nature. We are unknowing in things which fall under cognition, yet drive at that which is above our comprehension. We have a slender knowledge of ourselves, and much less of God, wherein we are like to rest until the advantage of another being; and therefore in vain we seek to satisfy our souls in close apprehensions and piercing theories of the divinity even from the divine word. Meanwhile we have a happy sufficiency in our own natures, to apprehend his good will and pleasure; it being not of our concern or capacity from thence to apprehend or reach his nature, the divine revelation in such points being not framed unto intellectuals of earth. Even the angels and spirits have enough to admire in their sublimer created natures; admiration being the act of the creature and not of God, who doth not admire himself."

blow which he gave his servant, who would not reach his sword unto him, his hand so swelled that he had much ado to effect his design. Hereby any one but a resolved stoic might have taken a fair hint of consideration, and that some merciful genius would have contrived his preservation. To be sagacious in such intercurrences is not superstition, but wary and pious discretion; and to contemn such hints were to be deaf unto the speaking hand of God, wherein Socrates and Cardan [3] would hardly have been mistaken.

SECT. XXX.—Break not open the gate of destruction, and make no haste or bustle unto ruin. Post not heedlessly on unto the *non ultra* of folly, or precipice of perdition. Let vicious ways have their tropics [4] and deflexions, and swim in the waters of sin but as in the Asphaltick lake,[5] though smeared and defiled, not to sink to the bottom. If thou hast dipped thy foot in the brink, yet venture not over Rubicon.[6] Run not into extremities from whence there is no regression. In the vicious ways of the world it mercifully falleth out that we become not extempore wicked, but it taketh some time and pains to undo ourselves. We fall not from virtue, like Vulcan from heaven, in a day. Bad dispositions require some time to grow into bad habits; bad habits must undermine good, and often repeated acts make us habitually evil: so that by gradual depravations, and while we are but staggeringly evil, we are not left without parenthesis of considerations, thoughtful rebukes, and merciful interventions, to recall us unto ourselves. For the wisdom of God hath methodized the course of things unto the best advantage of goodness, and thinking considerators overlook not the tract thereof.

SECT. XXXI.—Since men and women have their proper virtues and vices; and even twins of different sexes have not only distinct coverings in the womb, but differing qualities

---

[3] *Socrates and Cardan.*] Socrates and Cardan, perhaps in imitation of him, talked of an attendant spirit or genius, that hinted from time to time how they should act.—*Dr. J.*

[4] *tropics.*] The tropic is the point where the sun turns back.—*Dr. J.*

[5] *Asphaltick lake.*] The lake of Sodom; the waters of which being very salt, and therefore heavy, will scarcely suffer an animal to sink.—*Dr. J.*

[6] *Rubicon.*] The river, by crossing which Cæsar declared war against the senate.—*Dr. J.*

and virtuous habits after; transplace not their proprieties, and confound not their distinctions. Let masculine and feminine accomplishments shine in their proper orbs, and adorn their respective subjects. However, unite not the vices of both sexes in one; be not monstrous in iniquity, nor hermaphroditically vicious.

SECT. XXXII.—If generous honesty, valour, and plain dealing be the cognisance of thy family, or characteristic of thy country, hold fast such inclinations sucked in with thy first breath, and which lay in the cradle with thee. Fall not into transforming degenerations, which under the old name create a new nation. Be not an alien in thine own nation; bring not Orontes into Tiber;[7] learn the virtues not the vices of thy foreign neighbours, and make thy imitation by discretion not contagion. Feel something of thyself in the noble acts of thy ancestors, and find in thine own genius that of thy predecessors. Rest not under the expired merits of others, shine by those of thy own. Flame not like the central fire which enlighteneth no eyes, which no man seeth, and most men think there's no such thing to be seen. Add one ray unto the common lustre; add not only to the number but the note of thy generation; and prove not a cloud but an asterisk[8] in thy region.

SECT. XXXIII.—Since thou hast an alarum[9] in thy breast, which tells thee thou hast a living spirit in thee above two thousand times in an hour; dull not away thy days in slothful supinity and the tediousness of doing nothing. To strenuous minds there is an inquietude in over quietness, and no laboriousness in labour; and to tread a mile after the slow pace of a snail, or the heavy measures of the lazy of Brazilia,[1] were a most tiring penance, and worse than a race of some furlongs at the Olympics.[2] The rapid courses of the heavenly bodies are

---

[7] *Orontes into Tiber.*] In Tiberim defluxit Orontes: "Orontes has mingled her stream with the Tiber," says Juvenal, speaking of the confluence of foreigners to Rome.—*Dr. J.*

[8] *asterisk.*] A small star.—*Dr. J.*

[9] *alarum.*] The motion of the heart, which beats about sixty times in a minute; or, perhaps, the motion of respiration, which is nearer to the number mentioned.—*Dr. J.*

[1] *lazy of Brazilia.*] An animal called more commonly the sloth, which is said to be several days in climbing a tree.—*Dr. J.*

[2] *Olympics.*] The Olympic games, of which the race was one of the chief.—*Dr. J.*

rather imitable by our thoughts, than our corporeal motions ; yet the solemn motions of our lives amount unto a greater measure than is commonly apprehended. Some few men have surrounded the globe of the earth ; yet many in the set locomotions and movements of their days have measured the circuit of it, and twenty thousand miles have been exceeded by them. Move circumspectly not meticulously,[3] and rather carefully solicitous than anxiously solicitudinous. Think not there is a lion in the way, nor walk with leaden sandals in the paths of goodness ; but in all virtuous motions let prudence determine thy measures. Strive not to run like Hercules, a furlong in a breath : festination may prove precipitation ; deliberating delay may be wise cunctation, and slowness no slothfulness.

SECT. XXXIV.—Since virtuous actions have their own trumpets, and, without any noise from thyself, will have their resound abroad ; busy not thy best member in the encomium of thyself. Praise is a debt we owe unto the virtues of others, and due unto our own from all, whom malice hath not made mutes, or envy struck dumb. Fall not, however, into the common prevaricating way of self-commendation and boasting, by denoting the imperfections of others. He who discommendeth others obliquely, commendeth himself. He who whispers their infirmities, proclaims his own exemption from them ; and, consequently, says, I am not as this publican, or *hic niger*,* whom I talk of. Open ostentation and loud vainglory is more tolerable than this obliquity, as but containing some froth, no ink, as but consisting of a personal piece of folly, nor complicated with uncharitableness.[4] Superfluously

---

* Hic niger est, hunc tu Romane caveto.—*Hor.*
This man is vile ; here, Roman, fix your mark ;
His soul is black, as his complexion's dark.—*Francis.*

---

[3] *meticulously.*] Timidly.—*Dr. J.*
[4] *uncharitableness.*] Add from *MS. Sloan.* 1847 :—" They who thus closely and whisperingly calumniate the absent living, will be apt to strayn their voyce and be apt to be loud enough in infamy of the dead ; wherein there should be a civil amnesty and an oblivion concerning those who are in a state where all things are forgotten ; but Solon will make us ashamed to speak evil of the dead, a crime not actionable in Christian governments, yet hath been prohibited by Pagan laws and the old sanctions of Athens. Many persons are like many rivers, whose mouths are at a vast distance from their heads, for their words are as far from their thoughts as Canopus from the head of Nilus. These are of the former of those men, whose punish-

we seek a precarious applause abroad : every good man hath his plaudit [5] within himself; and though his tongue be silent, is not without loud cymbals in his breast. Conscience will become his panegyrist, and never forget to crown and extol him unto himself.

SECT. XXXV.—Bless not thyself only that thou wert born in Athens ; * but, among thy multiplied acknowledgments, lift up one hand unto heaven, that thou wert born of honest parents; that modesty, humility, patience, and veracity, lay in the same egg, and came into the world with thee. From such foundations thou may'st be happy in a virtuous precocity,[6] and make an early and long walk in goodness ; so may'st thou more naturally feel the contrariety of vice unto nature, and resist some by the antidote of thy temper. As charity covers, so modesty preventeth a multitude of sins ; withholding from noon-day vices and brazen-browed iniquities, from sinning on the house-top, and painting our follies with the rays of the sun. Where this virtue reigneth, though vice may show its head, it cannot be in its glory. Where shame of sin sets, look not for virtue to arise ; for when modesty taketh wing, Astrea † goes soon after.

SECT. XXXVI.—The heroical vein of mankind runs much in the soldiery, and courageous part of the world ; and in that form we oftenest find men above men. History is full of the gallantry of that tribe ; and when we read their notable acts, we easily find what a difference there is between a a life in Plutarch [7] and in Laertius.[8] Where true fortitude dwells, loyalty, bounty, friendship, and fidelity may be found.

---

* As Socrates did. Athens a place of learning and civility.
† Astrea, goddess of justice and consequently of all virtue.

ment in Dante's hell is to look everlastingly backward : if you have a mind to laugh at a man, or disparage the judgement of any one, set him a talking of things to come or events of hereafter contingency ; which elude the cognition of such an arrogate, the knowledge of them whereto the ignorant pretend not, and the learned imprudently faill ; wherein men seem to talk but as babes would do in the womb of their mother, of the things of the world which they are entering into.

[5] *plaudit.*] *Plaudite* was the term by which the ancient theatrical performers solicited a clap.—*Dr. J.*

[6] *precocity.*] A ripeness preceding the usual time.—*Dr. J.*

[7] *Plutarch.*] Who wrote the lives, for the most part, of warriors.—*Dr. J.*

[8] *Laertius.*] Who wrote the lives of philosophers.—*Dr. J.*

A man may confide in persons constituted for noble ends, who dare do and suffer, and who have a hand to burn for their country and their friend.[9] Small and creeping things are the product of petty souls. He is like to be mistaken, who makes choice of a covetous man for a friend, or relieth upon the reed of narrow and poltroon friendship. Pitiful things are only to be found in the cottages of such breasts; but bright thoughts, clear deeds, constancy, fidelity, bounty, and generous honesty are the gems of noble minds; wherein, to derogate from none, the true heroic English gentleman hath no peer.

PART THE SECOND.

SECT. I.—Punish not thyself with pleasure; glut not thy sense with palative delights; nor revenge the contempt of temperance by the penalty of satiety. Were there an age of delight or any pleasure durable, who would not honour Volupia? but the race of delight is short, and pleasures have mutable faces. The pleasures of one age are not pleasures in another, and their lives fall short of our own. Even in our sensual days, the strength of delight is in its seldomness or rarity,[1] and sting in its satiety: mediocrity is its life, and immoderacy its confusion. The luxurious emperors of old inconsiderately satiated themselves with the dainties of sea and land, till, wearied through all varieties, their refections became a study unto them, and they were fain to feed by invention: novices in true epicurism! which, by mediocrity, paucity, quick and healthful appetite, makes delights smartly acceptable; whereby Epicurus himself found Jupiter's brain in a piece of Cytheridian cheese,* and the tongues of nightingales in a dish of onions.[2] Hereby healthful and temperate poverty

---

* *Cerebrum Jovis*, for a delicious bit.

[9] *and their friend.*] Like Mutius Scævola.—*Dr. J.*

[1] *the strength, &c.*] Voluptates commendat rarior usus.—*Dr. J.*

[2] *tongues of nightingales, &c.*] A dish used among the luxurious of antiquity. —*Dr. J.*

hath the start of nauseating luxury; unto whose clear and naked appetite every meal is a feast, and in one single dish the first course of Metellus; [3*] who are cheaply hungry, and never lose their hunger, or advantage of a craving appetite, because obvious food contents it; while Nero,[†] half famished, could not feed upon a piece of bread, and, lingering after his snowed water, hardly got down an ordinary cup of Calda.[4‡] By such circumscriptions of pleasure the contemned philosophers reserved unto themselves the secret of delight, which the helluos[5] of those days lost in their exorbitances. In vain we study delight; it is at the command of every sober mind, and in every sense born with us: but nature, who teacheth us the rule of pleasure, instructeth also in the bounds thereof, and where its line expireth. And, therefore, temperate minds, not pressing their pleasures until the sting appeareth, enjoy their contentations contentedly, and without regret, and so escape the folly of excess, to be pleased unto displacency.

SECT. II.—Bring candid eyes unto the perusal of men's works, and let not Zoilism[6] or detraction blast well-intended labours. He that endureth no faults in men's writings must only read his own, wherein, for the most part, all appeareth white. Quotation mistakes, inadvertency, expedition, and human lapses, may make not only moles but warts in learned authors; who, notwithstanding, being judged by the capital matter, admit not of disparagement. I should unwillingly affirm that Cicero was but slightly versed in Homer, because in his work, *De Gloria,* he ascribed those verses unto Ajax, which were delivered by Hector. What if Plautus, in the account of Hercules, mistaketh nativity for conception? Who would have mean thoughts of Apollinaris Sidonius, who seems to mistake the river Tigris for Euphrates? and, though a good historian and learned bishop of Avergne, had the mis-

---

* His riotous pontifical supper, the great variety whereat is to be seen in Macrobius.
    † Nero, in his flight.   ‡ Caldæ gelidæque minister.

[3] *Metellus.*] The supper was not given by Metellus, but by Lentulus when he was made priest of Mars, and recorded by Metellus.—*Dr. J.*

[4] *Calda.*] Warm water —*Dr. J.*
[5] *Helluo's.*] Gluttons.—*Dr. J.*
[6] *Zoilism, &c.*] From Zoilus, the calumniator of Homer.—*Dr. J.*

fortune to be out in the story of David, making mention of him when the ark was sent back by the Philistines upon a cart; which was before his time. Though I have no great opinion of Machiavel's learning, yet I shall not presently say that he was but a novice in Roman history, because he was mistaken in placing Commodus after the Emperor Severus. Capital truths are to be narrowly eyed; collateral lapses and circumstantial deliveries not to be too strictly sifted. And if the substantial subject be well forged out, we need not examine the sparks which irregularly fly from it.

Sect. III.—Let well-weighed considerations, not stiff and peremptory assumptions, guide thy discourses, pen, and actions. To begin or continue our works like Trismegistus of old, "*verum certe verum atque verissimum est,*"[7] * would sound arrogantly unto present ears in this strict enquiring age; wherein, for the most part, 'probably' and 'perhaps' will hardly serve to mollify the spirit of captious contradictors. If Cardan saith that a parrot is a beautiful bird, Scaliger will set his wits to work to prove it a deformed animal. The compage of all physical truths is not so closely jointed, but opposition may find intrusion; nor always so closely maintained, as not to suffer attrition. Many positions seem quodlibetically[8] constituted, and, like a Delphian blade, will cut on both sides.[9] Some truths seem almost falsehoods, and some falsehoods almost truths; wherein falsehood and truth seem almost æquilibriously stated, and but a few grains of distinction to bear down the balance. Some have digged deep, yet glanced by the royal vein;[1] and a man may come unto the pericardium,[2] but not the heart of truth. Besides, many things are known, as some are seen, that is by parallaxis,[3] or at some distance from their true and proper beings, the superficial re-

* In Tabula Smaragdina.

[7] *verum certe, &c.*] It is true, certainly true, true in the highest degree. —*Dr. J.*

[8] *quodlibetically.*] Determinable on either side.—*Dr. J.*

[9] *like a Delphian blade, &c.*] The Delphian sword became proverbial, not because it cut on both sides, but because it was used to different purposes.—*Dr. J.*

[1] *royal vein.*] I suppose the main vein of a mine.—*Dr. J.*

[2] *pericardium.*] The integument of the heart.—*Dr. J.*

[3] *parallaxis.*] The parallax of a star is the difference between its real and apparent place.—*Dr. J.*

gard of thingshaving a different aspect from their true and
central natures. And this moves sober pens unto suspensory
and timorous assertions, nor presently to obtrude them as
Sibyl's leaves,[4] which after considerations may find to be but
folious appearances, and not the central and vital interiors of
truth.

SECT. IV.—Value the judicious, and let not mere acquests
in minor parts of learning gain thy pre-existimation. 'Tis an
unjust way of compute, to magnify a weak head for some
Latin abilities; and to undervalue a solid judgment, because
he knows not the genealogy of Hector. When that notable
king of France* would have his son to know but one sentence
in Latin; had it been a good one, perhaps it had been enough.
Natural parts and good judgments rule the world. States
are not governed by ergotisms.[5] Many have ruled well, who
could not, perhaps, define a commonwealth; and they who
understand not the globe of the earth, command a great part
of it. Where natural logic prevails not, artificial too often
faileth. Where nature fills the sails, the vessel goes smoothly
on; and when judgment is the pilot, the ensurance need not
be high. When industry builds upon nature, we may expect
pyramids: where that foundation is wanting, the structure
must be low. They do most by books, who could do much
without them; and he that chiefly owes himself unto himself,
is the substantial man.

SECT. V.—Let thy studies be free as thy thoughts and contemplations: but fly not only upon the wings of imagination;
join sense unto reason, and experiment unto speculation, and
so give life unto embryon truths, and verities yet in their chaos.
There is nothing more acceptable unto the ingenious world,
than this noble eluctation[6] of truth; wherein, against the
tenacity of prejudice and prescription, this century now pre-
vaileth. What libraries of new volumes aftertimes will behold, and in what a new world of knowledge the eyes of our
posterity may be happy, a few ages may joyfully declare; and

---

* Lewis the Eleventh.   Qui nescit dissimulare nescit regnare.

[4] *Sibyl's leaves.*] On which the Sybil   according to the forms of logic.—*Dr. J.*
wrote her oraculous answers.—*Virgil.*   [6] *eluctation.*] Forcible eruption.—
[5] *ergotisms.*] Conclusions deduced   *Dr. J.*

is but a cold thought unto those who cannot hope to behold this exantlation of truth, or that obscured virgin half out of the pit: which might make some content with a commutation of the time of their lives, and to commend the fancy of the Pythagorean metempsychosis;[7] whereby they might hope to enjoy this happiness in their third or fourth selves, and behold that in Pythagoras, which they now but foresee in Euphorbus.* The world, which took but six days to make, is like to take six thousand to make out: meanwhile, old truths voted down begin to resume their places, and new ones arise upon us; wherein there is no comfort in the happiness of Tully's Elisium,† or any satisfaction from the ghosts of the ancients, who knew so little of what is now well known. Men disparage not antiquity, who prudently exalt new enquiries; and make not them the judges of truth, who were but fellow enquirers of it. Who can but magnify the endeavours of Aristotle, and the noble start which learning had under him; or less than pity the slender progression made upon such advantages? while many centuries were lost in repetitions and transcriptions, sealing up the book of knowledge. And, therefore, rather than to swell the leaves of learning by fruitless repetitions, to sing the same song in all ages, nor adventure at essays beyond the attempt of others, many would be content that some would write like Helmont or Paracelsus ;[8] and be willing to endure the monstrosity of some opinions, for divers singular notions requiting such aberrations.

SECT. VI.—Despise not the obliquities of younger ways, nor despair of better things whereof there is yet no prospect. Who would imagine that Diogenes, who in his younger days was a falsifier of money, should in the after-course of his life be so great a contemner of metal? Some negroes who believe the resurrection, think that they shall rise white.‡ Even in this life, regeneration may imitate resurrection; our black

---

* Ipse ego, nam memini, Trojani tempore belli,
　　Panthoides Euphorbus eram.—OVID.
† Who comforted himself that he should there converse with the old philosophers.
　　‡ Mandelslo's travels.

[7] *Pythagorean metempsychosis.*]Transmigration of the soul from body to body.—*Dr. J.*

[8] *Helmont or Paracelsus.*] Wild and enthusiastic authors of romantic chymistry—*Dr. J.*

and vicious tinctures may wear off, and goodness clothe us with candour. Good admonitions knock not always in vain. There will be signal examples of God's mercy, and the angels must not want their charitable rejoices for the conversion of lost sinners. Figures of most angles do nearest approach unto circles which have no angles at all. Some may be near unto goodness, who are conceived far from it; and many things happen, not likely to ensue from any promises of ante-cedencies. Culpable beginnings have found commendable conclusions, and infamous courses pious retractations. Detestable sinners have proved exemplary converts on earth, and may be glorious in the apartment of Mary Magdalen in heaven. Men are not the same through all divisions of their ages: time, experience, self-reflections, and God's mercies, make in some well-tempered minds a kind of translation before death, and men to differ from themselves as well as from other persons. Hereof the old world afforded many examples, to the infamy of latter ages, wherein men too often live by the rule of their inclinations; so that, without any astral prediction, the first day gives the last :* men are commonly as they were: or rather, as bad dispositions run into worser habits, the evening doth not crown, but sourly conclude the day.

SECT. VII.—If the Almighty will not spare us according to his merciful capitulation at Sodom; if his goodness please not to pass over a great deal of bad for a small pittance of good, or to look upon us in the lump; there is slender hope for mercy, or sound presumption of fulfilling half his will, either in persons or nations: they who excel in some virtues being so often defective in others; few men driving at the extent and amplitude of goodness, but computing themselves by their best parts, and others by their worst, are content to rest in those virtues which others commonly want. Which makes this speckled face of honesty in the world; and which was the imperfection 9 of the old philosophers and great pre-

---

* Primusque dies dedit extremum.

9 *few men, &c.*] Instead of this passage, I find the following in *MS. Sloan.* 1874 :—" Persons, sects, and nations, mainly settling upon some Christian particulars, which they conceive most acceptable unto God, and

tenders unto virtue, who well declining the gaping vices of intemperance, incontinency, violence and oppression, were yet blindly peccant in iniquities of closer faces, were envious, malicious, contemners, scoffers, censurers, and stuffed with vizard vices, no less depraving the ethereal particle and diviner portion of man. For envy, malice, hatred, are the qualities of Satan, close and dark like himself; and where such brands smoke, the soul cannot be white. Vice may be had at all prices; expensive and costly iniquities, which make the noise, cannot be every man's sins: but the soul may be foully inquinated[1] at a very low rate; and a man may be cheaply vicious, to the perdition of himself.

Sect. viii.—Opinion rides upon the neck of reason; and men are happy, wise, or learned, according as that empress shall set them down in the register of reputation. However, weigh not thyself in the scales of thy own opinion, but let the judgment of the judicious be the standard of thy merit. Self estimation is a flatterer too readily intitling us unto knowledge and abilities, which others solicitously labour after, and doubtfully think they attain. Surely such confident tempers do pass their days in best tranquillity, who resting in the opinion of their own abilities, are happily gulled by such contentation; wherein pride, self-conceit, confidence, and opiniatry, will hardly suffer any to complain of imperfection. To think themselves in the right, or all that right, or only that, which they do or think, is a fallacy of high content; though others laugh in their sleeves, and look upon them as in a deluded state of judgment: wherein, notwithstanding, 'twere but a civil piece of complacency to suffer them to sleep who would not wake, to let them rest in their securities, nor by dissent or opposition to stagger their contentments.

---

promoting the interest of their inclinations, parties, and divisions; every one reckoning and preferring himself by the particulars wherein he excelleth, and decrying all others, though highly eminent in other Christian virtues. Which makes this speckled face of honesty in the world; whereas, if men would not seek themselves abroad; if every one would judge and reckon himself by his worst, and others by their best parts, this deception must needs vanish; humility would gain ground; charity would overspread the face of the church, and the fruits of the spirit not be so thinly found among us.

" This was the imperfection, &c."

[1] *inquinated.*] Defiled.—*Dr. J.*

SECT. IX.[2]—Since the brow speaks often truth, since eyes and noses have tongues, and the countenance proclaims the heart and inclinations; let observation so far instruct thee in physiognomical lines, as to be some rule for thy distinction, and guide for thy affection unto such as look most like men. Mankind, methinks, is comprehended in a few faces, if we exclude all visages which any way participate of symmetries and schemes of look common unto other animals. For as though man were the extract of the world, in whom all were "in coagulato,"[3] which in their forms were "in soluto"[4] and at extension; we often observe that men do most act those creatures, whose constitution, parts, and complexion, do most predominate in their mixtures. This is a corner stone in physiognomy, and holds some truth not only in particular persons but also in whole nations. There are, therefore, provincial faces, national lips and noses, which testify not only the natures of those countries, but of those which have them elsewhere. Thus we may make England the whole earth, dividing it not only into Europe, Asia, Africa, but the particular regions thereof; and may in some latitude affirm, that there are Egyptians, Scythians, Indians among us, who, though born in England, yet carry the faces and air of those countries, and are also agreeable and correspondent unto their natures. Faces look uniformly unto our eyes: how they appear unto some animals of a more piercing or differing sight, who are able to discover the inequalities, rubs, and hairiness of the skin, is not without good doubt: and, therefore, in reference unto man, Cupid is said to be blind. Affection should not be too sharp-eyed, and love is not to be made by magnifying glasses. If things were seen as they truly are, the beauty of bodies would be much abridged. And, therefore, the wise contriver hath drawn the pictures and outsides of things softly and amiably unto the natural edge of our eyes, not leaving them able to discover those uncomely asperities, which make oyster-shells in good faces, and hedgehogs even in Venus's moles.

---

[2] SECT. IX.—This is a very fanciful and indefensible section.—*Dr. J.*

[3] were "*in coagulato.*"] i. e. "In a congealed or compressed mass."—*Dr. J.*

[4] *in soluto.*] "In a state of expansion and separation."—*Dr. J.*

SECT. X.—Court not felicity too far, and weary not the favourable hand of fortune. Glorious actions have their times, extent, and non ultras. To put no end unto attempts were to make prescription of successes, and to bespeak unhappiness at the last: for the line of our lives is drawn with white and black vicissitudes, wherein the extremes hold seldom one complexion. That Pompey should obtain the surname of great at twenty-five years, that men in their young and active days should be fortunate and perform notable things, is no observation of deep wonder; they having the strength of their fates before them, nor yet acted their parts in the world for which they were brought into it; whereas men of years, matured for counsels and designs, seem to be beyond the vigour of their active fortunes, and high exploits of life, providentially ordained unto ages best agreeable unto them. And, therefore, many brave men finding their fortune grow faint, and feeling its declination, have timely withdrawn themselves from great attempts, and so escaped the ends of mighty men, disproportionable to their beginnings.[5] But magnanimous thoughts have so dimmed the eyes of many, that forgetting the very essence of fortune, and the vicissitude of good and evil, they apprehend no bottom in felicity; and so have been still tempted on unto mighty actions, reserved for their destructions. For fortune lays the plot of our adversities in the foundation of our felicities, blessing us in the first quadrate,[6] to blast us more sharply in the last. And since in the highest felicities there lieth a capacity of the lowest miseries, she hath this advantage from our happiness to make us truly miserable: for to become acutely miserable we are to be first happy. Affliction smarts most in the most happy state, as having somewhat in it of Belisarius at beggar's bush, or Bajazet in the

---

[5] *beginnings.*] *MS. Sloan.* 1874, proceeds thus :—" Wisely stopping about the meridian of their felicities, and unwilling to hazard the favours of the descending wheel, or to fight downward in the setting arch of fortune. " Sic longius ævium destruit ingentes animos, et vita superstes fortunæ, nisi summa dies cum fine bonorum affluit, et celeri prævertit tristia letho dedecori est fortuna prior quisquam ne secundis tradere se fatis audet nisi morte parcitâ.—*Lucan* 7."

[6] *quadrate, &c.*] That is, " in the first part of our time," alluding to the four quadratures of the moon.—*Dr. J.*

grate.[7]   And this the fallen angels severely understand ; who have acted their first part in heaven, are made sharply miserable by transition, and more afflictively feel the contrary state of hell.[8]

SECT. XI.—Carry no careless eye upon the unexpected scenes of things ; but ponder the acts of providence in the public ends of great and notable men, set out unto the view of all for no common memorandums.[9]   The tragical exits and unexpected periods of some eminent persons, cannot but amaze considerate observators ; wherein, notwithstanding, most men seem to see by extramission,[1] without reception or self-reflection, and conceive themselves unconcerned by the fallacy of their own exemption : whereas, the mercy of God hath singled out but few to be the signals of his justice,

---

[7] *Bellisarius, &c.*] Bellisarius, after he had gained many victories, is said to have been reduced, by the displeasure of the emperor, to actual beggary : Bajazet, made captive by Tamerlane, is reported to have been shut up in a cage. It may somewhat gratify those who deserve to be gratified, to inform them that both these stories are false.—*Dr. J.*

Lord Mahon, in his recent life of Bellisarius, has related the mendicity and loss of sight of this great man, and says in his preface that those facts, "which every writer for the last century and half has treated as a fable, may be established on firm historical grounds."

[8] *And this the fallen angels, &c.*] Instead of this passage, I find the following in *MS. Sloan.* 1874 :—" And this is the observable course ; not only in this visible stage of things, but may be feared in our second beings and everlasting selves ; wherein the good things past are seconded by the bad to come : and many to whom the embraces of fortune are open here, may find Abraham's arms shut unto him hereafter ; which wakes serious consideration, not so much to pity as envy some men's infelicities, wherein, considering the circle of both our beings, and the succession of good unto evil, tyranny may sometimes prove courteous, and malice mercifully cruel. Wherein, notwithstanding, if swelling beginnings have found uncomfortable conclusions, it is by the method and justice of providence equalizing one with the other, and re-

ducing the sum of the whole unto a mediocrity by the balance of extremities : that in the sum the felicities of great ones hold a truth and parity with most that are below them : whereby the minor favourites of fortune which incur not such sharp transitions, have no cause to whine, nor men of middle fates to murmur at their indifferences.

"By this method of providence the devil himself is deluded ; who maligning us at all points, and bearing felicity from us even in this earthly being, he becomes assistant unto our future happiness, and blessed vicissitude of the next. And this is also the unhappiness of himself, who having acted his first part in heaven, is made sharply miserable by transition, and more afflictively feels the contrary state of hell."

[9] *memorandums.*] This sentence is thus continued in *MS. Sloan.* 1874 :— "Whereof I, that have not seen the sixtieth part of time, have beheld great examples. Than the incomparable Montrose, no man acted a more fortunate part in the first scene of his adventures ; but courageous loyalty continuing his attempts, he quickly felt that fortune's favours were out ; and fell upon miseries smartly answering his felicities, which was the only accomplishment wanting before to make him fit for Plutarch's pen, and to parallel the lives of his heroic captains."

[1] *extramission.*] By the passage of sight from the eye to the object.—*Dr. J.*

leaving the generality of mankind to the pædagogy of example. But the inadvertency of our natures not well apprehending this favourable method and merciful decimation,[2] and that he sheweth in some what others also deserve; they entertain no sense of his hand beyond the stroke of themselves. Whereupon the whole becomes necessarily punished, and the contracted hand of God extended unto universal judgments: from whence, nevertheless, the stupidity of our tempers receives but faint impressions, and in the most tragical state of times holds but starts of good motions. So that to continue us in goodness there must be iterated returns of misery, and a circulation in afflictions is necessary.[3] And since we cannot be wise by warnings; since plagues are insignificant, except we be personally plagued; since also we cannot be punished unto amendment by proxy or commutation, nor by vicinity, but contraction; there is an unhappy necessity that we must smart in our own skins, and the provoked arm of the Almighty must fall upon ourselves. The capital sufferings of others are rather our monitions than acquitments. There is but one who died salvifically [4] for us, and able to say unto death, hitherto shalt thou go and no farther; only one enlivening death, which makes gardens of graves, and that which was sowed in corruption to arise and flourish in glory: when death itself shall die, and living shall have no period; when the damned shall mourn at the funeral of death; when life not death shall be the wages of sin; when the

---

[2] *decimation.*] The selection of every tenth man for punishment, a practice sometimes used in general mutinies.—Dr. J.

[3] *necessary.*] The following passage occurs here in *MS. Sloan.* 1874:— "Which is the amazing part of that incomprehensible patience, to condescend to act over these vicissitudes even in the despair of our betterments: and how that omnipotent spirit that would not be exasperated by our forefathers above 1600 years, should thus lastingly endure our successive transgressions, and still contend with flesh; or how he can forgive those sins which will be committed again, and accept of repentances, which must have after-penitences, is the riddle of his mercies.

"If God had not determined a settled period unto the world, and ordered the duration thereof unto his merciful intentions, it seems a kind of impossibility that he should have thus long continued it. Some think there will be another world after this. Surely God, who hath beheld the iniquity of this, will hardly make another of the same nature; and some wonder why he ever made any at all since he was so happy in himself without it, and self-sufficiently free from all provocation, wrath, and indignation, arising from this world, which sets his justice and his mercy at perpetual contention."

[4] *salvifically.*] "So as to procure salvation."—Dr. J.

second death shall prove a miserable life, and destruction shall be courted.

SECT XII.—Although their thoughts may seem too severe, who think that few ill-natured men go to heaven; yet it may be acknowledged that good-natured persons are best founded for that place; who enter the world with good dispositions and natural graces, more ready to be advanced by impressions from above, and christianized unto pieties; who carry about them plain and downright dealing minds, humility, mercy, charity, and virtues acceptable unto God and man. But whatever success they may have as to heaven, they are the acceptable men on earth, and happy is he who hath his quiver full of them for his friends. These are not the dens wherein falsehood lurks, and hypocrisy hides its head; wherein frowardness makes its nest; or where malice, hardheartedness, and oppression love to dwell; nor those by whom the poor get little, and the rich sometime lose all; men not of retracted looks, but who carry their hearts in their faces, and need not to be looked upon with perspectives; not sordidly or mischievously ingrateful; who cannot learn to ride upon the neck of the afflicted, nor load the heavy laden, but who keep the temple of Janus[5] shut by peaceable and quiet tempers; who make not only the best friends, but the best enemies, as easier to forgive than offend, and ready to pass by the second offence before they avenge the first; who make natural royalists, obedient subjects, kind and merciful princes, verified in our own, one of the best-natured kings of this throne. Of the old Roman emperors the best were the best-natured: though they made but a small number, and might be writ in a ring. Many of the rest were as bad men as princes; humourists rather than good humours; and of good natural parts rather than of good natures, which did but arm their bad inclinations, and make them wittily wicked.

SECT. XIII.—With what shift and pains we come into the world, we remember not: but 'tis commonly found no easy matter to get out of it. Many have studied to exasperate the

---

[5] *Janus.*] The temple of Janus among the Romans was shut in time of peace, and opened at a declaration of war.— *Dr. J.*

ways of death, but fewer hours have been spent to soften that necessity. That the smoothest way unto the grave is made by bleeding, as common opinion presumeth, beside the sick and fainting languors, which accompany that effusion, the experiment in Lucan and Seneca [6] will make us doubt; under which the noble stoic so deeply laboured, that, to conceal his affliction, he was fain to retire from the sight of his wife, and not ashamed to implore the merciful hand of his physician to shorten his misery therein. Ovid,[*] the old heroes, and the stoics, who were so afraid of drowning, as dreading thereby the extinction of their soul, which they conceived to be a fire, stood probably in fear of an easier way of death; wherein the water, entering the possessions of air, makes a temperate suffocation, and kills as it were without a fever. Surely many, who have had the spirit to destroy themselves, have not been ingenious in the contrivance thereof. 'Twas a dull way practised by Themistocles, to overwhelm himself with bull's blood,[†] who, being an Athenian, might have held an easier theory of death from the state potion of his country; from which Socrates in Plato seemed not to suffer much more than from the fit of an ague. Cato is much to be pitied, who mangled himself with poniards; and Hannibal seems more subtle, who carried his delivery, not in the point but the pummel of his sword.[‡]

The Egyptians were merciful contrivers, who destroyed their malefactors by asps, charming their senses into an invincible sleep, and killing as it were with Hermes's rod.[7]

---

[*] Demito naufragium, mors mihi munus erit.

[†] Plutarch's lives.

[‡] Pummel, wherein he is said to have carried something whereby, upon a struggle or despair, he might deliver himself from all misfortunes.

Juvenal says it was carried in a ring:

> Cannarum vindex, et tanti sanguinis ultor,
> Annulus. ———

> Nor swords at hand, nor hissing darts afar,
> Are doom'd t' avenge the tedious bloody war,
> But poison drawn thro' a ring's hollow plate.—DRYDEN.

[6] *that the smoothest way unto the grave, &c.*] Seneca, having opened his veins, found the blood flow so slowly, and death linger so long, that he was forced to quicken it by going into a warm bath.—Dr. J.

[7] *rod.*] Which procured sleep by a touch.—Dr. J.

The Turkish emperor,* odious for other cruelty, was herein a remarkable master of mercy, killing his favourite in his sleep, and sending him from the shade into the house of darkness. He who had been thus destroyed would hardly have bled at the presence of his destroyer : when men are already dead by metaphor, and pass but from one sleep unto another, wanting herein the eminent part of severity, to feel themselves to die; and escaping the sharpest attendant of death, the lively apprehension thereof. But to learn to die, is better than to study the ways of dying. Death will find some ways to untie or cut the most gordian knots of life, and make men's miseries as mortal as themselves; whereas evil spirits, as undying substances, are inseparable from their calamities; and, therefore, they everlastingly struggle under their *angustias*,[8] and bound up with immortality can never get out of themselves.

PART THE THIRD.

SECT. I.—'Tis hard to find a whole age to imitate, or what century to propose for example. Some have been far more approvable than others; but virtue and vice, panegyrics and satires, scatteringly to be found in all. History sets down not only things laudable, but abominable; things which should never have been, or never have been known; so that noble patterns must be fetched here and there from single persons, rather than whole nations; and from all nations, rather than any one. The world was early bad, and the first sin the most deplorable of any. The younger world afforded the oldest men, and perhaps the best and the worst, when length of days made virtuous habits heroical and immovable, vicious, inveterate and irreclaimable. And since 'tis said that the imaginations of their hearts were evil, only evil, and continually evil; it may be feared that their sins held pace with

---

* Solyman.

[8] *angustias*.] Agonies.—*Dr. J.*

their lives; and their longevity swelling their impieties, the longanimity of God would no longer endure such vivacious abominations. Their impieties were surely of a deep dye, which required the whole element of water to wash them away, and overwhelmed their memories with themselves; and so shut up the first windows of time, leaving no histories of those longevous generations, when men might have been properly historians, when Adam might have read long lectures unto Methuselah, and Methuselah unto Noah. For had we been happy in just historical accounts of that unparalleled world, we might have been acquainted with wonders; and have understood not a little of the acts and undertakings of Moses's mighty men, and men of renown of old; which might have enlarged our thoughts, and made the world older unto us. For the unknown part of time shortens the estimation, if not the compute of it. What hath escaped our knowledge, falls not under our consideration; and what is and will be latent, is little better than non-existent.[9]

SECT. II.—Some things are dictated for our instruction, some acted for our imitation; wherein 'tis best to ascend unto the highest conformity, and to the honour of the exemplar. He honours God, who imitates him; for what we virtuously imitate we approve and admire: and since we delight not to imitate inferiors, we aggrandize and magnify those we imitate; since also we are most apt to imitate those we love, we testify our affection in our imitation of the inimitable. To affect to be like, may be no imitation: to act, and not to be what we pretend to imitate, is but a mimical conformation, and carrieth no virtue in it. Lucifer imitated not God, when he said he would be like the highest; and he[1] imitated not Jupiter, who counterfeited thunder. Where imitation can go no farther, let admiration step on, whereof there is no end in the wisest form of men. Even angels and spirits have enough to admire in their sublimer natures; admiration being the act of the creature, and not of God, who doth not admire himself. Created natures allow of swelling hyperboles: nothing can be

---

[9] *non-existent.*] This sentence concludes thus:—"The world is not half itself, nor the moiety known of its occurrences, of what hath been acted."—*MS. Sloan.* 1848.

[1] *he.*] Salmoneus.—*Dr. J.*

said hyperbolically of God, nor will his attributes admit of expressions above their own exuperances.[2] Trismegistus's circle, whose centre is every where, and circumference no where, was no hyperbole. Words cannot exceed where they cannot express enough. Even the most winged thoughts fall at the setting out, and reach not the portal of divinity.

SECT. III.—In bivious theorems,[3] and Janus-faced doctrines, let virtuous considerations state the determination. Look upon opinions as thou dost upon the moon, and choose not the dark hemisphere for thy contemplation. Embrace not the opacous and blind side of opinions, but that which looks most luciferously or influentially unto goodness. 'Tis better to think that there are guardian spirits, than that there are no spirits to guard us; that vicious persons are slaves, than that there is any servitude in virtue; that times past have been better than times present, than that times were always bad; and that to be men it sufficeth to be no better than men in all ages, and so promiscuously to swim down the turbid stream, and make up the grand confusion. Sow not thy understanding with opinions, which make nothing of iniquities, and fallaciously extenuate transgressions. Look upon vices and vicious objects with hyperbolical eyes; and rather enlarge their dimensions, that their unseen deformities may not escape thy sense, and their poisonous parts and stings may appear massy and monstrous unto thee: for the undiscerned particles and atoms of evil deceive us, and we are undone by the invisibles of seeming goodness. We are only deceived in what is not discerned, and to err is but to be blind or dimsighted as to some perceptions.

SECT. IV.—To be honest in a right line,* and virtuous by epitome, be firm unto such principles of goodness, as carry in them volumes of instruction and may abridge thy labour. And since instructions are many, hold close unto those, whereon the rest depend: so may we have all in a few, and

---

* Linea recta brevissima.

[2] *exuperances.*]   Exaggerations.—   which open different tracks to the mind;
Dr. J.   which lead *two ways.—Dr. J.*
   [3] *bivious theorems.*]   Speculations

the law and the prophets in sacred writ in stenography,[4] and the Scripture in a nut-shell. To pursue the osseous and solid part of goodness, which gives stability and rectitude to all the rest; to settle on fundamental virtues, and bid early defiance unto mother-vices, which carry in their bowels the seminals of other iniquities; makes a short cut in goodness, and strikes not off an head, but the whole neck of Hydra. For we are carried into the dark lake, like the Ægyptian river into the sea, by seven principal ostiaries : the mother-sins[5] of that number are the deadly engines of evil spirits that undo us, and even evil spirits themselves ; and he who is under the chains thereof is not without a possession. Mary Magdalen had more than seven devils, if these with their imps were in her; and he who is thus possessed, may literally be named " Legion." Where such plants grow and prosper, look for no champian or region void of thorns; but productions like the tree of Goa,* and forests of abomination.

SECT. v.—Guide not the hand of God, nor order the finger of the Almighty unto thy will and pleasure ; but sit quiet in the soft showers of providence, and favourable distributions in this world, either to thyself or others. And since not only judgments have their errands, but mercies their commissions ; snatch not at every favour, nor think thyself passed by if they fall upon thy neighbour. Rake not up envious displacencies at things successful unto others, which the wise disposer of all thinks not fit for thyself. Reconcile the events of things unto both beings, that is, of this world and the next; so will there not seem so many riddles in Providence, nor various inequalities in the dispensation of things below.[6] If thou dost

---

* Arbor Goa de Ruyz, or Ficus Indica, whose branches send down shoots which root in the ground, from whence there successively rise others, till one tree becomes a wood.

---

[4] *stenography.*]   In short hand.— *Dr. J.*

[5] *mother-sins.*]   Pride, covetousness, lust, envy, gluttony, anger, sloth.— *Dr. J.*

[6] *below.*]   The following passage occurs here from *MS. Sloan.* 1847. " So mayst thou carry a smooth face, and sit down in contentation, without those cancerous commotions which take up every suffering, displeasing at things successful unto others ; which the arch-disposer of all thinks not fit for ourselves. To rejoice only in thine [own] good, exclusively to that of others, is a stiff piece of self-love, wanting the supplying oil of benevolence and charity."

not anoint thy face, yet put not on sackcloth at the felicities of others. Repining at the good, draws on rejoicing at the evils of others: and so falls into that inhuman vice,* for which so few languages have a name. The blessed spirits above rejoice at our happiness below: but to be glad at the evils of one another, is beyond the malignity of hell; and falls not on evil spirits, who, though they rejoice at our unhappiness, take no pleasure at the afflictions of their own society or of their fellow natures. Degenerous heads! who must be fain to learn from such examples, and to be taught from the school of hell.

SECT. VI.—Grain not thy vicious stains; [7] nor deepen those swart tinctures, which temper, infirmity, or ill habits have set upon thee; and fix not, by iterated depravations, what time might efface, or virtuous washes expunge. He, who thus still advanceth in iniquity, deepeneth his deformed hue; turns a shadow into night, and makes himself a negro in the black jaundice; and so becomes one of those lost ones, the disproportionate pores of whose brains afford no entrance unto good motions, but reflect and frustrate all counsels, deaf unto the thunder of the laws, and rocks unto the cries of charitable commisserators. He who hath had the patience of Diogenes, to make orations unto statues, may more sensibly apprehend how all words fall to the ground, spent upon such a surd and earless generation of men, stupid unto all instruction, and rather requiring an exorcist than an orator for their conversion!

SECT. VII.—Burden not the back of Aries, Leo, or Taurus,[8] with thy faults; nor make Saturn, Mars, or Venus, guilty of thy follies. Think not to fasten thy imperfections on the stars, and so despairingly conceive thyself under a fatality of being evil. Calculate thyself within; seek not thyself in the moon, but in thine own orb or microcosmical circumference.[9] Let celestial aspects admonish and advertise, not conclude and determine thy ways. For since good and bad stars moralize

* 'Επιχαιρεκακία.

[7] *vicious stains.*] See note [5], page 63.—*Dr. J.*

[8] *Aries, &c.*] The Ram, Lion, or Bull, signs in the Zodiack. — *Dr. J.*

[9] *microcosmical circumference.*] In the compass of thy own little world.—*Dr. J.*

not our actions, and neither excuse or commend, acquit or condemn our good or bad deeds at the present or last bar; since some are astrologically well disposed, who are morally highly vicious; not celestial figures, but virtuous schemes, must denominate and state our actions. If we rightly understood the names whereby God calleth the stars; if we knew his name for the dog-star, or by what appellation Jupiter, Mars, and Saturn, obey his will; it might be a welcome accession unto astrology, which speaks great things, and is fain to make use of appellations from Greek and barbarick systems. Whatever influences, impulsions, or inclinations there be from the lights above, it were a piece of wisdom to make one of those wise men who overrule their stars,* and with their own militia contend with the host of heaven. Unto which attempt there want not auxiliaries from the whole strength of morality, supplies from Christian ethics, influences also and illuminations from above, more powerful than the lights of heaven.

SECT. VIII.—Confound not the distinctions of thy life which nature hath divided; that is, youth, adolescence, manhood, and old age: nor in these divided periods, wherein thou art in a manner four, conceive thyself but one. Let every division be happy in its proper virtues, nor one vice run through all. Let each distinction have its salutary transition, and critically deliver thee from the imperfections of the former; so ordering the whole, that prudence and virtue may have the largest section. Do as a child but when thou art a child, and ride not on a reed at twenty. He who hath not taken leave of the follies of his youth, and in his maturer state scarce got out of that division, disproportionately divideth his days, crowds up the latter part of his life, and leaves too narrow a corner for the age of wisdom; and so hath room to be a man scarce longer than he hath been a youth. Rather than to make this confusion, anticipate the virtues of age, and live long without the infirmities of it. So may'st thou count up thy days as some do Adam's; † that is, by anticipation; so may'st thou be coetaneous unto thy elders, and a father unto thy contemporaries.

* Sapiens dominabitur astris.
† Adam, thought to be created in the state of man, about thirty years old.

SECT. IX.—While others are curious in the choice of good air, and chiefly solicitous for healthful habitations, study thou conversation, and be critical in thy consortion. The aspects, conjunctions, and configurations of the stars, which mutually diversify, intend, or qualify their influences, are but the varieties of their nearer or farther conversation with one another, and like the consortion of men, whereby they become better or worse, and even exchange their natures. Since men live by examples, and will be imitating something, order thy imitation to thy improvement, not thy ruin. Look not for roses in Attalus's garden,* or wholesome flowers in a venomous plantation. And since there is scarce any one bad, but some others are the worse for him; tempt not contagion by proximity, and hazard not thyself in the shadow of corruption. He who hath not early suffered this shipwreck, and in his younger days escaped this Charybdis, may make a happy voyage, and not come in with black sails into the port.[1] Self-conversation, or to be alone, is better than such consortion. Some school-men tell us, that he is properly alone, with whom in the same place there is no other of the same species. Nebuchadnezzar was alone, though among the beasts of the field; and a wise man may be tolerably said to be alone, though with a rabble of people little better than beasts about him. Unthinking heads, who have not learned to be alone, are in a prison to themselves, if they be not also with others: whereas, on the contrary, they whose thoughts are in a fair, and hurry within, are sometimes fain to retire into company, to be out of the crowd of themselves. He who must needs have company, must needs have sometimes bad company. Be able to be alone. Lose not the advantage of solitude, and the society of thyself; nor be only content, but delight to be alone and single with Omnipresency. He who is thus prepared, the day is not uneasy nor the night black unto him. Darkness may bound his eyes, not his imagination. In his bed he may lie, like Pompey and his sons,† in all quarters of

* Attalus made a garden which contained only venomous plants.
† Pompeios Juvenes Asia atque Europa, sed ipsum Terra tegit Libyes.

[1] black sails, &c.] Alluding to the story of Theseus, who had black sails when he went to engage the Minotaur in Crete.—Dr. J.

the earth; may speculate the universe, and enjoy the whole world in the hermitage of himself. Thus the old Ascetick Christians found a paradise in a desert, and with little converse on earth held a conversation in heaven; thus they astronomized in caves, and, though they beheld not the stars, had the glory of heaven before them.

SECT. X.—Let the characters of good things stand indelibly in thy mind, and thy thoughts be active on them. Trust not too much unto suggestions from reminiscential amulets,[2] or artificial memorandums. Let the mortifying Janus of Covarrubias * be in thy daily thoughts, not only on thy hand and signets. Rely not alone upon silent and dumb remembrances. Behold not death's heads till thou dost not see them, nor look upon mortifying objects till thou overlookest them. Forget not how assuefaction unto any thing minorates the passion from it; how constant objects lose their hints, and steal an inadvertisement upon us. There is no excuse to forget what every thing prompts unto us. To thoughtful observators, the whole world is a phylactery;[3] and every thing we see an item of the wisdom, power, or goodness of God. Happy are they who verify their amulets, and make their phylacteries speak in their lives and actions. To run on in despite of the revulsions and pull-backs of such remoras aggravates our transgressions. When death's heads on our hands have no influence upon our heads, and fleshless cadavers abate not the exorbitances of the flesh; when crucifixes upon men's hearts suppress not their bad commotions, and his image who was murdered for us withholds not from blood and murder; phylacteries prove but formalities, and their despised hints sharpen our condemnation.

* Don Sebastian de Covarrubias writ three centuries of moral emblems in Spanish. In the 88th of the second century he sets down two faces averse, and conjoined Janus-like; the one, a gallant beautiful face, the other, a death's head face, with this motto out of Ovid's Metamorphoses:—

> Quid fuerim, quid simque, vide.
> ————————You discern
> What now I am, and what I was shall learn.—ADDIS.

[2] *reminiscential amulets.*] Any thing worn on the hand or body, by way of monition or remembrance.—*Dr. J.*

[3] *phylactery.*] See page 69, note [7]. —*Dr. J.*

SECT. XI.—Look not for whales in the Euxine sea, or expect great matters where they are not to be found. Seek not for profundity in shallowness, or fertility in a wilderness. Place not the expectations of great happiness here below, or think to find heaven on earth; wherein we must be content with embryon felicities, and fruitions of doubtful faces : for the circle of our felicities makes but short arches. In every clime we are in a periscian state;[4] and with our light, our shadow, and darkness walk about us. Our contentments stand upon the tops of pyramids ready to fall off, and the insecurity of their enjoyments abrupteth our tranquillities. What we magnify is magnificent; but, like to the Colossus, noble without, stuft with rubbage and coarse metal within. Even the sun, whose glorious outside we behold, may have dark and smoky entrails. In vain we admire the lustre of any thing seen: that which is truly glorious is invisible. Paradise was but a part of the earth, lost not only to our fruition but our knowledge. And if, according to old dictates, no man can be said to be happy before death, the happiness of this life goes for nothing before it be over, and while we think ourselves happy we do but usurp that name. Certainly, true beatitude groweth not on earth, nor hath this world in it the expectations we have of it. He swims in oil,[5] and can hardly avoid sinking, who hath such light foundations to support him : 'tis, therefore, happy that we have two worlds to hold on. To enjoy true happiness, we must travel into a very far country, and even out of ourselves; for the pearl we seek for is not to be found in the Indian but in the Empyrean ocean.[6]

SECT. XII.—Answer not the spur of fury, and be not prodigal or prodigious in revenge. Make not one in the *Historia Horribilis ;** flay not thy servant for a broken glass,[7] nor

* A book so intitled, wherein are sundry horrid accounts.

[4] *periscian state.*] "With shadows all around us." The Periscii are those who, living within the polar circle, see the sun move round them, and, consequently, project their shadows in all directions.— *Dr. J.*

[5] *He swims in oil.*] Which being a light fluid, cannot support any heavy body.—*Dr. J.*

[6] *Empyrean ocean.*] In the expanses of the highest heaven.—*Dr. J.*

[7] *flay not thy servant, &c.*] When Augustus supped with one of the Roman senators, a slave happened to break a

pound him in a mortar who offendeth thee;[8] supererogate
not in the worst sense, and overdo not the necessities of evil;
humour not the injustice of revenge. Be not stoically mistaken in the equality of sins, nor commutatively iniquitous
in the valuation of transgressions; but weigh them in the
scales of heaven, and by the weights of righteous reason.
Think that revenge too high, which is but level with the offence. Let thy arrows of revenge fly short; or be aimed
like those of Jonathan, to fall beside the mark. Too many
there be to whom a dead enemy smells well, and who find
musk and amber in revenge. The ferity of such minds holds
no rule in retaliations, requiring too often a head for a tooth,
and the supreme revenge for trespasses which a night's rest
should obliterate. But patient meekness takes injuries like
pills, not chewing but swallowing them down, laconically suffering, and silently passing them over; while angered pride
makes a noise, like Homerican Mars,* at every scratch of of-
fences. Since women do most delight in revenge,[9] it may
seem but feminine manhood to be vindictive. If thou must needs
have thy revenge of thine enemy, with a soft tongue break
his bones,† heap coals of fire on his head, forgive him and
enjoy it. To forgive our enemies is a charming way of revenge, and a short Cæsarian conquest overcoming without a
blow; laying our enemies at our feet, under sorrow, shame,
and repentance; leaving our foes our friends, and sollicitously
inclined to grateful retaliations. Thus to return upon our
adversaries, is a healing way of revenge; and to do good for

---

* Tu miser exclamas, ut Stentora vincere possis
 Vel potius quantum Gradivus Homericus.—Juv.
Thus translated by Creech :—
 You rage and storm, and, blasphemously loud,
 As Stentor bellowing to the Grecian crowd,
 Or Homer's Mars.————
† A soft tongue breaketh the bones.—Prov. xxv. 15.

glass, for which his master ordered him
to be thrown into his pond to feed his
lampreys. Augustus, to punish his cruelty, ordered all the glasses in the house
to be broken.—Dr. J.

 [8] *nor pound him in a mortar, &c.*]
Anaxarchus, an ancient philosopher, was
beaten in a mortar by a tyrant.—Dr. J.

[9] *Since women, &c.*]
————————Minuti
Semper et infirmi est animi exiguique voluptas
Ultio————Sic collige, quod vindictâ
Nemo magis gaudet, quam fœmina.—Juv.

————Revenge! which still we find
The weakest frailty of a feeble mind.
Degenerous passion, and for man too base,
It seats its empire in the female race.—Creech.

evil a soft and melting ultion, a method taught from heaven,[1]
to keep all smooth on earth.   Common forceable ways make
not an end of evil, but leave hatred and malice behind them.[2]
An enemy thus reconciled is little to be trusted, as wanting
the foundation of love and charity, and but for a time restrained by disadvantage or inability.   If thou hast not mercy
for others, yet be not cruel unto thyself.   To ruminate upon
evils, to make critical notes upon injuries, and be too acute in
their apprehensions, is to add unto our own tortures, to
feather the arrows of our enemies, to lash ourselves with the
scorpions of our foes, and to resolve to sleep no more; for
injuries long dreamt on, take away at last all rest; and he
sleeps but like Regulus, who busieth his head about them.

SECT. XIII.—Amuse not thyself about the riddles of future
things.   Study prophecies when they are become histories,
and past hovering in their causes.   Eye well things past and
present, and let conjectural sagacity suffice for things to
come.   There is a sober latitude for prescience in contingencies of discoverable tempers, whereby discerning heads see
sometimes beyond their eyes, and wise men become prophetical.   Leave cloudy predictions to their periods, and let appointed seasons have the lot of their accomplishments.   'Tis
too early to study such prophecies before they have been
long made, before some train of their causes have already
taken fire, lay open in part what lay obscure and before
buried unto us.   For the voice of prophecies is like that of
whispering-places : they who are near, or at a little distance,
hear nothing; those at the farthest extremity will understand
all.   But a retrograde cognition of times past, and things
which have already been, is more satisfactory than a suspended knowledge of what is yet unexistent.   And the greatest
part of time being already wrapt up in things behind us; it's
now somewhat late to bait after things before us; for futurity
still shortens, and time present sucks in time to come.   What
is prophetical in one age proves historical in another, and so
must hold on unto the last of time ; when there will be no room

<hr/>

[1] *from heaven.*] " Not to be learned
elsewhere."—*MS. Sloan.* 1847.
[2] *behind them.*] "Quiet one party,
but leave unquietness in the other,—of a
seeming friend making but a close ad-
versary.."—*MS. Sloan.* 1847.

for prediction, when Janus shall lose one face, and the long beard of time shall look like those of David's servants, shorn away upon one side; and when, if the expected Elias should appear, he might say much of what is past, not much of what's to come.

SECT. XIV.—Live unto the dignity of thy nature, and leave it not disputable at last, whether thou hast been a man; or, since thou art a composition of man and beast, how thou hast predominantly passed thy days, to state the denomination. Un-man not, therefore, thyself by a bestial transformation, nor realize old fables. Expose not thyself by four-footed manners unto monstrous draughts, and caricature representations. Think not after the old Pythagorean conceit, what beast thou may'st be after death. Be not under any brutal metempsychosis, [3] while thou livest and walkest about erectly under the scheme of man. In thine own circumference, as in that of the earth, let the rational horizon be larger than the sensible, and the circle of reason than of sense: let the divine part be upward, and the region of beast below; otherwise, 't is but to live invertedly, and with thy head unto the heels of thy antipodes. Desert not thy title to a divine particle and union with invisibles. Let true knowledge and virtue tell the lower world thou art a part of the higher. Let thy thoughts be of things which have not entered into the hearts of beasts: think of things long past, and long to come: acquaint thyself with the choragium [4] of the stars, and consider the vast expansion beyond them. Let intellectual tubes give thee a glance of things which visive organs reach not. Have a glimpse of incomprehensibles; and thoughts of things, which thoughts but tenderly touch. Lodge immaterials in thy head; ascend unto invisibles; fill thy spirit with spirituals, with the mysteries of faith, the magnalities of religion, and thy life with the honour of God; without which, though giants in wealth and dignity, we are but dwarfs and pygmies in humanity, and may hold a pitiful rank in that triple division of mankind into heroes, men, and beasts. For though human souls are said to be equal, yet is there no small inequality in their operations;

[3] *metempsychosis, &c.*] See page 83, note [7].—*Dr. J.*   [4] *choragium.*] Dance.—*Dr. J.*

some maintain the allowable station of men; many are far below it; and some have been so divine, as to approach the apogeum[5] of their natures, and to be in the confinium of spirits.

SECT. XV.—Behold thyself by inward opticks and the crystalline of thy soul.[6] Strange it is, that in the most perfect sense there should be so many fallacies, that we are fain to make a doctrine, and often to see by art. But the greatest imperfection is in our inward sight, that is, to be ghosts unto our own eyes; and while we are so sharp-sighted as to look through others, to be invisible unto ourselves; for the inward eyes are more fallacious than the outward. The vices we scoff at in others, laugh at us within ourselves. Avarice, pride, falsehood lie undiscerned and blindly in us, even to the age of blindness; and, therefore, to see ourselves interiorly, we are fain to borrow other men's eyes; wherein true friends are good informers, and censurers no bad friends. Conscience only, that can see without light, sits in the areopagy[7] and dark tribunal of our hearts, surveying our thoughts and condemning their obliquities. Happy is that state of vision that can see without light, though all should look as before the creation, when there was not an eye to see, or light to actuate a vision: wherein, notwithstanding, obscurity is only imaginable respectively unto eyes; for unto God there was none: eternal light was ever; created light was for the creation, not himself; and, as he saw before the sun, may still also see without it. In the city of the new Jerusalem there is neither sun nor moon; where glorified eyes must see by the archetypal sun,[8] or the light of God, able to illuminate intellectual eyes, and make unknown visions. Intuitive perceptions in spiritual beings may, perhaps, hold some analogy unto vision: but yet how they see us, or one another, what eye, what light, or what perception is required unto their intuition, is yet dark unto our apprehension; and even how they see God, or how unto our glorified eyes the beatifical vision will be celebrated, another

---

[5] apogeum, &c.] To the utmost point of distance from earth and earthly things.—Dr. J.

[6] crystalline, &c.] Alluding to the crystalline humour of the eye.—Dr. J.

[7] areopagy.] The great court, like the Areopagus of Athens.—Dr. J.

[8] archetypal sun.] Original.—Dr. J.

world must tell us, when perceptions will be new, and we may hope to behold invisibles.

SECT. XVI.—When all looks fair about, and thou seest not a cloud so big as a hand to threaten thee, forget not the wheel of things : think of sullen vicissitudes, but beat not thy brains to foreknow them. Be armed against such obscurities, rather by submission than fore-knowledge. The knowledge of future evils mortifies present felicities, and there is more content in the uncertainty or ignorance of them. This favour our Saviour vouchsafed unto Peter, when he foretold not his death in plain terms, and so by an ambiguous and cloudy delivery damped not the spirit of his disciples. But in the assured fore-knowledge of the deluge, Noah lived many years under the affliction of a flood; and Jerusalem was taken unto Jeremy, before it was besieged. And, therefore, the wisdom of astrologers, who speak of future things, hath wisely softened the severity of their doctrines ; and even in their sad predictions, while they tell us of inclination not coaction from the stars, they kill us not with Stygian oaths and merciless necessity, but leave us hopes of evasion.

SECT. XVII.—If thou hast the brow to endure the name of traitor, perjured, or oppressor, yet cover thy face when ingratitude is thrown at thee. If that degenerous vice possess thee, hide thyself in the shadow of thy shame, and pollute not noble society. Grateful ingenuities are content to be obliged within some compass of retribution; and being depressed by the weight of iterated favours, may so labour under their inabilities of requital, as to abate the content from kindnesses. But narrow self-ended souls make prescription of good offices, and obliged by often favours think others still due unto them : whereas, if they but once fail, they prove so perversely ungrateful, as to make nothing of former courtesies, and to bury all that's past. Such tempers pervert the generous course of things ; for they discourage the inclinations of noble minds, and make beneficency cool unto acts of obligation, whereby the grateful world should subsist, and have their consolation. Common gratitude must be kept alive by the additionary fuel of new courtesies: but generous gratitudes, though but once well obliged, without quickening repetitions or expectation of new favours, have thankful minds for ever; for they write not their obligations in sandy but marble memories, which wear not out but with themselves.

SECT. XVIII.—Think not silence the wisdom of fools; but, if rightly timed, the honour of wise men, who have not the infirmity, but the virtue of taciturnity; and speak not out of the abundance, but the well-weighed thoughts of their hearts. Such silence may be eloquence, and speak thy worth above the power of words. Make such a one thy friend, in whom princes may be happy, and great counsels successful. Let him have the key of thy heart, who hath the lock of his own, which no temptation can open; where thy secrets may lastingly lie, like the lamp in Olybius's urn,* alive, and light, but close and invisible.

SECT. XIX.—Let thy oaths be sacred, and promises be made upon the altar of thy heart. Call not Jove † to witness, with a stone in one hand, and a straw in another; and so make chaff and stubble of thy vows. Worldly spirits, whose interest is their belief, make cobwebs of obligations; and, if they can find ways to elude the urn of the Prætor,9 will trust the thunderbolt of Jupiter: and, therefore, if they should as deeply swear as Osman to Bethlem Gabor;‡ yet whether they would be bound by those chains, and not find ways to cut such Gordian knots, we could have no just assurance. But honest men's words are Stygian oaths, and promises inviolable. These are not the men for whom the fetters of law were first forged; they needed not the solemness of oaths; by keeping their faith they swear, and evacuate such confirmations.§

SECT. XX.—Though the world be histrionical, and most men live ironically, yet be thou what thou singly art, and per-

---

* Which after many hundred years was found burning under ground, and went out as soon as the air came to it.

† Jovem lapidem jurare.

‡ See the oath of Sultan Osman, in his life, in the addition to Knolls's Turkish history.

§ Colendo fidem jurant.—CURTIUS.

9 *to elude the urn of the Prætor.*] condemnation or acquittal was cast.— The vessel, into which the ticket of *Dr. J.*

sonate only thyself. Swim smoothly in the stream of thy nature, and live but one man. To single hearts doubling is discruciating: such tempers must sweat to dissemble, and prove but hypocritical hypocrites. Simulation must be short: men do not easily continue a counterfeiting life, or dissemble unto death. He who counterfeiteth, acts a part; and is, as it were, out of himself: which, if long, proves so irksome, that men are glad to pull off their vizards, and resume themselves again; no practice being able to naturalize such unnaturals, or make a man rest content not to be himself. And, therefore, since sincerity is thy temper, let veracity be thy virtue, in words, manners, and actions. To offer at iniquities, which have so little foundations in thee, were to be vicious up-hill, and strain for thy condemnation. Persons viciously inclined, want no wheels to make them actively vicious; as having the elater and spring of their own natures to facilitate their iniquities. And, therefore, so many, who are sinistrous unto good actions, are ambi-dexterous unto bad; and Vulcans in virtuous paths, Achilleses in vicious motions.

Sect. xxi.—Rest not in the high-strained paradoxes of old philosophy, supported by naked reason, and the reward of mortal felicity; but labour in the ethics of faith, built upon heavenly assistance, and the happiness of both beings. Understand the rules, but swear not unto the doctrines of Zeno or Epicurus.[1] Look beyond Antoninus, and terminate not thy morals in Seneca or Epictetus.[2] Let not the twelve but the two tables be thy law: let Pythagoras be thy remembrancer, not thy textuary and final instructer: and learn the vanity of the world, rather from Solomon than Phocylides.[3] Sleep not in the dogmas of the Peripatus, Academy, or Porticus.[4] Be a moralist of the mount,[5] an Epictetus in the faith, and christianize thy notions.

Sect. xxii.—In seventy or eighty years, a man may have a deep gust of the world; know what it is, what it can afford,

[1] *Epicurus.*] The authors of the Stoical and Epicurean philosophy.—*Dr. J.*

[2] *Antoninus, &c.*] Stoical philosophers.—*Dr. J.*

[3] *Phocylides.*] A writer of moral sentences in verse.—*Dr. J.*

[4] *Peripatus, &c.*] Three schools of philosophy.—*Dr. J.*

[5] *mount.*] That is, according to the rules laid down in our Saviour's sermon on the mount.—*Dr. J.*

and what 't is to have been a man.   Such a latitude of years may hold a considerable corner in the general map of time; and a man may have a curt epitome of the whole course thereof in the days of his own life ; may clearly see he hath but acted over his forefathers ; what it was to live in ages past, and what living will be in all ages to come.

He is like to be the best judge of time, who hath lived to see about the sixtieth part thereof.   Persons of short times may know what 't is to live, but not the life of man, who, having little behind them, are but Januses of one face, and know not singularities enough to raise axioms of this world : but such a compass of years will shew new examples of old things, parallelisms of occurrences through the whole course of time, and nothing be monstrous unto him; who may in that time understand not only the varieties of men, but the variation of himself, and how many men he hath been in that extent of time.

He may have a close apprehension what is to be forgotten, while he hath lived to find none who could remember his father, or scarce the friends of his youth ; and may sensibly see with what a face in no long time oblivion will look upon himself.   His progeny may never be his posterity ; he may go out of the world less related than he came into it ; and considering the frequent mortality in friends and relations, in such a term of time, he may pass away divers years in sorrow and black habits, and leave none to mourn for himself; orbity may be his inheritance, and riches his repentance.

In such a thread of time, and long observation of men, he may acquire a physiognomical intuitive knowledge; judge the interiors by the outside, and raise conjectures at first sight; and knowing what men have been, what they are, what children probably will be, may in the present age behold a good part and the temper of the next; and since so many live by the rules of constitution, and so few overcome their temperamental inclinations, make no improbable predictions.

Such a portion of time will afford a large prospect backward, and authentic reflections how far he hath performed the great intention of his being, in the honour of his Maker : whether he hath made good the principles of his nature, and what he was made to be; what characteristic and special mark he hath left, to be observable in his generation; whether he hath lived to purpose or in vain; and what he hath added, acted, or performed, that might considerably speak him a man.

In such an age, delights will be undelightful, and pleasures grow stale unto him; antiquated theorems will revive, and Solomon's maxims[6] be demonstrations unto him; hopes or presumptions be over, and despair grow up of any satisfaction below. And having been long tossed in the ocean of this world, he will by that time feel the in-draught of another, unto which this seems but preparatory, and without it of no high value. He will experimentally find the emptiness of all things, and the nothing of what is past; and wisely grounding upon true Christian expectations, finding so much past, will wholly fix upon what is to come. He will long for perpetuity, and live as though he made haste to be happy. The last may prove the prime part of his life, and those his best days which he lived nearest heaven.

SECT. XXIII.—Live happy in the Elysium of a virtuously composed mind, and let intellectual contents exceed the delights wherein mere pleasurists place their paradise. Bear not too slack reins upon pleasure, nor let complexion or contagion betray thee unto the exorbitancy of delight. Make pleasure thy recreation or intermissive relaxation, not thy Diana, life, and profession. Voluptuousness is as insatiable as covetousness. Tranquillity is better than jollity, and to appease pain than to invent pleasure. Our hard entrance into the world, our miserable going out of it, our sicknesses, disturbances, and sad rencounters in it, do clamorously tell us we come not into the world to run a race of delight, but to perform the sober acts and serious purposes of man; which to omit were foully to miscarry in the advantage of humanity, to play away an uniterable life, and to have lived in vain. Forget not the capital end, and frustrate not the opportunity of once living. Dream not of any kind of metempsychosis[7]

[6] *Solomon's maxims.*] That all is vanity.—*Dr. J.*

[7] *metempsychosis.*] See note [7], page 83.—*Dr. J.*

or transanimation, but into thine own body, and that after a long time; and then also unto wail or bliss, according to thy first and fundamental life. Upon a curricle in this world depends a long course of the next, and upon a narrow scene here an endless expansion hereafter. In vain some think to have an end of their beings with their lives. Things cannot get out of their natures, or be or not be in despite of their constitutions. Rational existences in heaven perish not at all, and but partially on earth: that which is thus once, will in some way be always: the first living human soul is still alive, and all Adam hath found no period.

SECT. XXIV.—Since the stars of heaven do differ in glory; since it hath pleased the Almighty hand to honour the north pole with lights above the south; since there are some stars so bright that they can hardly be looked on, some so dim that they can scarce be seen, and vast numbers not to be seen at all, even by artificial eyes; read thou the earth in heaven, and things below from above. Look contentedly upon the scattered difference of things, and expect not equality in lustre, dignity, or perfection, in regions or persons below; where numerous numbers must be content to stand like lacteous or nebulous stars, little taken notice of, or dim in their generations. All which may be contentedly allowable in the affairs and ends of this world, and in suspension unto what will be in the order of things hereafter, and the new system of mankind which will be in the world to come; when the last may be the first, and the first the last; when Lazarus may sit above Cæsar, and the just, obscure on earth, shall shine like the sun in heaven; when personations shall cease, and histrionism of happiness be over; when reality shall rule, and all shall be as they shall be for ever.

SECT. XXV.—When the stoic said that life * would not be accepted, if it were offered unto such as knew it, he spoke too meanly of that state of being which placeth us in the form of men. It more depreciates the value of this life, that men would not live it over again; for although they would still live on, yet few or none can endure to think of being twice the same men upon earth, and some had rather never have lived

* Vitam nemo acciperet, si daretur scientibus.—*Seneca.*

than to tread over their days once more. Cicero in a prosperous state had not the patience to think of beginning in a cradle again.[8] Job would not only curse the day of his nativity, but also of his renascency, if he were to act over his disasters and the miseries of the dunghill. But the greatest underweening of this life is to undervalue that, unto which this is but exordial or a passage leading unto it. The great advantage of this mean life is thereby to stand in a capacity of a better; for the colonies of heaven must be drawn from earth, and the sons of the first Adam are only heirs unto the second. Thus Adam came into this world with the power also of another; not only to replenish the earth, but the everlasting mansions of heaven. Where we were when the foundations of the earth were laid, when the morning stars sang together, and all the sons of God shouted for joy,* He must answer who asked it; who understands entities of preordination, and beings yet unbeing; who hath in his intellect the ideal existences of things, and entities before their extances. Though it looks but like an imaginary kind of existency, to be before we are; yet since we are under the decree or prescience of a sure and omnipotent power, it may be somewhat more than a non-entity, to be in that mind, unto which all things are present.

SECT. XXVI.—If the end of the world shall have the same foregoing signs, as the period of empires, states, and dominions in it, that is, corruption of manners, inhuman degenerations, and deluge of iniquities; it may be doubted, whether that final time be so far off, of whose day and hour there can be no prescience. But while all men doubt, and none can determine how long the world shall last, some may wonder that it hath spun out so long and unto our days. For if the Almighty had not determined a fixed duration unto it, according to his mighty and merciful designments in it; if he had not said unto it, as he did unto a part of it, hitherto shalt thou go and no farther; if we consider the incessant and cutting

* Job xxxviii.

[8] *Cicero, &c..*] Si quis Deus mihi vagiam, valde recusem.—*Cic. de Senec-*
largiatur, ut repuerascam et in cunis *tute.—Dr. J.*

provocations from the earth; it is not without amazement, how his patience hath permitted so long a continuance unto it; how he, who cursed the earth in the first days of the first man, and drowned it in the tenth generation after, should thus lastingly contend with flesh, and yet defer the last flames. For since he is sharply provoked every moment, yet punisheth to pardon, and forgives to forgive again; what patience could be content to act over such vicissitudes, or accept of repentances which must have after-penitences, his goodness can only tell us. And surely if the patience of heaven were not proportionable unto the provocations from earth, there needed an intercessor not only for the sins, but the duration of this world, and to lead it up unto the present computation. Without such a merciful longanimity, the heavens would never be so aged as to grow old like a garment. It were in vain to infer from the doctrine of the sphere, that the time might come, when Capella, a noble northern star, would have its motion in the equator; that the northern zodiacal signs would at length be the southern, the southern the northern, and Capricorn become our Cancer. However, therefore, the wisdom of the creator hath ordered the duration of the world, yet since the end thereof brings the accomplishment of our happiness, since some would be content that it should have no end, since evil men and spirits do fear it may be too short, since good men hope it may not be too long; the prayer of the saints under the altar will be the supplication of the righteous world, that his mercy would abridge their languishing expectation, and hasten the accomplishment of their happy state to come.

SECT. XXVII.—Though good men are often taken away from the evil to come; though some in evil days have been glad that they were old, nor long to behold the iniquities of a wicked world, or judgments threatened by them; yet is it no small satisfaction unto honest minds, to leave the world in virtuous well-tempered times, under a prospect of good to come, and continuation of worthy ways acceptable unto God and man. Men who die in deplorable days, which they regretfully behold, have not their eyes closed with the like content; while they cannot avoid the thoughts of proceeding or growing enormities, displeasing unto that spirit unto whom they are then going, whose honour they desire in all times and throughout all generations. If Lucifer could be freed from his dismal place, he would little care though the rest were left behind. Too many there may be of Nero's mind,[9] who, if their own turn were served, would not regard what became of others; and when they die themselves, care not if all perish. But good men's wishes extend beyond their lives, for the happiness of times to come, and never to be known unto them. And, therefore, while so many question prayers for the dead, they charitably pray for those who are not yet alive; they are not so enviously ambitious to go to heaven by themselves; they cannot but humbly wish, that the little flock might be greater,' the narrow gate wider, and that, as many are called, so not a few might be chosen.

SECT. XXVIII.—That a greater number of angels remained in heaven, than fell from it, the school-men will tell us; that the number of blessed souls will not come short of that vast number of fallen spirits, we have the favourable calculation of others. What age or century hath sent most souls unto heaven, he can tell who vouchsafeth that honour unto them. Though the number of the blessed must be complete before the world can pass away; yet since the world itself seems in the wane, and we have no such comfortable prognosticks of latter times; since a greater part of time is spun than is to come, and the blessed roll already much replenished; happy are those pieties, which solicitously look about, and hasten to make one of that already much filled and abbreviated list to come.

SECT. XXIX.—Think not thy time short in this world, since the world itself is not long. The created world is but a small parenthesis in eternity, and a short interposition, for a time, between such a state of duration as was before it and may be after it. And if we should allow of the old tradition, that the world should last six thousand years, it could scarce have the name of old, since the first man lived near a sixth part thereof, and seven Methuselahs would exceed its whole

[9] *Nero's mind.*] Nero often had this saying in his mouth, Ἐμοῦ θάνοντος γαῖα μιχθήτω πυρι: "when I am once dead, let the earth and fire be jumbled together."—*Dr. J.*

duration. However, to palliate the shortness of our lives, and somewhat to compensate our brief term in this world, it's good to know as much as we can of it; and also, so far as possibly in us lieth, to hold such a theory of times past, as though we had seen the same. He who hath thus considered the world, as also how therein things long past have been answered by things present; how matters in one age have been acted over in another; and how there is nothing new under the sun; may conceive himself in some manner to have lived from the beginning, and to be as old as the world; and if he should still live on, 'twould be but the same thing.

SECT. xxx.[1]—Lastly;[2] if length of days be thy portion, make it not thy expectation. Reckon not upon long life: think every day the last, and live always beyond thy account. He that so often surviveth his expectation lives many lives, and will scarce complain of the shortness of his days. Time past is gone like a shadow; make time to come present. Approximate thy latter times by present apprehensions of them: be like a neighbour unto the grave, and think there is but little to come. And since there is something of us that will still live on, join both lives together, and live in one but for the other. He who thus ordereth the purposes of this life, will never be far from the next; and is in some manner already in it, by a happy conformity, and close apprehension of it. And if, as we have elsewhere declared,[3] any have been so happy, as personally to understand christian annihilation, extacy, exolution, transformation, the kiss of the spouse, and ingression into the divine shadow, according to mystical theology, they have already had an handsome anticipation of heaven; the world is in a manner over, and the earth in ashes unto them.

---

[1] SECT. xxx.] This Section, terminating at the words "and close apprehension of it," concludes the *Letter to a Friend.—Dr. J.*

[2] *Lastly.*]
Omnem crede diem tibi diluxisse supremum,
Grata superveniet quæ non sperabitur hora.
HORACE.

Believe, that ev'ry morning's ray
Hath lighted up thy latest day; ·
Then, if to-morrow's sun be thine,
With double lustre shall it shine.
FRANCIS.—*Dr. J.*

[3] *declared.*] In his treatise of *Urn-burial.* Some other parts of these essays are printed in a letter among Browne's Posthumous Works. Those references to his own books prove these essays to be genuine.—*Dr. J.*

In the present edition, the "other parts" here mentioned are pointed out, and some passages from *The Letter to a Friend*, are given, which were not included in *Christian Morals.*

Miscellany Tracts.

ORIGINALLY PUBLISHED IN

1684.

ALSO

Miscellanies.

ORIGINALLY PUBLISHED WITH HIS POSTHUMOUS WORKS IN

1712.

EDITOR'S PREFACE.

———◆———

Most of these Tracts were (as Archbishop Tenison remarks in his preface,) Letters, in reply to enquiries addressed to the author, by various, and some very eminent correspondents. The second, "*Of Garlands, &c.*," was written to Evelyn, as I find from his own hand-writing, in the margin of his copy of the original edition. On the same authority, (probably from the information of Sir Thomas himself,) we learn that the greater number were addressed to Sir Nicholas Bacon. *See MS. Note in first page.* The ninth, "*Of Artificial Hills*," was in reply to Sir William Dugdale.

Such enquiries he delighted to satisfy; and the immense stores of information amassed during a long life of curious reading, and inquisitive research, eminently qualified him for resolving questions on subjects the most dissimilar. Scarcely any could be brought before him, upon which he could not bring to bear the results of reiterated experiments, or of an extensive acquaintance with the most singular and recondite literature; and, where these treasures failed him, there remained the inexhaustible resources of his own matchless fancy.

The first and second Tracts have been collated with MS. Sloan. No. 1841; the eighth, tenth, and eleventh, with Nos. 1827 and 1839: the thirteenth with No. 1874; the twelfth with MS. Rawlinson, No. 58, in the Bodleian—and all the others with MS. Sloan. No. 1827. Whatever discrepancies seemed of sufficient importance have been preserved in notes.

The second edition were published with the folio edition of his works, in 1686; and none have since been re-printed, except *Museum Clausum*, which, with *Hydriotaphia*, and the *Letter to a Friend*, were published in a neat 18mo. volume, by Mr. Crossley, of Manchester.

For the sake of keeping distinct the whole of the unpublished works, I have added to the Miscellany Tracts, his remarks on *Iceland*, together with some miscellaneous observations, which made their appearance in that ill-assorted collection, the *Posthumous Works*, in 1712.

THE PUBLISHER TO THE READER.

THE papers from which these Tracts were printed, were, a while since, delivered to me by those worthy persons, the lady and son of the excellent author. He himself gave no charge concerning his manuscripts, either for the suppressing or the publishing of them. Yet, seeing he had procured transcripts of them, and had kept those copies by him, it seemeth probable, that he designed them for public use.

Thus much of his intention being presumed, and many who had tasted of the fruits of his former studies being covetous of more of the like kind; also these Tracts having been perused and much approved of by some judicious and learned men; I was not unwilling to be instrumental in fitting them for the press.

To this end, I selected them out of many disordered papers, and disposed them into such a method as they seemed capable of; beginning first with plants, going on to animals, proceeding farther to things relating to men, and concluding with matters of a various nature.

Concerning the plants, I did, on purpose, forbear to range them (as some advised) according to their tribes and families; because, by so doing, I should have represented that as a studied and formal work, which is but a collection of occasional essays. And, indeed, both this Tract, and those which follow, were rather the diversions than the labours of his pen: and, because he did, as it were, drop down his thoughts of a sudden, in those little spaces of vacancy which he snatched from those very many occasions which gave him hourly interruption. If there appears, here and there, any incorrectness in the style, a small degree of candour sufficeth to excuse it.

If there be any such errors in the words, I am sure the press has not made them fewer; but I do not hold myself obliged to answer for that which I could not perfectly govern.

However, the matter is not of any great moment: such errors will not mislead a learned reader; and he who is not such in some competent degree, is not a fit peruser of these letters. Such these Tracts are; but, for the persons to whom they were written, I cannot well learn their names from those few obscure marks which the author has set at the beginning of them. And these essays being letters, as many as take offence at some few familiar things which the author hath mixed with them, find fault with decency. Men are not wont to set down oracles in every line they write to their acquaintance.

There still remain other brief discourses written by this most learned and ingenious author. Those, also, may come forth, when some of his friends shall have sufficient leisure ; and at such due distance from these Tracts, that they may follow rather than stifle them.

Amongst these manuscripts there is one which gives a brief account of all the monuments of the cathedral of Norwich. It was written merely for private use: and the relations of the author expect such justice from those into whose hands some imperfect copies of it are fallen, that, without their consent first obtained, they forbear the publishing of it.

The truth is, matter equal to the skill of the antiquary, was not there afforded: had a fit subject of that nature offered itself, he would scarce have been guilty of an oversight like to that of Ausonius, who, in the description of his native city of Bordeaux, omitted the two famous antiquities of it, Palais de Tutele, and Palais de Galien.

Concerning the author himself, I choose to be silent, though I have had the happiness to have been, for some years, known to him. There is on foot a design of writing his life ; and there are already, some memorials collected by one of his ancient friends. Till that work be perfected, the reader may content himself with these present Tracts; all which commending themselves by their learning, curiosity, and bre-vity, if he be not pleased with them, he seemeth to me to be distempered with such a niceness of imagination, as no wise man is concerned to humour.

THOMAS TENISON.

𝔐iscellany 𝔗racts.

TRACT I.[1]

OBSERVATIONS UPON SEVERAL PLANTS MENTIONED IN SCRIPTURE.

SIR,

THOUGH many ordinary heads run smoothly over the Scripture, yet I must acknowledge it is one of the hardest books I have met with; and therefore well deserveth those numerous comments, expositions, and annotations, which make up a good part of our libraries.

However, so affected I am therewith, that I wish there had been more of it, and a larger volume of that divine piece, which leaveth such welcome impressions, and somewhat more, in the readers, than the words and sense after it. At least, who would not be glad that many things barely hinted were at large delivered in it? The particulars of the dispute between the doctors and our Saviour could not but be welcome to those who have every word in honour which proceeded from his mouth, or was otherwise delivered by him; and so would be glad to be assured, what he wrote with his finger on the ground: but especially to have a particular of that instructing narration or discourse which he made unto the disciples after his resurrection, where 'tis said: "And

---

[1] TRACT I.] "Most of these letters were written to Sir Nicholas Bacon."— *MS. Note, written in pencil, by Evelyn,* *in a copy formerly belonging to him, now in the Editor's possession.*

beginning at Moses, and all the prophets, he expounded unto them, in all · the Scriptures, the things concerning himself."

But, to omit theological obscurities, you must needs observe that most sciences do seem to have something more nearly to consider in the expressions of the Scripture.

Astronomers find herein the names but of few stars, scarce so many as in Achilles's buckler in Homer, and almost the very same. But in some passages of the Old Testament they think they discover the zodiacal course of the sun; and they, also, conceive an astronomical sense in that elegant expression of St. James "concerning the father of lights, with whom there is no variableness, neither shadow of turning:" and therein an allowable allusion unto the tropical conversion of the sun, whereby ensueth a variation of heat, light, and also of shadows from it. But whether the *stellæ erraticæ*, or wandering stars, in St. Jude, may be referred to the celestial planets or some metereological wandering stars, *ignes fatui, stellæ cadentes et erraticæ*, or had any allusion unto the impostor Barchochebas[2] or Stellæ Filius, who afterward appeared, and wandered about in the time of Adrianus, they leave unto conjecture.

Chirurgeons may find their whole art in that one passage, concerning the rib which God took out of Adam; that is, their διαίρεσις in opening the flesh; ἐξαίρεσις in taking out the rib; and σύνθεσις in closing and healing the part again.

Rhetoricians and orators take singular notice of very many excellent passages, stately metaphors, noble tropes and elegant expressions, not to be found or paralleled in any other author.

Mineralists look earnestly into the twenty-eighth of Job; take special notice of the early artifice in brass and iron,

---

[2] *Barchochebas.*] One of the impostors who assumed the character of Messias; he changed his true name, *Bar-Coziba*, son of a lie, to that of *Barchochebas*, son of a star! He excited a revolt against the Romans which led to a very sanguinary contest, terminating with his death, at the storming of Bither, by the Romans, under Julius Severus. Bossuet supposes him to be the star mentioned in the 8th chap. of Revelation.

The apostle Jude more probably alluded to the term 'star,' by which the Jews often designated their teachers, and applied it here to some of the Christian teachers, whose unholy motives, erroneous doctrines, or wandering and unsettled habits exposed them to his rebuke.

under Tubal Cain: and find also mention of gold, silver, brass, tin, lead, iron; beside refining, soldering, dross,[3] nitre, salt-pits, and in some manner also of antimony.*

Gemmary naturalists read diligently the precious stones in the holy city of the Apocalypse; examine the breast plate of Aaron, and various gems upon it; and think the second row[4] the nobler of the four. They wonder to find the art of engravery so ancient upon precious stones and signets; together with the ancient use of earrings and bracelets. And are pleased to find pearl, coral, amber, and crystal, in those sacred leaves, according to our translation. And when they often meet with flints and marbles, cannot but take notice that there is no mention of the magnet or loadstone, which in so many similitudes, comparisons, and allusions, could hardly have been omitted in the works of Solomon: if it were true that he knew either the attractive or directive power thereof, as some have believed.

Navigators consider the ark, which was pitched without and within, and could endure the ocean without mast or sails: they take special notice of the twenty-seventh of Ezekiel; the mighty traffic and great navigation of Tyre, with particular mention of their sails, their masts of cedar, oars of oak, their skilful pilots, mariners, and caulkers; as also of the long voyages of the fleets of Solomon; of Jehosaphat's ships broken at Ezion-Geber; of the notable voyage and shipwreck of St. Paul so accurately delivered in the Acts.

Oneirocritical diviners apprehend some hints of their knowledge, even from divine dreams; while they take notice of the dreams of Joseph, Pharaoh, Nebuchadnezzar, and the angels on Jacob's ladder; and find, in Artemidorus and Achmetes, that ladders signify travels, and the scales thereof preferment; and that oxen lean and fat naturally denote scarcity or plenty, and the successes of agriculture.

Physiognomists will largely put in from very many passages of scripture. And when they find in Aristotle, *quibus frons*

---

* *Depinxit oculos stibio.* 2 Kings ix, 30; Jerem. iv, 30; Ezek. xxiii, 40.

[3] *dross.*] *MS. Sloan.* 1841, adds, "sulphur."   [4] *second row.*] The emerald, sapphire, and diamond.

quadrangula commensurata, fortes, referuntur ad leones, cannot but take special notice of that expression concerning the Gadites; mighty men of war, fit for battle, whose faces were as the faces of lions.

Geometrical and architectonical artists look narrowly upon the description of the ark, the fabric of the temple, and the holy city in the Apocalypse.

But the botanical artist meets every where with vegetables, and from the fig leaf in Genesis to the star wormwood in the Apocalypse, are variously interspersed expressions from plants, elegantly advantaging the significancy of the text: whereof many being delivered in a language proper unto Judæa and neighbour countries, are imperfectly apprehended by the common reader, and now doubtfully made out, even by the Jewish expositor.

And even in those which are confessedly known, the elegancy is often lost in the apprehension of the reader, unacquainted with such vegetables, or but nakedly knowing their natures : whereof holding a pertinent apprehension, you cannot pass over such expressions without some doubt or want of satisfaction [5] in your judgment. Hereof we shall only hint or discourse some few which I could not but take notice of in the reading of holy Scripture.

Many plants are mentioned in Scripture which are not distinctly known in our countries, or under such names in the original, as they are fain to be rendered by analogy, or by the name of vegetables of good affinity unto them, and so maintain the textual sense, though in some variation from identity.

1. That plant which afforded a shade unto Jonah,* mentioned by the name of *kikaion,* and still retained, at least marginally, in some translations, to avoid obscurity Jerome rendered *hedera* or ivy; [6] which notwithstanding (except in

---

* Jonah, iv, 6. a gourd.

[5] *want of satisfaction.*] "Insatisfaction." *MS. Sloan.* 1841.

[6] *Jerome rendereth ivy.*] Augustine called it a gourd, and accused Jerome of heresy for the opinion he held. Yet they both seem to have been wrong. It was in all probability the *kiki* of the Egyptians, a plant of the same family as the *ricinus;* and according to Dioscorides, of rapid growth; bearing a berry from which an oil is expressed; rising to the height of ten or twelve feet, and furnished with very large leaves, like those of the plane-tree; so that the people of the East plant it before their shops for the sake of its shade.

its scandent nature) agreed not fully with the other, that is, to grow up in a night, or be consumed with a worm; ivy being of no swift growth, little subject unto worms, and a scarce plant about Babylon.

2. That hyssop [7] is taken for that plant which cleansed the leper, being a well scented and very abstersive simple, may well be admitted; so we be not too confident, that it is strictly the same with our common hyssop: the hyssop of those parts differing from that of ours; as Bellonius hath observed in the hyssop which grows in Judæa, and the hyssop of the wall mentioned in the works of Solomon, no kind of our hyssop; and may tolerably be taken for some kind of minor capillary, which best makes out the antithesis with the cedar. Nor when we meet with *libanotis*, is it to be conceived our common rosemary, which is rather the first kind thereof amongst several others, used by the ancients.

3. That it must be taken for hemlock, which is twice so rendered in our translation,* will hardly be made out, otherwise than in the intended sense, and implying some plant, wherein bitterness or a poisonous quality is considerable.

4. What Tremellius rendereth *spina*, and the vulgar translation *paliurus*, and others make some kind of *rhamnus*, is allowable in the sense; and we contend not about the species, since they are known thorns in those countries, and in our fields or gardens among us: and so common in Judæa, that men conclude the thorny crown [8] of our Saviour was made either of *paliurus* or *rhamnus*.

5. Whether the bush which burnt and consumed not, were properly a *rubus* or bramble, was somewhat doubtful from the original and some translations, had not the Evangelist, and St. Paul expressed the same by the Greek word βάτος, which, from the description of Dioscorides, herbarists accept

---

* Hosea, x, 4; Amos, vi, 2.

[7] *hyssop.*] A diminutive herb of a very bitter taste, which Hasselquist mentions as growing on the mountains near Jerusalem, as well as on the walls of the city. Pliny mentions it in connection with the *vinegar* and the *sponge. Nat. Hist.* lib. xxiii, c. 1.

[8] *thorny crown.*] Our Lord's crown was supposed by Bodæus and Theophylact to have been made of some species of *acacia.* Hasselquist considers it to have been the *rhamnus*, or *nubca paliurus Athenei.*

for *rubus;* although the same word βάτος expresseth not only
the *rubus* or kinds of bramble, but other thorny bushes, and
the hip-briar is also named κυνοσβάτος, or the dog-briar or
bramble.

6. That *myrica* is rendered heath,⁹* sounds instructively
enough to our ears, who behold that plant so common in barren plains among us: but you cannot but take notice that
erica, or our heath, is not the same plant with *myrica* or tamarice, described by Theophrastus and Dioscorides, and
which Bellonius declareth to grow so plentifully in the deserts
of Judæa and Arabia.

7. That the βότρυς τῆς κύπρου, *botrus cypri*, or clusters of cypress,¹† should have any reference to the cypress tree, according to the original, *copher*, or clusters of the noble vine of
Cyprus, which might be planted into Judæa, may seem to
others allowable in some latitude. But there seeming some
noble odour to be implied in this place, you may probably
conceive that the expression drives at the κύπρος of Dioscorides,
some oriental kind of *ligustrum* or *alcharma*, which Dioscorides and Pliny mention under the name of κύπρος and *cyprus*, and to grow about Egypt and Ascalon, producing a
sweet and odorate bush of flowers, and out of which was
made the famous *oleum cyprinum*.

But why it should be rendered camphor your judgment
cannot but doubt, who know that our camphor was unknown
unto the ancients, and no ingredient into any composition of
great antiquity: that learned men long conceived it a bituminous and fossil body, and our latest experience discovereth
it to be the resinous substance of a tree, in Borneo and China;
and that the camphor that we use is a neat preparation of
the same.

8. When 'tis said in Isaiah xli, " I will plant in the wilderness the cedar, the shittah tree, and the myrtle, and the oil

* *Myrica*, Cant. i, 14.   † Cant. i, 14.

⁹ *heath.*] " Be as the heath in the
wilderness."—*MS. Sloan.* 1847.

The lxx, in Jer. xlviii, 6, instead of
orur evidently read *orud*, 'a wild ass;'
which suits that passage (as well as Jer.
xvii, 6) better than "heath!"

¹ *cypress.*] Aquila, the lxx, Theodo-
tion, and others, consider the tree thus
called in Isa. xliv, 14, to be rather the
wild oak, or *ilex;* Bishop Lowth and
Parkhurst think the pine is intended.
But the wood of the cypress was more
adapted to the purpose specified.

tree, I will set in the desert, the fir tree, and the pine, and the box tree:" though some doubt may be made of the shittah tree,[2] yet all these trees here mentioned being such as are ever green, you will more emphatically apprehend the merciful meaning of God in this mention of no fading, but always verdant trees in dry and desert places.

9. "And they cut down a branch with one cluster of grapes,[3] and they bare it between two upon a staff, and they brought pomegranates and figs." This cluster of grapes brought upon a staff by the spies was an incredible sight, in Philo Judæus, seemed notable in the eyes of the Israelites, but more wonderful in our own, who look only upon northern vines. But herein you are like to consider, that the cluster was thus carefully carried to represent it entire, without bruising or breaking; that this was not one bunch, but an extraordinary cluster, made up of many depending upon one gross stalk. And, however, might be paralleled with the eastern clusters of Margiana and Caramania, if we allow but half the expressions of Pliny and Strabo, whereof one would lade a curry or small cart; and may be made out by the clusters of the grapes of Rhodes presented unto Duke Radzivil,* each containing three parts of an ell in compass, and the grapes as big as prunes.

10. Some things may be doubted in the species of the holy ointment [4] and perfume.† With amber, musk, and civet we meet not in the Scripture, nor any odours from animals; except we take the *onycha* of that perfume, for the covercle of a shell-fish, called *unguis odoratus*, or *blatta byzantina*, which Dioscorides affirmeth to be taken from a shell-fish of the Indian lakes, which feedeth upon the aromatical plants, is gathered when the lakes are dry. But whether that which

---

* Radzivil in his Travels.   † Exod. xxx, 34, 35.

[2] *shittah-tree.*] According to Dr. Shaw and others, it was the *acacia bera*, or *spina Egyptiaca*, which grows to about the size of the mulberry, and produces yellow flowers and pods like lupines.

[3] *cluster of grapes.*] Doubdan (*Voyage de la Terre Sainte*, ch. xxi) speaks of bunches weighing ten or twelve pounds. Forster, on the authority of a Religious, who had long resided in Palestine, says, that there grew in the valley of Hebron bunches so large that two men could scarcely carry one.

[4] *holy ointment.*] Frankincense was one of the ingredients therein; an aromatic gum produced by a tree not certainly known, called by the ancients *thurifera.*

we now call *blatta byzantina* or *unguis odoratus,* be the same
with that odorate one of antiquity, great doubt may be made;
since Dioscorides saith it smelled like *castoreum,* and that
which we now have is of an ungrateful odour.

No little doubt may be also made of *galbanum* [5] prescribed
in the same perfume, if we take it for *galbanum,* which is of
common use among us, approaching the evil scent of *assafœtida;* and not rather for *galbanum* of good odour, as the
adjoining words declare, and the original *chelbena* will bear;
which implieth a fat or resinous substance; that which is
commonly known among us being properly a gummous body
and dissoluble also in water.

The holy ointment of stacte or pure myrrh,[6] distilling from
the plant without expression or firing, of cinnamon, cassia,
and *calamus,* containeth less questionable species, if the cinnamon of the ancients were the same with ours, or managed
after the same manner. For thereof Dioscorides made his
noble unguent. And cinnamon was so highly valued by
princes, that Cleopatra carried it unto her sepulchre with her
jewels; which was also kept in wooden boxes among the rarities of kings: and was of such a lasting nature, that at his
composing of treacle for the Emperor Severus, Galen made
use of some which had been laid up by Adrianus.

11. That the prodigal son desired to eat of husks given
unto swine, will hardly pass in your apprehension for the
husks of pease, beans, or such edulious pulses; as well
understanding that the textual word κεράτιον, or *ceration,* properly intendeth the fruit of the *siliqua* tree, so common in
Syria, and fed upon by men and beasts; called also by some
the fruit of the locust tree, and *panis sancti Johannis,* as conceiving it to have been part of the diet of the baptist in the
desert. The tree and fruit is not only common in Syria and
the eastern parts, but also well known in Apuleia and the
kingdom of Naples; growing along the Via Appia, from

[5] *galbanum.*] A gum issuing from
an umbelliferous plant, growing in Persia and Africa;—when first drawn, white
and soft;—afterwards reddish;—of a
strong smell, bitter and acid, inflammable, and soluble in water.

[6] *myrrh.*] The gum of a tree growing in Egypt, Arabia, and Abyssinia :—
believed to possess the power of resisting
putrefaction, and therefore used by the
Jews and Egyptians in embalming.

Fundi unto Mola ; the hard cods or husks making a rattling noise in windy weather, by beating against one another : called by the Italians, *caróba* or *caróbala,* and by the French, *carouges.* With the sweet pulp hereof some conceive that the Indians preserve ginger, mirabolans, and nutmegs. Of the same (as Pliny delivers) the ancients made one kind of wine, strongly expressing the juice thereof; and so they might after give the expressed and less useful part of the cods and remaining pulp unto their swine : which, being no gustless or unsatisfying offal, might be well desired by the prodigal in his hunger.

12. No marvel it is that the Israelites, having lived long in a well-watered country, and been acquainted with the noble water of Nilus, should complain for water in the dry and barren wilderness. More remarkable it seems that they should extol and linger after the cucumbers[7] and leeks, onions and garlick of Egypt; wherein, notwithstanding, lies a pertinent expression of the diet of that country in ancient times, even as high as the building of the pyramids, when Herodotus delivereth, that so many talents were spent in onions and garlick, for the food of labourers and artificers ; and is also answerable unto their present plentiful diet in cucumbers, and the great varieties thereof, as testified by Prosper Alpinus, who spent many years in Egypt.

13. What fruit that was which our first parents tasted in Paradise, from the disputes of learned men, seems yet indeterminable.[8] More clear it is that they covered their nakedness or secret parts with fig leaves ;[9] which, when I read, I cannot but call to mind the several considerations which antiquity had of the fig tree, in reference unto those parts,

---

[7] *cucumbers.*] Hasselquist thus describes the *cucumis chate,* or queen of cucumbers. " It grows in the fertile earth round Cairo, after the inundation of the Nile, and not in any other place in Egypt, nor in any other soil. It ripens with water melons : its flesh is almost of the same substance, but is not near so cool. The grandees eat it as the most pleasant food they find, and that from which they have least to apprehend. It is the most excellent of this tribe of any yet known."—*Hasselquist's Trav.* p. 258.

[8] *yet indeterminable.*] Jewish tradition considers it to have been the *citron,* which, in all probability, was the fruit spoken of in Cant. ii, 13, rather than the *apple,* as it is translated.

[9] *fig leaves.*] The fig tree is called *taneh,* or the "grief tree," from its rough leaves. Hence the Rabbins and others represent Adam to have selected it as a natural sackcloth, to express his contrition.

particularly how fig leaves, by sundry authors, are described
to have some resemblance unto the genitals, and so were aptly
formed for such contection of those parts; how also, in that
famous statua of Praxiteles, concerning Alexander and Bu-
cephalus, the secret parts are veiled with fig leaves; how this
tree was sacred unto Priapus, and how the diseases of the
secret parts have derived their name from figs.

14. That the good Samaritan, coming from Jericho, used
any of the Judean balsam[1] upon the wounded traveller, is not
to be made out, and we are unwilling to disparage his charitable surgery in pouring oil into a green wound; and, therefore,
when 'tis said he used oil and wine, may rather conceive that
he made an *oinelæum*, or medicine of oil and wine beaten up
and mixed together, which was no improper medicine, and is
an art now lately studied by some so to incorporate wine and
oil, that they may lastingly hold together, which some pretend to have, and call it *oleum Samaritanum*, or Samaritan's
oil.

15. When Daniel would not pollute himself with the diet
of the Babylonians, he probably declined pagan commensa-
tion, or to eat of meats forbidden to the Jews, though common at their tables, or so much as to taste of their Gentile im-
molations, and sacrifices abominable unto his palate.

But when 't is said that he made choice of the diet of pulse[2]
and water, whether he strictly confined unto a leguminous
food, according to the vulgar translation, some doubt may be
raised from the original word *zeragnim*, which signifies *semi-
nalia*, and is so set down in the margin of Arias Montanus;
and the Greek word *spermata*, generally expressing seeds,
may signify any edulious or cerealious grains besides ὄσπρια or
leguminous seeds.

---

[1] *balsam*.] An evergreen, rising to
about fourteen feet high, indigenous in
Azab and all along the coast of Babel-
mandel; bearing but few leaves, and
small white flowers, like those of the
acacia. Three kinds of balsam were extracted from this tree:—1. The *opobal-
samum*, the most valuable sort, which
flowed, on incision, from the trunk or
branches. 2. *Carpobalsamum*, from pressure of the ripe fruit. 3. *Hylobalsa-*
mum, made by a decoction of the buds
and young twigs. The tree has entirely
disappeared from Palestine.

[2] *pulse*.] Parched peas or corn; both
of which make part of the food of the
Eastern people. "On the road from Acra
to Seide," says Hasselquist, "we saw a
herdsman eating his dinner, consisting of
half-ripe ears of wheat, which he toast-
ed, and ate with as good an appetite as
a Turk does his pillaus."

Yet, if he strictly made choice of a leguminous food, and water, instead of his portion from the king's table, he handsomely declined the diet which might have been put upon him, and particularly that which was called the *potibasis* of the king, which, as Athenæus informeth, implied the bread of the king, made of barley, and wheat, and the wine of Cyprus, which he drank in an oval cup. And, therefore, distinctly from that he chose plain fare of water, and the gross diet of pulse, and that, perhaps, not made into bread, but parched and tempered with water.

Now that herein (beside the special benediction of God) he made choice of no improper diet to keep himself fair and plump, and so to excuse the eunuch his keeper, physicians will not deny, who acknowledge a very nutritive and impinguating faculty in pulses, in leguminous food, and in several sorts of grains and corns, is not like to be doubted by such who consider that this was probably a great part of the food of our forefathers before the flood, the diet also of Jacob; and that the Romans (called, therefore, *pultifagi*) fed much on pulse for six hundred years; that they had no bakers for that time: and their pistours were such as, before the use of mills, beat out and cleansed their corn. As also that the athletic diet was of pulse, *alphiton, maza*, barley and water; whereby they were advantaged sometimes to an exquisite state of health, and such as was not without danger. And, therefore, though Daniel were no eunuch, and of a more fatning and thriving temper, as some have fancied, yet was he by this kind of diet sufficiently maintained in a fair and carnous state of body; and, accordingly, his picture not improperly drawn, that is, not meagre and lean, like Jeremy's, but plump and fair, answerable to the most authentic draught of the Vatican, and the late German Luther's bible.

The cynicks in Athenæus make iterated courses of lentils, and prefer that diet before the luxury of Seleucus. The present Egyptians, who are observed by Alpinus to be the fattest nation, and men to have breasts like women, owe much, as he conceiveth, unto the water of Nile, and their diet of rice, pease, lentils, and white cicers. The pulse-eating cynicks and stoicks are all very long livers in Laertius. And Daniel

must not be accounted of few years, who, being carried away
captive in the reign of Joachim, by King Nebuchadnezzar,
lived, by Scripture account, unto the first year of Cyrus.

16. "And Jacob took rods of green poplar, and of the
hazel, and the chesnut tree, and pilled white streaks in them,
and made the white appear which was in the rods, &c."
Men multiply the philosophy of Jacob, who beside the benediction of God, and the powerful effects of imagination, raised
in the goats and sheep from pilled and party-coloured objects,
conceive that he chose out these particular plants above any
other, because he understood they had a particular virtue
unto the intended effects, according unto the conception of
Georgius Venetus.*

Whereto you will hardly assent, at least till you be better
satisfied and assured concerning the true species of the
plants intended in the text, or find a clearer consent and uniformity in the translation: for what we render poplar, hazel,
and chesnut, the Greek translateth *virgam styracinam,*
nucinam, plantaninam, which some also render a pomegranate;
and so observing this variety of interpretations concerning
common and known plants among us, you may more reasonably doubt, with what propriety or assurance others less
known be sometimes rendered unto us.

17. Whether in the sermon of the mount, the lilies of the
field did point at the proper lilies,[3] or whether those flowers
grew wild in the place where our Saviour preached, some
doubt may be made; because κρίνον, the word in that place, is
accounted of the same signification with λείριον, and that in
Homer is taken for all manner of specious flowers; so received by Eustachius, Hesychius, and the scholiast upon

* G. Venetus, Problem. 200.

[3] *lilies.*] "At a few miles from
Adowa, we discovered a new and beautiful species of amaryllis, which bore
from ten to twelve spikes of bloom on
each stem, as large as those of the bella-
donna, springing from one common receptacle. The general colour of the
corolla was white, and every petal was
marked with a single streak of bright
purple, down the middle. The flower
was sweet scented, and its smell, though
much more powerful, resembled that of
the lily of the valley. This superb plant
excited the admiration of the whole
party; and it brought immediately to my
recollection the beautiful comparison used
on a particular occasion by our Saviour,
'I say unto you, that Solomon in all his
glory was not arrayed like one of these.'"
—*Salt's Voyage to Abyssinia,* p. 419.

Appollonius, Καθόλου τὰ ἄνθη λείρια λέγεται. And κρίνον is also received in the same latitude, not signifying only lilies, but applied unto daffodils, hyacinths, irises, and the flowers of colocynthis.

Under the like latitude of acception, are many expressions in the Canticles to be received. And when it is said "he feedeth among the lilies," therein may be also implied other specious flowers, not excluding the proper lilies. But in that expression, "the lilies drop forth myrrh," neither proper lilies nor proper myrrh can be apprehended, the one not proceeding from the other, but may be received in a metaphorical sense : and in some latitude may be made out from the roscid and honey drops observable in the flowers of martagon, and inverted flowered lilies, and, 't is like, is the standing sweet dew on the white eyes of the crown imperial, now common among us.

And the proper lily may be intended in that expression of 1 Kings, 7. that the brazen sea was of the thickness of a hand breadth, and the brim like a lily. For the figure of that flower being round at the bottom, and somewhat repandous, or inverted at the top, doth handsomely illustrate the comparison.

But that the lily of the valley, mentioned in the Canticles, "I am the rose of Sharon, and the lily of the valley," is that vegetable which passeth under the same name with us, that is *lilium convallium*, or the May lily, you will more hardly believe, who know with what insatisfaction the most learned botanists reduce that plant unto any described by the ancients; that Anguillara will have it to be the *œnanthe* of Athenæus, Cordus, the *pothos* of Theophrastus, and Lobelius, that the Greeks had not described it; who find not six leaves in the flower, agreeably to all lilies, but only six small divisions in the flower, who find it also to have a single, and no bulbous root, nor leaves shooting about the bottom, nor the stalk round, but angular. And that the learned Bauhinus hath not placed it in the classis of lilies, but nervifolious plants.

18. "Doth he not cast abroad the fitches,[4] and scatter the cummin seed, and cast in the principal wheat, and the ap-

---

[4] *fitches.*] There are two Hebrew *ketzach* and *kesmet;* the latter probably words rendered *fitches* by our translators, *rye*, the former is considered by Jerom,

pointed barley, and the rye in their place?" Herein though
the sense may hold under the names assigned, yet is it not so
easy to determine the particular seeds and grains, where the
obscure original causeth such differing translations. For in
the vulgar we meet with *milium* and *gith*, which our translation declineth, placing fitches for *gith*, and rye for *milium* or millet, which, notwithstanding, is retained by the
Dutch.

That it might be *melanthium, nigella*, or *gith*, may be allowably apprehended, from the frequent use of the seed
thereof among the Jews and other nations, as also from the
translation of Tremellius; and the original implying a black
seed, which is less than cummin, as, out of Aben Ezra, Buxtorfius hath expounded it.

But whereas *milium* or κέγχρος of the Septuagint is by ours
rendered rye, there is little similitude or affinity between
those grains; for *milium* is more agreeable unto *spelta* or
espaut, as the Dutch and others still render it.

That we meet so often with cummin[5] seed in many parts
of Scripture in reference unto Judæa, a seed so abominable
at present unto our palates and nostrils, will not seem strange
unto any who consider the frequent use thereof among the
ancients, not only in medical but dietetical use and practice:
for their dishes were filled therewith, and the noblest festival
preparations in Apicius were not without it; and even in
the *polenta*, and parched corn, the old diet of the Romans,
(as Pliny recordeth), unto every measure they mixed a small
proportion of linseed and cummin seed.

And so cummin is justly set down among things of vulgar
and common use, when it is said in Matthew 23. v. 23.
"You pay tithe of mint, anise, and cummin." But how to
make out the translation of anise we are still to seek, there
being no word in that text which properly signifieth anise:
the original being ἄνηθον, which the Latins call *anethum*, and
is properly Englished dill.

Maimonides, and the Rabbins to be *gith*,
in Greek μελανθων, in Latin *nigella*.
Parkhurst supposes it to have been
fennel.

[5] *cummin.*] An umbelliferous plant
resembling fennel; producing a bitterish,
warm, aromatic seed.

That among many expressions, allusions, and illustrations made in Scripture from corns, there is no mention made of oats, so useful a grain among us, will not seem very strange unto you, till you can clearly discover that it was a grain of ordinary use in those parts; who may also find that Theophrastus, who is large about other grains, delivers very little of it. That Dioscorides is also very short therein. And Galen delivers that it was of some use in Asia Minor, especially in Mysia, and that rather for beasts than men: and Pliny affirmeth that the *pulticula* thereof was most in use among the Germans. Yet that the Jews were not without all use of this grain seems confirmable from the Rabbinical account, who reckon five grains liable unto their offerings, whereof the cake presented might be made; that is, wheat, oats, rye, and two sorts of barley.

19. Why the disciples being hungry plucked the ears of corn, it seems strange to us, who observe that men half-starved betake not themselves to such supply; except we consider the ancient diet of *alphiton* and *polenta*, the meal of dried and parched corn, or that which was ὠμήλυσις, or meal of crude and unparched corn, wherewith they being well acquainted, might hope for some satisfaction from the corn yet in the husks; that is, from the nourishing pulp or mealy part within it.

20. The inhuman oppression of the Egyptian task-masters, who, not content with the common tale of brick, took also from the children of Israel their allowance of straw, and forced them to gather stubble where they could find it, will be more nearly apprehended, if we consider how hard it was to acquire any quantity of stubble in Egypt, where the stalk of corn was so short, that to acquire an ordinary measure it required more than ordinary labour; as is discoverable from that account which Pliny hath happily left unto us.* In the corn gathered in Ægypt the straw is never a cubit long: because the seed lieth very shallow, and hath no other nourishment than from the mud and slime left by the river; for under it is nothing but sand and gravel.

* Lib. 18. *Nat. Hist.*

So that the expression of Scripture is more emphatical than is commonly apprehended, when 't is said, " The people were scattered abroad through all the land of Ægypt to gather stubble instead of straw."   For the stubble being very short, the acquist was difficult; a few fields afforded it not, and they were fain to wander far to obtain a sufficient quantity of it.

21. It is said in the *Song of Solomon*, that " The vines with the tender grape give a good smell."   That the flowers of the vine should be emphatically noted to give a pleasant smell seems hard unto our northern nostrils, which discover not such odours, and smell them not in full vineyards ; whereas in hot regions, and more spread and digested flowers, a sweet savour may be allowed, denotable from several human expressions, and the practice of the ancients, in putting the dried flowers of the vine into new wine to give it a pure and flosculous race or spirit, which wine was therefore called οἰνάνθινον, allowing unto every *cadus* two pounds of dried flowers.

And therefore, the vine flowering but in the spring, it cannot but seem an impertinent objection of the Jews, that the apostles were "full of new wine at Pentecost," when it was not to be found.   Wherefore we may rather conceive that the word γλεύκυ in that place implied not new wine or must, but some generous strong and sweet wine, wherein more especially lay the power of inebriation.

But if it be to be taken for some kind of must, it might be some kind of αἰείγλευκος, or long lasting must, which might be had at any time of the year, and which, as Pliny delivereth, they made by hindering and keeping the must from fermentation or working, and so it kept soft and sweet for no small time after.

22. When the dove, sent out of the ark, returned with a green olive leaf, according to the original: how the leaf, after ten months, and under water, should still maintain a verdure or greenness, need not much amuse the reader, if we consider that the olive tree is αἰείφυλλον, or continually green; that the leaves are of a bitter taste, and of a fast and lasting substance. Since we also find fresh and green leaves among the olives which we receive from remote countries ; and since the plants

at the bottom of the sea, and on the sides of rocks, maintain a deep and fresh verdure.

How the tree should stand so long in the deluge under water, may partly be allowed from the uncertain determination of the flows and currents of that time, and the qualification of the saltness of the sea, by the admixture of fresh water, when the whole watery element was together.

And it may be signally illustrated from the like examples in Theophrastus * and Pliny † in words to this effect : even the sea affordeth shrubs and trees ; in the Red sea whole woods do live, namely of bays and olives bearing fruit. The soldiers of Alexander, who sailed into India, made report, that the tides were so high in some islands, that they over-flowed, and covered the woods, as high as plane and poplar trees. The lower sort wholly, the greater all but the tops, whereto the mariners fastened their vessels at high water, and at the root in the ebb ; that the leaves of these sea-trees while under water looked green, but taken out presently dried with the heat of the sun. The like is delivered by Theophrastus, that some oaks do grow and bear acorns under the sea.

23. "The kingdom of heaven is like to a grain of mustard-seed, which a man took and sowed in his field, which indeed is the least of all seeds ; but when 't is grown is the greatest among herbs, and becometh a tree, so that the birds of the air come and lodge in the branches thereof."

Luke xiii, 19. "It is like a grain of mustard-seed, which a man took and cast it into his garden, and it waxed a great tree, and the fowls of the air lodged in the branches thereof."

This expression by a grain of mustard-seed, will not seem so strange unto you, who well consider it. That it is simply the least of seeds, you cannot apprehend, if you have beheld the seeds of *rapunculus,* marjorane, tobacco, and the smallest seed of *lunaria.*

But you may well understand it to be the smallest seed among herbs which produce so big a plant, or the least of herbal plants, which arise unto such a proportion, implied in

---

* *Theophrast. Hist.* lib. iv, cap. 7, 8.   † *Pliny,* lib. xiii, cap. ultimo.

the expression; the smallest of seeds, and becometh the greatest of herbs.

And you may also grant that it is the smallest of seeds of plants apt to δενδρίζειν, *arborescere, fruticescere,* or to grow unto a ligneous substance, and from an herby and oleraceous vegetable, to become a kind of tree, and to be accounted among the *dendrolachana* or *arboroleracea :* as upon strong seed, culture, and good ground, is observable in some cabbages, mallows, and many more, and therefore expressed by γίνεται τὸ δένδρον and γίνεται εἰς τὸ δένδρον, it becometh a tree, or *arborescit,* as Beza rendereth it.

Nor if warily considered doth the expression contain such difficulty. For the parable may not ground itself upon generals, or imply any or every grain of mustard, but point at such a grain as, from its fertile spirit, and other concurrent advantages, hath the success to become arboreous, shoot into such a magnitude, and acquire the like tallness. And unto such a grain the kingdom of heaven is likened, which from such slender beginnings shall find such increase and grandeur.

The expression also that it might grow into such dimensions that birds might lodge in the branches thereof, may be literally conceived; if we allow the luxuriancy of plants in Judæa, above our northern regions; if we accept of but half the story taken notice of by Tremellius, from the Jerusalem Talmud, of a mustard tree that was to be climbed like a fig tree; and of another, under whose shade a potter daily wrought: and it may somewhat abate our doubts, if we take in the advertisement of Herodotus concerning lesser plants of *milium* and *sesamum,* in the Babylonian soil: *milium ac sesamum in proceritatem instar arborum crescere, etsi mihi compertum, tamen memorare supersedeo, probè sciens eis qui nunquam Babyloniam regionem adierunt perquam incredibile visum iri.* We may likewise consider that the word κατασκηνῶσαι doth not necessarily signify making a nest, but rather sitting, roosting, cowering, and resting in the boughs, according as the same word is used by the Septuagint in other places,* as the vulgate rendereth it in this, *inhabitant,*

* Dan. iv, 9. Psal. i, 14, 12.

as our translation, 'lodgeth,' and the Rhemish, 'resteth in the branches.'

24. " And it came to pass that on the morrow Moses went into the tabernacle of witness, and behold the rod of Aaron for the house of Levi was budded, and brought forth buds, and bloomed blossoms, and yielded almonds." *

In the contention of the tribes and decision of priority and primogeniture of Aaron, declared by the rod, which in a night budded, flowered, and brought forth almonds, you cannot but apprehend a propriety in the miracle from that species of tree which leadeth in the vernal germination of the year, unto all the classes of trees; and so apprehend how properly in a night and short space of time the miracle arose, and somewhat answerable unto its nature the flowers and fruit appeared in this precocious tree, and whose original name † implieth such speedy efflorescence, as in its proper nature flowering in February, and shewing its fruit in March.

This consideration of that tree maketh the expression in Jeremy more emphatical, when 't is said, " What seest thou? and he said, a rod of an almond tree. Then said the Lord unto me, thou hast well seen, for I will hasten the word to perform it." ‡ I will be quick and forward like the almond tree, to produce the effects of my word, and hasten to display my judgments upon them.

And we may hereby more easily apprehend the expression in Ecclesiastes; "when the almond tree shall 'flourish," § that is, when the head, which is the prime part, and first sheweth itself in the world, shall grow white, like the flowers of the almond tree, whose fruit, as Athenæus delivereth, was first called κάρηνον, or the head, from some resemblance and covering parts of it.

How properly the priority was confirmed by a rod or staff, and why the rods and staffs of the princes were chosen for this decision, philologists will consider. For these were the badges, signs, and cognisances of their places, and were a kind of sceptre in their hands, denoting their super-eminen-

---

* The Rod of Aaron, Numb. xvii, 8.
† Shacher, from Shachar festinus fuit or maturuit. ‡ Jer. i, 11.
§ Eccles. xii, 5.

cies. The staff of divinity is ordinarily described in the hands of gods and goddesses in old draughts. Trojan and Grecian princes were not without the like, whereof the shoulders of Thersites felt from the hands of Ulysses. Achilles in Homer, as by a desperate oath, swears by his wooden sceptre, which should never bud nor bear leaves again; which seeming the greatest impossibility to him, advanceth the miracle of Aaron's rod. And if it could be well made out that Homer had seen the books of Moses, in that expression of Achilles, he might allude unto this miracle.

That power which proposed the experiment by blossoms in the rod, added also the fruit of almonds; the text not strictly making out the leaves, and so omitting the middle germination; the leaves properly coming after the flowers, and before the almonds. And therefore if you have well perused medals, you cannot but observe how in the impress of many shekels, which pass among us by the name of the Jerusalem shekels, the rod of Aaron is improperly laden with many leaves, whereas that which is shewn under the name of the Samaritan shekel, seems most conformable unto the text, which describeth the fruit without leaves.

25. "Binding[6] his foal unto the vine, and his ass's colt unto the choice vine."

That vines, which are commonly supported, should grow so large and bulky, as to be fit to fasten their juments, and beasts of labour unto them, may seem a hard expression unto many: which notwithstanding may easily be admitted, if we consider the account of Pliny, that in many places out of Italy vines do grow without any stay or support: nor will it be otherwise conceived of lusty vines, if we call to mind how the same author * delivereth, that the statua of Jupiter was made out of a vine; and that out of one single cyprian vine a scale or ladder was made that reached unto the roof of the temple of Diana at Ephesus.

* *Plin.* lib. xiv.

[6] *Binding, &c.*] In some parts of Persia, it was formerly the custom to turn their cattle into the vineyards after the vintage, to browse on the vines, some of which are so large that a man can scarcely compass their trunks in his arms.

26. "I was exalted as a palm tree in Engaddi, and as a rose plant[7] in Jericho." That the rose of Jericho, or that plant which passeth among us under that denomination, was signified in this text, you are not like to apprehend with some, who also name it the rose of St. Mary, and deliver, that it openeth the branches, and flowers upon the eve of our Saviour's nativity: but rather conceive it some proper kind of rose, which thrived and prospered in Jericho more than in the neighbour countries. For our rose of Jericho is a very low and hard plant, a few inches above the ground; one whereof brought from Judæa I have kept by me many years, nothing resembling a rose tree, either in flowers, branches, leaves, or growth; and so improper to answer the emphatical word of exaltation in the text: growing not only about Jericho, but other parts of Judæa and Arabia, as Bellonius hath observed: which being a dry and ligneous plant, is preserved many years, and though crumpled and furled up, yet, if infused in water, will swell and display its parts.

27. *Quasi Terebinthus extendi ramos*, when it is said in the same chapter, "as a turpentine tree[8] have I stretched out my branches." It will not seem strange unto such as have either seen that tree or examined its description: for it is a plant that widely displayeth its branches: and though in some European countries it be but of a low and fruticeous growth, yet Pliny observeth that it is great in Syria* and so allowably, or at least not improperly mentioned in the expression of Hosea† according to the vulgar translation, *Su-*

---

* Terebinthus in Macedonia fruticat, in Syria, magna est, lib. xiiî, *Plin.*
† *Hos.* iv, 13.

---

[7] *rose plant in Jericho.*] Sir R. K. Porter gives the following description of the oriental rose trees probably here intended:—" On first entering this bower of fairy land, I was struck with the appearance of two rose trees; full *fourteen feet high*, laden with thousands of flowers, in every degree of expansion, and of a bloom and delicacy of scent, that imbued the whole atmosphere with the most exquisite perfume; indeed, I believe that in no country of the world, does the rose grow in such perfection, as in Persia, in no country is it so culti-vated, and prized by the natives. Their gardens and courts are crowded with its plants, their rooms ornamented with vases filled with its gathered bunches, and every bath strewed with the full blown flowers, plucked from the ever replenished stems."

[8] *turpentine tree.*] An evergreen of moderate size, with a top and branches large in proportion; leaves like the olive, but green, mixed with red and purple; the flowers purple, growing in branches, like the vine; fruit like that of the juniper, and of a ruddy purple.

per capita montium sacrificant, &c., sub quercu, populo, et terebintho, quoniam bona est umbra ejus. And this diffusion and spreading of its branches, hath afforded the proverb of *terebintho stultior*, appliable unto arrogant or boasting persons, who spread and display their own acts, as Erasmus hath observed.

28. It is said in our translation, "Saul tarried in the uppermost parts of Gibeah, under a pomegranate tree which is in Migron: and the people which were with him were about six hundred men." And when it is said in some Latin translations, *Saul morabatur fixo tentorio sub malogranato*, you will not be ready to take it in the common literal sense, who know that a pomegranate tree is but low of growth, and very unfit to pitch a tent under it; and may rather apprehend it as the name of a place, or the rock of Rimmon, or Pomegranate; so named from pomegranates which grew there, and which many think to have been the same place mentioned in Judges.*

29. It is said in the book of Wisdom, "Where water stood before, dry land appeared, and out of the red sea a way appeared without impediment, and out of the violent streams a green field;" or as the Latin renders it, *campus germinans de profundo:* whereby it seems implied that the Israelites passed over a green field at the bottom of the sea: and though most would have this but a metaphorical expression, yet may it be literally tolerable; and so may be safely apprehended by those that sensibly know what great number of vegetables (as the several varieties of *algæ*, sea lettuce, *phasganium, conferva, caulis marina, abies, erica*, tamarice, divers sorts of *muscus, fucus, quercus marina*, and corallines) are found at the bottom of the sea. Since it is also now well known, that the western ocean, for many degrees, is covered with *sargasso* or *lenticula marina*, and found to arise from the bottom of that sea; since, upon the coast of Provence by the isles of Eres, there is a part of the Mediterranean sea, called *la Prairie*, or the meadowy sea, from the bottom thereof so plentifully covered with plants: since vast heaps of weeds are found in the bellies of some whales taken in the

* Judges xx, 45, 47. ch. xxi, 13.

northern ocean, and at a great distance from the shore: and since the providence of nature hath provided this shelter for minor fishes; both for their spawn, and safety of their young ones. And this might be more peculiarly allowed to be spoken of the red sea, since the Hebrews named it *suph* or the weedy sea: and, also, seeing Theophrastus and Pliny, observing the growth of vegetables under water, have made their chief illustrations from those in the Red sea.

30. You will readily discover how widely they are mistaken, who accept the sycamore mentioned in several parts of Scripture for the sycamore or tree of that denomination with us; which is properly but one kind or difference of *acer*, and bears no fruit with any resemblance unto a fig.

But you will rather, thereby, apprehend the true and genuine sycamore or *sycaminus*, which is a stranger in our parts. A tree (according to the description of Theophrastus, Dioscorides, and Galen,) resembling a mulberry tree in the leaf, but in the fruit a fig;[9] which it produceth not in the twigs but in the trunk or greater branches, answerable to the sycamore of Egypt, the Egyptian fig or *giamez* of the Arabians, described by Prosper Alpinus, with a leaf somewhat broader than a mulberry, and in its fruit like a fig. Insomuch that some have fancied it to have had its first production from a fig tree grafted on a mulberry. It is a tree common in Judæa, whereof they made frequent use in buildings; and so understood, it explaineth that expression in Isaiah:*
"*Sycamori excisi sunt, cedros substituemus.* The bricks are fallen down, but we will build with hewen stones: the sycamores are cut down, but we will change them into cedars."

It is a broad spreading tree, not only fit for walks, groves, and shade, but also affording profit. And therefore it is said that King David† appointed Baalhanan to be over his olive trees and sycamores, which were in great plenty; and it is accordingly delivered, that "Solomon made cedars to be as the sycamore trees that are in the vale for abundance."‡

---

* Isaiah, ix, 10.   † 1 Chron. xxvii. 28.   ‡ 1 Kings, x, 27.

[9] *resembling in fruit a fig.*] In smell and figure, but not in the mode of growth; they grow in clusters at the end of a fruit stalk, not singly like figs.

That is, he planted many, though they did not come to perfection in his days.

And as it grew plentifully about the plains, so was the fruit good for food; and, as Bellonius and late accounts deliver, very refreshing unto travellers in those hot and dry countries : whereby the expression of Amos* becomes more intelligible, when he said he was an herdsman, and a gatherer of sycamore fruit.   And the expression of David † also becomes more emphatical; "He destroyed their vines with hail, and their sycamore trees with frost." That is, their *sicmoth* in the original, a word in the sound not far from the sycamore.

Thus, when it is said, " If ye had faith as a grain of mustard seed, ye might say unto this sycamine tree, be thou plucked up by the roots, and be thou placed in the sea, and it should obey you : " ‡ it might be more significantly spoken of this sycamore; this being described to be *arbor vasta*, a large and well-rooted tree, whose removal was more difficult than many others.   And so the instance in that text, is very properly made in the sycamore tree, one of the largest and less removable trees among them.   A tree so lasting and well-rooted, that the sycamore which Zaccheus ascended, is still shewn in Judæa unto travellers; as also the hollow sycamore at Maturæa in Egypt, where the blessed virgin is said to have remained : which though it relisheth of the legend, yet it plainly declareth what opinion they had of the lasting condition of that tree, to countenance the tradition ; for which they might not be without some experience, since the learned describer of the pyramids § observeth, that the old Egyptians made coffins of this wood, which he found yet fresh and undecayed among divers of their mummies.

And thus, also, when Zaccheus climbed up into a sycamore above any other tree, this being a large and fair one, it cannot be denied that he made choice of a proper and advantageous tree to look down upon our Saviour.

31. Whether the expression of our Saviour in the parable of the sower, and the increase of the seed unto thirty, sixty,

* *Amos*, vii, 14.   † *Psalm*, lxxviii, 47.
‡ *Luke*, xvii, 6.   § D. Greaves.

and a hundred fold, had any reference unto the ages of believers, and measure of their faith, as children, young and old persons, as to beginners, well advanced and strongly confirmed Christians, as learned men have hinted; or whether in this progressional ascent there were any latent mystery, as the mystical interpreters of numbers may apprehend, I pretend not to determine.

But, how this multiplication may well be conceived, and in what way apprehended, and that this centesimal increase is not naturally strange, you that are no stranger in agriculture, old and new, are not like to make great doubt.

That every grain should produce an ear affording an hundred grains, is not like to be their conjecture who behold the growth of corn in our fields, wherein a common grain doth produce far less in number. For barley, consisting but of two *versus* or rows, seldom exceedeth twenty grains, that is, ten upon each στοῖχος, or row; rye, of a square figure, is very fruitful at forty: wheat, besides the frit and *uruncus*, or imperfect grains of the small husks at the top and bottom of the ear, is fruitful at ten treble *glumi* or husks in a row, each containing but three grains in breadth, if the middle grain arriveth at all to perfection; and so maketh up threescore grains in both sides.

Yet even this centesimal fructification may be admitted in some sorts of *cerealia*, and grains from one ear: if we take in *triticum centigranum*, or *fertilissimum Plinii*, Indian wheat, and *panicum;* which, in every ear, containeth hundreds of grains.

But this increase may easily be conceived of grains in their total multiplication, in good and fertile ground, since, if every grain of wheat produceth but three ears, the increase will arise above that number. Nor are we without examples of some grounds which have produced many more ears, and above this centesimal increase: as Pliny hath left recorded of the Byzacian field in Africa.* *Misit ex eo loco procurator ex uno grano quadraginta paucis minus germina. Misit et Neroni similiter tercentum quadraginta stipulas ex uno grano. Cum centesimos quidem Leontini Siciliæ campi*

* *Plin. Hist. Nat.* lib. xviii, cap. 21.

fundunt, aliique, et tota Bætica, et imprimis Ægyptus. And
even in our own country, from one grain of wheat sowed in
a garden, I have numbered many more than an hundred.[1]

And though many grains are commonly lost which come
not to sprouting or earing, yet the same is also verified in
measure; as that one bushel should produce a hundred, as is
exemplified by the corn in Gerar; " Then Isaac sowed in
that land, and received in the same year an hundred fold." *
That is, as the Chaldee explaineth it, a hundred for one,
when he measured it. And this Pliny seems to intend, when he
saith of the fertile Byzacian territory before mentioned, *ex uno
centeni quinquaginta modii redduntur.* And may be favourably apprehended of the fertility of some grounds in Poland;
wherein, after the accounts of Gaguinus, from rye sowed in
August, come thirty or forty ears, and a man on horseback
can scarce look over it.

In the sabbatical crop of Judæa, there must be admitted a
large increase, and probably not short of this centesimal
multiplication : for it supplied part of the sixth year, the
whole seventh, and eighth until the harvest of that year.

The seven years of plenty in Egypt must be of high increase; when, by storing up but the fifth part, they supplied
the whole land, and many of their neighbours after: for it is
said, " the famine was in all the land about them." † And
therefore though the causes of the dearth in Egypt be made
out from the defect of the overflow of Nilus, according to the
dream of Pharaoh ; yet was that no cause of the scarcity in
the land of Canaan, which may rather be ascribed to the
want of the former and latter rains, for some succeeding
years, if their famine held time and duration with that of
Egypt; as may be probably gathered from that expression of
Joseph, " come down unto me (into Egypt) and tarry not,
and there will I nourish thee : for yet there are five years of
famine, lest thou and thy household, and all that thou hast,
come to poverty." ‡

* *Gen.* xxvi, 12.

† *Gen.* xli, 56.   ‡ *Gen* xlv, 9, 11.

[1] *many more than an hundred.*] The   "no less than three hundred stalks and
manuscript in the British Museum reads,   ears."—*MS. Sloan.* 1841.

How they preserved their corn so long in Egypt may seem hard unto northern and moist climates, except we consider the many ways of preservation practised by antiquity, and also take in that handsome account of Pliny; what corn soever is laid up in the ear, it taketh no harm keep it as long as you will, although the best and most assured way to keep corn is in caves and vaults under ground, according to the practice of Cappadocia and Thracia.

In Egypt and Mauritania above all things they look to this, that their granaries stand on high ground; and how dry soever their floor be, they lay a course of chaff betwixt it and the ground. Besides, they put up their corn in granaries and bins together with the ear. And Varro delivereth that wheat laid up in that manner will last fifty years; millet an hundred; and beans so conserved, in a cave of Ambracia, were known to live an hundred and twenty years; that is, from the time of King Pyrrhus, unto the Pyratick war under the conduct of Pompey.

More strange it may seem how, after seven years, the grains conserved should be fruitful for a new production. For it is said that Joseph delivered seed unto the Egyptians, to sow their land for the eighth year: and corn after seven years is like to afford little or no production, according to Theophrastus; " *ad sementem semen anniculum optimum putatur, binum deterius et trinum; ultra sterile fermè est, quanquam ad usum cibarium idoneum.**

Yet since, from former exemplifications, corn may be made to last so long, the fructifying power may well be conceived to last in some good proportion, according to the region and place of its conservation, as the same Theophrastus hath observed, and left a notable example from Cappadocia, where corn might be kept sixty years, and remain fertile at forty; according to his expression thus translated; *in Cappadociæ loco quodam Petra dicto, triticum ad quadraginta annos fœcundum est, et ad sementem percommodum durare proditum est, sexagenos aut septuagenos ad usum cibarium servari posse idoneum.* The situation of that conservatory, was, as he delivereth, ὑψηλὸν, εὔπνουν, εὔαυρον, high, airy, and exposed

* *Theoph. Hist.* lib. viii.

L 2

to favourable winds.   And upon such consideration of winds
and ventilation, some conceived the Egyptian granaries were
made open, the country being free from rain.   However it
was, that contrivance could not be without some hazard : for
the great mists and dews of that country might dispose the
corn unto corruption.*

More plainly may they mistake, who from some analogy of
name (as if pyramid were derived from πύρον, *triticum*), conceive the Egyptian pyramids to have been built for granaries,
or look for any settled monuments about the deserts erected
for that intention; since their store-houses were made in the
great towns, according to Scripture expression, " He gathered up all the food for seven years, which was in the land of
Egypt, and laid up the food in the cities : the food of the field
which was round about every city, laid he up in the same."†

32. " For if thou wert cut out of the olive tree, which is
wild by nature, and wert grafted, contrary to nature, into a
good olive tree, how much more shall these which be the natural branches, be grafted into their own olive tree ? "   In
which place, how answerable [2] to the doctrine of husbandry
this expression of St. Paul is, you will readily apprehend who
understand the rules of insition or grafting, and that way of
vegetable propagation; wherein it is contrary to nature, or
natural rules which art observeth : viz. to make use of scions
more ignoble than the stock, or to graft wild upon domestic
and good plants, according as Theophrastus hath anciently
observed,‡ and, making instance in the olive, hath left this
doctrine unto us ; *urbanum sylvestribus ut satis oleastris in-*
serere.   Nam si è contrario. sylvestrem in urbanos severis,
etsi differentia quædam erit, tamen bonæ frugis arbor nun-
quam profecto reddetur : § which is also agreeable unto our
present practice, who graft pears on thorns, and apples upon
crab stocks, not using the contrary insition.   And when it is
said, "how much more shall these, which are the natural

* Egypt ὁμιχλώδης, καὶ δρόσερος.   Vide *Theophrastum.*
† *Gen.* xli, 48.   ‡ *De Causis Plant.* lib. i, cap. 7.
                   § καλλικαρπεῖν οὐκ ἕξει.

[2] *how answerable.*]   " How geographically answerable."—*MS. Sloan.* 1841.

branches, be grafted into their own natural olive tree ? " this is also agreeable unto the rule of the same author; ἔστι δὲ βελτίων ἐγκεντǫρισμός ὁμοίων εἰς ὅμοια, *insitio melior est similium in similibus:* for the nearer consanguinity there is between the scions and the stock, the readier comprehension is made, and the nobler fructification. According also unto the later caution of Laurenbergius;* *arbores domesticæ insitioni destinatæ, semper anteponendæ sylvestribus.* And though the success be good, and may suffice upon stocks of the same denomination; yet, to be grafted upon their own and mother stock, is the nearest insition: which way, though less practised of old, is now much embraced, and found a notable way for melioration of the fruit, and much the rather, if the tree to be grafted on be a good and generous plant, a good and fair olive, as the apostle seems to imply by a peculiar word,† scarce to be found elsewhere.

It must be also considered, that the *oleaster,* or wild olive, by cutting, transplanting, and the best managery of art, can be made but to produce such olives as Theophrastus saith, were particularly named *phaulia,* that is, but bad olives; and that it was among prodigies, for the *oleaster* to become an olive tree.

And when insition and grafting, in the text, is applied unto the olive tree, it hath an emphatical sense, very agreeable unto that tree which is best propagated this way; not at all by surculation, as Theophrastus observeth,‡ nor well by seed, as hath been observed. *Omne semen simile genus perficit, præter oleam, oleastrum enim generat, hoc est sylvestrem oleam, et non oleam veram.*

"If, therefore, thou Roman and Gentile branch, which wert cut from the wild olive, art now, by the signal mercy of God, beyond the ordinary and commonly expected way, grafted into the true olive, the church of God; if thou, which neither naturally nor by human art canst be made to produce any good fruit, and, next to a miracle, to be made a true olive, art now by the benignity of God grafted into the proper olive; how much more shall the Jew, and natural branch, be grafted into its genuine and mother tree, wherein propinquity

---

* *De horticultura.*   † καλλιέλαιον.   *Rom.* xi, 24

‡ *Geoponic.* lib. x.

of nature is like, so readily and prosperously, to effect a coalition? And this more especially by the expressed way of insition or implantation, the olive being not successfully propagable by seed, nor at all by surculation."

33. "As for the stork, the fir trees are her house."* This expression, in our translation, which keeps close to the original *chasideh*, is somewhat different from the Greek and Latin translation; nor agreeable unto common observation, whereby they are known commonly to build upon chimneys, or the tops of houses and high buildings, which notwithstanding, the common translation may clearly consist with observation, if we consider that this is commonly affirmed of the black stork, and take notice of the description of *Ornithologus* in Aldrovandus, that such storks are often found in divers parts, and that they do *in arboribus nidulari, præsertim in abietibus;* make their nests on trees,[3] especially upon fir trees. Nor wholly disagreeing unto the practice of the common white stork, according unto Varro, *nidulantur in agris :* and the concession of Aldrovandus that sometimes they build on trees: and the assertion of Bellonius,† that men dress them nests, and place cradles upon high trees, in marish regions, that storks may breed upon them: which course some observe for herons and cormorants with us. And this building of storks upon trees, may be also answerable unto the original and natural way of building of storks before the political habitations of men, and the raising of houses and high buildings; before they were invited by such conveniences and prepared nests, to relinquish their natural places of nidulation. I say, before or where such advantages are not ready; when swallows found other places than chimneys, and daws found other places than holes in high fabricks to build in.

34. "And therefore, Israel said, carry down the man a present, a little balm, a little honey, and myrrh, nuts, and almonds."‡ Now whether this, which Jacob sent, were the proper balsam extolled by human writers, you cannot but make some doubt, who find the Greek translation to be ῥητίνη,

* *Psalm* civ, 17.   † *Bellonius de Avibus.*   ‡ *Gen.* xliii, 11.

[3] *make their nests on trees.*] Doubdan saw immense numbers of these birds in   Galilee resting in the evening on trees.— *Harmer's Observations*, vol. iii, p. 323.

that is, *resina*, and so may have some suspicion that it might be some pure distillation from the turpentine tree; which grows prosperously and plentifully in Judæa, and seems so understood by the Arabic; and was indeed esteemed by Theophrastus and Dioscorides, the chiefest of resinous bodies, and the word *resina* emphatically used for it.

That the balsam plant hath grown and prospered in Judæa we believe without dispute. For the same is attested by Theophrastus, Pliny, Justinus, and many more. From the commendation that Galen affordeth of the balsam of Syria, and the story of Cleopatra, that she obtained some plants of balsam from Herod the Great to transplant into Egypt. But whether it was so anciently in Judea as the time of Jacob; nay, whether this plant was here before the time of Solomon, that great collector of vegetable rarities, some doubt may be made from the account of Josephus, that the Queen of Sheba, a part of Arabia, among presents unto Solomon brought some plants of the balsam tree, as one of the peculiar estimables of her country.

Whether this ever had its natural growth, or were an original native plant in Judæa, much more that it was peculiar unto that country, a greater doubt may arise: while we read in Pausanias, Strabo, and Diodorus, that it grows also in Arabia, and find in Theophrastus,* that it grew in two gardens about Jericho in Judæa. And more especially while we seriously consider that notable discourse between Abdella, Abdachim, and Alpinus, concluding the natural and original place of this singular plant to be in Arabia, about Mecha and Medina, where it still plentifully groweth, and mountains abound therein; † from whence it hath been carefully transplanted by the Bashas of grand Cairo, into the garden of Matarea: where, when it dies, it is repaired again from those parts of Arabia, from whence the grand Signior yearly receiveth a present of balsam from the Xeriff of Mecha, still called by the Arabians *balessan;* whence they believe arose the Greek appellation balsam. And since these balsam plants are not now to be found in Judæa, and though purposely cultivated, are often lost in Judæa, but everlastingly live, and

---

* *Theophrast.* lib. ix, cap. 6.   † *Prosper Alpinus, de Balsamo.*

naturally renew in Arabia, they probably concluded, that those of Judæa were foreign and transplanted from these parts.

All which notwithstanding, since the same plant may grow naturally and spontaneously in several countries, and either from inward or outward causes be lost in one region, while it continueth and subsisteth in another, the balsam tree might possibly be a native of Judæa as well as of Arabia; which because *de facto* it cannot be clearly made out, the ancient expressions of scripture become doubtful in this point. But since this plant hath not for a long time grown in Judæa, and still plentifully prospers in Arabia, that which now comes in precious parcels to us, and still is called the balsam of Judæa, may now surrender its name, and more properly be called the balsam of Arabia. [4]

35. " And the flax and the barley was smitten ; for the barley was in the ear, and the flax was bolled, but the wheat and the rye were not smitten, for they were not grown up." [*] How the barley and the flax should be smitten in the plague of hail in Egypt, and the wheat and rye escape, because they were not yet grown up, may seem strange unto English observers, who call barley summer corn, sown so many months after wheat, and [who] beside (*hordeum polystichon*, or big barley), sow not barley in the winter to anticipate the growth of wheat.

And the same may also seem a preposterous expression unto all who do not consider the various agriculture, and different husbandry of nations, and such as was practised in Egypt, and fairly proved to have been also used in Judæa, wherein their barley harvest was before that of wheat; as is confirmable from that expression in Ruth, that she came into Bethlehem at the beginning of barley harvest, and staid unto the end of wheat harvest; from the death of Manasses the father of Judith, emphatically expressed to have happened in the wheat harvest, and more advanced heat of the sun; and from the custom of the Jews, to offer the barley sheaf of the first-fruits in March, and a cake of wheat flour but at the end of Pentecost, consonant unto the practice of the Egyptians,

* *Exod.* ix, 31.

[4] *Arabia.*] See note on the balsam, or Balm of Gilead, at page 130.

who (as Theophrastus delivereth) sowed their barley early in reference to their first-fruits; and also the common rural practice, recorded by the same author, *mature seritur triticum, hordeum, quod etiam maturius seritur;* wheat and barley are sowed early, but barley earlier of the two.

Flax was also an early plant, as may be illustrated from the neighbour country of Canaan. For the Israelites kept the passover in Gilgal, in the fourteenth day of the first month, answering unto part of our March, having newly passed Jordan: and the spies which were sent from Shittim unto Jericho, not many days before, were hid by Rahab under the stalks of flax, which lay drying on the top of her house; which sheweth that the flax was already and newly gathered. For this was the first preparation of flax, and before fluviation or rotting, which, after Pliny's account, was after wheat harvest.

"But the wheat and the rye were not smitten, for they were not grown up." The original signifies that it was hidden, or dark, the vulgar and septuagint that it was *serotinous* or *late*, and our old translation that it was late sown. And so the expression and interposition of Moses, who well understood the husbandry of Egypt, might emphatically declare the state of wheat and rye in that particular year; and if so, the same is solvable from the time of the flood of Nilus, and the measure of its inundation. For if it were very high, and over drenching the ground, they were forced to later seed-time; and so the wheat and the rye escaped; for they were more slowly growing grains, and, by reason of the greater inundation of the river, were sown later than ordinary that year, especially in the plains near the river, where the ground drieth latest.

Some think the plagues of Egypt were acted in one month, others but in the compass of twelve. In the delivery of Scripture there is no account of what time of the year or particular month they fell out; but the account of these grains, which were either smitten or escaped, makes the plague of hail to have probably happened in February. This may be collected from the new and old account of the seed-time and harvest in Egypt. For, according to the account of Radzivil,* the river rising in June, and the banks being cut in September, they sow about St. Andrew's, when the flood is retired, and the moderate dryness of the ground permitteth. So that the barley, anticipating the wheat, either in time of sowing or growing, might be in ear in February.

The account of Pliny † is little different. They cast their seed upon the slime and mud when the river is down, which commonly happeneth in the beginning of November. They begin to reap and cut down a little before the calends of April, or about the middle of March, and in the month of May their harvest is in. So that barley, anticipating wheat, it might be in ear in February, and wheat not yet grown up, at least to the spindle or ear, to be destroyed by the hail. For they cut down about the middle of March, at least their forward corns, and in the month of May all sorts of corn were in.

The "turning of the river into blood" shews in what month this happened not. That is, not when the river had overflown; for it is said, "the Egyptians digged round about the river for water to drink," which they could not have done if the river had been out and the fields under water.

In the same text you cannot, without some hesitation, pass over the translation of rye, which the original nameth *cassumeth*, the Greek rendereth *olyra*, the French and Dutch *spelta*, the Latin *zea*, and not *secale*, the known word for rye. But this common rye, so well understood at present, was not distinctly described, or not well known from early antiquity. And, therefore, in this uncertainty, some have thought it to have been the *typha* of the ancients. Cordus will have it to be *olyra*, and Ruellius some kind of *oryza*. But having no vulgar and well-known name for those grains, we warily embrace an appellation of near affinity, and tolerably render it rye.

While flax, barley, wheat, and rye are named, some may wonder why no mention is made of rice, wherewith, at present, Egypt so much aboundeth. But whether that plant grew so early in that country, some doubt may be made; for

* *Radzivil's Travels.*   † *Plin.* lib. xviii, cap. 18

rice is originally a grain of India, and might not then be transplanted into Egypt.

36. " Let them become as the grass growing upon the house top, which withereth before it be plucked up, wherewith the mower filleth not his hand, nor he that bindeth sheaves his bosom."*   Though the "filling of the hand," and mention of "sheaves of hay " may seem strange unto us, who use neither handfull or sheaves in that kind of husbandry, yet may it be properly taken, and you are not like to doubt thereof, who may find the like expressions in the authors *De Re Rustica*, concerning the old way of this husbandry.

Columella,† delivering what works were not to be permitted upon the Roman *feriæ*, or festivals, among others, sets down that upon such days it was not lawful to carry or bind up hay, *Nec fœnum vincire nec vehere per religiones pontificum licet*.

Marco Varro ‡ is more particular; *Primum de pratis herbarum cum crescere desiit, subsecari falcibus debet, et quoad peracescat furcillis versari, cum peracuit, de his manipulos fieri et vehi in villam.*

And their course of mowing seems somewhat different from ours.   For they cut not down clear at once, but used an after section, which they peculiarly called *sicilitium*, according as the word is expounded by Georgius Alexandrinus and Beroaldus, after Pliny : *Sicilire est falcibus consectari quæ fœnisecæ præterierunt, aut ea secare quæ fœnisecæ præterierunt.*

37. When 't is said that Elias lay and slept under a juniper tree, some may wonder how that tree, which in our parts groweth but low and shrubby, should afford him shade and covering.[5]   But others know that there is a lesser and a larger kind of that vegetable; that it makes a tree in its proper soil and region.   And may find in Pliny that in the temple of Diana Saguntina, in Spain, the rafters were made of juniper.

In that expression of David,§ "Sharp arrows of the mighty, with coals of juniper."   Though juniper be left out in

---

* *Psalm* cxxix, 7.   † *Columella*, lib. ii, cap. 22.
‡ *Varro*, lib. i, cap. 49.   § *Psalm* cxx, 4.

[5] *When 't is said, &c.*]   Parkhurst   this humble shelter *for want of a better.*
suggests that the prophet took up with

the last translation, yet may there be an emphatical sense from that word; since juniper abounds with a piercing oil, and makes a smart fire. And the rather, if that quality be half true, which Pliny affirmeth, that the coals of juniper raked up will keep a glowing fire for the space of a year. For so the expression will emphatically imply, not only the "smart burning but the lasting fire of their malice."

That passage of Job,* wherein he complains that poor and half-famished fellows despised him, is of greater difficulty; "For want and famine they were solitary, they cut up mallows by the bushes, and juniper roots for meat." Wherein we might at first doubt the translation, not only from the Greek text, but the assertion of Dioscorides, who affirmeth that the roots of juniper are of a venomous quality. But Scaliger hath disproved the same from the practice of the African physicians, who use the decoction of juniper roots against the venereal disease. The Chaldee reads it *genista*, or some kind of broom, which will be also unusual and hard diet, except thereby we understand the *orobanche*, or broom rape, which groweth from the roots of broom; and which, according to Dioscorides, men used to eat raw or boiled, in the manner of asparagus.

And, therefore, this expression doth highly declare the misery, poverty, and extremity of the persons who were now mockers of him; they being so contemptible and necessitous, that they were fain to be content, not with a mean diet, but such as was no diet at all, the roots of trees, the roots of juniper, which none would make use of for food, but in the lowest necessity, and some degree of famishing.

38. While some have disputed whether Theophrastus knew the scarlet berry, others may doubt whether that noble tincture were known unto the Hebrews, which, notwithstanding, seems clear from the early and iterated expressions of Scripture concerning the scarlet tincture, and is the less to be doubted, because the scarlet berry grew plentifully in the land of Canaan, and so they were furnished with the materials of that colour. For though Dioscorides saith it groweth in Armenia and Cappadocia; yet that it also grew in

* *Job* xxx, 3, 4.

Judæa, seems more than probable from the account of Bellonius, who observed it to be so plentiful in that country, that it afforded a profitable commodity, and great quantity thereof was transported by the Venetian merchants.

How this should be fitly expressed by the word *tolagnoth, vermis,* or worm, may be made out from Pliny, who calls it *coccus scolecius,* or the wormy berry; as also from the name of that colour called vermilion, or the worm colour: and which is also answerable unto the true nature of it. For this is no proper berry containing the fructifying part, but a kind of vesicular excrescence, adhering commonly to the leaf of the *ilex coccigera,* or dwarf and small kind of oak, whose leaves are always green, and its proper seminal parts acorns. This little bag containeth a red pulp, which, if not timely gathered, or left to itself, produceth small red flies, and partly a red powder, both serviceable unto the tincture. And, therefore, to prevent the generation of flies, when it is first gathered, they sprinkle it over with vinegar, especially such as make use of the fresh pulp for the confection of *alkermes;* which still retaineth the Arabic name, from the *kermes-berry;* which is agreeable unto the description of Bellonius and Quinqueranus. And the same we have beheld in Provence and Languedoc, where it is plentifully gathered, and called *manna rusticorum,* from the considerable profit which the peasants make by gathering of it.

39. Mention is made of oaks in divers parts of Scripture, which though the Latin sometimes renders a turpentine tree, yet surely some kind of oak may be understood thereby; but whether our common oak, as is commonly apprehended, you may well doubt; for the common oak, which prospereth so well with us, delighteth not in hot regions. And that diligent botanist, Bellonius, who took such particular notice of the plants of Syria and Judæa, observed not the vulgar oak in those parts. But he found the *ilex, chesne vert,* or evergreen oak, in many places; as also that kind of oak which is properly named *esculus:* and he makes mention thereof in places about Jerusalem, and in his journey from thence unto Damascus, where he found *montes ilice, et esculo virentes;* which in his discourse of Lemnos, he saith are always green.

And therefore when it is said of Absalom, that "his mule went under the thick boughs of a great oak, and his head caught hold of the oak, and he was taken up between the heaven and the earth," * that oak might be some *ilex* or rather *esculus.* For that is a thick and bushy kind, in *orbem comosa,* as Dalechampius; *ramis in orbem dispositis comans,* as Rene-almus describeth it.   And when it is said that " Ezechias broke down the images, and cut down the groves,"† they might much consist of oaks, which were sacred unto Pagan deities, as this more particularly, according to that of Virgil,

> —— Nemorumque Jovi quæ maxima frondet
> Esculus.——

And, in Judæa, where no hogs were eaten by the Jews, and few kept by others, 'tis not unlikely that they most cherished the *esculus,* which might serve for food for men.   For the acorns thereof are the sweetest of any oak, and taste like chesnuts ; and so, producing an edulious or esculent fruit, is properly named *esculus.*

They which know the *ilex* or evergreen oak, with some-what prickled leaves, named πρίνος, will better understand the irreconcileable answer of the two elders, when the one ac-cused Susanna of incontinency under a πρίνος or evergreen oak, the other under a σχῖνος, *lentiscus,* or mastic tree, which are so different in bigness, boughs, leaves, and fruit, the one bearing acorns, the other berries : and without the know-ledge, will not emphatically or distinctly understand that of the poet,

> Flavaque de viridi stillabant ilice mella.

40. When we often meet with the cedars of Libanus, that expression may be used, not only because they grew in a known and neighbour country, but also because they were of the noblest and largest kind of that vegetable : and we find the Phœnician cedar magnified by the ancients.   The cedar of Libanus is a *coniferous* tree, bearing *cones* or clogs, (not

---

* 2 *Sam.* xviii, 9, 14.   † 2 *Kings* xviii, 4.

berries) of such a vastness, that Melchior Lussy, a great
traveller, found one upon Libanus, as big as seven men could
compass. Some are now so curious as to keep the branches
and *cones* thereof among their rare collections. And, though
much cedar wood be now brought from America, yet 'tis
time to take notice of the true cedar of Libanus, employed
in the temple of Solomon: for they have been much destroyed and neglected, and become at last but thin. Bellonius could reckon but twenty-eight, Rowolfius and Radzivil
but twenty-four, and Bidulphus the same number. And a
later account of some English travellers* saith, that they
are now but in one place, and in a small compass, in
Libanus. [6]

*Quando ingressi fueritis terram, et plantaveritis in illa
ligna pomifera, auferetis præputia eorum. Poma quæ ger-
minant, immunda erunt vobis, nec edetis ex eis. Quarto
autem anno, omnis fructus eorum sanctificabitur, laudabilis
domino. Quinto autem anno comedetis fructus.* By this law
they were enjoined not to eat of the fruits of the trees which
they planted for the first three years: and, as the vulgar
expresseth it, to take away the *prepuces*, from such trees,
during that time; the fruits of the fourth year being holy
unto the Lord, and those of the fifth allowable unto others.
Now if *auferre præputia* be taken, as many learned men
have thought, to pluck away the bearing buds, before they
proceed unto flowers or fruit, you will readily apprehend the
metaphor, from the analogy and similitude of those sprouts
and buds, which, shutting up the fruitful particle, resembleth
the preputial part.

* *A Journey to Jerusalem,* 1672.

[6] *in a small compass, &c.*] Burck-
hardt thus describes the cedars of Libanus:—"They stand on uneven ground,
and form a small wood. Of the oldest
and best-looking trees, I counted eleven
or twelve; twenty-five very large ones:
about fifty of middling size; and more
than three hundred smaller and younger
ones. The oldest trees are distinguished,
by having the foliage and small branches
at the top only, and by four, five, or
even seven trunks springing from one
base; the branches and foliage of the
others were lower, but I saw none whose
leaves touched the ground, like those in
Kew Gardens. The trunks of the old
trees are covered with the names of travellers and other persons who have visited them: I saw a date of the seventeenth century. The trunks of the oldest trees seem to be quite dead; the
wood is of a grey tint."—*Travels in
Syria,* 19, 20.

And you may also find herein a piece of husbandry not mentioned in Theophrastus or Columella. For by taking away of the buds and hindering fructification, the trees become more vigorous, both in growth and future production. By such a way King Pyrrhus got into a lusty race of beeves, and such as were desired over all Greece, by keeping them from generation until the ninth year.

And you may also discover a physical advantage in the goodness of the fruit, which becometh less crude and more wholesome, upon the fourth or fifth year's production.

41. While you read in Theophrastus or modern herbalists, a strict division of plants, into *arbor, frutex, suffrutex et herba,* you cannot but take notice of the Scriptural division at the creation, into tree and herb: and this may seem too narrow to comprehend the class of vegetables; which, notwithstanding, may be sufficient, and a plain and intelligible division thereof. And therefore in this difficulty concerning the division of plants, the learned botanist, Cæsalpinus, thus concludeth, *clarius agemus si alterâ divisione neglectâ, duo tantum plantarum genera substituamus, arborem scilicet, et herbam, conjungentes cum arboribus frutices, et cum herba suffrutices; frutices* being the lesser trees, and *suffrutices* the larger, harder, and more solid herbs.

And this division into herb and tree may also suffice, if we take in that natural ground of the division of perfect plants, and such as grow from seeds. For plants, in their first production, do send forth two leaves adjoining to the seed; and then afterwards, do either produce two other leaves, and so successively before any stalk; and such go under the name of πόα, βοτάνη or herb; or else, after the two first leaves succeeded to the seed leaves, they send forth a stalk or rudiment of a stalk, before any other leaves, and such fall under the classes of δένδρον or tree. So that, in this natural division, there are but two grand differences, that is, tree and herb. The *frutex* and *suffrutex* have the way of production from the seed, and in other respects the *suffrutices* or *cremia*, have a middle and participating nature, and referable unto herbs.

42. "I have seen the ungodly in great power, and flourish-ing like a green bay tree."[7] Both Scripture and human writers draw frequent illustrations from plants. Scribonius Largus illustrates the old cymbals from the *cotyledon palus-tris* or *umbilicus veneris.* Who would expect to find Aaron's mitre in any plant? Yet Josephus hath taken some pains to make out the same in the seminal knop of *hyoscyamus* or henbane. The Scripture compares the figure of manna unto the seed of coriander. In Jeremy* we find the expression, "straight as a palm tree." And here the wicked in their flourishing state are likened unto a bay tree. Which, suffi-ciently answering the sense of the text, we are unwilling to exclude that noble plant from the honour of having its name in Scripture. Yet we cannot but observe, that the septu-agint renders it cedars, and the vulgar accordingly, *vidi impium superexaltatum, et elevatum sicut cedros Libani ;* and the translation of Tremellius mentions neither bay nor cedar ; *sese explicantem tanquam arbor indigena virens ;* which seems to have been followed by the last low Dutch transla-tion. A private translation renders it like a green self-grow-ing laurel.† The high Dutch of Luther's Bible retains the word laurel ; and so doth the old Saxon and Iceland transla-tion ; so also the French, Spanish, and Italian of Diodati : yet his notes acknowledge that some think it rather a cedar, and others any large tree in a prospering and natural soil.

But however these translations differ, the sense is allow-able and obvious unto apprehension : when no particular plant is named, any proper to the sense may be supposed ; where either cedar or laurel is mentioned, if the preceding words (exalted and elevated) be used, they are more appli-able unto the cedar ; where the word (flourishing) is used, it is more agreeable unto the laurel, which, in its prosperity, abounds with pleasant flowers, whereas those of the cedar

* *Jer.* x, 5.   † *Ainsworth.*

[7] *flourishing, &c.*] "Spreading him-self (is the English version) like a green bay tree :"—more accurately "like a *native* tree"—a tree growing in its native soil, not having suffered by trans-plantation, and therefore spreading itself luxuriantly.—*Psalm* xxxvii, 35.

are very little, and scarce perceptible, answerable to the fir, pine, and other coniferous trees.

43. "And in the morning, when they were come from Bethany, he was hungry; and seeing a fig tree afar off having leaves, he came, if haply he might find any thing thereon; and when he came to it, he found nothing but leaves: for the time of figs was not yet." Singular conceptions have passed from learned men to make out this passage of St. Mark which St. Matthew* so plainly delivereth; most men doubting why our Saviour should curse the tree for bearing no fruit, when the time of fruit was not yet come; or why it is said that the time of figs was not yet,[8] when, notwithstanding, figs might be found at that season.

Heinsius,† who thinks that Elias must salve the doubt, according to the received reading of the text, undertaketh to vary the same, reading οὐ γὰρ ἦν, καιρὸς σύκων, that is, for where he was, it was the season or time for figs.

A learned interpreter‡ of our own, without alteration of accents or words, endeavours to salve all, by another interpretation of the same, οὐ γὰρ καιρὸς σύκων, for it was not a good or seasonable year for figs.

But, because men part not easily with old beliefs or the received construction of words, we shall briefly set down what may be alleged for it.

And, first, for the better comprehension of all deductions hereupon, we may consider the several differences and distinctions both of fig trees and their fruits. Suidas upon the word ἰσχάς makes four divisions of figs, ὄλυνθος, φήληξ, σῦκον and ἰσχάς. But because φήληξ makes no considerable distinction, learned men do chiefly insist upon the three others;

---

* *Mark* xi, 13.   *Matt.* xxi, 19.   † *Heinsius in Nonnum.*
‡ Dr. Hammond.

[8] *for the time of figs, &c.*] The difficulty of this passage is simply and adequately solved, by reading, *though the fig harvest was not yet.* When it is considered that the fig tree produces its fruit before its leaves, our Saviour was justified in looking for fruit on a fig tree which was in leaf, and before the time *for gathering figs* had arrived. To find a tree which was, at that time, *without* figs, was, in fact, to find *a barren fig tree.*

In reference to the mode in which the fig tree vegetates, Jortin has the following beautiful remark:—" A good man may be said to resemble the fig tree; which, without producing blossoms and flowers, like some other trees, and raising expectations which are often deceitful, seldom fails to produce fruit in its season." —*Jortin's Tracts,* vol. 2, p. 537.

that is, ὄλυνθος, or *grossus,* which are the buttons, or small sort of figs, either not ripe, or not ordinarily proceeding to ripeness, but fall away at least in the greatest part, and especially in sharp winters, which are also named συκάδες, and distinguished from the fruit of the wild fig, or *caprificus,* which is named ἐρινεὸς, and never cometh unto ripeness. The second is called σῦκον or *ficus,* which commonly proceedeth unto ripeness in its due season. A third, the ripe fig dried, which maketh the ἰσχάδες or *carrier.*

Of fig trees there are also many divisions: for some are *prodromi* or precocious, which bear fruit very early, whether they bear once or oftner in the year; some are *protericæ,* which are the most early of the precocious trees, and bear soonest of any; some are *æstivæ,* which bear in the common season of the summer, and some *serotinæ* which bear very late.

Some are *biferous* and *triferous,* which bear twice or thrice in the year, and some are of the ordinary standing course, which make up the expected season of figs.

Again, some fig trees, either in their proper kind, or fertility in some single ones, do bear fruit or rudiments of fruit all the year long; as is annually observable in some kind of fig trees in hot and proper regions; and may also be observed in some fig trees of more temperate countries, in years of no great disadvantage, wherein, when the summer ripe fig is past, others begin to appear, and so standing in buttons all the winter, do either fall away before the spring, or else proceed to ripeness.

Now according to these distinctions, we may measure the intent of the text, and endeavour to make out the expression. For, considering the diversity of these trees and their several fructifications, probable or possible it is that some thereof were implied, and may literally afford a solution.

And first, though it was not the season for figs, yet some fruit might have been expected, even in ordinary bearing trees. For the *grossi* or buttons appear before the leaves, especially before the leaves are well grown. Some might have stood during the winter, and by this time been of some growth: though many fall off, yet some might remain on, and proceed towards maturity. And we find that good husbands had an art to make them hold on as is delivered by Theophrastus.

The σῦκον or common summer fig, was not expected; for that is placed by Galen among the *fructus horarii* or *horæi,* which ripen in that part of summer, called ὥρα, and stands commended by him above other fruits of that season. And of this kind might be the figs which were brought unto Cleopatra in a basket together with an asp, according to the time of her death, on the nineteenth of August. And that our Saviour expected not such figs, but some other kind, seems to be implied in the indefinite expression, " if haply he might find any thing thereon;" which in that country, and the variety of such trees, might not be despaired of, at this season, and very probably hoped for in the first precocious and early bearing trees. And that there were precocious and early bearing trees in Judæa, may be illustrated from some expressions in Scripture concerning precocious figs; *calathus unus habebat ficus bonas nimis, sicut solent esse ficus primi temporis;* " one basket had very good figs, even like the figs that are first ripe."* And the like might be more especially expected in this place, if this remarkable tree be rightly placed in some maps of Jerusalem; for it is placed, by Adrichomius, in or near Bethphage, which some conjectures will have to be the house of figs : and at this place fig trees are still to be found, if we consult the travels of Bidulphus.

Again, in this great variety of fig trees, as precocious, proterical, biferous, triferous, and always bearing trees, something might have been expected, though the time of common figs was not yet. For some trees bear in a manner all the year; as may be illustrated from the epistle of the Emperour Julian, concerning his present of Damascus figs, which he commendeth from their successive and continued growing and bearing, after the manner of the fruits which Homer describeth in the garden of Alcinous. And though it were then but about the eleventh of March, yet, in the latitude of Jerusalem, the sun at that time hath a good power in the

* *Jer.* xxiv, 2.

day, and might advance the maturity of precocious often-bearing or ever-bearing figs.   And therefore when it is said that St. Peter* stood and warmed himself by the fire in the judgment hall, and the reason is added ("for it was cold"†), that expression might be interposed either to denote the coolness in the morning, according to hot countries, or some extraordinary and unusual coldness, which happened at that time.   For the same Bidulphus, who was at that time of the year at Jerusalem, saith, that it was then as hot as at Mid-summer in England : and we find in Scripture that the first sheaf of barley was offered in March.

Our Saviour, therefore, seeing a fig tree with leaves well spread, and so as to be distinguished afar off, went unto it, and when he came, found nothing but leaves ; he found it to be no precocious or always-bearing tree : and though it were not the time for summer figs, yet he found no rudiments thereof ; and though he expected not common figs, yet some-thing might haply have been expected of some other kind, according to different fertility and variety of production ; but, discovering nothing, he found a tree answering the state of the Jewish rulers, barren unto all expectation.

And this is consonant unto the mystery of the story, wherein the fig tree denoteth the synagogue and rulers of the Jews, whom God having peculiarly cultivated, singularly blessed and cherished, he expected from them no ordinary, slow, or customary fructification, but an earliness in good works, a precocious or continued fructification, and was not content with common after-bearing ; and might justly have expostulated with the Jews, as God by the prophet Micah did with their forefathers ; ‡ *præcoquas ficus desideravit anima mea*, "my soul longed for (or desired) early ripe fruits, but ye are become as a vine already gathered, and there is no cluster upon you."

Lastly, in this account of the fig tree, the mystery and symbolical sense is chiefly to be looked upon.   Our Saviour, therefore, taking a hint from his hunger to go unto this spe-cious tree, and intending, by this tree, to declare a judgment

---

* *St. Mark* xiv, 67.   *St. Luke* xxii, 55, 56.
† *St. John* xviii, 18.   ‡ *Micah*, vii, 1.

upon the synagogue and people of the Jews, he came unto
the tree, and, after the usual manner, inquired, and looked
about for some kind of fruit, as he had done before in the
Jews, but found nothing but leaves and specious outsides, as
he had also found in them; and when it bore no fruit
like them, when he expected it, and come to look for it,
though it were not the time of ordinary fruit, yet failing when
he required it, in the mysterious sense, 't was fruitless longer
to expect it.   For he had come unto them, and they were
nothing fructified by it, his departure approached, and his
time of preaching was now at an end.

Now, in this account, besides the miracle, some things are
naturally considerable.   For it may be questioned how the
fig tree, naturally a fruitful plant, became barren, for it had
no show or so much as rudiment of fruit: and it was in old
time, a signal judgment of God, that " the fig tree should
bear no fruit: " and therefore this tree may naturally be conceived to have been under some disease indisposing it to such
fructification.   And this, in the pathology of plants, may be
the disease of φυλλομανία, ἐμφυλλισμὸς, or superfoliation mentioned by Theophrastus; whereby the fructifying juice is starved
by the excess of leaves; which in this tree were already so
full spread, that it might be known and distinguished afar off.
And this was, also, a sharp resemblance of the hypocrisy of
the rulers, made up of specious outsides, and fruitless ostentation, contrary to the fruit of the fig tree, which, filled with
a sweet and pleasant pulp, makes no shew without, not so
much as of any flower.

Some naturals are also considerable from the propriety of
this punishment settled upon a fig tree: for infertility and
barrenness seems more intolerable in this tree than any, as
being a vegetable singularly constituted for production ; so far
from bearing no fruit that it may be made to bear almost any.
And therefore the ancients singled out this as the fittest tree
whereon to graft and propagate other fruits, as containing a
plentiful and lively sap, whereby other scions would prosper :
and, therefore, this tree was also sacred unto the deity of fertility ; and the statua of Priapus was made of the fig tree ;

Olim truncus eram ficulneus inutile lignum.

It hath also a peculiar advantage to produce and maintain its fruit above all other plants, as not subject to miscarry in flowers and blossoms, from accidents of wind and weather. For it beareth no flowers outwardly, and such as it hath, are within the coat, as the later examination of naturalists hath discovered.

Lastly, it was a tree wholly constituted for fruit, wherein if it faileth, it is in a manner useless, the wood thereof being of so little use, that it affordeth proverbial expressions, *homo ficulneus, argumentum ficulneum,* or things of no validity.

44. "I said I will go up into the palm tree, and take hold of the boughs thereof."* This expression is more agreeable unto the palm than is commonly apprehended, for that it is a tall bare tree, bearing its boughs but at the top and upper part; so that it must be ascended before its boughs or fruit can be attained: and the going, getting, or climbing up, may be emphatical in this tree; for the trunk or body thereof is naturally contrived for ascension, and made with advantage for getting up, as having many welts and eminences, and so as it were a natural ladder, and staves by which it may be climbed, as Pliny observeth *palmæ teretes atque proceres, densis quadratisque pollicibus faciles se ad scandendum præbent,*† by this way men are able to get up into it. And the figures of Indians thus climbing the same are graphically described in the travels of Linschoten. This tree is often mentioned in Scripture, and was so remarkable in Judæa, that in after-times it became the emblem of that country, as may be seen in that medal of the Emperor Titus, with a captive woman sitting under a palm, and the inscription of *Judæa capta.* And Pliny confirmeth the same when he saith *Judæa palmis inclyta.*

45. Many things are mentioned in Scripture, which have an emphasis from this or the neighbour countries: for besides the cedars, the Syrian lilies are taken notice of by writers. That expression in the Canticles, "thou art fair, thou art fair, thou hast dove's eyes,"‡ receives a particular character,

---

* *Cant.* vii, 8.   † *Plin.* xiii, cap. 4.   ‡ *Cant.* iv, 1.

if we look, not upon our common pigeons, but the beauteous and fine eyed doves of Syria.

When the rump is so strictly taken notice of in the sacrifice of the peace offering, in these words, " the whole rump, it shall be taken off hard by the back-bone,"* it becomes the more considerable in reference to this country, where sheep had so large tails; which, according to Aristotle,† were a cubit broad ; and so they are still, as Bellonius hath delivered.

When 't is said in the Canticles, "thy teeth are as a flock of sheep which go up from the washing, whereof every one beareth twins, and there is not one barren among them ;" ‡ it may seem hard unto us of these parts to find whole flocks bearing twins, and not one barren among them; yet may this be better conceived in the fertile flocks of those countries, where sheep have so often two, sometimes three, and some- times four, and which is so frequently observed by writers of the neighbour country of Egypt. And this fecundity, and fruitfulness of their flocks, is answerable unto the expression of the psalmist, " that our sheep may bring forth thousands and ten thousands in our streets." § And hereby, besides what was spent at their tables, a good supply was made for the great consumption of sheep in their several kinds of sacri- fices ; and of so many thousand male unblemished yearling lambs, which were required at their passovers.

Nor need we wonder to find so frequent mention both of garden and field plants ; since Syria was notable of old for this curiosity and variety, according to Pliny, *Syria hortis operosissima ;* and since Bellonius hath so lately observed of Jerusalem, that its hilly parts did so abound with plants, that they might be compared unto mount Ida in Crete or Candia ; which is the most noted place for noble simples yet known.

46. Though so many plants have their express names in Scripture, yet others are implied in some texts which are not explicitly mentioned. In the feast of tabernacles or booths, the law was this, " thou shalt take unto thee boughs of goodly trees, branches of the palm, and the boughs of thick trees,

---

* *Levit.* iii, 9.   † *Arist. Hist. Animal.* lib. viii.   ‡ *Cant.* iv, 2.
§ *Psalm* cxliv, 13.

and willows of the brook." Now though the text descendeth not unto particulars of the goodly trees and thick trees; yet Maimonides will tell us that for a goodly tree they made use of the citron tree, which is fair and goodly to the eye, and well prospering in that country : and that for the thick trees they used the myrtle, which was no rare or infrequent plant among them. And though it groweth but low in our gardens, was not a little tree in those parts; in which plant also the leaves grew thick, and almost covered the stalk. And Curtius Symphorianus * in his description of the exotic myrtle, makes it *folio densissimo senis in ordinem versibus.* The paschal lamb was to be eaten with bitterness or bitter herbs, not particularly set down in Scripture : but the Jewish writers declare, that they made use of succory, and wild lettuce, which herbs while some conceive they could not get down, as being very bitter, rough, and prickly, they may consider that the time of the passover was in the spring, when these herbs are young and tender, and consequently less unpleasant : besides, according to the Jewish custom, these herbs were dipped in the *charoseth*, or sauce made of raisins stamped with vinegar, and were also eaten with bread ; and they had four cups of wine allowed unto them ; and it was sufficient to take but a pittance of herbs, or the quantity of an olive.

47. Though the famous paper reed of Egypt be only particularly named in scripture; yet when reeds are so often mentioned without special name or distinction, we may conceive their differences may be comprehended, and that they were not all of one kind, or that the common reed was only implied. For mention is made in Ezekiel † of "a measuring reed of six cubits ;" we find that they smote our Saviour on the head with a reed,‡ and put a sponge with vinegar on a reed, which was long enough to reach to his mouth,[9] while he was upon the cross. And with such differences of reeds, *vallatory, sagittary, scriptory*, and others they might be furnished in Judæa. For we find in the portion of Ephraim,§

---

* *Curtius de Hortis.*   † *Ezek.* xl. 5.
‡ *St. Matt.* xxvii. 30, 48.   § *Josh.* xvi. 17

[9] *A reed which was long enough to reach to his mouth.*] In the neighbourhood of Suez some reeds grow to the height of twelve yards.

vallis arundineti ; and so set down in the maps of Adricomius, and in our translation the river Kana, or brook of Canes. And Bellonius tells us that the river Jordan affordeth plenty and variety of reeds; out of some whereof the Arabs make darts and light lances, and out of others, arrows; and withal that there plentifully groweth the fine *calamus, arundo scriptoria,* or writing reed, which they gather with the greatest care, as being of singular use and commodity at home and abroad; a hard reed about the compass of a goose or swan's quill, whereof I have seen some polished and cut with a web [neb? or nib?]; which is in common use for writing throughout the Turkish dominions, they using not the quills of birds.

And whereas the same author, with other describers of these parts, affirmeth, that the river Jordan, not far from Jericho, is but such a stream as a youth may throw a stone over it, or about eight fathoms broad, it doth not diminish the account and solemnity of the miraculous passage of the Israelites under Joshua.   For it must be considered, that they passed it in the time of harvest, when the river was high, and the grounds about it under water, according to that pertinent parenthesis;—"As the feet of the priests, which carried the ark, were dipped in the brim of the water, for Jordan over-floweth all its banks at the time of harvest." *   In this consideration it was well joined with the great river Euphrates, in that expression in Ecclesiasticus, " God maketh the understanding to abound like Euphrates, and as Jordan in the time of harvest." †

48. The kingdom of heaven is likened unto a man which sowed good seed in his field, but while men slept, his enemy came and sowed tares," or as the Greek, *zizania,* " among the wheat."

Now, how to render *zizania,* and to what species of plants to confine it, there is no slender doubt; for the word is not mentioned in other parts of Scripture, nor in any ancient Greek writer: it is not to be found in Aristotle, Theophrastus, or Dioscorides.   Some Greek and Latin fathers have made use of the same, as also Suidas and Phavorinus; but probably they have all derived it from this text.

---

* *Josh.* iii, 15.   † *Eccles.* xxiv, 26.

And, therefore, this obscurity might easily occasion such variety in translations and expositions. For some retain the word *zizania*, as the vulgar, that of Beza, of Junius, and also the Italian and Spanish. The low Dutch renders it *oncruidt*, the German *oncraut*, or *herba mala*, the French *yuroye* or *lolium*, and the English *tares*.

Besides, this being conceived to be a Syriac word, it may still add unto the uncertainty of the sense. For though this gospel were first written in Hebrew or Syriac, yet it is not unquestionable whether the true original be any where extant. And that Syriac copy which we now have, is conceived to be of far later time than St. Matthew.

Expositors and annotators are also various. Hugo Grotius hath passed the word *zizania* without a note. Diodati, retaining the word *zizania*, conceives that it was some peculiar herb growing among the corn of those countries, and not known in our fields. But Emanuel de Sa interprets it *plantas semini noxias*, and so accordingly some others.

Buxtorfius, in his *Rabbinical Lexicon*, gives divers interpretations, sometimes for degenerated corn, sometimes for the black seeds in wheat, but withal concludes, *an hæc sit eadem vox aut species cum zizaniâ apud evangelistam, quærant alii.* But lexicons and dictionaries by *zizania* do almost generally understand *lolium*, which we call darnel, and commonly confine the signification to that plant. Notwithstanding, since *lolium* had a known and received name in Greek, some may be apt to doubt why, if that plant were particularly intended, the proper Greek word was not used in the text. For Theophrastus * named *lolium* αἶρα, and hath often mentioned that plant; and in one place saith, that corn doth sometimes *loliescere* or degenerate into darnel. Dioscorides, who travelled over Judæa, gives it the same name, which is also to be found in Galen, Ætius, and Ægineta; and Pliny hath sometimes Latinized that word into *æra*.

Besides, *lolium* or darnel shews itself in the winter, growing up with the wheat; and Theophrastus observed, that it was no vernal plant, but came up in the winter; which will

---

* οὐ ξαίρησθαι.   *Theophrast. Hist. Plant.* lib. 8.

not well answer the expression of the text, "And when the blade came up, and brought forth fruit," or gave evidence of its fruit, the *zizania* appeared. And if the husbandry of the ancients were agreeable unto ours, they would not have been so earnest to weed away the darnel; for our husbandmen do not commonly weed it in the field, but separate the seed after thrashing. And, therefore, Galen delivereth, that in an unseasonable year, and great scarcity of corn, when they neglected to separate the darnel, the bread proved generally unwholesome, and had evil effects on the head.

Our old and later translators render *zizania* tares, which name our English botanists give unto *aracus, cracca, vicia sylvestris,* calling them tares and strangling tares. And our husbandmen by tares understand some sorts of wild fitches, which grow amongst corn, and clasp unto it, according to the Latin etymology, *vicia a vinciendo.* Now in this uncertainty of the original, tares, as well as some others, may make out the sense, and be also more agreeable unto the circumstances of the parable. For they come up and appear what they are, when the blade of the corn is come up, and also the stalk and fruit discoverable. They have likewise little spreading roots, which may entangle or rob the good roots, and they have also tendrils and claspers, which lay hold of what grows near them, and so can hardly be weeded without endangering the neighbouring corn.

However, if by *zizania* we understand *herbas segeti noxias,* or *vitia segetum,* as some expositors have done, and take the word in a more general sense, comprehending several weeds and vegetables offensive unto corn, according as the Greek word in the plural number may imply, and as the learned Laurenbergius* hath expressed, *runcare, quod apud nostrates weden dicitur, zizanias inutiles est evellere.* If, I say, it be thus taken, we shall not need to be definite, or confine unto one particular plant, from a word which may comprehend divers. And this may also prove a safer sense,[1] in such obscurity of the original.

* *De Horti Cultura.*

[1] *This may also prove a safer sense.*] But the later commentators seem rather disposed, with Forskäl, to consider it to have been the darnel.

And, therefore, since in this parable the sower of the *zizania* is the devil, and the *zizania* wicked persons; if any from this larger acception will take in thistles, darnel, cockle, wild straggling fitches, bindweed, *tribulus*, restharrow and other *vitia segetum;* he may, both from the natural and symbolical qualities of those vegetables, have plenty of matter to illustrate the variety of his mischiefs, and of the wicked of this world.

49. When 't is said in Job, " Let thistles grow up instead of wheat, and cockle[2] instead of barley," the words are intelligible, the sense allowable and significant to this purpose: but whether the word cockle doth strictly conform unto the original, some doubt may be made from the different translations of it; for the vulgar renders it *spina*, Tremellius *vitia frugum*, and the Geneva *yuroye*, or darnel. Besides, whether cockle were common in the ancient agriculture of those parts, or what word they used for it, is of great uncertainty. For the elder botanical writers have made no mention thereof, and the moderns have given it the name of *pseudomelanthium, nigellastrum, lychnoides segetum*, names not known unto antiquity. And, therefore, our translation hath warily set down ' noisome weeds ' in the margin.

[2] *cockle.*] Celsius, and after him Michaelis, supposes this to have been the aconite.

TRACT II.

OF GARLANDS AND CORONARY OR GARLAND PLANTS.[1]

SIR,

THE use of flowery crowns and garlands is of no slender antiquity, and higher than I conceive you apprehend it.   For, besides the old Greeks and Romans, the Egyptians made use hereof; who, besides the bravery of their garlands, had little birds upon them to peck their heads and brows, and so to keep them [from] sleeping at their festival compotations.   This practice also extended as far as India: for at the feast of the Indian King, it is peculiarly observed by Philostratus, that their custom was to wear garlands, and come crowned with them unto their feast.

The crowns and garlands of the ancients were either gesta-tory, such as they wore about their heads or necks; portatory, such as they carried at solemn festivals; pensile or suspen-sory, such as they hanged about the posts of their houses in honour of their Gods, as Jupiter Thyræus or Limeneus; or else they were depository, such as they laid upon the graves and monuments of the dead.   And these were made up after

[1] In the margin of Evelyn's copy is this manuscript note:—" *This letter was written to me from Dr. Browne; more at large in the Coronarie Plants.*"

In order to preserve unaltered, as far as possible, the order of Sir Thomas Browne's published works, I have thought proper not to transplant into the " *Cor-respondence* " the present and several other Tracts, though they were, in fact, epistolary, and it has been ascertained to whom they were addressed.   In the preface to Evelyn's *Acetaria*, (re-printed by Mr. Upcott, in his *Collection of Eve-lyn's Miscellaneous Writings*,) we find his "Plan of a Royal Garden, in 3 Books."   It was in reference to this pro-jected work, (of which however *Acetaria* was the only part ever published,) that Browne's assistance was asked and given. Among the subjects named in that plan the following are referred to in the pre-sent Tract, and in other of Browne's Letters to Evelyn:—

Book II. chap. 6. Of a seminary; nur-series; and of propagating trees, plants, and flowers; planting and transplanting, &c.

Chap. 16. Of the coronary garden.

Chap. 18. Of stupendous and wonder-ful plants.

Book III. chap. 9. Of garden-burial.

Chap. 10. Of paradise, and of the most famous gardens in the world, an-cient and modern.

all ways of art, compactile, sutile, plectile; for which work there were ϛεφανοπλόκοι, or expert persons to contrive them after the best grace and propriety.

Though we yield not unto them in the beauty of flowery garlands, yet some of those of antiquity were larger than any we lately met with; for we find in Athenæus, that a myrtle crown, of one and twenty foot in compass, was solemnly carried about at the Hellotian feast in Corinth, together with the bones of Europa.

And garlands were surely of frequent use among them; for we read in Galen,* that when Hippocrates cured the great plague of Athens by fires kindled in and about the city: the fuel thereof consisted much of their garlands. And they must needs be very frequent and of common use, the ends thereof being many. For they were convivial, festival, sacrificial, nuptial, honorary, funebrial. We who propose unto ourselves the pleasures of two senses, and only single out such as are of beauty and good odour, cannot strictly confine ourselves unto imitation of them.

For, in their convivial garlands, they had respect unto plants preventing drunkenness, or discussing ² the exhalations from wine; wherein, beside roses, taking in ivy, vervain, melilote, &c. they made use of divers of small beauty or good odour. The solemn festival garlands were made properly unto their gods, and accordingly contrived from plants sacred unto such deities; and their sacrificial ones were selected under such considerations. Their honorary crowns triumphal, ovary, civical, obsidional, had little of flowers in them: and their funebrial garlands had little of beauty in them beside roses, while they made them of myrtle, rosemary, *apium*, &c. under symbolical intimations; but our florid and purely ornamental garlands, delightful unto sight and smell, nor framed according to any mystical and symbolical considerations, are of more free election, and so may be made to excel those of the ancients : we having China, India, and a new world to supply us, beside the great distinction of flowers unknown

* *De Theriaca ad Pisonem.*

² *discussing.*]   Dr. Johnson quotes   the word *discuss* in the sense of *dis-* this passage as his example of the use of   *perse.*

unto antiquity, and the varieties thereof arising from art and nature.

But, beside vernal, æstival and autumnal, made of flowers, the ancients had also the hyemal garlands; contenting themselves at first with such as were made of horn dyed into several colours, and shaped into the figures of flowers, and also of *æs coronarium* or *clincquant*, or brass thinly wrought out into leaves commonly known among us. But the curiosity of some emperors for such intents had roses brought from Egypt until they had found the art to produce late roses in Rome, and to make them grow in winter, as is delivered in that handsome epigram of Martial.

At tu Romanæ jussus jam cedere brumæ
Mitte tuas messes, accipe, Nile, rosas.

Some American nations, who do much excel in garlands, content not themselves only with flowers, but make elegant crowns of feathers, whereof they have some of greater radiancy and lustre than their flowers : and since there is an art to set into shapes, and curiously to work in choicest feathers, there could nothing answer the crowns made of the choicest feathers of some *tomineios* and sun birds.

The catalogue of coronary plants is not large in Theophrastus, Pliny, Pollux, or Athenæus: but we may find a good enlargement in the accounts of modern botanists; and additions may still be made by successive acquists of fair and specious plants, not yet translated from foreign regions, or little known unto our gardens; he that would be complete may take notice of these following,

Flos Tigridis.
Flos Lyncis.
Pinea Indica Recchi, Talama Ouiedi.
Herba Paradisea.
Volubilis Mexicanus.
Narcissus Indicus Serpentarius.
Helichrysum Mexicanum.
Xicama.
Aquilegia novæ Hispaniæ Cacoxochitli Recchi.
Aristochæa Mexicana.

Camaratinga sive Caragunta quarta Pisonis.

Maracuia Granadilla.

Cambay sive Myrtus Americana.

Flos Auriculæ Flor de la Oreia.

Floripendio novæ Hispaniæ.

Rosa Indica.

Zilium Indicum.

Fula Magori Garciæ.

Champe Garciæ Champacca Bontii.

Daullontas frutex odoratus seu Chamæmelum arborescens Bontii.

Beidelsar Alpini.

Sambuc.

Amberboi Turcarum.

Nuphar Ægyptium.

Lilionarcissus Indicus.

Bamma Ægyptiacum.

Hiucca Canadensis horti Farnesiani.

Bupthalmum novæ Hispaniæ Alepocapath.

Valeriana seu Chrysanthemum Americanum Acocotlis.

Flos Corvinus Coronarius Americanus.

Capolin Cerasus dulcis Indicus Floribus racemosis.

Asphodelus Americanus.

Syringa Lutea Americana.

Bulbus unifolius.

Moly latifolium Flore luteo. [3]

Conyza Americana purpurea.

Salvia Cretica pomifera Bellonii.

Lausus Serrata Odora.

Ornithogalus Promontorii Bonæ Spei.

Fritillaria crassa Soldanica Promontorii Bonæ Spei.

Sigillum Solomonis Indicum.

Tulipa Promontorii Bonæ Spei.

Iris Uvaria.

Nopolxock sedum elegans novæ Hispaniæ.

---

[3] *Moly latifolium Flore luteo.*]   Sir
Thomas, in a subsequent letter, (see
Correspondence, p. 380,) corrects this name; —" for *Moly Flore luteo,*" he says,
" you may please to put in *Moly Hondianum novum.*"

More might be added unto this list; [4] and I have only taken the pains to give you a short specimen of those, many more which you may find in respective authors, and which time and future industry may make no great strangers in England. The inhabitants of *nova Hispania,* and a great part of America, Mahometans, Indians, Chinese, are eminent promoters of these coronary and specious plants; and the annual tribute of the King of Bisnaguer in India, arising out of odours and flowers, amounts unto many thousands of crowns.

Thus, in brief, of this matter.   I am, &c.

---

[4] *More might be added unto this list.*] Which Sir Thomas sent me a catalogue of from Norwich.—*MS. note of Evelyn's.* This list has not been found.

TRACT III.

OF THE FISHES EATEN BY OUR SAVIOUR WITH HIS DISCIPLES
AFTER HIS RESURRECTION FROM THE DEAD.

SIR,

I HAVE thought a little upon the question proposed by you
[viz. what kind of fishes those were,[1] of which our Saviour
ate with his disciples after his resurrection?*] and I return
you such an answer, as, in so short a time for study, and in
the midst of my occasions, occurs to me.

The books of Scripture (as also those which are apocryphal) are often silent or very sparing, in the particular names
of fishes; or in setting them down in such manner as to leave
the kinds of them without all doubt and reason for farther
inquiry. For, when it declareth what fishes were allowed the
Israelites for their food, they are only set down in general which
have fins and scales: whereas, in the account of quadrupeds
and birds, there is particular mention made of divers of them.
In the book of Tobit that fish which he took out of the river
is only named a great fish, and so there remains much uncertainty to determine the species thereof. And even the fish
which swallowed Jonah, and is called a great fish, and commonly thought to be a great whale, is not received without
all doubt; while some learned men conceive it to have been
none of our whales, but a large kind of *lamia*.

And, in this narration of St. John, the fishes are only expressed by their bigness and number, not their names, and
therefore it may seem undeterminable what they were: notwithstanding, these fishes being taken in the great lake or
sea of Tiberias, something may be probably stated therein.

* *St. John* xxi, 9, 10, 11—13.

[1] *what kind, &c.*]   *MS. Sloan.* 1827,   were, which fed the multitude in the
reads, "of what kind those little fish   wilderness, or, &c."

For since Bellonius, that diligent and learned traveller, informeth us, that the fishes of this lake were trouts, pikes, chevins, and tenches; it may well be conceived that either all or some thereof are to be understood in this Scripture. And these kind of fishes become large and of great growth, answerable unto the expression of Scripture, "one hundred fifty and three great fishes;" that is, large in their own kinds, and the largest kinds in this lake and fresh water, wherein no great variety, and of the larger sort of fishes, could be expected. For the river Jordan, running through this lake, falls into the lake of Asphaltus, and hath no mouth into the sea, which might admit of great fishes or greater variety to come up into it.

And out of the mouth of some of these forementioned fishes might the tribute money be taken, when our Saviour, at Capernaum, seated upon the same lake, said unto Peter, "go thou to the sea, and cast an hook, and take up the fish that first cometh; and when thou hast opened his mouth thou shalt find a piece of money; that take and give them for thee and me."

And this makes void that common conceit and tradition of the fish called *faber marinus*, by some, a peter or penny fish; which having two remarkable round spots upon either side these are conceived to be the marks of St. Peter's fingers or signatures of the money: for though it hath these marks, yet is there no probability that such a kind of fish was to be found in the lake of Tiberias, Gennesareth, or Galilee, which is but sixteen miles long and six broad, and hath no communication with the sea; for this is a mere fish of the sea and salt water, and (though we meet with some thereof on our coast) is not to be found in many seas.

Thus having returned no improbable answer unto your question, I shall crave leave to ask another of yourself concerning that fish mentioned by Procopius,* which brought the famous King Theodorick to his end: his words are to this effect: "the manner of his death was this; Symmachus and his son-in-law Boëthius, just men and great relievers of the poor, senators, and consuls, had many enemies, by whose

* *De Bello Gothico*, lib. i.

false accusations Theodorick being persuaded that they plot-
ted against him, put them to death, and confiscated their
estates.   Not long after his waiters set before him at supper
a great head of a fish, which seemed to him to be the head of
Symmachus lately murdered: and with his teeth sticking out,
and fierce glaring eyes to threaten him: being frighted, he
grew chill, went to bed, lamenting what he had done to
Symmachus and Boëthius; and soon after died." What fish
do you apprehend this to have been? I would learn of you;
give me your thoughts about it.

I am, &c.

TRACT IV.

AN ANSWER TO CERTAIN QUERIES RELATING TO FISHES, BIRDS, AND INSECTS.

SIR,

I RETURN the following answers to your queries, which were these:—

1. What fishes are meant by the names, *halec* and *mugil?*

2. What is the bird which you will receive from the bearer, and what birds are meant by the names *halcyon, nysus, ciris, nycticorax?*

3. What insect is meant by the word *cicada?*

ANSWER 1. The word *halec* we are taught to render an herring, which, being an ancient word, is not strictly appropriable unto a fish not known or not described by the ancients; and which the modern naturalists are fain to name *harengus:* the word *halecula* being applied unto such little fish out of which they are fain to make pickle; and *halec* or *alec*, taken for the *liquamen* or liquor itself, according to that of the poet,

—— Ego fæcem primus et alec
Primus et inveni album——

And was a conditure and sauce much affected by antiquity, as was also *muria* and *garum.*

In common constructions *mugil* is rendered a mullet, which, notwithstanding, is a different fish from the *mugil* described by authors;[1] wherein, if we mistake, we cannot so closely apprehend the expression of Juvenal,

——Quosdam ventres et mugilis intrat.

And misconceive the fish whereby fornicators were so opprobriously and irksomely punished; for the *mugil*, being some-

---

[1] *authors.*] *MS. Sloan.* proceeds thus: "for which I know not, perhaps, whether we have any proper name in English; and other nations nearly imitate the Latin, wherein, &c."—*MS. Sloan.* 1827.

what rough and hard skinned, did more exasperate the guts
of such offenders: whereas the mullet was a smooth fish, and
of too high esteem to be employed in such offices.

ANSWER 2. I cannot but wonder that this bird you sent
should be a stranger unto you, and unto those who had a sight
thereof; for, though it be not seen every day, yet we often
meet with it in this country. It is an elegant bird, which
he that once beholdeth can hardly mistake any other for it.
From the proper note it is called an hoopebird with us; in
Greek *epops*, in Latin *upupa*. We are little obliged unto
our school instruction, wherein we are taught to render *upupa*
a lapwing, which bird our natural writers name *vannellus;* for
thereby we mistake this remarkable bird, and apprehend not
rightly what is delivered of it.

We apprehend not the hieroglyphical considerations which
the old Egyptians made of this observable bird; who, considering therein the order and variety of colours, the twenty-
six or twenty-eight feathers in its crest, his latitancy, and
mewing this handsome outside in the winter: they made it an
emblem of the varieties of the world, the succession of times
and seasons, and signal mutations in them. And, therefore,
Orus, the hieroglyphic of the world, had the head of an hoopebird upon the top of his staff.

Hereby we may also mistake the *duchiphath*, or bird forbidden for food in Leviticus; * and, not knowing the bird,
may the less apprehend some reasons of that prohibition;
that is, the magical virtues ascribed unto it by the Egyptians,
and the superstitious apprehensions which that nation held of
it, whilst they precisely numbered the feathers and colours
thereof, while they placed it on the heads of their gods, and
near their Mercurial crosses, and so highly magnified.this
bird in their sacred symbols.

Again, not knowing or mistaking this bird, we may misap-
prehend, or not closely apprehend, that handsome expression
of Ovid, when Tereus was turned into an *upupa*, or hoopebird :—

> Vertitur in volucrem cui sunt pro vertice cristæ,
> Protinus immodicum surgit pro cuspide rostrum
> Nomen epops volucri, facies armata videtur·

* *Levit.* xi, 19.

For, in this military shape, he is aptly fancied even still re-
vengefully to pursue his hated wife, Progne : in the propriety
of his note crying out, *pou, pou, ubi, ubi* ; or, Where are you?

Nor are we singly deceived in the nominal translation of
this bird : in many other animals we commit the like mistake.
So *gracculus* is rendered a jay, which bird, notwithstanding,
must be of a dark colour according to that of Martial,

> Sed quandam volo nocte nigriorem
> Formica, pice, gracculo, cicada.

Halcyon is rendered a kingfisher,* a bird commonly known
among us, and by zoographers and naturals the same is named
ispida, a well coloured bird, frequenting streams and rivers,
building in holes of pits, like some martins, about the end
of the spring ; in whose nests we have found little else than
innumerable small fish bones, and white round eggs of a
smooth and polished surface, whereas the true *halcyon* is a sea
bird, makes an handsome nest floating upon the water, and
breedeth in the winter.

That *nysus* should be rendered either an hobby or a spar-
row-hawk in the fable of Nysus and Scylla in Ovid, because
we are much to seek in the distinction of hawks according to
their old denominations, we shall not much contend, and may
allow a favourable latitude therein : but that the *ciris* or bird
into which Scylla was turned should be translated a lark, it
can hardly be made out agreeable unto the description of
Virgil, in his poem of that name,

> Inde alias volucres mimoque infecta rubenti crura——

But seems more agreeable unto some kind of *hæmantopus* or
redshank ; and so the *nysus* to have been some kind of hawk,
which delighteth about the sea and marishes, where such prey
most aboundeth, which sort of hawk, while Scaliger deter-
mineth to be a merlin, the French translator warily expound-
eth it to be some kind of hawk.

Nycticorax we may leave unto the common and verbal
translation of a night-raven, but we know no proper kind of

---

* See *Vulg. Err.* b. iii, c. 10.

raven unto which to confine the same, and, therefore, some take the liberty to ascribe it unto some sort of owls, and others unto the bittern; which bird, in its common note, which he useth out of the time of coupling and upon the wing, so well resembleth the croaking of a raven, that I have been deceived by it.[2]

ANSWER 3. While *cicada* is rendered a grasshopper, we commonly think that which is so called among us to be the true *cicada;* wherein, as we have elsewhere declared,* there is a great mistake: for we have not the *cicada* in England,[3] and, indeed, no proper word for that animal, which the French nameth *cigale.* That which we commonly call a grasshopper, and the French *saulterelle,* being one kind of locust, so rendered in the plague of Egypt, and, in old Saxon, named *gersthop.*[4]

I have been the less accurate in these answers, because the queries are not of difficult resolution, or of great moment: however, I would not wholly neglect them or your satisfaction, as being, Sir,   Yours, &c.

* *Vulg. Err.* b. v, c. 3.

[2] *Nycticorax, &c.*] Very possibly the night-raven, *ardea nycticorax*, Lin.

[3] *we have not the* cicada *in England.*] Of the true Linnæan *cicadæ (Tettigonia Fabr.),* the first British species was discovered in the New Forest, by Mr. Bydder, a collector whom I employed there for a considerable period, nearly twenty years since. It has been named *C. Anglica*, and is figured by Samouelle, *Comp.* pl. 5, fig. 2, and by Curtis, *British Entomology,* Feb. 1st, 1832, No. 392.

[4] *gersthop.*] " Gerstrappa," in *MS. Sloan.* 1827.

TRACT V.

OF HAWKS AND FALCONRY, ANCIENT AND MODERN.

SIR,

IN vain you expect much information, *de re accipitraria*, of falconry, hawks, or hawking, from very ancient Greek or Latin authors; that art being either unknown or so little advanced among them, that it seems to have proceeded no higher than the daring of birds: which makes so little thereof to be found in Aristotle, who only mentions some rude practice thereof in Thracia; as also in Ælian, who speaks something of hawks and crows among the Indians; little or nothing of true falconry being mentioned before Julius Firmicus, in the days of Constantius, son to Constantine the Great.

Yet, if you consult the accounts of later antiquity left by Demetrius the Greek, by Symmachus and Theodotius, and by Albertus Magnus, about five hundred years ago, you, who have been so long acquainted with this noble recreation, may better compare the ancient and modern practice, and rightly observe how many things in that art are added, varied, disused, or retained, in the practice of these days.

In the diet of hawks, they allowed of divers meats which we should hardly commend. For beside the flesh of beef,[1] they admitted of goat, hog, deer, whelp, and bear. And how you will approve the quantity and measure thereof, I make some doubt; while by weight they allowed half a pound of beef, seven ounces of swines' flesh, five of hare, eight ounces of whelp, as much of deer, and ten ounces of he-goats' flesh.

In the time of Demetrius they were not without the practice of phlebotomy or bleeding, which they used in the thigh and pounces;[2] they plucked away the feathers on the thigh,

---

[1] *beef.*] Lamb, mutton, beef.—*MS. Sloan.* 1827.

[2] *pounces.*] The pounce is the talon or claw of a bird of prey.

and rubbed the part; but if the vein appeared not in that part, they open the vein of the fore talon.

In the days of Albertus, they made use of cauteries in divers places : to advantage their sight they seared them under the inward angle of the eye; above the eye in distillations and diseases of the head; in upward pains they seared above the joint of the wing, and in the bottom of the foot, against the gout; and the chief time for these cauteries they made to be the month of March.

In great coldness of hawks they made use of fomentations, some of the steam or vapour of artificial and natural baths, some wrapt them up in hot blankets, giving them nettle seeds and butter.

No clysters are mentioned, nor can they be so profitably used; but they made use of many purging medicines. They purged with aloe, which, unto larger hawks, they gave in the bigness of a Greek bean; unto lesser, in the quantity of a *cicer*,[3] which notwithstanding I should rather give washed, and with a few drops of oil of almonds: for the guts of flying fowls are tender and easily scratched by it; and upon the use of aloe both in hens and cormorants I have sometimes observed bloody excretions.

In phlegmatic cases they seldom omitted stavesaker,[4] but they purged sometimes with a mouse, and the food of boiled chickens, sometimes with good oil and honey.

They used also the ink of cuttle fishes, with smallage, betony, wine, and honey. They made use of stronger medicines than present practice doth allow. For they were not afraid to give *coccus baphicus;*[5] beating up eleven of its grains unto a *lentor*,[6] which they made up into five pills wrapt up with honey and pepper : and, in some of their old medicines, we meet with scammony and *euphorbium*. Whether, in the tender bowels of birds, infusions of rhubarb, agaric and *mechoachan*, be not of safer use, as to take of agaric two drachms, of cinnamon half a drachm, of liquorice a scruple, and, infusing them in wine, to express a part into

---

[3] *cicer.*] The seed of a vetch.
[4] *stavesaker.*] Or *stave's-acre*, a plant; *Delphinium staphisagria*, Lin.

[5] *coccus baphicus.*] Or mezerion.— *MS. Sloan.* 1827.
[6] *lentor.*] A stiff paste.

the mouth of the hawk, may be considered by present practice.

Few mineral medicines were of inward use among them: yet sometimes we observe they gave filings of iron in the straightness of the chest, as also lime in some of their pectoral medicines.

But they commend unguents of quicksilver against the scab: and I have safely given six or eight grains of *mercurius dulcis* unto kestrils and owls, as also crude and current quicksilver, giving the next day small pellets of silver or lead till they came away uncoloured: and this, if any [way], may probably destroy that obstinate disease of the filander or back-worm.

A peculiar remedy they had against the consumption of hawks. For, filling a chicken with vinegar, they closed up the bill, and hanging it up until the flesh grew tender, they fed the hawk therewith: and to restore and well flesh them, they commonly gave them hog's flesh, with oil, butter, and honey; and a decoction of cumfory to bouze.[3]

They disallowed of salt meats and fat; but highly esteemed of mice in most indispositions; and in the falling sickness had great esteem of boiled bats: and in many diseases, of the flesh of owls which feed upon those animals. In epilepsies they also gave the brain of a kid drawn through a gold ring; and, in convulsions, made use of a mixture of musk and *stercus humanum aridum.*

For the better preservation of their health they strewed mint and sage about them; and for the speedier mewing of their feathers, they gave them the slough of a snake, or a tortoise out of the shell, or a green lizard cut in pieces.

If a hawk were unquiet, they hooded him, and placed him in a smith's shop for some time, where, accustomed to the continual noise of hammering, he became more gentle and tractable.

They used few terms of art, plainly and intelligibly expressing the parts affected, their diseases and remedies. This heap of artificial terms first entering with the French

---

[3] *bouze.*] MS. *Sloan.* 1827, reads "drink; and had a notable medicine against the inflammation of the eyes, by juice of purslain, opium, and saffron."

artists: who seem to have been the first and noblest falconers in the western part of Europe; although, in their language, they have no word which in general expresseth an hawk.

They carried their hawks in the left hand, and let them fly from the right. They used a bell, and took great care that their jesses should not be red, lest eagles should fly at them. Though they used hoods, we have no clear description of them, and little account of their lures.

The ancient writers left no account of the swiftness of hawks or measure of their flight: but Heresbachius* delivers, that William Duke of Cleve had an hawk, which in one day, made a flight out of Westphalia into Prussia. And upon good account, an hawk in this county of Norfolk made a flight at a woodcock near thirty miles in one hour. How far the hawks, merlins, and wild fowl which come unto us with a north-west wind in the autumn, fly in a day, there is no clear account: but coming over sea their flight hath been long or very speedy. For I have known them to light so weary on the coast, that many have been taken with dogs, and some knocked down with staves and stones.

Their perches seemed not so large as ours: for they made them of such a bigness that their talons might almost meet: and they choose to make them of sallow, poplar, or lime tree.

They used great clamours and hallowing in their flight, which they made by these words, *ou loi, la, la, la;* and to raise the fowls, made use of the sound of a cymbal.

Their recreation seem more sober and solemn than ours at present, so improperly attended with oaths and imprecations. For they called on God at their sitting out, according to the account of Demetrius, τὸν Θεὸν ἐπικαλέσαντες, in the first place calling upon God.

The learned Rigaltius thinketh, that if the Romans had well known this airy chase, they would have left or less regarded their Circensial recreations. The Greeks understood hunting early, but little or nothing of our falconry. If Alexander had known it, we might have found something of it and more of hawks in Aristotle; who was so unacquainted with that way, that he thought that hawks would not feed

* *De Re Rustica.*

upon the heart of birds.   Though he hath mentioned divers
hawks, yet Julius Scaliger, an expert falconer, despaired to
reconcile them unto ours.   And 't is well if among them, you
can clearly make out a lanner, a sparrow hawk, and a kestril,
but must not hope to find your gier falcon there, which is the
noble hawk; and I wish you one no worse than that of Henry
King of Navarre; which, Scaliger saith, he saw strike down
a buzzard, two wild geese, divers kites, a crane, and a swan.

Nor must you expect from high antiquity the distinctions
of eyes and ramage hawks, of stores and entermewers, of
hawks of the lure and the fist; nor that material distinction
into short and long winged hawks : from whence arise such
differences in their taking down of stones; in their flight,
their striking down or seizing of their prey, in the strength
of their talons, either in the heel and fore talon, or the middle and the heel: nor yet what eggs produce the different
hawks, or when they lay three eggs, that the first produceth
a female and large hawk, the second of a middler sort, and
the third a smaller bird, tercellene, or tassel, of the male sex;
which hawks being only observed abroad by the ancients,
were looked upon as hawks of different kinds, and not of the
same eyrie or nest.   As for what Aristotle affirmeth, that
hawks and birds of prey drink not; although you know that
it will not strictly hold, yet I kept an eagle two years, which
fed upon cats, kitlings, whelps, and rats, without one drop
of water.

If anything may add unto your knowledge in this noble art,
you must pick it out of later writers than those you enquire
of.   You may peruse the two books of falconry writ by that
renowned Emperor, Frederick the Second; as also the works
of the noble Duke Belisarius, of Tardiffe, Francherius, of
Francisco Sforzino of Vicensa; and may not a little inform or
recreate yourself with that elegant poem of Thuanus.*   I
leave you to divert yourself by the perusal of it, having, at
present, no more to say but that I am, &c.

* *De Re Accipitraria,* in 3 books. †

† Or more of late by P. Rapinus in verse.—*MS. Note of Evelyn's.*

TRACT VI.

OF CYMBALS, ETC.

Sir,

With what difficulty, if possibility, you may expect satisfaction concerning the music, or musical instruments of the Hebrews, you will easily discover if you consult the attempts of learned men upon that subject: but for the cymbals, of whose figure you enquire, you may find some described in Bayfius, in the comment of Rhodius upon Scribonius Largus, and others.

As for κύμβαλον ἀλαλάζον mentioned by St. Paul,* and rendered a tinkling cymbal, whether the translation be not too soft and diminutive, some question may be made: for the word ἀλαλάζον implieth no small sound, but a strained and lofty vociferation, or some kind of hallowing sound, according to the exposition of Hesychius, ἀλαλάξατε ἐνυψώσατε τὴν φωνήν. A word drawn from the lusty shout of soldiers, crying ἀλαλά at the first charge upon their enemies, according to the custom of the eastern nations, and used by the Trojans in Homer; and is also the note of the chorus in Aristophanes ἀλαλαί ἡ παιών. In other parts of scripture we read of loud and high sounding cymbals; and in Clemens Alexandrinus, that the Arabians made use of cymbals in their wars instead of other military music; and Polyænus in his *Stratagems* affirmeth that Bacchus gave the signal of battle unto his numerous army, not with trumpets but with tympans and cymbals.

And now I take the opportunity to thank you for the new book sent me, containing the anthems sung in our cathedral and collegiate churches: 't is probable there will be additions, the masters of music being now active in that affair. Beside my naked thanks I have yet nothing to return you but this

* 1 *Cor.* xiii, 1.

enclosed, which may be somewhat rare unto you, and that is a Turkish hymn, translated into French out of the Turkish metre, which I thus render unto you.

" O what praise doth he deserve, and how great is that Lord, all whose slaves are as so many kings !

"Whosoever shall rub his eyes with the dust of his feet, shall behold such admirable things that he shall fall into an ecstacy.

" He that shall drink one drop of his beverage, shall have his bosom like the ocean, filled with gems and precious liquors.

" Let not loose the reins unto thy passions in this world: he that represseth them shall become a true Solomon in the faith.

" Amuse not thyself to adore riches, nor to build great houses and palaces.

" The end of what thou shalt build is but ruin.

" Pamper not thy body with delicacies and dainties; it may come to pass one day that this body may be in hell.

"Imagine not that he who findeth riches, findeth happiness. He that findeth happiness is he that findeth God.

" All who prostrating themselves in humility shall this day believe in Vele,* if they were poor, shall be rich; and if rich, shall become kings."

After the sermon ended, which was made upon a verse in the Alcoran containing much morality, the Dervises in a gallery apart sung this hymn, accompanied with instrumental music, which so affected the ears of Monsieur du Loir, that he would not omit to set it down, together with the musical notes, to be found in his first letter unto Monsieur Bouliau, prior of Magny.

Excuse my brevity : I can say but little where I understand but little.   I am, &c.

* Vele, the founder of the convent.

TRACT VII.

OF ROPALIC OR GRADUAL VERSES, ETC.

Mens mea sublimes rationes præmeditatur.

SIR,

THOUGH I may justly allow a good intention in this poem presented unto you, yet I must needs confess, I have no affection for it; as being utterly averse from all affectation in poetry, which either restrains the fancy, or fetters the invention to any strict disposure of words. A poem of this nature is to be found in *Ausonius*, beginning thus,

> Spes Deus æternæ stationis conciliator.

These are verses *ropalici* or *clavales*, arising gradually like the knots in a ῥοπάλη or club; named also *fistulares* by Priscianus, as Elias Vinetus * hath noted. They consist properly of five words, each thereof encreasing by one syllable. They admit not of a *spondee* in the fifth place, nor can a golden or silver verse be made this way. They run smoothly both in Latin and Greek, and some are scatteringly to be found in Homer.

> ῏Ω μάκαρ 'Ατρείδη μοιρηγενὲς ὀλβιοδαίμον,

> Libere dicam sed in aurem, ego versibus hujusmodi ropalicis, longo syrmate protractis, Ceraunium affigo.

He that affecteth such restrained poetry, may peruse the long poem of Hugbaldus the monk, wherein every word beginneth with a C, penned in the praise of *calvities* or baldness, to the honour of Carolus Calvus, King of France,

> Carmina clarisonæ calvis cantate Camænæ.

The rest may be seen at large in the *Adversaria* of Barthius: or if he delighteth in odd contrived fancies, may he please himself with antistrophes, counterpetories, retrogrades,

---

* *El Vinet. in Auson.*

rebuses, leonine verses, &c. to be found in *Sieur des Accords*. But these and the like are to be looked upon, not pursued. Odd work might be made by such ways; and for your recreation I propose these few lines unto you.[1]

> Arcu paratur quod arcui sufficit.
>
> Misellorum clamoribus accurrere non tam humanum quam sulphureum est.
>
> Asino teratur quæ asino teritur.
>
> Ne asphodelos comedas, phœnices manduca.
>
> Cœlum aliquid potest, sed quæ mira præstat papilio est.

Not to put you unto endless amusement, the key hereof is the homonomy of the Greek made use of in the Latin words, which rendereth all plain. More enigmatical and dark expressions might be made if any one would speak or compose them out of the numerical characters or characteristical numbers set down by Robertus de Fluctibus.[2] *

As for your question concerning the contrary expressions of the Italians and Spaniards in their common affirmative answers, the Spaniard answering *cy Sennor*, the Italian *Signior cy*, you must be content with this distich,

> Why saith the Italian *Signior cy*, the Spaniard *Sy Sennor* ?
> Because the one puts that behind, the other puts before.

And because you are so happy in some translations, I pray return me these two verses in English,

> Occidit heu tandem multos quæ occidit amantes,
> Et cinis est hodiè quæ fuit ignis heri.[3]

My occasions make me to take off my pen.   I am, &c.

* *Tract 2, part lib.* i.

---

[1] *and, &c.*] MS. *Sloan.* reads thus, "And I remember I once pleased a young hopeful person with a dialogue between two travellers, beginning in this manner: well drunk, my old friend, the famous King of Macedon; that is, well overtaken, my old friend Alexander, your friend may proceed. With another way I shall not omit to acquaint you, and for your recreation I present these few lines."

[2] *More enigmatical, &c.*] These are more largely noticed in *MS. Sloan.* 1837: thus, "One way more I shall mention, though scarce worth your notice:—Two pestels and a book come short of a retort, as much as a spear and an ass exceed a dog's tail. This to be expounded by the numerical characters, or characteristical numbers set down by Robertus de Fluctibus, and speaks only this text:—two and four come short of six, as much as ten exceed six; the figure of an ass standing for a cipher."

[3] *Occidit heu tandem, &c.*] In *MS. Sloan.* 1827, is the following translation

> " She is dead at last, who many made expire
> Is dust to day which yesterday was fire."

TRACT VIII.

OF LANGUAGES, AND PARTICULARLY OF THE SAXON
TONGUE.

SIR,

THE last discourse we had of the Saxon tongue recalled to my mind some forgotten considerations.[1] Though the earth were widely peopled before the flood, (as many learned men conceive) yet whether, after a large dispersion, and the space of sixteen hundred years, men maintained so uniform a language in all parts, as to be strictly of one tongue, and readily to understand each other, may very well be doubted. For though the world preserved in the family of Noah before the confusion of tongues might be said to be of one lip, yet even permitted to themselves their humours, inventions, necessities, and new objects (without the miracle of confusion at first), in so long a tract of time, there had probably been a Babel. For whether America were first peopled by one or several nations, yet cannot that number of different planting nations answer the multiplicity of their present different languages, of no affinity unto each other, and even in their northern nations and incommunicating angles,[2] their languages are widely differing. A native interpreter brought from California proved of no use[3] unto the Spaniards upon the neighbour shore. From Chiapa to Guatemala, S. Salvador, Honduras, there are at least eighteen several languages; and so numerous are they both in the Peruvian and Mexican regions, that the great princes are fain to have one common language, which, besides their vernaculous and mother tongues, may serve for commerce between them.

And since the confusion of tongues at first fell only upon those which were present in Sinaar at the work of Babel,

---

[1] *forgotten considerations.*] " Both of that and other languages."—*MS. Sloan.*

[2] *angles.*] "Where they may be best

conceived to have most single originals."

[3] *of no use.*] "Of little use."—*MS. Sloan.*

whether the primitive language from Noah were only preserved in the family of Heber, and not also in divers others,
which might be absent at the same, whether all came away,
and many might not be left behind in their first plantations
about the foot of the hills, whereabout the ark rested, and
Noah became an husbandman,[4] is not absurdly doubted.

For so the primitive tongue might in time branch out into
several parts of Europe and Asia, and thereby the first or
Hebrew tongue, which seems to be ingredient into so many
languages, might have larger originals and grounds of its
communication and traduction than from the family of Abraham, the country of Canaan, and words contained in the
Bible, which come short of the full of that language. And
this would become more probable from the Septuagint or
Greek Chronology strenuously asserted by Vossius; for
making five hundred years between the deluge and the days
of Peleg, there ariseth a large latitude of multiplication and
dispersion of people into several parts, before the descent of
that body which followed Nimrod unto Sinaar from the east.

They who derive the bulk of European tongues from the
Scythian and the Greek, though they may speak probably
in many points, yet must needs allow vast difference or corruptions from so few originals, which, however, might be
tolerably made out in the old Saxon, yet hath time much
confounded the clearer derivations. And as the knowledge
thereof now stands in reference unto ourselves, I find many
words totally lost, divers of harsh sound disused or refined
in the pronunciation, and many words we have also in common use not to be found in that tongue, or venially derivable
from any other from whence we have largely borrowed, and
yet so much still remaineth with us that it maketh the gross
of our language.

The religious obligation unto the Hebrew language hath
so notably continued the same, that it might still be under-

---

[4] *husbandman.*]   *MS. Sloan.* 1827,
adds here the following clause ; " whether
in that space of 150 years, according to
common compute, before the conduct of
Nimrod, many might not expatriate
northward, eastward, or southward, and
many of the posterity of Noah might not
disperse themselves before the great migration unto Sinaar, and many also afterwards ; is not, &c."

stood by Abraham, whereas by the Mazorite points and Chaldee character the old letter stands so transformed, that if Moses were alive again, he must be taught to read his own law.[5]

The Chinese, who live at the bounds of the earth, who have admitted little communication, and suffered successive incursions from one nation, may possibly give account of a very ancient language: but, consisting of many nations and tongues, confusion, admixtion, and corruption in length of time might probably so have crept in, as, without the virtue of a common character and lasting letter of things, they could never probably make out those strange memorials which they pretend, while they still make use of the works of their great Confucius many hundred years before Christ, and in a series ascend as high as Poncuus, who is conceived our Noah.

The present Welch, and remnant of the old Britons, hold so much of that ancient language, that they make a shift to understand the poems of Merlin, Enerin, Telesin, a thousand years ago, whereas the Herulian *Pater Noster*, set down by Wolfgangus Lazius, is not without much criticism made out, and but in some words ; and the present Parisians can hardly hack out those few lines of the league between Charles and Lewis, the sons of Ludovicus Pius, yet remaining in old French.

The Spaniards in their corruptive traduction and romance, have so happily retained the terminations from the Latin, that, notwithstanding the Gothic and Moorish intrusion of words, they are able [6] to make a discourse completely consist-

---

[5] *law.*] In *MS. Sloan.* 1827, the following additional paragraph occurs ;— " Though this language be duly magnified, and always of high esteem, yet if, with Geropius Becanus, we admit that tongue to be most perfect which is most copious or expressive, most delucid and clear unto the understanding, most short, or soon delivered, and best pronounced with most ease unto the organs of speech, the Hebrew now known unto us will hardly obtain the place ; since it consisteth of fewer words than many others, and its words begin not with vowels, since it is so full of homonymies, and words which signify many things, and so ambiguous, that translations so little agree ; and since, though the radices consist but of three letters, yet they make two syllables in speaking ; and since the pronunciation is such, as St. Jerome, who was born in a barbarous country, thought the words anhelent, strident, and of very harsh sound.

[6] *they are able.*] " This will appear very unlikely to a man that considers the Spanish terminations ; and Howel, who was eminently skilful in the three provincial languages, declares, that after many essays he never could effect it."—*Dr. Johnson.*

ing of grammatical Latin and Spanish, wherein the Italians and French will be very much to seek.[7]

The learned Casaubon conceiveth that a dialogue might be composed in Saxon, only of such words as are derivable from the Greek, which surely might be effected, and so as the learned might not uneasily find it out. Verstegan made no doubt that he could contrive a letter which might be understood by the English, Dutch, and East Frislander, which, as the present confusion standeth, might have proved no very clear piece, and hardly to be hammered out : yet so much of the Saxon still remaineth in our English, as may admit an orderly discourse and series of good sense, such as not only the present English, but Ælfric, Bede, and Alfred might understand after so many hundred years.

Nations that live promiscuously under the power and laws of conquest, do seldom escape the loss of their language with their liberties; wherein the Romans were so strict, that the Grecians were fain to conform in their judicial processes;[8] which made the Jews lose more in seventy years dispersion in the provinces of Babylon, than in many hundred in their distinct habitation in Egypt; and the English which dwelt dispersedly to lose their language in Ireland, whereas more tolerable reliques there are thereof in Fingall, where they were closely and almost solely planted; and the Moors which were most huddled together and united about

---

[7] *seek.*]   The following paragraphs occur here, in *MS. Sloan.* 1827.

   "The many mother tongues spoke in divers corners of Europe, and quite different from one another, are not reconcileable to any one common original; whereas the great languages of Spain, France, and Italy, are derivative from the Latin; that of Greece and its islands from the old Greek; the rest of the family of the Dutch or Schlavonian. As for the *lingua Fullana,* spoken in part of Friuli, and the *lingua Curvallea* in Rhætia, they are corruptions of the Italian, as that of Sardinia is also of the Spanish.

   "Even the Latin itself, which hath embroiled so many languages of Europe, if it had been the speech of one country, and not continued by writers, and the

consent and study of all ages since, it had found the same fate, and been swallowed like other languages ; since, in its ancient state, one age could scarce understand another, and that of some generations before must be read by a dictionary by a few successions after ; as, beside the famous pillar of Quillius, may be illustrated in these few lines, ' Eundo omnibus honestitudo præterbitunda nemo escit. Quianam itaque istuc effexis hauscio, temperi et toppertutemet tam hibus insegne, quod ningribus potestur aut ruspare nevolt. Sapsam saperdæ seneciones sardare nequinunt cuoi siemps et socienum quissis sperit?' "

   [8] *to conform in their, &c.*]   "To conform, and make use of Latin in their, &c." —*MS. Sloan.*

Granada have yet left their *Arvirage* among the Granadian Spaniards.

But shut up in angles and inaccessible corners, divided by laws and manners, they often continue long with little mixture, which hath afforded that lasting life unto the Cantabrian and British tongues, wherein the Britons are remarkable, who having lived four hundred years together with the Romans, retained so much of the British as it may be esteemed a language; which either they resolutely maintained in their cohabitation with them in Britain, or retiring after in the time of the Saxons into countries and parts[9] less civilized and conversant with the Romans, they found the people distinct, the language more entire, and so fell into it again.

But surely no languages have been so straitly locked up as not to admit of commixture. The Irish, although they retain a kind of a Saxon character,[1] yet have admitted many words of Latin and English. In the Welch are found many words from Latin, some from Greek and Saxon. In what parity and incommixture the language of that people stood, which were casually discovered in the heart of Spain, between the mountains of Castile, no longer ago than in the time of Duke D'Alva, we have not met with a good account; any farther than that their words were Basquish or Cantabrian: but the present Basquensa, one of the minor mother tongues of Europe, is not without commixture of Latin and Castilian, while we meet with *santifica, tentationeten, gloria, puissanea,* and four more [words] in the short form of the Lord's prayer, set down by Paulus Merula: but although in this brief form we may find such commixture, yet the bulk of their language seems more distinct, consisting of words of no affinity unto others, of numerals totally different, of differing grammatical rules, as may be observed in the Dictionary and short Basquensa Grammar, composed by Raphael Nicoleta, a priest of Bilboa.

And if they use the auxiliary verbs of *equin* and *ysan,*

---

[9] *into countries, &c.*] "Into Wales, and countries, &c."—*MS. Sloan.*

[1] *The Irish, although they, &c.*] The Irish using the same characters with the Anglo-Saxons, does not prove any affinity of language, nor does it exist. They both took their alphabet from the Roman.—*G.*

answerable unto *hazer* and *ser*, to have, and be, in the Spanish, which forms came in with the northern nations into the Italian, Spanish, and French, and if that form were used by them before, and crept not in from imitation of their neighbours, it may shew some ancienter traduction from northern nations,[2] or else must seem very strange: since the southern nations had it not of old, and I know not whether any such mode be found in the languages of any part of America.

The Romans, who made the great commixture and alteration of languages in the world, effected the same, not only by their proper language, but those also of their military forces, employed in several provinces, as holding a standing militia in all countries, and commonly of strange nations; so while the cohorts and forces of the Britons were quartered in Egypt, Armenia, Spain, Illyria, &c., the Stablæsians and Dalmatians here, the Gauls, Spaniards, and Germans, in other countries, and other nations in theirs, they could not but leave many words behind them, and carry away many with them, which might make, that, in many words of very distinct nations, some may still remain of very unknown and doubtful genealogy.

And if, as the learned Buxhornius contendeth,[3] the Scythian language as the mother tongue runs through the nations of Europe, and even as far as Persia, the community in many words, between so many nations, hath a more reasonable original traduction, and were rather derivable from the common tongue diffused through them all, than from any particular nation, which hath also borrowed and holdeth but at second hand.

The Saxons, settling over all England, maintained an uniform language, only diversified in dialects, idioms, and minor differences, according to their different nations which came in unto the common conquest, which may yet be a cause of

---

[2] *traduction from northern nations.*] Adelung considers the Basque to be *radically* different from any European *tribe* of languages—though many words are Teutonic borrowed from the Visigoths.

The great Danish philologist, Rask, also classes it by itself.— *G.*

[3] *And if, &c.*] Dr. Jamieson has discussed this subject in his Hermes Scythicus, the object of which work is to connect the Goths and Greeks, through the Pelasgi and Scythians.— *G.*

the variation in the speech and words of several parts of England, where different nations most abode or settled, and having expelled the Britons, their wars were chiefly among themselves, with little action with foreign nations until the union of the heptarchy under Egbert: after which time, although the Danes infested this land, and scarce left any part free, yet their incursions made more havoc in buildings, churches, and cities, than [in] the language of the country,[4] because their language was in effect the same, and such as whereby they might easily understand one another.

And if the Normans, which came into Neustria or Normandy with Rollo the Dane, had preserved their language in their new acquists, the succeeding conquest of England, by Duke William of his race, had not begot among us such notable alterations; but having lost their language in their abode in Normandy, before they adventured upon England, they confounded the English with their French, and made the grand mutation, which was successively increased by our possessions in Normandy, Guien, and Acquitain, by our long wars in France, by frequent resort of the French, who, to the number of some thousands, came over with Isabel, Queen to Edward the Second, and the several matches of England with the daughters of France before and since that time.

But this commixture, though sufficient to confuse, proved not of ability to abolish the Saxon words, for from the French we have borrowed many substantives, adjectives, and some verbs, but the great body of numerals, auxiliary verbs, articles, pronouns, adverbs, conjunctions, and prepositions, which are the distinguishing and lasting part of a language, remain with us from the Saxon, which, having suffered no great alteration for many hundred years, may probably still remain, though the English swell with the inmates of Italian, French, and Latin. An example whereof may be observed in this following:—

[4] *yet their incursions, &c.*] Yet the Danes had a great effect upon the Saxon language. The portion of the Saxon Chronicle written during their sway in England, is quite in a different dialect from the former part, and it is called the Dano-Saxon—it is not, however, so marked a departure from the early Anglo-Saxon, as the next dialect—the Norman-Saxon.—*G.*

ENGLISH I.—The first and foremost step to all good works is the dread and fear of the Lord of heaven and earth, which through the Holy Ghost enlightneth the blindness of our sinful hearts to tread the ways of wisdom, and leads our feet into the land of blessing.

SAXON I.—The erst and fyrmost stæp to eal gode weorka is the dræd and feurt of the Lauord of heofan and eorth, whilc thurh the Heilig Gast onlihtneth the blindnesse of ure sinfull heorte to træd the wæg of wisdome, and thone læd ure fet into the land of blessung.

ENGLISH II.—For to forget his law is the door, the gate, and key to let in all unrighteousness, making our eyes, ears, and mouths to answer the lust of sin, our brains dull to good thoughts, our lips dumb to his praise, our ears deaf to his gospel, and our eyes dim to behold his wonders, which witness against us that we have not well learned the word of God, that we are the children of wrath, unworthy of the love and manifold gifts of God, greedily following after the ways of the devil and witchcraft of the world, doing nothing to free and keep ourselves from the burning fire of hell, till we be buried in sin and swallowed in death, not to arise again in any hope of Christ's kingdom.

SAXON II.—For to fuorgytan his laga is the dure, the gat, and cæg to let in eal unrightwisnysse, makend ure eyge, eore, and muth to answare the lust of sin, ure brægan dole to gode theoht, ure lippan dumb to his preys, ure earen deaf to his gospel, and ure eyge dim to behealden his wundra, whilc ge witnysse ongen us that wee œf noht wel gelæred the weord of God, that wee are the cilda of ured, unwyrthe of the lufe and mænigfeald gift of God, grediglice felygend æfter the wægen of the deoful and wiccraft of the weorld, doend nothing to fry and cæp ure saula from the byrnend fyr of hell, till we be geburied in synne and swolgen in death, not to arise agen in ænig hope of Christes kynedome.

ENGLISH III.—Which draw from above the bitter doom of the Almighty of hunger, sword, sickness, and brings more sad plagues than those of hail, storms, thunder, blood, frogs, swarms of gnats and grasshoppers, which ate the corn, grass, and leaves of the trees in Egypt.

SAXON III.—Whilc drag from buf the bitter dome of the Almagan of hunger, sweorde, seoknesse, and bring mere sad plag, thone they of hagal, storme, thunner, blode, frog, swearme of gnæt and gærsupper, whilc eaten the corn, gærs, and leaf of the treowen in Ægypt.

ENGLISH IV.—If we read his book and holy writ, these, among many others, we shall find to be the tokens of his hate, which gathered together might mind us of his will, and teach us when his wrath beginneth, which sometimes comes in open strength and full sail, oft steals like a thief in the night, like shafts shot from a bow at midnight, before we think upon them.

SAXON IV.—Gyf we ræd his boc and heilig gewrit, these gemong mænig othern, we sceall findan the tacna of his hatung, whilc gegatherod together miht gemind us of his willan, and teac us whone his ured onginneth, whilc sometima come in open strength and fill seyle, oft stæl gelyc a theof in the niht, gelyc sceaft scoten fram a boge at midneoht, befor an we thinck uppen them.

ENGLISH V.—And though they were a deal less, and rather short than beyond our sins, yet do we not a whit withstand or forbear them, we are wedded to, not weary of our misdeeds, we seldom look upward, and are not ashamed under sin; we cleanse not ourselves from the blackness and deep hue of our guilt; we want tears and sorrow, we weep not, fast not, we crave not forgiveness from the mildness, sweetness and goodness of God, and with all livelihood and steadfastness to our uttermost will hunt after the evil of guile, pride, cursing, swearing, drunkenness, over-eating, uncleanness, all idle lust of the flesh, yes many uncouth and nameless sins, hid in our inmost breast and bosoms, which stand betwixt our forgiveness, and keep God and man asunder.

SAXON V.—And theow they wære a dæl lesse, and reither scort thone begond oure sinnan, get do we naht a whit withstand and forbeare them, we eare bewudded to, noht werig of ure agen misdeed, we seldon loc upweard, and ear not ofschæmod under sinne, we cleans noht ure selvan from the blacnesse and dæp hue of ure guilt; we wan teare and sara, we weope noht, fæst noht, we craft noht foregyfnesse fram the mildnesse, sweetnesse and goodnesse of God, and mit eal lifelyhood and stedfastnesse to ure uttermost will hunt æfter the ufel of guile, pride, cursung, swearung, druncennesse, overeat, uncleannesse and eal idle lust of the flæsc, yis mænig uncuth and nameleas sinnan, hid in ure inmæst brist and bosome, whilc stand betwixt ure foregyfnesse, and cæp God and man asynder.

ENGLISH VI.—Thus are we far beneath and also worse than the rest of God's works; for the sun and moon, the king and queen of stars, snow, ice, rain, frost, dew, mist, wind, fourfooted and creeping things, fishes and feathered birds, and fowls either of sea or land, do all hold the laws of his will.

SAXON VI.—Thus eare we far beneoth and ealso wyrse thone the rest of Gods weorka; for the sun and mone, the cyng and cquen of stearran, snaw, ise, ren, frost, deaw, miste, wind, feower fet and crypend dihga, fix yefetherod brid, and fælan auther in sæ or land do eal heold the lag of his willan.

Thus have you seen in few words how near the Saxon and English meet.[5]

Now of this account the French will be able to make nothing; the modern Danes and Germans, though from several words they may conjecture at the meaning, yet will they be much to seek in the orderly sense and continued construction thereof. Whether the Danes can continue such a series of sense out of their present language and the old Runick, as to be intelligible unto present and ancient times, some doubt may well be made; and if the present French would attempt a discourse in words common unto their present tongue and the old *Romana Rustica* spoken in elder times, or in the old language of the Francks, which came to be in use some suc-

---

[5] *how near the Saxon, &c.*] Johnson observes, "the words are, indeed, Saxon, but the phraseology is English; and, I think, would not have been understood by Bede or Ælfric, notwithstanding the confidence of our author. He has, however, sufficiently proved his position, that the English resembles its parental language more than any modern European dialect." This opinion exactly coincides with that of a still higher authority, Miss Gurney, of Northrepps Cottage, the translator of the Saxon Chronicle; on whose recommendation I have preferred to reprint the Saxon passages as they stand, rather than to adopt any additions or variations from partial transcripts of them in the British Museum and Bodleian.

cessions after Pharamond, it might prove a work of some trouble to effect.

It were not impossible to make an original reduction of many words of no general reception in England, but of common use in Norfolk, or peculiar to the East Angle countries; as, bawnd, bunny, thurck, enemmis, sammodithee, mawther, kedge, seele, straft, clever, matchly, dere, nicked, stingy, noneare, feft, thepes, gosgood, kamp, sibrit, fangast, sap, cothish, thokish, bide owe, paxwax:[6] of these and some

---

[6] *Bawnd, &c.*] Some time before the appearance of "*The Vocabulary of East Anglia, by the Rev. W. Forby,*" I had been favoured with valuable illustrations of this curious list of words in common use in Norfolk during Sir Thomas's life, by Miss Gurney, and Mr. Black, of the British Museum, of which I have availed myself in the following notes.

Bawnd;—swollen. Not in present use; at least, not known to be so. Isl. *bon,* tùmidus.—*Forby.*

Bunny;—a common word for a rabbit, especially among children.—*Blk.*——A small swelling caused by a fall or blow. Perhaps a diminutive *bump.* One would be glad to derive it from the Greek βουνος, a hillock. It may be so through the Gothic.—*Forby.*

Thurck;—appears to mean dark, if it be the same as in the *Promptorium Parvulorum Clericorum.*—*MS. Harl.* 221. "*Therke* or *dyrk,* tenebrosus, caliginosus; terknesse or derknesse."—*Blk.*——Dark. So say Hickes and Ray; may have been for ought we can say to the contrary.—*Forby.*

Enemmis;—Qu. *et neqnmoins?*—*G.*—— I will not say that this is the, old word *anempst* for *anenst (anent* in modern Scottish), about, concerning; because I know not its proper collocation.—*Blk.* ——Of very obscure and doubtful meaning, like most of Sir Thomas Browne's words. Hickes says it means *lest* (ne forte), and he derives it from Isl. *einema,* an adv. of exclusion, as he says. It may mean, notwithstanding, N. Fr. *nemis.* Or it may be an adjective, signifying variable, as *emmis* is in L. sc. which JAM. derives from Isl. *ymiss,* varius. But as the word is quite extinct, it is impossible to decide upon its meaning, when it was in use.—*Forby.*—— The word is not extinct, but still used in

Norfolk in the sense of *lest:* though its usual sound would rather lead us to spell it *enammons.*

Sammodithee;—Samod o 'thi; the like of that.—*G.*——*Sammodithee* is an old oath or asseveration, *sá môt I thé,* so may I thrive. "*Als mote I the* " is common in ancient English, and "*So the ik* " in Chaucer. See Tyrwhitt's and other Glossaries, in v. *The,* which is the A. S. *dean,* to thrive.—*Blk.*——This uncouth cluster of little words (for such it is) is recorded by Sir Thomas Browne as current in his time. It is now totally extinct. It stands thus in the eighth tract, "On Languages." Dr. Hickes has taken the liberty of changing it to *sammoditha,* and interprets it, "Say me how dost thou; " in pure Saxon "*sæg me hu dest thu.*" "Say me," for "tell me," is in use to this day in some counties. It is in the dialect of Sedgmoor. Ray adduces, as a sort of parallel to this jumble of words, one which he says was common in his time; *muchgoodite,* "much good do it thee."—*F.*

Mawther;—the same as the vulgar *mawkes,* a wench—*Blk.*——A girl. Tusser uses it. So does B. Johnson:—" You talk like a foolish *mauther,*" says Restive to Dame Pliant, in the Alchemist. It seems peculiarly an East Anglian word. So at least it was considered by Sir Henry Spelman. It is highly amusing to find so grave an antiquary endeavouring earnestly, and at no inconsiderable length, to vindicate the honour of his mother-tongue; and to rescue this important word from the contempt with which some, as it seems, through their ignorance, were disposed to treat it. " Quod rident cæteri Angli," says he, " vocis nescientes probitatem." He assures us that it was applied by our very early ancestors, even to the noble virgins who

others of no easy originals, when time will permit, the resolution may be attempted; which to effect, the Danish language

were selected to sing the praises of heroes. They were called *scald-moers*, q. d. *sing-ing mauthers!* "En quantum in spretâ jam voce antiquæ gloriæ!" He complains that the old word *moer* had been corrupted to *mother*, and so confounded with a very different word. We distinguish them very effectually by pronunciation, and, what is more, we actually come very near to the original word in the abbreviated form we use in addressing a *mauther*. We commonly call her *mau'r*. Dan. *moer*. Belg. *modde*, innupta puella.—*Forby*.

Kedge;—I should rather think is the "*Kygge* or Joly, Jocundus, Hillaris," of *Prompt.* than "*cadge*, to carry, of *Wilbr. Appendix.*" — *Blk.* —— Brisk, active. This is Sir Thomas Browne's spelling. We pronounce it *kidge*, and apply it exclusively, or nearly so, to hale and cheerful old persons. In Ray, the word CADGE has the same meaning. It is by mere change of vowels *cadge, kedge, kidge*. Dan. *kaud*, lascivus. Lowland Scotch *kedgie* and *caigie.*—*Forby*.

Seele ;—is this our sell, haysell, or seel time?—*G.*——Take these from *Prompt.* "*sele*, horsys harneys, arquillus." "*Selle*, stoddyng howse cella." "*Sylle* of an howse. Silla Solma." I cannot offer any thing else.—*Blk.*——Seal, time, season. Hay-*seal*, wheat-*seal*, barley-*seal*, are the respective seasons of mowing or sowing those products of the earth. But it goes as low as hours. Of an idle and dissipated fellow, we say that he "keeps bad *seals*," of poachers, that they are out at all *seals* of the night; of a sober, regular, and industrious man, that he attends to his business at all *seals*," or that "he keeps good *seals* and meals." Sir Thomas Browne spells it seele ; but we seem to come nearer to the Saxon *sæl*, opportunitas.—*Forby*.

Straft ;—Iratus, irâ exclamans, vox in agro Norf. usitata. Hickes derivat ab Is. *straffa*, objurgere, corripere, increpare. *L. Junius Etymol.* I cannot find the passage on a cursory examination of Hickes in his little *Dict. Islandicum.* In the 2nd vol. of the Thesaur. p. 89, Hickes gives "Straff, gannitus," but the usual meaning is punishment, and this is the meaning given by Biorn Halderson.-*G.* ——I will adduce a word from *Wachter's German Glossary.* "Straff, rigidus, du-

rus, astrictus, severus."— *Blk.* —— A scolding bout; an angry strife of tongues. Isl. *straffa*, iratus.—*Forby.*

Clever ;—perhaps some unusual meaning of our present adj. unless the first vowel should be pronounced long.—*Blk.* ——Dextrous, adroit ; Ray says, neat, elegant: in either sense it is so very common and general, and appears so to have been for so many years, that it seems difficult to conceive how Sir Thomas Browne should have been struck with it as a provincialism, and still more, how Ray, long afterwards, should have let it pass as such without any remark. If not when Sir Thomas wrote his tract, certainly long before the second edition of Ray, S.E.C., published by the author, it had been used by Butler, L'Estrange, and South. In L'Estrange, indeed, it might be positively provincial ; in Butler low, ludicrous, or even burlesque ; in South too familiar and undignified for the pulpit ; but in neither provincial. But what shall we say of Addison, who had also used it ? In Todd's Johnson it is said to be low, and scarcely ever used but in burlesque, and in conversation. A colloquial and familiar term it certainly is ; but assuredly not provincial, nor even low. Sir Thomas Browne is the only guarantee of its insertion here. And if it must be ours, let it by all means be taken with our own rustic pronunciation, *claver.* — *Forby.* —— My friend Mr. Black's suggestion,—that there is some unusual meaning attached in Norfolk to this word, which justifies its insertion among provincialisms,—is correct. The poor in this county, speaking of any one who is kind and liberal towards them, say very commonly, "He is a *claver* gentleman !" "'Twas a *claver* thing he did for us !" "He always behave very *claver* to the poor."——Moor says that it means handsome, good-looking ;—e. g. a *clever* horse, a *clever* gal (girl).

Matchly ;—perhaps may mean proportionately, or corresponding. — *Blk.* ——Exactly alike, fitting nicely. Another of Sir Thomas Browne's words, happily explained by modern pronunciation, *mackly*. A. S. *maka*, par.—*Forby.*

Dere ;—dire, sad. But it is Old English. Chaucer has it, and Shakspeare, in "Love's Labour Lost:"—"Deaf'd with the clamour of their own *dear*

new and more ancient may prove of good advantage: which
nation remained here fifty years upon agreement, and have

groans." Dr. Johnson observes that
dear is for *dere*. And yet the words
"own *dear*" may seem to come very
nearly to the sense of the adjective φίλος
in Homer; φίλον ἦτορ, φίλον ὄμμα,
φίλα γούνατα.' It is a sense of close
and particular endearment, in which certainly we often use those two words, in
speaking of any thing we particularly
cherish, as our beloved kindred or friends,
or, as in Homer, the limbs or organs of
our bodies.—*Forby*.

Nicked ;—cheated, as yet among the
vulgar. I think to have seen (in Wachter) *nicken*, obstinate.—*Blk*.——Exactly
hit; in the very nick: at the precise
point. Another of Sir Thomas Browne's
words, at which one cannot but marvel.
The very same authorities are produced
by Johnson, for the verb *nick* in this
sense, as for the adjective CLEVER ;—
those of Butler, L'Estrange, and South.
It is not possible to conceive that the
word had at that time any other sense in
which it might be considered as a provincial word. Ray explains it thus : *Nick-
led*, beaten down and intricately entangled, as growing corn or grass by rain
and wind. Might not this be the word
meant by Sir Thomas Browne, and imperfectly heard ?—*Forby*.——Both these
are wrong; the following is the correct
explanation:—To *nick* is to notch the
under part of a horse's tail, to make it
stand out or erect. An instance occurs
in the Monthly Mag. for 1812, part I, p.
28, in the memoir of John Fransham ;
who, when at Norwich, could not bear
"the cruel practices there carried on of
cropping, *nicking*, and docking horses."
I transcribe this from a more recent communication from Mr. Black. But that a
Norfolk man (Mr. Forby) should have
been ignorant of the meaning of so common a provincialism, seems singular.

Stingy ;—with a soft *g*, commonly
means parsimonious.—*Blk*.——This is
its commonly received sense. Its provincial acceptation is given by Forby :—
1. Cross, ill-humoured ; 2. Churlish, biting ; as applied to the state of the air. It
was most probably in one or in both these
senses in which Sir Thomas Browne remarked it as provincial. He must surely
have been acquainted with it in its commonly current sense. That, indeed,

seems to be perverted from another word,
of very different origin. This of ours, in
both its senses, is very clearly from A.S.
stinge, aculeus.—*Forby*. —— Moor remarks that, "in bees the propensity to
hoard and *resent* is proverbial;" here
the two principal meanings of the word
stingy equally apply.

Noneare ;—Lye thus explains this
word between brackets, marking it as an
addition of his own to Junius's Etymol.
Angl. [Modò—vox Norf. etiamnum in
usu, ab Isl. *nunœr* idem significante, ut
monet Hickesius. L.] I cannot find it in
Hickes. Nor is the compound word
nunœr in Biorn Halderson's Ice. Dict.
but it is, in fact, *now-near*, anon.—*G*.
——Not till now. So says Ray. But
we know nothing of the word whatever.
Sir Thomas Browne might. Isl. *nunœr*.
modo.—*Forby*.

Feft ;—Prompt. feffyd, feofatus ; but
not likely to be the right word.—*Blk*.
——To persuade, or endeavour to per-
suade, says Ray in pref. to N. C. W.
Yet he adds that in his own county,
Essex, it meant, to "put off wares ;"
but that he was to seek for an etymon.
So are we. But it is of no importance.
It is one of Sir Thomas Browne's words
become obsolete.—*Forby*.

Thepes ;—or rather *thapes*. *Gooseberries*.
I cannot find any word resembling this as
a fruit; but *Tap* in Danish is the *uvula* of
the throat. V. FAPES.—*Forby*, p. 110.

Gosgood ;—A vulgar London word for
a gooseberry is goosgog.—*Blk*.——Yeast.
Ray says, that in his time, it was in use
also in Kent. But he does not say, nor
is it possible to conceive, how it is entitled
to so exalted an interpretation as he be-
stows upon it—*God's Good !* A meaning
much more suitable and seemly, and
surely not improbable, may be conjectured. It may have had its origin from
A. S. *gos*, anser. In Norfolk, if not in
every part of East Anglia, yeast dump-
lings have been immemorially associated
with a roasted goose ; and when properly soaked in the natural gravy of the
fowl, are of a very delicious savour to a
true East Anglian palate. In this sense
yeast may be said to be *good with goose*,
and called *goose-good*, or in the most ancient form, *gos-good*. But the word is
now utterly extinct. The taste remains.
—*Forby*.

left many families in it, and the language of these parts had surely been more commixed and perplext, if the fleet of Hugo

Kamp ;—May, perhaps, be the game of foot-ball, from these words in *Prompt.* "*Camper*, or player at foot-ball," also "*camping.*" I suppose so named by reason of the space required for this game. —*Blk.*

Sibrit ;—or *Sibberet*, means the bands of marriage; "sibberidge" in *Wilbr.* and "sybrede banna" in *Prompt.*—*Blk.*
——It is one of Sir Thomas Browne's words, and in full use at this day. It is explained by Hickes, A. S. *syb*, cognatio, and *byrht*, manifestus, q. d. a public announcing or proclamation of an intended affinity. This is unquestionably preferable to the unfounded notion, that the word is corrupted from "*Si quis sciverit,*" the supposed first words of the publication of banns in the Roman Latin service. —*Forby.*——This word has been derived from *sib*, said to mean akin; and to imply, that by banns the parties have a *right* to become akin, that is, *sib-right.* Some say it is *rib-right*, the right to take a rib. Ray has this proverb :—As much *sibb'd* as sieve and riddle that grew in the same wood. p. 225. And he says that "*sibb'd* means akin, and that in Suffolk the banns of matrimony are called sibberidge," which is correct; though *sibrit* be most common. Both are in extensive use. *Sib* is also Scottish. It occurs twice in the sense of relationship in Scottish colloquialism in Guy Mannering, ii, 183, 219. It occurs also in the Antiquary, iii, 75;—"By the religion of our holy church they are ower sibb thegither." Again, "They may be brought to think themselves sae sibb as on Christian law will permit them wedlock." I do not find, however, that *sibrit* or *sibridge* is Scottish.—*Moor.*

Fangast ;—A marriageable maid. The word is not now known, and is, therefore, given with Ray's interpretation and etymon. A. S. *fangan*, capere, and *gast*, amor.—*Forby.*

Sap ;—*sapy, foolish ;* perhaps only *sappy*, ill pronounced.—*G.*——Mr. Forby was unacquainted with the meaning suggested by Miss Gurney, and in which I have often heard the word used :—a silly fellow is called a *sap*; he is also termed *sapy* or *sappy.* The comparison intended is possibly to the sap in timber, which is of little value, and soon becomes unsound and useless.

Cothish ;—is likely to be an adj. from this noun in *Prompt.* "*cothe*, or swowning, sincopa."—*Blk.*——*Cothish, cothy,* adj. faint, sickly, ailing. There can surely be no doubt of the identity of these words; the former is Sir Thomas Browne's, the latter the modern form. Yet in the pref. to R. N. C. it is interpreted *morose*, without a word of explanation or proof. It never could have been used in that sense. Its derivation is so very obvious, that it is wonderful it escaped Ray. It is amply justified by modern and very frequent use. A dog is said to be *cothy* when he is meek and delicate. A. S. *cothe*, morbus.

Thokish ;—*thoke*, as on-sadde (*sad* meant firm) fysh, humorosus, insolidus, *Prompt.* applied to boggy land.—*Blk.*
——Slothful: sluggish. This is Ray's interpretation, and may be right for ought we know.—*Forby.*——The sense suggested by Mr. Black I believe to be the true one.

Bide-owe ;—interpreted by Ray (Pr. to N. C.) "*poenas dare.*" It may be so. It is impossible to assent or gainsay, as it is totally extinct. It is one of Sir Thomas Browne's words.—*Forby.*——Let us, in such failure of authorities, hazard a conjecture; that it means "wait a while,"—*bide a wee.*

"*Pax wax;*—synewe," *Prompt.* It is still used dialectically for our *pathwax* or *packwax.*—*Blk.*——The strong tendon in the neck of animals. It is a word which has no proper claim to admission here, for it is quite general; yet must be admitted, because it is on Sir Thomas Browne's list. It must certainly have been in use in his time. And it is very strange he should not have heard it till he came into Norfolk. Ray, in the preface to N. C., makes no remark to this effect, but takes this as he finds it with the other words. Yet he had himself used it in his great work on the Creation, and to all appearance as a word well known. He spells it *pack-wax*, indeed, but that can surely make no difference. He not only gives no derivation, but declines giving one, at the same time declaring his own knowledge of the very extensive, if not general, use of the word. The fact is, that it is not even confined to the English language. It is used by Linnæus, somewhere in the Upsal Amœ-

de Bones had not been cast away, wherein threescore thousand soldiers out of Britany and Flanders were to be wafted
over, and were by king John's appointment to have a settled
habitation in the counties of Norfolk and Suffolk.[7]

But beside your laudable endeavours in the Saxon, you are
not like to repent you of your studies in the other European
and western languages, for therein are delivered many excellent historical, moral, and philosophical discourses, wherein
men merely versed in the learned languages are often at a
loss: but although you are so well accomplished in the
French, you will not surely conceive that you are master of
all the languages in France, for to omit the Briton, Britonant
or old British, yet retained in some part of Britany, I shall
only propose this unto your construction.

Chavalisco d'aquestes Boemes chems an freitado lou cap
cun taules Jargonades, ero necy chi voluiget bouta sin tens

nitates Academicæ. A friend, who undertook the search, has not been able to
find the passage; but it is not likely that
any thing explanatory would be found.
Indeed, it is a sort of *crux etymologorum.*
They, very reasonably, do not care to
come near it. And they might all
frankly avow, as Ray does, that they
"have nothing to say to it." Br. has
fix-fax.—Forby.

[7] *the Danish language, &c.*] I do not
see the Danish original of most of the
Norfolk words here given; but there are
several which can be traced to no other,
and I have found several which are, I
suspect, peculiar to the coast:—

Hefty;—stormy. Dan. *heftig*, angry.
Swale;—shade. Dan. or Ice. *svala,*
cold.
Willock;—a guillemot, or any sea
bird of the awk or diver kind.
Roke;—fog or sea haze. —— *Rak,*
wet, Ice., "With cloudy gum and rak
ouerquhelmst the are."—*Gawin Douglas.*
To shrepe;—used by the fishermen in
the sense of "to clear." "The fog begins
to *shrepe* yonder." Ice. *skreppa.* Dila-
bi, se subducere.
Lum;—the handle of an oar. Icel.
hlummr. In other parts of England,
however, it is called the *loom* of an oar.
Rooms; — the spaces between the
thwarts of a boat. Ice. *rum,* used only
in this sense.
To go driving;—to go fishing: chiefly

applied to the herring fishers, I think.—
G.

I have added, from a list of *Norfolk
words* furnished me by the same correspondent, the following, which are either
new to Forby, or with different derivations:—

" *Wips and strays,*" not *waifs and
strays,* but "wipper and straae." Dan.
"heads and straws of corn," odds and
ends. I found this expression in a list of
provincialisms of the Danish island of
Zealand.
To lope;—to stride along. Ger. *hlaup-
en,* to run.
Unstowly;—applied to children; unruly.
Car;—a low marshy grove. Alder
car, osier car. *Kior,* Ice., marsh.
Skep or skip;—a basket; toad's skep,
(not *cap,* I think). *Skieppe* is a Danish
half bushel measure.
Pottens;—crutches.
Hobby;—small horse. Dan. *hoppe,* a
mare.
Wunt;—to sit as a hen. Sax. *wuni-
an,* to abide.
Shacking. In German *yechen* is to
club—and "zur yeche gehen," literally,
"to go to shack" is an expression in use,
meaning to take a common share. The
essence of our shacking is that the pigs
and geese run in common over the fields
to pick up the remains of the harvest.
—*G.*

embè aquelles. Anin à lous occells, che dizen tat prou ben
en ein voz L' ome nosap comochodochi yen ay jes de plazer,
d' ausir la mitat de paraulles, en el mon.

This is a part of that language which Scaliger nameth
Idiotismus Tectofagicus or Langue d'oc, counterdistinguish-
ing it unto the Idiotismus Francicus or Langue d'ouy, not
understood in a petty corner or between a few mountains, but
in parts of early civility, in Languedoc, Provence and Cata-
lonia, which put together will make little less than England.

Without some knowledge herein you cannot exactly understand the works of Rabelais : by this the French themselves
are fain to make out that preserved relique of old French,
containing the league between Charles and Lewis the sons of
Ludovicus Pius. Hereby may tolerably be understood the several tracts, written in the Catalonian tongue ; and in this is
published the Tract of Falconry written by Theodosius and
Symmachus ; in this is yet conserved the Poem Vilhuardine
concerning the French expedition in the holy war, and the
taking of Constantinople, among the works of Marius Æqui-
cola an Italian poet. You may find in this language, a pleasant dialogue of love ; this, about an hundred years ago, was
in high esteem, when many Italian wits flocked into Provence ;
and the famous Petrarcha wrote many of his poems in Vau-
cluse in that country.[8]

[8] *country.*] In the *MS. Sloan.* 1827,
I find the following very odd passage ;
respecting which, most certainly, the
author's assertion is incontrovertible,
that "the sense may afford *some trouble.*" I insert it, not expecting that many
readers will take that trouble—but it appeared too characteristic to be omitted.

"Now having wearied you with old languages or little understood, I shall put
an end unto your trouble in modern
French, by a short letter composed by
me for your sake, though not concerning
yourself ; wherein, though the words be
plain and genuine, yet the sense may
afford some trouble.

"MONSIEUR,—Ne vous laisses plus
manger la laine sur le dors. Regardes
bien ce gros magot, lequel vous voyez de
si bon œil. Assurement il fait le mitou.
Monsieur, vous chausses les lunettes de
travers, ne voyant point comme il prati-

que vos dependants. Il s'est desïa queri
de mal St. Francois, et bride sa mule
a vostre despens. Croyez moi, il ne
s'amusera pas a là moutarde ; mais,
vous ayant miné et massacré vos affaires,
au dernier coup il vous rendra Monsieur
sans queue.

"Mais pour l'autre goulafie et benueur
a tire la rigau, qui vous a si rognement
fait la barbe, l'envoyes vous a Pampe-
lune. Mais auparavant, a mon advis, il
auroit a miserere jusques a vitulos, et je
le ferois un moutton de Berry. En le
traittant bellement et de bon conseil,
vous assuyes de rompre un anguille sur
les genoux. Ne lui fies poynt : il ne
rabbaissera le menton, et mourra dans
sa peau. Il scait bien que les belles
paroles n'escorchent pas la guele, les
quelles il payera a sepmaine de deux
Jeudies. Chasses le de chez vous a
bonne heure, car il a estè a Naples sans

For the word (Dread) in the royal title (Dread sovereign) of which you desire to know the meaning, I return answer unto your question briefly thus.

Most men do vulgarly understand this word dread after the common and English acceptation, as implying fear, awe, or dread.

Others may think to expound it from the French word *droit* or *droyt*. For, whereas, in elder times, the presidents and supremes of courts were termed sovereigns, men might conceive this a distinctive title and proper unto the king as eminently and by right the sovereign.

A third exposition may be made from some Saxon original, particularly from *Driht, Domine,* or *Drihten, Dominus,* in the Saxon language, the word for *Dominus* throughout the Saxon Psalms, and used in the expression of the year of our Lord in the Decretal Epistle of Pope Agatho unto Athelred King of the Mercians, *anno* 680.

Verstegan would have this term *Drihten* appropriate unto God. Yet, in the constitutions of Withred King of Kent,* we find the same word used for a Lord or Master, *si in vesperâ præcedente solem servus ex mandato Domini aliquod opus servile egerit, Dominus (Drihten) 80 solidis luito.* However, therefore, though *Driht, Domine,* might be most eminently applied unto the Lord of heaven, yet might it be also transferred unto potentates and gods on earth, unto whom fealty is given or due, according unto the feudist term

* *V. Cl. Spelmanni Concil.*

passer les monts ; et ancore que parle en maistre, est patient de St. Cosme.

" Soucies vous aussi de la garcionaire, chez vous, qu'elle n'ayst le mal de neuf mois. Assurement elle a le nez tourné a la friandise, et les talons bien courts. Elle jouera volontiers a l'Home ; et si le hault ne defend le bas, avant la venue des cicoignes, lui s'enlevera la juppe.

" Mais, pour le petit Gymnosophiste chez vous, caresses le vous aux bras ouverts. Voyez vous pas comme a toutes les menaces de Fortune il branle comme la Bastille ? Vrayment il est Stoic a vingt-quatre carrats, et de mesme calibre avec les vieux Ascetiques. Al-

loran* lui vault autant que l'isle de France, et la tour de Cordan † lui vault le mesme avec la Louvre.

" Serviteur très-humble,
" THOMAS BROUNE."

* *Note ;*—"Alloran, Allusama, or Insula Erroris ; a small desolate barren island, whereon nothing liveth but coneys, in the Mediterranean sea, between Carthagena and Calo-de-tres-furcus, in Barbary."

† *Note ;*—" A small island or rock, in the mouth of the river Garonne, with one tower in it, where a man liveth, to take care of lights for such as go to, or come from, Bordeaux."

ligeus,[9] *à ligando,* unto whom they were bound in fealty.
And therefore from *Driht, Domine,* dread sovereign, may,
probably, owe its original.

I have not time to enlarge upon this subject: pray let this
pass, as it is, for a letter and not for a treatise.   I am,

Yours, &c.

[9] *ligeus.*]   " Or liege lord."—*MS. Sloan.* 1827.

TRACT IX.

OF ARTIFICIAL HILLS, MOUNTS, OR BURROWS,
IN MANY PARTS OF ENGLAND: WHAT THEY ARE, TO WHAT END RAISED, AND BY WHAT NATIONS.

My Honoured Friend Mr. W. D.'s [1] *Query.*

IN my last journey through Marshland, Holland, and a great part of the Fens, I observed divers artificial heaps of earth of a very large magnitude, and I hear of many others which are in other parts of those countries, some of them are at least twenty foot in direct height from the level whereon they stand. I would gladly know your opinion of them, and whether you think not that they were raised by the Romans or Saxons, to cover the bones or ashes of some eminent persons?

My Answer.

WORTHY SIR,

CONCERNING artificial mounts and hills, raised without fortifications attending them, in most parts of England, the most considerable thereof I conceive to be of two kinds; that is, either signal boundaries and land marks, or else sepulchral monuments or hills of interment for remarkable and eminent persons, especially such as died in the wars.

[1] *Mr. W. D.*] "The initials, in both the preceding editions, are "E. D.:" but it has been clearly ascertained that this is an error. The query was Sir William Dugdale's; and his reply to the present discourse will be found vol. i, p. 381. A reference to Dugdale's History of Embanking and Draining, will shew that he availed himself of the reply he obtained to his enquiry: for he has transcribed the quotations from Leland and Wormius in illustration of the Saxon and Danish mode of sepulture; and has given almost *verbatim* the passage referring to Germanicus.

As for such which are sepulchral monuments, upon bare and naked view, they are not appropriable unto any of the three nations of the Romans, Saxons, or Danes, who, after the Britons, have possessed this land; because upon strict account, they may be appliable unto them all.[2]

For that the Romans used such hilly sepultures, beside many other testimonies, seems confirmable from the practice of Germanicus, who thus interred the unburied bones of the slain soldiers of Varus ; and that expression of Virgil, of high antiquity among the Latins,

—— facit ingens monte sub alio
Regis Dercenni terreno ex aggere bustum.

That the Saxons made use of this way is collectible from several records, and that pertinent expression of Lelandus,* *Saxones, gens Christi ignara, in hortis amœnis, si domi forte ægroti moriebantur ; sin foris et bello occisi, in egestis per campos terræ tumulis, (quos burgos appellabant) sepulti sunt.*

That the Danes observed this practice, their own antiquities do frequently confirm, and it stands precisely delivered by Adolphus Cyprius, as the learned Wormius † hath observed.   *Dani olim in memoriam regum et heroum, ex terra coacervata ingentes moles, montium instar eminentes, erexisse, credibile omnino ac probabile est, atque illis in locis ut plurimum, quo sæpe homines commearent, atque iter haberent, ut in viis publicis posteritati memoriam consecrarent, et quodammodo immortalitati mandarent.*   And the like monuments are yet to be observed in Norway and Denmark in no small numbers.

* *Leland in Assertione Regis Arthuri.*
† *Wormius in Monumentis Danicis.*

[2] *appliable unto them all.*] Mr. Pegge, in a paper published in the Archæologia, on the Arbour Lows, in Derbyshire, expresses the same opinion ; — ascribing these burrows or *tumuli* to Britons, Romans, Saxons, and Danes,—and not to any one of those people exclusively. Some he supposes to be British, from their being dispersed over moors, and usually on eminences ; not placed with any regard to roads, as the Roman *tu-* *muli* generally are. The Danish lows would frequently exhibit a circle of stones round their base. But the contents would furnish the best and perhaps the only sure criterion to judge by ; kist-vaens and stone coffins, rings, beads, and other articles, peculiar to the Britons, being found in some ; Roman coins, urns, and implements in others, and the arms and utensils of the Saxons or Danes in others.—*Archæologia*, vii, 131, &c.

So that upon a single view and outward observation they may be the monuments of any of these three nations: although the greatest number, not improbably, of the Saxons; who fought many battles with the Britons and Danes, and also between their own nations, and left the proper name of burrows for these hills still retained in many of them, as the seven burrows upon Salisbury plain, and in many other parts of England.

But of these and the like hills there can be no clear and assured decision without an ocular exploration, and subterraneous enquiry by cutting through one of them either directly or cross-wise. For so with lesser charge discovery may be made what is under them, and consequently the intention of their erection. For if they were raised for remarkable and eminent boundaries, then about their bottom will be found the lasting substances of burnt bones of beasts, of ashes, bricks, lime, or coals.

If urns be found, they might be erected by the Romans before the term of urn-burying or custom of burning the dead expired: but if raised by the Romans after that period, inscriptions, swords, shields, and arms, after the Roman mode, may afford a good distinction.

But if these hills were made by Saxons or Danes, discovery may be made from the fashion of their arms, bones of their horses, and other distinguishing substances buried with them.

And for such an attempt there wanteth not encouragement. For a like mount or burrow was opened in the days of King Henry the Eighth upon Barham Down, in Kent, by the care of Mr. Thomas Digges, and charge of Sir Christopher Hales; and a large urn with ashes was found under it, as is delivered by Thomas Twinus, *de Rebus Albionicis,* a learned man of that country, *sub incredibili terræ acervo, urna cinere ossium magnorum fragmentis plena, cum galeis, clypeis æneis et ferreis rubigine fere consumptis, inusitatæ magnitudinis, eruta est: sed nulla inscriptio nomen, nullum testimonium tempus, aut fortunam exponebant:* and not very long ago, as Camden delivereth,* in one of the mounts of Barklow hills, in Essex,

* *Camd. Brit p.* 326.

being levelled, there were found three troughs, containing broken bones, conceived to have been of Danes : and in later time we find, that a burrow was opened in the Isle of Man, wherein fourteen urns were found with burnt bones in them; and one more neat than the rest, placed in a bed of fine white sand, containing nothing but a few brittle bones, as having passed the fire ; according to the particular account thereof in the description of the Isle of Man.* Surely many noble bones and ashes have been contented with such hilly tombs ; which neither admitting ornament, epitaph, or inscription, may, if earthquakes spare them, out-last all other monuments. *Suæ sunt metis metæ.* Obelisks have their term, and pyramids will tumble, but these mountainous monuments may stand, and are like to have the same period with the earth.

More might be said, but my business of another nature, makes me take off my hand. I am,

Yours, &c.

* *Published* 1656, *by Dan. King.*

TRACT X.

OF TROAS, WHAT PLACE IS MEANT BY THAT NAME.
ALSO, OF THE SITUATIONS OF SODOM, GOMORRHA, ADMAH,
ZEBOIM, IN THE DEAD SEA.

SIR,

To your geographical queries, I answer as follows:—

In sundry passages of the New Testament, in the Acts of the Apostles, and Epistles of St. Paul, we meet with the word Troas; [1] how he went from Troas to Philippi, in Macedonia, from thence unto Troas again: how he remained seven days in that place: from thence on foot to Assos, whither the disciples had sailed from Troas, and, there taking him in, made their voyage unto Cæsarea.

Now, whether this Troas be the name of a city or a certain region of Phrygia seems no groundless doubt of yours: for that it was sometimes taken in the signification of some country, is acknowledged by Ortelius, Stephanus, and Grotius; and it is plainly set down by Strabo, that a region of Phrygia in Asia minor, was so taken in ancient times; and that at the Trojan war, all the territory which comprehended the nine principalities subject unto the King of Ilium Τροίη λεγουμένη, was called by the name of Troja. And this might seem sufficiently to solve the intention of the description, when he came or went from Troas, that is some part of that region; and will otherwise seem strange unto many how he should be said to go or come from that city which all writers had laid in the ashes about a thousand years before.

---

[1] *Troas.*] Troas was a small country lying to the west of Mysia, upon the sea. It took this name from its principal city, Troas, a sea-port, and built, as is said, about some four miles from the situation of old Troy, by Lysimachus, one of Alexander the Great's captains, who peopled it from the neighbouring cities, and called it Alexandria, or Troas Alexandri, in honour of his master Alexander; who began the work, but lived not to bring it to any perfection. But in following times it came to be called simply Troas. The name may be understood as taken by the sacred writers to denote the country as well as city so called, but chiefly the latter.

All which notwithstanding,—since we read in the text a particular abode of seven days, and such particulars as leaving of his cloak, books, and parchments at Troas, and that St. Luke seems to have been taken in to the travels of St. Paul at this place, where he begins in the Acts to write in the first person—this may rather seem to have been some city or special habitation, than any province or region without such limitation.

Now, that such a city there was, and that of no mean note, is easily verified from historical observation. For though old Ilium was anciently destroyed, yet was there another raised by the relicts of that people, not in the same place, but about thirty furlongs westward, as is to be learned from Strabo.

Of this place Alexander, in his expedition against Darius, took especial notice, endowing it with sundry immunities, with promise of greater matters, at his return from Persia; inclined hereunto from the honour he bore unto Homer, whose earnest reader he was, and upon whose poems, by the help of Anaxarchus and Callisthenes, he made some observations : as also much moved hereto upon the account of his cognation with the Æacides and Kings of Molossus, whereof Andromache, the wife of Hector, was Queen. After the death of Alexander, Lysimachus surrounded it with a wall, and brought the inhabitants of the neighbour towns unto it; and so it bore the name of Alexandria; which, from Antigonus, was also called Antigonia, according to the inscription of that famous medal in Goltsius, *Colonia Troas Antigonia Alexandrea, legio vicesima prima.*

When the Romans first went into Asia against Antiochus, it was but a κωμόπολις, and no great city; but, upon the peace concluded, the Romans much advanced the same. Fimbria, the rebellious Roman, spoiled it in the Mithridatick wars, boasting that he had subdued Troy in eleven days, which the Grecians could not take in almost as many years. But it was again rebuilt and countenanced by the Romans, and became a Roman colony, with great immunities conferred on it; and accordingly it is so set down by Ptolemy. For the Romans, deriving themselves from the Trojans, thought no favour too great for it; especially Julius Cæsar, who, both in imitation of Alexander, and for his own descent from Julus, of the posterity of Æneas, with much passion affected it, and in a discontented humour,* was once in mind to translate the Roman wealth unto it ; so that it became a very remarkable place, and was, in Strabo's time,† one of the noble cities of Asia.

And, if they understood the prediction of Homer in reference unto the Romans, as some expound it in Strabo, it might much promote their affection unto that place ; which being a remarkable prophecy, and scarce to be paralleled in Pagan story, made before Rome was built, and concerning the lasting reign of the progeny of Æneas, they could not but take especial notice of it. For thus is Neptune made to speak, when he saved Æneas from the fury of Achilles.

> Verum agite hunc subito præsenti à morte trahamus
> Ne Cronides ira flammet si fortis Achilles
> Hunc mactet, fati quem lex evadere jussit.
> Ne genus intereat de læto semine totum
> Dardani ab excelso præ cunctis prolibus olim,
> Dilecti quos è mortali stirpe creavit,
> Nunc etiam Priami stirpem Saturnius odit,
> Trojugenum post hæc Æneas sceptra tenebit
> Et nati natorum et qui nascentur ab illis.

The Roman favours were also continued unto St. Paul's days ; for Claudius,‡ producing an ancient letter of the Romans unto King Seleucus concerning the Trojan privileges, made a release of their tributes ; and Nero elegantly pleaded for their immunities, and remitted all tributes unto them. §

And, therefore, there being so remarkable a city in this territory, it may seem too hard to lose the same in the general name of the country ; and since it was so eminently favoured by emperors, enjoying so many immunities, and full of Roman privileges, it was probably very populous, and a fit abode for St. Paul, who being a Roman citizen, might live more quietly himself, and have no small number of faithful well-wishers in it.

Yet must we not conceive that this was the old Troy, or re-built in the same place with it : for Troas was placed about thirty furlongs west, and upon the sea shore : so that, to hold

---

* *Sueton.*　　† ἐλλογίμων πόλεων.　　‡ *Sueton.*　　§ *Tacit. Ann.* l. 13.

a clearer apprehension hereof than is commonly delivered in the discourses of Troy, we may consider one inland Troy, or old Ilium, which was built farther within the land, and so was removed from the port where the Grecian fleet lay in Homer; and another maritime Troy, which was upon the sea coast, placed in the maps of Ptolemy, between Lectum and Sigæum or Port Janizam, southwest from the old city, which was this of St. Paul, and whereunto are appliable the particular accounts of Bellonius, when, not an hundred years ago, he described the ruins of Troy with their baths, aqueducts, walls, and towers, to be seen from the sea as he sailed between it and Tenedos; and where, upon nearer view, he observed some signs and impressions of his conversion in the ruins of churches, crosses, and inscriptions upon stones.

Nor was this only a famous city in the days of St. Paul, but considerable long after. For, upon the letter of Adrianus, Herodes, Atticus,* at a great charge, repaired their baths, contrived aqueducts and noble water courses in it. As is also collectible from the medals of Caracalla, of Severus, and Crispina; with inscriptions, *Colonia Alexandria Troas*, bearing on the reverse either an horse, a temple, or a woman; denoting their destruction by an horse, their prayers for the emperor's safety, and, as some conjecture, the memory of Sibylla Phrygia, or Hellespontica.

Nor wanted this city the favour of christian princes, but was made a bishop's see under the archbishop of Cyzicum; but in succeeding discords was destroyed and ruined, and the nobler stones translated to Constantinople by the Turks to beautify their mosques and other buildings.

Concerning the Dead Sea, accept of these few remarks.

In the map of the Dead Sea we meet with the figure of the cities which were destroyed: of Sodom, Gomorrah, Admah, and Zeboim; but with no uniformity; men placing them variously, and from the uncertainty of their situation, taking a fair liberty to set them where they please.

For Admah, Zeboim, and Gomorrah, there is no light from the text to define their situation. But, that Sodom could not be far from Segor which was seated under the

* *Philostrat. in Vita Herodis Attici.*

mountains near the lake, seems inferrible from the sudden arrival of Lot, who coming from Sodom at day break, attained to Segor at sun rising; and therefore Sodom is to be placed not many miles from it, not in the middle of the lake, which against that place is about eighteen miles over, and so will leave nine miles to be gone in so small a space of time.

The valley being large, the lake now in length about seventy English miles, the river Jordan and divers others running over the plain, 'tis probable the best cities were seated upon those streams; but how the Jordan passed or winded, or where it took in the other streams, is a point too old for geography to determine.

For, that the river gave the fruitfulness unto this valley by over-watering that low region, seems plain from that expression in the text,* that it was watered, *sicut Paradisus et Ægyptus*, like Eden and the plains of Mesopotamia, where Euphrates yearly overfloweth; or like Egypt where Nilus doth the like; and seems probable also from the same course of the river not far above this valley where the Israelites passed Jordan, where 't is said that " Jordan overfloweth its banks in the time of harvest."

That it must have had some passage under ground in the compass of this valley before the creation of this lake, seems necessary from the great current of Jordan, and from the rivers Arnon, Cedron, Zaeth, which empty into this valley; but where to place that concurrence of waters or place of its absorbition, there is no authentic decision.

The probablest place may be set somewhat southward, below the rivers that run into it on the east or western shore: and somewhat agreeable unto the account which Brocardus received from the Saracens which lived near it, *Jordanem ingredi mare mortuum et rursum egredi, sed post exiguum intervallum a terra absorberi.*

Strabo speaks naturally of this lake, that it was first caused by earthquakes, by sulphureous and bituminous eruptions, arising from the earth. But the Scripture makes it plain to have been from a miraculous hand, and by a remarkable ex-

* *Gen.* xiii, 10.

pression, *pluit dominus ignem et sulphur à domino.*[2] See also Deut. 29, *in ardore salis:* burning the cities and destroying all things about the plain, destroying the vegetable nature of plants and all living things, salting and making barren the whole soil, and, by these fiery showers, kindling and setting loose the body of the bituminous mines, which shewed their lower veins before but in some few pits and openings, swallowing up the foundation of their cities; opening the bituminous treasures below, and making a smoke like a furnace able to be discerned by Abraham at a good distance from it.

If this little may give you satisfaction, I shall be glad, as being, Sir,   Yours, &c.

---

[2] *But the Scripture, &c.*] Dr. Wells supports this opinion at considerable length and by a series of very satisfactory arguments. See *Geography of the Old and New Testament,* i, 153.

TRACT XI.

OF THE ANSWERS OF THE ORACLE OF APOLLO AT DELPHOS
TO CRŒSUS KING OF LYDIA.

SIR,[1]

AMONG the oracles of Apollo * there are none more celebrated than those which he delivered unto Crœsus King of
Lydia;† who seems of all princes to have held the greatest
dependence on them. But most considerable are his plain and
intelligible replies which he made unto the same king, when
he sent his chains of captivity unto Delphos, after his overthrow by Cyrus, with sad expostulations why he encouraged
him unto that fatal war by his oracle, saying προλέγουσαι Κροίσῳ,
ἢν στρατεύηται ἐπὶ Πέρσας, μεγάλην ἀρχήν μιν καταλύσειν, Crœsus, if
he wars against the Persians, shall dissolve a great empire.‡
Why, at least, he prevented not that sad infelicity of his devot-
ed and bountiful servant, and whether it were fair or honourable

---

* *See Vul. Err.* l. vii, c. 12
† *Herod.* l. i, 46, 47, &c. 90, 91.   *Herod.* ibid. 54.

---

[1] *Sir.*] The copy of this tract in
MS. Sloan. is thrown more into the form
of an essay, by the following introductory passage:—"Men looked upon ancient
oracles as natural, artificial, demoniacal,
or all. They conceived something natural of them, as being in places affording exhalations, which were found to
operate upon the brains of persons unto
raptures, strange utterances, and divinations; which being observed and ad-
mired by the people, an advantage was
taken thereof; an artificial contrivance
made by subtle crafty persons confeder-
ating to carry on a practice of divination;
pretending some power of divinity therein; but because they sometimes made
very strange predictions, and above the
power of human reason, men were inclined to believe some demoniacal co-
operation, and that some evil spirit

ruled the whole scene; having so fair an
opportunity to delude mankind, and to
advance his own worship; and were
thought to proceed from the spirit of
Apollo or other Heathen deities; so that
these oracles were not only apprehended
to be natural, human, or artificial, but
also demoniacal, according to common
opinion, and also of learned men; as
Vossius hath declared:—"Constitere
quidem oracula fraudibus vatum, sed
non solis; solertia humana, sed sæpe
etiam diabolica. Cum multa predixerint,
ad quæ nulla ratione humana mentis
acumen perlegisset in natura humana
non est subsistendum, sed assurgendum
ad causas superioris naturæ, quales sunt
dæmones." According to which sense
and opinion we shall enlarge upon this
following oracle of Delphos."

for the gods of Greece to be ungrateful: which being a plain and open delivery of Delphos, and scarce to be paralleled in any ancient story, it may well deserve your farther consideration.

1. His first reply [2] was, that Crœsus suffered not for himself; but paid the transgression of his fifth predecessor, who killed his master, and usurped the dignity unto which he had no title.

Now whether Crœsus suffered upon this account or not, hereby he plainly betrayed his insufficiency to protect him; and also obliquely discovered he had a knowledge of his misfortune; for knowing that wicked act lay yet unpunished, he might well divine some of his successors might smart for it: and also understanding he was like to be the last of that race, he might justly fear and conclude this infelicity upon him.

Hereby he also acknowledged the inevitable justice of God; that though revenge lay dormant, it would not always sleep; and consequently confessed the just hand of God punishing unto the third and fourth generation, nor suffering such iniquities to pass for ever unrevenged. [3]

Hereby he flatteringly encouraged him in the opinion of his own merits, and that he only suffered for other men's transgressions: meanwhile he concealed Crœsus his pride, elation of mind and secure conceit of his own unparalleled felicity, together with the vanity, pride, and height of luxury of the Lydian nation, which the spirit of Delphos knew well to be ripe and ready for destruction.

2. A second excuse was, that it is not in the power of God to hinder the decree of fate. A general evasion for any falsified prediction founded upon the common opinion of fate, which impiously subjecteth the power of heaven unto it; widely discovering the folly of such as repair unto him con-

---

[2] *His first reply.*] This is a mistake; the oracle began his answer by alleging the impossibility of avoiding the determination of fate. It was the second observation, that Crœsus was expiating the crimes of Gyges, his ancestor in the fifth descent. (Ardys, Sadyattes, and Atyattes, were the intervening descendants.)

[3] *unrevenged.*] In *MS. Sloan.* occurs here this passage:—"The devil, who sees how things of this nature go on in kingdoms, nations, and families, is able to say much on this point; whereas, we, that understand not the reserved judgments of God, or the due time of their executions, are fain to be doubtfully silent."

cerning future events: which, according unto this rule, must go on as the fates have ordered, beyond his power to prevent or theirs to avoid; and consequently teaching that his oracles had only this use to render men more miserable by foreknowing their misfortunes; whereof Crœsus himself had sensible experience in that dæmoniacal dream concerning his eldest son, that he should be killed by a spear, which, after all care and caution, he found inevitably to befall him.

3. In his third apology he assured him that he endeavoured to transfer the evil fate and to pass it upon his children; and did, however, procrastinate his infelicity, and deferred the destruction of Sardis and his own captivity three years longer than was fatally decreed upon it.

Wherein while he wipes off the stain of ingratitude, he leaves no small doubt whether, it being out of his power to contradict or transfer the fates of his servants, it be not also beyond it to defer such signal events, and whereon the fates of whole nations do depend.

As also, whether he intended or endeavoured to bring to pass what he pretended, some question might be made. For that he should attempt or think he could translate his infelicity upon his sons, it could not consist with his judgment, which attempts not impossibles or things beyond his power; nor with his knowledge of future things, and the fates of succeeding generations: for he understood that monarchy was to expire in himself and could particularly foretell the infelicity of his sons, and hath also made remote predictions unto others concerning the fortunes of many succeeding descents, as appears in that answer unto Attalus,

> Be of good courage, Attalus, thou shalt reign,
> And thy sons' sons, but not their sons again.

As also unto Cypselus, King of Corinth.

> Happy is the man who at my altar stands,
> Great Cypselus, who Corinth now commands.
> Happy is he; his sons shall happy be;
> But for their sons, unhappy days they'll see.

Now, being able to have so large a prospect of future things, and of the fate of many generations, it might well be granted he was not ignorant of the fate of Crœsus's sons, and well understood it was in vain to think to translate his misery upon them.

4. In the fourth part of his reply, he clears himself of ingratitude, which hell itself cannot hear of; alleging that he had saved his life when he was ready to be burnt, by sending a mighty shower, in a fair and cloudless day, to quench the fire already kindled, which all the servants of Cyrus could not do. Though this shower might well be granted, as much concerning his honour, and not beyond his power;[4] yet whether this merciful shower fell not out contingently, or were not contrived by an higher power,[5] which hath often pity upon Pagans, and rewardeth their virtues sometimes with extraordinary temporal favours ; also, in no unlike case, who was the author of those few fair minutes, which, in a showry day, gave only time enough for the burning of Sylla's body, some question might be made.

5. The last excuse devolveth the error and miscarriage of the business upon Crœsus, and that he deceived himself by an inconsiderate misconstruction of his oracle ; that if he had doubted, he should not have passed it over in silence, but consulted again for an exposition of it. Besides, he had neither discussed, nor well perpended his Oracle concerning Cyrus, whereby he might have understood not to engage against him.

Wherein, to speak indifferently, the deception and miscarriage seems chiefly to lie at Crœsus's door, who, if not in-

---

[4] *not beyond his power.*] *MS. Sloan.* adds 'when countenanced by divine permission or decree.'

[5] *or were not contrived by an higher power.*] —i. e. ". that of the devil." The whole course of these observations on the Delphian oracle reminds us of what in his former works Sir Thomas had declared to be his opinion—viz. that it was a Satanic agency. And several passages of *Religio Medici* betray this sentiment—(see §§ 13 and 46) : and in his larger work, *Pseud. Epid.* he devotes a chapter (the 13th of book 7) to the subject of the " cessation of oracles ;" in which he takes no pains to *prove* them to have existed in any other way than by

the mere juggle of the priests, imposing on the ignorance and superstition of the people ; but, *assuming* the fact that a real divination, through the agency of Satan, was permitted to exist in Pagan antiquity, he only discusses the question how and when such permission was withdrawn and oracles ceased to exist.

Since the preceding remarks were written, I turned to Dr. Johnson's brief account of these *Miscellany Tracts*, in his life of the author, and find the following observation:—" In this tract nothing deserves notice, more than that Browne considers the oracles as evidently and indubitably supernatural, and founds all his disquisition upon that postulate."

fatuated with confidence and security, might justly have
doubted the construction; besides, he had received two
Oracles before, which clearly hinted an unhappy time unto
him: the first concerning Cyrus.

> Whenever a mule shall o'er the Medians reign,
> Stay not, but unto Hermus fly amain.

Herein, though he understood not the Median mule, or Cyrus,
that is, of his mixed descent from Assyrian and Median
parents, yet he could not but apprehend some misfortune from
that quarter.

Though this prediction seemed a notable piece of divination, yet did it not so highly magnify his natural sagacity or
knowledge of future events as was by many esteemed; he
having no small assistance herein from the prophecy of
Daniel concerning the Persian monarchy, and the prophecies
of Jeremiah and Isaiah, wherein he might read the name of
Cyrus, who should restore the captivity of the Jews, and
must, therefore, be the great monarch and lord of all those
nations.

The same misfortune was also foretold when he demanded
of Apollo if ever he should hear his dumb son speak.

> O foolish Crœsus! who hast made this choice,
> To know when thou shalt hear thy dumb son's voice ;
> Better he still were mute, would nothing say ;—
> When he first speaks, look for a dismal day!

This, if he contrived not the time and the means of his
recovery, was no ordinary divination: yet how to make out
the verity of the story, some doubts may yet remain. For,
though the causes of deafness and dumbness were removed,
yet since words are attained by hearing, and men speak not
without instruction, how he should be able immediately to
utter such apt and significant words, as Ἄνθρωπε, μὴ κτεῖνε Κροῖσον,
"O man! slay not Crœsus," * it cannot escape some doubt;
since the story also delivers, that he was deaf and dumb, that
he then first began to speak, and spake all his life after.

Herod. l. i, 85.

Q 2

Now, if Crœsus [6] had consulted again for a clearer exposition of what was doubtfully delivered, whether the Oracle would have spake out the second time, or afforded a clearer answer, some question might be made from the examples of his practice upon the like demands.

So, when the Spartans had often fought with ill success against the Tegeates, they consulted the Oracle, what God they should appease, to become victorious over them. The answer was, " That they should remove the bones of Orestes." Though the words were plain, yet the thing was obscure, and like finding out the body of Moses. And, therefore, they once more demanded in what place they should find the same; unto whom he returned this answer,

> When in the Tegean Plains a place thou find'st
> Where blasts are made by two impetuous winds,
> Where that that strikes is struck, blows follow blows,
> There doth the earth Orestes' bones enclose.

Which obscure reply the wisest of Sparta could not make out, and was casually unriddled by one talking with a smith, who had found large bones of a man buried about his house; the Oracle implying no more than a smith's forge, expressed by a double bellows, the hammer and anvil therein.

Now, why the Oracle should place such consideration upon the bones of Orestes, the son of Agamemnon, a mad man and a murderer, if not to promote the idolatry of the Heathens, and maintain a superstitious veneration of things of no activity, it may leave no small obscurity.

Or why, in a business so clear in his knowledge, he should affect so obscure expressions it may also be wondered; if it were not to maintain the wary and evasive method in his answers: for, speaking obscurely in things beyond doubt within his knowledge, he might be more tolerably dark in matters beyond his prescience.

Though EI were inscribed over the gate of Delphos, yet was there no uniformity in his deliveries. Sometimes with that obscurity as argued a fearful prophecy; sometimes so plainly as might confirm a spirit of divinity; sometimes moral-

---

[6] *Now, if Crœsus.*] *MS. Sloan.* reads " Now, notwithstanding this plausible apology and evasion, if Crœsus."

ly, deterring from vice and villany; another time vitiously, and in the spirit of blood and cruelty; observably modest in his civil ænigma and periphrasis of that part which old Numa would plainly name,* and Medea would not understand, when he advised Ægeus not to draw out his foot before, until he arrived upon the Athenian ground; whereas another time he seemed too literal in that unseemly epithet unto Cyanus, King of Cyprus,† and put a beastly trouble upon all Egypt to find out the urine of a true virgin.

Sometimes, more beholding unto memory than invention, he delighted to express himself in the bare verses of Homer. But that he principally affected poetry, and that the priest not only nor always composed his prosal raptures into verse, seems plain from his necromantical prophecies, whilst the dead head in Phlegon delivers a long prediction in verse; and at the rising of the ghost of Commodus unto Caracalla, when none of his ancestors would speak, the divining spirit versified his infelicities; corresponding herein unto the apprehensions of elder times, who conceived not only a majesty but something of divinity in poetry, and, as in ancient times, the old theologians delivered their inventions.

Some critical readers might expect in his oraculous poems a more than ordinary strain and true spirit of Apollo; not contented to find that spirits make verses like men, beating upon the filling epithet, and taking the licence of dialects and lower helps, common to human poetry; wherein, since Scaliger, who hath spared none of the Greeks, hath thought it wisdom to be silent, we shall make no excursion.

Others may wonder how the curiosity of elder times, having this opportunity of his answers, omitted natural questions; or how the old magicians discovered no more philosophy; and if they had the assistance of spirits, could rest content with the bare assertions of things, without the knowledge of their causes; whereby they had made their acts iterable by sober hands, and a standing part of philosophy. Many wise divines hold a reality in the wonders of the Egyptian magicians, and that those *magnalia* which they performed before Pharaoh were not mere delusions of sense. Rightly to under-

* *Plut. in Thes.* † *V. Herod.*

stand how they made serpents out of rods: frogs, and blood of water, were worth half Porta's magic.

Hermolaus Barbarus was scarce in his wits, when, upon conference with a spirit, he would demand no other question than an explication of Aristotle's *Entelecheia*. Appion, the grammarian, that would raise the ghost of Homer to decide the controversy of his country, made a frivolous and pedantic use of necromancy, and Philostratus did as little, that called up the ghost of Achilles for a particular of the story of Troy. Smarter curiosities would have been at the great elixir, the flux and reflux of the sea, with other noble obscurities in nature; but, probably, all in vain: in matters cognoscible and framed for our disquisition, our industry must be our Oracle, and reason our Apollo.

Not to know things without the arch of our intellectuals, or what spirits apprehend, is the imperfection of our nature, not our knowledge, and rather inscience than ignorance in man. Revelation might render a great part of the creation easy, which now seems beyond the stretch of human indagation; and welcome no doubt from good hands might be a true almagest, and great celestial construction; a clear system of the planetical bodies of the invisible and seeming useless stars unto us; of the many suns in the eight sphere; what they are; what they contain; and to what more immediately those stupendous bodies are serviceable. But being not hinted in the authentic revelation of God, nor known how far their discoveries are stinted; if they should come unto us from the mouth of evil spirits, the belief thereof might be as unsafe as the enquiry.[7]

This is a copious subject; but having exceeded the bounds of a letter, I will not now pursue it further. I am,

Yours, &c.

.[7] *enquiry.*] *MS. Sloan.* adds this sentence, "and how far to credit the father of darkness and great obscurer of truth, might yet be obscure unto us." Here the *MS.* terminates.

TRACT XII.[1]

A PROPHECY CONCERNING THE FUTURE STATE OF SEVERAL
NATIONS, IN A LETTER WRITTEN UPON OCCASION OF AN
OLD PROPHECY SENT TO THE AUTHOR FROM A FRIEND
WITH A REQUEST THAT HE WOULD CONSIDER IT.

SIR,

I TAKE no pleasure in prophecies so hardly intelligible, and
pointing at future things from a pretended spirit of divination; of which sort this seems to be which came unto your
hand, and you were pleased to send unto me. And therefore, for your easier apprehension, divertisement, and con-

---

[1] TRACT XII.] Dr. Johnson remarks, that in this tract the author plainly dis-covers his expectation to be the same with that entertained lately with more confidence by Dr. Berkley, " that Ame-rica will be the seat of the fifth em-pire."

If this alludes to Berkley's favourite " Scheme for Converting the Savage Americans to Christianity," no just com-parison can be drawn between it and Browne's speculations on the possible advancement of the New World in poli-tical consequence. I can, however, find nothing in Berkley about " America be-coming the seat of the fifth *empire*," un-less it be in his " Verses on the prospect of planting arts and learning " there ;— which he closes, after an allusion to the four *ages*, (viz. of gold, silver, brass, and iron,) by anticipating the arrival of a second age of gold, which he terms the " fifth act in the course of em-pire."

Many of the more important specula-tions of our author, respecting the New World, remain, after a lapse of nearly two centuries, matter of speculation still ; —though, perhaps, to judge from the course of events since Sir Thomas wrote, we may not unreasonably look forward to their more complete fulfilment.

A very spirited writer in our own days has indulged himself (in the specimen number of *The Argus* newspaper,) with a similar anticipation of events yet (if ever) to come.—By the provisions of that abomination—in a land of liberty and literature—the STAMP ACT, it was forbidden to relate real incidents, unless on stamped paper.—He therefore filled his paper with imaginary events. Some of his paragraphs relating to " Foreign Affairs" may afford an amusing parallel to the present tract.

" Despatches have been this morning received at the Foreign Office, from the allied Greek and Polish army before Mos-cow, announcing a truce between the al-lies and the besieged, under the media-ation of the federative republic of France. Negociations for a final pacification are to be immediately entered on, under the joint mediation of Great Britain, France, and Austria ; and it is confidently hoped that the united efforts of these powers to put an end to the destructive five years' war, will be finally successful, and will end in the acknowledgement, by the Emperor Nicholas, of the independence of the crown of Warsaw, in the person of Constantine."

" As we gather these facts from what may be considered official sources, we give them this prominent place, out of the general order of our foreign news, on which we now enter, however, in de-tail, having carefully examined all the

sideration, I present you with a very different kind of prediction : not positively or peremptorily telling you what shall
come to pass, yet pointing at things not without all reason or
probability of their events; not built upon fatal decrees or
inevitable designations, but upon conjectural foundations,
whereby things wished may be promoted, and such as are
feared may more probably be prevented.

The Prophecy.

WHEN New England shall trouble[2] New Spain;
When Jamaica shall be lady of the isles and the main ;
When Spain shall be in America hid,
And Mexico shall prove a Madrid ;
When Mahomet's ships on the Baltic shall ride,
And Turks shall labour to have ports on that side;[3]

letters of this morning's mail, from our
established and exclusive correspondents;
not doubting but that many will be a
little surprised at the extent and variety,
to say nothing of the novelty and interest, of the facts thus, for the first time,
made public."

" *United Empire of America.*—Since
the last census of the United Empire of
North and South America, it has been
found that the population now amounts
to 180,620,000 inhabitants, including
the whole country, from Cape Horn to
the Frozen Sea; Upper and Lower Ca-
nada, as well as Peru and Patagonia,
being now incorporated in the Union.
The General Senate still holds its Parliament in the magnificent city of Columbus, which reaches quite across the Isth-
mus of Darien, and has its fortifications
washed by the Atlantic on one side, and
the Pacific on the other, while the two
Provincial Senates are held at Washing-
ton for the north, and at Bolivar for the
south, thus preserving the memory of the
first great discoverer, and the two greatest patriots, of this magnificent quarter
of the globe."

" *Turkey.*—Since the elevation of
Count Capo d'Istria to the throne of the
New Greek Kingdom of the East, tran-
quillity reigns at Constantinople, and

that city promises again to be the centre
of commerce and the arts."

" *China.*—Letters from the capital of
China state, that there are now not less
than fifty commission-houses of Liver-
pool merchants established at Pekin alone,
besides several agents from London es-
tablishments, and a few depôts for Bir-
mingham and Manchester goods. The
English nankeens are much preferred by
the Chinese over their own, and Staffordshire porcelain is sold at nearly twice
the price of the original china manufacture, in the bazaars."

" *Syria.*—Lady Hester Stanhope had
left her beautiful residence between Tyre
and Sidon, as well as her summer retreat
amid the snows and cedars of Lebanon,
and taken up her new abode in the valley
of Jehoshaphat, between the Mount of
Olives and Mount Zion, at Jerusalem.
Her ladyship, though growing old, still
retained all her benevolence and vivacity;
and her house was the chief resort of all
the intelligent visitors to the Jewish capital, which was increasing in splendour
every day."

[2] *trouble.*] ' Terrify.'—*MS. Rawl.*
58.

[3] *And Turks, &c.*] ' When we shall
have ports on the Pacific side.'—*MS.
Rawl.* 58.

When Africa shall no more sell out their blacks,
To make slaves and drudges to the American tracts; [4]
When Batavia the Old shall be contemn'd by the New;
When a new drove of Tartars shall China subdue;
When America shall cease to send out [5] its treasure,
But employ it at home in [6] American pleasure;
When the new world shall the old invade,
Nor count them their lords but their fellows in trade;
When men shall almost pass to Venice by land,
Not in deep water but from sand to sand;
When Nova Zembla shall be no stay
Unto those who pass to or from Cathay;—
Then think strange things are come to light,
Whereof but few [7] have had a foresight.

The Exposition of the Prophecy.

When New England shall trouble New Spain;

THAT is, when that thriving colony, which hath so much encreased in our days, and in the space of about fifty years,
that they can, as they report, raise between twenty and thirty
thousand men upon an exigency, shall in process of time be
so advanced, as to be able to send forth ships and fleets, and
to infest [8] the American Spanish ports and maritime dominions
by depredations or assaults; for which attempts they are not
like to be unprovided, as abounding in the materials for shipping, oak and fir.   And when length of time shall so far encrease that industrious people, that the neighbouring country
will not contain them, they will range still farther and be
able, in time, to set forth great armies, seek for new possessions, or make considerable and conjoined migrations, ac-

---

[4] *To make slaves, &c.*] 'But slaves
must be had from *incognita* tracts.'—
MS. Rawl. 58.
   [5] *out.*] 'Forth.'—*MS. Rawl.* 58.

[6] *in.*] 'For.'—*MS. Rawl.* 58.
   [7] *few.*] 'Few eyes.'—*MS. Rawl.* 58.
   [8] *infest.*] 'Be a terror to.'—*MS.
Rawl.* 58.

cording to the custom of swarming northern nations; wherein
it is not likely that they will move northward, but toward the
southern and richer countries, which are either in the dominions or frontiers of the Spaniards : and may not improbably
erect new dominions in places not yet thought of, and yet,
for some centuries, beyond their power or ambition.

When Jamaica shall be lady of the isles and the main;

That is, when that advantageous island shall be well peopled, it may become so strong and potent as to overpower the
neighbouring isles, and also a part of the main land, especially the maritime parts.　And already in their infancy they
have given testimony of their power and courage in their
bold attempts upon Campeche and Santa Martha; and in
that notable attempt upon Panama on the western side of
America: especially considering this island is sufficiently
large to contain a numerous people, of a northern and warlike descent, addicted to martial affairs both by sea and land,
and advantageously seated to infest their neighbours both of
the isles and the continent, and like to be a receptacle for colonies of the same originals from Barbadoes and the neighbour isles.

When Spain shall be in America hid,
And Mexico shall prove a Madrid ;

That is, when Spain, either by unexpected disasters or
continued emissions of people into America, which have already thinned the country, shall be farther exhausted at
home ; or when, in process of time, their colonies shall grow
by many accessions more than their originals, then Mexico
may become a Madrid, and as considerable in people, wealth,
and splendour: wherein that place is already so well advanced,
that accounts scarce credible are given of it.　And it is so advantageously seated, that, by Acapulco and other ports on the
south sea, they may maintain a communication and commerce
with the Indian isles and territories, and with China and
Japan, and on this side, by Porto Bello and others, hold correspondence with Europe and Africa.

When Mahomet's ships in the Baltic shall ride,

Of this we cannot be out of all fear; for if the Turk should master Poland, he would be soon at this sea. And from the odd constitution of the Polish government, the divisions among themselves, jealousies between their kingdom and re-public; vicinity of the Tartars, treachery of the Cossacks, and the method of Turkish policy, to be at peace with the Em-peror of Germany when he is at war with the Poles, there may be cause to fear that this may come to pass. And then he would soon endeavour to have ports upon that sea, as not wanting materials for shipping. And, having a new acquist of stout and warlike men, may be a terror unto the confiners on that sea, and to nations which now conceive themselves safe from such an enemy.[9]

When Africa shall no more sell out their blacks,[1]

That is, when African countries shall no longer make it a common trade to sell away their people to serve in the drud-gery of American plantations. And that may come to pass whenever they shall be well civilized, and acquainted with arts and affairs sufficient to employ people in their countries: if also they should be converted to Christianity, but especially unto Mahometism; for then they would never sell those of their religion to be slaves unto Christians.[2]

When Batavia the old shall be contemn'd by the new;

When the plantations of the Hollander at Batavia in the East Indies, and other places in the East Indies, shall, by

[9] *enemy.*] MS. Rawl. 58, proceeds thus;—"When we shall have ships, &c. on the Pacific side, or west side of Ame-rica, which may come to pass hereafter, upon enlargement of trade or industrious navigation, when the streights of Magel-lan, or more southerly passages be well known, and frequently navigated."

[1] *When Africa, &c.*] The abolition of the slave trade, and the American ef-forts to colonize and evangelize Africa, may be regarded as two important steps towards the fulfilment of this prophecy. One measure remains to be adopted,—

the emancipation of the slaves in the West Indies:—a measure of equity—which, if not carried by legislation, will, ere long, be effected by means far less desirable.—Dec. 1832.

[2] *Christians.*] MS. Rawl. adds this sentence;—"then slaves must be sought for in other tracts, not yet well known, or perhaps from some parts of *terra in-cognita,* whenever hereafter they shall be discovered and conquered, or else when that trade shall be left, and slaves be made from captives, and from male-factors of the respective countries.

their conquests and advancements, become so powerful in the Indian territories; then their original countries and states of Holland are like to be contemned by them, and obeyed only as they please. And they seem to be in a way unto it at present by their several plantations, new acquists, and enlargements: and they have lately discovered a part of the southern continent, and several places which may be serviceable unto them, whenever time shall enlarge them unto such necessities.

And a new drove of Tartars shall China subdue;

Which is no strange thing if we consult the histories of China, and successive inundations made by Tartarian nations. For when the invaders, in process of time, have degenerated into the effeminacy and softness of the Chinese, then they themselves have suffered a new Tartarian conquest and inundation. And this hath happened from time beyond our histories: for, according to their account, the famous wall of China, built against the irruptions of the Tartars, was begun above a hundred years before the incarnation.

When America shall cease to send forth its treasure,
But employ it at home in American pleasure;

That is, when America shall be better civilized, new policied and divided between great princes, it may come to pass that they will no longer suffer their treasure of gold and silver to be sent out to maintain the luxury of Europe and other parts: but rather employ it to their own advantages, in great exploits and undertakings, magnificent structures, wars, or expeditions of their own.

When the new world shall the old invade,

That is, when America shall be so well peopled, civilized, and divided into kingdoms, they are like to have so little regard of their originals, as to acknowledge no subjection unto them: they may also have a distinct commerce between themselves, or but independently with those of Europe,[3] and may hostilely and piratically assault them, even as the Greek and Roman colonies after a long time dealt with their original countries.

> When men shall almost pass to Venice by land,
> Not in deep waters but from sand to sand ;

That is, when, in long process of time, the silt and sands shall so choke and shallow the sea in and about it. And this hath considerably come to pass within these fourscore years: and is like to encrease from several causes, especially by the turning of the river Brenta, as the learned Castelli hath declared.

> When Nova Zembla shall be no stay
> Unto those who pass to or from Cathay ;

That is, when ever that often sought for north-east passage [4] unto China and Japan shall be discovered; the hindrance whereof was imputed to Nova Zembla; for this was conceived to be an excursion of land shooting out directly, and so far northward into the sea, that it discouraged from all navigation about it. And therefore adventurers took in at the southern part at a strait by Waygatz next the Tartarian shore: and sailing forward they found that sea frozen and full of ice, and so gave over the attempt. But of late years, by the diligent enquiry of some Muscovites, a better discovery is made of these parts, and a map or chart made of them. Thereby Nova Zembla is found to be no island extending very far northward, but, winding eastward, it joineth to the Tartarian continent, and so makes a peninsula: and the sea

---

[3] *Europe.*]   Here ends the *MS. Rawl.* 58.

[4] *North-east passage.*]   These speculations may well be contrasted with some observations of Mr. Barrow on the same subject, in his *Chronological History of Voyages into the Arctic Regions*, p. 370. " Of the three directions in which a passage has been sought for from the Atlantic to the Pacific, that by the north-east holds out the least encouraging hope; indeed the various unsuccessful attempts by the English and the Dutch on the one side, and by the Russians on the other, go far to prove the utter impracticability of a navigable passage round the northern extremity of Asia; though the whole of this coast, with the exception perhaps of a single point, has been navigated in several detached parts, and at different times."

between it which they entered at Waygatz, is found to be but a large bay, apt to be frozen by reason of the great river of Oby, and other fresh waters, entering into it; whereas the main sea doth not freeze upon the north of Zembla except near unto shores; so that if the Muscovites were skilful navigators, they might, with less difficulties, discover this passage unto China; but, however, the English, Dutch, and Danes are now like to attempt it again.

But this is conjecture, and not prophecy: and so (I know) you will take it.   I am,   Sir, &c.

TRACT XIII.[1]

MUSÆUM CLAUSUM, OR, BIBLIOTHECA ABSCONDITA: CONTAIN-
ING SOME REMARKABLE BOOKS, ANTIQUITIES, PICTURES, AND
RARITIES OF SEVERAL KINDS, SCARCE OR NEVER SEEN BY
ANY MAN NOW LIVING.

SIR,

WITH many thanks I return that noble catalogue of books,
rarities, and singularities of art and nature, which you were
pleased to communicate unto me.   There are many collections
of this kind in Europe.   And, besides the printed accounts
of the Museum Aldrovandi, Calceolarianum, Moscardi, Wor-
mianum; the Casa Abbellita at Loretto, and Tresor of St.
Dennis, the Repository of the Duke of Tuscany, that of the
Duke of Saxony, and that noble one of the Emperor at
Vienna, and many more, are of singular note.   Of what in
this kind I have by me I shall make no repetition, and you
having already had a view thereof, I am bold to present you
with the list of a collection, which I may justly say you have
not seen before.

The title is as above :—*Musæum Clausum*, or *Bibliotheca
Abscondita;* containing some remarkable books, antiquities,
pictures, and rarities of several kinds, scarce or never seen by
any man now living.

---

[1] TRACT XIII.]   This curious Tract is
well characterised by Mr. Crossley, as
" the sport of a singular scholar.   Warburton, in one of his notes on Pope, is
inclined to believe that this list was
imitated from Rabelais's Catalogue of the
Books in the library of St. Victor; but
the design of the two pieces appears so
different, that this suggestion seems entitled to little regard."—*Preface to Tracts*,
18mo. Edin. 1822.

Bishop Warburton's opinion seems to
me, nevertheless, highly probable.   It
had been suggested to me by a passage
in *Religio Medici* (Part I, § 21); and
seems to be in perfect consonance with
Sir Thomas's character as a writer.   He
delighted, perhaps from the very origi-
nality of his own mind, to emulate the
singularities of others.   The preceding
Tract was occasioned by some similar
production which had been submitted to
his criticism.   His *Christian Morals* appears to have been written on the model
of the *Book of Proverbs;* see an allusion,
in his 21st section, p. 107.

1. *Rare and generally unknown Books.*[2]

1. A Poem of Ovidius Naso,[3] written in the Getick language,* during his exile at Tomos; found wrapt up in wax, at Sabaria, on the frontiers of Hungary, where there remains a tradition that he died in his return towards Rome from Tomos, either after his pardon or the death of Augustus.

2. The Letter of Quintus Cicero, which he wrote in answer to that of his brother, Marcus Tullius, desiring of him an account of Britany, wherein are described the country, state and manners of the Britans of that age.

3. An ancient British Herbal, or description of divers plants of this island, observed by that famous physician Scribonius Largus, when he attended the Emperor Claudius in his expedition into Britany.

4. An exact account of the Life and Death of Avicenna, confirming the account of his death by taking nine clysters together in a fit of the cholic, and not as Marius, the Italian poet, delivereth, by being broken upon the wheel: left with other pieces, by Benjamin Tudelensis, as he travelled from Saragossa to Jerusalem, in the hands of Abraham Jarchi, a famous Rabbi of Lunet, near Montpellier, and found in a vault when the walls of that city were demolished by Lewis the Thirteenth.

5. A punctual relation of Hannibal's march out of Spain into Italy, and far more particular than that of Livy: whereabout he passed the river Rhodanus, or Rhone; at what place he crossed the Isura, or L'Isere; when he marched up towards the confluence of the Soane and the Rhone, or the place where the city of Lyons was afterward built: how wisely he decided the difference between King Brancus and

---

* Ah pudet et scripsi Getico sermone libellum.

[2] *Books.*] The Irish antiquaries mention *public libraries* that were before the flood: and Paul Christian Ilsker, with profounder erudition, has given an exact catalogue of Adam's!— *Dr. Israeli's Cur. of Lit.* 7th edit. *vol.* ii, 250.

[3] *A Poem of Ovidius, &c.*] Mr. Taylor, in his *Historic Survey of German Poetry*, has a curious section on this Poem of Ovid, whom he considers as the earliest German Poet on record.—*See vol.* i, § 2.

his brother; at what place he passed the Alps; what vinegar he used; and where he obtained such a quantity as to break and calcine the rocks made hot with fire.

6. A learned comment upon the Periplus of Hanno the Carthaginian; or his navigation upon the western coast of Africa, with the several places he landed at; what colonies he settled; what ships were scattered from his fleet near the Æquinoctial Line, which were not afterward heard of, and which probably fell into the trade winds, and were carried over into the coast of America.

7. A particular Narration of that famous Expedition of the English into Barbary, in the ninety-fourth year of the Hegira, so shortly touched by Leo Africanus, whither called by the Goths, they besieged, took and burnt the city of Arzilla possessed by the Mahometans, and lately the seat of Guyland; with many other exploits, delivered at large in Arabic, lost in the ship of books and rarities which the King of Spain took from Siddy Hamet, King of Fez, whereof a great part were carried into the Escurial, and conceived to be gathered out of the relations of Hibnu Nachu, the best historian of the African affairs.

8. A Fragment of Pythæas, that ancient traveller of Marseilles; which we suspect not to be spurious; because, in the description of the northern countries, we find that passage of Pythæas mentioned by Strabo; that all the air beyond Thule is thick, condensed and gellied, looking just like sea lungs.

9. A Submarine Herbal, describing the several vegetables found on the rocks, hills, vallies, meadows, at the bottom of the sea, with many sorts of *alga, fucus, quercus, polygonum, gramen,* and others not yet described.

10. Some Manuscripts and Rarities brought from the libraries of Æthiopia, by Zaga Zaba, and afterwards transported to Rome, and scattered by the soldiers of the Duke of Bourbon, when they barbarously sacked that city.

11. Some Pieces of Julius Scaliger, which he complains to have been stolen from him, sold to the Bishop of Mende, in Languedoc, and afterward taken away and sold in the civil wars under the Duke of Rohan.

12. A Comment of Dioscorides upon Hippocrates, procured from Constantinople by Amatus Lusitanus, and left in the hands of a Jew of Ragusa.

13. Marcus Tullius Cicero his Geography; as also a part of that magnified piece of his, *De Republica*, very little answering the great expectation of it, and short of pieces under the same name by Bodinus and Tholosanus.

14. King Mithridates his *Oneirocritica*.

Aristotle, *De Precationibus*.

Democritus, *de his quæ fiunt apud orcum, et oceani circumnavigatio*.[4]

Epicurus *De Pietate*.

A Tragedy of Thyestes, and another of Medea, writ by Diogenes the Cynick.

King Alfred, upon Aristotle *de Plantis*.

Seneca's Epistles to St. Paul.

King Solomon, *de Umbris Idæarum*, which Chicus Asculanus, in his comment upon Johannes de Sacrobosco, would make us believe he saw in the library of the Duke of Bavaria.

15. *Artemidori Oneirocritici Geographia*.

Pythagoras, *de Mare Rubro*.

The works of Confutius, the famous philosopher of China, translated into Spanish.

16. Josephus, in Hebrew, written by himself.

17. The Commentaries of Sylla the Dictator.

18. A Commentary of Galen upon the Plague of Athens, described by Thucydides.

19. *Duo Cæsaris Anti-Catones*, or the two notable books writ by Julius Cæsar against Cato; mentioned by Livy, Sallustius, and Juvenal; which the Cardinal of Liege told Ludovicus Vives were in an old library of that city.

Mazhapha Einok or the prophecy of Enoch, which Ægidius Lochiensis, a learned eastern traveller, told Peireschius that he had found in an old library at Alexandria, containing eight thousand volumes.

---

[4] *Democritus, &c.*] *MS. Sloan.* 1847, adds the following article:—A defence of Arnoldus de Villa Nova, whom the learned Postellus conceived to be the author of *De Tribus Impostoribus*.

20. A collection of Hebrew Epistles, which passed between the two learned women of our age, Maria Molinea of Sedan, and Maria Schurman of Utrecht.

A wondrous collection of some writings of Ludovica Saracenica, daughter of Philibertus Saracenicus, a physician of Lyons, who, at eight years of age, had made a good progress in the Hebrew, Greek, and Latin tongues.

2. Rarities in Pictures.

1. A picture of the three remarkable steeples or towers in Europe, built purposely awry, and so as they seem falling. Torre Pisana at Pisa, Torre Garisenda in Bononia, and that other in the city of Colein.

2. A draught of all sorts of sistrums, crotaloes, cymbals, tympans, &c. in use among the ancients.

3. Large submarine pieces, well delineating the bottom of the Mediterranean sea; the prairie or large sea-meadow upon the coast of Provence; the coral fishing; the gathering of sponges; the mountains, valleys, and deserts; the subterraneous vents and passages at the bottom of that sea.[5] Together with a lively draught of Cola Pesce or the famous Sicilian swimmer, diving into the Voragos and broken rocks by Charybdis, to fetch up the golden cup, which Frederick, King of Sicily, had purposely thrown into that sea.

4. A moon piece, describing that notable battle between Axalla, General of Tamerlane, and Camares the Persian, fought by the light of the moon.

5. Another remarkable fight of Inghimmi, the Florentine, with the Turkish galleys, by moonlight; who being for three hours grappled with the Basha galley, concluded with a signal victory.

6. A delineation of the great fair of Almachara in Arabia, which, to avoid the great heat of the sun, is kept in the night, and by the light of the moon.

---

[5] *passages, &c.*] *MS. Sloan.* 1874, reads—'the passage of Kircherus in his *Iter Submarinus* when he went down about Egypt, and rose again in the Red Sea.'

7. A snow piece, of land and trees covered with snow and ice, and mountains of ice floating in the sea, with bears, seals, foxes, and variety of rare fowls upon them.

8. An ice piece, describing the notable battle between the Jaziges and the Romans, fought upon the frozen Danubius; the Romans settling one foot upon their targets to hinder them from slipping; their fighting with the Jaziges when they were fallen; and their advantages therein, by their art in volutation and rolling contention or wrestling, according to the description of Dion.

9. Socia, or a draught of three persons notably resembling each other. Of King Henry the Fourth of France and a miller of Languedoc; of Sforza, Duke of Milan, and a soldier; of Malatesta, Duke of Rimini, and Marchesinus the jester.[6]

10. A picture of the great fire which happened at Constantinople in the reign of Sultan Achmet. The janizaries in the mean time plundering the best houses, Nassa Bassa, the vizier, riding about with a symetre in one hand and a janizary's head in the other to deter them; and the priests attempting to quench the fire, by pieces of Mahomet's shirt dipped in holy water and thrown into it.

11. A night piece of the dismal supper and strange entertain of the senators by Domitian, according to the description of Dion.

12. A vestal sinner in the cave, with a table and a candle.

13. An elephant dancing upon the ropes, with a negro dwarf upon his back.

14. Another describing the mighty stone falling from the clouds into Ægospotamos or the goats' river in Greece; which antiquity could believe that Anaxagoras was able to foretel half a year before.

15. Three noble pieces; of Vercingetorix, the Gaul, submitting his person unto Julius Cæsar; of Tigranes, King of Armenia, humbly presenting himself unto Pompey; and of Tamerlane ascending his horse from the neck of Bajazet.

16. Draughts of three passionate looks; of Thyestes when he was told at the table that he had eaten a piece of his own

---

[6] *jester.*] " Of Charles the First, and one Osburn, an hedger, whom I often   employ."—*MS. note by Evelyn.*

son; of Bajazet when he went into the iron cage; of Œdipus when he first came to know that he had killen his father and married his own mother.

17. Of the Cymbrian mother in Plutarch, who, after the overthrow by Marius hanged herself and her two children at her feet.

18. Some pieces delineating singular inhumanities in tortures. The Scaphismus of the Persians. The living truncation of the Turks. The hanging sport at the feast of the Thracians. The exact method of flaying men alive, beginning between the shoulders, according to the description of Thomas Minadoi, in his Persian war. Together with the studied tortures of the French traitors at Pappa, in Hungaria: as also the wild and enormous torment invented by Tiberius, designed according unto the description of Suetonius. *Excogitaverunt inter genera cruciatús, ut largâ meri potione per fallaciam oneratos repentè veretris deligatis fidicularum simul urinæque tormento distenderet.*

19. A picture describing how Hannibal forced his passage over the river Rhone with his elephants, baggage, and mixed army; with the army of the Gauls opposing him on the contrary shore, and Hanno passing over with his horse much above to fall upon the rear of the Gauls.

20. A neat piece describing the sack of Fundi by the fleet and soldiers of Barbarossa, the Turkish admiral, the confusion of the people and their flying up to the mountains, and Julia Gonzaga, the beauty of Italy, flying away with her ladies half naked on horseback over the hills.

21. A noble head of Franciscus Gonzaga, who being imprisoned for treason, grew grey in one night, with this inscription,

O nox quam longa est quæ facit una senem.

22. A large picture describing the siege of Vienna by Solyman the Magnificent, and at the same time the siege of Florence, by the Emperor Charles the Fifth and Pope Clement the Seventh, with this subscription,

Tum vacui capitis populum Phæaca putares ?

23. An exquisite piece properly delineating the first course of Metellus's pontificial supper, according to the description of Macrobius; together with a dish of *Pisces Fossiles*, garnished about with the little eels taken out of the backs of cods and perches; as also with the shell fishes found in stones about Ancona.

24. A picture of the noble entertain and feast of the Duke of Chausue at the treaty of Collen, 1673, when in a very large room, with all the windows open, and at a very large table he sat himself, with many great persons and ladies; next about the table stood a row of waiters, then a row of musicians, then a row of musketeers.

25. Miltiades, who overthrew the Persians at the battle of Marathon, and delivered Greece, looking out of a prison grate in Athens, wherein he died, with this inscription,

> Non hoc terribiles Cymbri non Britones unquam,
> Sauromatæve truces aut immanes Agathyrsi.

26. A fair English lady drawn *Al Negro*, or in the Ethiopian hue excelling the original white and red beauty, with this subscription,

> Sed quandam volo nocte nigriorem.

27. Pieces and draughts in *caricatura*, of princes, cardinals, and famous men; wherein, among others, the painter hath singularly hit the signatures of a lion and a fox in the face of Pope Leo the Tenth.

28. Some pieces *a la ventura*, or rare chance pieces, either drawn at random, and happening to be like some person, or drawn for some, and happening to be more like another; while the face, mistaken by the painter, proves a tolerable picture of one he never saw.

29. A draught of famous dwarfs with this inscription,

> Nos facimus Bruti puerum nos Lagona vivum.

30. An exact and proper delineation of all sorts of dogs upon occasion of the practice of Sultan Achmet; who in a

great plague at Constantinople, transported all the dogs
therein unto Pera, and from thence into a little island, where
they perished at last by famine : as also the manner of the
priests curing of mad dogs by burning them in the forehead
with Saint Bellin's key.

31. A noble picture of Thorismund, King of the Goths,
as he was killed in his palace at Tholouze, who being let
blood by a surgeon, while he was bleeding, a stander by took
the advantage to stab him.

32. A picture of rare fruits with this inscription,

Credere quæ possis surrepta sororibus Afris.

33. An handsome piece of deformity expressed in a notable hard face, with this inscription,

—— Ora
Julius in Satyris qualia Rufus habet.

34. A noble picture of the famous duel between Paul Manessi and Caragusa the Turk, in the time of Amurath the Second ;
the Turkish army and that of Scanderbeg looking on ; wherein
Manessi slew the Turk, cut off his head, and carried away
the spoils of his body.

3. *Antiquities and Rarities of several sorts.*

1. Certain ancient medals with Greek and Roman inscriptions, found about Crim Tartary : conceived to be left in those
parts by the soldiers of Mithridates, when overcome by Pompey, he marched round about the north of the Euxine to
come about into Thracia.

2. Some ancient ivory and copper crosses found with many
others in China ; conceived to have been brought and left
there by the Greek soldiers who served under Tamerlane in
his expedition and conquest of that country.

3. Stones of strange and illegible inscriptions, found about
the great ruins which Vincent le Blanc describeth about Ce-
phala in Africa, where he opinioned that the Hebrews raised

some buildings of old, and that Solomon brought from there-about a good part of his gold.

4. Some handsome engraveries and medals of Justinus and Justinianus, found in the custody of a Banyan in the remote parts of India, conjectured to have been left there by the Friars mentioned in Procopius, who travelled those parts in the reign of Justinianus, and brought back into Europe the discovery of silk and silk worms.

5. An original medal of Petrus Aretinus, who was called *flagellum principum*, wherein he made his own figure on the obverse part with this inscription,

Il Divino Aretino.

On the reverse sitting on a throne, and at his feet ambassadors of kings and princes bringing presents unto him, with this inscription,

I Principi tributati dai Popoli tributano il Servitor loro.

6. *Mummia Tholosana;* or the complete head and body of father Crispin, buried long ago in the vault of the cordeliers at Tholouse, where the skins of the dead so dry and parch up without corrupting, that their persons may be known very long after, with this inscription,

Ecce iterum Crispinus.

7. A noble *quandros* or stone taken out of a vulture's head.

8. A large ostrich's egg, whereon is neatly and fully wrought that famous battle of Alcazar, in which three kings lost their lives.

9. An *Etiudros Alberti* or stone that is apt to be always moist: useful unto dry tempers, and to be held in the hand in fevers instead of crystal, eggs, lemons, cucumbers.

10. A small vial of water taken out of the stones therefore called *Enhydri*, which naturally include a little water in them, in like manner as the Ætites or Eagle stone doth another stone.

11. A neat painted and gilded cup made out of the *con-fiti di Tivoli,* and formed up with powdered egg-shells; as Nero is conceived to have made his *piscina admirabilis,* singular against fluxes to drink often therein.

12. The skin of a snake bred out of the spinal marrow of a man.

13. Vegetable horns mentioned by Linschoten, which set in the ground grow up like plants about Goa.

14. An extract of the ink of cuttle fishes reviving the old remedy of Hippocrates in hysterical passions.

15. Spirits and salt of Sargasso, made in the western ocean covered with that vegetable; excellent against the scurvy.

16. An extract of *Cachunde* or *Liberans,* that famous and highly magnified composition in the East Indies against melancholy.

17. *Diarrhizon mirificum;* or an unparalleled composition of the most effectual and wonderful roots in nature.

   ℞ Rad. Butuæ Cuamensis.

    Rad. Moniche Cuamensis.

    Rad. Mongus Bazainensis.

    Rad. Casei Bazainensis.

    Rad. Columbæ Mozambiguensis.

    Gim. Sem. Sinicæ.

    Fo. Lim. lac. Tigridis dictæ.

    Fo. seu Cort. Rad. Soldæ.

    Rad. Ligni Solorani.

    Rad. Malacensis madrededios dictæ an. ℥ij.

M. fiat pulvis, qui cum gelatina Cornu Cervi Moschati Chinensis formetur in massas oviformes.

18. A transcendent perfume made of the richest odorates of both the Indies, kept in a book made of the Muschie stone of Niarienburg, with this inscription,

      —— Deos rogato,
    Totum ut te faciant, Fabulle, Nasum.

19. A *Clepselæa,* or oil hour glass, as the ancients used those of water.

20. A ring found in a fish's belly taken about Gorro; conceived to be the same wherewith the Duke of Venice had wedded the sea.

21. A neat crucifix made out of the cross bone of a frog's head.

22. A large agath, containing a various and careless figure, which looked upon by a cylinder representeth a perfect centaur. By some such advantages King Pyrrhus might find out Apollo and the nine Muses in those agaths of his whereof Pliny maketh mention.

23. *Batrachomyomachia,* or the Homerican battle between frogs and mice, neatly described upon the chisel bone of a large pike's jaw.

24. *Pyxis Pandoræ,* or a box which held the *unguentum pestiferum,* which by anointing the garments of several persons begat the great and horrible plague of Milan.

25. A glass of spirits made of æthereal salt, hermetically sealed up, kept continually in quick-silver; of so volatile a nature that it will scarce endure the light, and therefore only to be shewn in winter, or by the light of a carbuncle, or bononian stone.

He who knows where all this treasure now is, is a great Apollo. I 'm sure I am not he. However, I am,

Sir, Yours, &c.

𝔐iscellanies.

CONCERNING THE TOO NICE CURIOSITY OF CENSURING THE PRESENT, OR JUDGING INTO FUTURE DISPENSATIONS.[1]

[POSTHUMOUS WORKS, p. 23.   MS. SLOAN. 1885 & 1869.]

WE have enough to do rightly to apprehend and consider things as they are, or have been, without amusing ourselves how they might have been otherwise, or what variations, consequences, and differences might have otherwise arisen upon a different face of things, if they had otherwise fallen out in the state or actions of the world.

The learned King Alphonso would have had the calf of a man's leg placed before rather than behind : and thinks he could find many commodities from that position.

If, in the terraqueous globe, all that now is land had been sea, and all that is sea were land, what wide difference there would be in all things, as to constitution of climes, tides, disparity of navigation, and many other concerns, were a long consideration.

If Sertorius had pursued his designs to pass his days in the Fortunate Islands, who can tell but we might have had many noble discoveries of the neighbouring coasts of Africa; and perhaps America had not been so long unknown to us.

---

[1] *Concerning, &c.*]   This most incorrect title I strongly incline to suspect is not genuine.

This piece and the following are mere extracts from Sir Thomas's Common Place Book.—Different copies of the first occur in two volumes of MSS. in the Sloanian Collection, from which I have inserted several additional passages.

If Nearchus, Admiral to Alexander the Great, setting out from Persia, had sailed about Africa, and come into the Mediterranean, by the straits of Hercules, as was intended, we might have heard of strange things, and had probably a better account of the coast of Africa than was lost by Hanno.

If King Perseus had entertained the barbarous nations but stout warriors, which in so great numbers offered their service unto him, some conjecture it might be, that Paulus Emilius had not conquered Macedon.

If [Antiochus?] had followed the counsel of Hannibal, and come about by Gallia upon the Romans, who knows what success he might have had against them?

If Scanderbeg had joined his forces with Hunniades, as might have been expected before the battle in the plains of Cossoan, in good probability they might have ruined Mahomet, if not the Turkish empire.

If Alexander had marched westward, and warred with the Romans, whether he had been able to subdue that little but valiant people, is an uncertainty: we are sure he overcame Persia; histories attest, and prophecies foretell the same. It was decreed that the Persians should be conquered by Alexander, and his successors by the Romans, in whom Providence had determined to settle the fourth monarchy, which neither Pyrrhus nor Hannibal must prevent; though Hannibal came so near it, that he seemed to miss it by fatal infatuation: which if he had effected, there had been such a traverse and confusion of affairs, as no oracle could have predicted. But the Romans must reign, and the course of things was then moving towards the advent of Christ, and blessed discovery of the Gospel: our Saviour must suffer at Jerusalem, and be sentenced by a Roman judge; St. Paul, a Roman citizen, must preach in the Roman provinces, and St. Peter be Bishop of Rome, and not of Carthage.

UPON READING HUDIBRAS.

[POSTHUMOUS WORKS, p. 24.]

THE way of Burlesque Poems is very ancient, for there was a ludicrous mock way of transferring verses of famous poets into a jocose sense and argument, and they were called Ωδίαι, or *Parodiæ;* divers examples of which are to be found in Athenæus.

The first inventor hereof was Hipponactes, but Hegemon, Sopater and many more pursued the same vein; so that the Parodies of Ovid's Buffoon, Metamorphoses, Burlesques, Le Eneiade Travastito, are no new inventions, but old fancies revived.

An excellent Parody there is of both the Scaligers upon an Epigram of Catullus, which Stephens hath set down in his Discourse of Parodies: a remarkable one among the Greeks is that of Matron, in the words and epithets of Homer, describing the feast of Xenocles, the Athenian Rhetorician, to be found in the fourth book of Athenæus, page 134, Edit. Casaub.

AN ACCOUNT OF ISLAND, *alias* ICELAND, IN THE YEAR
MDCLXII.[1]

[POSTHUMOUS WORKS, p. 1.]

GREAT store of drift-wood or float-wood, is every year cast up on their shores, brought down by the northern winds, which serveth them for fuel and other uses, the greatest part whereof is fir.

Of bears there are none in the country, but sometimes they are brought down from the north upon ice, while they follow seals, and so are carried away. Two in this manner came over and landed in the north of Island, this last year, 1662.

No conies or hares, but of foxes great plenty, whose white skins are much desired, and brought over into this country.

The last winter, 1662, so cold and lasting with us in England, was the mildest they have had for many years in Island.

Two new eruptions, with slime and smoke, were observed the last year in some mountains about Mount Hecla.

Some hot mineral springs they have, and very effectual, but they make but rude use thereof.

The rivers are large, swift, and rapid, but have many falls, which render them less commodious; they chiefly abound with salmons.

They sow no corn, but receive it from abroad.

They have a kind of large lichen, which dried, becometh hard and sticky, growing very plentifully in many places;

---

[1] AN ACCOUNT, &c.] The following brief notices respecting Iceland were collected at the request of the Royal Society. They were partly obtained through correspondence with Theodore Jonas, a Lutheran minister, resident in the Island;—three of whose letters have been preserved in the British Museum. These letters I have preferred to place immediately after the paper to which they relate, rather than in the Correspondence.

whereof they make use for food, either in decoction or powder, some whereof I have by me, different from any with us.

In one part of the country, and not near the sea, there is
a large black rock, which, polished, resembleth touchstone,
as I have seen in pieces thereof, of various figures.

There is also a rock, whereof I received one fragment,
which seems to make it one kind of *pisolithes* or rather *oro-
bites*, as made up of small pebbles, in the bigness and shape
of the seeds of *ervum* or *orobus*.

They have some large well-grained white pebbles, and
some kind of white cornelian or agath pebbles, on the shore,
which polish well. Old Sir Edmund Bacon, of these parts,
made use thereof in his peculiar art of tinging and colouring
of stones.

For shells found on the sea shore, such as have been
brought unto me are but coarse, nor of many kinds, as ordinary turbines, chamas, aspers, læves, &c.

I have received divers kinds of teeth and bones of cetaceous fishes, unto which they could assign no name.

An exceeding fine russet down is sometimes brought unto
us, which their great number of fowls afford, and sometimes
store of feathers, consisting of the feathers of small birds.

Beside shocks and little hairy dogs, they bring another sort
over, headed like a fox, which they say are bred betwixt
dogs and foxes; these are desired by the shepherds of this
country.

Green plovers, which are plentiful here in the winter, are
found to breed there in the beginning of summer.

Some sheep have been brought over, but of coarse wool,
and some horses of mean stature, but strong and hardy; one
whereof kept in the pastures by Yarmouth, in the summer,
would often take the sea, swimming a great way, a mile or
two, and return the same: when its provision failed in the
ship wherein it was brought, for many days fed upon hoops
and cask; nor at the land would, for many months, be
brought to feed upon oaths.

These accounts I received from a native of Island, who
comes yearly into England; and by reason of my long acquaintance and directions I send unto some of his friends

against the *elephantiasis*, (leprosy,) constantly visits me before
his return; and is ready to perform for me what I shall desire
in his country; wherein, as in other ways, I shall be very ambitious to serve the noble society, whose most honouring servant I am,

THOMAS BROWNE.

Norwich, January 15, 1663.

Theodore Jonas to Dr. Browne.

[MS. SLOAN. 3418, fol. 189.]

PRIMA, qvam instituit Auctor, ζήτησις difficilis mihi et sub-
obscura videtur.

1. De Arboribus et Herbis in Islandia quales vulgò occurrant, qva ratione cum Anglicis conveniant, qva discrepent?
Cum nunquam contigit olim felicem illam Terram Anglicam
adire ac lustrare, nedum in pernoscendis discernendisque
istius soli proventibus operæ qvicqvam sumere, frustra meo
judicio, de Arborum aut Herbarum convenientia cum nostratibus, compelletur. Verum ne videar, vel faciendo inhumanus, vel in patria recensendo, qvas fert Islandia, [primum]
sejungam, deinde etiam illas, non omnes qvidem sed præcipuas
et mihi visas, succincte memorem.

Multi patriam nostram, præter solam Betulam, ne qvicqvam arborum sunt procreare rati, sed falso: proveniunt vero
hic Arbusculæ permultæ, et qvidem frugiferæ; ut Morus,
Buxus, Juniperus, Rubus, Myrtillus, cum suis qvælibet baccis: qvanquam libenter do has arborum species non altius
assurgere qvam ut Virgulta merito dicantur; impediuntur
vero frigore, et assiduis opprimuntur nivibus, qvò minus ad
excellentem et justam qvantitatem naturaliter possint per-
venire. Abundat etiam Islandia Salice, nec unius tantum-
modo generis sed cum Punicea, qvæ Plinio Viminalis, tum
Candida, eidem Vitellina, tum Cinerea. Habet præterea
qvoddam Arboris Genus, nostratibus Reyner dictum, Sam-
buci nomine à nonnullis insignitum, nec refragabor tantisper

dum Auctores et herbarios cum ipsa confero experientia. Spinas, vepres, sentesque prudens omitto ; nec ejus generis nimium ferax hæc terra.

2. Num hyems hic aut æstas virescat, qvave alia facie tellus gaudeat ? Prior pars τῆς ζητήσεως vix est vestigationis nomine digna, cum ubique locorum æstas inducat viriditatem terræ, et hyems contra marcorem ac flaccedinem. Posterior scriptionis est longioris : id saltem nunc significabo, ab æqvinoctio autumnali procellis et imbribus ut plurimum nos concuti, Kalendas usque Novembrias, circa Solstitium brumale nivosissimam esse cœli constitutionem. Sole [autem] peragrante signa Aqvarii et Piscium frigus vehementer affligere et intendi, raroque hyems se remittet ante Kal. April. Æstas plerumque siccior initio, ac ver ipsum, media calidior, fine pluviosa et turbida. Nox fere nulla aut notabilis umbra in nostro hemisphærio sentitur æstivali solstitio præsertim in septentrionali plaga. Et tamen brumali die brevissimo, duarum nempe horarum, aut fere trium, solem, sereno cælo, clare conspicimus, terras collustrantem, caloremque sentimus ; ut pro commento sit habendum qvod Cosmographi et Astronomi qvidam de Islandia scripserunt, corpus solare bruma non videri nobis, nec verum diem oriri.

3. Qvi flores aut herbæ in littore aut alibi reperiantur ?— qvamvis animo intendam annotare, vix tamen vacat, sed libelli alicujus paginis inserere qvæ commode ad vos integræ veniant : operam omnino luderam, si tentarem herbas ac olera, ut jam sunt matura, foliis floribusque gravia, libro involvere, in Angliam usque perferenda. Nominatim vero recensebo nonnullas, qvæ hic nascuntur herbæ vulgatiores, et qvæ usibus humanis esse solent, alioqvi multitudine et varietate obruerer. Seqvar autem ordinem D. Adami Leoniceri Medico-Physici Francfurt : Herbarii non contemnendi, qvo cum sedulo species arborum et herbarum contuli, atque ex lib. 2do didici, seqventes H. Islandiam nostram producere. Sempervivam seu Sedum majus et minus, cap. 8. delineatum. Trixaginem et Teucrion, c. 15. Lapathi et Rumicis genera varia, c. 62, 63, 64. Chrysanthemum, c. 65. Buphthalmum, 66. Calthum, c. 67. Chamomillum, c. 68. Hieracium seu Traxacon majus et minus, c. 71. Auriculum

Muris, vulgo Pilosellam, c. 80. Tithymalum Myarinites seu
fæminam et Tithymalium paralium, seu Esulam marinam, c.
82. Melissam, c. 99. Calamintham, c. 100. Mentham, c. 101.
Serpillum, c. 109. Bellem seu Solidaginem minimam; Lysi-
machiam seu Salicariam, herbam pedicularem, sive Staphi-
sagriam, c. 146. Tanacetum, c. 175. Geranium rostrum-
ciconiæ. Ibid. Chelidonium seu Gratiam Dei, c. 177.
Ranunculum, c. 197. Asinen seu morsum Gallinæ, c. 204.
Arundinem, c. 217. Gramen et Caricem, c. 218. Holosteon,
vel denticulum canis, c. 219. Eqvisetum, c. 223. Rapunculum
Rapum, c. 244, 245. Cepas, c. 248. Bulbos, 249. Porrum, et
c. 250. Allium, c. 251. Fragariam, c. 275. Tormentillam et
Pentaphyllum, c. 277. Saniculam, c. 278. Ledum Leonis, c.
279. Filicis genera nonnulla, c. 291. Gyllitem seu lingvam
cervinam, c. 294. Angelicam, c. 302. Petroselinum, c. 316.
Millefolium, 321. Potentillam, 322. Gallium, c. 326. Aperi-
nens vulgo Aspergulam, c. 327. Matrisylvam seu herbam
stellarem, c. 328. Crithmnm vulgo cretam marinam, c. 330.
Ornithogalum, c. 337. Vicia, c. 364, et Lentem, 366. Alias-
que innumeras, qvæ licet non omnimodo et vsque qvoque
congruant cum herbariorum descriptionibus et pigmentis,
specie tamen easdem esse nulli dubitamus, ideoque et depictis annumerandas. Multas, ut ubique obvias prudens prætereo; plurimæ quoque neglectæ, nobis etiam non visæ, qvas
patrium fert solum, sunt omissæ. Nonnullas, in iisque igno-
tas haud paucas, libello et fasciculo involvi, Dno Literatiss.
perferendas, si fortasse nativam repræsentent arefactæ figu-
ram et innotescant. Nemini vero videbitur mirum si tum
qvantitate tum forma utcunque et qvalitate nonnihil nostræ
dissideant ab Anglicis, aut exoticis, et ob soli sterilitatem
et aeris asperitatem. Adjunxi etiam Culmos cum spica, in
australi Islandiæ plaga sponte nascentes, qvos resectos et are-
factos nostrates quotannis concutiunt et copiosum eliciunt
frumentum, qvale sacculo inclusum mittimus. Sed et alibi
tritico simile frumentum provenit, ab incolis annuatim resec-
tum, arefactum, molaque subactum, panibus et pulmentariis
utiliter aptatum, terreni quidem saporis, eò qvod non seritur,
nihilo tamen minus frugaliter atque ad satietatem alere fertur.
Hæc autem quæ intuenda mittuntur, eo exhibentur fine, ut

et sagaci indagatori fiat satis, et nos in pleniorem harum rerum notitiam, per amicam vestram informationem, mutuam-
que collationem, si Diis placet, perducamnr.

4. Crustulum vel placentam panis istius qvi fit è pulvere
confusorum piscium, non habemus Pisc . . . . siccatus aut
sole induratus funditur hic communiter (qvemadmodum etiam
Rasa, salmo etc. indurati) et qvidem in superficiarium ut ita
dicam, pulverem, sed qvi vel mox cum butyro et sale comme-
ditur vel ex lacte aut alio jure pro obsonio habetur. Estque
hic piscium apparatus Islandicæ plebi cocti panis instar,
qvanqvam ditiores et nobiliores, eo non contenti, pane exotico
ut plurimum bis cocto mensas solent adornare suas. Interim
non obliviscendum reor, moris esse vulgi nautici, ad levandam
panis penuriam, ova piscium advectitio frumento ut admis-
ceant, depsant in formam placentæ, et pro pane utantur
escarito.

5. Chylus stomachis vitulorum contentus, hic ut in aliis
regionibus usui qvidem est, omni parte anni, ad lac coagulan-
dum, quò tum in caseum, tum in oxygalas concrescat, qvales
nec Anglia nec Dania vidit, utpote crassas, pingves, consis-
tentes et sine singulari aciditate perdurantes in annum, ut
non Islandis solum, sed extraneis etiam, cibum gratissimum
et fere dixerim Jovis cerebrum esse censendum.

6. Qvid rerum ferat Hekla mons pene friget referre, prop-
ter variorum scriptorum commenta et aniles [fabulas], qvibus
Heklam Islandiæ modo Orcum, modo glacialem Infernvm
esse, petulanter astruere, imperitisque persvadere velle videntur. Verissime Dns Arngrinus Jonas Islandus de monte hoc
mirabili scripsit, Apologet. suo, par. I, § 6, 7, ubi commenta
solide refutavit et explosit. Mons Hekla sulphure et bitu-
mine dives ardorem in cavernis ab exhalationum et ventorum
motu conflictuque concipiens sæpenumero fumum flammamque
eructavit. Prima hæc ignis eruptio legitur, Anno Dni 1106,
facta; qvam variæ, per dissimilia temporum intervalla, sunt
subsecutæ, nec tantum ex Hekla, sed aliis etiam sublimiori-
bus montibus et alpibus, australis et maxime orientalis Islandiæ
partis, imo et ex mari, prope promontorium Reylianes, plæ-
risque Anglis qvi huc velificati sunt pernotum, flamma non
semel erupit, et ignis per aliqvot dies arsit. Imprimis fuit

memorabilis ignis eruptio, Ao. 1625, cum aqvarum et cineris, pumicisque ingenti eluvie, ex alpium ruptura et commotione prope Heklam, concomitantibus fragoribus tremendis et terræ motu, cœlo cinere, ceu nubilissimo imbre, aut eclipsi, obducto et obscurato ; unde magnus orientalis Islandiæ tractus, diffugientibus hominibus et pecoribus est evastatus. Nec multo remissior fuit ignis vis Anno 1636, cum Hekla ipsa jam octavum (ut habent annales) tremere et conflagrare cœpit idibus Maijs ad vesperam, erumpente flamma, prima ad austrum ex montis illius barathro, deinde per bina, tandem sena, septena, vel octona spiracula se vis effudit ignea, large diffundens fumum, cineres, et pumices, atros seu lapideos carbones, qvibus terra circumqvaque obducta, pabulum denegat armentis in hunc usque diem.   In hac eruptione tellus itidem tremuit, flamma longe conspecta, fragores eminus auditi, maximo cum stupore et consternatione incolarum ad remotiora tutioraque loca dilabentium ; lux etiam diurna favillis et fumo intercepta, cinis in nubem coactus ad loca remotissima, prout venti flaverunt, deferebatur, ipse mons ignivomus, alioqui cum alpibus nive certans, ab hac eruptione denigratus magnitudinem rei diu testatus est, tota illa æstate ignes in monte conspecti sunt, sub initium hyemis paulatim se remiserunt et qvanquam rarius postea apparuerunt, primo tamen vere tandem ex defectu materiei, imo ex divina dispensatione penitus deferbuerunt; nec indidem ab ullo hactenus animadversi.   Atque hæc de Monte mirabili scripsisse sat sit.

7. De Noctuis, Vespertilionibus, Ranis, et Talpis eò brevior ero qvo in Islandia sunt animalcula rariora, mihi . . . .* neque visa hic neque audita.   Animalia quæ habent nostrates omnis generis castrant, è jumentis, eqvos et boves, ex pecudibus, oves, imo canes, feles, etc., adeo ut parcè ministrent admissarios, cuique gregi sobolis procreandæ gratia.

8. Morborum genere vario vexantur Islandi.   Universalis et vernaculus esse videt morbus pustularum, quo plerique in adolescentia et juventute semel tantum corripiunter, paucissimi in senectute, idque lethaliter ; recurrit autem fere vicenorum annorum interstitio, diramque falcem in nostram solet immit-

---

* The paper is torn here.

tere messem. Cephaleâ multi utriusque sexus et catarrho gravantur, Plevritis, peripneumonia et ossium, ut vocant, dolor, haud paucos deijcit. Interim Morbus Comitialis, Cholera, Dysenteria, Spasmus, Ophthalmia, Odontalgia, Angina, Asthma, Morbus regius, Dysuria, Hydrops, Gangræna ; Erysipelas non nullos affligit, sed raro ad mortem ducit. Nullus Elephantiasi, vel abominabilior vel pestilentior hic existimatur, et tamen postremo hoc seculo pavendus se diffundit. Fluentem morbum non agnoscimus alium, Febris itidem species prorsus ignoramus, nisi medicos evolvamus.

9. De Canitie et Calvitio nihil habeo notabile scribere, nisi diverse nostrates afficiantur prout cujusque ferat complexio. Alii ante 30 annum πολιας conseqvuntur, alii vix 80m canescunt. Qvidam septimo lustro calvescunt, qvidam bene criniti promissoque capillo seculum simul et vitam absolvunt, tam longævos namque senes vidimus.

10. Ætites an in nidis aqvilarum aliqvando fuerit repertus, nescio, nostra certe memoria Islandis, etiam inqvirentibus non contigit invenisse qvare in fabulis habendum.

11. Cervos Islandia non vidit, nedum decidua eorum cornua autumamus.

13. Minutula testaceorum conchyliorumque genera qvæ apud nos reperiuntur sigillatim indigitare aut describere, non opis est nostræ, qvippe qvi mediterranea incolimus et hoc studium liberale otium et industriam poscit. Qvæ vero poteram obiter ac quasi in transcursu conqvirere collecta mittuntur, precor amanter et qua par est observantia, Rev. et Doct. Lectorem in qvemcunque perfunctus hæc inciderit epistola, ut dexter, qvæ scripsi candido animo, accipiat, nec existimet ullus honori proprio me velificari voluisse, dum nude strictimque res patrias memoro rogatus ; malui autem honestæ, viri Naturæ studiosi φιλόσοφου καὶ φιλόφρονος Islandiæque nostræ bene cupientis petitioni, accedente Charissimi Sympatriotæ mei in Anglia degentis appellatione morem gerere laconico et rudi responso, qvam vel inciviliter abnuere, vel occupationes meas laboriosissimo hoc anni tempore, inhumanitati obtendere. Qvod si D.no Literat. qvi qvæsita huic transferri voluit, qvibus utcunque respondi, porrò libuerit, super his vel aliis disqvirere, nosque suis propriis dignari literis, habebit me, Deo vitam

prorogante, facilem et sibi, pro mea tenuitate, gratificandi studiosissimum.

Christus Jesus, æterni Sapientia Patris suo nos collustret spiritu, ut, qvæ nobis saluti maxime sunt, impense sectemur, fidem veram retinentes, et charitatem non fucatam invicem exercentes, donec in pleniorem Salvatoris nostri cognitionem transformemur et æternam consequamur hæreditatem in cœlis. Amen.

Dabam Hitterdalæ, 2 ids. Julias, Anno 1651.

THEODORUS JONAS, ISLANDUS,

Ecclesiæ Hitterd. Pastor.

The first account from Island, T. Jona: 1651.*

Theodore Jonas to Dr. Browne.

[MS. SLOAN. 3418, fol. 191.]

SALVE VIR HUMANISSIME,

QVANTI amicam tuam compellationem faciam, vir eruditissime et solertissime, D. Thoma Broune, et affatum tuum amicum, facilius sentio qvam exprimo. Beneficium enim est, sic interpretor, meliores istas mentes ad me sub extremo fere cæli climate constitutum, inclinare et ignotum complecti. Pauci hodie ita comparati, saltem in aliqvo honoris apice, et blandientis fortunæ cumulo, vel sub apricante sole viventes, ut in sterili Musarum contubernio qværant qvem amicitia sua dignentur. Opum aut dignitatum splendor passim affectum conciliat; & ut solem orientem omnes adorant, sic crescentem fortunam minorum gentium homunculi, vappæ fere apud eos, qvi se et sua tantum suspiciunt. Tu melius, Vir Humanissime, qvi virum non purpurâ et pecuniæ censu metiri didicisti, sed doctrinæ et virtutis, qvanqvam ego mihi ipse neutrum fere arrogo, aliorum benevolentiâ abblandiente qvidem, verum non titillante: quâ certe inductus, D. Broune, non semel me, de uno atque altero, per literas sciscitando consuluisti, sed irrito conatu, cum ab occupationibus meis anniversariis, hoc

* The indorse.

potissimum tempore usque ad adultam æstatem qvotannis in-
cumbentibus, tum ab imperitiâ meâ et ignorantiâ rerum de
qvibus qværitur. Et qvantum ad proximas D. Thomæ literas, a viro probo sympatriota meo Jona Aruæo mihi redditas,
cvm adjuncto munusculo, ad unciæ argenteæ plus-minus pretium, qvorum utrumque longe nobis gratissimum. Non us-
qveqvaqve difficile videbitur, qvæ sitis, respondere, si plus otii
nunc haberemus. De Avibus, qvas vocas migratorias, an sint
in Islandia, nullus dubitat, et qvidem variarum specierum; qvo
vero nomine insigniendæ, qvove exulent, magis in dubio re-
linqvitur. Anseres agrestes habemus duum generum : sunt
quos appellant Tardam, Tetracem; Anatumque varia, qvæ
vocantur, Boscas, Penelops, Qverqvedula, et Anas torqvata.
Commorantur nobiscum, magno numero Alaudæ, sed sine
crista; item Motacilla, annuus et certus exterarum nationum
præsertim Anglicarum . . . .; tum Fringilla, Cuculus,
et id genus; aliæ aviculæ, qvorum latina nomina non ex-
acte nunc memini: hæ vero omnes verno terram nostram
tempore assiliunt, primo autem autumno, vel exeunte æstate,
nemine advertente avolant. Qvo? disqvirant ingenia acutiora,
et otio abundantiora. Continue nobiscum inhabitant insulam
Aqvila, olor, corvus, perdix, Falco, Æsalo seu merillus, passer, curruca : nec multo pluras memini nobiscum hyemantes,
in mediæ hujus insulæ regione : de maritimis enim volatilibus
cum adventitijs, tum permanentibus, hactenus non fui sollicitus. Longiorem qvippe disqvisitionem præ varietate et multitudine postulant. Habito autem in meditullio hujus insulæ,
vallem saltuosam Hitterdal, qvam in bonis allodiabus numera-
mus, beneficio Serenissimi Danorum et Norvegorum Regis
patri meo, venerando seniori (nunc μαχαϱίτῃ :) mihique succes-
sori concessam. Qvare mari navigatoribusque remotior ex-
istens, postulatis tuis, qvanqvam æqvissimis et jucundis, tem-
pestive non qveo facere satis. Cætera qvæsitorvm qvod attinet, nescit nostra terra Serpentes, id est Colubros, Ranas,
Talpas. A morborum variis generibus, Divinâ disponente
clementiâ, liberi qvidem sunt Islandi, non tamen omnibus, ut
nec à morbillis et variolis, qvæ ut pituitosæ aut biliosæ erup-
tiones, ceu congenita scabies, plurimis hic accidunt in pueritia
vel in cunabulis : rarò adultis : præterqvam qvod ætati decri-

pitæ sua Psora adheret. Plantas, qvas φυτα, herbas nempe et
frutices intelligo, olim a nobis designatas, expetivisti, sicco
pede nunc transeo; tot enim hic suppetunt genera, forma,
flore, fructu, usu varia, ut vel ipsi Chironi negotium facerent:
interim diversas, et contrarias etiam facultates habere nemo
nostrum nescit.   Maxima autem difficultas, de his scribere vo-
lenti metuenda, ab auctorum dissensu, discrepantiaque, cum
circa nomenclaturam cujusvis plantæ, tum multo-maxime formam et efficaciam, quorum litem si qvis suam facit, omnium
Aristarchus audiat necesse est. Verum antequam manum de
tabula, dominum meum et amicum D. Thomam Brounium
cupio rogatum, velit anno seqvente, vitam Deo prorogante,
distincte mihi significare per literas et statum suarum rerum,
ætatis, professionis, habitationis, conjugii: et Anglicanæ Rei-
publicæ formam, administrationem, [itemque] religionem. Tunc
qvæ floreant Academiæ, qvi Doctores seu professores celeberrimi vel sint vel habeuntur ? qvot Episcopi, Archiepiscopi, qvæ
eorum authoritas, et vis sive in religione propaganda et refor-
manda, sive in rebus civilibus administrandis dijudicandisque.
Hæc enim omniaque: somnium nobis enarrant à morte Regis
Caroli I. vestrates, qvare commentarium rerum Anglicarum
latino idiomate à D.no Amico, nisi est molestum, expeterem :
[cui] vicissim pro meo modulo, qvà possim gratificaturus.
Qvod restat, Deum patrem omnis misericordiæ obsecro, nos
in sui cognitione et amore æternum conservet, vitam et valetu-
dinem nobis pro suo beneplacito protollat, et in cælestem patriam, qvos fide hic et charitate conjunxit, olim benigne susci-
piat. Vale vir Humanissime; dabam Hitterdalæ idib. Jul.
Tibi addictissimus.   Anno 1656.

THEODORUS JONAS, ISL.

Verbi M.

Viro Virtute et Doctrinâ præstantissimo, Humaniss :
   D. Thomæ Brounio, Artis Machaonicæ peritissimo,
   in Norvick ad Caurrum in Anglia D.no et Amico
   meo, dentur L.
To Noruic in England.

Indorsed.—Read at a meeting of the Royal Society,
   Feb. 7th, 1711-12—the second letter, 1656—the
   third and last miscaryed, the shippe being taken.

Theodore Jonas to Dr. Browne.

[MS. SLOAN. 3418, fol. 205.]

SALVE PLURIMUM, VIR REVERENDE ET DOCTISSIME DOMINO
THOMA BROUNE .... QVA CHRISTO ..... NORVICI
IN ANGLIA .... ET MODERATOR ....[1]
DOMINE ET AMICE CUM PRIMIS OBSERVANDE,

ET ipsæ tuæ literæ, Vir honorande, mihi gratissimæ, et gratior
causa qvæ te impulit ad scribendum, amor enim humanitas-
que [erat], qvemque nisi amem mutuum, [haurientem] a tam pu-
ro fonte, durus sim et inhumanus. Atque ego te, mi Broune
(vere et [sinc] blanditiis dicam) jam ante inter junctos habebam
et inter charos, ita multa de virtute tua audiebam, et ex alto
adorabam studium sapientiæ et doctrinæ tuæ, qvod rarum in
hoc ancipiti statu rerum et tumultuum. Nunc autem merito
te colloco inter familiarissimos, postqvam non semel legi et manibus versavi nuncium affectus tui in nos benevoli et constantis:
intermisimus sane ad tempus officium illud invicem compellan-
di alterum, et fortasse culpa in me reciderit, verum haud obli-
vione tui, sed mera dulcedine cessationis, qva facillime scri-
bendi occasio nobis abscinditur tam procul disjunctis. Tu
autem redintegras amicitiæ vices, et defectum gratis resarcis,
non modo blanda et docta tua epistola, per virum probum nos-
tratem Sigvardum Jugemundi (vobis forte Ingramum) missa,
sed simul etiam trigemina prole recentium motuum in Magna Britannia, quorum Historiam admodum desideravimvs et
nunc tandem tuo dono nacti sumus, qvo nos habeo tibi ob-
strictiores. Quamvis autem hæc opuscula Doctissimi Viri,
Georgii Batei Med: luculente nos edoceant, tristia fata, va-
riamque fortunam duorum M. Britanniæ Regum; optarem
tamen adhuc potiri, superis faventibus, uno opusculo ejusdem
farinæ, qvod in lucem jam prodijsse nullus dubito, nempe de
introductione et plenaria ab exilio exaltatione Augustissimi
Regis Caroli II. Et qvæ pœnæ manserint immanes regicidas
ac persecutores hujus jam regnantis. Qvæ et qvantæ rerum ac

[1] QUA CHRISTO, &c.] These words are struck out in MS.

statuum mutationes sint subsecutæ. Tum imprimis aveo videre formulam vestræ reformatæ religionis, qvæ in Regno
Angliæ nunc obtinet. Summam puta fidei et cercmoniarum,
qvam Ecclesiæ Anglicanæ, cum cathedrales, et universitates,
tum oppidani et suburbani cœtus profitentur et sectantur : Qvot
et qvæ sectæ apud vos tolerentur ? Qvid Præsbyteriani ab
aliis differant ? Hæc ante libuit Domino Amico vota significare, qvam ad ejus ζητημαζα devenirem, qvorum brevem et
simplicem ἀνάλυσιν subjungam. 1. Qvæ Historia vel traditio
extet de Frislandia, Insula non longe à nobis remota ? Uno
verbo absolvam ; nulla qvæ vel aures vel oculos nostros per-
strinxerit. Habemus qvidem Frislandiam, insulam in tabulis
hydrographicis delineatam, sed qvod sciam, nec nostra nec
patrum memoria ulli visam, nedum calcatam. Navarchæ etiam, qvi qvotannis hæc maria sulcant (ut verbo utar poetico)
dictam insulam vel ex industria ne qvierunt invenire ; qvam
ob rem hanc, aut nunquam exstitisse, aut, qvod verisimilius,
jamdudum insanis obrutam aqvis, et oceano absorptam arbi-
trantur. Et frustra sunt, qvi hanc Frislandiam, eandem ac
Winlandiam bonam seu felicem, qvo nonnulli ex primoribus
nostræ terræ incolis olim migraverint et coloniam deduxerint,
rati sint. Autumarem potius Winlandiam illam, sive insulam
sive continentem, partem fuisse Gronlandiæ lybonotum versus, feliciore gleba et mitiore tempestate qvam Meditullium
tunc temporis habitatæ Gronlandiæ, ac propterea dictam vete-
ribus illis, felicem. Sunt et qvi hanc Gronlandiæ partem ipsi
Americæ boreali cohærentem, et qvasi continentem et con-
tiguamt erram esse fluctuent, nec absimile vero.

  Gronlandiæ historia dudum est divulgata, qvamvis jam
aliqvot retro seculis nil novi de illa percrebuit. Dani vero
nostri, non ita multis ante annis eo cursum instituentes, naves
appulerunt : homines, lustrata terra, prædati, si modo id homines licebit nuncupare, qvibus nec Deus, nec religio, nec
discrimen honestorum et turpium, neque ratio æqvi bonique
ulla est ; vescuntur crudis et sangvinolentis carnibus avium,
animalium et piscium, qvorum copiam illud mare suppeditat,
præsertim Balænas et Phocas. Lingvam illorum aut orati-
onem ncc audiverunt, nec murmur aut nutationes intellexerunt
Dani, qvanqvam ultra bimatum apud se captos retinuerint,

sperantes benevolentia et blanda conversatione tandem ho-
mulos illos mansvefieri, sed frustra fuerunt.

2. Qvæstio. Ligna fluctuantia qvæ ad terræ nostræ cre-
pidines feruntur, Gronlandia avulsa plurimi censent. Cum
qvod ventorum vi, qvi exinde spirant, Septentrionis, Aqvilonis
et Cori plurimum agitentur, et Islandiam appellant tum qvia
mare illud glaciale navigantes, inter Islandiam et Gronl. mul-
titudinem lignorum fluitantium, imo et glaciei inhærentium et
concomitantium sæpiuscule reperierunt.   Potius tamen ad-
ducor ut credam, istiusmodi ligna a Norvegia seu Finnmar-
chia nostro bono affluere, utpote terra sylvarum feracissima,
insignis denique magnitudinis, et ad arctum longissime expor-
recta, ultra scilicet 70 gr. ut Aqvilo vel Corus exinde nullo
negotio ligna ferat Islandiæ ; divina sic dispensante provi-
dentia, cum sylvis ad extruendas domus destituamur. Gron-
landiam autem prædivitem esse sylvarum non videtur vero
simile.   Porro an inundatione et æstu maris subinde terris
aliqvid abscindatur, an vero fluvialium vel pluvialium aqvarum
immoderata violentia et eluvie, qvibus qvævis obvia in declivi
potissimum rapi solent, hujusmodi ligna eradicentur, et nostro
bono in mare proijciantur, in dubio relinquo.   Species lignorum qvod attinet, duum vel plurium suut : unum Abietis,
Alni alterum, denique et Piceæ seu potius Piceastri.

3. Qv. An veneficis abundet Islandia et qva dignosci com-
periantur ? Dolet nobis serio, patriam eo nomine male audi-
visse.   Et qvanqvam non negamus adhuc temporis tales aliqvando depræhendi (nunqvam enim desistit Diabolus, hostis
divini cultus et hominum salutis, omnibus vijs suas extendere
plagas et agro Christiano sua inserere si potest zizania) multum tamen malum illud remisit et elanguit: cum ex mera Dei
bonitate, puram doctrinæ vocem apud nos conservante et
adjuvante, tum ex severiore Magistratus sententia et inquisi-
tione, atrocissima pœna talibus Diaboli mancipiis irrogata.

4, 5, 6. Quæstio. Sciuros, Lutras et talia animalcula non
alit Islandia. Neque Asinos, qvamobrem an ferre possint
brumam Isl. nec ne, incertum est. An boves omnes excornes,
uti refert Ortelius ? Sensus est, an viderit Islandia vel habue-
rit boves cornutos ? quasi vero omnes hic carerent cornibus !
Id autem, in gratiam Doctiss: Ortelii, affirmamns, duplo vel

triplo majus esse sine cornibus hic armentum, qvam bicorne :

7. Qvæstio. Qvid sentias per animalia aliqva endemica et propria non satis asseqvor. Huic antea regioni animalia aliqva esse peculiaria, qvasi connata, nec ullus hominum [denegare est] ausus, de Ursis, lupis, vulpibus et id genus animalibus, nocuis qvam utilibus, qvæ majores nostri hic antea se reperierunt, non est, ut videtur quæstio.

8. Q. An pisces in lacubus congelatis supervivant? an majori ex parte depereant. Rotunda est solutio, mori pisces constrictis omnino, et in glaciem conversis funditis aquis. Sin autem pro cortice aut crustulo glacies saltem innatet et obtegat aqvas, nihil detrimenti, forsan et non nihil recrementi piscibus affert, unde etiam, qvi tunc per fenestras ab hamiotis venantur, dulciores et pingviores æstimantur.

9. Q. Febribus raro vexantur Islandi, adeo ut nec species, nec paroxysmum febris qvisqvam hic observet.

10. Q. Elevationem Poli qvod spectat, et situm Islandiæ cosmographicum. Qvanqvam variant, inter nos qvi Astronomicæ rei operam aliqvam navarunt, a naucleris seu τῶν κυβερνήτιχων, qvi Islandiam freqventer et summa cum attentione circum quaque naves adpellunt, tamen ut de horum autoritate et sententia aliqvid scribam ; ponunt isti Insulas Westmannorum, qvæ ad austrum, vel verius evronotum ab hac terra distant circiter 10 mill. Latitudinis ab Æqvatore, 63 grad. 25 m. Reitenes, qvod est Promontorium Islandiæ australe latit. 64 gr. 0 m. atq. fere ejusdem latit. statuimus Skalholtiam sedem Episcopalem Isl. australis, ut et Heklam montem satis famosum à sulphurea flamma, qvi hinc non longe versus orientem, 2 fortasse mill. distat. Aliud Isl. promontorium ab altissimis Alpibus et continua nive omnibus huc navigantibus pernotum, Snæfelsnef dictum lybonotum respiciens, scribitur latit. 65 g. 0 m. Latitudo Ejafiord, qvi est sinus Islandiæ Septentrionalis, ab astronomicis depræhensa, gr. 66 m. 8. arguit. Holas, sedem alteram Episcopalem, Islandiæ Borealis ab Æqvatoris circulo, non distare plus 66 gr. atque adeo gr. 67 Islandia non excedit, Arctum versus.

11. Q. Fristas aut grana segetis spontaneæ transmittere (quod est postremum Epistolæ postulatum) in præsentiarum duxi supervacaneum.

Reliqvum est ut Doctissimum Dn. Amicum obnixe rogem, [ut] levem hanc animi mei significationem, et proletariam qvæstionum ejus solutionem in dextram accipiat partem. Certum jubeo ac spondeo me ad omnia illi obseqvia fore paratissimum. Cujus rei testimonium erint Biblia SS. vernaculo idiomate translata, et à nostrate bibliopego qvalitercunque adornata, qvæ rogo Dns. Amicus, à me missa, serena fronte dignetur accipere et boni consulere. Valeat in Christo Jesu, rever. et literatissimus D. Amicus meus (cum uxore lectissima, liberis dulcissimis, et tota sua familia) Deo Triuni æternum commendatus.

Dabam Hitterdalæ in Islandia, Idibus Julijs, Anni à nato Xo. 1664. Rev. tuam dign. amans et colens.

THEODORUS JONAS,
Hitterdalæ Parœcus et Ecclesiæ Christi mystes indignus.

Viro Eximio, qva virtute, qvá doctrina, Domino
  Thomæ Brounio, Norvici in Anglia, dimissio Verbi
  dei fidelissimo, D.no Amico et ¹ fratri in Christo
  conjunctis°. Dentur [L.]
Of Norwitz in England.

---

¹ *Norvici, &c.*] These words are blotted out in MS.

Unpublished Papers.

𝔘npublished 𝔓apers.

FRAGMENT ON MUMMIES.

[FROM A COPY IN THE HAND WRITING OF J. CROSSLEY, ESQ.[1]]

WISE Egypt, prodigal of her embalmments, wrapped up her princes and great commanders in aromatical folds, and, studiously extracting from corruptible bodies their corruption, ambitiously looked forward to immortality; from which vainglory we have become acquainted with many remnants of the old world, who could discourse unto us of the great things of yore, and tell us strange tales of the sons of Misraim, and ancient braveries of Egypt. Wonderful indeed are the preserves of time, which openeth unto us mummies from crypts and pyramids, and mammoth bones from caverns and excavations; whereof man hath found the best preservation, appearing unto us in some sort fleshly, while beasts must be fain of an osseous continuance.

In what original this practice of the Egyptians had root, divers authors dispute; while some place the origin hereof in the desire to prevent the separation of the soul, by keeping the body untabified, and alluring the spiritual part to remain by sweet and precious odours. But all this was but fond inconsideration. The soul, having broken its * * * *, is not stayed by bands and cerecloths, nor to be recalled by Sabæan odours, but fleeth to the place of invisibles, the *ubi* of spirits, and needeth a surer than Hermes's seal to imprison

---

[1] *J. Crossley, Esq.*] I have given this fragment on the authority of. Mr. Crossley; but have not been able to find the vol. in the British Museum which contained it, nor could he inform me; having transcribed it himself in the Museum, but omittted to note the volume in which he met with it.

it to its medicated trunk, which yet subsists anomalously in its indestructible case, and, like a widow looking for her husband, anxiously awaits its return.

*　　*　　*　　*　　*

Of Joseph it is said, that they embalmed him ; and he was put in a coffin in Egypt. When the Scripture saith that the Egyptians mourned for him three score and ten days, some doubt may be made, from the practices as delivered by Herodotus, who saith that the time allowed for preserving the body and mourning was seventy days. Amongst the Rabbins, there is an old tradition, that Joseph's body was dried by smoke, and preserved in the river Nile, till the final departure of the children of Israel from Egypt, according to the Targum of Uzziel. Sckichardus delivereth it as the opinion of R. Abraham Seba, that this was done in contempt of Egypt, as unworthy of the depositure of that great patriarch; also as a type of the infants who were drowned in that river, whereto Sckichardus subjoineth that it was physically proper to prevent corruption. The Rabbins likewise idly dream that these bones were carried away by Moses about a century after, when they departed into Egypt, though how a coffin could be preserved in that large river, so as to be found again, they are not agreed; and some fly after their manner to Schem-hamphorasch, which most will regard as vain babblings.

That mummy is medicinal, the Arabian Doctor Haly delivereth and divers confirm ; but of the particular uses thereof, there is much discrepancy of opinion. While Hofmannus prescribes the same to epileptics, Johan de Muralto commends the use thereof to gouty persons ; Bacon likewise extols it as a stiptic : and Junkenius considers it of efficacy to resolve coagulated blood. Meanwhile, we hardly applaud Francis the First, of France, who always carried mummies with him as a panacea against all disorders; and were the efficacy thereof more clearly made out, scarce conceive the use thereof allowable in physic, exceeding the barbarities of Cambyses, and turning old heroes unto unworthy potions. Shall Egypt lend out her ancients unto chirurgeons and apothecaries, and Cheops and Psammitticus be weighed unto us for drugs ? Shall we eat of Chamnes and Amosis in electuaries and pills, and be cured by cannibal mixtures? Surely such diet is dismal vampirism; and exceeds in horror the black banquet of Domitian, not to be paralleled except in those Arabian feasts, wherein Ghoules feed horribly.

But the common opinion of the virtues of mummy bred great consumption thereof, and princes and great men contended for this strange panacea, wherein Jews dealt largely, manufacturing mummies from dead carcasses, and giving them the names of kings, while specifics were compounded from crosses and gibbet leavings. There wanted not a set of Arabians who counterfeited mummies so accurately, that it needed great skill to distinguish the false from the true. Queasy stomachs would hardly fancy the doubtful potion, wherein one might so easily swallow a cloud for his Juno, and defraud the fowls of the air while in conceit enjoying the conserves of Canopus.

*   *   *   *   *

Radzivil hath a strange story of some mummies which he had stowed in seven chests, and was carrying on ship board from Egypt, when a priest on the mission, while at his prayers, was tormented by two ethnic spectres or devils, a man and a woman, both black and horrible; and at the same time a great storm at sea, which threatened shipwreck, till at last they were enforced to pacify the enraged sea, and put those demons to flight by throwing their mummy freight overboard, and so with difficulty escaped. What credit the relation of the worthy person deserves, we leave unto others. Surely if true, these demons were Satan's emissaries, appearing in forms answerable unto Horus and Mompta, the old deities of Egypt, to delude unhappy men. For those dark caves and mummy repositories are Satan's abodes, wherein he speculates and rejoices on human vain-glory, and keeps those kings and conquerors, whom alive he bewitched, whole for that great day, when he will claim his own, and marshal the kings of Nilus and Thebes in sad procession unto the pit.

Death, that fatal necessity which so many would overlook, or blinkingly survey, the old Egyptians held continually before their eyes. Their embalmed ancestors they carried about at their banquets, as holding them still a part of their families, and not thrusting them from their places at feasts. They wanted not likewise a sad preacher at their tables to admonish them daily of death, surely an unnecessary discourse while they banqueted in sepulchres. Whether this were not making too much of death, as tending to assuefaction, some reason there is to doubt, but certain it is that such practices would hardly be embraced by our modern gourmands who like not to look on faces of *morta*, or be elbowed by mummies.

Yet in those huge structures and pyramidal immensities, of the builders whereof so little is known, they seemed not so much to raise sepulchres or temples to death, as to contemn and disdain it, astonishing heaven with their audacities, and looking forward with delight to their interment in those eternal piles. Of their living habitations they made little account, conceiving of them but as *hospitia*, or inns, while they adorned the sepulchres of the dead, and planting thereon lasting bases, defied the crumbling touches of time and the misty vaporousness of oblivion. Yet all were but Babel vanities. Time sadly overcometh all things, and is now dominant, and sitteth upon a sphinx, and looketh unto Memphis and old Thebes, while his sister Oblivion reclineth semisomnous on a pyramid, gloriously triumphing, making puzzles of Titanian erections, and turning old glories into dreams. History sinketh beneath her cloud. The traveller as he paceth amazedly through those deserts asketh of her, who builded them? and she mumbleth something, but what it is he heareth not.

Egypt itself is now become the land of obliviousness and doteth. Her ancient civility is gone, and her glory hath vanished as a phantasma. Her youthful days are over, and her face hath become wrinkled and tetrick. She poreth not upon the heavens, astronomy is dead unto her, and knowledge maketh other cycles. Canopus is afar off, Memnon resoundeth not to the sun, and Nilus heareth strange voices. Her monuments are but hieroglyphically sempiternal. Osiris and Anubis, her averruncous deities, have departed, while Orus yet remains dimly shadowing the principle of vicissitude and the effluxion of things, but receiveth little oblation.

*　　*　　*　　*　　*

DE PESTE.

[MS. SLOAN. 1827.]

THE learned Kircherus in his book, *De Peste*, cap. 7, particularly delivers what medicines Hippocrates made use of in the great plague of Athens, and particularly mentions sulphur, assafœtida, and vipers, as may be seen in that tract; which being not to be found in the works of Hippocrates, the question is, "What is to be said herein?"

When I had read the seventh chapter of Kircherus abovementioned, I found it very singular; nor could I confirm it by any ancient author. And since, upon inquiry, I find his own expression true, that they are *parum cognita;* for I meet not therewith in any author which might most probably mention the same; not in Hippocrates, Galen, Ætius, Ægineta, Massarias, Jordanus, and others, who have particularly written *De Peste;* not in Paulinus, who hath largely commented upon the narration of Thucydides, concerning the plague of Athens. Not in Nardius, or any comment upon Lucretius, where he makes a large description of this plague, conceived to be the same wherein Hippocrates exercised this cure.

Franciscus Rota, a learned Italian, having read in Marini, an eminent poet of Italy, that Averrhoes was put to death by the cruel death of the wheel, consulted many learned men in Europe where such a passage might be found in any other writer; and none could satisfy his question. But this learned author,[1] yet living, is able to afford a resolution, and may probably do it in following editions of this or some other work, which he shall hereafter publish, though he hath not performed it in his *Mundus Subterraneus,* wherein he largely discourses upon sulphur.

Meanwhile referring unto further inquiry, this account may be taken from some unusual manuscript, from some ancient comment on Hippocrates or some work ascribed unto him or

[1] *author.*] Kircherus.

his successors, known only to some libraries, or else from some Arabic writer; the Arabians being very careful to preserve the works of ancient Greeks, which they often translated, and sometimes fathered other works upon the best of them, which are now very rare or quite lost among us.

Now, although the whole relation be allowed, and the remedies to be approved, yet, whether these were the secrets of Hippocrates in the plague of Athens, or whether they were so successful in that pestilence, some doubt may be allowed; for Thucydides, who passed the same disease,[2] affirmeth that there was no remedy (probably meaning inward) that did any good; but that which did profit one did hurt another: "nec ullum prorsus remedium repertum est[3] quod adhibitum prodesset; nullumque corpus, sive firmæ sive infirmæ valetudinis esset, tanti mali violentiæ resistere potuit; sed omnia absumpsit." From which description some doubt may arise whether Hippocrates came not to Athens rather in the declination than in the raging time of the disease.

Galen, "*De Theriaca ad Pisonem*,"[4] ascribeth this cure of Hippocrates only unto his fires. "Vehementer laudo admirandum Hippocratem, quod pestem illam quæ ex Æthiopia Græcos invasit non alia ratione curavit quam aerem immutando. Jussit igitur per totam civitatem accendi ignem, qui non simplicem incendii materiam habeat, sed coronas et flores odore fragrantissimos. Hæc consuluit ad ignem alendum, et ipsi etiam inspergere unguenta delibata et suavissimi odoris." And the same course they put in practice at Venice, in the great plague which happened under Duke Foscaro, about two hundred years ago.

Again, if this account of the cure of Hippocrates, set down by Kircherus, be ancient, and in times when it might have best been known, some wonder it is how it escaped the pen of Galen, a superlative admirer of him, and who had good opportunity to know what elder times had delivered on this subject; for Thessalus, the son of Hippocrates, left expositions upon his epidemics. Lycus, Sabinus, Satyrus, and Quintus, the preceptors of Galen, had also left tracts upon the

---

[2] *who passed, &c.*] Αὐτός τε νοσήσας.—Thuc. B. μή.

[3] *nec,&c.*] οὐδὲν κατέστη ἴαμα.-Ib. νά.

[4] *De Theriaca, &c.*] Cap. 16.

narration of Thucydides; and Galen himself had written a discourse upon the same, as he testifies in his work,[5] περὶ δὑσπνοιας.

Actuarius, an author of good esteem, who wrote many hundred years ago, undertakes to set down the antidote of Hippocrates, which he used against the plague ; which he believed to be this :—℞. Calami aromatici, junci odorati, sabinæ, ana ʒiii ; cardamomi, cyperi, crocomagmatis, ana ʒv ; nardi Celtici, lib. 5 ; aspalathi, ʒvii ; cupressi ros. an. ʒiii. Ladani, myrrhæ, thuris, an. lib. 1 ; bac. junip. 40 ; mastic. ʒiiii ; nardi spicæ lib. 5 ; costi, ʒiiii ; fol.[6] ʒviii ; cassiæ. lib. 5 ; amomi, ʒiii ; styracis ʒx ; terebinthinæ, lib. 3 ; mellis Attici, lib. 5 ; vini veteris, q. s. This he affirmeth to be the same which he used at the plague of Athens ; et cujus causa coronatus fuit. This, however learned by him, is admitted by Massarias and others ; and is a very different medicine from those so highly commended by Kircherus, who in all equity is obliged to make use of some author of equal credit and authority with him.

Now, while I discourse of this obscurity, some others arise which I cannot omit to propound unto you ; particularly, why Hippocrates left no distinct description of this plague, together with his remedies ? Why Thucydides, in his large description of the plague of Athens, makes no mention of Hippocrates ; and may[7] also consider that this cure of the plague by fires, and even in Athens itself, was elder than Hippocrates, and practised by Acron Agrigentinus, (as testified by Pliny, Ætius, Paulus,) and also made use of by Jachen the Egyptian physician, who lived in the days of Senies, King of Egypt, as is delivered by Suidas, and may be gathered from the practice afterwards of the Egyptian priests, to kindle their fire at the tomb of Jachen, and so to diffuse it through the city ; and from what is delivered by Plutarch,[8] concerning the Egyptian priests ;—de nocte soliti consurgere et inquinatum aerem odoratis incendiis purgare ; to emit their purifying fumes of the great and lesser cyphi, or odorate composition, containing twenty-eight and thirty-six ingredients, which they used in their daily sacrifices unto the sun and moon.

---

[5] *work.*] Hist. lib. 5, cap. 6.
[6] *fol.*] Folium indicum or malabathri. —*Gr.*

[7] *and may.*] Sic. in MS. *you* is doubtless the word left out by a Latinism.—*Gr.*
[8] *Plutarch.*] De Iside et Osir.

But before I dismiss you I shall not omit to entertain you with a few other queries, whereof perhaps you have not taken much notice.

An pestis sit ex lege naturæ, ut dubitat Cardanus; id est, ne terra hominum numero non sufficeret?

An detur pestis artificialis, "uti fertur de pulvere et unguento pestifero in peste Mediolanensi?"

An pisces sint a peste immunes?

An ignis sit maxima pesti pestis?

An pestis fuerit ante diluvium?

An a mundo condito plures occiderit pestis an gladius?

An atomi pestiferi sint animalia, ut vult Kircherus?

An dentur temperamenta aloimodea pesti parum aut nihil subdita?

Cur inter maximas Europæ urbes pestis Lutetiæ minus grassetur?

Cum pestis sudoribus optimè discutiatur, cur detur pestis sudatoria, ut sudor Anglicus?

An pestis sit perpetuo ambulatoria, nunquam ubique extincta?

An ubicunque grassetur pestis, quatuor tempora, id est, principii incrementi status et declinationis, manifeste absolvet?

An non æque mirum sit, quomodo desinat quam quomodo inciperit pestis?

Cur in peste Hebraica nulla fiat mentio de separatione sanorum ab infectis, quæ tamen specialiter notatur in lepra?

Unde verbum *plague*, emphatice pestem significans apud Anglos?

An musica conferat in sananda peste? Questio oritur a praxi Thaletis Cretensis, qui pestem Spartanam musica curasse dicitur? *Plutarch.*

An qui carbunculis et bubonibus liberantur a peste, sanantur simul a lue venerea?

An quis variolis et peste simu laboret?

An aeri infecto purgando sulphurata non præstent aromaticis; quibus tamen maxime secundum Galenum usus est Hippocrates?

An balsamum sulphuris non sit addendum Theriacis?

An alexipharmacis absq. opio compositis sit nimis fidendum?

A BRIEF REPLY TO SEVERAL QUERIES.

[MS. SLOAN. 1827.]

"An Irish soldier who died phrenitical, in the hospital of Paris, made great vociferations, always having in his mouth words of this sound, *bebeithe, bebaithe, bekelle;* scarce affording any other words to any question or proposal; and therefore some, conceiving it had been his native language, brought one of his country unto him, who could make nothing of it."

This account of yours seemed not at first very strange unto me, as I conceived them to be some fantastical words, proceeding from his phrenzy: nor could I afford any sense or solution thereof, till I fell upon the Epistle of Johannes Milesius unto Georgius Sabinus, *De Funeribus Borussorum;* whereof I found this description. "Cum ad sepulchrum effertur cadaver, plerique in equis funus prosequuntur, et currum obequitant quo cadaver vehitur, eductisque gladiis verberant auras, vociferantes, *geygeithe, begaithe, pekelle;* id est, aufugite, vos dæmones, in infernum!"

Now, therefore, this person, having been a soldier about Russia, and under the Poles in Prussia, might probably have heard of this custom; and so, in the delirium and suggestion from his inflamed spirits, might fall into like apprehension of evil spirits, which produced this iterated conjuration from him.

Upon an old picture of a man riding upon a bear, and a dead torn horse lying by.

He that would amuse himself about odd pictures, especially of bears, may have enough to do to interpret the prophetical figures of Anselmus, and Abbot Joachim, which have sometimes passed under the name of the magical figures of Paracelsus, and after set forth by Paulus de la Scala; wherein you may meet with no less than three bears in one figure, one upon the pope's shoulders, and two by his sides.

But, as for this picture, I am not of your opinion, that it is some emblematical piece, but rather historical, and made out of the legend of St. Corbinian, bishop of Freisingen, in Bavaria, who, travelling towards Rome, and coming late to a town in the Alps, when the gates were shut, was fain to lodge abroad, and his horse, straying, was killed and torn by a bear; which news being brought unto him by his servant Ansericus, he bade him go boldly on, and put the saddle of the horse upon the bear: which being done, St. Corbinian rode upon the bear to Rome, and then dismissed him.

As to your other question, how the common expression, 'to tell noses,' implying the number of persons, came up, I can return you no distinct original, either for the time or occasion; and perhaps there needed no other than to account by the most visible and extant part of the face, except it had some such original as is to be met with in the history of Cuspinianus, concerning the great slaughter which Bajazet the second made of the Christian Hungarians and Croatians. "Maxima clades illata est, et septem millia hominum uno prelio interfecta. Victor hostis ut cæsorum numerus commodius iniretur, nares jacentium exsectas baltheolisque insertas secum extulit;" and so in a short way, by telling the number of the noses which were brought to him, he knew how many he had slain in that battle.

But, before I conclude, give me leave to propose these few queries concerning epitaphs unto you.

Whether the epitaph of . . . . . [1] in Herodotus be not the most ancient in good history or record?

Though Joshua be said by Rabbins to have had the sun upon his tomb, and we find, in the annals of Saliom,[2] an epitaph of Abel, yet whether, from any good account, the ancient Hebrews used epitaphs?

[1] . . . .] Left blank in original.   [2] *Saliom.*] "Salian."—*Crossley.*

Whither *siste viator* be not improperly used in church epithets; that form being proper unto sepulchres placed of old by highways, and where travellers daily passed?

Whether jocular and enigmatical epitaphs be allowable?

What to think of epitaphs upon brutes, as that upon Boristhenes, the horse of Adrian? and that upon Roldano, Prince Doria's dog, still to be seen and read in his garden at Genoa?

When that form of ἐνθάδε κεῖται, or *hic jacet,* came up, or where the most ancient to be met with in that form?

What to think, that in the great number of old epitaphs and inscriptions collected by Gruterus, there are so few persons above fifty or sixty years old?

What to think of that inscription set down by Procopius,[3] upon a pillar not far from Tingis, "Nos Maurisi sumus qui fugimus a facie Jehoschuæ filii Nunis predatoris?"

As for the other queries concerning John Port, Lammas, and *O sapientia!* upon the 16th of December, I must crave your patience till another opportunity.

Upon the picture of a learned physician, Mr. S. of Bury, not drawn at large, but to the waist, was this obscure inscription,

> Hic meus Nausiphanes
>
> > ut abortivus fuit olim
> > Sisyphus.

The first part I remember to have read either in the Fragments of Lucillius, or some ancient poet, in this order:

> > hic meus esto
>
> Nausiphanes.

The second is in the third Satire of Horace,

> > ...... strabonem
>
> Adpellat Pætum pater; et Pullum, male parvus
> Si cui filius est, ut abortivus fuit olim
> Sisyphus.

Nausiphanes I find mentioned as a philosopher in Cicero, *De Natura Deorum.* It is a name not easily to be met with,

---

[3] *Procopius.*] This epitaph is also mentioned by Bochart.—*Gr.*

either historically for any person, or grammatically for any signification; but literally expresseth "appearing in ships." Sisyphus was a person of short and low stature, and a famous dwarf of Marc Antony, *Staturæ vix bipedalis*, as Torrentius upon that place.

And therefore this inscription seems to refer unto the picture, name, stature, or all; that is, "this my Nausiphanes, this curtailed and small piece which you behold drawn scarce to the waist, and as a man appearing, or as far as a man appeareth, above the deck of a ship, is such another as was Sisyphus, the dwarf of Antonius, of short and abortive stature, or much about the same measure."

A thick piece of lead, about the compass of half a crown, found near North Walsham, in Norfolk.

This piece upon one side containeth the heads of St. Peter and St. Paul, with their names. On the other side this inscription: Bonifacius VIII.

This seems to have been the seal of a papal bull. Boniface VIII was the first pope who introduced the solemn celebration of jubilees at Rome; and, to attract the greater concourse, sent bulls abroad into most part of Christendom, with indulgences and pardons unto such as should resort unto Rome. Of some of these bulls this might be the seal.

Upon a copper medal sent me, of the compass of a shilling, but the figures much embossed. Upon the obverse side it representeth the head of Malatesta, with this inscription: Sigismundus Pandulphus Malatesta. Upon the reverse an arm extended out of the sky, with a rod in the hand. The inscription: Pontificii exercitus Imp. MCCCCXLVII.

This piece seems to have been made in honour of Pandulphus Malatesta, the Venetian general against the Bohemians, Istrians, and Furlans; [4] more particularly for a great overthrow given them at Udine, where he took about seven hundred prisoners; for which the Venetians highly honoured him, and purchased for him the house of Luigi Taneri, in

---

[4] *Furlans.*] Malatesta defeated the Lord of Forli, in Italy, along with Sforza. These are probably the Furlans here meant.

Venice, at the price of twelve thousand ducats. He was brother to Carlo Malatesta. I have seen a noble medal of gold in this country, of the value of fifty pounds, with the figure of a soldier completely armed, and kneeling before a crucifix, with this inscription: MALATESTA DUX EQUITUM PRÆSTANS. Whether pertaining to this Pandulfo, or Carlo, when I behold the piece again, I may be able to determine.

Many noble large ponderous medals of gold are to be seen in the custody of princes and great ones, but I doubt whether any to be compared with the noble medallion of gold in the treasury of the emperor at Vienna, with the figures of the emperor and Imperial arms upon it. It exceedeth a round trencher plate in compass, and esteemed in value 2200 ducats, or a thousand pounds English, as I am informed by an ocular witness, who had a sight thereof, at Vienna, in 1669.

Of ancient medals, the largest I have, or have seen, is that of the Emperor Heraclius, of about two inches diameter, and containing his triumph for the reduction of the holy cross, with many Greek and Latin inscriptions, which you may see and read in Lipsius, Casalius, and others.

Upon a medal of gold, of the value of six pounds, in the hands of a most worthy person, and my honoured friend, of this country. This piece upon the obverse or face side, hath the head of King Henry VIII with this inscription: HENRICUS OCTAVUS ANGLIÆ FRANCIÆ ET HIB. REX FIDEI DEFENSOR, ET IN TERRA ECCLESIÆ ANGLIÆ ET HIBERNIÆ SUB CHRISTO CAPUT SUPREMUM. On the reverse an inscription of the same sense in Greek and Hebrew: Ἑνριχος ογδοος τρισβασιλευς πιστεως προστατης εν τη εκκλησια της Αγγλιας και Ιβερνιας υπο Χριστω αχρη η κεφαλη. Londini, 1545. About the same an Hebrew inscription to the same effect.

This is a memorial piece, coined by King Henry, when, having disclaimed the power of the pope, he assumed the style of supreme head of the church in his dominions. This piece is now become rare; not easily to be met with, and omitted by Luckius in his description of medals of the last century.[5]

[5] *Luckius, &c.*] Luckii Sylloge nummorum clariorum ab anno 1500 ad 1600.

Sir,

Whereas you find yourself obliged by the articles of your tenures, to pay a mark yearly unto the crane's-pot of the abbey of Ramsey, and you have not obtained satisfaction concerning that crane's-pot, till you meet with better information, I shall offer this unto you.[6] In former times there were many gold and silver utensils belonging unto rich and well-endowed abbeys and churches, chiefly employed about the high altar. Hereof some were made in the figure and form of cranes, with long and extended necks, serving especially for fumigation or perfuming with sweet perfumes conveyed into their bellies, which being fired, or heated, exhaled out of their mouths, and afforded a pleasant odour.

Of these we find clear mention in the enumeration of the list of the precious treasure of the church of Mentz, in a description thereof about four hundred years ago, observed by Rhenanus, in his notes upon Tertullian, in these words :— " *Calyces aurei, grues argenteæ impositorum in cavo ventre thymiamatum per rostra ac collum mira arte exhalentes, juxta aram maximam.* Now these being vessels consuming costly odours, and often used, required some revenue to maintain them. And therefore this, whether by fee, donation, or charge, whether from the bounty of the first donor, or otherwise, was probably the first occasion of your rent.

---

[6] *unto you.*] Probably to Sir Nicholas L'Estrange, lord of the manor of Ringstead.

NAVAL FIGHTS.[1]

[MS. SLOAN. 1827.]

IN most naval fights, some notable advantage, error, or un-expected occurrence, hath determined the victory. The great fleet of Xerxes was overthrown by the disadvantage of a narrow place for battle. In the encounter of Duillius, the Roman, with the Carthaginian fleet, a new invention of the iron *corvi* made a decision of the battle on the Roman side. The unexpected falling off of the galleys of Cleopatra, lost the battle of Actium. In the fight between King Philip and Attalus, the great excursion which Attalus made from his squadron, unto the loss of his galley, made the victory disputable; though Philip suffered so great a loss and destruction of his men, that he had but two arguments left to pretend unto the victory :—that he had kept his station, and taken the galley of Attalus.

Even in the battle of Lepanto, which you particularly enquire of, if Caracoza had given unto the Turks orders not to narrow on account of the number of the Christian galleys, they had, in all probability, declined the adventure of a battle: and, even when they came to fight the unknown force, an advantage of the eight Venetian galleasses gave the main stroke unto the victory; otherwise the whole rencounter was stoutly performed, and in no passage with derogation unto the Turkish valour. An account hereof you may read in Sabellicus, in Peruzzi " of Famous Islands," and in the Turkish History of Knollis in English, which, since you take most notice of, I shall propose unto you these queries and observations, grounded upon his account.[2]

---

[1] NAVAL FIGHTS.] I suspect this to be a passage from a letter to his younger son Thomas, who was in the naval service. [2] *account.*] Knollys, Vol. I, p. 589-599.

How the patience of Don John is to be justified, who, having hidden four hundred valiant men under the hatches, for a reserve in extremity, would be thrice repulsed after he had boarded the Turkish admiral, before he called up that reserve.

And, though it succeeded well upon a tired enemy, yet, whether it was handsomely done to cut off Ali Bassa, the admiral's head, and fastening it on the top of a pole, to erect it in his own galley?

How to justify the noble Andreas Doria, in being so far off in the fight, till a great part of his confederates suffered? Why our Turkish historian, speaking so often of the eight galleasses which did such signal service, should not so much as mention their commander, and whom Peruzzi nameth Dodo?

Whether it were not here verified that bad news flieth apace, since, in eight days' space, Selimus, being at Adrianople, understood of this defeat?

Whether it be commendable in great generals to carry their sons or noble young relations with them, in adventurous and hazardous actions, whose miscarriages may blot their victories or add unto their overthrows; since, in this fight, both Ali Bassa's sons were taken, and one of them but thirteen years of age, who was presented to the Pope?

What different effects bad news hath on the spirits of men, dejecting some, and fairly inflaming others; for, upon going unto the fight, the Christian fleet received news that the Turks had taken Cyprus, which, nevertheless, was so far from discouraging them, that it the more enraged them to revenge?

How you like that argument of Mahomet Bassa, whereby he somewhat pacified the enraged Selimus, and saved a general massacre of the Christians, when he told him the battle was not lost by the valour of the Christians, but by some fatal and unknown cause unto them? Or whether Selimus would have thought there had been any force in such words, if the Venetians had so flattered themselves upon the loss of Cyprus unto him?

Though Selimus threatened a general massacre of the Christians in his dominions, yet, whether he himself or any of his successors, and seriously perform the same, especially in their European dominions, since thereby he would so much weaken his power, leave scarce people to cultivate his grounds, pay his rents, and continue his revenues, may very well be doubted?

Whether the Christians committed not a great error in not pursuing so signal a victory without any considerable advantage but that of honour? Or what considerable benefit may hereafter be expected from the auxiliary forces of Christian princes united against the Turk in any expedition; since they are commonly long in drawing together, and after the attempt or exploit, are ready to return into their respective countries?

AMICO OPUS ARDUUM MEDITANTI.

[MS. SLOAN. 1827, fol. 61—64.]

DE Opusculo quod meditaris, iterum atque iterum cogita: scias quid valeant humeri; ut sis natator bonus, immo Delius, in
hoc tamen procelloso pelago, noli sine cortice natare; enucle-
andi sunt tibi libelli non proletarii, immo ἔμψυχοι.

Nosti quam petulca sit tribus literaria, quam ad commissi-
ones prona, ut non temere profecto κυνομυίας hinc inde expa-
vescas.   Quod candidiores animæ utroque pollice collaudant,
φίλαυτοι tristiores obducta·fronte aspicient.   Nasuti[1] sunt, immo nasi, literionum plurimi, non tantum tuberibus,[2] sed ne
verrucis parcituri.   Si rem minus attigeris, abundè cachinno-
rum est; sin ad amussim, invidiæ plus quam satis.

Nonnulli vocibus inhiantes rem ipsam laxa cervice inspici-
ent; alii (quod caput rei est) ad sensum potius intenti vocabula et voces sicco pede prætereunt.   Quod Prasini ad cœlum
evehunt, Veneti[3] sannis accipient.   Geniorum varietas, studiorum discordia, partes, αἱρέσεις, lucubrationum clarissimarum
fata dividunt: quibus omnibus ut facias satis, frustra sis, ni
ultra Jovem sapias.

Dum itaque huic opellæ insudas, nolim te credas[4] Aspara-
gos coquere.   Dele, reple, incudi redde, Annalibus Volusii[5]
Cinnæ Smyrnam antepone.   Viro tamen erudito, cui ingenium in numerato, cui otii et secessus impendio satis, seram coronidem et cunctationem manuum vix indulsero.

---

[1] *Nasuti.*] Vid. *Martialis Epigram.*
Lib. xiii, 2, I.—"Nasutus sis usque licet, sis denique nasus."

[2] *tuberibus.*] "—— ne tuberibus propriis —— ignoscet verrucis illius."—Hor.
S. i, 3, 73.

[3] *Veneti.*] Mart. *Epigr* xiv, 131, 1.

"Si Veneto Prasinove faves, &c."—
Vide etiam *Suet. Cæs. Aug.* 87 ;—*Calig.*
55.

[4] *credas.*] Vid. *Suet. in Vit. Cæs.*
Aug. 87.

[5] *Volusii.*] "Annales Volusi cacata
charta." *Catull.* 37—20.

Nudæ veritati oleum atque operam spondens, videris tamen ne dum veritati officium prætexas, propriæ gloriolæ inservias. Authores neotericos, per quos profeceris, nequaquam perstringas. Si quid erraverint, omisso nomine rem corripias, nec præclaros viros honorifice hinc inde compelles, ut alibi inculpatam vellices. Et, quamvis[6] nulli gravis est percussus Achilles, antiquis tamen nominibus, et ævi veteris scriptoribus, terram optes faciasque levem.[7] Dandum est ætati ad tam longinqua cæcutienti, clarissimus eorum quisque ―――― nostrum dilatus in ævum[8] detereret sibi multa.

Quod undiquaque sartum tectum est animitus amplectere, de dubiis cunctare, immo rebus reapse aut specie falsis indicto die noli illico renunciare, ne dum ob primævam rerum imperitiam σφάλματα nonnulla, aut ἄτοπα paginis interjecta, veneranda nomina in solidum damnare, aut integris operibus iniquissimum Theta præfigere.

Ut sis acerrimus veritatis hyperaspistes et jaculator optimus, rem tamen, non hostem jugules. Scommata, cavillas,[9] dicteria, longe amoveas, immo salibus urbanis, et intra pomœria natis,[1] parce et invitus indulgeas, nedum genuinum etiam, vel læsus, infigas.

De summa cavea sollicitus non sis, orchestræ et podio studeas. Itaque ut sis parcus in paralogis desi[2] oculis tamen et lippis nota ne congeras; et ut rationum momenta pro numero transigant, quod Achilleum est duntaxat efferas; levicula et notæ minoris reculas summis digitis attingas.

In suspensa rerum veritate, ubi Sibyllæ folia literatores potius quam literati quæritant, videris ne Φοιβάζειν præ te feras. Quicquid libuerit effutire, a fonte relatum Ammonis reputare, leviculi est animi, et in naturæ strophis parum exercitati, sciolisque potius solenne, qui, ut nihil non sapiant, haud aliquid in dubio relinquunt.

Leviculæ fidei historiolas, et quas in re aliena insuper habeas, cave ne in rem tuam tranferas, ne propriæ sententiæ ancillantior tittivillitia asserere quam causa cadere malis.

---

[6] *Quamvis.*] Vid. *Juvenal. Sat.* 1, 163.
[7] *levem.*] Vid. *Mart. Epigr.* Lib. ix, 30, 10, "sit tibi terra levis. . . . . ."
[8] *ævum.*] *Horat.* S. i, 10, 69.

[9] *cavillas.*] Cavilla, MS.
[1] *natis.*] " Et salibus vehemens intra pomœria natis." *Juven. Sat.* 9, 11.
[2] *desi.*] Sic MS. qu. desis si?

Argumenta domi nata mutuatis adjicias, nec analectis, syllabis, collectaneis multum debeas, ne summo improperio pyrata Cilicum audias.

Nec gyris brevioribus rem amplam coerceas; nec ut millesima pagina [3] crescat, prolixo syrmate in re tenui excurras. Quod ut felicius præstes, unilinguis fere sit quam pingis tabella. Ἀλλόφυλα et e dialectis alienis notanda in oram pagellæ transferas, cum ut eruditis orexim expleas, tum ne sciolis fastidio fueris.

Itaque nec verbis humidis et lapsantibus diffluas, nec aciem sententiæ curto sermone stringas. Et ne te Allobroga [4] dicant, qui ad numeros Tullianos tantum saltant, purissimæ sermonis ætatulæ cum primis studeas. Si quæ tamen occurrant vocabula extra classem petita, sensui tamen magis accommoda, ne te stigmaticis annumerent animi liberiores. Ludo critico non ita demisse inservias, ut vel Plautina, Apuleiana, vel domi nata respuas.

Phraseologia modo materiæ non impar, compta an libera perinde erit; sed cum sis Isæo torrentior, ne verborum cataclysmo rem obruas, etiam atque etiam cures; et ne quid liberius excidat, Stradano periculo caveas.

Quod si in hoc opere texendo, (uti vix aliter operandum,) obscura aliquot et spinosa te fatigent, liberè et subinde studia nostra exerceas. Is sanè non sum qui benefacta imputem, aut ea in rationibus et meriti loco numerem, ἐπίλυσιν qualemqualem sub manum remissurus. Opusculo denique ad umbilicum ducto, illimatum, nec virgula censoria notatum, me authore,

Nulla taberna tuum videat neque pila libellum.[5]

Nec hoc officium privatis tantum et continuis in rebus amicorum omissioribus,[6] sed et egregiis et publicæ famæ viris submissè deputandum, qui minus accurate dictis, κρύφια, κρίσιμα, etiam ceraunia affigant, maculasque [7] quas aut incuria fudit,

---

[3] *pagina.*] Vid. *Juv.* 7, 100. "Namq. oblita modi millesima pagina surgit."

[4] *Allobroga.*] "Ciceronem Allobroga dixit." *Juv. Sat.* 7, 214.

[5] *libellum.*] *Hor. Sat.* Lib. i. 4, 71.

"Nulla taberna meos habeat neque pila libellos."

[6] *omissioribus.*] Sic MS. qu. remissioribus?

[7] *maculasque.*] *Horatii Ars Poet.* 352.

aut humana parum cavit natura, omni cura et curatura emendent. Quando denique ingenium, igne literario tentatum, venale destinaveris, summo viro et Mæcenati tuo inscribas. Quo vindice nec Probum timebis;[8] quicquid scripseris, cœlum[9] sit precor. Vale, et quæ nos limpidissimo viro,[1] ingenio pomeridiano, et spirante Austro scripsimus, æqui precor consules ac boni.

THOMAS BROWNE.

[8] *timebis.*] *Mart.* L. iii, 2, 12.— "Illo vindice nec Probum timeto."— Vid. *Sueton. De Illust. Grammat.* 24.

[9] *cœlum.*] Sic MS. qu. cœlatum?
[1] *viro.*] Sic MS. qu. vino?

NAUMACHIA.

[*Description of a Sea-Fight.*[1]]

[MS. SLOAN. 1827, fol. 65—68.]

LABILIS rerum memoria, ætas, tempus, averticula,[2] plurima oblivioni tradunt; parandi itaque mature commentarii, qui tanto malo subveniant. Non qui sententias authorum in loca communia disponant, (quod erit actum agere,) sed a recenti librorum lectione, libero filo schedam exarare, quæ difficilia quæque et notatu digna contineat. Qualia vel author ipse, similium memoria, vel propria Minerva suppeditat. Exemplo sit inter alia, Naumachia ista, a lectione Bayfii,[3] Revii,[4] Schefferi,[5] illico a me depicta.

Peracta lustratione, votis nuncupatis, facto deinde Neptuno, Zephyris, et Tempestatibus, sacrificio, fausta ominante multitudine in littoribus adstante, solvit e portu sub præfectura Cornelii procinctissima Romanorum classis. Sed chelis vix superatis, dum ventos aucuparet et brevia exploraret proreta navarchalis, classem Græcorum, constructissimam sub stolarcho Mentore conspexit.

Aderant e partibus Græcorum inhabilis fere magnitudinis hepteres duæ, hexeres quatuor, triremes, gauli, pistres, hemiolia[6] pentecontori plures, dromonum, myoparonum, hip-

---

[1] *Description, &c.*] "Appears to be a fictitious one, and to have been written for the purpose of exercising himself with the Latin naval terms, from these words: pugnatum est juxta manum, &c." —*Cr.*

[2] *averticula.*] Sic MS. qu. diverticula?

[3] *Bayfii.*] Referring probably to a little work entitled, "*De Re Navali Libellus, in Adolescentulorum bonarum Literarum Studiosorum Favorem, ex Bayfii Vigiliis excerpta, &c.*" 8vo. *Paris. apud*

Franciscum Stephanum, 1537, 12mo.; or to *Lazari Bayfii Annotationes in L. II. de Captivis et Postliminis reversis, in quibus tractatur de Re Navali, Lutetiæ, ex Officina Roberti Stephani,* 1549, 4to.

[4] *Revii.*] This seems the reading of the MS. but I have not been able to find any writer, on naval affairs, of that name.

[5] *Schefferi.*] *Joannis Schefferi, Argentoratensis, de militia Navali Veterum, libri quatuor,* 4to. *Upsal.* 1654.

[6] *hemiolia.*] Sic MS. qu. hemiolæ?

paginum[7] præter acatia, dicrota, et catascopia, ingens numerus.

Classem Romanam magna mole et numero constituerunt quinqueremes, quadriremes, triremes, actuariæ longæ, e sylvis publicis cæsæ lignisque tempestivis fabricatæ, præter onerarias, speculatorias, et liburnas, relicta in naustathmo, navalibus, et textrinis, non levi navium vi.

Classes in propinquo positæ armamenta componunt, vela contrahunt, malos dimittunt, tubicines classicum insonant polemicum, et pæanem multitudo utrinque tollit.

Initio prætoria Romana in Navarchidem Græcam irruit, et Imperator aciem præcedens strenuè cum hoste conflixit. Primo missilibus telis, rutris demum, drepanis, et gladiis res acta est. Romani magnum bello diem imponere satagentes cædibus insistunt, ictus densant, ora mucronibus quærunt. Sed cum virtutem propugnatorum in turribus et catastromatis minus feliciter lacesserent, rostris et chalcembolis impetus in hostem faciendos imperator publico signo indicavit.

Acriter exinde pugnatum est; inter triremes acerrima concertatio. Tarentina in Rhodiam a latere impetum faciens, remos detersit, hypozomata et spondas concussit, encopum quassavit, peritonæum confregit, et thalamitarum versus pessundedit.

Huic extemplo succurrens Græcorum altera, cui parasemon equus, tutela Neptunus erat, magno conatu in prumnam hostilem irruit, pedalium dextrum inter clavum . . . . dimidiavit, parexiresiam concussit, parodum, fores, et hedolia contrivit, omniaque puppis ornamenta cestro aut viriculo facta comminuit, stylum cum tænia, anserculi medium cum aplustre sustulit. Fractisque remis zygitas et thranitas posteriores per columbaria clibanarii confoderunt.

Sed dum illa Romanos male mulctat, occurrit ocyus subpræfectoria Romanorum magnoque impetu. Rostro tridente, et chalcomatis proram hostilem feriens illam inter embolidem et stiram terebravit, parasemon, epotides, tutelam comminuit, stolum cum acrostolio et oculo laxavit, adeo ut epibatæ et classiarii in encopum confugerint, classiarii et milites in puppim se receperint. Sed ictu exitiali aqua per vulnus succe-

---

[7] *hippaginum.*] Sic MS. qu. hippagogarum?

dens, frustra nitentibus antliariis et naupegis triremem præcipitio demersat.

Sed dum utrinque secus dubio Marte certaretur tollenonibus, manibus ferreis, corvis, harpagonibus, etiam maricibus frustra tentatis, Romani missilia ignita, faces ardentes, ollas pice et carbone refertas conjiciunt, quæ in corbitam strategidis impingentes carchesia, trachelum, orloremque omnem usque ad carcheriam concremaverunt. Faciliori incendio tumices omnes, calones, protones, hyperæ, ceruchi, funes chalatorii, et propedes absumpti.

Exinde omnia in confuso esse, quodlibet officii munus a quovis obvio obiri. Harmeneus,[8] celeustes per interscalmia decurrere, classiarii in encelia confugere. Sed irrito conatu. Solis cubistis salus. Ignis enim non tantum statumina corripuit, sed et dryochum combamque ipsam occupavit, virosque omnes tanquam in rogo combussit.

Reliquæ navium incendio perculsæ et de fuga sollicitæ sublatis dolonibus effuse confugerunt. Samiorum tres laceræ, dehiscentes, succinctæ, et fluctibus impares, tumultuoso remigio nec monitis pausarii morigero, venilibus[9] adjutæ ad littus vicinum contendunt.

Nonnullæ φεγγομαχουσαι, crebris ictibus et vento non suo tandem Piræum dilabuntur; ubi natantibus oculis et vultuosè accepti acerbas rerum vices et funesta Neptunalia enunciant.

Romanus, parta victoria, militibus strenuè se gerentibus præmia, ignavis pænas statuit, sequebatur inde cum funibus castigatio, per thalamum trajectio, in aquam immersio, cum saliva et sputis incessatio, manuum præcisio, exilium, in insulam deportatio, mors, ut cujusque αἱαμαχειου demeritum postulavit.

Ducibus perclare se gerentibus collatæ coronæ navales rostratæ, militibus donativum, subsidiales et exteri jure civitatis donati, honesta missione, exemptione a tributis, aut singulari sepulturæ loco accepti.

Decretus Imperatori titulus et triumphus navalis, quem obvium in curru accipiebat senatus. Præcedebant tubicines, fidicines, navium devictarum imagines, spolia navalia, rostra,

[8] *harmeneus*] Sic MS. qu. harmenistes?   [9] *venilibus*.] Sic MS. qu. ventis?

acrostolia plaustris vecta, et captiva pecunia. Rostra navium integra in Campo Martio servata. Erecti denique arcus triumphales et columnæ rostratæ, nec minora honoramenta Cornelio quam olim Duillio a senatu collata.

Captæ Græcorum triremes undecem, flammis absumptæ quatuor, septem fundo datæ. Capta et remulco ducta thalamegus unica deliciis jocisque triumphalibus sub propitio Marte destinata. Spolia ampla et præda non levis præter commeatum nauticum. Denique littus omne exuviis, armamentis, et cadaveribus crepidatis oppletum. Romanorum interierunt triremes quatuor, mutilatæ plures, cæsa volonum pars non exigua; classiariorum manus (præter mediastinos, caculas, et metellos,) passa non ultra cladem Fabianam.

Inchoata acies luna maxima, sole minimo, vento afflatili et Græco, circa horam Græcorum fortissimo funestam, et die quasi ad umbilicum ducto eversa.

Pugnatum est juxta manum Gigantis non longe a Rupe Fæminea et fabuloso mari, ubi Syrius[1] ostentat admirabilem morganam.

Causa hujus belli eadem quæ omnium, nimia felicitas. Gliscentibus opibus crevere animi, unde libido et ardor dominandi: exinde nihil modicum sentire, alienam felicitatem ægris oculis introspicere, irrequieta animo volvere, composita turbare; ne firmiter constent aliena, propria in lubrico statuere; tandemque, (ut in humanis fieri amat,) ne pariant, servire, et quam reverenter fortunam habere, ima experiri.

---

[1] *Syrius.*] Sic MS. qu. Sirius?

DE ASTRAGALO AUT TALO.

[MS. SLOAN, 1827, 69.]

ARISTOT. DE HISTORIA ANIMALIUM LIB. 2, CAP. 1. VERSIONIS
SCALIGERIANÆ.

Quod est pronum, foris; quod est supinum, introrsum spectat: ita ut quæ Coa et felicia dicuntur, intus inter se obversa; quæ Chia et infelicia, foris; quæ Antennæ sive cornua dicuntur, superne.

Quod est pronum, id est pars gibba seu Ternio in Ludo dicta foris versus caudam spectat.

Quod est supinum seu pars cava suppa Quaternio in Ludo Talorum dicta introrsum versus crus anterius spectat.

Ita ut Coa et felicia latera quorum unum auriculam referens et Venus in Ludo dictum et crus compar aspiciens, aliud item Quaternio dictum introrsum inter se obversa sunt.

Item χῖα Chia et in ludo infausta latera quorum unum canis dicitur pars Veneri contraria exterius laterorsum spectans, alterum Ternio seu pars prona versus caudam aspiciens foris, sibimet obversa sunt, sive ut Aristoteles, εἰς ἄλληλα ἐστραμμένα, non enim situ contraria, sed fausta infaustis opposita, felicia felicibus, infelicia infelicibus obversa.

PLAUTUS IN CURCUL. (ii, 3, 79.)

——— "Facit Vulturios quatuor,
Talos abripio, invoco almam meam nutricem Heram,
Jacto basilicum."

Dictum hoc Plautinum de Ludo Talorum composito, sicut de simplici Astragalismo dictum illud Aristotelicum. Lusere primum veteres talo simplici, postea multiplici, numero plerumque quaternario: ubi facierum concordia jactus infaustissimus,

et Vulturius dictus, ubi omnium discordia felicissimus et Ba-
silicus. Facit Vulturios quatuor jactus infelix. Ego Talos
abripio, jacto basilicum, id est omnes dispari facie, itaque omnia vinco, totum depositum tollo.

MARTIALIS, (EPIGR. xiv, 14.)

"Cum [1] steterit nullus vultu tibi talus eodem,
Munera me dices magna dedisse tibi."

Id est, Munusculum hoc est quod tibi e Talis offero, quod
si felicissimus tibi jactus contigerit et omnes tali diverso
vultu tibi in ludo steterint, poterit tibi in lucrum non par-
vum cedere et magni muneris vices explere.

Sed ut omnia de Talo simplici physice aut ludicre dicta melius capias, attente consulas hosce versiculos in tui gratiam a
me compositos; ubi Lusor felicem Astragalismum et faustam
manum precatur;—

Astragalisme fave, non Chi, sed da mihi Kappa,
Non uncum, gibbum, sed suppum, sed sinuosum,
Externas remove facies, monstra interiores.
Da jactu haud facilem dubio fulcimine nixam,
Da quod in horrendo tortè protuberat urso,
Quodque refert mutila et facies monstrosa Caballi,
Aspiciam Conchas, Helicem, pterygomata Lobum,
Auritam et Venerem . . . . quæ nectitur ossi,
Da Cotylam, latum atque ubi tibia sistitur antrum,
Quodque situs primum ludus statuitque secundum,
Cornua nec videam nisi majus cerno supernum,
Non Dorsuosum calcis sub ventre locatum,
Non quod multifidis facie stat dimidiata,
Quodque stat in talo nutans recubansque suillo,
Quodque Canis dictum canibus male competit uncum,
Nec latus ossiculo quod vix annectitur uni.

1 *Cum.*] "Si" in MS.

NONNULLA A LECTIONE ATHENÆI SCRIPTA.

[MS. SLOAN. 1827, f. 71—77.]

UTINAM extaret pars multo minima scriptorum, e quibus egregia, paradoxa, et jucundissime dicta sparsim hinc illinc interserit, et lectori inhianti quasi salivam commovet Athenæus. Quis Parodum matronis legens prcsopolepsiam temporis non incusat? Quis in Antiphanis, Antigoni, Alexidis, aliorumque libris deperditis mitiorem non desideret χρόνου κατάτριψιν? cum ut acutissimam nancisceremur Græcorum indolem, tum ut nudatam spectaremus Latinam corniculam, quæ nunc assumentis Græcis ornata, nullo ævo denudabitur. Quid dicæ super hac re inter Græcos Latinosque apud inferos sit, optime diceret Lucianus, sed cum sic fata volunt, et operum egregiorum non pauca oblivioni debentur, plures optamus Athenæos, plures Græcorum Plinios. Condonamus Homero Mantuano luxuriantem transferendi genium, cui unice debemus oraculum Sibyllinum ; cuperem et plura transtulisset, cum pleraque meliora reddiderit. Utinam vel sub quovis nomine superesset pars aliquotula librorum Aristotelis, quos expes lego relegoque in Catalogo Laertiano ; fertur et vir summus nonnihil in poesin retulisse, quam ego certe poesi Ciceroniana non gravate redimerem.

Omnifariæ lectionis vir Ulpianus cum de singulis vocibus κεῖται ἢ οὐ κεῖται, extarentne an non apud quempiam scriptorum, disquireret, Κειτούκειτος a Dipnosophistis dictus est ; liberrimo improperio et Græcis, quibus nihil est negatum, impune concesso. Idem fere priscæ Latinorum scholæ indultum. Antiquiores enim in componendis fingendisque vocabulis libere Græcissant, quibus voces sensui accommodatissimas proferre

non erat barbare et cum Evandro loqui. Facetissimus Plautus[1] plagipatidas et[2] ferritribaces plaudente Roma dixit; nunc
carceribus Nizolianis inclusum, pecus Latinum, nisi per Mæ-
andros, nihil audet novi, et allophyliam metuens, frigide
περιφράζει. Interim decompositissimos Hegesandri Delphici
versiculos, Lucillianis verbis reddidit criticorum princeps Scaliger; et elegantiorum plerosque etiamnum videas διγλωττίζειν.

Nolim sane ego quempiam in verborum copia, antiqua ve-
nari, nova aut novata decerpere; justo satis discrimine Latinæ
linguæ ætates partimur; sed dum a rebus vocabula superan-
tur, et nemo authorum omnia complectitur, brevissima classi-
cæ Latinitatis epocha frustra claudimur, uniusqne vel scripto-
ris, vel ætatulæ Augustilis, iniqua lege mancipamur. Plurima occurrunt vocabula apud authores extra classem positos,
quæ avidissimos captus explent animique recessus intrant, quorum ego nonnulla amplector in Sidonio, Apuleio, &c. quæ in
maximo oratorum desidero.

Græcæ Latinæque linguæ peritum Laurentium Asteropæ-
um sive ambidextrum dixit Athenæus. Δίγλωττος sane apud
Galenum mirus homo, immo miraculum ἄνθρωπος ἀκριβῶν διαλέ-
κτους δύω. Barbarorum tamen reperiuntur polyglotti plurimi.
Quotilinguis enim Ponti rex, qui viginti dialectis loquacem ma-
sculum exercuit; aut Ægypti regina celebris fluvii sui ostiis
ἰσόγλωσσος. Inter Judæos legas non tantum Ἀττικίζοντα Philonem
et Josephum, sed et septuaginta seniores Græcæ callentissi-
mos necnon ante Imperium Græcorum sacerdotes Hebræos
vaticinium Danielis Alexandro Magno exponentes. Et certe
Græcanicæ linguæ apud Judæum notitiæ imputandum, si quæ,
uti fertur, philosophiæ arcana a Clearcho Judæo perceperit
Stagirites.

Ipsi tamen Græci etiam Romæ Atticissant, quod in Galeno
mirum et Plutarcho, qui, cum res Romanas fuse traderet Latine non magis quam forte philo-Hebraice potuit, cum nisi Punice etiam Philo Biblius, oblivioni deberetur clarissimum San-
choniathonis monumentum.

Interim Romani mire Græcam coluerunt, cum etiam Græciæ
concumberent. Laudandus poetarum facetissimus, quod et

---

[1] *Plautus.*] *Capt.* iii, **1**, 12.   [2] *et.*] *Plaut. Most.* ii, 1, 9.

Punice aliqua dixerit.　Unde de lingua Cananæa Hebrææ
consentanea judicium utinam etiam Herodotus, rerum Egy-
ptiarum callentissimus, inscriptiones et monumenta non tantum
Græce, sed et Ægyptiace protulisset; eo enim adminiculo tria
tantum linguæ Ægyptiacæ vocabula in sacro Codice relicta non
adeo anxie exercuerint polyglottos.

Vereor tamen ne ab authoribus Latinis in transferendis vocabulis non corrumpantur plurima, et instar Anchiali apud
Martialem Orientalium verborum non pauca efferantur.　Quod
etiam Græcis commune; Delio³ natatore interdum indigent
Celticæ et Punicæ apud Dioscoridem nomenclaturæ.　Antiquissimus Chærilus Judæos ita παραφράζει, ut Syros an Arabes velit,
in medio relinquat.　Hellanicus et Græci antiquiores, qui vel
lectura vel tralatione aliqua Ptolemaicam præeunte Hebraica-
rum rerum notitiam habuerunt, ita plerumque verba et voces
transformant, ut notariaco et temula⁴ indigeant, ut non mirum
sane falli potuisse Spartanos in Machabaica ad Judæos
Epistola, ab Abrahamo originem ducentes.

Sit suus polyglossiæ honos; multilinguæ tamen par est, qui
unicam Græcam ἀκριβεῖ.　In simplicitate sermonis ne deficiat
critice non est quod vereantur Grammatici.　Consule in unica
dialecto criticorum principem Galenum, nec non minutientem
in Cratylo Platonem.

Duo supra septuaginta glossemata a συγχύσει Babelis statuunt
eruditi.　Utinam non excurreret iste numerus vel unico in
orbe novo.　Millesima minor ætas gentibus Babelem reddit,
unde majores nobis barbari, futuri etiam nosmetipsi posteris
nostris Scythæ.

Amœnissimus est ille Charmi Syracusani convivandi mos,
ut versiculi et adagia singulis cœnarum ferculis lepide accom-
modata apponantur.　Lepidiora tamen apponi posse non
dubito quam quæ notantur apud Athenæum.　Mimi, moriones,
Gnathones, psaltriæ, tolerabilia sunt, nec ἀπροσδιόνυσα sym-
posiorum ludicra.　Sed prodigiorum convivalium Coryphæum
est illud apud veteres jocosi homicidii genus Ἀγχώνην παίζειν
dum atrocissima ἐπιχαιρεκακίας specie homines ante mensas

---

³ *Delio.*]　Vid. *Epist. Amico Opus*
Arduum meditanti ;—antea, page 290.
⁴ *notariaco et temula.*]　Sic MS.

Rev. J. Mitford happily conjectures,
"notario coetaneo."

ludicre illaqueatos risu et cachinno accipiunt.[5] Mos iste
Thracibus conviviis proprius, Scythicum omne superat. His
ego flammulam et apium risus in postcœnio apponerem ut et
ipsi ridicule plecterentur. Quo etiam sannæ genere dignus
Thracici nominis imperator Nero, cum lugubre Homericum
canens ardentem Romam, quod vultu non audebat, animo
subrisit. His ego sane barbarorum epulis, Plutonias cœnas
aut nocturnas Domitiani dapes antefero.

Lepidissima est illa apud Athenæum de adolescentibus in
pandocheo Agrigentino fabula. Temulenti adeo dementantur,
ut horrenda tempestate jactari et in triremi navigare se cre-
dant. Exonerandæ itaque navis causa, stragula, vasa omnia
foras ejiciunt, magistratus Tritones appellant, objurgantibus
soteria vovent, nec a populo spectante et bona deripiente, ad
sanam mentem redeunt.

Mirum unde totuplici capiti unica delirii facies, ut eandam
puram putam insaniam omnes insanirent. Sed ita stultitias
luunt, qui liberum invitum quatiunt, et a doloso luctatore parum cavent, qui Baccho recto non faciunt, et ἀμυστὶ potantes,
inclusos utribus Euros non cogitant.

Triremis ista Agrigentina mundus est. In quo quotus quisque non desipit. Cui ita cerebrum affabre ab Jove concinnatum est, ut παράκρουσιν aliqualem non prodat. Vanas rerum
species imbibimus, imagunculis enutrimus, serio deliramus;
et, (quod Heraclito dignum,) dementati juvenes helleborum
non ferunt senes. Frustra temulentiam aut vini venenum
causamur, siccos circumagit ἄοινος μέθη et citra vinum ebrietas.
Somnia hominum sunt et somnambulones plurimi,[8] vigilantes
stertunt, apertis oculis peragunt, quæ clausis palpebris sobrii
delirant. Per tempestates, turbellas, et procellosa errorum
sufflamina sic mimus vitæ transagitur, sic in circo rerum de-
curritur, ubi debacchantium instar non sine famæ, fortunæ,
vitæ, dispendio, magno molimine nugas canoras agimus, et
(quod infortunii caput,) ambiguo ævi curriculo, vitæ prius
quam virtutis metam attingimus.

Agonistice dicam: vita nostra curriculum est, ad quod e
carceribus fati sortibus evocati, sive in summa sive in ima
quadriga statuti, funalibus equis male imperamus. Sæpe

5 *accipiunt.*] Vid. *Horat.*

ante delphinos impingimus, raro obeliscum a tergo relinquimus, plerumque ante ova sistitur, vix unquam missus peragitur.

Magna colluvione in theatrum vitæ effundimur, nec inani-
bus spectaculis sufficiunt vomitoria, viæ, διαζώματα, cunei. A
summa cavea ad imam pauci subselliis acquiescunt. Equestria
orchestræ, equestribus popularia se immiscent. Nemo lec-
tium curat, vix quispiam oceanum cogitat. A foraminibus
ad podium omnes eadem fronte ludicra juxta ac sæva aspi-
ciunt, pauci digitum tollunt, plures premunt. Ipsi denique
in arena mortis serias amentiæ vices rependentes, morbis lani-
ati multis telis saucii, nulla missionis spe in spoliarium Ditis
subtrahimur.

NONNULLA,
A LECTIONE ATHENÆI, PLATINÆ, APICII,
DE RE CULINARIA, CONSCRIPTA.

[MS. SLOAN. 1827, fol. 77—81.]

Quibus præter famem condimentis usa sit ætas illa herbivora
et diluvium prægressa, utinam dicerent Columnæ Sethianæ.
Condimentorum Coryphæum negant, qui acetum tollunt. Idque faciunt severiores, qui vinum inventum Noæ tribuunt.
Interim a pomis, palmarum fructibus, uvis, succisque acescen-
tibus fieri vix potuit, quin vel casu acetum innotesceret.
Quin et sicarorum genera aliquot et fructibus, baccis, aut fru-
gibus, quibus incalesceret primæva severitas, olim confecta
fuisse, cui non ignota multifaria Americanorum temeta, quis
neget? ut non sit purum putum a diluvio vitium, sed ex pec-
catis cataclysmum provocantibus etiamsi citra vinum vineale,
ebrietas. Zythi insuper sive vini ex cerealibus confecti extat
apud Ægyptios usus antiquissimus, Osiridi authori adscriptus.
Quod si Osiris non alius quam Mizraim, uti doctissimi conjiciunt, quid ni hoc a Chamo patre traditum nec orbi demerso
incognitum?

Utinam clarius innotescerent antiquorum columina, gara,
oxygara, laserata, oxypora, gusta, succidia, apotherma, et
muriarum genera omnia. Nescio tamen an ὠᾶ τάριχα sturionum,
encrasicholi liquamen, aut murias regales nostras, post se
relinquerent.

Sylvestre quiddam et virus sapiunt pleraque priscorum
condimenta, quæ ligusticum, rutam, fœnugræcum, viride cori-
andrum, immo cuminum, capiunt, ut mihi sane, qui culices
pati rotundos inter equuleos habeo, et cimices redolentia
grana cumini a mensa longe amoveo, stomachum conquassent
lucanica, volvuli, offellæ et olus smaragdinum Apicii, æque

mihi ferenda regis Zeilani mensa, qui patinas assa fœtida con-
fricat, aut simuli moretum cum vel allium spiret.

Famelicæ nomen sortitur apud veteres Zoroastri in deserto
mensa, quæ non nisi melle et caseo constabat. Cum tamen
mel et caseus farcimina Parthica, Numidica, Eleogara, Hypo-
trimmata impleant Apicii ; nec non Cyceonem Homericum, et
celebrem Victoris Attici calicem, pentaploon dictam.

Empedocles equis in Olympico certamine victor, Pythagori-
cus et animalis abstemius, bovem e myrrha, thure, et aromatibus
compactum occurrentibus in conventu distribuit. Huic certe
curricænarum pauci manum porrigerent, qui ventrem, non
nares pascere in delitiis habent.

Isiciis de sepia et loligine quis non prætulerit Bononiensia,
aut minutalibus Apicianis Hispanorum ollas putres! Lentes
et cicerum omne genus Stoicorum dapes, coloni nostri præ-
sepibus damnant. Ab Asphodelo nescio quid magnum spon-
det Hesiodus ; nos inferorum fercula posthabentes, sisaris
batatis vescimur. Struthiones, grues, ciconias, hirundines,
longo apparatu inferunt Platina et Apicius, quas tamen deli-
catuli nostrates ne summis quidem labiis attingerent. Anseris
exta, (quibus olim nepotatum est,) hodie inter plebeia fercula.
Et cum callos aprugnos nullus non ministret December, im-
brices, sumina, et contusa scrofarum ubera canibus aman-
dantur.

Torta de anguillis, ova in veru quis ferret ? ad primam
pontificis Metelli mensam hodiernæ gulæ contremiscerent.
Cristas gallorum, capita psittacorum, ungulas mulorum, quas
nequissimus helluonum apposuit nemo vel famelicus gustaret.
Quid gula insanius ? a centum aviculis unica patella congestis
esurit Æsopus, oleribus et caseo satiatur Epicurus. Adsit
quod orexim leniat, et naturæ satisfaciat ; stulte ultro expectamus quid parturiat porcus Trojanus.*

Pipiones exossatos Apicio laudatos tanquam edentulorum
cibos hodie non moramur. Nobis tergus bovillum cœnæ
caput ; quod et Heroibus Homericis solenne. Hoc post con-
gressum cum Hectore, Ajaci dono misit Agamemnon ; quod
et Menelao Telemachus apposuit. Alcinous etiam delicatis-

---

* A hog roasted with great variety of other flesh in the belly ; so called from
the Trojan horse, which concealed so many men in its cavity.

simæ vitæ vir bubula vescitur; proci itidem et Antinous pede
bovino e mensa rapto Ulyssem adstantem iratus petit. Carnem fere assutam eamque bubulam, pisces vero aut fructus
mensis Heroum inferri nusquam prodidit Homerus; quan-
tumvis mare piscosum dicat, et hortos Alcinoi ampliter cele-
braverit. Nec proci Penelopes petulantes et voluptate dissoluti, piscibus, avibus, aut mellitis vescuntur.

Cerebrum suillum mensis veterum interdictum eoque pari
flagitio vescebantur ac si fabam roderent, omnibusque capiti-
bus, in quibus sensus vigent, abstinebant, cum tamen quidquid
delicatulum est cerebrum Jovis dicerent: interim porcelli
cerebrum cum sale et salvia nostratibus mirum sapit, nec pe-
riodum Hippocratis religiose expectamus, qui ante, senioris
victimæ ætatem porcellos mensis non apponit. Cerebra vola-
tilium ὀλιγύωνα et sicca a struthiocamelo ad passerculum Tur-
conum mensis illata sæpius legimus; piscium vero paucissima,
cum a coctione vix oculos adæquent. Cerebra cuniculorum
nobis in deliciis, medicorum nonnullis minus commendata.
Quod animal εὐκνημίδα et pelle ocreatum ne pro fele imponant,
cauponæ Gallici inferunt, cum tamen dentes et spina impo-
sturam satis prodant. Caput polypi veteres a mensis amovent,
cautela abundante; cum id nemo nostratium attingeret.
Caput jecinoris ejusque pars familiaris et hostilis Aruspeini
non culinarii discriminis est. Illud enim in συκωτῷ seu jecore
ficato non distinguunt ganeones.

Inepta sunt omnia et animo luxurianti et opsoniorum avido
magis quam sensuum delectamento commoda, quæ dicuntur
de Philoxeno, Melanthio, de collo gruino, linguis item et digitis, thecis et elytris coopertis, ut calidissima opsonia prævo-
rent. Frivola item dubio procul, necnon perditissima erat
Apicii cupedia quæ locustas vægrandes et toto orbe quæsitas
maximo pretio comparavit. Edulius siquidem mediocrium
genus et coctu facilius ; sed omnium fatuissima Nicomedis
Bithyniæ regis gula, cui procul a mari dissito, rapam incisam
et culinariter confectam cum oleo, sale, et papaveris nigri
semine, coquus pro pisciculo apposuit.

Bacchum noviter natum nymphæ lavantes vinum aqua tem-
perandum pulchre innuunt. Heroes certe apud Homerum
magna mensura diluunt, et Hector egressurus ad pugnam et

rediens omnino vinum respuit.　Agamemnon gravi improperio
οἰνοβαρὴς ab Achille dictus est.　An vina veterum nostra longe
antecellant in medio relinquimus.　In ætate certe aut potandi
termino non leviter discrepant.　Vinum Falernum apud veteres ab anno decimo quinto usque ad vigesimum potui tempe-
stivum : Albano ab anno decimo vigor, Surrentinum post viges-
simum quintum incipit esse πότιμον.　Horatii pia testa consule
Manlio sibimet connata longe annosior.　Jam vini veteris apud
nos nomen sortitur triennale.　Oleum etiam Ulyssei canis
ætatem dimidians antiquum audit.　Interim pharmaca quædam medicorum oleum vetus centum annorum postulant.
Quod an alibi quam in sepulcris antiquorum reperiatur, vide-
rint pharmacopœi.

　　Nectar et ambrosia laudatissimæ deorum dapes quid sint, e
cœlo delapsus nondum edidit Vulcanus.　Nectar divinum
Homerus pater potulentum quid describit, esculentum diserte
asserit Alcman cum Alexandride, sed cum ambrosiam melle
novies dulciorem dicat Ibycus apud Athenæum, habeant suam
sibi Glyceram cælestes gulæ, Chiam malo ficum.

AMICO CLARISSIMO, DE ENECANTE GARRULO SUO.

[MS. SLOAN. 1827, fol. 83-86.]

QUINTO me foramine* distendit, et acerbissimo equuleo torquet glossogastor ille tuus, Ligurinus† et viæ sacræ Ardelio,‡ qui me secessus quæritantem, fabellis, nugaculis, et importunis verborum tricis enecat, nec dormiturienti parcens, semisomnem Cadmo tradit.§

Cruento verborum tædio diem ad umbilicum duco, lunas insomnes ago, naso vigilanti frustra sterto. Citius silebit Luna quam lunaticus iste; quem nisi Caduceo demulserit aut piscem fecerit Mercurius, exspes somnum cogito.

Frustra a te struuntur mensæ, temere advocantur convivæ; ubi ciceris iste ac nucis emptor cœnitat, Transtiberinus ambulator aut aliquis de ponte negabit. Emortualem umbram quam tuam minus fugiunt, etiam qui umbram decempedam colunt. Domicœnium[1] famelici quam hujus ineptias malunt; et nisi huic in cœna obstrepenti, modimperator insiliat, incœnati aufugient, etiam qui domi salem lingunt.

In scena rerum novitius trita pro novis venditat. Quibus effutiendis terram cælo miscet, Araxi Tiberim, Ligeri Tagum maritat. Ut ganniendi ansam arripiat de cometis, diluviis, terræ motibus gaudet, ostenta, prodigia, τερατίσματα[2] quæ deprecantur alii, ipse gratulanter aspicit. Quæ si defecerint, fabulonum avias, menalogorum liras effundit. Aut quid sibi

---

* The utmost stretch or rack, in the old *equuleus*, or tormenting engine, was at the fifth hole. Vide *Magium de Equuleo*.

† The great prater in Martial, of whom the Epigram.

‡ See *Horace*, Sat ix, " Ibam forte via sacra."

§ Cadmus, the hangman in Juvenal, " dejicere e saxo cives et tradere Cadmo."

[1] *Domicœnium.*] Vide *Martial* 12, lxxvii, 6.   [2] τερατίσματα.] Sic MS. qu. τερατεύματα?

vagienti olim acciderit, quid heri in somniis viderit importunè obtrudens, figuligerulus et famigerator effutilis astantibus febrem facit.

Quod numero dicendum est, amplo fasce complectitur, nunquam nisi fodiam latus de tribus capellis dicturus: dum horam diei sciscito, si ad clepsydram dimidiam sileat, pro Laconismo reputo; si forte de ætate quærito, vitæ annales exaudio; ubi ut trivialia acciderint, longo syrmate diducens, languente tandem sole, tædio me confossum et ranam Seriphiam³ dimittit.

'Εχεμυθίαν, et taciturnitatem Pythagoricam, rabiosa silentia et ægroti somnia reputat. Harpocrati laqueum mandat, ante aras gannit, et sibimet ipsi Siren, etiam surdis canit. Fustibus ogganiendum est, si voles obmutescat, quo solo argumento habet.

Phonasco indiget λαρυγγίζων iste et Gradivus Homericus, qui mihi assidue intonat: Cui ego vocem nigram, fuscam, Neronianam imprecor, ut vel Ulysseo commento evadam, aut molliori fato cedam.

Nescit nugivendulus linguulaca καχλάζων et littore loquacior quantos loquatur lapides,⁴ dum me multiloquio captat, nec quas comica facie tragœdias agat, dum renidente ore jugulat.

Vappæ verborum splendidam suspendens complacendi hederam amici specie jugi sermone diffluit. Interim ruris plenus et inficetiarum, insulso verborum stromate, salibus paganis et extra pomæria natis, bilem mihi ac stomachum commovet homunculus iste palmo et sago dignus, necnon sudore quasi Anglico me perfundit.

Nec mihi tantum crux. Solitudinem in circo facit μαψιδάκας iste, et Alpha blateratorum, quo cornicante præsto elabitur quicquid uspiam est bucconum: Tibicines, Ascaules, næniatrices, et quæ laboranti lunæ acclamant, fuga sibi consulunt.

Nec lingua tantum, sed et calamo furit Ardelio iste, loquax scribaxque eadem vi. Cujus mihi nugas legere, nedum exigere libet, quare dum eas oscitanter percurro, semper ἐσχατο-

---

³ *Seriphiam.*] Vid. *Plin. Histor. Natural.* 8, 68.

⁴ *lapides.*] Vid. *Plaut. Aulul.* 2, 1, 30, "lapides loqueris."

κωλικὸν specto, sæpius interjungo. Quantumlibet enim chartæ speciem exaret, me opisthographis, et in aversa scriptis male mulctat. Nec chartæ sinu satiatus oram plagulæ replet, campum hinc inde et inane spatium sulcat. Nec semper integro vocum ductu, sed et notulis minutis scriptitat. A quorum omnium fastidio flamma et ferro unice me expedio: atque ita codicillorum tyrannidem et Cassiani martyrium * effugio.

Nec tantum missilibus nugis, tricisque epistolicis, sed et schedarum cumulis serâ coronide metuendis, (quod a locuteleis fieri amat,) amicorum optimos lacessit. Hujus autem ego ossa potius quam scripta legerem, quæ veratro [5] ebria, nulloque Apolline concinnata, Attalicis conditionibus non evolverem; illa itaque aut cloacinæ devoveo aut circum, tonstrinas, turbamque si quam habet Pompeius, vel Agenoris puella otiosiorem,[6] ablego.

Serò miselli illicet exaudiunt, qui huic bombylio aures mancipant, dictum enim dicere potius quam sermoni colophonem statuere satagens nunquam ita verborum decoctor est ut conturbet, nonunquam ita prodigus ut proterviam faciat nihilque dicendum relinquat. Invisentibus itaque de plebe amiculis,[7] utramque auriculam nequiter flagellat; obvios quosque devorato pudore fabulamentis atterit, nec nisi elumbes et varicosos dubio sole dimittit. Nec tantum vitrea fracta, sed et venena loquitur Niger iste et rimosissimus Ardelio, dúm (quod linguacibus solenne est,) susurro nequissimus, et in aurem garrulus, convitia hinc inde serit, lites nectit, arcana eliminat, quibus mutiendis amicos una ac diem lacerat. Luscis invideat, qui reculas amicorum tam acute inspicit, ut suas inepte pervideat; nec semet ipsum concutiens aliena resupinet.

Si quis commento Pythagorico locus, hunc ego cuculum exuentem hominem subiisse, nec tamen humano indumento vocalem posuisse characterem autumo. In cicadam denuo diis iratis migraturus; ut in deviis fritinniens arbusta potius quam

---

* Sanctus Cassianus, qui codicillis et stylis discipulorum confossus et contusus interiit.

[5] *veratro.*] Vid. *Persii,* 1, 51.—"non hic est Ilias Actî Ebria veratro."   *Martialis Epigr.* lib. ii, 1. 10.

[6] *turbamque si quam habet, &c.*] Vid.   Turbam non habet. otiosiorem Pompeius, vel Agenoris puella.

auriculas humanas rumpat. Ex eo forte numero, qui in
utero materno ante ortum vagiunt, qui in somniis ganniunt,
Anginosi strepunt, nullo Gorgone obmutescunt. In custodi-
endis Capitoliis omnibus certe anseribus potior. Quo presente
nemo in excubiis, nedum in contuberniis dormitat. Spartam,
non Anticyram me authore religandus, ut vel polymythiam
Laconismo commutet, aut flagris ante aras cæsus fortem taciturnitatem ediscat.

Dimissis manibus et grandi gradu frustra hunc effugio, quem
ludis vix evaserit. Huc aliquis incitatum Achilles sane aut
sub Delphino natus sit oportet, cui spem fuga fecerit. Sed
chiragra ferocius manum mihi corripiens, vinculis quasi Vulca-
niis fugam mihi sistit, quam dum anhelanter tento, dum chla-
myde excussa mercari satago, deridiculo sum et astantibus
scenam præsto.

Totus itaque in fermento Scythicam solitudinem expeto,
beatos ad Catadupas Nili natos prædico, et surdos in cœlis
statuo. Latibula misellus quærito, ad tenebras confugio; solem tamen citius quam Aturopum huncce lateo. Nisi me
nube involutum subduxerit dea quæpiam Homerica, illico ad
plures propero.

Desperabundus itaque, fractus, ilia ducens, et ut ipsa me
salvet salus, nullo thure litaturus, temere ᾿Αλεξίκακον invoco,
frustra cœlum peto, quæ me liberabit Innocentia aut Mica
Aurea? * Ursis, tigribus, elephantis, ultro nec auctoratus
adsto, arenas insuper habeo, qui in unico Ardelione tot peril-
los reperio.

Sed glandium satis. Importunum hunc abige, aut postico
falle. Ocyus Norvicum advola, ubi te opperiuntur animæ
candidæ juxta ac literatæ. Quare si sapias, viam vorabis.
Vale !

THOMAS BROWNE.

---

* Alluding unto the two bears, which Constantius, the Emperor, kept; the one
named Innocentia, the other Mica Aurea; which he purposely kept, to set upon
such as displeased him, as Ammianus Marcellinus recordeth; whereby I might be
delivered from the tediousness of this prater.

[AN ACCOUNT OF BIRDS FOUND IN NORFOLK.]

[MS. SLOAN. 1830, fol. 5—22; & 31.]

I WILLINGLY obey your command; in setting down such birds, fishes, and other animals, which for many years I have observed in Norfolk.

Besides the ordinary birds, which keep constantly in the country, many are discoverable, both in winter and summer, which are of a migrant nature, and exchange their seats according to the season. Those which come in the spring, coming for the most part from the southward; those which come in the autumn or winter, from the northward; so that they are observed to come in great flocks, with a north-east wind, and to depart with a south-west: nor to come only in flocks of one kind, but teal, woodcocks, fieldfares, thrushes, and small birds, to come and light together; for the most part some hawks and birds of prey attending them.

The great and noble kind of eagle, called *aquila Gesneri*,[1] I have not seen in this country; but one I met with in this country, brought from Ireland, which I kept two years, feeding with whelps, cats, rats, and the like; in all that while not giving it any water; which I afterward presented unto my worthy friend Dr. Scarburgh.

Of other sorts of eagles, there are several kinds, especially of the *halyætus* or fen eagles; some of three yards and a quarter from the extremity of the wings;[2] whereof one being taken alive, grew so tame, that it went about the yard feeding on fish, red herrings, flesh, and any offals, without the least trouble.

[1] *aquila Gesneri.*] *Falco chrysætos*, the golden eagle; the largest of the genus, known to breed in the mountainous parts of Ireland.

[2] *some, &c.*] *Haliætus nisus,—falco ossifragus*, Lin. The sea eagle. Few specimens, however, measure more than seven or eight feet from the extremities of the wings.

A specimen of *F. fulvus*, the ring-tailed eagle, has been caught at Cromer. —G.

There is also a lesser sort of eagle, called an osprey,[3] which hovers about the fens and broads, and will dip his claw, and take up a fish, ofttimes; for which his foot is made of an extraordinary roughness, for the better fastening and holding of it; and the like they will do unto coots.

Aldrovandus takes particular notice of the great number of kites[4] about London and about the Thames. We are not without them here, though not in such numbers. Here are also the grey[5] and bald[6] buzzard; of all which the great number of broad-waters and warrens make no small number, and more than in woodland counties.

Cranes are often seen here in hard winters, especially about the champian and fieldy part. It seems they have been more plentiful; for, in a bill of fare, when the mayor entertained the Duke of Norfolk, I met with cranes in a dish.[7]

In hard winters, elks,[8] a kind of wild swan, are seen in no small number; in whom, and not in common swans, is remarkable that strange recurvation of the wind pipe through the sternon—and the same is also observable in cranes.[9] It is probable they come very far; for all the northern discoverers have observed them in the remotest parts; and like divers and other northern birds, if the winter be mild, they commonly come no farther southward than Scotland; if very hard, they go lower, and seek more southern places; which is the cause that, sometimes, we see them not before Christmas or the hardest time of winter.

A white large and strong-billed fowl, called a ganet,[1] which seems to be the greater sort of *larus;* whereof I met with one killed by a greyhound, near Swaffham; another in Marshland, while it fought, and would not be forced to take wing: another entangled in a herring-net, which, taken alive, was fed with herrings for a while. It may be named *larus*

---

[3] *osprey.*] *Falco haliætus*, Lin. The osprey. Sometimes met with near Cromer.—*G.*

[4] *kites.*] F. *milvus.* L.

[5] *grey.*] Probably F. *buteo.*

[6] *bald.*] The bald buzzard is a name usually given to the osprey. Dr. Browne, however, having just spoken of the osprey, must here refer to some other species—perhaps F. *æruginosus.*

[7] *dish.*] Cranes are no longer met with in this country.

[8] *elks.*] Elk; one of the popular names given to the wild swan, A. *cygnus.*

[9] *cranes.*] Willoughby.

[1] *ganet.*] *Pelecanus bassanus*, L.

major, leucophæopterus; as being white and the top of the wings brown.

In hard winters I have also met with that large and strong-billed fowl, which Clusius describeth by the name of *skua Hoyeri,*[2] sent him from the Faro Islands, by Hoierus, a physician; one whereof was shot at Hickling, while two thereof were feeding upon a dead horse.

As also that large and strong-billed fowl, spotted like a starling, which Clusius nameth *mergus major Farrensis,*[3] as frequenting the Faro Islands, seated above Shetland; one whereof I sent unto my worthy friend Dr. Scarburgh.

Here is also the *pica marina,*[4] or sea-pie.

Many sorts of *lari,* sea-mews, and cobs. The *larus major,*[5] in great abundance, in herring time, about Yarmouth.

Larus alba[6] or pewits, in such plenty, about Horsey, that they sometimes bring them in carts to Norwich, and sell them at small rates; and the country people make use of their eggs in puddings, and otherwise, great plenty thereof have bred about Scoulton Meers, and from thence sent to London.

Larus cinereus,[7] greater and smaller, but a coarse meat, commonly called sterns.

Hirundo marina[8] or sea-swallow, a neat white and forked-tail bird; but much longer than a swallow.

The *ciconia* or stork, I have seen in the fens; and some have been shot in the marshes between this and Yarmouth.

The platea or shovelard,[9] which build upon the tops of high trees. They have formerly built in the Hernery, at Claxton

[2] *skua Hoyeri.*] *Larus catarractes,* L. *Lestris catarractes,* Temm. *Skua gull,* Latham, Pennant, and Bewick.

[3] *mergus major Farrensis.*] Doctor Browne's description leaves little doubt that he refers to *colymbus glacialis,* L. the great northern diver; though his synonym is not correctly given. It is called by Clusius, *colymbus maximus ferroensis, seu arcticus;*—by Willoughby, *mergus maximus faroensis.*

[4] *pica marina.*] *Hæmatopus ostralegus,* L. The oyster-catcher.

[5] *larus major.*] This name was given long after, by Catesby, to *L. atricilla,* L. Dr. Browne, quoting from memory, may probably refer to *L. fuscus,* L. *L. cinereus maximus,* Will. The wagel gull.

[6] *larus alba.*] *Larus ridibundus,* L. The pewit gull.

[7] *larus cinereus.*] It seems not very easy to determine the species here referred to:—certainly not the "greater and lesser" terns, *sterna hirundo* and *minuta,* the former of which is certainly the bird next mentioned; and neither of which is called the stern, which is *sterna fissipes.* He may refer to *S. minuta* and *fissipes;* or possibly, but not so probably, to *L. cinerarius* and *canus,* L. the red-legged and common gulls, *L. cinereus major* and *minor* of Aldrovandus.

[8] *hirundo marina.*] *Sterna hirundo,* L.

[9] *shovelard.*] *Platalea leucorodia,* L. Spoonbill.

and Reedham; now at Trimley, in Suffolk. They come in March, and are shot by fowlers, not for their meat, but the handsomeness of the same; remarkable in their white colour, copped crown, and spoon or spatule-like bill.

Corvus marinus,[1] Cormorants; building at Reedham, upon trees, from whence King Charles the First was wont to be supplied. Beside the rock cormorant,[2] which breedeth in the rocks, in northern countries, and cometh to us in the winter, somewhat differing from the other in largeness and whiteness, under the wings.

A sea-fowl called a sherewater,[3] somewhat billed like a cormorant, but much lesser; a strong and fierce fowl, hovering about ships when they cleanse their fish. Two were kept six weeks, cramming them with fish which they would not feed on of themselves. The seamen told me they had kept them three weeks without meat; and I, giving over to feed them, found they lived sixteen days without taking anything.

Bernacles, brants, *(branta)*[4] are common.

Sheldrakes. *Sheledracus Jonstoni.*

Barganders, a noble-coloured fowl *(vulpanser)*[5] which herd in coney-burrows about Norrold and other places.

Wild geese. *Anser ferus.*[6]

Scotch goose. *Anser scoticus.*

Goosander. *Merganser.*[7]

Mergus acutirostris speciosus or loon, a handsome and specious fowl, cristated,[8] and with divided fin feet placed very backward, and after the manner of all such which the Dutch call *arsvoote.* They have a peculiar formation in the leg bone, which hath a long and sharp process extending above the thigh bone. They come about April, and breed in the broadwaters; so making their nest on the water, that their eggs are seldom dry while they are set on.

[1] *corvus marinus.*] *Pelecanus carbo,* L. The cormorant.

[2] *rock cormorant.*] Probably the crested cormorant, thought to be but a variety of the preceding.

[3] *sherewater.*] *Procellaria puffinus,* L. The shearwater.

[4] *branta.*] *Anas erythropus* and *bernicla,* L. The bernacle and brent goose.

[5] *vulpanser.*] *Anas tadorna,* L.

Vulpanser, Gesner and Aldrov. Sheldrake or burrow duck. "Barganders," the name given this species by Dr. Browne, may possibly be a corruption of *burrow-ganders.*

[6] *anser ferus.*] *Anas anser ferus,* L. the grey lag or grey leg.

[7] *merganser.*] *Mergus merganser,* L.

[8] *cristated.*] *Podiceps cristatus,* Lath. *Colymbus,* L.

Mergus acutirostris cinereus,[9] which seemeth to be a difference of the former.

Mergus minor,[1] the smaller divers or dab-chicks, in rivers and broad waters.

Mergus serratus,[2] the saw-billed diver, bigger and longer than a duck, distinguished from other divers by a notable saw-bill, to retain its slippery prey, as living much upon eels, whereof we have seldom failed to find some in their bellies.

Divers other sorts of dive-fowl; more remarkable the *mustela fusca*,[3] and *mustela variegata*,[4] the grey dun, and the variegated or party-coloured weasel, so called from the resemblance it beareth unto a weasel in the head.

Many sorts of wild ducks which pass under names well-known unto fowlers, though of no great signification, as smee, widgeon, arts, ankers, noblets:—

The most remarkable are, *anas platyrhinchos*[5] a remarkably broad-billed duck.

And the sea-pheasant,[6] holding some resemblance unto that bird in some feathers in the tail.

Teals, *querquedula*,[7] wherein scarce any place more abounding. The condition of the country, and the very many decoys, especially between Norwich and the sea, making this place very much to abound in wild fowl.

Fulicæ cottæ,[8] coots, in very great flocks upon the broad waters. Upon the appearance of a kite or buzzard, I have seen them unite from all parts of the shore, in strange numbers; when, if the kite stoops near them, they will fling up, and spread such a flash of water with their wings, that they will endanger the kite, and so keep him off again and again in open opposition; and a handsome provision they make about their nest against the same bird of prey, by bending and

---

[9] *mergus acutirostris cinereus.*] *Podiceps urinator,* Lath.

[1] *mergus minor.*] *Podiceps minor,* Ib.

[2] *mergus serratus.*] Probably *mergus serrator,* L.

[3] *mustela fusca.*] *Mergus castor,* L. The dun diver?

[4] *mustela variegata.*] Probably *mergus albellus,* L. The smew; which Gesner calls *M. mustelaris.*

[5] *platyrhinchos.*] *A. clypeata,* L. The Shoveller.

[6] *sea-pheasant.*] *A. acuta,* L. The pintail duck. Sometimes taken in the Hempstead decoy.—*G.*

[7] *querquedula.*] *A. crecca,* L. *Querquedula* of Gesner. Aldrovandus and Ray scarcely distinguished the *teal* from the *gargany, A. querquedula,* L.

[8] *fulicæ cottæ.*] *F. atra,* L. The coot.

twining the rushes and reeds so about them, that they cannot stoop at their young ones, or the dam while she sitteth.

Gallinula aquatica,[9] moor hen, and a kind of *ralla aquatica,*[1] or water rail.

An *onocrotalus,* or pelican, shot upon Horsey Fen, May 22, 1663, which, stuffed and cleansed, I yet retain. It was three yards and a half between the extremities of the wings; the chowle and beak answering the usual description; the extremities of the wings for a span deep brown; the rest of the body white; a fowl which none could remember upon this coast. About the same time I heard one of the king's pelicans was lost at St. James's;[2] perhaps this might be the same.

Anas arctica Clusii,[3] which though he placeth about the Faro islands, is the same we call a puffin, common about Anglesea, in Wales, and sometimes taken upon our seas, not sufficiently described by the name of *puffinus;* the bill being so remarkably differing from other ducks, and not horizontally, but meridionally, formed, to feed in the clefts of the rocks, of insects, shell-fish, and others.

The great number of rivers, rivulets, and plashes of water makes herns and herneries to abound in these parts; young herns being esteemed a festival dish, and much desired by some palates.

The *ardea stellaris, botaurus,* or bitour, is also common, and esteemed the better dish. In the belly of one I found a frog in a hard frost at Christmas. Another, kept in a garden two years, feeding it with fish, mice, and frogs; in defect whereof, making a scrape[4] for sparrows, and small birds, the bitour made shift to maintain herself upon them.

Bistardœ, or bustards, are not unfrequent in the champian and fieldy part of this country. A large bird, accounted a dainty dish, observable in the strength of the breast-bone and short heel. Lays an egg much larger than a turkey.

---

[9] *gallinula aquatica.*] The moor hen is *gallinula chloropus,* Lath. *(fulica,* L.*)*
[1] *ralla aquatica.*] *Rallus aquaticus,* L. *G. aquatica,* of some authors.
[2] *St. James's.*] But for this information, the pelican might probably have been added to our *Fauna* on the authority of Dr. Browne.—See *Bray's Evelyn,* i, 373.
[3] *anas arctica Clusii.*] *Alca arctica,* L.
[4] *scrape.*] A scrape, or *scrap,* is a term used in Norfolk, for a quantity of chaff, mixed with grain, frequently laid as a decoy to attract small birds, for the purpose of shooting or netting them.

Morinellus,[5] or dotterell, about Thetford, and the champian, which comes unto us in September and March, staying not long, and is an excellent dish.

There is also a sea dotterell somewhat less but better coloured than the former.

Godwyts; taken chiefly in marshland; though other parts are not without them; accounted the daintiest dish in England; and, I think, for the bigness, of the biggest price.

Gnats, or knots,[6] a small bird, which, taken with nets, grow excessively fat, being mewed and fed with corn. A candle lighted in the room, they feed day and night; and when they are at their height of fatness, they begin to grow lame, and are then killed, as at their prime, and apt to decline.

Erythropus, or red-shank;[7] a bird common in the marshes, and of common food, but no dainty dish.

A may chit,[8] a small dark grey bird, little bigger than a stint, of fatness beyond any. It comes in May into Marshland and other parts, and abides not above a month or six weeks.

Stints [9] in great number about the sea shore and marshes, about Stiffkey, Burnham, and other parts.

Another small bird, somewhat larger than a stint, called a *churr*,[1] and is commonly taken among them.

Pluvialis, or plover,[2] green and grey, in great plenty about Thetford, and many other heaths. They breed not with us, but in some parts of Scotland, and plentifully in Iceland.

The lapwing or *vanellus*,[3] common over all the heaths.

Cuckoos of two sorts; the one far exceeding the other in bigness.[4] Some have attempted to keep them in warm rooms all the winter, but it hath not succeeded. In their migration they range very far northward; for in the summer they are to be found as high as Iceland.

Avis pugnans;[5] ruffe; a marsh bird of the greatest variety of colours, every one therein somewhat varying from other.

[5] *morinellus.*] *Charadrius morinellus*, L.

[6] *knots.*] *Tringa canutus*, L.

[7] *red-shank.*] *Scolopax calidris*, L.

[8] *a may chit.*] Probably one of the genus *tringa*.

[9] *stints.*] *Tringa cinclus.*

[1] *churr.*] Or *purre?*

[2] *plover.*] *Charadrius pluvialis*, L.

[3] *vanellus.*] *Tringa vanellus*, L.

[4] *bigness.*] Differing only in age or sex.

[5] *avis pugnans.*] *Tringa pugnax.* L.

The female is called a reeve, without any ruff about the neck, lesser than the other, and hardly to be got. They are almost all cocks, and, put together, fight and destroy each other; and prepare themselves to fight like cocks, though they seem to have no other offensive part but the bill. They lose their ruffs about the autumn, or beginning of winter, as we have observed, keeping them in a garden from May till the next spring. They most abound in Marshland, but are also in good number in the marshes between Norwich and Yarmouth.

Of *picus martius*,[6] or wookspeck, many kinds. The green, the red,[7] the *leucomelanus*,[8] or neatly marked black and white, and the *cinereus*[9] or dun-coloured little bird, called a nut-hack. Remarkable, in the larger, are the hardness of the bill and skull, and the long nerves which tend unto the tongue, whereby it shooteth out the tongue above an inch out of the mouth, and so licks up insects. They make the holes in trees without any consideration of the winds or quarters of heaven; but as the rottenness thereof best affordeth convenience.

Black heron.[1] Black on the sides, the bottom of the neck, with white grey on the outside, spotted all along with black on the inside. A black coppe of small feathers some a span long; bill pointed and yellow, three inches long; back, heron-coloured, intermixed with long white feathers; the strong feathers black; the breast black and white, most black; the legs and feet not green, but an ordinary dark cock colour.

The number of rivulets, becks, and streams, whose banks are beset with willows and alders, which give occasion of easier fishing and stooping to the water, makes that handsome-coloured bird abound, which is called *alcedo ispida*, or the king-fisher. They build in holes about gravel-pits, wherein is to be found a great quantity of small fish-bones; and lay very handsome round and, as it were, polished eggs.

---

[6] *picus martius.*] The black wood-pecker, extremely rare in this country. "*Habitat vix in Anglia,*" says Linnæus.

[7] *red.*] Probably *P. major*, L.

[8] *leucomelanus.*] *P. minor*, L.

[9] *cinereus.*] *Sitta Europea*, Lin. Nut-hatch.

[1] *black heron.*] No British species appears to correspond so nearly with Dr. Browne's description as *Ardea Purpurea*.

An hobby-bird;[2] so called because it comes either with, or a little before, the hobbies, in the spring. Of the bigness of a thrush, coloured and paned like a hawk; marvellously subject to the vertigo, and are sometimes taken in those fits.

Upupa, or hoopebird, so named from its note; a gallant marked bird, which I have often seen, and it is not hard to shoot them.

Ringlestones,[3] a small white and black bird, like a wagtail, and seems to be some kind of *motacilla marina*, common about Yarmouth sands. They lay their eggs in the sand and shingle, about June, and, as the Eringo diggers tell me, not set them flat, but upright, like eggs in salt.

The *arcuata*[4] or curlew, frequent about the sea-coast.

There is also a handsome tall bird, remarkably eyed, and with a bill not above two inches long, commonly called a stone curlew;[5] but the note thereof more resembleth that of a green plover, and breeds about Thetford, about the stone and shingle of the rivers.

Avoseta called [a] shoeing-horn, a tall black and white bird, with a bill semicircularly reclining or bowed upward; so that it is not easy to conceive how it can feed; answerable unto the *avoseta Ibalorum*, in Aldrovandus, a summer marshbird, and not unfrequent in Marshland.

A yarwhelp,[6] so thought to be named from its note, a grey bird intermingled with some whitish yellowish feathers, somewhat long-legged, and the bill about an inch and a half; esteemed a dainty dish.

Loxias[7] or *curvirostra*, a bird a little bigger than a thrush, of fine colours and pretty note, differently from other birds, the upper and lower bill crossing each other; of a very tame nature; comes about the beginning of summer. I have known them kept in cages; but not to outlive the winter.

---

[2] *hobby-bird.*] Surely this may be *yunx torquilla*, L. the wryneck; the singular motion of its head and neck was probably attributed to vertigo.

[3] *ringlestones.*] *Charadrius hiaticula*, L. The ring dotterel. Plentiful near Blakeney.—*G.*

[4] *arcuata.*] *Scolopax arquata*, L.

[5] *curlew.*] *Charadrius œdicnemus*, L. The great or Norfolk plover, or thick-kneed bustard.

[6] *yarwhelp.*] *Scolopax Ægocephala*, L. is called the yarwhelp:—but the bill is four inches long.

[7] *loxias.*] The crossbill. *Loxia curvirostra*, L.

A kind of *coccothraustes*,[8] called a coble-bird, bigger than a thrush, finely coloured and shaped like a bunting. It is chiefly seen in summer, about cherry-time.

A small bird of prey, called a birdcatcher, about the big-ness of a thrush, and linnet-coloured, with a longish white bill, and sharp; of a very fierce and wild nature, though kept in a cage, and fed with flesh;—a kind of *lanius*.

A dorhawk[9] or kind of *accipiter muscarius*, conceived to have its name from feeding upon flies and beetles; of a wood-cock colour, but paned like a hawk; a very little pointed bill; large throat; breedeth with us; and lays a marvellous hand-some spotted egg. Though I have opened many, I could never find any thing considerable in their maws. *Caprimulgus.*

Avis trogloditica[1] or chock, a small bird, mixed of black and white, and breeding in coney-burrows; whereof the war-rens are full from April to September; at which time they leave the country. They are taken with an hobby and a net; and are a very good dish.

Spermalegous rooks, which, by reason of the great quantity of corn-fields and rook groves, are in great plenty. The young ones are commonly eaten; sometimes sold in Norwich market, and many are killed for their livers, in order to the cure of the rickets.

Crows, as every where; and also the *corvus variegatus*,[2] or pied crow, with dun aud black interchangeable. They come in the winter, and depart in the summer; and seem to be the same which Clusius describeth in the Faro Islands, from whence perhaps these come. I have seen them very common in Ireland; but not known in many parts of England.

Corvus major; ravens; in good plenty about the city; which makes so few kites to be seen hereabout. They build in woods very early, and lay eggs in February.

Among the many *monedulas* or jackdaws, I could never in these parts observe the *pyrrhocorax* or Cornish chough, with

[8] *coccothraustes.*] *Loxia coccothraus-tes,* L. The grossbeak.

[9] *dorhawk.*] *Caprimulgus Europæus,* L. The goat-sucker.

[1] *avis trogloditica.*] By the term *avis trogloditica,* Dr. Browne probably in-tended a kind of wren. He refers very possibly to the wheatear, *Motacilla œnanthe,* L.

[2] *corvus variegatus.*] *Corvus cornix,* L. The hooded crow.

red legs and bill, to be commonly seen in Cornwall; and, though there be here very great store of partridges, yet the French red-legged partridge is not to be met with.[3] The *ralla* or rail, we have counted a dainty dish; as also no small number of quails. The heathpoult,[4] common in the north, is unknown here, as also the grouse; though I have heard some have been seen about Lynn. The calandrier or great-crested lark, *(galerita)* I have not met with here,[5] though with three other sorts of larks;—the ground-lark, wood-lark, and tit-lark.

Stares or starlings, in great numbers. Most remarkable in their numerous flocks, which I have observed about the autumn, when they roost at night in the marshes, in safe places, upon reeds and alders; which to observe, I went to the marshes about sunset; where standing by their usual place of resort, I observed very many flocks flying from all quarters, which, in less than an hour's space, came all in, and settled in innumerable numbers in a small compass.

Great variety of finches and other small birds, whereof one very small, called a whin-bird, marked with fine yellow spots, and lesser than a wren. There is also a small bird, called a chipper, somewhat resembling the former, which comes in the spring, and feeds upon the first buddings of birches and other early trees.

A kind of *anthus*, goldfinch, or fool's coat, commonly called a draw-water, finely marked with red and yellow, and a white bill, which they take with trap-cages, in Norwich gardens, and, fastening a chain about them, tied to a box of water, it makes a shift, with bill and leg, to draw up the water in to it from the little pot, hanging by the chain about a foot below.

On the 14th of May, 1664, a very rare bird was sent me, killed about Crostwick, which seemed to be some kind of jay. The bill was black, strong, and bigger than a jay's; somewhat yellow claws, tipped black; three before and one claw behind. The whole bird not so big as a jay.

---

[3] *French, &c.*] Our Norfolk sportsmen can bear witness that this species is now to be found in various parts of the county.

[4] *heathpoult.*] Or black grouse.

[5] *here.*] Nor any one else, in England, if he refers to *alauda cristata*, which is the *A. sylvestris galerita* of Frisch.

The head, neck, and throat, of a violet colour; the back and upper parts of the wing, of a russet yellow; the fore part of the wing, azure; succeeded downward by a greenish blue; then on the flying feathers, bright blue; the lower parts of the wing outwardly, of a brown; inwardly, of a merry blue; the belly, a light faint blue; the back, toward the tail, of a purple blue; the tail, eleven feathers of a greenish colour; the extremities of the outward feathers thereof, white with an eye of green.—*Garrulus argentoratensis.*[6]

[6] *garrulus argentoratensis.*] *Coracias garrula,* L. The roller.

[AN ACCOUNT OF FISHES, ETC. FOUND IN NORFOLK AND ON THE COAST.]

[MS. SLOAN. 1830, fol. 23—30, & 32—38; & 1882,[1] fol. 145, 6.]

IT may well seem no easy matter to give any considerable account of fishes and animals of the sea; wherein, 't is said, that there are things creeping innumerable, both small and great beasts, because they live in an element wherein they are not so easily discoverable. Notwithstanding, probable it is that after this long navigation, search of the ocean, bays, creaks, estuaries, and rivers, that there is scarce any fish but hath been seen by some man; for the large and breathing sort thereof do sometimes discover themselves above water, and the other are in such numbers that at one time or other they are discovered and taken, even the most barbarous nations being much addicted to fishing; and in America and the new discovered world the people were well acquainted with fishes of sea and rivers, and the fishes thereof have been since described by industrious writers. Pliny seems too short in the estimate of their number in the ocean, who reckons up but one hundred and seventy-six species; but the seas being now farther known and searched, Bellonius much enlargeth; and in his book of birds thus delivereth himself:—" Although I think it impossible to reduce the same unto a certain number, yet I may freely say, that 't is beyond the power of man to find out more than five hundred species of fishes, three

---

[1] 1882.] The first paragraph of this paper I met with in 1882 MS. SLOAN. preceded by the words " *I willingly obey your co . . . . .* " which were left unfinished, and struck through with the pen. The author probably at one time intended the account of fishes, &c., to be distinct from that of birds, and wrote this as an introductory paragraph. I have therefore so preserved it; though both subjects are mentioned in the first paragraph of the tract on birds.

hundred sorts of birds, more than three hundred sorts of four-footed animals, and forty diversities of serpents."[2]

Of fishes sometimes the larger sort are taken or come ashore. A spermaceti whale, of sixty-two feet long, near Wells; another of the same kind, twenty years before, at Hunstanton; and, not far off, eight or nine came ashore, and two had young ones after they were forsaken by the water.[3]

A grampus, above sixteen feet long, taken at Yarmouth, four years ago.[4]

The *Tursio,* or porpoise,[5] is common. The dolphin[6] more rare, though sometimes taken, which many confound with the porpoise; but it hath a more waved line along the skin; sharper toward the tail; the head longer, and nose more extended; which maketh good the figure of Rondeletius; the flesh more red, and, well cooked, of very good taste to most palates, and exceedeth that of porpoise.

The *vitulus marinus,*[7] sea-calf, or seal, which is often taken sleeping on the shore. Five years ago, one was shot in the river of Norwich, about Surlingham Ferry, having continued in the river for divers months before. Being an amphibious animal, it may be carried about alive, and kept long if it can be brought to feed. Some have been kept for many months in ponds. The pizzell, the bladder, the *cartilago ensiformis,* the figure of the throttle, the clustered and racemose form of the kidneys, the flat and compressed heart, are remark-

[2] *serpents.*] Naturalists now enumerate 800 species of beasts; and at least 50,000 of insects.—*Gray.*

[3] *sometimes, &c.*] A whale, 58 feet long, was cast ashore at Overstrand, in the spring of 1822 (I think); and another went spouting past Cromer, in the autumn of the same year.

Towards the end of 1829, a whale, only 24 feet long, was cast ashore and killed at Runton. He was of the *Balæna* division, with a whale-bone mouth, and no teeth; and, as far as I could make out, I think it was one of the *boops balæna* species—as the man who made the capture told me, the nose was very sharp pointed—but it was much hacked before I saw it. I found the extreme width of the tail was 3 feet 11 inches. It was dark, nearly black on the back, and white be-

low in folds. There were two spout-holes close together, in the middle of the head. Almost an inch and half thickness of blubber; and the oil which has been made from it is remarkably fine. The *whale-bone fringe* in its mouth was nearly white: the length of the jaw-bones, 3 feet 7 inches. It did not look tempting enough to make me bring any of the meat away; but at Northrepps hall, a steak was cooked, and tasted like tender beef.—*G.*

[4] *grampus, &c.*] Oct. 1827, the fishermen saw a fish which they called a grampus.—*G.*

[5] *tursio or porpoise.*] *Delphinus phocæna,* L.

[6] *dolphin.*] *D. Delphis,* L.

[7] *vitulus marinus.*] *Phoca vitulina,* L.

able in it. In stomachs of all that I have opened, I have found many worms.

I have also observed a *scolopendra cetacea* of about ten [inches] long, answering the figure in Rondeletius, which the mariners told me was taken in these seas.

A *pristis serra*,[8] or saw-fish, taken about Lynn, commonly mistaken for a sword-fish, and answers the figure in Rondeletius.

A sword-fish, (*iphias*, or *gladius*,[9]) entangled in the herring-nets at Yarmouth, agreeable unto the *icon* in Johnstonus, with a smooth sword, not unlike the *gladius* of Rondeletius, about a yard and a half long; no teeth; eyes very remarkable; enclosed in a hard cartilaginous covercle, about the bigness of a good apple; the vitreous humour plentiful; the chrystalline larger than a nutmeg, remaining clear, sweet, and untainted, when the rest of the eye was under a deep corruption, which we kept clear and limpid many months, until an hard frost split it, and manifested the foliations thereof.

It is not unusual to take several sorts of *canis*, or dog-fish, great and small, which pursue the shoal of herrings and other fish; but this year [1662] one was taken entangled in the herring-nets, about nine feet in length, answering the last figure of Johnstonus, lib. 7, under the name of *canis carcharias alter*; and was, by the teeth and five gills, one kind of shark, particularly remarkable in the vastness of the optic nerves and three conical hard pillars, which supported the extraordinary elevated nose, which we have reserved with the skull. The seamen called this kind, a scrape.

Sturio, or sturgeon, so common on the other side of the sea, about the mouth of the Elbe, come seldom into our creeks, though some have been taken at Yarmouth, and more in the great Ouse, by Lynn; but their heads not so sharp as represented in the *icons* of Rondeletius and Johnstonus.

Sometimes we meet with a *mola*, or moon-fish,[1] so called from some resemblance it hath of a crescent in the extreme part of the body from one fin unto another. One being ta-

[8] *pristis serra*.] *Squalus pristis*, L.
[9] *iphias or gladius*.] *Xiphias gladius*, L.

[1] *mola, or moon-fish*.] *Tetraodon mola*, L. Sun-fish.

ken near the shore at Yarmouth, before break of day, seemed to shiver, and grunt like a hog, as authors deliver of it. The flesh being hard and nervous, it is not like to afford a good dish; but from the liver, which is large, white, and tender, somewhat may be expected. The gills of these fish we found thick beset with a kind of sea-louse. In the year 1667, a *mola* was taken at Monsley, which weighed 200 pounds.

The *rana piscatrix*, or frog-fish,[2] is sometimes found in a very large magnitude, and we have taken the care to have them cleaned and stuffed, wherein we observed all the appendices whereby they catch fishes, but much larger than are described in the *icons* of Johnstonus, lib. xi, fig. 8.

The sea-wolf,[3] or *lupus nostras*, of Schoneveldus, remarkable for its spotted skin and notable teeth,—*incisores*, dog-teeth and grinders. The dog-teeth, both in the jaws and palates, scarce answerable by any fish of that bulk, for the like disposure, strength, and solidity.

Mustela Marina;[4] called by some a weazel ling, which, salted and dried, becomes a good Lenten dish.

A lump, or *lumpus anglorum;*[5] so named by Aldrovandus, by some esteemed a festival-dish, though it affordeth but a glutinous jelly, and the skin is beset with stony knobs, after no certain order. Ours most answereth the first figure in the 13th table of Johnstonus, but seems more round and arcuated than that figure makes it.

Before the herrings, there commonly cometh a fish, about a foot long, by fishermen called a horse, resembling, in all points the *trachurus*[6] of Rondeletius, of a mixed shape, between a mackerel and a herring; observable from its green eyes, rarely sky-coloured back, after it is kept a day, and an oblique bony line running on the outside from the gills unto the tail: a dry and hard dish, but makes a handsome picture.

The *rubelliones*, or rochets, but thinly met with on this coast. The *gornart cuculus*, or *lycæ species*,[7] more often;

[2] *frog-fish.*] *Lophius piscatorius,* L.
[3] *sea-wolf.*] *Anarhichas lupus,* L.
[4] *mustela marina.*] Perhaps *gadus mustela,* L. or *petromyzon marinus,* L. The lamprey.
[5] *lumpus anglorum.*] *Cyclopterus lum-*

pus, L. The lump-fish, or lump-sucker.
[6] *trachurus.*] *Scomber Trachurus,* L. The scad or horse mackerel: caught with the mackerel.—*G.*
[7] *lycæ species.*] *Trigla cuculus,* L. The red gurnard.

which they seldom eat, but bending the back and spreading the fins into a large posture, do hang them up in their houses.

Beside the common *mullus*, or mullet,[8] there is another not unfrequent, which some call a cunny-fish, but rather a red mullet,[9] of a flosculous red, and somewhat rough on the scales, answering the description and *icon* of Rondeletius, under the name of *mullus ruber asper;* but not the taste of the usually-known mullet, as affording but a dry and lean bit.

Several sorts of fishes there are which do or may bear the names of sea-woodcocks; as the *acus major, scolopax,* and *saurus*.[1] The *saurus* we sometimes meet with young. Rondeletius confesseth it a very rare fish, somewhat resembling the *acus* or needle-fish before, and mackerel behind. We have kept one dried many years ago.

The *acus major*,[2] called by some a garfish, and greenback, answering the figure of Rondeletius, under the name of *acus prima species*, remarkable for its quadrangular figure, and verdigrease-green backbone.

A *scolopax*[3] or sea woodcock, of Rondeletius, was given me by a seaman of these seas. About three inches long, and seems to be one kind of *acus* or needle-fish, answering the description of Rondeletius.

The *acus* of Aristotle,[4] lesser, thinner, corticated, and sexangular; by divers called an addercock, and somewhat resembling a snake; ours more plainly finned than Rondeletius describeth it.

A little corticated fish, about three or four inches long, answering that which is named *piscis octangularis*, by Wormius; *cataphractus*, by Schoneveldeus. *Octagonius versus caput; versus caudam hexagonius*.[5]

The *faber marinus*,[6] sometimes found very large, answering the figure of Rondeletius, which though he mentioneth as a

---

[8] *mullet.*] *Mugil cephalus*, L.
[9] *red mullet.*] *Mullus barbatus*, L. Sur-mullet. Sometimes caught at Cromer.—*G.*
[1] *saurus.*] *Esox sanrus*, L. ?
[2] *acus major.*] *Syngnathus acus*, L. Needle-fish.

[3] *scolopax.*] *Centriscus scolopax*, L.
[4] *acus of Aristotle.*] *Syngathus typhle*, L. ?
[5] *hexagonius.*] Possibly a gurnard, *trigla cataphracta*, L.
[6] *faber marinus.*] *Zeus faber*, L. John Dorée or Dory.

rare fish, and to be found in the Atlantic and Gaditane
ocean, yet we often meet with it in these seas, commonly
called a peter-fish, having one black spot on either side the
body; conceived the perpetual signature, from the impression
of St. Peter's fingers, or to resemble the two pieces of money
which St. Peter took out of this fish; remarkable also from
its disproportionable mouth, and many hard prickles about
other parts.

A kind of *scorpius marinus;* [7] a rough, prickly, and monstrous headed fish, six, eight, or twelve inches long, answerable unto the figure of Schoneveldeus.

A sting-fish, wiver, or kind of opthidion,[8] or araneus; slender; narrow-headed; about four inches long, with a sharp,
small, prickly fin along the back, which often venemously
pricketh the hands of fishermen.

Aphia cebites marina, or a sea-loche.

Belennus; a sea miller's thumb.

Funduli marini; sea gudgeons.

Alosæ, or chads; [9] to be met with about Lynn.

Spirinches, or smelt,[1] in great plenty about Lynn; but
where they have also a small fish, called a priame, answering
in taste and shape a smelt, and perhaps are but the younger
sort thereof.

Aselli, or cod, of several sorts.—*Asellus albus,* or whitings,[2]
in great plenty.—*Asellus niger, carbonarius,* or coal-fish.[3]—
Asellus minor Schoneveldei (callarias Plinii), or haddocks; [4]
with many more. Also a weed-fish, somewhat like a had-
dock, but larger, and drier meat. A basse,[5] also much resembling a flatter kind of cod.

Scombri are mackerel; in great plenty. A dish much
desired; but if, as Rondeletius affirmeth, they feed upon sea-
stars and squalders, there may be some doubt whether their
flesh be without some ill quality. Sometimes they are of a
very large size; and one was taken this year, 1668, which

---

[7] *scorpius marinus.*] *Cottus scorpio,* L. Father Lasher?

[8] *opthidion.*] Probably *trachinus draco,* L. The sting-bull or common weaver.

[9] *chads.*] *Clupea alosa,* L. Shad.

[1] *smelt.*] *Salmo eperianus,* L. Smelt.

[2] *whitings.*] *Gadus merlangus,* L.

[3] *coal-fish.*] *G. carbonarius,* L.

[4] *haddocks.*] *G. æglesinus,* L.

[5] *basse.*] *Perca labrax,* L.

was by measure an ell long; and of the length of a good salmon, at Lowestoft.

Herrings departed, sprats, or *sardæ*, not long after succeed in great plenty, which are taken with smaller nets, and smoked and dried like herrings, become a sapid bit, and vendible abroad.

Among these are found bleak, or *blicæ*,[6] a thin herring-like fish, which some will also take to be young herrings. And though this sea aboundeth not with pilchards, yet they are commonly taken among herrings; but few esteem thereof, or eat them.

Congers are not so common on these coasts as in many seas about England; but are often found upon the north coast of Norfolk, and in frosty weather left in pulks and plashes upon the ebb of the sea.

The sand eels *(Anglones* of Aldrovandus, or *Tobianus* of Schoneveldeus) commonly called smoulds,[7] taken out of the sea-sands with forks and rakes about Blakeney and Burnham: a small round slender fish, about three or four inches long, as big as a small tobacco-pipe; a very dainty dish.

Pungilius marinus, or sea-bansticle, having a prickle on each side. The smallest fish of the sea, about an inch long, sometimes drawn ashore with nets, together with weeds and fragments of the sea.

Many sorts of flat-fishes. The *pastinaca oxyrinchus,* with a long and strong aculeus in the tail, conceived of special venom and virtues.

Several sorts of *raias* (skates), and thornbacks. The *raia clavata oxyrinchus; raia oculata, aspera, spinosa, fallonica.*

The great rhombus, or turbot,[8] *aculeatus et levis.*

The *passer,* or place.

Butts, of various kinds.

The *passer squamosus;* bret, bretcock, and skulls; comparable in taste and delicacy unto the sole.

---

[6] *blicæ.*] *Cyprinus alburnus,* L. Bleak.

[7] *smoulds.*] *Ammodytes tobianus,* L. Sand launce.

[8] *turbot.*] In *MS. Sloan.* 1784, I find this distich, with the subsequent explanatory notes attached:—

Of wry-mouth'd fish! give me the left side black,[*]
Except the sole,[†] which hath the noblest smack.

[*] *As turbot, bret, bret-cock, skulls.*
[†] *Which is black on the right side; as also butts, sandaps, and flounders.*

The *buglossus solea,* or sole, *plana et oculata;* as also the *lingula,* or small sole; all in very great plenty.

Sometimes a fish about half a yard long, like a butt or sole, called *asprage,* which I have known taken about Cromer.

Sepia, or cuttle-fish, and great plenty of the bone or shelly substance, which sustaineth the whole bulk of that soft fish found commonly on the shore.

The *loligo sleve,* or *calamar,*[9] found often upon the shore, from head to tail sometimes about an ell long, remarkable for its parrot-like bill ; the *gladiolus* or *celanus* along the back, and the notable crystalline of the eye, which equalleth, if not exceedeth, the lustre of oriental pearl.

A polypus, another kind of the mollia, sometimes we have met with.

Lobsters in great number, about Sherringham and Cromer, from whence all the country is supplied.

Astacus marinus pediculi marini facie, found also in that place.   With the advantage of the long fore claws about four inches long.

Crabs, large and well-tasted ; found also on the same coast.

Another kind of crab, taken for *canis fluvialis;* little, slender, and of a very quick motion, found in the river running through Yarmouth, and in Bliburgh river.

Oysters exceeding large about Burnham and Hunstanton, like those of Pool, St. Mallows, or Civita Vecchia, whereof many are eaten raw ; the shells being broken with cleavers ; the greater part pickled, and sent weekly to London and other parts.

Mituli, or muscles, in great quantity, as also chams or cockles, about Stifkay and the north-west coast.

Pectines pectunculi varii, or scallops of the lesser sort.

Turbines, or smaller wilks, *leves, striati,* as also *trochi, trochili,* or sea tops, finely variegated and pearly.   Likewise *purpuræ minores, nerites, cochleæ, tellinæ.*

---

[9] *loligo, &c.*] In digging for soles and shrimps, I have taken numbers of little *sepiæ,* an inch or two in length, in July and August, and have seen others (I believe of the species *loligo*), about twelve or eighteen inches long in the *sleeve* or *trunk,* in the autumn ; *Cromer.—G.*

Lepades, patellæ : limpets, of an univalve shell, wherein an animal like a snail cleaving fast unto the rocks.

Solenes, " cappe lunge" *Venetorum;* commonly a razor-fish; the shell thereof *dentalia,* by some called pin-patches, because the pin-meat thereof is taken out with a pin or needle.

Cancellus turbinum et neritis. Bernard the hermit of Rondeletius. A kind of crab, or *astacus;* living in a forsaken wilk or *nerites.*

Echinus Echinometrites, sea hedgehog, whose neat shells are common on the shore. The fish alive often taken by the drags among the oysters.

Balani, a smaller sort of univalve growing commonly in clusters. The smaller kinds thereof to be found ofttimes upon oysters, wilks, and lobsters.

Concha anatifera, or *ansifera,* or barnacle-shell, whereof about four years past were found upon the shore no small number by Yarmouth, hanging by slender strings of a kind of *alga* unto several splinters or cleavings of fir-boards, unto which they were severally fastened, and hanged like ropes of onions ; their shell flat, and of a peculiar form, differing from other shells; this being of four divisions ; containing a small imperfect animal, at the lower part divided into many shoots or streams, which prepossessed spectators' fancy to be the rudiment of the tail of some goose or duck to be produced from it. Some whereof in the shell, and some taken out and spread upon paper, we still keep by us.

Stellæ marinæ, or sea-stars, in great plenty, especially about Yarmouth. Whether they be bred out of the urticus, squalders, or sea-jellies, as many report, we cannot confirm ; but the squalders in the middle seem to have some lines or first draughts not unlike. Our stars exceed not five points, though I have heard that some with more have been found about Hunstanton and Burnham ; where are also found *stellæ marinæ testaceæ,* or handsome crusted and brittle sea-stars, much less.

The *pediculus* and *culex marinus,* the sea louse and fly, are also no strangers.

Physsalus Rondeletii, or *eruca marina physsaloides,* ac-

cording to the *icon* of Rondeletius, of very orient green and
purple bristles.

Urtica marina of divers kinds ; some whereof called squalders.   Of a burning and stinging quality, if rubbed in the
hand.   The water thereof may afford a good cosmetic.

Another very elegant sort there is often found cast up by
shore in great numbers, about the bigness of a button, clear
and welted, and may be called *fibula marina crystallina*.

Hirudines marini, or sea-leeches.

Vermes marini, very large worms, digged a yard deep out
of the sands at ebb, for bait.   It is known where they are to
be found by a little flat over them, on the surface of the
sand.   As also *vermes in tubulis testacei.*   Also *tethya,* or
sea-dogs; some whereof resemble fritters.   The *vesicaria
marina* also, and *fanago,* sometimes very large; conceived to
proceed from some testaceous animals, and particularly from
the *purpura* ; but ours more probably from other testaceous,
we have not met with any large *purpura* upon this coast.

Many river fishes also and animals.   Salmon no common
fish in our rivers, though many are taken in the Ouse ; in the
Bure or North river; in the Waveney or South river; in the
Norwich river but seldom, and in the winter.   But four years
ago fifteen were taken at Trowse mill, at Christmas, whose
mouths were stuck with small worms or horseleaches, no bigger than fine threads.   Some of these I kept in water three
months.   If a few drops of blood were put to the water, they
would in a little time look red.   They sensibly grew bigger
than I first found them, and were killed by a hard frost freezing the water.   Most of our salmon have a recurved piece of
flesh in the end of the lower jaw, which, when they shut
their mouths, deeply enters the upper, as Scaliger hath noted
in some.

The rivers, lakes, and broads, abound in the *lucius* or
pikes of a very large size, where also is found the *brama* or
bream, large and well tasted.   The *tinca* or tench ; the *au-
lecula,* roach; as also rowds and dare or dace ; *perca* or perch,
great and small; whereof such as are taken in Breydon, on
this side Yarmouth, in the mixed water, make a dish very
dainty ; and, I think, scarce to be bettered in England.   But

the blea, the chubbe, the barble, to be found in divers other
rivers in England I have not observed in these.   As also fewer
minows than in many other rivers.

The *trutta* or trout; the *gammarus* or crawfish; but scarce
in our rivers; but frequently taken in the Bure or North river,
and in the several branches thereof.   And very remarkable
large crawfishes to be found in the river which runs by Castle-
acre and Nerford.

The *aspredo perca minor*, and probably the *cernua* of Cardan, commonly called a ruff; in great plenty in Norwich
river, and even in the stream of the city; which though Camden appropriates unto this city, yet they are also found in the
rivers of Oxford and Cambridge.

Lampetra, lampreys, great and small, found plentifully in
Norwich river, and even in the city, about May; whereof
some are very large; and, well cooked, are counted a dainty
bit collared up, but especially in pies.

Mustela fluviatilis or eel-poult, to be had in Norwich river,
and between it and Yarmouth, as also in the rivers of Marshland; resembling an eel and a cod; a very good dish; and the
liver whereof well answers the commendations of the ancients.

Gudgeons or *funduli fluviatiles;* many whereof may be
taken within the river in the city.

Capitones fluviatiles or millers' thumb; *pungitias fluviatilis*
or stanticles.   *Aphia cobites fluviatilis* or loches.   In Norwich river, in the runs about Heveningham Heath, in the
North river and streams thereof.

Of eels, the common eel, and the glot, which hath somewhat a different shape in the bigness of the head, and is affirmed to have young ones often found within it; and we
have found an *uterus* in the same, somewhat answering the
icon thereof in Senesinus.

Carpiones, carp; plentiful in ponds, and sometimes large
ones in broads.   Two of the largest I ever beheld were taken
in Norwich river.

Though the woods and drylands abound with adders and
vipers, yet are there few snakes about our rivers or meadows;
more to be found in Marshland.   But ponds and plashes
abound in lizards or swifts.

The *gryllotalpa* or fen cricket, common in fenny places; but we have met with them also in dry places, dunghills, and churchyards, of this city.

Besides horseleaches and periwinkles, in plashes and standing waters, we have met with *vermes setacei* or hard worms; but could never convert horsehairs into them by laying them in water. As also the great *hydrocantharus* or black shining water-beetle, the *forficula, squilla, corculum,* and *notonecton,* that swimmeth on its back.

Camden reports that in former time there have been beavers in the river of Cardigan in Wales. This we are too sure of, that the rivers, great broads, and carrs, afford great store of otters with us; a great destroyer of fish, as feeding but from the vent downwards; not free from being a prey itself; for their young ones have been found in buzzards' nests. They are accounted no bad dish by many; are to be made very tame; and in some houses have served for turnspits.

ON THE OSTRICH.[1]

[MS. SLOAN. 1830, fol. 10, 11; 1847.]

THE Ostrich hath a compounded name in Greek and Latin—
Struthio-Camelus, borrowed from a bird and a beast, as being
a feathered and biped animal, yet in some ways like a camel;
somewhat in the long neck; somewhat in the foot; and, as some
imagine, from a camel-like position in the part of generation.

It is accounted the largest and tallest of any winged and
feathered fowl; taller than the gruen or cassowary. This
ostrich, though a female, was about seven feet high, and some
of the males were higher, either exceeding or answerable unto
the stature of the great porter unto King Charles the First.
The weight was a[2]   in grocer's scales.

Whosoever shall compare or consider together the ostrich
and the tomineio, or humbird, not weighing twelve grains,
may easily discover under what compass or latitude the creation of birds hath been ordained.

The head is not large, but little in proportion to the whole
body. And, therefore, Julius Scaliger, when he mentioned
birds of large heads (comparatively unto their bodies), named
the sparrow, the owl, and the woodpecker; and, reckoning up
birds of small heads, instanceth in the hen, the peacock, and
the ostrich.*

The head is looked upon by discerning spectators to resemble that of a goose rather than any kind of σρούθος, or
passer: and so may be more properly called *cheno-camelus,*
or *ansero-camelus.*

There is a handsome figure of an ostrich in Mr. Willoughby's and Ray's *Ornithologia:* another in Aldrovandus

---

* See Scaliger's *Exercitations.*

[1] ON THE OSTRICH.] This was drawn
up for his son Edward, to be delivered in
the course of his lectures. It occurs in
the middle of the paper on Birds; but

evidently was inserted by mistake in the
binding; it is written on larger paper.
[2] *a* . . . . .] Utterly undecypherable
in the original.

and Jonstonus, and Bellonius; but the heads not exactly agree-
ing. "Rostrum habet exiguum, sed acutum," saith Jonstoun;
"un long bec et poinctu," saith Bellonius; men describing
such as they have an opportunity to see, and perhaps some
the ostriches of very distant countries, wherein, as in some
other birds, there may be some variety.

In Africa, where some eat elephants, it is no wonder that
some also feed upon ostriches. They flay them with their
feathers on, which they sell, and eat the flesh. But Galen
and physicians have condemned that flesh, as hard and indigestible.[3] The Emperor Heliogabalus had a fancy for the
brains, when he brought six hundred ostriches' heads to one
supper, only for the brains' sake; yet Leo Africanus saith that
he ate of young ostriches among the Numidians with a good
gust; and, perhaps, boiled, and well cooked, after the art of
Apicius, with peppermint, dates, and other good things, they
might go down with some stomachs.

I do not find that the strongest eagles, or best-spirited
hawks, will offer at these birds; yet, if there were such gyr-
falcons as Julius Scaliger saith the Duke of Savoy and Henry,
king of Navarre, had, it is like they would strike at them, and,
making at the head, would spoil them, or so disable them,
that they might be taken.*

If these had been brought over in June, it is, perhaps,
likely we might have met with eggs in some of their bellies,
whereof they lay very many; but they are the worst of eggs
for food, yet serviceable unto many other uses in their country; for, being cut transversely, they serve for drinking cups
and skull-caps; and, as I have seen, there are large circles of
them, and some painted and gilded, which hang up in Turkish
mosques, and also in Greek churches. They are preserved
with us for rarities; and, as they come to be common, some
use will be found of them in physic, even as of other egg-
shells and other such substances.

* See Scaliger's *Exercitations*, and in his *Comment.* on *Arist. De Historia Animal.*

[3] *as hard and indigestible.*] " And, therefore, when, according to Lampridius, the Emperor Heliogabalus forced the Jews to eat ostriches, it was a meat not only hard of digestion to their stomachs, but also to their consciences, as being a for-bidden meat food."—*Addition from MS. Sloan.* 1847.

When it first came into my garden, it soon ate up all the gilliflowers, tulip-leaves, and fed greedily upon what was green, as lettuce, endive, sorrell; it would feed on oats, barley, peas, beans; swallow onions; eat sheeps' lights and livers. Then you mention what you know more.[4]

When it took down a large onion, it stuck awhile in the gullet, and did not descend directly, but wound backward behind the neck; whereby I might perceive that the gullet turned much; but this is not peculiar unto the ostrich; but the same hath been observed in the stork, when it swallows down frogs and pretty big bits.

It made sometimes a strange noise; had a very odd note, especially in the morning, and, perhaps, when hungry.

According to Aldrovandus, some hold that there is an antipathy between it and a horse, which an ostrich will not endure to see or be near; but, while I kept it, I could not confirm this opinion; which might, perhaps, be raised because a common way of hunting and taking them is by swift horses.

It is much that Cardanus should be mistaken with a great part of men, that the coloured and dyed feathers of ostriches were natural; as red, blue, yellow, and green; whereas, the natural colours in this bird were white and greyish. Of [the] fashion of wearing feathers in battles or wars by men, and women, see Scaliger, *Contra Cardan. Exercitat.* 220.

If wearing of feather-fans should come up again, it might much increase the trade of plumage from Barbary. Bellonius saith he saw two hundred skins with the feathers on in one shop of Alexandria.

---

[4] *Then you mention, &c.*] This must be considered as spoken " aside " to his son.

BOULIMIA CENTENARIA.[1]

[MS. SLOAN. 1833, & MS. RAWL. LVIII.]

THERE is a woman now living in Yarmouth, named Elizabeth Michell, an hundred and two years old; a person of four feet and half high, very lean, very poor, and living in a mean room with pitiful accommodation. She had a son after she was past fifty.[2] Though she answers well enough unto ordinary questions, yet she apprehends her eldest daughter to be her mother; but what is most remarkable concerning her is a kind of *boulimia* or dog-appetite; she greedily eating day and night what her allowance, friends, or charitable persons afford her, drinking beer or water, and making little distinction or refusal of any food, either of broths, flesh, fish, apples, pears, and any coarse food, which she eateth in no small quantity, in so much that the overseers for the poor have of late been fain to augment her weekly allowance. She sleeps indifferently well, till hunger awakes her; then she must have no ordinary supply, whether in the day or night. She vomits not, nor is very laxative. This is the oldest example of the *sal esurinum chymicorum,* which I have taken notice of; though I am ready to afford my charity unto her, yet I should be loth to spend a piece of ambergris I have upon her, and to allow six grains to every dose till I found some effect in moderating her appetite; though that be esteemed a great specific in her condition.

---

[1] BOULIMIA.] Brutus was attacked with this disease on his march to Durrachium.—*Plutarch.*

[2] *She had a son, &c.*] A duplicate copy of this paper in the Bodleian (*MS. Rawl.* lviii,) reads "her youngest son is forty-five years old."

UPON THE DARK THICK MIST HAPPENING
ON THE 27TH OF NOVEMBER, 1674.

[MS. SLOAN. 1833, fol. 136.]

THOUGH it be not strange to see frequent mists, clouds, and rains, in England, as many ancient describers of this country have noted, yet I could not [but] take notice of a very great mist which happened upon the 27th of the last November, and from thence have taken this occasion to propose something of mists, clouds, and rains, unto your candid considerations.

Herein mists may well deserve the first place, as being, if not the first in nature, yet the first meteor mentioned in Scripture and soon after the creation, for it is said, Genesis ii, that " God had not yet caused it to rain upon the earth, but a mist went up from the earth, and watered the whole face of the ground," for it might take a longer time for the elevation of vapours sufficient to make a congregation of clouds able to afford any store of showers and rain in so early days of the world.

Thick vapours, not ascending high but hanging about the earth and covering the surface of it, are commonly called mists; if they ascend high they are termed clouds. They remain upon the earth till they either fall down or are attenuated, rarified, and scattered.

The great mist was not only observable about London, but in remote parts of England, and as we hear, in Holland, so that it was of larger extent than mists are commonly apprehended to be ; most men conceiving that they reach not much beyond the places where they behold them. Mists make an obscure air but they beget not darkness, for the atoms and particles thereof admit the light, but if the matter thereof be very thick, close, and condensed, the mist grows considerably obscure and like a cloud, so the miraculous and palpable darkness of Egypt is conceived to have been effected by an extraordinary dense and dark mist or a kind of cloud spread over the land of Egypt, and also miraculously restrained from the neighbour land of Goshen.

Mists and fogs, containing commonly vegetable spirits, when they dissolve and return upon the earth, may fecundate and add some fertility unto it, but they may be more unwholesome in great cities then in country habitations; for they consist of vapours not only elevated from simple watery and humid places, but also the exhalations of draughts, common sewers, and fœtid places, and decoctions used by unwholesome and sordid manufactures: and also hindering the sea-coal smoke from ascending and passing away, it is conjoined with the mist and drawn in by the breath, all which may produce bad effects, inquinate the blood, and produce catarrhs and coughs. Sereins, well known in hot countries, cause headache, toothache, and swelled faces, but they seem to have their original from subtle, invisible, nitrous, and piercing exhalations, caused by a strong heat of the sun, which falling after sun-set produce the effects mentioned.

There may be also subterraneous mists, when heat in the bowels of the earth, working upon humid parts, makes an attenuation thereof and consequently nebulous bodies in the cavities of it.

There is a kind of a continued mist in the bodies of animals, especially in the cavous parts, as may be observed in bodies opened presently after death, and some think that in sleep there is a kind of mist in the brain; and upon exceeding motion some animals cast out a mist about them.

When the cuttle fish, polypus, or loligo, make themselves invisible by obscuring the water about them; they do it not by any vapourous emission, but by a black humour ejected, which makes the water black and dark near them: but upon excessive motion some animals are able to afford a mist about them, when the air is cool and fit to condense it, as horses after a race, so that they become scarce visible.

[ORATIO ANNIVERSARIA HARVEIANA.¹]

[MS. SLOAN. 1833, fol. 146—150 ; COLLATED WITH 1839, fol. 299—316.]

Commentaturo mihi insignes benefactorum munificentias, nobilesque Patronorum ἐνεργησίας, liceat, colendissime Præses, collegæ ornatissimi, et auditores humanissimi, liceat inquam prudentissimo Cardani * consilio ejusque de civili prudentiâ verbis præfari. " Maximum est in humanâ vitâ beneficia bene collocasse, ideoque ingratos cavere oportet. Ingrati autem sunt pueri, mulieres, rustici, utpote parvi sensus ; invidi, avari, sibi quippe tantum prospiciunt ; perfidi, inconstantes aut stupidi, qui beneficia non sentiunt."

Summà itaque prudentiâ beneficia collocasse beneficentissimos viros et Mæcenates nostros memorandissimos, solennitas hodierna satis dictat, immo clamitat. Quorsum etenim conventus hic solennis Panegyris anniversaria, et oratio laudatoria, quorsum inquam tot gratitudinis μνημεῖα et χαριστήρια, quibus benefactores meritissimos et dignos laude viros recognitionum symbolis gratissimis celebramus ? Neque certe conatu perfunctorio, aut ἀχαριστίας infamiam tantum vitantes, diem hunc gratulatorium observamus, sed uti viros probos decet, debitum virtuti officium præstantes quicquid est hodiernæ solennitatis, quicquid encomiastici honoris, illud tantorum virorum memoriæ gratissime dicamus, et ne quæ hodie apud nos vigent, interjecto spatio apud alios absolescant, ea institutis et consuetudine clavo quasi trabali figimus.

Laudes sane postulant,† non precibus petunt, egregia opera, præclara facta ; etiamsi laudatores non inveniant, non esse minus pulchra ultro profitemur. Æquissimum tamen censemus,

---

* The works of Cardanus are printed in ten volumes : in the moral volumes there is a tract *De civili prudentia*, where these words here quoted are to be found.

† Imperio posco, precibus peto, postulo jure.

1 ORATIO, &c.] This is the oration mentioned in the first volume, page 291, note.

ut præclare merentibus suus reddatur honos, et quos bona opera sequuntur eos etiam gratissimâ memoriâ et laudibus prosequamur. Laudibus itaque digni et laudationibus effer-endi sunt hodie munificentissimi viri de Collegio medico Lon-dinensi et Societate præclarè meriti. Hi licet viritim cele-brandi, quia tamen celeberrimi Harvei institutioni solennem hujus diei conventum primario debemus, clarissimi ejusdem viri memoriæ encomiorum initia et laudum primitias deferimus.

Quo de viro consummatissimo dicturus, in laudes ejus am-plissimas tanquam in oceanum descendo, ubi initium facilius est quam exitum reperire. Hic itaque, si unquam alibi plures sunt poscendæ clepsydræ, hic implorandus charitum et mu-sarum omnium chorus, huc in auxilium advocandus disertis-simus Millingtonus, doctissimus Charltonus, aliique facundis-simi oratores, olim hoc in loco et themate perpolite versati : est enim sublimis vir nostra panegyri major, sive eximias animi dotes, sive indulta nobis beneficia, sive in literatorum orbem merita pensitemus.

Sibi nasci, sibi tantum vivere, rebusque propriis inhiare in-dolis arctioris et ingenii angustioris indicium est. Animi erectiores et divino propiores, charius sibi nihil habent quam ut diffusa bonitate aliis insuper liberali manu prospiciant. Quibus sanè virtutibus cumulatus incomparabilis Harveus, alienæ felicitati munifice prospexit ; nec rebus tantum propriis sed et publicis generose consuluit : ne quid etenim benefac-torum memoriæ et pulchre de nobis meritorum honori, ne quid mutuæ inter nos amicitiæ fovendæ deesset, diem hunc nobis solennem et festivum fecit, favores favoribus, munera muneribus cumulavit, et post tot collata beneficia, ne patri-monio quidem proprio parcens, societatem hanc hæredem ex asse reliquit, atque ita sapientissimus vir fortunæ bona extra fortunam * statuit.

Plurima in lucem eruunt et in apricum proferunt, multa in-veniunt, aut inventis superaddunt, Naturæ curiosi et quasi Philosophi nati, qui sagaci scrutinio et industria perspicaci res ipsas, non rerum simulachra, penetrant ; qui non ex dog-matibus traditis, aut aliorum dictatis, sed ex iterata observa-tione et experimentis sensatis, de rebus optime dijudicant.

* Extra fortunam est quicquid largitur amicis.—*Martialis.*

Fecundam et vere philosophicam hanc animi crasin Harve-
anam, ut alia præteream, nobilitarunt duo nunquam satis
collaudanda heuremata,* sanguinis scilicet περικύκλωσις, atque
ex ovo genesis. Ad primam circulationis tubam fremuerunt
universæ Europæ scholæ: quam statim lapillo nigro notarunt,
nec non communibus suffragiis damnarunt, paulatim vero
dies diem docuit, et magni viri vicit sententia; eaque tandem
a clarissimis medicis recepta et confirmata, adeo ubique cla-
ruit admirandus inventor, ut maximi nominis anatomicus † in
tam præclaræ inventionis consortium admitti, honorem partiri,
particepsque aliquomodo fieri, ambiverit, novam circulationis
regulam commentus, illamque argumentis et scriptis propa-
gare, sed Diis iratis,‡ satagens.

Improles denuo et in ætate effœta, prolem immortalem, ob-
servationibus admirandis novis, incognitis, fecundam genuit;
sanguinisque circulo orbi prius demonstrato, miram ex ovo
genesin superaddidit, duoque naturæ magnalia experimentis
inauditis et ratione irrefragabili explicuit: atque ita tandem
prætermissam ab Angliæ rege § primam Americæ sive novi or-
bis noticiam, inventis domi natis, et scientiæ thesauris, Po-
tosianis certe præferendis, Anglus compensavit. Exile quiddam famæ est quod tanto viro conferre patria poterat, qui tot
honoribus patriam cumulavit. Cumulata superaddunt sym-
bola omni ex orâ exteri. Scriptis oscula litant. Serta, coronas, tumulo inspergunt, terramque exoptant levem, Galli,
Itali, Germani; laudant quotquot sub Aquilone, et Jove fri-
gido, musas severiores colunt; 'norunt et Tagus et Ganges;
forsan et Antipodes.'‖

Revera et in sese vir ille magnus, cui tot debentur magnalia, immo rigidissimi stoici sententia magnus, si voles veram
hominis æstimationem inire et scire qualis sit, nudum aspice;
ponat patrimonium, ponat honores et alio fortunæ mendacia,
corpus ipsum exuat; animum intuere, ut scias qualis quan-
tusque sit, alieno an suo magnus. Harveus certe, si quispiam

* Inventa.   † Riolanus.
‡ Diis iratis; unsuccessfully, unfortunately.
§ Henry the Seventh, unto whom Columbus first applied, but was refused.
‖ "Johannes jacet hic Mirandula; cætera norunt et Tagus et Ganges, forsan et
Antipodes:" the epitaph of the learned Joh. Mirandula, in Paulus Jovius his
Elogia virorum illustrium, capite de Johanne Mirandula.

alius se sibi debuît, sine Theseo Hercules, nullo fultus adminiculo, et Minerva propria, tot tantaque præstitit, errorum
tenebras dissipavit, veritatem Orco latentem eruit.　Naturæ
denique omnia explorare, nihil ignorare, Harveanum erat.
Libet itaque tanto Heroi, quod olim vir eruditus celebri phi-
losopho, occinere;

> Naturæ rerum si quid te forte latebat,
> Hoc legis in magno nunc Gulielme Deo.*

Posthuma contenti fama mortalium multi ætatem transigunt
et . . . . si post fata venit gloria non properant.　Vixisti autem Harvee magna vitæ parte annisque plurimis δακτυλόδεικτος,†
digitis et ore fere omnium honoratus; vixisti, inquam, octo-
genarius ideoque cæteris aliquanto beatius, ut scilicet immortalitati tuæ justa gloria plenus interesses.　Quid enim majus
dare poterant cælestia numina, quam ut diu in terris vivus et
incolumis, inusitatæ, nec nisi post fata obvenientis gloriæ,
fructum perciperes? ‡

Vixere fortes ante Agamemnona et præclari, § sane ante
Harveum benefactores, quorum celeberrimæ memoriæ elogia
et pergrata recognitio meritissime debentur.　Rex enim
Regalissimus et μεγαλοπρεπης, Henricus Octavus, ob tot Pala-
tia, Xenodochia,² et Collegia fundata illustris, societatem
etiam hanc medicam instituit nec non privilegiis exornavit,
principem nempe dignitati metropolitanæ a patre designatum,‖
ideoque literis imbutum, latere non potuit regum sapientissimi
dictatum, "in multitudine populi dignitas Regis et in pauci-
tate plebis ignominia Principis."　Prudenter itaque cavere
voluit, ne vitæ subditorum prorogandæ debita deessent subsi-
dia, nec præceps Agyrtarum ³ inscitia stragem peste funesti-

---

* These verses are in Paulus Jovius his *Elogia doctorum, capite de Lenonico
Thomæo,* a noted Philosopher.

† δακτυλόδεικτος, digitis monstratus.

‡ This is borrowed from Paulus Jovius in his *Elogia doctorum—capite de Alberto
Magno.*

§ Vixere—this is in Horace and here used to another intention.

‖ H. 8. designed by H. 7. his father to be Archbishop of Canterbury; Prince
Arthur his elder brother then living.

² *Xenodochia.*] Ξενοδοχεῖα; more pro-
perly, inns; but used here in the sense of　hospitals or other charitable institutions.

³ *Agyrtarum.*] Ἀγύρτης, a quack.

orem ederet; quo etiam nomine Serenissimæ tanti Regis filiæ, Maria et Elizabetha, cum clarissimis successoribus, patrociniis et favoribus collegium cohonorarunt.

Inter Mecænates insignes Harveo antiquiores, prætermittendus non est Thomas Linacrus, vir doctorum elogiis et Epitaphio olim in Æde Paulina celebratus. Principis nempe Arthuri, Henrici septimi filii primogeniti, præceptor, Regis Henrici octavi medicus, qui collegium medicorum Londinense sua industria fieri curavit, ejusque Præses primus electus est, qui etiam Medicinæ studiosis Oxonii lectiones duas, Cantabrigiæ * unam, in perpetuum stabilivit. Græce et Latine eruditissimus, multa Galeni opera singulari facundia vertit; vir fraudes dolosque mire perosus, amicis fidus, omnibus ordinibus juxta charus, clarissimo Angelo Politiano et Hermolao Barbaro notissimus.†

Sequenti serie commemorandi viri benefici Harveo σύγχρονοι, aut aliquæ saltem ætatis parte contemporanei. Doctor Johannes Atkinsius, Collegii Medicorum Præses, olim meritissimus. Foxius, cujus Bibliotheca insignis, collegio medicorum a generossissimo viro forte designata, a belli civilis prædonibus direpta atque dissipata est. Theodorus Gulstonus, vir Praxi medica et egregiis in Aristotelem commentariis ‡ clarus. Readus peritia Anatomica et Chirurgica celebris. Doctor Otwellus, Meverellus, et Nathan Pagetus, medici humanissimi et nulla non laude efferendi.

Clarissimus denique Doctor Baldwinus Hamæus, auditorum plerisque non ignotus, nobisque in perpetuum celebrandus. Collegium etenim Medicum, iniquis temporibus quasi sub hasta positum, pro mercale et pretio alienandum, benignissimus patronus, λυτρῳ voluntario et nummis numeratis redimens, quasi ex lupinis faucibus eripuit. Quo itaque sostro [4] et salutis præmio, quibus gratiarum cumulis beneficentissimum virum, et quasi fundatori comparem, celebrabimus? Corona

---

* If exception be taken for naming Oxford before Cambridge, it is so in his epitaph, and he was an Oxford man.

† Angelo Politiano, etc., as appears by Paulus Jovius in *Elogia virorum doctorum capite de Thoma Linacro.*

‡ Upon Aristotelis Rhetorica.

[4] *sostro.*] Σῶστρον, a fee.

certe querna ob cives servatos dignissimus: quique monumentis marmoreis et statuis æreis, non imaginibus depictis (uti
nunc in senaculo nostro), honoretur. Neque tamen animus
ad beneficia natus hic constitit; Collegii ædificium magnis
sumptibus ornando, reditus augendo, plurima legando, animos
pergratos in perpetuum devinxit. Tantæ certe virtutes soli-
tariæ non ambulant; non illo melior quisquam nec amantior
æqui vir fuit. Mellita morum suavitate, et humanitate gra-
tissima, omnium amorem et benevolentiam promeritus, nusquam clariora bonitatis indicia, nemo virtutibus ornatior, nullus cumulatior, quem, certe medicorum ornamentum, in dubiis oraculum, in arduis asylum, in honestis exemplum, merito
recognoscimus.

Fautoribus nostris dignissimis annumerandus deinde est
multis nominibus honorabilis, Dominus Henricus Dorchestriæ
Marchio, vir meritis propriis et literatura quam titulis ornatior,
in hoc sane præclaros aliquot veteris prosapiæ viros sapienter
imitatus. Julius Cæsar Scaliger, medicus φιλοσοφότατος, familiæ
suæ nobilitatem, capta frequenter occasione, summis laudibus
attollit, atque urbe Cairina antiquiorem prædicat. Ille vero
talis tantusque vir, nisi rerum omnium scientiam et incompa-
rabilem doctrinam honorificis natalibus adjecisset, cum ma-
joribus suis dominio et potestate claris in oblivionis tumu-
lum una descendisset. Nunc autem Agenni Nitiobrigum in
Gallia sepultus, non absconditus, ubique terrarum claret,
similisque gemmæ electro inclusæ et latet et lucet. Pari fere
modo Nobilissimus Henricus, avis licet proavis, abavis, illustris, solis tamen stemmatibus * decorari aut longo sanguine
censeri, velut alienum quiddam nec satis fidum honoris sem-
piterni fundamentum ducens, fortunæ bonis animi thesauros
addidit, titulos insignes propriis virtutibus ornavit, rerum omnium scientiæ et liberali cognitioni incubuit, Philosophiæ
adyta et medicinæ arcana penetravit, authores eximios et
classici nominis indefessa manu versans, honorem mori nesci-
um, nec perituram virtutis famam bonorum omnium calculo ob-
tinuit. Prudenter itaque insignissimus vir verborum insigni-
bus propriis et scuto militari adscriptorum *(Pie repone te)* †

---

* Juvenal. Sat. 8. Stemmata quid faciunt, etc.
† *Pie repone te* is the motto of his coat of arms, alluding to his name.

continuo memor, ætate ingravescente, a strepitu et colluvie mundana, a moribus vitiisque publicis, se subducens, studiis privatis, eleemosynis, pauperum sublevationibus, precibus et divini numinis cultui, se fere totum dicavit.

Quid itaque ab animo benevolo et Principe dignissimo sperare nobis non licuit, qui pro singulari in medicinam ejusque mystas benevolentia, catalogo collegarum nomen suum honorificum, literisque aureis dignum adscribi voluit? Qui libros selectissimos nec levi pretio comparatos Collegio jam flammis absumpto impertivit, plures etiam auroque contra æstimandos et bibliotheca nostra hodie inclusos donavit, damnumque illud funestum animo planè regio resarcivit. Qui meliori, uti speramus, fato, tanti Mæcenatis munificentiam prædicabunt, nobisque ac posteris in emolumentum cedent.

Bibliotheca Fessana* a celeberrimo rege Almanzore aliisque compilata, erat, uti ferunt, manuscriptis Mauritanicis refertissima. Cum vero Fezzæ monarcha victus, fugiens rebusque suis male fidens, libros in tutiorem Regni sedem transferendos navi commisisset, capta nave et librorum parte aliqua hinc inde dispersa, reliqua in Hispanorum manus pervenit, hi, uti ex auditu accepi, in Bibliotheca sancti Laurentii in Escuriali hodie conservantur, ubi a paucis legibiles, a paucioribus lecti, a nullis bene intellecti, rarioris supellectilis vicem magis quam studiorum emolumentum præstant et ornamento potius quam utilitati inserviunt. In Bibliotheca Durnovariana et libris Petrapontanis dispar omnino ratio est; sint enim licet et isti ornatu et specie decori, in recessu tamen habent, quod nullo ornatu pensatur. Linguis et dialectis constant orbi literato non incognitis; editionibus optimis: subjectis etiam lectoribus pergratis, adeo ut animos scientiæ avidos et alliciant et expleant, nunquam certe blattarum et tinearum sed doctorum epulæ futuræ.

Generossimi Cutleri nomen hoc in loco silentio præterire, absurdissima certe oblivionis species, et monstrum αχαρισίας horrendum foret. Hic enim præclari viri beneficentiam et famam, si homines tacerent, lapides loquerentur. Hujus si-

---

* This in some accounts of Barbary; and I have heard it long ago from old merchants; and that library is mentioned by divers writers.

quidem munificentiæ speciosum hoc in quo convenimus theatrum gratulanter agnoscimus, huic uni debemus. Noverat
quippe vir cordatus medicorum hujusce societatis solertiam,
et indefessum in corporibus dissecandis scrutinium. Senserat
vir sensatus inventa nova et omnibus retro sæculis ignota, hac
ex societate prodiisse. Ut itaque non deesset theatrum tantis
ausibus, talibus inventionibus, et futuris sectionibus, apprime
accommodatum, sumptibus propriis et μεγαλοπρεπεία singulari,
hoc ipsum exstruendum curavit. Hoc, inquam, adeo affabre
fabricatum, muniisque publicis concinnatum, ut omnium in
Europa quæ mihi videre contigit longe sit pulcherrimum;
quod ne gratis dixisse videar, favore vestro fretus, auditores
humanissimi, instantias aliquot adjiciam.

Theatrum Anatomicum Viennense forma est satis humili,
nec fornice nec tholo superbum, neque ducentorum auditorum capax. Altorphinum propè Norinbergum, quod primo et
ante alia in Germania exstructum fuisse, præsenti mihi narra-
vit clarissimus professor Doctor Mauritius Hoffmannus; ejusdem ferè dignitatis cum Viennensi est, neque auditores multo
plures capit. Leydense ædificio satis eleganti, lectoribus eruditis et auditoribus peregrinis clarum, Londinensi nequaquam
æquiparandum. Theatrum Patavinum antiquitate et lectoribus præclaris nobile, a Theatro nostro licet Tramontano se
superari, Palladio vel Scamozzio judice facile fatebitur. Mon-
speliense ex lapide quadrato fabricatum, formæ est arctioris,
pro numero tamen auditorum satis amplum. Theatrum Pa-
risiense, sectionum frequentia et prælectionibus egregiis clarum, maximæ tamen Europæ civitati minime congruum, nec
cum Cutleriano conferendum. Ne vos tædio afficiam, Romanum, Pisanum, Lovaniense, lubens prætereo, unum pro cunctis fama loquatur opus.* Vivas itaque munificentissime Cut-
lere, meritò sanè viventi tibi præsentes largimur honores,
qui non solibus tantum sed et beneficiis annos metiris, qui
anteactæ vitæ fruitione bis vivis,† etiam cum vivere desinis
gloria immortalis etiamnum victurus, laudibus et encomiis a

---

* Omnis Cæsareo cedat labor Amphitheatro,
   Unum pro cunctis fama loquatur opus.—*Martial.*
† Ampliat ætatis spatium sibi vir bonus: hoc est, Vivere bis, vita posse priore
frui.—*Martial.*

virtutis cultoribus non tantum quotannis sed quotidie cele-
brari dignissimus.

Veram certe virtutis et gloriæ sempiternæ semitam calca-
runt qui virtutes beneficas coluerunt, virtutisque cultoribus,
donariis et liberali manu prospexerunt. Nullum virtuti sepulchrum est, nullibi sepelitur quæ nunquam moritur, ubique
decantatur quæ undiquaque colitur. Diuturnum certe hunc
honorem non donant statuæ, non marmora conferunt. Tunc
enim, cum marmora Messalæ findet caprificus :* cum Curios
jam dimidios, cum Galbam auriculis nasoque carentem, edax
annorum reddiderit, tunc, inquam, perennabunt illustria nomina, et immortalis Heroum memoria vitabit Libitinam.†

Nos interim in vivis tantorum virorum muneribus beati, ad
grati animi officia, pares laudes et encomia, nostro præunte
exemplo, posteros incitabimus. Ita enim futura sæcula non
solum fautores nostros munificos, sed et nosmetipsos nostra-
que hæc instituta collaudabunt, neque nos tantorum bonorum
immemores censebunt aut ingratitudinis infamia mulctabunt.

Quandoquidem verò beatius est dare quam accipere, lau-
dari itidem quam laudare, nunquam uti speramus deerunt
animi generosi, qui beatorum hunc numerum expleant, etiam-
que in hac societate ornatissima genii publici viri, qui laudan-
dorum catalogum adaugeant. Hoc enim erit, colendissime
Præses et Collegæ honoratissimi, non tantum luce aliena, sed,
cum Apolline medicorum patre, propriis radiis fulgere.

Det bonorum omnium Largitor, ut quibus benefaciendi
animus non deest, iisdem et facultates suppetant, quibus vero
facultates suppetunt, iisdem animus non deficiat. Ut vero
beneficiis non indigni, aut ea minus promereri videamur, benefactorum non tantum memoriam, sed et virtutes colamus.
Justitia quæ regnum firmat, collegium etiam Regia authori-
tate munitum, stabiliat. Præsidi Colendissimo reverentiam
et obsequium præstemus, mutuam inter nos amicitiam et con-

---

* Marmore Messalæ findet caprificus. *Juvenal.* When a wild fig tree shall
cleave the monument of Messala the great family of Rome : as we see elders and
wall flowers and shrubby plants with us in the clefts of old walls and spoil them.

† Libitina the goddess of funerals, from whose temple they provided funeral
necessaries, taken figuratively for death itself; as Horace, " Pars mei vitabit Libitinam." and Juvenal, "quando Libitinam evaserit æger."

cordiam amplectamur, præclaris collegarum inventis nova ad-
jicere conemur, humanitate, comitate, et morum suavitate,
ornemur : nihil denique Æsculapio indignum, nihil a dignitate
medica alienum perpetremus.   Ita enim, Amplissime Præses,
et Collegæ ornatissimi, in sæculo generoso et civitate munifi-
centissima erit certe, erit inquam, cur præclara additamenta,
immo et montes speremus.*

* Montes, great matters : " promittere montes."

[ACCOUNT OF A THUNDER STORM AT NORWICH, 1665.]

[MS. SLOAN. 1866, fol. 96.]

June 28, 1665.

AFTER seven o'clock in the evening there was almost a continued thunder until eight, wherein the *tonitru* and *fulgur*, the
noise and lightning were so terrible, that they put the whole
city into an amazement, and most unto their prayers. The
clouds went low, and the cracks seemed near over our heads
during the most part of the thunder. About eight o'clock,
an *ignis fulmineus, pila ignea fulminans, telum igneum ful-
mineum,* or fire-ball, hit against the little wooden pinnacle
of the high leucome window of my house, toward the market-
place, broke the flue boards, and carried pieces thereof a
stone's cast off; whereupon many of the tiles fell into the
street, and the windows in adjoining houses were broken.
At the same time either a part of that close-bound fire, or
another of the same nature fell into the court-yard, and whereof no notice was taken till we began to examine the house,
and then we found a freestone on the outside of the wall of
the entry leading to the kitchen, half a foot from the ground,
fallen from the wall; a hole as big as a foot-ball bored through
the wall, which is about a foot thick, and a chest which stood
against it, on the inside, split and carried about a foot from
the wall. The wall also, behind the leaden cistern, at five
yards distance from it, broken on the inside and outside; the
middle seeming entire. The lead on the edges of the cistern
turned a little up; and a great washing-bowl, that stood by
it, to recover the rain, turned upside down, and split quite
through. Some chimneys and tiles were struck down in other
parts of the city. A fire-ball also struck down the walk in
the market-place. And all this, God be thanked! without
mischief unto any person. The greatest terror was from the

noise, answerable unto two or three cannon. The smell it left was strong, like that after the discharge of a cannon. The balls that flew were not like fire in the flame, but the coal; and the people said it was like the sun. It was *discutiens, terebrans,* but not *urens.* It burnt nothing, nor any thing it touched smelt of fire; nor melted any lead of window or cistern, as I found it do in the great storm, about nine years ago, at Melton hall, four miles off, at that time when the hail broke three thousand pounds worth of glass in Norwich, in half-a-quarter of an hour. About four days after, the like fulminous fire killed a man in Erpingham church, by Aylsham, upon whom it broke, and beat down divers which were within the wind of it. One also went off in Sir John Hobart's gallery, at Blickling. He was so near, that his arm and thigh were numbed about an hour after. Two or three days after, a woman and horse were killed near Bungay; her hat so shivered that no piece remained bigger than a groat, whereof I had some pieces sent unto me. Granades, crackers, and squibs, do much resemble the discharge, and *aurum fulminans* the fury thereof. Of other thunderbolts or *lapides fulminei,* I have little opinion. Some I have by me under that name, but they are *è genere fossilium.*

THOMAS BROWNE.

Norwich, 1665.

[ON DREAMS.]

[MS. SLOAN. 1874, fol. 112, 120.]

HALF our days we pass in the shadow of the earth; and the brother of death exacteth a third part of our lives. A good part of our sleep is peered out with visions and fantastical objects, wherein we are confessedly deceived. The day supplieth us with truths; the night with fictions and falsehoods, which uncomfortably divide the natural account of our beings. And, therefore, having passed the day in sober labours and rational enquiries of truth, we are fain to betake ourselves unto such a state of being, wherein the soberest heads have acted all the monstrosities of melancholy, and which unto open eyes are no better than folly and madness.

Happy are they that go to bed with grand music, like Pythagoras, or have ways to compose the fantastical spirit, whose unruly wanderings take off inward sleep, filling our heads with St. Anthony's visions, and the dreams of Lipara in the sober chambers of rest.

Virtuous thoughts of the day lay up good treasures for the night; whereby the impressions of imaginary forms arise into sober similitudes, acceptable unto our slumbering selves and preparatory unto divine impressions.[1] Hereby Solomon's sleep was happy. Thus prepared, Jacob might well dream of angels upon a pillow of stone. And the best sleep of Adam might be the best of any after.[2]

That there should be divine dreams seems unreasonably doubted by Aristotle. That there are demoniacal dreams

---

[1] *Virtuous thoughts, &c.*] See an exquisite passage, in *Religio Medici*, p. 113.

[2] *the best sleep of Adam, &c.*] The only sleep of Adam recorded, is that which God caused to fall upon him, and which resulted in the creation of woman. It does not very clearly appear whether Sir Thomas calls it the *best* sleep of Adam, in allusion to its origin, or its result.

we have little reason to doubt. Why may there not be an-
gelical? If there be guardian spirits, they may not be in-
actively about us in sleep; but may sometimes order our
dreams: and many strange hints, instigations, or discourses,
which are so amazing unto us, may arise from such foundations.

But the phantasms of sleep do commonly walk in the great
road of natural and animal dreams, wherein the thoughts or
actions of the day are acted over and echoed in the night.
Who can therefore wonder that Chrysostom should dream
of St. Paul, who daily read his Epistles; or that Cardan,
whose head was so taken up about the stars, should dream
that his soul was in the moon! Pious persons, whose
thoughts are daily busied about heaven, and the blessed state
thereof, can hardly escape the nightly phantasms of it, which
though sometimes taken for illuminations, or divine dreams,
yet rightly perpended may prove but animal visions, and natural night-scenes of their awaking contemplations.

Many dreams are made out by sagacious exposition, and
from the signature of their subjects; carrying their interpretation in their fundamental sense and mystery of similitude,
whereby, he that understands upon what natural fundamental
every notion dependeth, may, by symbolical adaptation, hold
a ready way to read the characters of Morpheus. In dreams
of such a nature, Artemidorus, Achmet, and Astrampsichus,
from Greek, Ægyptian, and Arabian oneiro-criticism, may
hint some interpretation: who, while we read of a ladder
in Jacob's dream, will tell us that ladders and scalary ascents
signify preferment; and while we consider the dream of Pharaoh, do teach us that rivers overflowing speak plenty, lean
oxen, famine and scarcity; and therefore it was but reasonable in Pharaoh to demand the interpretation from his magicians, who, being Ægyptians, should have been well versed
in symbols and the hieroglyphical notions of things. The
greatest tyrant in such divinations was Nabuchodonosor,
while, besides the interpretation, he demanded the dream itself; which being probably determined by divine immission,
might escape the common road of phantasms, that might
have been traced by Satan.

When Alexander, going to besiegè Tyre, dreamt of a Satyr, it was no hard exposition for a Grecian to say, "Tyre will be thine." He that dreamed that he saw his father washed by Jupiter and anointed by the sun, had cause to fear that he might be crucified, whereby his body would be washed by the rain, and drop by the heat of the sun. The dream of Vespatian was of harder exposition; as also that of the emperor Mauritius, concerning his successor Phocas. And a man might have been hard put to it, to interpret the language of Æsculapius, when to a consumptive person he held forth his fingers; implying thereby that his cure lay in dates, from the homonomy of the Greek, which signifies dates and fingers.

We owe unto dreams that Galen was a physician, Dion an historian, and that the world hath seen some notable pieces of Cardan; yet, he that should order his affairs by dreams, or make the night a rule unto the day, might be ridiculously deluded; wherein Cicero is much to be pitied, who having excellently discoursed of the vanity of dreams, was yet undone by the flattery of his own, which urged him to apply himself unto Augustus.

However dreams may be fallacious concerning outward events, yet may they be truly significant at home; and whereby we may more sensibly understand ourselves. Men act in sleep with some conformity unto their awaked senses; and consolations or discouragements may be drawn from dreams which intimately tell us ourselves. Luther was not like to fear a spirit in the night, when such an apparition would not terrify him in the day. Alexander would hardly have run away in the sharpest combats of sleep, nor Demosthenes have stood stoutly to it, who was scarce able to do it in his prepared senses. Persons of radical integrity will not easily be perverted in their dreams, nor noble minds do pitiful things in sleep. Crassus would have hardly been bountiful in a dream, whose fist was so close awake. But a man might have lived all his life upon the sleeping hand of Antonius.[3]

[3] *sleeping hand of Antonius.*] Who, awake, was *open-handed* and liberal, in contrast with the *close-fistedness* of Crassus, and therefore would have been munificent in his dreams.

There is an art to make dreams, as well as their interpretations; and physicians will tell us that some food makes turbulent, some gives quiet, dreams. Cato, who doated upon cabbage, might find the crude effects thereof in his sleep; wherein the Ægyptians might find some advantage by their superstitious abstinence from onions. Pythagoras might have [had] calmer sleeps, if he [had] totally abstained from beans. Even Daniel, the great interpreter of dreams, in his leguminous diet, seems to have chosen no advantageous food for quiet sleeps, according to Grecian physic.

To add unto the delusion of dreams, the phantastical objects seem greater than they are; and being beheld in the vaporous state of sleep, enlarge their diameters unto us; whereby it may prove more easy to dream of giants than pigmies. Democritus might seldom dream of atoms, who so often thought of them. He almost might dream himself a bubble extending unto the eighth sphere. A little water makes a sea; a small puff of wind a tempest. A grain of sulphur kindled in the blood may make a flame like Ætna; and a small spark in the bowels of Olympias a lightning over all the chamber.

But, beside these innocent delusions, there is a sinful state of dreams. Death alone, not sleep, is able to put an end unto sin; and there may be a night-book of our iniquities; for beside the transgressions of the day, casuists will tell us of mortal sins in dreams, arising from evil precogitations; meanwhile human law regards not noctambulos; and if a nightwalker should break his neck, or kill a man, takes no notice of it.

Dionysius was absurdly tyrannical to kill a man for dreaming that he had killed him; and really to take away his life, who had but fantastically taken away his. Lamia was ridiculously unjust to sue a young man for a reward, who had confessed that pleasure from her in a dream which she had denied unto his awaking senses: conceiving that she had merited somewhat from his fantastical fruition and shadow of herself. If there be such debts, we owe deeply unto sympathies; but the common spirit of the world must be ready in such arrearages.

If some have swooned, they may have also died in dreams, since death is but a confirmed swooning. Whether Plato died in a dream, as some deliver, he must rise again to inform us. That some have never dreamed, is as improbable as that some have never laughed. That children dream not the first half year; that men dream not in some countries, with many more, are unto me sick men's dreams; dreams out of the ivory gate,[4] and visions before midnight.

---

[4] *the ivory gate.*] The poets suppose two gates of sleep, the one of horn, from which true dreams proceed; the other of ivory, which sends forth false dreams.

[NOTÆ IN ARISTOTELEM.]

[MS. SLOAN. 1874, fol. 81.]

LIBELLUM edidit, non ita pridem, Johannes de Launoy, Theologus Parisiensis, de varia Aristotelis fortuna; unde celeberrimum philosophum, interdum publice combustum, interdum restitutum, nunc decretis solennibus damnatum, alias iterum honoratum, octonam denique varietatem passum, in eadem Academia, constat.

Habuerunt sane antiqui Christiani, Justinus, Clemens, Tertullianus, Augustinus, aliique plurimi, quæ scriptis tanti viri opponerent. Qui hodie a neotericis acrius et ad vivum sectus, tantum non animam agit: ut videatur mihi peripatetica jam quasi ad incitas redacta, et vix aut ne vix eluctatura.

Sed cum in Aristotele multa deficiant, multa fallant, multa itidem contradicant, non pauca tamen prosunt. Noli itaque integro operi valedicere; sed dum physica parum teris et metaphysica oscitanter legis, cætera quidem magni facias, et indefessa manu verses.

Problemata Aristotelis magno labore, sed successu impari, illustraverunt Petrus Aponensis et Alexander Aphrodisæus; præclarius sane Petrus Septalius, magni nominis medicus. Sed cum genio minus libero, nec nova philosophia imbuto, ad mentem philosophi omnia fere exponat, sæpe sæpius rem minus attingit, nec animum veritatis avidum explet.

Itaque ut quæsitorum veritas et ratio melius constet, operæ pretium erit ea ad examen revocare, et, ubi fallunt antiqui canones, ad nova theoremata transire. Quod ut faciliori negotio præstes, en tibi selectiora aliquot, quibus intelligendis, examinandis, elucidandis, operam præ ceteris impendas.

Sect. i. Prob. 17.

A Vergiliis ad Zephyrum usque, qui longis morbis laborant, tolluntur e medio; id est, ab occasu pleiadum, circa 14 Novembris,—ad principium veris, cum spirare solent Zephyri. Sive brevius, ab initio hyemis medicæ ad veris initium.

In locis humidis, ulcera in capite cito sanantur, in tibiis ægre.

Hyems Borealis cum vere Austrino et pluvia, et sicca æstate, lethales facit Autumnos, potissimum pueris, aliis autem dysenteriæ et quartanæ fiunt.

Si quis ære vuleneretur citius sanatur quam si ferro.

Dentium stuporem (αἱμωδίαν) solvunt portulaca et sal.

Æstivi labores balneo, hyemales inunctionibus, curandi.

Odorata urinam movent, tam semina quam plantæ.

Ad sanitatem carnem densare non oportet, sed rarefacere.

In febribus paulatim, et sæpe potio dari debet.

In quartanis oportet non extenuare, sed ignem in corporibus adaugere.

Sect. ii.

Sudamus magis tergo quam anteriore parte; superiores magis sudant quam inferiores partes; in aqua etiamsi calida non sudant; sudores in capite [minus] gravis odoris; maxime sudamus in facie.

Sect. [iv.]

Moriens oculos sursum vertit, dormiens deorsum.

Albi homines et quia maxima ex parte glauci, colorem corporis oculi color sequitur.[1]

Sect. vi.

Inflexo corpore cubare melius.

Surgentibus vertigo magis evenit quam sedentibus: ova cruda nequeunt circumvolvi.

Super dextram cubantibus facilius somnus advenit.

Sect. vii.

Juxta ignem stantes non mingimus, si juxta fluvium irritamur.

---

[1] *Albi, &c.*] This passage is almost illegible in MS.

Ad tristium auditum exhorrescimus, ut cum serra acuitur aut pumex secatur.

Oscitantibus contra oscitamus.

Sect. ix.

Medium carnis ferula percussum album redditur, extremum rubrum; ligno vero rubicundius medium.

Spleneticorum cicatrices nigræ.

Cæteræ cicatrices nigræ, in oculo albæ.

Æs et cyathus applicatus sugillata dissolvunt.

Sect. x.

1. Animalium alia tussiunt, alia non, ut homo, non autem bos.

2. Homini soli, inter alia animalia, sanguis e naribus fluit.

5. Homo tantum habet vitiliginem λευκην.

12. Proles cæterorum animantium, magis quam hominum, similem parentibus gerit naturum.

17. Inter animalia homo habet minimum intervallum oculorum, pro suo magnitudine.

19. Quæ collum non habent, caput non movent.

20. Homo inter animantia maxime sternutat.

21. Lingua nulli animali pinguis.

23. Animalia quæ non volant deponunt hymales pilos, præter suem. Oves et homines, bos et canis, et equi, deponunt.

24. Ovibus expilatis molliores pili subnascuntur, homini duriores.

25. Ovis pili quanto longiores tanto duriores, homini molliores.

27. Homo jubam non habet, quia barbam.

28. Omnia animalia pares pedes habent.

33. Minori tempore animalia dormiunt, quam vigilant.

36. Ubi vitiligo ibi canities.

40. Omnium animalium homo maxime a nativitate claudus.

42. Animalium solus homo calculo laborat.

43. Non eructant jumenta, non boves et cornigera, nec etiam aves.

45. Hominibus umbilici magni, aliis non manifesti.

48. Quicunque sectionem, quæ est per manum, habent per totam traductam, longævi.

50. Animalium homo maxime fumo afficitur.

52. Bipeda in anterioribus pilosiora, quadrupeda in posterioribus.

63. Quibus sub umbilicum majores sunt partes, quam quæ sunt versus pectus, iis brevis vita et imbecillis.

Sect. xi.

Sensibus a nativitate maxime auditu privamur.

Surdi per nares loquuntur.

Magna voce præditi natura calidi.

Melius exaudiri quæque nocte solent.

Si quis dolia et fictilia vasa vacua sepeliat, magis sonant ædificia quam si puteas aut fovea fuerit in domo.

Aqua frigida ex eodem vase effusa, acutiorem sonum reddit quam calida.

Plorantes acutiorem vocem edant, ridentes graviorem.

Voces hyeme graviores.

Oscitantes minus audiunt.

Lingua hæsitantes (ἰσχόφωνοι) melancholici.

Melius audimus, spiritum continentes, quam emittentes.

Sect. xv.

Omnes Barbari quam Græci in decem numerant.

Sol per quadrilatera transiens, non rectilineas figuras sed circulares, ut in cratibus.

Parelius non fit neque in medio cœlo constituto sole, neque supra nec infra sed ad latus.

Extremum umbræ solis tremere videtur.

Sect. xvi.

Bullæ hæmisphæricæ.

Sect. xix.

Æqualium doliorum et similium si unum sit vacuum, diapason consonat echo.

Sect. xx.

Cur irrigant mane, nocte, aut occidente sole?

Cur citius excaulescat olus, quod e semine vestustiore, bimo aut trimo, quam quo de nova producitur ?

Cur cepe solum tam acriter oculos mordet, origanus autem non ; atque alia acria?

Quæ frigida aqua irrigantur dulciora evadunt, quam quæ calida.

Sect. xxi.

Panes albidiores videntur frigidi, quam calidi.

Cur panes non saliti plus ponderant quam saliti, cum sal aqua gravius?

Frigidi panes madefacti, si se invicem tangunt, non cohærent, calidi autem cohærent.

Farina aqua subacta melius coit quam oleo.

Sect. xxii.

Dulcia minus dulcia videntur calida, quam frigida.

Sect. xxiii.

Mare albius est in Ponto, quam in Ægæo.

Mare, etiamsi crassius, εὐδιόπτερα, perspectius, aqua potabili.

In Borealibus perspectius, quam in regionibus Australibus.

Salem prius liquefacit aqua salsa, quam dulcis.

In mare lavantes citius resiccantur.

Maris partes prope terram dulciores.

In lacubus arena non fit, ut in mari et fluviis.

In mari lapides et testæ rotundæ fiunt.

Sect. xxiv.

Fundus vasorum non urit cum aquam bullientem contineat.

Non super effervescit (ὑπερζεῖ) aqua hyeme perinde ac æstate.

Aqua ebulliens non exilit, ut pulmentum ex pisis et elixis leguminibus, et argentum cum aqua injicitur.

Pede quiescente in aqua calida, cur minus calida sentiatur quam mota.

Calida in sole magis quam in umbra refrigeratur.

Sect. xxv.

Media in nocte et meridie maxima fit tranquillitas.

Noctu serenitas magis fit quam interdiu.

Noctibus æstus præfocatiores (πνιγηρότεραι.)

Sect. xxvi.

Cur dicitur, "Tertia lux nunquam nocturno aquilone calorat, laborat?"

Auster fœtidus.

Ventus ante eclipses, magna ex parte.

Auster non incipiens, sed finiens pluvius.

Venti hyeme ab oriente, æstate ab occidente.

Spirantibus austris, gravius se habent, et imbecillius, homines.

Auster incipiens parvus, finiens magnus, Boreas e contra; unde proverbium, "bonum est navigare incipiente Austro et finiente Aquilone."

Post Austrum cito Aquilo, post hunc non cito Auster spirat.

Austri sicci, et inaquosi, febriculosi.

Ventus mane incipiens, durat magis.

Aquilo interdiu vehemens, noctu autem cadit.

Sect. xxvii.

Fortes et plurimum vinosi.

Timentes maxime tremunt voce, manibus, et labro inferiori.

Timentes sitiunt et algent, alvo solvuntur, mingunt, et testes contrahuntur.

Sect. xxxi.

Perfricato oculo cessat sternutatio.

Irati oculis maxime rubore tentantur, pudefacti auribus.

Hominibus solis inter animalia oculi pervertuntur.

Sect. xxxii.

Cur urinatores sibi dissecant aures et nares.

Aliqui, dum aures scalpunt, tussiunt.

Sinistra auris ocius consolidatur magna ex parte cum perforatur.

Sect. xxxiii.

Sternutatio singultum solvit ; eructatio autem non sedat.
Singultum solvit sternutatio, spiritus cohibitio, acetum.
Sternutatio dormientibus non fit.

End of Problems.

[OBSERVATIONS ON GRAFTING.[1]]

[MS. SLOAN. 1848, fol. 44—48; 1882, fol. 136, 137; AND ADDITIONAL MSS. NO. 5233, fol. 58.]

IN the doctrine of all insitions, those are esteemed most successful which are practised under these rules :—

That there be some consent or similitude of parts and nature between the plants conjoined.

That insition be made between trees not of very different barks ; nor very differing fruits or forms of fructification ; nor of widely different ages.

That the scions or buds be taken from the south or east part of the tree.

That a rectitude and due position be observed ; not to insert the south part of the scions unto the northern side of the stock, but according to the position of the scions upon his first matrix.

Now, though these rules be considerable in the usual and practised course of insitions, yet were it but reasonable for searching spirits to urge the operations of nature by conjoining plants of very different natures in parts, barks, lateness, and precocities, nor to rest in the experiments of hortensial plants in whom we chiefly intend the exaltation or variety of their fruit and flowers, but in all sorts of shrubs and trees applicable unto physic or mechanical uses, whereby we might alter their tempers, moderate or promote their virtues, exchange their softness, hardness, and colour, and so render them considerable beyond their known and trite employments.

[1] OBSERVATIONS, &c.] " *Generation of Plants,*" was the title given by Dr. Ayscough to this paper: which, in all probability, was written for and addressed to Evelyn.

To which intent curiosity may take some rule or hint from these or the like following, according to the various ways of propagation:—[2]

> Colutea upon anagris
> Arbor judæ upon anagris
> Cassia poetica upon cytisus
> Cytisus upon periclymenum rectum
> Woodbine upon jasmine
> Cystus upon rosemary
> Rosemary upon ivy
> Sage or rosemary upon cystus
> Myrtle upon gall or rhus myrtifolia
> Whortle-berry upon gall, heath, or myrtle
> Coccygeia upon alaternus
> Mezereon upon an almond
> Gooseberry and currants upon mezereon, barberry, or
>   blackthorn
> Barberry upon a currant tree
> Bramble upon gooseberry or raspberry
> Yellow rose upon sweet briar
> Phyllerea upon broom
> Broom upon furze
> Anonis lutea upon furze
> Holly upon box
> Bay upon holly
> Holly upon pyracantha
> A fig upon chesnut
> A fig upon mulberry
> Peach upon mulberry
> Mulberry upon buckthorn
> Walnut upon chesnut
> Savin upon juniper
> Vine upon oleaster, rosemary, ivy

---

[2] *propagation.*] A brief memorandum occurs here in the original, in these words:—" *To insert the Catalogue,*" evidently showing that the author intended the list of his proposed experiments to be here introduced. Having met with such a Catalogue (in *MS. Sloan.* 1843, fol. 44—48) I have not hesitated to transplant it hither as the one intended. Several of the names are so illegible, that it is impossible not to fear they may be incorrectly given.

An arbutus upon a fig
A peach upon a fig
White poplar upon black poplar
Asp upon white poplar
Wych elm upon common elm
Hazel upon elm
Sycamore upon wych elm
Cinnamon rose upon hipberry
A whitethorn upon a blackthorn
Hipberry upon a sloe, or skeye, or bullace
Apricot upon a mulberry
Arbutus upon a mulberry
Cherry upon a peach
Oak upon a chesnut
Katherine peach upon a quince
A warden upon a quince
A chesnut upon a beech
A beech upon a chesnut
An hornbeam upon a beech
A maple upon an hornbeam
A sycamore upon a maple
A medlar upon a service tree
A sumack upon a quince or medlar
An hawthorn upon a service tree
A quicken tree upon an ash
An ash upon an asp
An oak upon an ilex
A poplar upon an elm
A black cherry tree upon a tilea or lime tree
Tilea upon beech
Alder upon birch or poplar
A filbert upon an almond
An almond upon a willow
A nux vesicaria upon an almond or pistachio
A cerasus avium upon a nux vesicaria
A cornelian [3] upon a cherry tree
A cherry tree upon a cornelian
An hazel upon a willow or sallow

[3] *Cornelian.*] Cornel-tree.

  A lilac upon a sage tree
  A syringa upon lilac or tree-mallow
  A rose elder upon syringa
  An water elder upon rose elder
  Buckthorn upon elder
  Frangula upon buckthorn
  Hirga sanguinea upon privet
  Phyllerea upon vitex
  Vitex upon evonymus
  Evonymus upon viburnum
  Ruscus upon pyracantha
  Paleurus upon hawthorn
  Tamarisk upon birch
  Erica upon tamarisk
  Polemonium upon genista hispanica
  Genista hispanica upon colutea.

  Nor are we to rest in the frustrated success of some single experiments, but to proceed in attempts in the most unlikely unto iterated and certain conclusions, and to pursue the way of ablactation or inarching. Whereby we might determine whether, according to the ancients, no fir, pine, or picea, would admit of any insition upon them ; whether yew will hold society with none ; whether walnut, mulberry, and cornel cannot be propagated by insition, or the fig and quince admit almost of any, with many others of doubtful truths in the propagations.

  And while we seek for varieties in stocks and scions, we are not to omit the ready practise of the scion upon its own tree. Whereby, having a sufficient number of good plants, we may improve their fruits without translative conjunction, that is, by insition of the scion upon his own mother, whereby an handsome variety or melioration seldom faileth—we might be still advanced by iterated insitions in proper boughs and positions. Insition is also made not only with scions and buds, but seeds, by inserting them in cabbage stalks, turnips, onions, &c., and also in ligneous plants.

  Within a mile of this city of Norwich, an oak groweth upon the head of a pollard willow, taller than the stock, and about half a foot in diameter, probably by some acorn falling or fastening upon it. I could shew you a branch of the same willow which shoots forth near the stock which beareth both willow and oak twigs and leaves upon it. In a meadow I use in Norwich, beset with willows and sallows, I have observed these plants to grow upon their heads; bylders,[4] currants, gooseberries, *cynocrambe,* or dog's mercury, barberries, bittersweet, elder, hawthorn.

[4] *Bylders.*] Qu. bilberry?

[FRAGMENTS.[1]]

[BIBL. BODL. MS. RAWL. LVIII, 5 & 15.]

[*Part of a Lecture.*]

CETACEOUS animals, as whales, grampusses, dolphins, though they live in water are not without lungs. I shall instance in the dolphin, as having had the opportunity to be at the dissection of two of them. The lungs are in situation and figure like those of viviparous quadrupeds, but not so spongy, and of a thicker and flesh-like substance, and probably they may have a strong and forcible respiration. And because they live and feed in the water, Providence hath provided them with an Αὐλος, fistula, or spout, by which both air may be admitted and water ejected, which hath been taken in at the mouth; so that if they be kept too long under water they perish. Now because this remarkable passage is so variously delivered by writers, it may not be improper from ocular view to state something in this point.

Pliny delivers that this fistula is on the back; Aristotle, in his History of Animals, placeth it also in the back. Julius Scaliger, in his comment upon that place, hath these words. "Aut delphinum ignoravit Aristoteles aut nos; nam quos in Adriatico quos in oceano Britannico vidimus fistulam versus occiput habent," have the fistula toward the occiput. Bellonius saith it is between the eyes, and Rondeletius above the rostrum or snout.

---

[1] FRAGMENTS.] The first of these "Fragments" was evidently intended for a passage in one of his son's lectures. The second was very probably a suggestion to Evelyn—as a passage in his proposed "*Chapter on Echoes.*"

Now that you may experimentally behold who is in the truth, and who widest from it; that you may see that sight is the best judge; and indeed that you may doubt no more, I shall produce the skull of a dolphin; wherein you may observe this passage contrived by nature and its situation; not on the back as Aristotle and Pliny affirmed; not clearly enough expressed by Scaliger, when he saith 'versus occiput;' nor sufficiently by Bellonius between the eyes; but rather as Rondeletius de piscibus; "post rostrum sive supra rostrum fistulam habet geminam quæ ad caput asperæ arteriæ pertingit interius:" you may see its situation about the rostrum, but the ductus is double and divided by a septum osseum, that it somewhat resembleth the foramina descending from the nostrils unto the palate. This ductus is filled with a soft carnous substance, which openeth on the outside with a single orifice, resembling an old Greek sigma, or our letter C, at which the water is spouted out.

(In the Chapter of Echoes, &c.)

It would be of no small moment and curiosity to contrive a whispering place; for if the arching be elliptical, made by a line of a double centre, denoting the two foci of the ellipsis, these whispering places may be made. For in the longest diameter of an ellipsis there are two points, named the foci, always equi-distant from the centre, from one whereof if a line be drawn unto the circumference so reflecting, that the angle of reflection be equal unto that of incidence, they will reflect unto the other focus, and so the sound be conveyed unto him whose ear lieth at it. And therefore if we whisper at one focus, all the vocal rays which are carried unto the circumference of the ellipsis, are, by reflexion, all ended in the other focus; and by the multitude and union of these reflected rays, the voice be strongly heard at the other extreme, or focus; not easily in the middle, unto which one . . . . the ray only arriveth.

Nor to rest in the bare . . . . or fabric, but upon the same to inscribe the mechanical draught, wherein lie the causes and reasons of this admirable effect; the figure being drawn in red or blue, extending the whole length of the arch, and each focus denoted by some mark or special colour, whereat may stand two figures of cupids, boys, or handsome draughts, with the mouth to one focus, the ear unto the other, according to the rule which containeth the mystery of this effect.

OF GREENLAND.[1]

[MS. RAWLINSON. CCCXCI.]

IF any trees grow in the country, and what sorrel and scurvy grass said to grow there: what others either on the land or sea shore: what shells likewise or other substances commonly or rarely found.

To put the leaves of those few herbs which may be found in some book, so preserving their figure between the leaves of the book.

Whether any bees, flies, and the like insects, and to bring some thereof.

Whether any such birds as we have here.

Whether any snakes, worms or snails: whether any kinds of shell fish, what, either agreeable to ours or not.

Whether all or any of their whales have teeth—to bring one of the least: what is found in their stomachs; whether herbs, fish, both or neither: what is also found in the stomachs of sea horses or morses: what herb it is they are said to feed on at the bottom of the sea: to bring a leaf thereof if it may be gotten.

To bring the white of a whale's eye made hard by boiling.

Whether the country be plane or mountainous: how the tides to ours: whether it raineth often, thundereth and lighteneth often: what winds most common.

What quantity of salt a gallon or any other greater measure of sea water affordeth, if taken up at flowing water.

What use they make of the stones or seed of whales.

To bring the bladder of a whale or morse, cleansed and dried so that it may be blown up.

The bigness of the stones and kidneys of whales, if not too big, to bring one dried, or one of a sea horse.

---

[1] OF GREENLAND.] These queries were in all probability instructions for some friend, by whom Sir Thomas was desirous of obtaining information respecting Greenland.

[EXTRACTS FROM COMMON PLACE BOOKS.]

[MS. SLOAN, 1843.]

Verses which I made upon several occasions.[1]

To one, to study and enquire into the occult and inside of his
gold, not only to please himself in looking on it.

Opto tibi Daricos, obryzos [2] opto Philippos,
   Cæsareos necnon opto tibi aureolos;
Sed præter faciem nosce interiora metalli,
   Ingenio nec sit ditior arca tuo.

O my love! when shall it be
That these eyes those eyes shall see,
And in them once more discover
The image of thy truest lover?
But since thou hast inconstant been,
   Inconstant still remain,
For so perhaps by changing still,
   Thou may'st be mine again.

Upon a covetous person in the jaundice.

Aurescat deformi aurigine qui colit aurum;
   Auratus non sis, aureus esse velis.

Alloquitur podagram nanus podagricus;—
Quid sedere in presso nanorum pollice figis,
   Cogeris hic parvâ nempe habitare casâ.
Latius ut regnes, magna et domineris in aula,
   Quære Giganteos Herculeosque pedes.

---

[1] *Verses which, &c.*] The arrangement of the extracts from this volume
have been slightly altered, in order to collect all the verses together under this title.
   [2] *obryzos.*] Aurum obryzam, finest
gold. *Plin.* 33, 3.

Optans optat podagræ paroxysmum brevem.
Dum meus Ætnæo sufflamine dactylus ardet;
    Ut mihi dactylicus sit precor iste dolor
    Sit brevis exopto dactylicusque dolor.

    Sum Davus pulchre [3] vates, non Oedipus, inquit.
    Oedipus haud fiam, sim quoque Davus ego.

One in the gout wishing for King Pyrrhus's toe, which
could not be burnt at his funeral pyre.
    O for a toe, such as the funeral [4] pyre
    Could make no work on—proof 'gainst flame and fire;
    Which lay unburnt when all the rest burnt out,
    Such amianthine toes might scorn the gout;
    And the most flaming blast the gout could blow
    Prove but an *ignis lambens* to that toe.

An inscription upon a silver cup given to a physician for
his free cure.
        Vendere quam poteras malles donare salutem.
        Mutua donatæ dona salutis habe.

Being in the country, a few miles from Norwich, I observed a
handsome bower of honey-suckles over the door of a cottage of
a right good man; which bower I fancied to speak as followeth:
        Hic humilem et sanum potius recreare colonum
            Mallem, quam nasos pascere patritios,
        Et nares muliebre lue turpesque mephyti,
            Gallia quam peperit fædave Parthenope.
        Nec fauces olidas perjuraque guttura carpo
            Decocto ex foliis atque limare meis.
        Sed neque magnatum crudelia limina cingo,
            Et queis collatus Cerberus agnus erit.
        At domini dominæque meæ pia limina adorno
            Et quam non intrant visque dolusque domum.
        Talem, si peterent de cœlo numina terras,
            Jupiter intraret Mercuriusque casam.

---

[3] *pulchre.*] "Placide." *MS. Sloan.* 1874.   [4] *funeral.*] "Regal." *MS. Sloan.* 1874.

[*Miscellanies.*]

THE charnel house of St. Paul's, of London, was under a chapel on the north side of the church-yard. When that chapel was demolished, the bones which lay in the vault, amounting to more than a thousand cart-loads, were conveyed into Finsbury fields, and there laid in a moorish place,[5] with so much soil to cover them as raised the ground for three windmills, which have since been built there, which J. Stowe hath delivered in his Survey of London.

To make an epigram or a few verses upon this subject, or of a windmill upon a mount of bones.

The picture of Signor Verdero in a proper habit:—
A suit of a mandrake or nightshade green,
A cloak of a thistle-colour, faced with holly-green,
A burdock-green hat, with a hatband of poppy-leaf, vert,
    set with emeralds and beryls, and a plume of parrot-green
    feathers,
Stockings of an ivy-green, with sage-coloured garters,
A rue-coloured sash or girdle, with brake-green fringe,
Pantoffles of cabbage-colour, laced with sea-holly or eryngo
    green,
Ribands all about, of fig-laurel and box green.

In yellow meadows I take no delight;
Let me have those which are most red and white.

That which makes meadows look so yellow, is the great abundance of ranunculus or crow-foot flowers. But of this burning and blistering plant neither horse nor cow will feed; which made me the more observe it, when I have seen peacocks crop the flowers of it. Meadows are also yellow by the flowers of *caltha palustris* or marsh marigold, of which

---

[5] *into Finsbury fields, &c.*] This spot is now covered with a beautiful square, taking its name from the manor of Fins- bury; and this gives the title of Lord Mayor, as Lord of the Manor of Finsbury. —*Gray.*

cattle will not eat, nor also of *argentina*, which leaves a yellow flower, nor of *jacobæa* or ragweed, which overruns some grounds. But the flowers of sorrel are reddish, of clover-grass red, of sweet trefoil or suckling three-leaved grass, red or white; of *ulmaria* or meadow-sweet white, as also of saxifrage, chervill, cow-parsley, *cardamine lactea* or meadow-cresses, as also of *lingua passerina;* of all which cattle will feed.

What way King Mithridates took when being overcome by Pompey, he marched with his army, and took a strange and unknown journey on the north side of the Euxine sea, to come round about into Thracia, and so to war upon the Romans. Again, whether he went by the north of the Mæotis Palus, crossing the Tanais, or made a short cut, crossing the Bosphorus Cimmerius, and so marching through the Taurica Chersonesus, which is a much shorter cut.

I cannot fancy unto myself a more acceptable representation or state of things, than if I could see all my best friends and worthy acquaintance of forty years last past upon the stage of the world at one time.

I attained my purpose, and came to reach this port by a bare wind, much labour, great pains, and little assistance.

A way to know men from boys, or boyish men and manly boys, deducible from the character in Homer.

A dialogue between an inhabitant of the earth and of the moon.

A dialogue between two twins in the womb, concerning the world they were to come into.

Question—Why do you give so much unto the poor?
Answer—I have no less for what I give unto the poor, and I am also still indebted to them.

A woodcock, in the total, weighed twelve ounces; and the feathers weighed three quarters of an ounce.

A goose weighed three pounds ten ounces in the total; the feathers, ten ounces.

A turkey weighed, in the total, twelve pounds eleven ounces; the feathers weighed eleven ounces.

A wild duck weighed, in the total, two pounds six ounces; the feathers, in all, two ounces.

A partridge, in the whole, weighed ten ounces; the feathers weighed half an ounce.

Robert Huchinson, at the Wheatsheaf, in St. Peter's, in Norwich, drank a gallon of brandy, burnt and sweetened, in the month of June, 1675, in the space of fourteen hours; he drank it hot, fell into a fever, and complained of an extraordinary burning in the stomach, but recovered in seven days, with a great loathing of brandy after: he is aged fifty-six. Another man who drank with him drank also a gallon of burnt brandy for his share, and rode home into the country after it, and seemed not to suffer any more than a burning heat in his stomach for some days. He drunk a good quantity of beer after he had made an end of his gallon of brandy.

------◆------

[MS. SLOAN. 1848.]

[*Scripture Criticism.*]

"And they brought unto him one that was deaf," &c. unto "dumb to speak." [*Mark* vii, 32.]

One that was deaf, and had an impediment in his speech; μογιλάλον. That is, one that suffered in both the nerves; the primary whereby he was chiefly deaf, and the other branching into the tongue and larynx, whereby his speech was very imperfect; so that what words he could utter were abrupt, and dissonantly delivered.

He put his fingers into his ears, and touched his tongue. He applied the visible way of cure unto both the suffering parts.

And his ears were opened, and the string of his tongue
was loosed. His ears were opened when the obstruction of
the auditory nerve was relieved. The string of his tongue,
the *vinculum* of his speech, was released when the second
branch descending upon the larynx and tongue, implicated
with the motive nerve of the seventh conjugation, was opened
and restored to its natural function.

So that he spake plain, as he did before he was deaf.
For, if he had been born deaf, we must multiply the miracle
to conceive him to speak without instruction.

————◆————

[MS. SLOAN. 1869, fol. 12—60,62—118, COLLATED WITH 1874 & 1885.]

[Hints and Extracts; to his Son, Dr. Edward Browne.]

Several hints which may be serviceable unto you and not
ungrateful unto others I present you in this paper; they are
not trite or vulgar, and very few of them any where to be
met with. I set them not down in order, but as memory,
fancy, or occasional observation produced them; whereof you
may take the pains to single out such as shall conduce unto
your purpose.

That Elias was a type of our Saviour, and that the mock-
ing and railing of the children had reference unto the deri-
sion and reviling of our Saviour by the Jews, we shall not deny,
but whether their calling of him bald pate, crying, *ascende
calve*, had any relation unto Mount Calvary, we shall not be
ready to affirm.

That Charles the Fifth was crowned upon the day of his
nativity carrieth no remarkable consideration, but that he also
took King Francis prisoner upon that day, was a concurrence
of accidents which must make that day observable.

Antipater that died on his birth-day, had an anniversary
fever all his life upon the day of his nativity, needed not an

astrological revolution of his nativity to know the day of his death.

Who will not commend the wit of astrology;—Venus born out of the sea hath her exaltation in Pisces.

Whosoever understandeth the fructifying quality of water will quickly apprehend the congruity of that invention which made the cornucopia to be filled with flowers by the naiades or water nymphs.

Who can but wonder that Fuchsius should doubt the purging quality of manna, or derive *aloe sucotina* from *succus citrinus*, which every novice now knows to be from Socotara, an island from whence 't is brought.

Take heed of confidence and too bold an opinion of your work: even the famous Phidias so erred in that notable statua of Jupiter made in a sitting posture, yet so that if he had risen up he had borne up the top of the temple.

Transcriptional erratas, ignorance in some particulars, expedition, inadvertency, make not only moles but wens in learned works, which notwithstanding being judged by their better parts admit not of reasonable disparagement. I will not say that Cicero was slightly versed in Homer, because in his books *De Gloria* he ascribeth those verses unto Ajax which were delivered by Hector. In the account of Hercules, Plautus mistakes nativity for conception. Pliny, who was well seen in Homer, denieth the art of picture in the Trojan war, and whereas it is plainly said, *Iliad* Σ, 483, that Vulcan engraved in the arms of Achilles the earth and stars of heaven. And though I have no great opinion of Machiavell's learning, yet am I unwilling to say he was but a weak historian, because he commonly exemplified in Cæsar Borgia and the petty princes of Italy ; or that he had but a slight knowledge in Roman story, because he was mistaken in placing Commodus after the emperor Severus.

Wonderful without doubt and of excellent signification are the mysteries, allegories, and figures of Holy Scripture, had we a true intelligence of them, but whether they signified any such thing as Gamaliel, Rampegnoli, Venetus, and others, do put upon them, is a great obscurity and Urim and Thummim unto me.

That the first time the Creator is called the Lord, in Holy Scripture, was twenty-eight times after he was called God, seems an excellent propriety in Scripture; which gave him the relative name after the visible frame and accomplishment of the creation, but the essential denomination and best agreeable unto him before all time or ere the world began.

Whether there be any numerical mystery in the omission of the benediction of the second day, because it was the first recess from unity and beginning of imperfection: and according to which mystery three angels appeared unto Abraham to bring him happy tidings, but two at the destruction of Sodom.

Whether Tubal Cain, the inventor of smith's work, be therefore joined with Jubal, the father of musicians, because musical consonances were first discovered from the stroke of hammers upon anvils, the diversities of their weights discovering the proportion of their sounds as is also reported from the observation of Pythagoras, is not readily to be believed.

The symbolical mysteries of Scripture sacrifices, cleansings, feasts, and expiations, is tolerably made out by Rabbins and ritual commentators, but many things are obscure, and the Jews themselves will say that Solomon understood not the mystery of the red cow. Even in the Pagan lustration of the people of Rome, at the *palilia*, why they made use of the ashes of a calf taken out of the belly of the dam, the blood of an horse, and bean straw, hath not yet found a convincing or probable conjecture.

Certainly most things are known as many are seen, that is,

by parallaxes, and in some difference from their true and proper beings; the superficial regard of things being of different aspect from their central natures; and therefore following the common view, and living by the obvious track of sense, we are insensibly imposed upon by consuetude, and only wise or happy by coestimation; the received apprehensions of true or good having widely confounded the substantial and inward verity thereof, which now only subsisting in the theory and acknowledgement of some few wise or good men, are looked upon as antiquated paradoxes or sullen theorems of the old world : whereas indeed truth, which is said not to seek corners, lies in the centre of things; the area and exterous part being only overspread with legionary vanities of error, or stuffed with the meteors and imperfect mixtures of truth.

Discoveries are welcome at all hands; yet he that found out the line of the middle motion of the planets, holds an higher mansion in my thoughts than he that discovered the Indies, and Ptolemy, that saw no further than the feet of the centaur, than he that hath beheld the snake by the southern pole. The rational discovery of things transcends their simple detections, whose inventions are often casual and secondary unto intention.

Cupid is said to be blind; affection should not be too sharp-sighted, and love not to be made by magnifying glasses; if things were seen as they are, the beauty of bodies would be much abridged ; and therefore the wisdom of God hath drawn the pictures and outsides of things softly and amiably unto the natural edge of our eyes, not able to discover those unlovely asperities which make oystershells in good faces, and hedgehogs even in Venus' moles.

When God commanded Abraham to look up to heaven and number the stars thereof, that he extraordinarily enlarged his sight to behold the host of heaven, and the innumerable heap of stars which telescopes now shew unto us, some men might be persuaded to believe. Who can think that

when 't is said that the blood of Abel cried unto heaven, Abel
fell a bleeding at the sight of Cain, according to the observation of men slain to bleed at the presence of the murderer?

The learned Gaspar Schottus dedicates his Thaumaturgus
Mathematicus unto his tutelary or guardian angel; in which
epistle he useth these words: *cui, post Deum conditorem Dei-
que magnam matrem Mariam, omnia debeo.* Now,[1] though
we must not lose God in good angels, and because they are
always supposed about us, hold lesser memory of him in our
prayers, addresses, and consideration of his presence, care,
and protection over us, yet they which do assert them have
both antiquity and Scripture to confirm them; but whether
the angel that wrestled with Jacob were Esau's good angel;
whether our Saviour had one deputed him, or whether that
was his good angel which appeared and strengthened him
before his passion; whether antichrist shall have any; whether all men have one, some more, and therefore there must
be more angels than ever were men together; whether angels
assist successively and distinctly, or whether but once and
singly to one person, and so there must be a greater number
of them than ever of men or shall be; whether we are under
the care of our mother's good angel in the womb, or whether
that spirit undertakes us when the stars are thought to concern us, that is, at our nativity, men have a liberty and latitude to opinion.

Aristotle, who seems to have borrowed many things from
Hippocrates, in the most favourable acceptation, makes mention but once of him, and that by the bye, and without reference unto his doctrine. Virgil so much beholding unto Homer hath not his name in his works; and Pliny, that seems to
borrow many authors out of Dioscorides, hath taken no notice
of him. Men are still content to plume themselves with
others feathers. Fear of discovery, not single ingenuity, makes
quotations rather than transcriptions; of which, notwithstanding, the plagiarism of many holds little consideration, where-

[1] *The learned Gaspar Schottus, &c.*]   present paragraph in *MS. Sloan.* 1874
This passage is from a duplicate of the

of, though great authors may complain, small ones cannot but take notice. Mr. Philips, in his *Villare Cantianum*, transcribes half a side of my *Hydrotaphia, or Urn Burial*, without mention of the author.[2]

Many things are casually or favourably superadded unto the best authors, and the lines of many made to contain that advantageous sense which they never intended. It was handsomely said, and probably intended by Virgil, when on every word of that verse he laid a significant emphasis, *una dolo divum si fæmina capta duorum;* and 'tis not unlikely that in that other, consisting altogether of slow and heaving spondees, he intended to humour the massive and heaving strokes of the gigantic forgers, *illi inter sese magna vi brachia tollunt;* but in that which admitteth so numerous a transposition of words, as almost to equal the ancient number of the noted stars, I cannot believe he had any such scope or intention, much less any numerical magic in another, as to be a certain rule in that numeration practised in the handsome trick of singling Christians and Turks, which is due unto later invention; or that Homer any otherwise than casually began the first and last verse of his Iliad with the same letter.

Some plants have been thought to have been proper unto peculiar countries, and yet upon better discovery the same have been found in distant countries and in all community of parts.

Jul. Scalig. in *Questionibus Familiaribus;*—
Extra fortunam est quicquid donatur amicis.

Many things are casually or favourably superadded unto the best authors, and sometimes conceits and expressions common unto them with others, and that not by imitation but coincidence, and concurrence of imagination upon harmony of production. Scaliger observes how one Italian poet fell upon

---

[2] *Mr. Philips, &c.*] This paragraph has a mark of erasure in the original.

the verse of another, and one that understood not metre, or
had ever read Martial, fell upon one of his verses. Thus it
is not strange that Homer should Hebraise, and that many
sentences in human authors seem to have their original in
Scripture. In a piece of mine, published long ago,[3] the learned annotator hath parallelled many passages with others of
Montaigne's Essays, whereas, to deal clearly, when I penned
that piece, I had never read three leaves of that author, and
scarce any more ever since.

Truth and falsehood hang almost equilibriously in some
assertions, and a few grains of truth which bear down the
balance.

To begin our discourses like Trismegistus of old, with
" verum certe verum atque verissimum est," would sound arrogantly unto new ears, in this strict enquiry of things;
wherein, for the most part, *probably and perhaps*, will hardly
serve the turn, or serve to mollify the spirits of positive contradictors.

If Cardan saith a parrot is a beautiful bird, Scaliger will
set his wits on work to prove it a deformed animal.

Few men expected to find so grave a philosopher of Po-
lemo, who spent the first part of his life in all exorbitant
vices. Who could imagine that Diogenes in his younger
days should be a falsifier of money, who in the aftercourse of
his life was so great a contemner of metal, as to laugh at all
that loved it? But men are not the same in all divisions of
their ages: time, experience, contemplation, and philosophy,
make in many well rooted minds a translation before death,
and men to vary from themselves as well as other persons.
Whereof old philosophy made many noble examples, to the
infamy of later times: wherein men merely live by the line of
their inclinations ; so that without any astrall prediction, the
first day gives the last, " primusque dies dedit extremum."
Seneca. Men are as they were; and according as evil dis-

---

[3] *in a piece of mine.*] Viz. *Religio*
Medici; see page 10, where this pas-

sage has been introduced in a note.

positions run into worse habits, being bad in the first race, prove rather worse in the last.

In vain we seek to satisfy our souls in narrow theories and close apprehensions of the divine essence, even from the revealed word, since we have a happy sufficiency in our own natures to apprehend the will and pleasure of God delivered in Holy Scripture ; it being neither of our concern nor capacity to comprehend or reach his nature. The divine revelation in such points being not framed unto intellectuals of earth. Even the best of creatures have enough to admire in their higher created natures. Admiration being the act of the creature and not of God, who doth not admire himself.

We consider not sufficiently the good of evils, nor fairly compare the mercy of providence, in things that are afflictive at first hand. The famous Andreas D'Oria invited to a feast by Aloisio Fieschi, with intent to dispatch him, fell opportunely into a fit of the gout, and so escaped that mischief. When Cato intended to kill himself, with a blow which he gave his servant that would not bring him his sword, his hand so swelled that he had much ado to effect it, whereby any but a resolved stoic might have taken a hint of consideration and that some merciful genius would have contrived his preservation.

The virtues, parts, and excellencies both of men and nations are allowable by aggregation, and must be considered by coacervation as well as single merit. The Romans made much of their conquests by the conquered; and the valour of all nations, whose acts went under their names, made up the glory of Rome. So the poets that writ in Latin built up the credit of Latium, and passed for Roman wits ; whereas if Carthage deducted Terence, Ægypt Claudian, if Seneca, Lucan, Martial, Statius, were restored unto Spain, if Marseilles should call home Petronius, it would much abridge the glory of pure Italian fancy ; and even in Italy itself, if the Cisalpine Gauls should take away their share, if Verona and Mantua should challenge Catullus and Virgil, and if in other parts out of Campagna di Roma, the Venusine Apulians should pull away their Horace, the Umbrians their Plautus, the Aquinatians Juvenal, Volaterrani Persius, and the Pelignians of Abruzzo their Ovid, the rest of Rome or Latium would make no large volume.

Where 'tis said in the book of Wisdom that the earth is unto God but as a sand, and as a drop of morning dew, therein may be implied the earth and water or the whole terraqueous globe; but when 't is delivered in the Apocalypse that the angel set his right foot upon the sea and his left upon the earth, what farther hidden sense there is in that distinction may farther be considered.

Of the seven wise men of Greece 'twas observed by Plutarch, that only Thales was well versed in natural things, the rest obtained that name for their wisdom and knowledge in state affairs.

Whether the ancients were better architects then their successors many discourses have passed. That they were not only good builders, but expedite and skilful demolishers, appears by the famous palace of Publicola, which they pulled down and rased to the ground by his order in one day.

We are no way doubtful that there are witches, but have not been always satisfied in the application of their witchcrafts, or whether the parties accused or suffering have been guilty of that abomination, or persons under such affliction suffered from such hands. In ancient time we read of many possessed and probably there are many still; but the common cry and general opinion of witches hath confounded that of possession; men salving such strange effects from veneficial agents and out of the party suffering. Many strange things have been done beyond the salvo of human reason, which might proceed as well from possession as venefication. If the man in the gospel had now lived, who would not have said he had been bewitched, which few or none might then suspect? Or who now sayeth that Saul was bewitched? Many examples may occur of the like nature among us; wherein, whether possession be not sometimes mistaken for venefication, may well be considered.

Whether it might not be fitly added unto the *questiones peregrinæ* of Bartholomæus;—how tender conceptions shall be ordered at the last day, and whether those before animation shall be improved unto perfection?

Whether that fiction be elegantly contrived, when Somnus is made to make Endymion sleep with his eyes open, that Luna might look upon them? since there is no beauty in open sleeping eyes, but a seeming deformity in them.

Whether it were not more dulness in Polyphemus to omit to praise the eyes of his Mrs. Galatea, while he commendeth her other parts, than weariness to pass them over, lest he should consequently condemn his own?

Whether it be general that lepers have no lice?

Whether great ear'd persons have short necks, long feet, and loose bellies?

Whether in voracious persons and gourmands the distance between the navel and the sternon be greater than from the sternon unto the neck?

" An misericordes sint θηλυγόνοι, fæminigenitores;" how verified by your observation and historical example? since pity and mercy are affections of generosity, and generous persons are commonly of a masculine temper.

How to make out those physiognomical notes of Aristotle concerning soft and effeminate persons; " genuflexibilitas, inclinatio capitis ad dextram, ambulationes duplices, oculorum circumspectiones?"

Whether haloes be so rare betwixt May and September

as Gassendus delivereth from his observations in France, and whether his observation there be verified in other climates?

To observe that little spot behind the ear whereof Omnibonus Ferrarius takes notice and makes it a mortal sign in dysenterical persons; and is also mentioned in the book *De Pustulis*, ascribed unto Hippocrates, and translated by Golius, as Bartholinus hath delivered. *Centur. 6ta.*

To observe whether animals drowned have no water in their lungs and weason.

Whether, as there be most female witches, so most females are bewitched and why?

Whether, if observable occurrences were strictly taken notice of before the appearance of comets, they may not prove as remarkable as those that follow after, an equal space of time being taken before as after?

Whether as remarkable and great occurrences have not happened without the appearance of comets as any with, or some after them?

Whether northern comets or on this side of the equator have proved more fatal than southern, and whether smaller not sometimes more ominous than greater?

Since there be two major remedies in physic, bleeding and purging, which thereof deserves the preeminency; since in the general purging cures more diseases: since the whole nation of the Chinese use no phlebotomy, and many other nations sparingly, but all some kind of purgative evacuation: and since besides in man there are so few hints for bleeding from any natural attempt in horses, cows, dogs, birds, and other creatures.

Whether it be safe for obtaining a bass or deep voice to make frequent use of vitriol, and whether it hath such an effect?

Whether posssession be not often mistaken for witchcraft, and many thought to be bewitched which are indeed possessed ?

If in the terraqueous globe all that now is land were sea, and all that is sea were land, to discover what great differences there would be in all things, as to constitution of climes, tides, navigation, and many other considerables.

To observe whether the juice of the fruit of *ficus Indica*, taken inwardly, will cause the urine to have a red and bloody colour, as is delivered by some and commonly received in parts of Italy where it plentifully groweth ; and whether the juice of the prickly fig from America will not do the like?

Whether ice be to be found in subterraneous cavities and deep caves in the earth?

To observe the gangleon in birds that are apt to imitate the speech of man, and what advantage they have by any such like part?

What to be hoped from that feminine practice, which I have known in pearl of the eye, to put a louse into the eye at night?

Whether mare's milk be properly used against worms, or sow's milk to procure sleep, to which end many women among us give it unto children?

Whether thistle apples, that is the bunches found upon the common small thistle, running into knops without flower or seed, do any thing to the intent that they are so much sought for by many?

The left rib of roasted beef powdered, a sovereign remedy against fluxes.

That if a woman with child looks upon a dead body, the child will be pale complexioned.

Why little lap dogs have a hole in their heads, and often other little holes out of the place of the sutures?

Why a pig's eyes drop out in roasting rather than other animals?

Why a pig held up by the tail leaves squeaking?

Why a low signed horse is commonly a stumbler?

What is the use of dew claws in dogs?

Whether that will hold, which I have sometimes observed, that lice combed out of the head upon a paper, will turn and move towards the body of the party, and so as often as the paper is turned about?

An pestis sit ex lege naturæ, ut quærit Cardanus?

An detur pestis artificialis?

An detur unguentum pestiferum, ex cadaveribus peste mortuorum confectum, ut in historia pestis Mediolanensis?

An pestis unquam grassetur inter pisces?

Whether services and cornel-trees be so dangerous unto persons which have been bit by a mad dog, as Codronchi and others mention.

What kind of motion natation or swimming is, and to which to be referred; whether not compounded of a kind of salition, and volation, the one performed by the hands, the other by the legs and feet? What kind of motion sliding is; whether it imitateth not the *motus projectorum* upon a plane, wherein the *corpus motum* is not separated *a motore?*

An foculi portatiles Belgarum sint monstrifici?

An Lastaurocacabus Athenæi sit olla patris (olla podrida) Hispanorum?

Whether the name of a *palatium*, or palace, began first to be used for prince's houses in the time of Augustus, when he dwelt in *Monte Palatino*, as Dion delivereth, or whether the word is not to be found in authors before his time?

Whether the heads of all mummies have the mouth open, and why?

Why solipeds, or whole hoofed animals, arise with their fore legs first, bisulcous with their hinder?

If a child dieth and the neck groweth not stiff, but continueth flaccid many hours after, another will not long after die in the same house; a groundless opinion of many women with us.

Whether, where it is said (*Wisdom* 7.), "Deus dedit mihi horum quæ sunt veram cognitionem," that text implieth his knowledge in the metaphysics, that being a science *de ente*, as the other expressions imply his natural and moral knowledge?

Whether Noah might not be the first man that compassed the globe? Since, if the flood covered the whole earth, and no lands appeared to hinder the current, he must be carried with the wind and current according to the sun, and so in the space of the deluge, might near make the tour of the globe. And since, if there were no continent of America, and all that tract a sea, a ship setting out from Africa without other help, would at last fall upon some part of India or China.

Whether that of David, "convertentur ad vesperam et famem patientur ut canes," may be prophetically applied to the late conversion of the wild Americans, as it is delivered in *Gloriosus Franciscus Redivivus*, or the *Chronicles of the Acts of the Franciscans*, lib. 3.

Hesiod delivers that none who planted the olive gathered of the fruit thereof.

Theophrastus affirmeth, that the olive grew not, except near the sea or within forty miles of it.

Fenestella delivereth that olives were not to be found in Africa, Spain, France, nor Italy.

How the Macrocephali, or long-headed people, arose, Hippocrates hath instructed us. How the Chinese come to have such little feet, every history of that country delivereth. But how the people of Rovigno come to be lame, so that among seven thousand of that city, about a third part are lame, as Du Loir hath observed, is yet to be enquired.

Diogenes, the Cynick, being asked what was the best remedy against a blow, answered a helmet. This answer he gave, not from any experience of his own, who scarce wore any covering on his head; yet he that would see how well a helmet becometh a cynick, may behold it in that draught of Diogenes, prefixed to his life, in the new edition of the *Epitome of Plutarch's Lives*, in English; wherein, in the additional lives, he is set forth, soldier-like, with a helmet and a battle axe.

Aristotle, lib. animal.

Whether till after forty days, children, though they cry, weep not; or, as Scaliger expresseth it, " vagiunt sed oculis siccis."

Whether they laugh not upon tickling?

Why though some children have been heard to cry in the womb, yet so few cry at their birth, though their heads be out of the womb?

Traitte de la politique de France. In this French discourse, a hard character is given of the English, and this among the rest;—a people fit only for handy strokes, and ready execution, but incapable of managing a war with discretion. To refute this by many examples, and even in our wars with the French.

Whether there be any such consent between the horns

and the hoofs in oxen, that the anointing of the horns may
be of effect in the diseases of the hoofs, as Aristotle delivers,
and Scaliger directly rejecteth not, lib. 8, *Hist. Animal.* "In
podagra pedes tument verum non intereunt, sed ungulas
amittant, melius continent delibatis pice calida cornibus."

That a horse is a ζωον φιλολουτρον και φιλυδρον, may be granted;
that, farther considered, which Scaliger addeth in his comment, "Gaudent lavacris equi praesertim nigri, et maxime qui
in fine aestatis nati sunt:" lib. 8.

"Faeniculorum umbellae, antequam comedantur, aperiantur
et diligenter concutiantur, ut a vermibus emundentur, a quorum esu, pessima deveniunt symptomata;" *ex Balthasaro Pi-
sanello.* Enquire more diligently after these worms in due
season.

Observe farther the effect of Jacobus Doviretus's remedy
against the *elephantiasis,* by a *decoctio ulmi,* used for many
days in common drink and a little white wine.

Observe farther the remedy of Marquardus against angi-
nas and aposthemes of the throat; "observatum est come-
dentem ex cochleari hederae ligneo, et bibentem in aliquo
vase ligneo hederae, nunquam vel raro in gutturis vel uvulae
apostema incurrere."

Whether the feeding on carp be so apt to bring on fits of
the gout, as Julius Alexandrinus affirmeth?

"Mespili lignum collo appensum, mire ab abortu gravidas
defendere. Confiteor in pleurisi tale remedium fuisse a me
expertum idque certum et sanum remedium semper invenisse." *Baricellus.* This is an *euporeston,* and worth the
trying; the like we have known often to succeed upon the
wearing of a girdle of sea horse leather, and the eaglestone.

Cardanus, to try the alteration of the air, exposeth a
sponge, which groweth dark when the air is inclined to moisture. Another way I have made more exact trial; by putting
a dry piece of sponge into one balance of a gold scale, so

equally poised, with weights in the other balance, that it will hang without inclining either way. For then upon alteration of the air to moisture, the scale with the sponge will fall, and when the air grows hot and dry will rise again. The like may be done by *favago marina*, found commonly on the sea shore. The change of the weather I have also observed by hanging up a dry *aplyssalus marinus*, which grows moist and dry according to the air; as also *phasganium marinum*, sea laces, and others.

To observe that *carbo odoratus, qui sub arthemisiæ radicibus solstitio æstivo colligitur*, because it is so highly commended by Hugenius, for a remedy against the epilepsy, if given forty days; and Baricellus confirmeth it by his own experience.

Syrupus de spina cervina is of frequent and excellent use. Try it in *tenesmo*, which was the experienced medicine of Baricellus in that case, in the quantity of ʒi *aut* ʒii *in vino albo aut aqua:* the patient to eat sparingly after it, and to sleep.

To observe that insect which a countryman shewed Baricellus, found in the flowers of *Eryngium cichoreum*, which readily cure warts; *est coloris Thalassini cum maculis rubris, et assimulatur proportione corporis cantharidi, licet parvulum sit. Acceperat ea rusticus, et singula in singulis verrucis digitis expressit unde exibat liquor.*

Whether the flowers of *verbascum* or mullein shake and fall most in the morning; *illius enim plantæ hæc est proprietas, ut sole accedente flores decidant.*

To make trial of this; whether live crawfish put into spirits of wine will presently turn red, as though they had been boiled, and taken out walk about in that colour.

In the head of the reddish grey snails without shells, I have often found stones or flat testaceous substances. To acquire some quantity of them; to make trial of those qualities in them, as against quartans, by way of amulet; in the strangury, and for easy delivery if taken inwardly; and against dryness and thirst, if held in the mouth in distempers.

'T is a ludicrous experiment in Baricellus; to rub napkins and handkerchiefs with powder of vitriol for such as sweat or have used to wipe their faces; for so they become black and sullied. Whether shirts thus used may not do something against itch and lice. Whether shirts washed or well rubbed in quicksilver would not be good to that end.

Since you are so much unsatisfied with the many rational medicines which you say you have tried for the gout, you have leisure enough to make trial of these empirical medicines:—

Wear shoes made of a lion's skin.

Wear a plaster of montacana upon your feet.

Try the way of transplantation; give poultices taken from the part unto dogs, and let a whelp lie in the bed with you.

Use an ointment of ostrich, vulture, and hern's grease.

Suffocate an eel or frog in your wine, to make thee little affected to wine.

If you are not afraid to be lame without pain, try the remedy of Agrippa, to put your feet in vinegar.

Try the magnified amulet of Muffetus, of spider's legs worn in a deer's skin; or of tortoise's legs cut off from the living tortoise, and wrapped up in the skin of a kid.

Since you find no benefit in the noble plasters of the Duke of Wirtemberg, of King James and of Charles the Fifth, try the *empl. ciconiæ* made up of *stercus ciconiæ*.

If you have a mind to proceed farther you may see what cure may be had from transplantation. And may also consider of the sigil of Paracelsus.

To consider that of Cardan in his *Encomium Podagræ*, whether the gout freeth and preserveth from the stone in the bladder and the pthysis of the lungs, which he reckons in many the *dona podagræ*.

Yet Sir Arthur Jenny, who had often fits of the gout, died

of the stone in the bladder. He had a remarkable cough above forty years, but no proper pthysis when he died.

Whether podagrical persons have the best palates, and are the choicest tasters of wine, and commonly discursive persons.

Cur claudi venerei, gibbosi dolosi, strabi fraudulenti, calvi in actionibus prompti?

The emperor Severus, Budæus, Erasmus, Julius Scaliger, great examples of the gout.

Erasmus e cubili podagræ quicquid legi meretur exprompsit: præclarissima scriptorum monumenta podagræ debemus.

Three magnified plasters set down by Zozelius de podagra: one of the Duke of Wirtemberg, another of King James, a third of Charles the Fifth; to examine these well, and whether a plain anodyne cataplasm affordeth not better relief in red and inflamed gouts, which so impatiently endure plasters.

Eat partridge's eggs.

To consider and try the two notable amulets in that case, one . . . . from the feet of a tortoise cut off alive and worn in kid's skin; the other of Muffetus from spider's legs worn in a deer's skin.

To examine the success and cures said to be wrought by transplantation in that disease.

To try that way of purging by lapis lazuli, unto which Brasavolus, *de medicamentis purgantibus,* so much encourageth. ℞ Lap. lazuli prepar. ℨj camphoræ, anisi, cin. zinzib. mastick; ana gr. vj. cum suc. salviæ, vel diacatholicon, q. s. fiant pilulæ x. ℭ. first trying l. laz. jij, which is also commended by Gioravanti to try also what effect it hath by infusion.

Whether purging pomanders may prove of any effectual use.

Gaddius in Scriptores upon William the Conqueror, writes that he wrote a book *de Supremo puniendi Judicio;* whether hereby be any more meant than that register which is called Doomsday Book.

To cleanse and clear pearls by washing or steeping them in May dew taken from lettuces. *Boet.*

Whether a true emerald feels colder in the mouth than another.

Whether the way of Amatus Lusitanus be to be followed, to clip the leeches after they are fastened unto the hæmorrhoids or other parts. *Centuria 5ta.*

Whether aloe be so powerful a fœcundating medicine as he confidently promiseth. *5ta.*

Whether his test of fœcundity which he peculiarly commended, be to be insisted upon; *coaguli leporis 3j. aqua calida dissoluti, et mulieri in balneo existenti exhibiti; si ventri dolores accidant fæcunda est, si non, infæcunda. Cent. 6ta.*

How far to rely upon his remedy for the increase of milk, from the powder of hippocampe, or *cavallo marino*, found in many shores of Italy. *Centuria 4ta.* Since neither Diascorides, Mathiolus, nor others mention such quality, and chiefly receive it as remedy against the biting of a mad dog.

Since these few observations please you, for your farther discourse and consideration, I would not omit to send you a larger list, scatteringly observed out of good authors, relating unto medical enquiry, and whereof you may single out one daily to discourse upon it; which may be a daily recreation unto you, and employ your evening hours, where your affairs afford you the conversation of studious and learned friends.

Plut: in vita Tim.

Timoleon his sight beginning to fail he lost it at last altogether. Athanæus writes that as he was in his camp at Mylles, there came a white spot in his eyes that dimmed [his] eyes somewhat, so that every one perceived that he should lose his sight altogether.

Plut. in vita Cleomenis.

It chanced that Cleomenes marching thither, being very hot, drank cold water, and fell on such a bleeding withal that his voice was taken from him and he almost stifled.

Hippotus pricked Cleomenes in the heel, to see if he were yet alive; whether this were not a good way of trial upon so sensible a part.

Now a disease took Antigonus, King of Macedon, whereon he died, which appeared a phthisis mixed with a sore catarrh, and fiercely crying in the fight, he tore his lungs worse than they were before.

In vita Pyrrhi.

Men hold opinion that he did heal those that were sick of the spleen, by sacrificing a white cock, and touching the place of the spleen with his right foot, they lying on their backs. There was none so poor that he denied that remedy, and took the cock he sacrificed for a reward, which pleased him very well.

Ammianus Marcellinus in vita Juliani.

A horseman's javelin pierced within his short ribs and stuck fast in the nether lappet or fillet of his liver : and by reason the wound opened very wide, and the tumour of the veins and arteries stopped his spirits, as also with drinking of a draught of cold water, he was easily dispatched this life.

Ammianus Marcellinus in vita Joviani.

He was found dead in his bed. It is said he could not endure the smell of his bedchamber newly plastered with mortar made of lime, or that he came to his end occasioned by an huge fire kindled of coals, others that he crammed his belly so full that he died of a surfeit. Whether all these causes be not allowable?

Plut. in vita Julii Cæsaris.

There fell a pestilent disease among them, which came by ill meats which hunger drove them to eat; but after he had taken the city of Gomphes, in Thessalie, he met not only with plenty of victuals, but strangely did rid them of that disease; for the soldiers meeting with plenty of wine, drank hard, and making merry, drank away the infection of the

pestilence: in so much that drinking drunk they overcame
their disease and made their bodies new again.   The soldiers
were driven to take sea weeds, called alga, and washing away
the brackishness thereof with sea water, putting to it a little
herb, called dogstooth, to cast it to their horses to eat.

The country of Thessaly became the more considerable
unto me, because it hath produced many famous persons, and
been the seat of many notable actions: and more especially
because the famous Hippocrates, and father of physicians,
lived and practised in it, as may be collected from the oration
of his son Thessa unto the Athenians, and the description of
his life, by Soranus, annexed unto his works; wherein 't is
delivered that he was admonished by dream to live in Thessaly, that he had an habitation in Thessaly, that the princes
and rulers of the barbarian nation of Illyria and Pæonia sent
unto him, as also the King of Macedonia, that he died in or
about Larissa; that he was buried between Gyrton and Larissa, and has had of old a monument in those parts.   And it
may be also observed that in the books of Hippocrates, where
he sets down the particular progress of diseases of his patients,
unto life and death, together with their names and places of
habitation, it may be observed that he mentions many places
of Thessaly, but of any one place the greatest number of
his patients were of Larissa.

That America was peopled of old, not from one, but several nations, seems probable from learned discourses concerning their originals: and whether the Tyrians and Carthaginians had not a share therein may be well considered;
and if the periplus of Hanno or his navigation about Africa
be warily perpended, it may fortify that conjecture; for he
passed the straits of Hercules with a great fleet and many
thousand persons of both sexes; founded divers towns, and
placed colonies in several parts of that shore; and sailed in
tolerable account as far about as that place now called Cabo
de Tres Puntas.

To these there is little question but the Carthaginians
sometimes repaired, and held communication with them.

The colonies also being a people of civility could not but continue the use of navigation; so that either the Carthaginians in their after researches might be carried away by the trade winds between the tropics, or finding therein no difficult navigation might adventure on such a voyage; and also their colonies left on so convenient a shore might casually, if not purposely, make the same adventure.

The Chinese also could hardly avoid, at least might easily have, a part in their originals. For the east winds being very rare, and the west almost constantly blowing from their shore, being once at sea they were easily carried to the back part of America.

If there were ever such a great continent in the western ocean, as was hinted of old by Plato, and the learned Kircherus considers might by subterraneous eruptions be partly swallowed up and overthrown, and partly leave the islands yet remaining in the ocean, it is not impossible or improbable that from great antiquity some might be carried from thence upon the American coast, or some way be peopled from those parts.

While Attahualpa, King of Peru, and Montezuma, King of Mexico, might owe their originals unto Asia or Africa.

Since the Indian inhabitants are found, at least conceived, to have peopled the southern continent, whether these, after debating over *terra incognita*, might not pass or be carried over into Magellanica or the south of America, may also be enquired, and some might not come in at this door.

If any plantations of civil nations were ever made from civil nations, how it comes to pass that letters and writing was unknown unto all the parts of America.

Why no wonder is likewise made how the Islas de los Ladrones, or islands of thieves, were peopled, since they are so far removed from any neighbour continent.

Strabo, lib. 4.

Garumna et Ligeris.—Hi duo fluvii quodammodo parallel

2 D 2

sunt respectu Pyrenes, ac cum ea duas includunt parallel-
ogrammas areas, quarum reliqua latera oceano et Cemmenis
montibus describuntur.

Whether Strabo rightly understood the whole current of
these rivers while he illustrates their content by two parallel-
ograms, which must be made out with so great a latitude,
especially if you take not in the river Tarne, which runs into
the Garonne, and whether this illustration be not more agreeable unto the Isara and Druentia, the Lisere, and the Durance, and the Mediterranean sea, the two other sides being
made by the Rhodanus and the Alps?

To reconcile the differences between Hippocrates, de aere,
aquis, et locis, and Avianus de Periplo Ponti Euxini, about
the description of the river Phasis; which the one makes
a stagnant, the other a swift river; Hippocrates a corrupting water, Avianus affirms it will keep uncorrupted many
years.

Aristot. lib. 8, cap. 22, de hist. Animalium.

How to make out that of Aristotle that all creatures bit by
a mad dog become mad, excepting man: since by unhappy
experience so many men have been mischieved thereby; or
whether it holdeth not better at second than at first hand, so
that if a dog bite a horse, and that horse a man, the evil
proves less considerable, as we seem to have observed in
many. Whether St. Bellin's priests cure any after the hy-
drophobia; whether hellebore, tin, garlick, treacle, and *pulvis
palmarii* be the prime remedies against this poison; and why
the use of *alyssum galeni* is not more in request; and how the
cornel and service tree become such mischievous promoters
of that venom; and how far this venom takes place in Ireland,
where they have no venomous creature, and not long ago very
few quartan agues.

What intent or what advantage the Helvetians might have,
when quitting their country in Cæsar's time, being hindered
from coming into Province, they designed to march into Xan-
toigne a country so remote from them.

How to make out that of Strabo, that the river Rhine runs parallel to that of Seine whereon Paris standeth, or that from the mouth of Rhine a man may see a part of Kent.

Urbs Nemansus Arecomicorum caput. Sita est urbs in via quæ ex Hispania in Italiam ducit per æstatem commoda, hyeme et vere lutosa ac fluviorum eluvie molesta, fluviorum quidam scaphis trajiciuntur, alii pontibus instrati." How this to be construed when 't is seated in a dry soil, and the ordinary rivers of the Vidurle, and the Gardon eight miles from it, and since for the commodity of water they were fain to convey it by a subterraneous aqueduct, about ten miles off, conveying the water over the Gardon, by an unparalleled bridge, yet standing, and making that famous antiquity of Port du Gard, near Remolins, not far out of the way between Avignon and Nismes.

When Strabo delivereth that Nismes exceeded Narbona in dominion but not in populosity, whether it must not be understood in order to his time, who lived in the reign of Augustus; and not so verifiable in the reign of Domitian, Adrian, and Antoninus, who being born in that place, added all advantages unto it, as did also Adrian in raising . . . . . . to his empress. And since he that beholds the circuit of the old ruined wall, will hardly conceive it to have been much less than Paris, and larger at least than any other city in Gallia; and bearing still for its arms the crocodile bound to a palm tree, so often to be met with in ancient medals, whether it doth not retain as ancient arms as any city in Europe?

Whether the Romans had not as many or more theatres and amphitheatres in a piece of Gallia, than in all their other conquests of Europe, out of Italy; since southward of the Loir they left no less than fourteen; as namely, at Poictiers, Pont de Sey, Sainctes, Perigueux, Bourdeaux, Bourges, Lyons, Vienne, Aurange, Tholouse, Nismes, Arles, Antibes, and Narbonne.

When Annibal marched out of Spain for Italy, no mention

is made how he passed the river Atax or Aude with his elephants; whether he declined the Vidurle, or forded the Gardon; no mention I say is made of passing the rivers till he arrived at the Rhosne, which with great artifice, labour, and unquietness of his elephants, and also opposition of the Gauls on the other side, he got over; how he passed the Isere, a great and rapid river, is not at all delivered; at what part he crossed the Rhosne is not directly specified; but since the Volcæ and Arecomici which had fled to the other side opposed him, 't is most probable he passed over from Vivarez, between Valence and Orange, or below the great and swift river of Isara, or L'Isere. For Hanno went twenty-five miles above, and crossed the Rhosne with his horse, to fall upon the rear of the Gauls, which faced Annibal's camp below, and where he was to pass; so that they passed below the Isere to prevent a second trouble and have a better retreat. 'T is also said by Livy, that Annibal being got over, sent a party of Numidian scouts to discover the Roman army, whereof the main body lay in Province; which he probably would not have done if he had been encamped above the Isere. It is likewise delivered, that Cornelius Scipio, marching out of Province unto the place of Annibal's camp, found him gone three days, so that probably concluding he must be passed the Isere, he thought it not safe to force his pass over the river against so strong a power, which was now beyond his approach. And whereas it is affirmed by Livy and Plutarch, that in four encampings he arrived to the concurrence of the river Soane and Rhosne, where Lyons now standeth, it may be conceived he made speedy marches to avoid Scipio behind him, and by all means declined battle, until he might come into Italy, when he hoped to have the Cisalpine Gauls to join with him.

And surely though the longest this was the wisest way, to decline the maritime Alps, or march through Province, where the Roman army must have met him; wherein Scipio seemed to have committed the oversight; for if he had hastened to join with the many thousand Gauls which opposed Annibal's passing over the Rhosne, he had probably prevented the ensuing calamity of Italy; whereas having lost that opportunity,

he made hard shift to return into Italy, and could not meet
with Annibal before he came to the Tesin by Pavia, where
himself was like to lose his life, and the Romans lost the
battle.

'T was surely a noble sight to behold that numerous and
mixed army, with elephants and baggage to force their way
over this impetuous river, and only second unto the siege of
Alexia, and confederate strength of Gallia. Though the
memorable battle of Charles Martel with the Saracens and
numerous forces of Atius the Roman general, and Attila the
Hun, and his great defeat by Tholouse, [be of high consideration.

Which way Annibal took towards the Alps or over them,
is very uncertain, till we more clearly understand that passage
of Livy, that parting towards them he marched not the direct
way, but took the left hand toward the Tricastines, and so on
the borders of the Vocontians unto the Tricorians; and had
no impediment till he came at the river Druentia, which is
rendered the Durance. Now if he took the left hand in reference unto Gallia, he could not well come at the Vocontians
and the Durance; if the left accounting from Rome, he could
not well pass at the Pennine Alps, and mount Bernard, as is
commonly conceived, nor fall upon the Durance.

Whether the commodity of situation have not always been
the great advantage of places, and especially that of Lyons.
When Hannibal marched to the concurrence of the Soane and
the Rhosne, where that city now standeth, there was no mention of Lyons, which upon the best record was built by Lucius Munacius Plancus; and yet not longer after than in the
time of Strabo, it was in his expression the most populous
place of all Gallia, except Narbonne. And by this convenience, it still maintaineth the second place of France, as making the passage from England, France, Italy, Spain, and Germany; and had been more advanced if the lieutenant of Nero
had gone through with his design to unite the Soane and the
Moselle, and so to have made a water passage from the mid-
land sea unto the German ocean; and the like some of the

kings of France have seriously designed between the Aude and the Garonne.

How to make good the account of Benjamin Tudelensis, the Jew, concerning Montpellier, or as he calls it, Montpeslier, who passing that way from Spain unto Jerusalem, about five hundred years ago, hath thus delivered himself. " Locus est quo ex omni loco ad mercaturam confluunt Christianorum et Mohammedanorum plurimi, e regionibus Algarbiæ, Lombardiæ, et regno magno illius Romæ, universo Regno Ægyptio, terra Israelitica, et Græcia, Gallia, Hispania et Anglia, adeo ut ex omnium linguarum populo ibidem reperientur, una cum Gervensibus et Pisanis." Whether this may be made out from history or probability since it hath no port nor any considerable river, and Marseilles not far off hath carried a main trade as the same author delivers, " hæc civitas maritima celeberrima est commerciis."

Whether after all the mutations of Gallia, by nations, laws, and customs, the temper of the present Gauls makes not good that of the old, as Strabo hath set it down. " Animosi, stolidi, arrogantes, ornatus studiosi."

Whether the Burgundians, who possessed both Burgundies, Lyonois, Dauphiny, and much of Provence, did politically place the seat of their kingdom at Arles?

Whether the observation of Strabo concerning Gallia hold true in all nations, that the maritime inhabitants are the most fighting men?

How to salve that of Ptolemy who placeth the mouth of Rhenus in the latitude of 54, which is rather agreable unto the mouth of the river Elbe or Albis.

Whether it must not be rather taken for an extraordinary then ordinary course of passage when 'tis delivered by Strabo, lib. 5. " A Placentia autem Ravennam secundo Pado navigatur, duobus diebus naturalibus," as Xilander hath rendered it?

Since Italy at first view so tolerably resembleth a leg, whether if the ancients had handsome or tolerable maps, it be not somewhat strange how Pliny should compare it unto an oak leaf, or Eustathius to an ivy?

Since a great part of Gallia Cisalpina was confessedly over-run and inhabited by Gallic nations, and the Galli, Senones, and Cenomani, are brought as far as from the countries about Sens and Lemaine, whether it be not more probable that the Heneti or Veneti came rather from the Gallic Veneti in Britanie, when Vannes yet retains their name, than from the ancient Trojans, as Strabo hath left some account, may well admit of doubt.

How Ausonius, in a large description of Burdeaux, his own native city, omitteth any mention of the two famous antiquities, thereof Palais de Tutele and Palais de Galien, or the Amphitheatre, the ruins thereof are yet to be seen in that ,city?

How Strabo, who mentioneth many ordinary rivers in Gallia, should omit the considerable streams of the Mosa and the Scaldis, the Maze and the Scheldt, and mention none between the Sequana and the Rhine.

How Strabo can be made out, when he delivereth that that part of Britany which lieth against Gallia is the largest side thereof; or whether the Romans well understood the dimensions of this island before the time of Vespasian, when Agricola his lieutenant caused some ships to sail about the island.

When Strabo saith that the old Britans paid for tribute "fræna eburnea," whether this must not be rather taken for such as were made of the teeth of cetaceous and great fishes, rather resembling than proper ivory or elephant's teeth, since Solinus observeth that they made use of such and made hafts of swords therewith, as they still do in more northern regions.

Whether Corah, Dathan, and Abiram, were swallowed up

in the earth as 'tis commonly conceived, or rather Dathan and Abiram, and yet not Corah; who was burnt, if we strictly consult the original. And what in that point is alleged for it by Estius?

Whether that passage of *Deut.* 28, *verse* 68, " classibus reducet in Ægyptum," be not sufficiently made out by the record of Josephus, when Titus, after the taking of Jerusalem, sent all or most under seventeen years of age into Egypt.

If the prophet Jonah were contemporary unto Jeroboam and Osias, as good commentators determine, it is in vain to think he was the woman of Sareptha's son.

Whether, when he intended from Joppa unto Tarsis, he was bound for Tarsis in Cilicia, Tartessus in Bætica, of Spain, or Tarsis by which sometimes Carthage is called, it is not of moment to decide. 'T is plain that they were strangers of the ship, since every one called upon his God, and since they demanded from whence he was; which, although they did not by an interpreter, yet if they were of the colonies of the Phænicians, either of Tartessus or Carthage, their language having no small affinity with the Hebrew, they might have been understood.

The story of Jonah might afford the hint unto that of Andromeda and the sea monster, that should have devoured her; the scene being laid at Joppa by the fabulists: as also unto the fable of Hercules out of Lycophron, three nights in the whale's belly, that is of Hercules Phœnicius.

Some nations of the Scythians affected only or chiefly to make use of mares in their wars, because they do not stop in their course to stale like horses. Quære.

Plutarch.—He that killed Caius Gracchus and cut off his head, was to be rewarded with the weight thereof in gold; to advance the weight thereof he took out the brains and putting

lead into it, made it weigh seventeen pounds and the third part
of a pound. How much this exceedeth the ordinary weight
of a head?

Plutarch.—To render their iron money unserviceable to
other uses, the Lacedæmonians quenched it in vinegar. This
way might make it brittle, but withal very apt to rust. Inquire farther of their drinking cup named *cothon*.

Whether that rigid commonwealth were not more strict in
the rule and order, than measure, of their diet, or how their
provision cometh short of a regular and collegian diet, when
every one brought monthly into the hall one bushel of meal,
eight gallons of wine, five pounds of cheese, and two pounds
and half of figs, beside money for sudden and fresh diet.

What to judge of that law that permitted them not to have
lights to guide them home from the common hall in the night,
that so they might be emboldened to walk and shift in the dark.

Though many things in that state promoted temperance,
fortitude, and prudence; yet were there many also culpable
to high degrees; as justifying theft, adultery, and murder:
while they encouraged men to steal, and the grand crime
thereof was to be taken in the action: while they admit of
others to lie with their wives, and had not the education of
their own children: while they made no scruple to butcher
their slaves in great numbers : and while they had apothetes
or places to make away with their children which seemed
weak or not to strongly shapen as to promise lusty men : and
therefore well needed that Pagan fallacy that these ways were
confirmed and ratified by the oracle of Delphos.

It was the custom of their midwives not to wash their children with water but with wine and water, whereby, if they were
weak, they extenuated and much pined. Which whether a
reasonable test of constitutions may be doubted.

Cato Utican being to convey a great treasure from Cyprus
unto Rome, he made divers little chests and put into every
one two talents and five hundred drachms, and tied unto each
a long rope with a large piece of cork, that, if the ship should

miscarry, the corks might shew where the chests laid at the
bottom of the sea. A good piece of providence, and done
like Cato.   Whether not still to be practiced, if the make of
our ships, with deck upon deck, would admit of it.

Upon the 16th day of October, Cæpio was overcome by
the Cambrians, and Lucullus obtained a battle over Tigranes
and the Asian forces, scarce to be matched since.   From this
and the like a hint may be taken to compose an historical calendar, affixing unto each day the famous battles, actions,
events, and occurrences, which authentic accounts and best
records afford from ancient and not too late delivery.   Which
may daily serve to revive to mind, the greatest memorials of
time ; wherein may be observed how thin some days, how full
some others have been, in the great concerns of the world, and
some days sufficient to afford the discourse of a volume.

How the ancients made the north part of Britain to bend
so unseasonably eastward, according to the old map, agreeable unto Ptolemy?   Or how Pliny could so widely mistake
as to place the Isle of Wight between Ireland and England,
if it be not mistaken for the Isle of Man or Anglesea.

Julius Cæsar being hard put to it near Alexandria, leaped
into the sea, and, laying some books on his head, made shift
to swim a good way with one hand.   Sertorius being wounded in a battle with the Cambrians, with his corslet and target
swam over the river Rhosne.   He that hath seen that river
may doubt which was the harder exploit.

Upon the memorable overthrow of the Cambrians, not far
from Verona, by Marius and Catullus, the contention arose
whose soldiers were most effective to the victory.   For that
decision Catullus conducted the ambassadors of Parma, then
in the camp, to view the bodies of the dead, where they might
behold the pila, or Roman javelots, in their bodies, which
Plutarch saith had Catullus's name upon them.   Whether
this were not extraordinary, for we read not of such a constant custom to set their leader's names upon them.

The apology of Socrates in Plato, concludeth thus, when he was to drink the cup of poison. "Verum jam abeundi tempus et mihi morituro, vobis autem victuris: utri autem nostrum sit melius, omnibus quidem incognitum, soli autem deo notum, existimo." Whether this be fairly rendered by Cicero (*Tusculan Quæst*. lib. i.). "Utrum sit melius dii immortales sciunt, hominum autem neminem existimo?" For herein for *deus* he puts in *dii immortales*, whereas his charge was that he contemned the gods of Athens; and in his last words, when men speak freely and without fear, he delivers himself not plurally, but, according as he believed, makes mention but of one God.

When Julius Cæsar, after a hard siege, took the city of Marseilles, he spared the same, and would not demolish it for the antiquity thereof. And whether it be not the most ancient city of Gallia, as having a known erection by a colony of the Phocenses, about the reign of Tarquinius Priscus, some doubt may be made. For though these may be more ancient habitations, yet none of that continued story, civility, place, and walled; especially if that be true which Justin delivereth, that the Massilians first taught the Gauls to wall their towns.

Whether not also the place of most ancient civility, since Cæsar delivers that the Belgians were the most fierce and warlike nation of Gallia, as being less civilized and most remote *a cultu Provinciæ*. Which country was civilized, and much peopled by the Massilians, and who extended their colonies along that shore from Arles to Niza and Antibes. And though it be no university at present, whether it hath not been the most ancient place of study, in this western part of Europe; since in Strabo's time not only the Gauls but the Romans resorted thither rather than unto Athens.

Upon a very great exclamation of a multitude, at the plays and shows, some crows flying at that time over, fell unto the ground, as Plutarch delivereth in the life of Titus Flamminius. Whether the reasons alledged by him attain the cause thereof? *Plutarch. in vita Titi Flamminii.*

At the city of Gratianopolis, or Grenoble, in Dauphine, upon the swift river L'Isere, there is a bridge of boats, somewhat like that of Rouen in Normandy ; contrived at first with great cost and pains. In the like kind the Roman labours were more notably carried on. Plancus, the Roman general, made a bridge over it in one day. What time was taken in building the admirable bridge of Trajan over the Danube, whose ruins are to be seen near Severin, in the confines of Valachia and Transylvania; it is not delivered in Dion, who so wonderingly writeth of it. But Cæsar's bridge over the Rhine was raised in ten days, after that the materials were brought. In not many days they could build a large fleet, since we read in Valerius, that in sixty days the same trees made both a wood and a complete navy. Among the many strange and stupendous bridges of China, that of Phogen were worth the sight; which being made over the river Croceus, from one hill unto another, consisted but of one arch of no less than four hundred cubits over.

The rivers of countries may commodiously be divided into principal, capital, or sea rivers, which immediately discharge into the sea; or else into accessionary, or such as are discharged into main rivers, and so immediately enter the sea.

To exemplify in France : where are considerable, four less principal streams, Charente, Some, the river of Baiona, the Atax or Aude at Narbona ; four also main principal rivers, the Sequana or Seine, Ligeris or La Loire, the Rhodanus or Rhone, and the Garumna or Garonne.

The considerable accessionary rivers run into one of the four great ones.

Into the Seine run the Marne, the Oyse, the Yonne.

Into the Loire on the south runneth the Allier, the Cher, La Crease, Vienne. On the north Le Loire, Sarire.

Into the Rhone passeth the Araris or Soane, (having before received into itself the Doubis or Dou) the Isare or Lisere, and the Druentia or Durance.

Into the Garonne are discharged the Dordanne, the Loch, and the Tarne.

The advantages of these rivers were not neglected by the

old Gauls and Romans in the conveyance of their commodities; which as Strabo delivers they sent up by the Atax, and so over land unto the Garunna, and likewise up the Rhosne, and so over land to the Seine, and so into the ocean. But when Diodorus Siculus delivers that the Romans brought their tin out of Cornwall into Gaul, and so by horses in thirty days, either unto the heads of the Po, or to the city Narbona; they undertook a hard journey, and with little or no advantage of rivers.

The considerable cities of countries are likewise commodiously divided into three magnitudes, subdividing every magnitude into as many degrees.

To exemplify in France. In the first magnitude, and the first degree of that magnitude, Paris; in the second degree of that magnitude, Lyons; and the third, Rouen, Tholouse, Poictiers.

In the second magnitude, and first degree thereof, Orleans, Bourdeaux, Angiers.

In the second degree, Aix, Nantes;

In the third, Dijon, Grenoble, Marseilles, Avignon, Nevers, Tours.

In the third magnitude, and first degree thereof, Rennes, Carcassonne, Rochelle;

In the second of the third magnitude, Troies, Montpellier, Amiens;

In the third, Agen, Vienne, Valance, Sainctes.

St. Vincent, whose name the noble cathedral of Lisbon beareth, was a courageous and undaunted martyr in the persecution of Dioclesianus and Maximianus. Attacked at Evora, by Dacianus the Roman governor, and afterwards racked and tortured to death at Abyla, the Moors dispersed his bones at St. Vincent's, a place upon the *Promontorium Sacrum* of Ptolemy, now called the Cape of St. Vincent, the most western head-land of Europe. Upon my print of St. Vincent these few lines may be inscribed,

> Extorque, si potes, fidem,
> Tormenta, carcer, ungulæ,
> Stridensque flammis lamina,

Atque ipsa pœnarum ultima,
Mors, Christianis ludus est.
Prudentius in hymno St. Vincentii.

Though in point of devotion and piety, physicians do meet with common obloquy, yet in the Roman calendar we find no less than twenty-nine saints and martyrs of that profession, in a small piece expressly described by Bzovius (in his *Nomenclatura sanctorum professione medicorum*). A clear and naked history of holy men, of all times and nations, is a work yet to be wished. Many persons there have been, of high devotion and piety, which have no name in the received canon of saints; and many now only live in the names of towns, wills, tradition, or fragments of local records. Wherein Cornwall seems to exceed any place of the same circuit, if we take an account of those obscure and probably Irish saints to be found in Carew's survey of that country, affording names unto the churches and towns thereof; which clearly to historify might prove a successless attempt. Even in France, many places bear the names of saints, which are not commonly understood. St. Malo, is Maclovius; Disier, Desiderius; St. Arigle, St. Agricola; St. Omer, St. Audomarus. Many more there are, as St. Chamas, St. Urier, St. Loo, Saincte Menehoud, St. Saulye, St. Trouve, St. Riquier, St. Papoul, St. Oaen; and divers others which may employ your enquiry.

Plutarch in the Life of Agesilaus.

Menecrates, the physician, arrogantly usurped the name of Jupiter, presuming, in a letter, he wrote unto Agesilaus, to subscribe in this manner, "Menecrates Jupiter unto King Agesilaus, greeting." Agesilaus wrote again unto him, "Agesilaus unto Menecrates, health."

Whether this translation be not made rather unto the present practise, to subscribe names unto our letters, than unto the ancient mode either above or at the beginning of the letter, according as we may observe from many in Laertius, the epistolary works of Greek authors, and the epistle of Festus unto Felix, may be doubted. Or whether ἐπιστεῖλαι, in the

original, ought to be translated, to subscribe ; and when the
present manner of subscribing names began, and what ancient
copy might be produced for our practise, may also be enquired.

Agesilaus was going up into the counsel house in the castle,
where suddenly took him a great cramp in his left leg, that
swelled extremely and put him to great pain. Men thinking
it had been but blood which filled the vein, a physician being
there opened a vein under the ancle of his foot, which made
the pain to cease, but there came such abundance of blood
that they could not stanch it, so that he swooned often, and
was in danger of present death. In fine a way was found to
stop it, and they carried him to Lacedæmon; where he lay
sick a long time, so that he was past going to the wars any
more. Herein to consider the nature of the disease, the ra-
tionality of the cure, and by what way probably they stanched
the bleeding.

Xenophon writes that his daughter's *canathrum* was nothing more sumptuous than any others were. A *canathrum*
in Lacedæmon, is a kind of coach or chariot, after the like-
ness of griffins, harts, or goats, upon which they carried young
wenches in solemn procession in the city. To make an icon,
figure, or draught, of a *canathrum*, according to the best accounts which are left thereof.

The punishment of such as fled from the battle, whom they
called at Sparta *trepidantes,* was this. They can bear no
office in the commonwealth ; it is a shame and reproach to
give them any wives, and also to marry any of theirs; whosoever meeteth them may lawfully strike them, and they must
abide it, not giving them any word again ; they are compelled
to wear poor tattered cloth gowns, patched with cloth of divers
colours; and worst of all, to shave one side of their beards
and the other not. Whether the severity of this law of Lacedæmon, and which sometimes they durst not put in execution, were ingenious, rational, and commodious, or to be drawn
into example.

Whether Pompey committed not two great oversights in the war against Julius Cæsar; the one in not returning out of Greece with his army into Italy, while Cæsar was gone into Spain; the other in deferring battle, and not setting upon Cæsar when he was so distressed for victuals.

In the city of Padua, Cornelius, an excellent soothsayer, was by chance, at that time when the battle of Pharsalia was fought, set to behold the flying of birds. He, as Livy reporteth, knew the very time when the battle began, and told them that were present, even now they give the onset on both sides, and after cried out, O Cæsar, the victory is thine. And every man wondering, he took the crown from his head, and said he would never put it on again, till the event had proved his art true.

Plut. in vita Julii C.—Si questa relatione non si debbia riporre fra farfalloni degl' istorichi antichi di Lancellotto.

In vita Alexandri.

He understood, by the countrymen, that the river Ganges was two-and-thirty furlongs over, and an hundred fathoms deep. Whether this may not be made out upon comparison with the river of Amazons, according unto the late description thereof translated out of French.

Thither came Nearchus's admiral unto him, who made report of what he had seen and done in his navigation. Alexander was so glad of that, as he was desirous to sail by sea himself, and so entering into the ocean by the mouth of Euphrates, to compass in all the coasts of Arabia and Africa, and thence into the Mediterranean sea, by the straights of the pillars of Hercules. Who can but wish this had been performed, although not by himself. A bold design it may seem in those days, and yet seeming far greater unto us than unto them, who might hope the coast of Africa ran nothing near so far southward as we now find it; nor how the coast of Africa bore out to make a large sail before they could attain the straits of Hercules. Yet Herodotus reports the same was done before; that Necho, King of Egypt, by the help of Phœnicians, sailed from the Red Sea, round about Africa, unto Cadiz.

A Macedonian, as he digged in a certain place by the river of Oxus, to set up the king's tent, he found a certain fat and oily vein, which, after he had drawn out the first, there came out also another clearer, which differed nothing, either in smell, taste, or savour, from natural oil, having the gloss and fatness so like, as there could be discerned no difference between them; the which was so much the more to be wondered at, because that in all that country there were no olives: nor needed there any, this being a kind of *petroleum* spring and natural oil, not vegetable and artificial.

Alexander, having won the city of Susa, he found to the value of five thousand talents weight of purple Hermione silk, which they had locked up safe, and kept the space of two hundred years, and yet the colour kept as fresh as if it had been newly made. Some say the cause why it was so well kept, came by means of the dying of it with honey in silks which before had been dyed red, and with white oil in white silks, which before had been dyed red. For there are silks seen of that colour that keep colour as long as the other. (To be farther considered by inquiries into tinctures).

Plutarch in vita Crassi.

Hyrodes the king fell into a disease that became a dropsy after he had lost his son Pacorus. Phraates, his second son, thinking to set his father forwards, gave him drink of the juice of *aconitum.* The dropsy received the poison, and one drove the other out of Hyrodes' body, and set him on foot again.

Plut. in vita Themist.

Upon the difference of the Athenians with the Lacedæmonians, before the sea fight with Xerxes, Themistocles said unto them, "If you will needs go your ways and forsake us, you shall hear, ere it be long, that the Athenians have another

free city, and have possessed again as much free land as they
have already lost."

Sir Walter Raleigh, lib. iii, *History of the World;* here
withal he mentions a town in Italy belonging of old to the
state of Italy, of which town he said, an oracle had foretold
that the Athenians in process of time should build it anew;
" and here," quoth he, "will we plant ourselves, leaving unto
you a sorrowful remembrance of my words."

What city this was of Italy which he meaneth in his speech.

To [1] be sure that no day pass, without calling upon God in
a solemn formed prayer, seven times within the compass thereof; that is, in the morning, and at night, and five times between; taken up long ago from the example of David and
Daniel, and a compunction and shame that I had omitted it
so long, when I heedfully read of the custom of the Mahometans to pray five times in the day.

To pray and magnify God in the night, and my dark bed,
when I could not sleep; to have short ejaculations when ever
I awaked, and when the four o'clock bell [2] awoke me, or my
first discovery of the light, to say the collect of our liturgy,
"Eternal God, who hath safely brought me to the beginning
of this day, &c."

To pray in all places where privacy inviteth; in any house,
highway, or street; and to know no street or passage in this
city which may not witness that I have not forgot God and
my Saviour in it; and that no parish or town where I have
been, may not say the like.

To take occasion of praying, upon the sight of any church,
which I see or pass by, as I ride about.

Since the necessities of the sick, and unavoidable diversions

[1] *To be sure, &c.*] This, and the following nine paragraphs, seem to have
been inserted in this volume by mistake.
They were evidently not intended for the
perusal of his son, or of any one else.

[2] *four o'clock bell.*] A bell which
tolls (or ought to toll, if the old sexton
does not oversleep himself) in pursuance
of the will of a person who, after wandering about for a considerable time on
Mousehold Heath, having lost his way
in a winter night's storm, at length was
directed to the city, by the tolling of a bell
in this church of St. Peter Mancroft, the
residence of Sir Thomas Brown, when he
wrote this passage, and that of his editor,
when he writes this note.

of my profession, keep me often from church, yet to take all possible care that I might never miss sacraments upon their accustomed days.

To pray daily and particularly for sick patients, and in general for others, wheresoever, howsoever, under whose care soever; and at the entrance into the house of the sick, to say, " The peace and mercy of God be in this place."

After a sermon, to make a thanksgiving, and desire a blessing, and to pray for the minister.

In tempestuous weather, lightning, and thunder, either night or day, to pray for God's merciful protection upon all men, and his mercy upon their souls, bodies, and goods.

Upon sight of beautiful persons, to bless God in his creatures, to pray for the beauty of their souls, and to enrich them with inward graces to be answerable unto the outward. Upon sight of deformed persons, to send them inward graces, and enrich their souls, and give them the beauty of the resurrection.

Marcus Antoninus Philosophus wanted not the advice of the best physicians; yet how warrantable his practice was, to take his repast in the night, and scarce any thing but treacle in the day, may admit of great doubt.

Why Commodus, heated in the theatrical recreations, would drink his refrigerated wine only from the hand of a woman. If not for being over heated by the hotter hands of men.

How to make out the effect, or what antidotal property there might be in the bodies of eunuchs, who only were able to bear that bituminous exhalation at Hieropolis, which proved mortal unto other men and animals, as is positively delivered by Dion.

Every tenth day, the young Spartan striplings were presented unto the Ephori, and such as were found to be fat were punished, as conceiving they used not sufficient exercise; whether this rigour of Lycurgus were tolerable, or not too generally extended upon all constitutions, to punish thus indefinitely, and such which might probably be only peccant by constitution.

Plutarch in vita Alexandri.

They found Darius laid on a couch, having many wounds ; and being almost at the last gasp, he called for cold water, and drank it ; and after a few words gave up the ghost. Gravitur vulneratos et multum sanguinem effundentes admodum sitire notissimum.

After Philip, the physician, had given the potion unto Alexander, the medicine beginning to work, overcame the disease, and drove for the time all his natural strength and powers into the lowest parts of his body, insomuch that his strength failed him, and his pulse did scarce beat, &c. An hoc satis medice dictum ?

Callisthenes, being kept a prisoner, and being very fat, was eaten in the end by lice, and so died.

Of others, who fell to quaffing who should drink most, there died forty-one persons, of an extreme cold that took them in their drunkenness. Eodem funguntur fato ebriones plurimi apud nos.

Hephestion fell sick of an ague, but being a young man of war, he did not regard his mouth, but having spied an opportunity, when his physician was gone unto the theatre to see sports and pastimes, he went to dinner and ate a roasted capon whole, and drank a great pot full of wine, which he had caused to be set in water, whereupon his fever took him so sorely that he lived not long after.

Lysippus, of all others, hath perfectly drawn Alexander, holding his neck somewhat hanging downwards towards the left side : which was more agreeable to a person of a generous temper; *inclinatio capitis ad dextram* being, according to Aristotle, among the physiognomical notes of an effeminate temper ; and how well this is observed in the picture and statue made of him.

Plut. in vita Antonii.

In the end they were compelled to live on herbs and

roots, but they found few of them that men do commonly eat,
and were enforced to taste of them that were never eaten before, among the which there was one that killed them, and
made them out of their wits ; for he that had once eaten of
it, his memory was gone from him, and knew no manner of
thing, but only busied himself in digging and hurling of
stones from one place to another, as though it had been a
great weight, and to be done with all possible speed. All
the camp over were busily stooping to the ground, digging
and carrying of stones from one place to another. But at
last they cast up a great deal of choler and died suddenly,
because they lacked wine which was the only sudden remedy
to cure that disease.

What plant this might be, considerable from the symptoms
and cure by wine.

Turkish History, in the Life of Morah, p. 1483.

Count Mansfield died : the news whereof coming to Duke
John Ernestus, already weakened with a fever fourteen days,
he fell into an apoplexy. His body was opened, and not one
drop of blood found, but his heart withered to the smallness
of a nut.

Plutarch in Demosthene.

Touching the stammering of his tongue, which was very
fat, and made him that he could not pronounce all syllables
distinctly, he did help it by putting of little pebble stones into
his mouth, which he found upon the sands by the river side,
and so pronounced with open mouth the orations he had
without book. How this might not produce the effect upon
the causes of *balbuties* or blæsity assigned by Sanctorius,
De vitandis erroribus in medicina.

He went into the temple, as though he would dispatch
some letters, and put the end of the quill into his mouth and
bit it as his manner was, when he did use to write, and
held the quill in his mouth a pretty while together ; then feeling the poison to work, he spoke unto Archias, after which
he prayed them to stay him up by the arm holes, for his feet
began already to fail him, and as he passed by the altar of

Neptune, he fell down, and giving one gasp, gave up the ghost.

What poison this was; whether the common and state poison of Athens, made out of the hemlock, whereof a drachm of the juice inspissated was a sufficient dose, as appears in the life of Phocion, whereby Socrates perished, and the effects seem to have been somewhat like in Demosthenes.

Suet. in vita Calig. sect. 23.

Tiberius's brother he surprised and killed, because he smelled strongly of a preservative or antidote, as if he had taken the same to prevent his poisons; whereas, for a continual cough that grew still upon him, he used a medicine.

Life of Dion. Plutarch.

The surgeons were to search the wound of Sothis, who found that it was rather a scratch than any violent wound given him, for the wounds or cuts of a sword are ever deeper in the middest; whether this may not be solved from the fashion and make of their swords, different from ours.

Olearius.

In the travels of Olearius, and in his description of Persia, he delivers that the Persians commonly cure the sting of a scorpion by applying a piece of copper upon the wound; and that himself, being stung in the throat by a scorpion, was cured by the application of oil of scorpions, and taking treacle inwardly; but that for some years after he was troubled with a pricking in that part, when the sun was in Scorpius.

The princess of Coreski, taken prisoner by the Tartars, received a precious stone of rare virtue, which applied unto the eyes of the brother of the Tartar, whose prisoner she was, in a short time recovered his sight. Whether any such virtue probable or possible by that means. *Turk. Hist. in the Life of Achmet.*

Ameida, intending to take away the sight of his father, Mulleasses, with a hot knife cut the sight of his eyes: the manner of this operation would be farther enquired.

Whether that of Psalm viii, may not be literally verified and fulfilled, when Christ entered Jerusalem, since according to that of Maccabees vii, "lac triennio dedi," the Jewish women suckled their children three years, and they could speak before, or at that age.

[MS. SLOAN. 1875.] [1]

[*On the Laws of Motion and Gravitation.*]

Two very considerable qualities there are, concerning the natural motion of bodies in the universe, which order all bodies in due place and situation.

That which disposes the situation and fastens them to the poles is the quality magnetical, which is discoverable in iron and loadstone, and some few others, beyond which nothing is strictly magnetical; as is also discovered in the globe of the earth, whereby it is tied unto its poles, and making a constant elevation of every place, the pole constant, and the latitude and longitude of each region invariable; whether the same dispositive quality or dispositive power unto one situation, be not in the stars of heaven is very questionable; nor altogether without reason that this power maintains the spots of the moon in one constant face, unto all eyes, and makes the moles in the western cheek invariably to regard us. Whether the natures of things have not something magnetical, whereby disturbed from themselves they still return into their former point; and whether temperamental inclinations stay not so firm by this or anatomical quality, may be also considered.

The other doth order and dispose every body to take up his proper place; that is, in order to the centre, nearer or far-

---

[1] MS. SLOAN. 1875.] This volume contains many very curious, and some erroneous and fallacious experiments, and observations. It appears both from the hand writing and spelling, and from occasional dates, to have been written earlier than other of his Common Place Books, but, being principally on scientific subjects, it has been printed as a fit companion to No. 1869, which is almost entirely literary. It should be observed that the hand-writing in this volume is so bad, that it cannot but be apprehended that many errors will remain.

ther from it, which is by gravity and levity, or rather less gravity; for things are not absolutely light, but comparatively to each other, ascending or descending according to their conjunction with other bodies. Wood will descend in the air, but bear from the centre in water. In this motion all heavy bodies bear not to the centre, as greedy of that position, every body remaining content in that place which is below a less heavy body, that could not sustain [it,] and ready to give place to another if not hindered; and therefore the centre properly is due unto the heaviest body, and gold may challenge that place, which is the simply heavy, and never light in reference to other bodies. And though there lay a circle of a globe of liquefied gold, and such as were penetrate and drossive of other bodies, though the earth were perforated nothing would reach the centre, because the centre would ...... and all things swim in gold, and the central relation would not break the rule of nature which ordereth every thing its place according to its gravity.[2] But things useful unto man were set where man might come at them, nor is it likely any thing lies at the centre but what is subservient unto the earth, ... through it fire, which men are so far from placing the heaviest body that they have placed it the lightest; that is, fire, inservient to the generation of all things under the earth, and the greater circulation of nature without; and if the earth be divided into three orbs, two thereof contain but little of what we know and may only serve the other.

They speak reason who say, if the earth were perforated and a bullet let fall, it would not rest immediately at the centre, but by the impetus it conceiveth, move almost as far as the opposite surface.

Clymical earth, as being lightest, hath least title unto the centre; for though the elementated earth, as it stands impregnated with other principles, be the heaviest body in the universe, yet resolved near its element it proves the lightest part of any body except the oil or inflammable part, as will be

---

2 *and though, &c.*] There are several words in this sentence very illegible. He probably means that supposing the centre of the earth occupied by a globe of liquid gold nothing could displace it, because every other body, being lighter, would remain on its surface.

evident unto any that shall separate the salt and ashes, shall so urge a body as to disturb the volate principles, oil, water, and then having the earth shall extract all salt from it; for the dry and discontinued carcase remaining will weigh less in an equal ratio than so much water, but come very short of salt which maketh ashes heavy, so many bodies that abound in earth are lighter than others which have it in smaller quantity. So are we deceived in buying of ashes, conceiving we have especial pennyworths if we have a great bulk and measure, although in some there is much earth that greatens the bulk without store of salt which is the expected principle.

Tanner's stuff having been long infused in their pits burns well dried, but makes a weak lye, unfit for cleansing of linen.

[*On Coagulation.*]

So many coagulations there are in nature; and though we content ourselves with one in the running of milk, yet many will perform the same.

The maws or stomachs of other animals, as of pigeons.

The inner coat of the gizzard of wild ducks and teal, not the pike, or maw of a pike, which seems of strong digestion.

Several seeds may do it, the best the seeds of carthamus, not too much dried.

Many others not, as not the seed of pæony. Myrobalans powdered do it.

The milk of spurge doth it actively; the milk of fig; that of lettuce; succory; tragopogon; apocinon. Whether salerdine?

Whereby whey and cheese might be made more medical; milk of lettuce and sowthistle will not hold the colour, but grow black and gummy, yet strongly coagulate milk.

The opium and scammony.

The inward skin of the gizzard of turkies will actively coagulate; so will the crop; the chylus or half digested matter in the crop did the like, and strongly. That in the gizzard was too dry.

The milk of a woman full of the jaundice, that nursed a child, infected the same; yet the milk was blue and a laudable colour, and would not be coagulated by runnet, nor after long stirring did manifest any colour or febrical tincture.

To try and observe the several sorts of coagulations or runnets; whether any will turn all kinds of milk, or whether they be appropriate. That of a hare we find will turn that of the cow. To observe further whether it will coagulate that of a mare or ass, or woman, and how the coagulum stands in multifidous animals; as in whelps and kittens, and also in swine and bats. The runnet of cows is strong, for it co-agulates the milk of herbs. The milk in whelps' maws did the milk of cows, but the runnet of cows, as we have tried in several womens' milk, will not coagulate the same. The run-net of rabbit coagulates well the milk of a cow. Neither that nor calf's runnet did make a good coagulum of mare's milk, leaving only a gross thickness therein, without serous separa-tion.

Of the several sorts of milk and lacical animals; of the several sorts of coagulums; of all kinds of mineral coagula-tion.

> of tin with aquafortis
> of . . . . . . antimony
> of soap
> of the coagulum of blood
> . . . . of milk

How several sayings concerning coagulum in authors may be understood?

How in the Scripture " sicut lac coagulasti me ?"

How far the coagulating principle operateth in generation is evident from eggs which will never incrassate without it; from the incrassation upon incubiture, when heat diffuseth the coagulum, from the *chalaza* or gellatine, which sometime . . . . three nodes, the head, heart, and liver.

How its qualities made good in physic?

How in natural observations?

What runnet the Scythians used to separate mare's milk is uncertain; cow's runnet we have not found to do it, but the same we have effected by the maws of turkies. Whether the buttons of figs or the milk of spurge which are strong coagulators? Quære.

Coagulum in the first digestion, in the second or blood, whether not also in the last digestion or stomach, of every particular part, when the coagulate parts become fine and next to flesh, and the rest into cambium and gluten.

Whether the first mass were but a coagulation, whereby the water and earth lay awhile together, and the watery or serous part was separated from the sole and continuating substance, the . . . . . . separated by coagulation, and the inner part flowing about them.

The practice of the . . . . seems convenient unto experiment; for the blood of man and pig, falling upon vinegar, would not coagulate, but lie thin and turn of the colour of muscadell.

Bled upon aquavitæ, it did coagulate, though weaker, and maintained its colour.

Upon vinegar, it keeps long without corruption, and becometh blackish.

Bled upon a solution of saltpetre in water, it coagulates not, keeps long, and shoots into nitrous branched particles, which separated, it lasteth long, and contracteth the smell of storax liquida, and the glass or urinal being inclined, it strokes long figures . . . . conjoined by right lines.

White dung of hens and geese coagulates milk.

Mare's milk very serous, not equally running with coagulum [of] fig, except some cow's milk be added; perhaps the Scythians used a mixture of goat's milk. Spirits of salt poured upon mare's milk, makes a curdling which in a little space totally dissolved into serum.

Woman's milk will not coagulate with common runnet, try whether the milk of nurses that are concerned may be run.

Mrs. King's milk, Octob. 23, (1650) would not run, but only curdled in small roundles like pin's heads, as vinegar will curdle milk.

The semichylus or half-digested humour of young lobsters, in a cod's stomach, did it very well.

The entrails of soles coagulated milk, so also the stomach of sandlings. The stomach of a tench would not, nor of a rat, nor of a whiting or gudgeon; and that of smelts did it in winter; the maw of a cod did it well; the appendages about the maw indifferently also of smelts.

Milk of different nature according to the different times of gestation, which is to be observed to know the differences of milk in several seasons, it being so commonly ordered, that cows come in the spring, so that milk grows thick about Christmas.

Camborgia, which some suspect to be the juice of . . . . . . coloured with saffron or other yellow tincture, would not coagulate.

The *verum coagulum* seems seated in the inner skin of the gizzard, for the outward and carnous part would not do it.

The maw of a bittern did it well.

The mutings also of a bittern and a kestrell.

The inward skin in the maws of partridges, or the substance contained therein, not yet fully digested.

Sow's milk run very well with runnet and skin of green figs; even ripe do it well.

Runnet beat up with the whites of eggs, seems to perform nothing, nor will it well incorporate, without so much heat as will harden the egg.

The peculiar coagulum of stomachs to make stones, as bezoar.

Milk of poppy runs milk.

The stomachs of turkies dry and powdered doth it well; so also the dry and chaffy substance in the gizzard after some months, but the carnous substance not.

The buttons of figs, which prove figs the next year, doth it very well, either green or dried; salt alone will do it if plentiful; whether saltpetre, salt upon saltpetre, or sal-gemmæ; vide.

The curdled milk in the stomach of a pig coagulates cow's milk.

Adding salt cleanly, runnet may be made out of milk put into the maw of a turkey.

As also a pig will do it very well.

The appendages below the lower orifice of the stomach will coagulate milk, when the substance will not do it; as tried in cods, these are filled with a little thick humour, very

remarkable in salmon, wherein they are of exceeding largeness.

Buttermilk, or churn milk, will not be turned with runnet,
but being warm will run itself, as will also milk in the summer.

Try whether the inward part of the duodenum will do it,
as the inward tunicle of the stomach.

Whether if in quadrupeds ruminant the three former stomachs, and not only the . . . . . or last division next the guts.

That . . . . of a sheep coagulated strong and soon ; the
parcels of the great stomach not at all, or very slowly and
weakly, the upper part of the duodenum did also coagulate
milk.

The milk of mares is very serous, and will not run with the
cow's runnet; in the summer we made it run with turkies gizzard, and fig's buttons ; the same in October we could not effect, neither with Turkey figs, cow's, nor pig's runnet ; whether it be so serous that the caseous parts cannot hold together
the other, may be doubted; although, if unto an ounce of
cow's milk you add an ounce of water, it will, notwithstanding,
coagulate in the caseous part, leaving the whey asunder.

And if you mix equal parts of mare's and cow's milk, the
runnet will take place.

The skin of a peacock's gizzard very well.

As also the dried milk of spurge and lettuce, above a year
old; the chylus of animals ; the chylus of plants; the stomach
of an horse, and chylus contained in it, did very well coagulate.

Beef taken out of the paunch of a kestrell four hours after,
turned very strongly.

A clean and neat seeming runnet may be made in the crop
of a turkey, and milk and salt put therein will coagulate and
grow hard like runnet ; but surely the same must be old to
be effectual, for after a month upon trial, we could not find it
to run cows' milk.

The strawy substances in the stomach of a pig, turned milk
well in October, also the fresh white dung of a goose did very
well, that best which is whitest probably.

The inward skin of a duckling, six days old, as also the
hard and chaffy substances in the same did it very well.

Spirits of salt and aquafortis, gently poured on milk, will strongly coagulate; but in a woman's milk we find it not effectual, which would not coagulate upon a large quantity, nor would salt in gross body effect it, nor the other common coagulums.

Try whether the milk of children vomited will do it.

The dung of chickens in some degree.

The shells and half-digested fragments in a lobster's stomach that had nearly cut the skin did it.

How butchers make sheep's blood to hold from concretion; whether by agitation when it is fresh, and so dispersing the fibres which are thought to make the concretion? Unto such, a great quantity of runnet added could make no concretion.

Eggs seem to contain within themselves their own coagulum, evidenced upon incubation, which makes incrassation of parts before very fluid.

Rotten eggs will not be made hard by incubation or decoction, as being destitute of that spirit; or having the same vitiated. They will sooner be made hard if put in before the water boileth.

They will be made hard in oil, but not so easily in vinegar, which by the attenuating quality keeps them longer from concretion; for infused in vinegar they lose the shell, and grow big and much heavier than before.

Salt seems to be the principal agent in this coagulation, for bay salt will run milk alone if strongly mixed, and so it will, though mixed with some vinegar. Vinegar alone will curdle it, not run it.

In the ovary, or second cell of the matrix, the white comes upon the yolk, and in the later and lower part, the shell is made or manifested. Try if the same parts will give any coagulation unto milk. Whether will the ovary best?

The whites of eggs drenched in saltpetre will shoot forth a long and hairy saltpetre, and the egg become of a hard substance; even in the whole egg there seems a great nitrosity, for it is very cold, and especially that which is without a shell, (as some are laid by fat hens,) or such as are found in the egg poke or lowest part of the matrix, if an hen be killed a day or two before she layeth.

Several hens produce eggs commonly of the same form, some round, some long, neither strictly distinguishing the sex.

The proper uses of the shell; for the defence of the chicken in generation, promotion of heat upon incubation, and protection therein least it be broken by the hen, either upon incubation or treading with her claws upon them, as also to keep and restrain the chicken until due time, when the hen often breaks the shell.

Difference between the sperm of frogs and eggs.

Spawn though long boiled, would not grow thick or coagulate.

In the eggs of skates or thornbacks, upon long decoction the yolk coagulates, not the greatest part of the white.

If in spawn of frogs the little black specks will concrete, though not the other.

The white part of the mutings of birds dried run milk, not leaving any ill savor. Try in that of cormorants, hens, turkeys, geese, kestrels.

The chylus in the stomach of a young hen strongly coagulated, the stomach also itself though washed.

The white and cretaceous mutings of a bittern made a sudden coagulation, the like hath the dung of ducks and hens.

The coagulate stomach of kittens would not convert women's milk, nor cows, though in good quantity; which after coagulated by addition of calf's runnet.

The chylus in a young rabbit run cow's and bitch's milk, 1653.

The seeds of the silver or milk thistle run milk also.

Mucilaginous concretions are made by liquid infusions and decoctions, imbibing the gum and tenacious parts, until they fix and determine their fluidity.

As is observable in gums, hartshorn, and seeds, especially lentous natures, as quince, psyllium, mallows, &c., when these tenacious parts are forced out by ignition, they afford no farther concretion, as in burnt hartshorn, wherein there are lost most of the separable parts, and so little of salt as makes the preparation questionable, if given with the same intentions with the other.

Wherein it is presumable the water may also imbibe some part of the volatile salt, as is manifested sometimes when it is exposed to congelation, and standeth long in pewter dishes; some part fastening upon the crown or upper circle, and also discolouring the pewter.

But whether the mucilages or jellies do answer our expectation of their quantities, while we think we have a decoction made of two ounces and half which affordeth a jelly of almost a pint; the horns again after they were dried wanted not a drachm, the jelly dried left little but a small gummy substance.

Half an ounce of *ichthyocolla* or isinglass, will fix above a pint of water; and in half a pint of jelly of hartshorn there is not above two drachms.

Much hartshorn is therefore lost in the usual decoction of hartshorn in shavings or raspings, where the greatest part is cast away.

For the same may be performed from the solid horn sawed into pieces of two or three ounces or less, and the same pieces will serve for many jellies.

The calcination of hartshorn by vapour of water is a neat invention, but whether very much of the virtue be not impaired, while the vapour insinuating into the horn hath carried away the tenacious parts and made it butter, and hath also dissolved those parts which make the jelly; which may be tried if a decoction be made of the water from whence the vapour proceedeth, and especially if the calcination hath been made in vessels not perspirable.

[*On Congelation.*]

NATURAL bodies do variously discover themselves by congelation.

Bodies do best and [most] readily congelate which are aqueous, or water itself.

Of milk the wheyish part, in eggs we observe the white, will totally freeze, the yolk, with the same degree of cold, grow thick and clammy like gum of trees, but the sperm or tread hold its former body, the white growing stiff that is nearest it.

The spirits of things do not freeze; if they be plentiful, they keep their bodies from congelation; as spirits of wine, *aquavitæ*, nor is it easy to freeze such, when French wine cannot resist it. But congelation seems to destroy or separate the spirits, for beer or wine are dead and flat after freezing, and in glasses ofttimes the most flying salts will settle themselves above the surface of the water.

Waters freezing do carry a vegetable crust foliated surface upon them, representing the leaves of plants, and this they do best which carry some salt or vegetable seminals in them. Rain water which containeth seminal atoms, elevated by exhalations, making the earth fruitful where it falleth. Snow water will also do, as containing these seeds, and salt nitrous coagulum, whereby it was formerly concreted. The lyes or lixivium of herbs will do it well, but the juices of herbs or waters wherein these essential salts have been dissolved, far better, as we have tried in that of scurvy grass, chalie, nettles. Jellies of flesh will do the like, as we have tried in that of cow's and calf's foot, wherein, though the surface be obscured, yet will there be several glaciations intermixed, and so excellently foliated, that they will leave their impression or figure in the next part of the jelly which remaineth uncongealed, and being beheld in a magnifying glass, either in the day or night against a candle, affordeth one of the most curious spectacles in nature, nor will these little conglaciated plates so easily dissolve as common ice, as carrying perhaps a greater portion of carnel nitre in them.

But, what is remarkable most of congelations, simple or compounded, they seem to carry in their surface a leaf of one figure, which somewhat representeth the leaf of a fern or brake,* from a middle and long rib spreading forth jagged leaves; so a lixivium of nettles, wormwood, wild cucumber, scurvy grass, will shoot in the same shapes; a solution of salt or sugar will do the like and also a decoction of hartshorn, and the salt distilled of the blood of a deer and dissolved in water, carried the same shape upon calcination; but the shoot-

---

* There is some *regent* salt which carrieth them into the form of brake or long rib jagged plant.

ings in the jellies of flesh carry smaller branches and like twigs without that exact distinction of leaves.

But the exact and exquisite figurations, and such as are produced above the surface of the liquor, in the side of glasses by exhalation from the liquor compounded with, is best discoverable in urinals and long bellied glasses, and often happeneth over urines, where the figures are very distinct arising from a root, and most commonly resembling coralline mosses of the sea, and sometimes larger plants, whereof some do rise in so strong a body, as to hold their shapes many months, and some we have kept two or three years entire.

Water and oil behave differently from congelation; a glassful of water frozen swells above the brim, oil congelated subsideth.

Congelation is a rare experiment; is made by a mixture of salt and snow strongly agitated in a pewter pot, which will freeze water that's poured about it. But an easier way there is, by only mixing salt and snow together in a basin, and placeing therein a cup of water, for when the snow doth thaw and the congealing spirits fly away, they freeze the neighbour bodies which are congealable; and, if the vessel wherein the snow melteth stand in water, it freezeth the water about it, which is excellently discerned by mixing snow and salt in an urinal, and placing it in water.

This way liquors will suddenly freeze which a long time resist the diffused causes in the air, as may be experienced in wine, and urine, and excellently serveth for all figurations; this way will in a short time freeze rich sack, and crust *aquavitæ* about the side of the cup or glass, if weak and with a light addition of water.

A small quantity of *aquavitæ*, mingled with water, is not able to resist this way of congelation; but therein the ice will not be so hard and compact, and hollow spaces will be left at the surface.

That the sea was salt from the beginning, when that principle was cast into the whole mass of this globe, and not occasioned by those ways the ancients dreamt of, seems almost beyond doubt: wherein . . . . salt was so tenderly sprinkled as not to make that part inhabitable, and therefore, how-

ever some seas near the tropic where the same is strongest
be conceived so to contain more salt, the seas with us do
hardly make good five in the hundred.

It is no easy effect to condense water and make it take up
a lesser space than in its fluid body; congealed into ice it
seems to lose nothing, but rather acquireth a greater space
and swelleth higher, as is manifestible in water frozen in eaures[1] and glasses.

This way eggs will suddenly freeze through their whole
bodies.

Eyes will freeze through all the humours and become in
short time like stones. By this way upon . . . . only the
watry humour will congelate under the cornea, and shew like
a cataract or *albugo*, the iris also loses its colour, and this way
the humours may be taken out distinctly; the hardest to freeze
is the crystalline, yet laid upon snow and salt it groweth hard
and dim, as though it had been boiled.

Whether such a congealing spirit be not the raiser of catar-
acts, *gutta serena*, apoplexies, catalepsies, and the like may
be inquired.

In the congelation of snow there is much space required,
and dissolved it will not occupy half the space it possessed
before, for it is congealed in a vapourous body and in some
rarefaction from its original of water.

Mineral water or quicksilver . . . . by taking off the
fluidity, takes up a greater space than before, although allowance be made for the body that forceth it.

Salt and snow pursue their operations most actively, while
it freezeth : and in coldest weather dissolve sooner, for when
it begins to thaw, the operation is troublesome; the snow
loseth his tenacity, grows hard and brittle, and salt thrown
upon it makes it harder for a little space, and is longer in dissolving it. Salt answereth awhile to send back the parting
spirit upon itself, and mixing with it while it holdeth fast,
makes a little congelation.

Lime unslaked mixed with snow would dissolve it; not
freeze water set into it.

---

1 *eaures.*] This may be *pannes* in   meant ewers—spelt, according to French
MS. but I am inclined rather to think he   derivation, *caures.*

Snow dissolved, without salt, would not freeze water set in it. Herein we may also sometimes observe the very motion and stroke of the coagulum; for when the snow and salt are aptly conjoined, and the liquor to be congealed be put in a flat thin cup of silver, if it chance to dissolve at that time, in any quantity, it will instantly run curdled whey; the spirit separated will make a curdled cloud at the bottom or side of the cup, and fix that part first; for, contrary unto common congelation, if the cup standeth upon snow, and that at the bottom thaweth it, the liquor first freezeth at the bottom, and while the liquor in the flat cup freezeth within the basin, the outside of the basin will be thick frosted, and if it stands will adhere unto the table.

It is observable in this way of congelation, that the liquor freezeth last in the middle of the surface, as being furthest from the action of the snow and flying spirit; nor is this only effected by snow and salt, but by snow and saltpetre or alum; but the quickest congelation [is] by snow and salt, the other mixture remaining longer without dissolution: and therefore, on some earth snow lieth longest, and seldom long near the sea side; and if two vessels be filled, the one with snow alone, the other with a mixture of salt, the salt snow will dissolve in half the time, and ice in the like manner.

This way it is possible to observe the rudiments and progress of congelation; it beginning first with *striæ*, and having shoots like the filamental shoots of pure nitre, and the interstitial water becomes after conjoined.

The same is also effected by ice powdered or broken like sugar between dry bodies, and mixed with salt; and is also performable without mixture of salt bodies, by snow alone, as it falleth to solution, and the congelating spirit separateth; so water in a very thin glass set in a porringer of snow, and set upon salt will freeze, the salt being able to dissolve it through the pewter. And, therefore, catarrhs and colds are taken and encreased upon thaws; the leaves of trees withered and blasted where snow dissolves upon them; and something more than mere water fixed, because it spoileth leather, and alters the colour thereof to walk long in snow, especially when it melteth: and this congelative spirit, that penetrateth glass and metal, is probably the same which is felt so penetrating and cutting in winds, and according to frequent relations, hath left whole bodies of men rigid and stiff, even to petrification, in regions near the pole; and may assign some reason of that strange effect on our men, some that were left in Greenland, when they touched iron it seemed to stick to the fingers like pitch, the same being mollified and made in the same temper as it is, by the acid spirits of sulphur, if a red hot iron be thrust into a roll thereof.

In the congealing of tinctures, as . . . . . and saffron, if we narrowly observe it, there still remaineth whiteness, and the tincture seemeth to lie distant and less congealed. Starch, a strong congelation may be made, wherein the atoms of the powder may be distinguished, and sensibly observed to cast their colour upon parts, which they do not corporally attain.

To freeze roughly, or make ice with elevated superficies, the water must be exposed warm, and the liquor thick, the better as in jellies, while the exhalation elevating the surface, is held in and frozen in its passage.

Oil put upon snow, in an open mouth glass, and sharp at the bottom, makes a curdling which lasts a long time, and gives a mixed taste of snow and oil, pleasant unto the palate, and excellent against burning.

Snow upon a thaw freezeth itself, while the spirits of some parts dissolved, flying out, do fix the neighbour parts unto them.

Snow closely pressed, dissolves into about half its measure ; lying loose, and as it falleth, dissolving, takes up little more than a fifth part.

Snow upon a thaw needeth no addition, and ice at that time will freeze, the pot being melted in it.

Salt maketh snow to melt; so may you bore a hole through ice with salt laid thereon, with armoniac. Sugar will also do the like but in a slower manner ; the like dully with pepper.

To make ice crack, throw salt upon it.

Ice splits star-wise.

In the making of ice with snow and salt, we find little variety in practice, and the reasons drawn peculiar upon the

salt; but this we have observed to be effected by other bodies, of no probability to produce such an effect, as without
salt to effect it in a pot of snow, with ginger, pepper, liquorice,
sugar, chalk, white-lead, wheat-flour, sulphur, husk of almonds, charcoal.

Water that is easily rarified will hardly or not at all admit
of pressure, or be made to take up a lesser space than its natural body, and as it stands in its natural consistence.

In snow it takes up a very much larger space than in water;
even in ice, which takes off the fluidity, and is a kind of fixation, it will not be contained in the same circumference as
before in its fluid body, a glass filled with water and frozen in
salt and snow, will manifestly rise above the brim. Eggs
frozen, the shell will crack, and open largely, and there will
be found no hollow space at the top or blunter part which
comes first out upon exclusion of the hen, and yet it will remain of the same weight upon exact ponderation. Ice is
spongy and porous, as may be observed upon breaking, and
in glasses wherein it is frozen and seems not to be so close
and continued as in its liquid form. Beside there are many
bubbles ofttimes in it, which though condensed, are not of the
congelable parts, and take up a room in the congelation;
which may be air mixed with the water, or the spirits thereof,
which will not freeze, but separating from the pure water, set
themselves in little cells apart, which upon the liquation make
the spaws and froth which remaineth after, in standing vessels thawed, which makes all things frozen lose their quickness; the spirits chased into several conservations, flying away
upon liquefaction, and not returning to an intrinsical and close
mixture with their bodies again; and therefore an apple froz-
en, and thawed in warm water, the spirits are called out, and
giving a sudden exhalation, the same never tastes well after;
whereas put into cold water, they are kept in, and while they
raise themselves through the mass again, and are not carried
out by a warm thaw; and this way are noses and cheeks preserved in cold regions, by a sudden application of snow unto
them.

The same assertion is verified in metallical water, or quicksilver, which is closer in its own body than by any fixation;

for either mortified or fixed, it takes up a much larger space than in its fluid body.

Quære how oil;—and whether metal, silver, and gold, liquefied, takes not up lesser room than when it is cold and congealed again : but these having attained their natural consistence and closeness, seem to take up a larger space when they are forced from it, and therefore seem to shrink as in moulds; and then in their cruding before solution to stretch and dilate themselves ; as is observable in iron pierced, which smoothly admitting a nail when it is cold, will not so easily admit it being red hot.

Why the snow lies not long near the sea side ; by reason it is dissolved by salt exhalation of the sea, or from the like in the earth near the sea, which partaketh of that temper.

Why it is so cold upon a thaw ; by reason of the exhaling of those freezing parts which lie quiet in the snow before.

Why snow maks a fruitful year and is good for corn ; because it keeps in the terreous evaporatives, concentrates the heat in seeds and plants, destroys mice and the principles of putrefaction in the earth, which breedeth vermin.

Why it changeth the colour of leather, making black shoes russet, which water doth not; by reason of the admixture of nitrous and saline parts, which drink in the copperas parts which made the deep colour.

The common experiment of freezing is made by salt and snow ; where salt dissolving the snow sends out the congealing spirit thereof, which actively is able to fix the fluid element about it.

But the same effect will follow from other conjunctions, from vitriol, nitre, alum ; and what is remarkable, from bodies which promise no such effect, as we have tried in pepper, ginger, chalk, white lead, charcoal-powder, liquorice.

And from ice itself stirred and beaten in a pint pot.

[*On Bubbles.*]

THAT the last circumference of the universe is but the bubble of the chaos and pellicle arising from the grosser foundation of the first matter, containing all the higher and diaphanous bodies under it, is no affirmation of mine; but that bubbles on watery or fluid bodies are but the thin gumbs of air, or a diaphanous texture of water arising about the air, and holding it awhile from eruption. They are most lasting and large in viscous humidities, wherein the surface will be best extended without dissolving the continuity, as in bladders blown out of soap. Wine and spirituous bodies make bubbles, but not long lasting, the spirit bearing through and dissolving the investiture. Aqua-fortis upon concussion makes few, and soon vanishing, the acrimonious effluvia suddenly rending them: some gross and windy wines make many and lasting, which may be taken away by vinegar or juice of lemon. And therefore the greatest bubbles are made in viscous decoctions, as in the manufacture of soap and sugar, wherein there is nothing more remarkable than that experiment, wherein not many grains of butter cast upon a copper of boiling sugar, presently strikes down the ebullition and makes a subsidence of the bubbling liquor.

Boiling is literally nothing but bubbling; any liquor attenuated by decoction sends forth evaporous and attenuated parts, which elevate the surface of the liquor into bubbles; even in fermentations and putrefactions wherein attenuation of parts are made, bubbles are raised without fire.

Glass is made by way of bubble, upon the blowing of the artificer.

Blisters are bubbles in leaves, wherein the exhalation is kept in by the thickness of the leaf, and in the skin, when the [membrane] thereof holds in the attenuated or attracted humour under it.

Fire blisters even dead flesh, forcibly attenuating the water in the skin and under it; and cantharides and crowfoot raise blisters by a potential fire and armoniac salt in them, attenuating the humour in the skin and under, which stretches and dilateth the parts, prohibiting its evolution.

Bubbles are white, because they consist of diaphanous humour or air fermented; and air under ice a thicker *tergunt* makes a grosser and stronger white, but in icterical and jaundiced urine the bubbles are yellow, according to the tincture diffused through the water, which investeth the airy contents of its bubbles. Even man is a bubble, if we take his consideration in his rudiments, and consider the *vesicula* or *bulla pulsans*, wherein begins the rudiment of life.

Froth or spume is but a coagulation or conglobation of bubbles, and gross skins are but the coats of bubbles subsiding, or at least bodies which are fat and subphureous, keeping the surface, are apt to make them, and therefore are not without the active parts as is observable in the spume of iron and steel.

Pitch and resinous bodies have also their bubbles, but they rise highest at the first, whilst the aqueous parts are attenuated, do copiously and crowdingly fly up, do elevate the viscous parts which largely dilate before their division, for that being spirit these bubbles are less, and if water be thrown upon it recover their force again; as is also discernable in the ebullition of soap, till the aqueous parts be spent, and the salt of the lixivium and oil and tallow entirely mixed.

The bubbles of oil will not last, the air pierceth, opening or perspiring their thin coats ; water under oil makes not bubbles into the oil, but at the side or bottom.

Water and oil do best concur to the making of bubbles, air or exhalation included in a watery coat, or air in an oily habit, as in oil boiled wherein there are some watery parts or vaporous attenuations that are invested in their eruption.

Fire makes none, for that is too subtle to be contained and too fluid and moving to be contained ; not affecting a circle but a piramidal ascension, which destroys inclusion; the nearest resemblance thereof is in water thrown upon strong oil, wherein the water suddenly rising seemeth to carry up a strong bubble about it.

Quicksilver seems to have bubbles, being shaken together, but they are but small spherical bodies like drops of water, which hold in some bodies, to avoid discontinuation.

[*On Vegetation, &c.*]

To manifest how lasting the seminal principles of bodies are, how long they will lie incorrupted in the earth, or how the earth that hath been once impregnated therewith, may retain the power thereof, unto opportunity of actuation, or visible production,—a remarkable garden where many plants had been, being digged up, and turned a fruitless ground, after ten years being digged up, many of the plants returned which had laid obscure; the plants were blattaria, stramonium, hyoscyamus flore albo, &c.; and little less have we observed that some plants will maintain their seminality out of the earth, as we have tried in one of the least of seeds, that is of marjorum.

How little snails or perriwinkles rely upon the water, and how duck-weed is bred, some light may be received from this experiment. In April we took out of the water little herbs of crow-foot and the like, whereon hung long cods of jelly; this put in water, and so into an urinal exposed unto the sun, many young perriwinkles were bred sticking to the side of the glass, some aselli, or sows, which fled from the water, and much duck-weed grew over, which, cleared once or twice, now hath grown again.

That water is the principle of all things, some conceive; that all things are convertible into water, others probably argue; that many things which seem of earthly principles were made out of water the Scripture testifieth, in the genealogy of the fowls of the air; most insects owe their original thereto, most being made of dews, froths, or water; even rain water, which seemeth simple, contains the seminals of animals. This we observed, that rain water in cisterns, growing green, there ariseth out of it red maggots, swimming in a labouring and contortile motion, which after leaving a . . . . . case behind them, turn into gnats and ascend above the water.

When the red worm tends to transformation, it seems to acquire a new case, and continues most at the surface of the water; two motions are observable, the one of the red worm by a strong and laborious contorsion, the other, a little before it comes to a gnat, and that is by jaculation or sudden spring, which if it use not, it ariseth to the surface, and soon after ariseth into a gnat.

Little red worms and less than threads are found in great numbers in ditches and muddy places, where the water is almost forsaken; whereof having taken a large number included in a glass, they would stir and move continually in fair weather like eels, pulling some part of their bodies above the mud, and upon the least touch of the glass would all disappear and contract into the mud. They lived that remaining part of summer, and after a hard winter, showed themselves again in the succeeding summer. Therein I observed two things, the exquisite sense and vivacity of these imperfect animals, which extended unto two years.

All solid bodies are rendered liquid before they are qualified for nutriment; and the solidest bodies seem to be sustained by the thin bodies of waters, as is very remarkable in trees, especially oak, and birch, and sycamore, wherein the nutriment ascendeth in a mere body of water, as by wounding them at the spring is very discernible.

Thus we also observe that plants will be nourished long in rain water, as is very observable in mint, basil, and other plants, which being cropped, will shoot out roots, which will augment them by mere attraction of watery nutriment.

Whether the quantities of plants may not this way be sensibly altered deserves experiment; whether the liquor impregnated with colours may not communicate the same upon necessity of this single aliment; whether smells may not be impressed; whether when it purges corrected, and purgative qualities imbibed.

If others answer, mint and basil, though they sprout largely, yet they will hardly afford flowers, much less seed;—senecio, or groundswell, seems best to promise it.

Groundswell, put into water in December, lived, was frozen in January, sent forth flowers in the end of February, flowered and vanished in the beginning of May.

Bulbous roots, once shot, will flower there, and no wonder therein, for some will flower being hung up, having a sufficient stock of moisture for flowers that are precocious.

Plants will not only grow in the summer, but also in the winter if they be such as then continue green, as scurvy grass and groundswell. They will hold best which are put into the water with their roots, otherwise they will either not shoot them forth in the winter, or be long about it; as we tried in scurvy grass. Rue stood almost three months, without putting any roots forth, fresh and verdant; spurge stood well with the root, as chamomile, and featherfew, and parsley. Mint and scordium, put in about July, stood and grew all summer, shot plentiful roots, from whence came fresh sprouts out of the glass when the other decayed, and some now stand under water, Feb. 17. Mint grew up in several branches in April, and now groweth, June 28. Mint, set in water in May, grew up, and seemed to die, but sprouted again about October, stood all winter, and grew up in many branches the next spring.

Rue, set in October, without shooting any roots, grew about two inches in the winter, shot forth above forty roots in the spring, and grew much all the summer, flowered July and August.

Scurvy grass grew all winter, flowered in the spring, but seeded not, other put in in February, near to flower, shot roots, flowered and seeded in May, and shot new leaves under water.

Try how they will thrive in aqua vitæ, wine, vinegar, oil, salt water.

Many were put in, none grew or thrived, but suddenly decayed in aqua vitæ, wine, vinegar, salt water; oil draweth not at all, and so it dieth.

Mint would not grow in water and sugar, nor in strong rose water, but, unto two ounces of water adding but two or three spoonfulls, it thrived and acquired a richer smell. Seeds of plants which seed in the water of glasses, prove fruitful, as tried in those of scurvy and spurge, which now grow at the spring, being sowed about September before.

Asarum which had stood about two years in water, and twice cast the leaves; of these the leaves given maintained their vomitive quality,

How little, beside water alone, will support or maintain the growth of plants, beside the experiment of Helmont we have seen in some which have lived six years in glasses; and asarum which grew two years in water and lived; cast the leaves, maintained its vomiting quality.

Fertile seeds sink, but when they germinate they rise up and come up to the top of the water, for then the seed ferments and swells, and breaks the closure or covering.

The seed of an almond or plum, at first when it is hollow and windy swimmeth, afterward sinketh, yet take out the nib and it sinketh.

In bay leaves commonly used at funerals, we unknowingly hold in our hands a singular emblem of the resurrection; for the leaves that seem dead and dry, will revive into a perfect green, if their root be not withered ; as is observable in bay trees after hard winters, in many leaves half, in some almost wholly withered, wherein though the alimental and aqueous juice be exhausted the radical and balsamical humour remaining though in a slender quantity is able to refresh itself again, the like we have observed in dead and withered furze.

[*On Tobacco.*]

ALTHOUGH of ordinary use in physic, the anatomy of tobacco is not discovered, nor hath Hoffmanus in his work of thirty years relieved us. That which comes fermented and dyed unto us affords no distinct account, in regard it is infected with a decoction or lixivium, which is diverse according to different places, and some ascend no higher than urine. Adulterations proceed further, adding euphorbium or pepper, and some do innocently temper it with gum of guaiacum.

The herb simply in itself and green or dried, is but flat, nor will it hold fire well upon ordinary exsiccation. Other plants are taken in the pipe but they want quickness and hold not fire only prick and draw . . . . . . by their fuligo, which all smoke will do ; and probably other herbs might be made quick and fire well, if prepared the same way, that is by fermentation, for in that alteration the body is opened, the fixed parts attenuated by the spirit, the oily parts diffused and the salt raised from the earthly bed wherein it naturally lieth obscure and heavy.

It containeth three eminent qualities, sudorific, narcotic, and purgative; from the subtle spirits and flying salt, sweat seems to proceed, for the ashes will not do it. The narcotic depends on the *humor impurus ;* for the vapour thereof contains it, and the burnt part loseth it, as in opium. Poppy seeds dried are ineffectual, and the green heads work most powerfully; the same is observable in the *mandichoca* root, which being a strong poison, is harmless, being dried. The purgative quality lieth in the middle principle, which goes not away by a gentle heat; for the water purgeth not, the smoke but very doubtfully, and seldom in clysters of the smoke of three or four pipefuls, nor in the salt thereof, neither incineration, but in the middle principles of the nitrous salt, and such parts as are to be extracted by tincture, infusion, or decoction, whose actives remain in the menstruum, and therefore that which is decocted, and after dried, grows faint in the purgative quality, if it returneth.

Of tobacco there is the male and female; the male the best. Yellow rhubard is often taken for the true plant.

Tobacco may be made or cured without a *caldo*, and will ferment and grow brown long laid together, and hung up will grow brown. To advance the same the caldo may be added before the rolling up, for then it will have a quicker taste and sweeter smell.

The leaves first ripe make the best when they grow gummy and brittle; they must be often cleared of the sprouts that grow upon the same stem, and the *baschros* left out.

To make the best tobacco, these to be taken, and of the male; and a good caldo used, and kept awhile, till time digest remaining crudities.

[*On the Ivy.*]

CONCERNING ivy these remarkable:—The leaves less indented, scarce angular toward the top; like many herbs which laciniate at the lower leaves, little at the upper.

It beareth twice a year, spring and . . . . It groweth not about every tree; most about oak, ash, elm, thorn; less about wich hasel; hardly observed about firs, pine, yew.

Whether it will not delight about trees that are perpetually green may be inquired. It seldom ariseth about holly or not to great bigness; the perpetual leafing prevents the arise, or hindring the growth or twisting of . . . . to provide for themselves.

Whether there be not also a dissimilitude in their motions, not one enduring the approximation of the other.

That they follow the sun in their windings is hard to make out upon impartial observation; hops do it more clearly, which nothing turning are commonly directed that way by the husbandman.

Inquire how it ariseth from the primary root.

Try whether ivy will bear when cut from the root; whether it may have sufficient stock remaining for once, or whether it may not attract somewhat by the *cerni*.

[*On the Fig Tree.*]

CONCERNING the fig tree, some things are remarkable from its proper nature; that it is a tree of plentiful sap and milk diffused throughout, which will drop from the trunk and branches if seasonably cut at the spring.

That it is the general plant for admission of insition, engrafting; and though misletoe seldom or never groweth thereon, yet it becomes a fit stock for most plants.

That it was the coagulum or runnet of the ancients, wherewith they turned their milk and made cheese, as is remarkable from Aristotle *de Animal.* and illustrates that passage in Homer and Euripides, and might frustrate all the use of other herbs, and hath its name from thence and which we find so great effect; and might therefore be medically used in the place of coagulum, which having that virtue may serve for dissolution of blood coagulated.

That they have fruits without any flower, as jessamine flowers without fruit or seeds; that these are the forerunners of fruit the year following, and stay in buttons all the winter, making figs the year after.

Of this, two parables, remarkable in the Scripture.

Cursed for barrenness, as being less tolerable in that tree than any, which is the stock of all other trees, and therefore more considerable that nothing grew upon it, on which all other trees will grow, and in this consideration probably the *phallus* or *virile neuter* and the image of Priapus the god of fertility and semblance of fecundation was formed out of a fig tree. And whether in the Hebrew notation there be any natural fertility implied, whilst we find it from a word that signifieth twins and plural generations, may admit of consideration.

That our first parents covered their secret parts with fig-leaves, which tree was after sacred unto Priapus, I shall not deduce upon genteel imagination.

[*Scripture Criticism.*]

How properly the priority was conferred unto Aaron by a rod or staff, and why the staff and sceptre of the princes were chosen for this intention, philologists may conjecture; in that they were the bodies and cognizances of their places, and were a kind of sceptre in their hands, denoting their power and supremacy, without which we find the princes of the Trojans, and which rod was ready in the hand of Ulysses. Thersites' shoulders felt it from the hand of Ulysses; and Achilles, as the deepest oath, swears by his sceptre, that should never bud nor bear leaves again, as a thing impossible. This lash of divinty is in the hands of gods and goddesses.

Whether there be any such implied in the vision of Jeremy, *video virgam vigilantem* or *amygdalinum*, as it is translated, may be considered, for thereby the power and staff of the Assyrian king is implied. But in the contention of the children of Israel, and miraculous decision of priority testified by the rod of Aaron, which flowered and brought forth almonds, you cannot but discern a look at the propriety of the miracle in that species of tree which is the first that blossometh, and leadeth in the vernal geniture unto all the body of trees. That most famous allegory of Scripture implies the head in that expression, " when the almond tree shall flourish," that is, " the head grow white like the flowers of almonds," whose fruit was anciently called Καρυον, or the head.

God that proposed the experiment only by blossoms, added also the fruit of almonds, the text not clearly making out leaves, but the buds of flowers, open flowers, and almonds; and, therefore, if you have perused medals, you cannot but observe how derogatory unto the miracle the Jews have described in them, shewing the rod of Aaron laden only with leaves, and whether the . . . . have attained it best, and done it after the original when they describe it only almonds, and the fruit without leaves.

How the dove sent out of the ark should bring in a green olive leaf according to the original, hath nothing of such wonder as to amaze expositors, how after ten months it should maintain that verdure, since the tree is continually green, the leaves dry, thick, and lasting, since plants at the bottom of the sea maintain that verdure, and since we receive the leaves fresh among the olives which come from far countries and very late unto us.

How it should stand thus long under water, may partly be allowed from the uncertain detention of the currents, and ebbs and flows at that time, and the mixture of the fresh water from the whole ocean of that element, and notably illustrated from like examples in Theophrastus and Pliny. *Theophrasti Hist.* iv, cap. 7. *Plin.* lib. xiii, cap. ult.

[*On Chiromancy.*]

To make further inquiry into that chiromantical doctrine of Bartholomeus Cocles, that the acuteness of the *linea mensalis* denotes the acuteness of fevers, and great disposition thereto, in persons where it extendeth high and near the fore finger, *Chiromanticæ parvæ*, lib. vi, cap. 28.

Great variety there is in the lines of the hand; almost no strict conformity. In the palm, they seem to be made by the articulation of the *metacarpus*, or middle hand, from whence the fingers begin. The inflexion of the little and fourth finger makes the table of the . . . . . and middle the natural line, that of the thumb the line of life. The other lines are made out of the ligaments or ties of the broad tendons unto the bones, or of divers lines of fibres under the skin.

Of the first sort there are also master and principal lines, in some analogy to these, in creatures of five divisions of foot, as apes, monkeys, in frogs, with like lesser also, and in great variety.

These are also observed in most digitate animals, and variously disposed, as in dogs, cats, &c.; in fin-footed birds, swans, geese, ducks.

[*Experiments on Animals.*]

OBSERVE how purges and narcotics, aloe and opium, do work with other animals; in what quantity purges work well with hawks; whether they will with hens, and birds with craws and gizzards ; what they will do with herons and cormorants, that seem to have but one gut, what they will do with fishes, as a pickerel or carp or eel.

Three grains of opium works strongly upon a dog. Observe how much will take place with a horse, which subsisteth with little sleep. Fishes are quickly intoxicated with baits ; in what quantity with opium ? What quantity will take, in birds and animals with little heads ?

From two grains unto five we have given unto a cockerel, without any discernible sopition. Observe what place it will take in birds without craws ; where, falling into the maw, the heat may quicklier liquate it.

Four unto a crow, without visible effect.

Six and eight unto dogs, making them dull, not profoundly to sleep.

Ten grains of aloe given unto a cock, produce bloody excretions, carrying off the mucus of the guts; which in birds are tender, and might be employed in puddings.

Five grains we have also given unto turkeys without effect of sleep; four unto a crow, and as much unto cocks and hens.

Two grains given a pickerel, above a quarter long; died in twelve hours, stooled not; another, who had nothing given, survived.

Six grains of white hellebore given unto a young quail produced vertigo, but it survived. Ten of black hellebore unto another produced no sensible alteration, but only frequent ejections or mutings.

We entered a mole, a toad, and a viper, in one glass : within half an hour the mole eat up half the viper, leaving the tail and harder parts; destroyed the toad, eat part of the entrails ; died the next day; which I imputed not unto eating so large a meal, for they will not commonly live above a day or two out of the earth.

Fifteen grains of opium given unto a young cormorant, it

seemed for some hours to be a little vertiginous and to go but weakly, but seemed not to sleep at all.

Five grains unto a young kestrel, did seem the like vertiginous and a little more sleepy; not profoundly.

Five unto a young heron did nothing; given in paste it was excluded in an hour.

Twenty-one grains of aloes powdered, given unto a young cormorant, wrought often, thin and yellow, the bird well after it.

Two drachms of hemlock given unto a cormorant; died in two hours after, vertiginous.

Of *crocus metallorum*, a drachm given unto a cormorant; lived a week after, vomited much; being dead it was found still remaining in the bottom of the maw.

[*Receipts.*]

Two neat pickles may be contrived, the one of oysters stewed in their own vinegar, with thyme, lemon peel, onion, mace, pepper; adding Rhenish wine, elder vinegar, three or four pickled cucumbers.

Another with equal parts of the liquor of oysters, and the liquor that runs from herrings newly salted, dissolving anchovy therein, or pickling therein a few smelts, or garlick, especially the seeds thereof.

High esteem was made of *garum* by the ancients, and was used in sauces, puddings, &c. If simply made with aromatic mixture, as is delivered, it cannot but have an ungrateful smell, however a haut gout, for it was the liquor or the resolution of guts of fishes, salt and insolated.

This same way may be tried by us yearly, and is still continued in Turkey.

And may be made out of the entrails of mackarel, the liquor that runs from the herrings which may dissolve anchovies, and with a mixture of oysters and limpets and the testaceous fishes, whereof every one makes his own pickle, and varieth the taste of sea water.

The neatest way is to have pickles always ready, wherein we may make additions at pleasure, or use them simply in sauces. The ancients loaded their pickles with cummin seed and the like, distateful unto our senses.

[MS. SLOAN. 1882, FOL. 143.]

[*Fossil Remains found in Norfolk.*][1]

THIS bone was found about a year past, by Winterton, on the sea shore, in Norfolk.

The cliff had been much broken by high tides and the rage of the sea, many hundred loads falling down as it often doth upon this coast, the cliffs being not rock but earth.

Upon the same coast, but at some miles distance, divers great bones are said to have been found, and I have seen one side of a lower jaw containing very large teeth petrified, far exceeding the teeth of the biggest ox.

It was found after a great flood near to the cliff, some thousand loads of earth being broken down by the rage of the sea.

That it came not out of the sea it might be conjectured, because it was found so far from it, and from the colour, for if out of the sea it would have been whiter.

When the outward crust is taken off, it answereth the grain of the bones of whales and other cetaceous animals, comparing it with a piece of whale's scull that I have by me.

This last month in a grave of Earsham churchyard, were found sixteen large teeth but of a different bigness, whereof this is one brought me and taken for a giant's tooth, but it very well resembleth the tooth of an ox, as you may observe by comparing it.

[MS. SLOAN. 1862 AND 1866.]

[*Classical passages selected for mottoes.*][2]

Boletus domino.—*Juvenal.*   *The best meat for the best.*

---

[1] And presented to the Royal Society, 1666.—*Hooke's Posthumous Works*, p. 313.

[2] In *MS. Sloan.* 1843, there occur several *Anagrams sent me by my ever honored friend Sir Philip Wodehouse*, and others; some, however, are not altogether fit for publication; and Sir Thomas's own exclamation immediately following, *Valete anagrammata! Nil mihi vobiscum!* —shows his estimation of such things. The following sentences are selected from Nos. 1862-1866, (which form but one volume) in order to shew one of the uses to which Browne turned his classical reading.

. . . . . . refert,
Quo gestu lepores, et quo gallina secetur.   *Juv. Sat.* v, *l.* 124.
In small matters a decorum is to be observed.

. . . . . . Plurima sunt, quæ
Non audent homines pertusâ dicere lænâ.   *Ib. l.* 130.
Poor men dare not speak what they think;
Or must not, if you make it debent.

Oppida tota canem venerantur, nemo Dianam.   *Ib.* xv, *l.* 8.
The servant more honoured than the master—
The man honored; the lord neglected.

Nefas illic fœtum jugulare capellæ: *Ib. lin.* 13.
Carnibus humanis vesci licet. . . .
They strain at a gnat, and swallow a camel.

Quis gremio Encladi, doctique Palæmonis adfert
Quantum grammaticus meruit labor?   *Ib.* viii, *l.* 215.
Upon the Free school door at Norwich.

Qui nunquam visæ flagrabat amore puellæ.
                          Juv. lib. i, *Sat.* iv, *l.* 114.
A blind man in love.

Pocula adorandæ rubiginis.   *Ib.* xiii, *l.* 148.
Upon an antique vessel.

Hoc pretio squamæ?   *Ib.* iv, *l.* 25.
Who would give such high prices for trifles?

Quare si sapies viam vorabis.   *Catul.* xxxvi, 7.
To a friend to come in haste.

. . . nimis uncis
Naribus indulges.   *Ib. l.* 40.
Upon one that exceedeth in scoffing.

Tenerum et laxa cervice legendum.   *Pers.* i, 98.
Upon a smooth and easy poem.

Et qui cœruleum dirimebat Nerea delphin.   *Pers.* i, 94.
Upon my picture of a dolphin.

Per me equidem sint omnia protinus alba.   *Pers.* i, 110.
All is well for me.

Qui sale multo
Urbem defricuit.   *Horat. S.* i, x. 4.
Ben Jonson.

Hoc meruit fundi de Ganimede merum.   *Mart.* 13, cviii.
Upon super-excellent wine.

Libros non legit ille, sed libellos.   *Ib.* xi, i, 5.
Upon a book dedicated to a prince.

Qui scribit nihil, et tamen pöeta est.   *Ib.* x, cii.
Upon a stolen piece, or piece of plagiarism.

Hæredem scripsit me Numa: convaluit.
Upon one whose hopes are unexpectedly and narrowly disappointed.

Neronianas hic refrigerat thermas.   *Mart.* iii, xxv, 4.
Upon one of a very cold temper.

O nox, quam longa est, quæ fecit una senem.
Upon Gonzaga imprisoned, who in one night grew grey.

Et mare percussum puero, fabrumque volantem. *Juv.* i, *l.* 54.
Upon my large picture of Icarus and Dœdalus.

Unde epulum possis centum dare Pythagoræis. *Ib.* iii, *l.* 229.
An inscription upon the kitchen-garden door.

Omnes tanquam ad vivaria currunt.   *Ib. l.* 303.
Whither all sharking or shifting people resort, as it were their pasture, to London.

Dr. Thomas Browne's Journey

WITH

DR. PLOT.

[MS. SLOAN. NO. 1899.]

Auguste the 15*th,* 1693.

THIS morninge I went to Greenwhiche with Dr. Plot; from the landing place wee went directly up to Blackeheath. A little beyonde the bowlingreen, Watlingstreet, one of the Roman highways, appeard very conspicuous, running directly to the corner of the parke, where we loste it, but recoverd it againe in lesse then halfe a mile, where it passes by two tumuli in a pointe of lande between Dover roade and an other running towards Liegh; and some of the present roade going up Shooters hill is parte of it. Upon the heathe between Wellinge and Crayforde it passes on the righte hand of the great roade, and somtimes between two horse ways. Att Crayforde wee inquired for some deep perpendicular pits, mentiond by Lambert? and placed in this parishe, thoughe wee coulde finde none here: in halfe a mile of Dartforde and in that parishe wee met with several, some of chalke and some of sand. I had not the opportunity of being lett downe into any of them, but as far as I can perceive they are of the same forme of some others in Chadwell wood, in Essex, about three miles from Grayes. There are two cuts of them in Camden, and he supposes that the Britains dug chalke out of them, but surely that was not theire purpose, for it seems improbable that they shoulde dig several fathom deep for chalke when they might haue it neer the surface of the earth, and I was in one which was 9 fathoms deep which had nothing but sande in it; this pit was scarce a fathom broade till I came within three yards of the botom where it expatiates itselfe and is of a circular form,* belieue the Britains upon an incursion of the enemie hid themselves, their cattle, goods, and corne, in these caverns, as Tacitus says the Germans did, and as the Hungarians doe at present, when they are invaded by the Turkes; the countrey people in Essex call them the Danes holes: att Dartforde they haue noe name for them, one John Lowe who liues nearest them tells us that in Dartforde and neer it there are about fortie of these pits.

On the sixteenth, on Dartforde Brent, we perceived the Roman waye running on the righte hande of the great roade; it strikes downe a lane, and passes on the ***** hand of a farme, called Woodcocks hall, and an other named Blacke sole; some remains of wee found in stone wood, and these led us to Bettysham, a hamlet in Southfleet: here we left the Roman waye and went to Swanscombe, which takes its name from Swaine, the Dane; who, in one of his invasions, came up Ebsfleet, now a rivulet, which passes under Stone bridge; he incamped here or very neer it. Lamberte says it was att Greenhithe; but after a stricte inquiry att both these places, wee coulde neither hear of or see any remains of Swains intrenchments, or Swanscombe castle, which Philpot says was an honour: perhaps Mr. Weldons house stands on the castle, and the Danishe fortifications ar dug away att Greenhithe.

On the seventeenth wee found something of the way at Chinglewell, and on the north side of Cobham parke, they haue taken the advantage here to set the parke pale on it. Cobham house is an antient noble bricke building; the rooms are stately and well furnished; the chymney pieces are moste of them marble, well carvde and polished; in order to finde where the Roman way passed the Medway at Durobrovis, now Rochester, it was rational to enquire for the moste fordable, and were informed that att the pointe of lande over against Friendsbury church, att lowe water, it was not aboue three or foure foote water and that in our grandfathers days,

* Sic.

by the helpe of an horses head, any one might passe the river; we coulde finde nothing of the waye att either of these places; in the afternoone going up Chatham hill wee coulde perceive nothing of the waye, but aboue the hill it runs on the left hand hedge going to Raynham, the burying place of the Tuftons Earles of Thanet; on the right hand of the waye to Newington it passes on the right hand of the waye, and neer the towne it seems to fall into the Dover-roade about halfe a mile from Newington; on the left hand is a fielde called Crockefielde (from the infinite number of urns that have been found here) Burton says that some thousand of urns were here dug up, and will haue this to bee Durolevum, though the distance between that and Durovernum, now Canterbury, does not agree, and I belieue that these bones were reposited here after some suddain ingagement, and that it was never a Roman station. About two miles from hence there is a hill called Standarde hill, and is saide to haue been once graced with the Roman eagle. Watling street falls into the roade at Caicolhill, between that and Greenstreet; it is much demolished but fair enough in this village. On the left hand about a mile from hence in Castlewoode, wee founde some trenches running one into an other, and perhaps mighte bee the olde Durolevum, the distance between that and Durovernum agree better then any other place that we haue met with. Att Ospringe beacon wee met with some of it again, att Ospringe beacon nothing of it appears between that and Feversham, it being worne away here as it is in all valleys; here wee sought for the chalke pits as Dr. Childery supposes they doe not resemble those att Crayforde, but are as broade att the top as any where ard containe a good compasse of grounde; it is likely that the Britains might builde their hovels or place their tents in these bottoms to protect them from ill weather: the next daye till wee came to the lower end of Bougton street it appeard not att all; but here is prittie plaine on the right hand of the roade, thence running to the beacon, and so to be seen at divers places between that and Harble downe. About a quarter of a mile from hence, on the left hand, is a round hill steep and high, on all sides but the easte. Wee haue met with several such, but whether they

bee fortified by art or nature is disputable.   Between this and
Canterbury the waye is worne out.   At Canterbury there
are two remarkable things not taken notice of by Sumner,
viz. in the N. E. staircase in the castle are several verses
of the psalms curiously cut in Hebrew characters, yet visible
in the stone worke.   Mrs. Elizabeth Moore, daughter to Sir
Thomas Moore, Chancellour of England, after his fathers
execution kept his head in her closet till her death, and then
orderd it to bee inclosed in lead and placed on her coffin.
She married one Mr. Roper, whose successours are now living in St. Dunstans parishe, in Canterbury, in the vaulte of
which family, her body and Sir Thomas's head are reposited.
Wee made an excursion to Chilham to view the burial place
of Quintus Durus Laberius, a Roman tribune, slaine by the
Britains; his tumulus is not rounde as all other Roman ones I
have yet met with, but is a ridge of earth, much resemblinge
a Roman waye, seventy paces long and twentie broad, it is in
a fielde of Mr. Diggs's neer a mill, and within a   * of a
mile of his house, which was raised out of the ruins of Chilham
castle, whose trenches incompasse moste of the towne, and
the keep is att present Mr. Diggs's brewhouse.   Three mile
and an halfe from Canterbury, in Iffin wood, wee founde a
fortification on a rising grounde, the possession of John Le
Mot Honeywoode, Esq. of Cogshul, in Essex; it has two
trenches; the innermoste contains two acres and the other
seven att least.   If we coulde distinguish the Britishe for-
tresses from others, wee might conclude that this was one,
and that to which Cæsar forced the Britains to retire to, for
after he had left his navy (which laye then wide of Sand-
whiche) under the commande of Q. Atrius, says thus of him-
selfe, *progressus millia passuum circiter duodecim hostium
copias conspicatus est illi esse dis ad flumen progressi ex
loco superiore nostros prohibere, et prælium committere
cœperunt repulsi ab equitatu in silvis se abdiderunt locum
nacti egregie naturâ et opere munitum quod domestici belli
causâ ut videatur ante præparaverant.*   This fortification is
the exact distance from his navy, which he assigns it is neer
a river, and has several wells neer it which must bee requisite

* Sic.

for such an intrenchment.   Aug. 27, wee went to Sandwhich, and in our waye founde the Roman Watling street, on the left hand of the roade where my Lorde Winchelsheas parke-wall stands upon; it is conspicuous att Fishepoole hill and Little Bourne, but moste aparent by Wyngham churche in the mill medowe; and on a green about halfe a mile on this side of Ashe, it is prittie plain, having a large tumulus neer it.   On the left hand of the green it pointed S. E. by S., and was worne awaye between that and Richboroughe.

From Sandwhich wee went to Richborowe, the olde Rutupium, the ruins of which station are of a square forme contaning about fiue acres of land.   The northe wall is 168 paces longe, the southe 126, and the weste 160, the easte wall is fallen away and overgrowne with bushes tho' the other three are loftie, and thicke composed of flinte, and double ridges of Roman bricke, compacted together with a mortar made of cockleshells and sand; the chief entrance was on the weste side; in the northe wall there is a little posterne.   Neer this is an other fortification of earth having foure entrances to it; it takes up about an acre of lande.   Some authers giue an accounte K. Ethelberte received St. Augustine in his palace of Richboroughe in the Isle of Thanet, whether Richboroughe was in that islande is not certaine; though possible, for the Stowre might formerly haue its course over Goshall and Fleet marshes, that parte of the countrie being as lowe as the channel in which the river now runs, and upon the digging of ditches in this parte of the level great quantities of cockles, periwinkles, and other shels are found.   Whilste wee were here wee gathered some from the surface of the earthe, which is no small argument to proue that Richboroughe was once in the isle of Thanet.   Neer the ferry from Sandwiche is a rounde risinge ground, including neer thirtie acres; here stood Stonar, by some thought to bee Lapis Tituli.   The foundations of buildings are turnde up by the plowe every daye. Peter Van Slade who had one of the farms here, raised the bancke that lies between the two farms with parte of the foundation he dug up here.   In our returne to Canterbury wee sawe Wingham churche, it is in very good repair, and amongst other monuments has one very beautifull erected in memory of several of that branch of the Oxendine family, which is now seated att Deane here in this parishe, this tombe is in a neat chappel paved with blacke and white marble, here is an other handsome tombe for Sir Ed. Palmer and his lady.

On Iffindowne about halfe a mile beyond Stubbington, that part of Watlingstreet which is paved and raisd high with flinte is to bee seen, it runs by Eye and Divels courte hall, leaving it on the right hand as it had done Stubbington before and goes to Harmansoale and points.* It is yet so entire that passeingers is for the ease of their horses, where they can, leaue this waye, and choose the sof ground ; so that in divers places the Roman waye is overgrowne with bushes; att Hempton hill, within lesse then three miles of Hyde, it turns to the right hand and winds about to the left againe, going downe that hill to Stanforde where it is quite worne out; between this and Hyde, is an antient seat called Oustern hanger parke, builte by Oeske King of Kent, and as tradition goes his sworde was kepte here in succeeding ages, and gaue name to the house.   Halfe a mile from hence is Saltwood castle the firste builte by Vske a Kinge of Kent, and much repaired by William Montforde, constable of Dover castle, and afterwards by William Courtney, archbishop of Canterbury, his arms are over the easte gate, the only parte of the castle which is inhabited, tis of an oval forme from easte to weste, it is twentie five rods in lengthe, in 1580 it suffered much by an earthquake.

* Sic.

AN ACCOUNT OF

The Manuscript Collections

OF

SIR THOMAS & DR. E. BROWNE.

Sir Thomas Browne left a very considerable mass of letters and manuscripts, principally his own, but including also some which he had collected;—especially the MSS. of Dr. Arthur Dee. A small portion found their way into the Bodleian Library, through the medium of Dr. Rawlinson; but how or when he obtained them, I have not been able to ascertain. They are in Nos. 58, 108, 390, and 391, of the Rawlinson MSS. No. 58 is composed very largely of fragments and letters relating to Dr. Edward Browne's travels; but bound up without any arrangement. I have printed several of the letters, and one or two fragments from it. From No. 108 I have printed about 20 letters: it contains also some extracts, probably by Dr. Edward Browne, from various authors, and some *memoranda* and *commonplaces* by Sir Thomas. From No. 390 has been obtained the "*Catalogue of MSS. &c.*" which has enabled me to determine, with some degree of certainty, what unpublished papers Browne left, and thus to satisfy myself, that the present is a COMPLETE COLLECTION OF HIS WORKS. No. 391 is occupied almost entirely with letters;—of which I have printed about 25. The fragment *Of Greenland*, vol. iv, p. 375, is from this volume; which contains, besides, copies of *Sir K. Digby's Letter to Browne*, and the *Brampton Urns*, both which have been collated with the printed editions.

But the far greater portion of the Browne MSS. comprising those of the father, son, and grandson, with large medical and miscellaneous collections which had fallen into their hands, were disposed of, soon after the death of the latter, to Sir Hans Sloane. On his decease, they ultimately reached the National Library in the British Museum; where they are now contained in about 100 volumes, occupying, with few exceptions, the consecutive numbers from 1825 to 1923, inclusive, besides some other numbers.[1]

In order to exhibit these collections with some degree of clearness, I have printed the Rawlinson catalogue,—drawn up, in all probability, but just before they were sold;—and have attached to each article the number which I have ascertained it to bear at present. Some, however, have escaped my search. Of the 100 consecutive numbers between 1824 and 1924, some are blank, not attached to any volume;[2] some refer to MSS. not belonging to the Browne collection;[3] and some to articles which, though they belong to it, are not included in the Rawlinson catalogue. Among the latter are some volumes of correspondence,[4] two MSS. of the younger Dr. T. Browne,[5] and several commonplace books,[6] whereas

---

[1] Nos. 1745, 3418, and 4039, contain letters; and No. 1797, a catalogue of plants, and a number of Medical Observations in Dr. Edward Browne's handwriting. No. 2, among the *Miscellaneous Papers, &c.* of the catalogue, is No. 5233, of the *Additional MSS.* of the British Museum.

[2] 1849, 1855, 1879.

[3] 1829, 1831, 1832, 1835, 1840, 1850, 1858, 1871.

[4] 1847, 1911, 1912, 1913.

[5] Nos. 1845 and 1846. The former contains *Extracts and Medical Exercises, by Dr. Thomas Browne, Jun.* The latter is the volume spoken of Mr. D'Israeli, in his *Curiosities of Literature,* as " the imperfect MS. collection made by the celebrated Sir Thomas Browne,"—and from which he has given some extracts. Mr. D'Israeli relied (as the consulter of these MSS. ought to be able *safely* to rely) on the description given in Ayscough's catalogue of them, at p. 882, viz. "SIR THOMAS BROWNE. *Extracts from Books, and Miscellaneous Observations:*"—whereas, the volume is in the handwriting of his grandson. In his first edition, Mr. D'Israeli was led to refer his extract to *Plot's Staffordshire,* by the fact of the MS. opening with two pages of transcript from that work: but the passage was from *Hacket's Memorial of Abp. Williams,* p. 213, fol. Lond. 1693. The volume is a jumble (sadly confused in the binding) of extracts from Thomas of Walsingham, Bartolomeus de Cotton, Mat. Paris, and a score others.

[6] For example, 1843; See Rawl. Cat. No. 7, 4to.—1848; which is, in truth, a mere mass of rough papers, bound together; from which I have gleaned nothing but the collation of one or two passages, in the *Tracts,* a *Catalogue,* at p. 368, and a criticism, at p. 380, vol. iv.—1862; see No. 25, 4to.—1865; No. 31, 4to.—1869; 36, 4to.—1874. Several portions of which are enumerated in the catalogue, Nos. 40—44; but a considerable part is, in fact, a commonplace book.—1882 and 1885, also contain similar rough drafts, and hints for passages in his various works. —The fact is that when the collection passed into Sir Hans Sloane's possession, it contained a number of letters and miscellaneous papers, which were so mentioned in his own MS. catalogue, and were not bound up till after he had them.

the catalogue names but one, which I have referred to *MS. Sloan.* 1866.[7] In several instances I find that a volume containing one or more of the articles enumerated in the catalogue, also contains some not in it.[8]

But my great object in making so careful an analysis of the present catalogue has been, to ascertain whether any of the works which Sir Thomas left in manuscript, had escaped me. Of the 112 numbers contained in the catalogue, there are but 16 which I have not either found or accounted for; and of these one only (No. 23, 4to.) is ascribed to Browne. Another article (No. 7, 4to.) for some time eluded my search : yet I was satisfied that the two dialogues there mentioned must have been written, or they would not have been described so fully : but a reference to Sir Hans Sloane's own catalogue at length satisfied me that such was not the fact, and that the article in question was *MS. Sloan.* No. 1843; in which the *titles* only, and not the dialogues, are to be found :—he calls the volume " *Subjects for* Tracts, Sir T. B. &c." The only remaining article (No. 23, 4to.—*Tractatus Varii per T. Browne, M.D.*) appears certainly to have passed into Sir Hans Sloane's possession, for he mentions it and ascribes it to Sir Thomas Browne : but, as certainly, it is no longer to be found; and my consolation is, the probability that it was the " duplicate in 4to." of the Latin Tracts contained in No. 1827, and printed in my fourth volume.—(See No. 5, fol. and No. 23, 4to.) Supposing this conjecture to be true, and supposing that the following catalogue comprises a complete list of the works of Sir Thomas, which remain in MS. excepting those in the Bodleian Library,—then it follows, that I may safely assure my readers, that the present is a COMPLETE COLLECTION of the works of that distinguished writer.

[7] See *Rawl. Cat.* No. 32, 4to.
[8] In No. 1828, for example, the last two, *on the Philosopher's Stone*, and on *the Art of Navigation*, (*Aysc.* p. 510 and 701.) Again at fols. 207 to 296 of *MS. Sloan*, 1839, *Moral Essays*, (*Aysc.* Nos. 9 to 14 :) and in No. 1844, *Astronomical Tables*, (No. 2. *Aysc.*)

[BIBL. BODL. MSS. RAWLINSON. 390. NO. 11.]

A Catalogue of MSS. written by and in the possession of Sir Thomas Browne, M.D. late of Norwich, and of his Son, Dr. Edward Browne, late President of the College of Physicians, London.

FOLIO.

No. 1. A very ancient MS. (Poetry) upon vellum, finely illuminated.

> *MS. Sloan.* 1825 :—thus described in *Ayscough's Catalogue*, p. 819;—1825, 1. *Thos. Occleve, De Regimine Principis. Aug. In Perg.* Ib. p. 832;—1825, 2. *An Old Poem on Death, on vellum.*

No. 2. Relatione del Clariss⁰· Vincentio d'Alessandri, Ambasciadore al Re di Persia, per la Serᵐᵃ· Republica di Venetia.

> *MS. Sloan.* 1826. *Aysc.* p. 364.—Besides this article, (the only one mentioned either in Ayscough's or the present catalogue,) which occupies but 9 folios, the volume contains narratives of embassies to, or particulars respecting, the Papal States, Tuscany, Savoy, Ferrara, the Venetian Republic, Spain, France, Poland, Muscovy and Tartary.

No. 3. Some Anatomical Lectures.

> These Lectures were probably bound up with other papers; perhaps in *MS. Sloan.* 1833. Nos. 1914 and 1915 contain Dr. E. Browne's Lectures, from 1675 to 1678; and 2 vols. entitled *Syllabus Musculorum Corporis humani;* 1687 to 1698. But these volumes are 4to. not folio.

No. 4. Mr. Thos. Browne's (second son of Sir Thomas) Account of his journey from Bordeaux to Paris.—Letters on several occasions.—Sea-coasts described and neatly drawn.

> *MS. Sloan.* 1745. Now first printed :—vol. i, p. 17-22, and 128-149.

No. 5. Miscellanies, by Sir Thos. Browne.—1. Discourse upon the Ancient Oracles. 2. Observations upon the place Troas, so often mentioned by St. Paul, in his Epistles. 3. Some remarks upon the Impropriety, Falsity, or Mistakes in Pictural Draughts. 4. De Re Accipitraria, or a Discourse of Falconry, Hawks, or Hawking. 5. Of Languages. 6. Remarks upon several Texts of Scripture;—with several other Tracts on various subjects.

> *MS. Sloan.* 1827. Upon the fly-leaf of this volume are fastened two slips of parchment, (probably cut from the original cover,) thus labelled, in Sir Thomas's hand writing :—*Of Oracles. De Re Accipitra. &c. (also in 4to.) Amico Ardua Med. (Ys in 4to. also.)* The duplicate of the former portion was very possibly the copy from which Abp. Tenison printed the *Miscellany Tracts.* That of the latter portion, (the Latin Tracts,) I suppose may have been No. 23, 4to. of the present catalogue, which I cannot discover in Br. Mus. The present volume (like most of the other Browne MSS. in the Br. Mus.) has been so deranged in the binding, and Ayscough's catalogue

of it is so inaccurate, that I shall give a fresh sketch of its contents, stating what use has been made of them.

FOL. 1——9. On Oracles—*Collated with Tract* xi.

  10—13. On Troas—*Collated with Tr.* x.

  14—16. On Impropriety or Falsity, &c.—*Now first printed*, vol. iii, p. 157-160.

  17, 18. On the Dead Sea—*Collated with Tract* x.

  19. Of what kind those little fishes—*Collated with Tr.* iii.

  20—22. On Haman hanged—*Collated with Ps. Ep.* v, 21.

  23—26. On Hawks and Hawking—*Collated with Tr.* v.

  27—40 and 50. On Languages, but intermixed in the binding—*Collated with Tr.* viii, *and various readings given*, vol. iv, p. 195-212.

  40—43. On Tumuli—*Collated with Tr.* ix.

  44—48. De Peste—*Now first Printed*, iv, 277-380.

  49—55 and 57. Brief Reply to Queries—*Ditto* iv, 281-286.

  55—57. Ditto, *On the Hoopi bird.—Aysc.—A part of Tr.* iv.

  58, 59. Musick of the Ancients, &c.—*Collated with Tr.* vi, and vii.

  59, 60. Naval Fights—*Now first printed*, iv, 287-289.

  60—86. To the end of the volume extend the Latin Tracts—*And are now first printed*, vol. iv, 290-312.

No. 6. A Genealogical Account of the Families in Suffolk, with their arms variously drawn and illuminated.

Does not seem to have passed into the Sloanian Collection; at least I have not been able to trace it.

No. 7. Modo breve a prender la lengua Biscayna. Compuesto por ell^{do.} Rafael Nicoleta, presby^{to.} de la muy leal y noble Villa de Bilboa, 1653.

Neither can I find this in Mus. Br. See it mentioned, vol. iv, 199.

No. 8. Receipts for making Syrupi et Pilulæ Alterantes et purgantes.

MS. Sloan. 1828, (No. 4, *Aysc.)* is headed as above, with "*Gualteri Charlton*," in addition. Ayscough calls it, *Pharmacopœia Londinensis, correct. à Gualt. Charlton.*

No. 9. An Account of the Bishops and Deans of Norwich.

Not found in Mus. Br. This was probably sold, together with "Repertorium," (No. 9, 4to.) to Curll, for the *Posthumous Works.* I have not reprinted it, as it was not written by Sir Thomas. It is mentioned in the 4th Vol. of *Ballard's MS. Letters* in *the Bodleian Library*, p. 58; as having been printed in the *Posthumous Works*, by permission of the Dean of Norwich, then Dr. Prideaux.

No. 10. Original Letters written by King Charles I.

MS. Sloan. 1828, (No. 3, *Aysc.)* This is called by Ayscough, *K. James I, Letter to his Parliament, &c. &c.* It is entered in Sr. Hans Sloane's MS. Cat., *Letters by King James and King Charles the First to the Parliament.*

No. 11. A Genealogical Account of the Family of Norfolk.
MS. Sloan. 1928?

No. 12. Zoroastres, a Tragedy, written by the late **Earl of** Orrery, also a Comedy.

MS. Sloan. 1828, (Nos. 1 and 2, *Aysc.)*

No. 13. Missale Romanum, upon vellum.

Numbered 1829, in the MS. Sloanian Catalogue; but not now bearing that No., which is attached to an 8vo. vol. of *Remarks on French Poetry, &c.*

No. 14. Sir Thos. Browne's Observations upon uncommon Birds, Fish, and other animals discovered in Norfolk.

MS. Sloan. 1830. Besides the papers on Birds, Fishes, and the Ostrich, (printed in our 4th vol. pp. 313-339,) this vol. contains 3 letters to, and 2 from, Dr. Merrett, (printed vol. i, pp. 395-403;) and on the last leaf a memorandum on the comparative height of Antwerp and Utrecht Steeples, and St. Peter's at Rome.

No. 15. Mr. Thomas Browne's Journal with Sir Jeremy Smith, anno 1661, to Alicant, Tangier, &c. with curious draughts.

MS. Sloan. 1910, fol. 1-45—The date however is 1665.—Printed, vol. i, p. 119-128. The vol. also contains Miscel. No. 4, No. 7, and 4to. No. 26, of the present catalogue, *qu. vide.*

No. 16. An account of Ancient Medals.

The Sloanian MS. Cat. adds *in two parts,* and numbers it 1832: which number however is now attached to a small oblong 4to. vol. (see *Aysc.* p. 384.) I am inclined to think the present article may be *MS. Sloan.* 1828, No. 5, *Aysc. ;)* which is a catalogue of 120 Roman Coins, in two parts.

No. 17. Anatomical Dissections of several creatures; with exact draughts, and some Physical Tracts.

I am persuaded that this article has been cut up, and bound, here a bit and there a bit, *(comme à l'ordinaire,)* in *MS. Sloan.* 1833, amidst other and various subjects;—viz. lists of places visited by Dr. E. B., books which he had read, Latin Orations, Collections for his lectures, recipes and prescriptions, medical cases, letters, &c. I have printed a very small portion of the vol. viz. *Letters ;* four to his son Edward, one to Dr. Merrett, and one to Mr. Talbot, in vol. i, pp. 222, 231, 291, 309, 393, and 415. *Boulimia Centenaria; Upon the dark thick mist, &c.;* and *Oratio, &c.* vol. iv, pp. 340-352.

No. 18. Relatione della Republica di Venetia fatta dal Marchese di Bedmare, Ambasc. del Re Catt^lca.·presso della Republica.

MS. Sloan. 1834.

No. 19. An account of Europe.

See the next article.

No. 20. An account of Africa.

MSS. Sloan. 1836, 1837. The vols. comprise accounts of Europe, Africa, and Asia, and their principal states and countries, in 1675.

QUARTO.

No. 1. Excerpta e Procli Elementis, &c.

MS. Sloan. 1838. A large 4to. called by Ayscough a folio.—*Proclus, Elementa Theologica.* Very probably by Dr. Lushington: see vol. i, p. 467, *Letter from Browne to Aubrey.*

No. 2. Miscellany Tracts, by Sir Thos. Browne.

MS. Sloan. 1839, fol. 1-48—Tracts 11, 10, 8—*Collated with the former edition.* For the remaining contents of No. 1839, see articles, 4to. 14, 4, 15, 16, 3, and 37. The 90 pages intervening between the last two numbers are occupied by a series of Moral Essays, which seem not enumerated in the present catalogue.

No. 3. Physical Receipts.

MS. Sloan. 1839, fol. 176-206.

No. 4. Observations on Sir Thomas Browne's Vulgar Errors.

MS. Sloan. 1839, fol. 104-145. This was written by Sir Hamon L'Estrange, and sent by him to Sir Thos. Br. with a letter dated Jan. 16, 1653 ; which I have printed (vol. i, p. 369, from *MS. Rawl.* 391.) See notice of the MS. vol. ii, p. 173.

No. 5. Critical notes upon several texts of Scripture, by Sir Thomas Browne.

MS. Sloan. 1841, fol. 191-262 ; *Collated with Tract* i.

No. 6. Chemical and Alchemical Receipts.

MS. Sloan. 1842. See Sir Thomas's detail of contents of the volume among *Dee's MSS.*—vol. ii, p. 464.

No. 7. Tracts by Sir Thomas Browne : viz. 1. A Dialogue between an Inhabitant of the Earth and of the Moon. 2. A Dialogue between two twins in the womb, concerning the world they were to come into, and other pieces.

Who would have believed that a volume so distinctly described as containing Tracts on these two most curious subjects, would be found, on examination, to contain nothing more than the *titles* of them ? Yet such is the fact. Surely the catalogue must have been drawn up either with intention to mislead, or by some one utterly incompetent to the task. Sir Hans Sloane has described the volume as containing " *Subjects for Tracts, &c. &c.*" and it is numbered 1843 :—correctly.

MS. Sloan. 1843 is a commonplace book, a very thin volume, containing Anagrams, Epigrams, Mottoes, and detached sentences, among which occur the two in question, as if memoranda for tracts to be written ; see vol. iv, 379. The latter of the two subjects is mentioned in *Hydriotaphia* as affording an opportunity " handsomely to illustrate our ignorance of the next world, &c."—see vol. iii, 486.

No. 8. Differentia Verborum [?] usuve similium, una cum diversis ejusdem vocabuli significationibus, per E. Browne, M.D.

MS. Sloan. 1844, (1, *Aysc.*)

No. 9. Repertorium, or some account of the Tombs and Monuments in the Cathedral Church of Norwich, 1680.

Not in Mus. Br. Probably the copy used in printing the *Posthumous Works.*

No. 10. A Diary of the Conferences and Proceedings in the Treaty at London, 1604, between King James I, King Philip III, of Spain, and Albertus Archduke of Austria.

MS. Sloan. 1851.

No. 11. Physical and Chirurgical Receipts.

MS. Sloan. 1852.

No. 12. A Poetical Paraphrase on the VII Penitential Psalms, finely written upon vellum.

MS. Sloan. 1853.

No. 13. Speculum Philosophiæ, Johannis Dastini.

MS. Sloan. 1854.   Mentioned by Browne, among Dee's MSS. vol. i, p. 465.

No. 14. Travels in Bohemia, Austria, &c. by Sir Tho. Browne.

MS. Sloan. 1839, fol. 50-103, probably.—From the name attached to this article, it is clear that the catalogue was drawn up by some one ignorant of the history of the family, or he would not have ascribed these Travels to the father instead of the son.

No. 15. Tractatus de Peste, &c.

MS. Sloan. 1839, fol. 146-161.   This is not a duplicate of the paper on the plague, printed vol. iv, p. 277.   Ayscough has called the article *Quæstiones Medicæ.*

No. 16. Fraus Pia, Comoedia. Lat. Elegant.

MS. Sloan. 1839, fol. 162-175.

No. 17. Miscellaneous Tracts, written by the Lord Bacon, Sir Walter Raleigh, Oliver St. John's, &c.   Also Speeches in the House of Lords, in the Reign of Charles I, with other papers.

MS. Sloan. 1856, (Nos. 1-11, *Aysc.*)

No. 18. Theriaca Divina Benedicti; scripsit Anno 1599.

MS. Sloan. 1857.   Among Dee's MSS. see vol. i, p. 464.

No. 19. A Course of Chemistry.

Not found in the museum.   The Sloanian catalogue numbers it 1858; but *MS. Sloan.* 1858 is a very different thing.

No. 20. An Historical and Chorographical Description of Suffolk, written in the year 1602.

Not found.

No. 21. Moral Discourses, English, upon vellum, very ancient.

MS. Sloan. 1859.

No. 22. A Game at Chesse, a Comedy, written by Tho. Middleton, an. 1620.

Not found.

No. 23. Tractatus Varii, per T. Browne, M.D.

In the Sloanian catalogue this is said to be *per Sir Thos. Browne, M.D.* and is numbered 1860 ; which however is not to be found in Mus. Brit. See the remarks under the next article.

No. 24. An Account of a Voyage to East India. Also several Letters from Dr. Edward Browne to Sir Thomas, relating to Antiquities, &c. in foreign parts, never printed.

In *Cat. Sloan.* numbered 1861. In Mus. Br. I found a vol. numbered 1860-1861, containing the articles in the present number, but not the *Tractatus Varii*, which therefore is missing. Ayscough however catalogues 1860 as containing the *Voyage of M. Escaliot* (which is printed, vol. iv, p. 43) and the letters, some few of which also are printed; i, pp. 154, 158, 169, 174, 186 : but of 1861, he says *deest* : but erroneously ; for it is 1860 which *deest.*

No. 25. Concerning some Urns found in Brampton Field in Norfolk, 1667.

In my preface to *Garden of Cyrus, Hydriotaphia, and Brampton Urns*, I have conjectured the copy of the latter, contained in 1862, fol. 26-37, to have been that from which Curll printed. Perhaps however it is more probable that it was a duplicate, as well as those in 1869, p. 60—and *MS. Rawl.* 391.—No. 1862 now contains mere sketches of passages for several of his works—viz. *Hydriotaphia* and *Christian Morals*, fol. 1-8, and 38-94 ; *Letter to a Friend*, 8-25 ; *Brampton Urns*, 26-37. It forms one volume with 1866, and is in fact, a Commonplace Book.

No. 26. The Diary of George Weldon and Abraham Navarro's Journey to the Court of the Great Mogul, anno 1688, with the account of an Expedition to Carthagena.

MS. Sloan. 1910, fol. 89—fin.

No. 27. An Historical and Chorographical Description of Norfolk.

Probably with No. 20.

No. 28. Chymical Experiments.

MS. Sloan. 1863?

No. 29 and 30. Traité de l'Euchariste.

MS. Sloan. 1864.

No. 31. Treatise of Geography and other Tracts.

MS. Sloan. 1865 ? It is possible that this may be the volume ; but I strongly doubt it, and if it be, it is very ill described. It contains in Dr. Ed. B's hand writing, Prescriptions, Anatomical Observations, many pages of Extracts from various authors, Hobbes's *De Mirabilibus Pecei*, a paper of 36 pages, *Institutiones Logicæ*, and Flamstead's Account of the Comet of 1680. Besides these, is an account of Europe, in the early part of the volume, and this is the only geographical paper it contains.

No. 32. Commonplace Book, by Sir Thomas Browne.

Sir Hans Sloane's catalogue determines this to be the *MS. Sloan.* No. 1866 : yet I have preferred to select my specimens of his Commonplace Books from 1869, 1874, and 1875—only comparing 1866 with the others in similar passages. The only extract I have printed from it, is the *Account of a Thunderstorm,*"—at p. 353, vol. iv, and some latin passages at p. 453.

No. 33. Holy Bible Epitomized, in latin verse, upon vellum.

MS. Sloan. 1870.

No. 34. Verses, Epigrams, &c. English and Latin.

MS. Sloan. 1867.

No. 35. Letters from Dr. Edward Browne in his Travels.

MS. Sloan. 1868.   Many printed in the early part of vol. i, from page 60 to 114.

No. 36. Essays upon several subjects, by Sir Thos. Browne.

MS. Sloan. 1869? This number has supplied a considerable portion of the Commonplace Books which I have printed; see iv, p. 381. It contains a copy of Brampton Urns, fol. 60.

No. 37. Oratio Celeberrima Dom T. Browne, coram Prs. Coll. Med.

MS. Sloan. 1839, fol. 299-316 and 1833, fol. 146-150, See vol. iv, 343.

No. 38. Probationes ex Grotio. Græce.

MS. Sloan. 1872.

No. 39. Thomas Norton's Ordinal, being a Treatise of Alchymie in Verse; very ancient; neatly written.

MS. Sloan. 1873.   Among Dee's MSS. vol. i, 464.

No. 40. A Book of the Use of the Crosse Staffe, by Thos Golding; written in 1660.

MS. Sloan. 1874, fol. 1-17.

No. 41. Ordinances made by the Lord Keeper Coventry, with the advice and assistance of Sir Julius Cæsar, master of the Rolles, for the Redress of Sundry Errors, Defaults and Abuses in the High Court of Chancery.

MS. Sloan. 1874, fol. 18-20.

No. 42. Brevis Animalium Adumbratio ad mentem et methodum Peripatheticam.

MS. Sloan. 1874, fol. 21-37.

No. 43. Fragmenta Miscellanea, by Sir T. Browne.

MS. Sloan. 1874, fol. 38-91.   For *Notæ in Aristotelem,*—a portion of these "Fragmenta," See vol iv, 360.

No. 44. Museum Clausum; or Bibliotheca Abscondita; containing some remarkablè things, Books, Antiquities, Pictures, Rarities of several kinds, scarce or never seen by any man living. By Sir Thos. Browne.

MS. Sloan. 1874, fol. 92-110—*Collated with Tract* xiii, vol. iv, p. 239.

No. 46.[2] Arca Arcanorum, abstrusæ Hermeticæ Scientiæ Ingres-

----

[2] No 45 is omitted in MS.

sum, Progressum, Coronidem, verbis apertissimis explicans. Ex selectissimis, et celeberrimis Authoribus collecta, et antehac a nemine hac methodo distributa. Opera et Studio Arthuri Dee, Magni Imperatoris totius Russiæ, per annos bis septem, Archiatri.

MS. Sloan. 1876.

No. 47. Physical receipts by Dr. Ponder.

MS. Sloan. 1877.

No. 48. *(Left Blank in MS.)*

Note. No 1878 is a volume of Medical instructions apparently from Dr. E. B. to his Son. But we have no other ground for placing it here than the order of its number.

No. 49. Occasional Reflections on Several Subjects by Sir. Thos. Browne.

MS. Sloan. 1874, fol. 111-167. *On Dreams*, fol. 111-120, vol iv, 355—*Collated with* 1869, *Commonplace Book*, iv, 381, &c.

No. 50. An Account of the Emperor's Curiosities, by Sir. T. Browne.

MS. Sloan. 1874, fol. 168-177. By Dr. E. B. and printed in his Travels.

No. 51. A Volume of Italian Poetry, *neatly written.*

MS. Sloan. 1880.

No. 52. The Golden Rotation, Conversion, Circulation, Purification, and Concatenation of the Elements.

MS. Sloan. 1881.

No. 53. A Treatise of Generation. By Sir Thomas Browne.

MS. Sloan. 1882, fol. 125-151. The title ought to have been *A treatise on the Generation of Plants*:—or, as Sir Thomas would have called it, *On the doctrine of Insitions.* In the middle of this paper occurs a memorandum of some fossil bones dug up at Winterton, printed, vol. iv, p. 454: and at fol. 145-6, the first paragraph of the *Account of Fishes*, printed at p. 325, vol. iv.

No. 54. Antiquities in the City of Norwich, by Sir Thos. Browne.

MS. Sloan. 1885, fol. 1-4? This is but a slight sketch for the *Repertorium :* and the Volume consists of similar *brouillons* for his other works, *Christian Morals* especially.

No. 55. Physical Receipts by Dr. Ponder.

MS. Sloan. 1883?

Octavo.

No. 1. Observations upon several parts of France, &c.

MS. Sloan. 1886, fol. 1-11 and 32-52. The rest of the Volume consists of French exercises, and Medical receipts, extracts, and memoranda.

No. 2. Physical receipts by Dr. Tearne.

MS. Sloan. 1887.

No. 3. Speculum Salutiferum, Boni et Mali, upon Vellum.

MS. Sloan. 1888.

No. 4. Old English Epigrams.

MS. Sloan. 1889.

No. 5. A Treatise of Anatomy, by Dr. Tearne.

MS. Sloan. 1890.

No. 6. Algebra and Analytical Arithmetick, in two Books, by Thos. Golding, 1660.

MS. Sloan. 1891.

No. 7. The Alcoran, in Arabic, on Persian Paper, pointed and ruled with gold.

Not found in Br. Museum.

No. 8. Physical Receipts, by Dr. Edward Browne.

MS. Sloan. 1892.

No. 9. The Investigation of Causes, neatly written.

Written on large 8vo. paper, bound in a 4to. vol. No. 1893. One of Dee's Mss.—see vol. i, 464.

No. 10. Chirurgical Receipts, by I. S. Surgeon.

MS. Sloan. 1894.

No. 11. Physical Receipts, by Sir Theodore Mayerne, &c.

1895. This Vol. is all in Dr. E. B's. hand-writing. Besides Sir T. Mayerne's, it contains a vast number of the receipts of other medical men: some for the Plague, with the initials T. B. attached; many used at St. Thomas's and Bartholomew's Hospitals: among a number of Dr. E. B's patients, are mentioned some persons of rank.

No. 12. Poems written by Robert Smith, &c. Sufferers in Q. Mary's Day.

MS. Sloan. 1896.

No. 13. Methodus curand. Morbis, per C. Tearne, M.D.

MS. Sloan. 1897.

No. 14. Tractatus varii: viz. 1. Series Regum West-Saxonum. 2. Diarium Itineris Gall. 3. Inscriptiones Antiquæ, &c.

MS. Sloan. 1898.

No. 15. Dr. Thos. Browne's journal of his Travels to several parts of England, in Company with Dr. Robert Plot. Anno 1693.

MS. Sloan. 1899. The Vol. is in the younger Dr. T. Browne's hand-writing, and contains at the close some inscriptions from gravestones, in pencil. The our will be found vol. iv, p. 457.

No. 16. Remarks on several parts of England, anno 1662.

MS. Sloan. 1900:—printed vol. i, p. 22-42. It contains also bills of expences, a list of plays, prescriptions, &c.

No. 17. Statuta Collegii Medicorum Londinensium.

MS. Sloan. 1901.

No. 18. Hermeticæ Philosophiæ Medulla, upon vellum.

MS. Sloan. 1902. Called by Ayscough, *Arthur Dee's collections, &c. in Astrology, with figures of some nativities.* Yet the title given in the present cat. occurs in the volume. Among the Nativities I find *Johannis Dee, natus* 1606, with some others of his family—see vol. i, 464.

No. 19. Oratio Dom. C. Tearne, coram Præs. Coll. Med. in laudem G. Hervei, M.D.

MS. Sloan. 1903.

No. 20. Statuta Nova Collegii Medicorum, Lond. 1687.

MS. Sloan. 1904.

No. 21. Observations on several parts of Turkey, by Dr. E. Browne.

MS. Sloan. 1905.

No. 22. Dr. Edw. Browne's Journal of his Travels through France, &c.

MS. Sloan. 1906: printed vol. i, p. 65.

No. 23. Icon Basilike. Vers. Lat. neatly written.

MS. Sloan. 1907.

No. 24. Dr. Ponder's Journal of his Travels though France.

MS. Sloan. 1908, is called by Ayscough, *Dr. E. T's. Journal of his Travels through France in* 1668 : I have little doubt of its identity with this article. Though (on that supposition) the present catalogue is wrong both in the traveller's name and the scene of his travels. Ayscough has corrected the former but retained the latter error. The whole volume is written by Dr. E. B. and is a regular Journal of his travels in Holland, Germany and Austria from Aug. 26, 1668, to July 21, 1669. See vol. i, 464. pp. 154-191. It contains the Greek letter to Dr. Pearson and others at Cambridge; see p. 171.

No. 25. Collection of Romish Missals, Lat. upon Vellum.

MS. Sloan. 1909.

No. 26. .... Scriptus fuit, 1205, a quodum Monacho Monasterii Rochiensis in Comitat. Eboracensi nomine Britom, critico maximo.

I cannot find this in Mus. Brit. In Sir H. L's MS. Cat. it is called *Glossarium.*

Miscellaneous Papers, &c.

No. 1. Nouvelles Figures de Proportion et d'Anatomie du Corps Humain.

Not found in Br. Museum.

No. 2. A collection of 90 very curious drawings (some in colours) of public buildings, habits, fishes, mines, rocks, tombs, and other antiquities, observed by Sir Thos. and Dr. Edwd. Browne, in their travels.

MS. Addit. 5233; large folio.

No. 3. A large draught, (in colours) of the Island of Jamaica, presented by Captain Hacke to King Charles II, done on a skin of parchment.

No. 4. An account of Persia, 16 sheets.   English.

MS. Sloan. 1910, fol. 46-76.

No. 5. Draught of a strange bird (in colours,) on a large sheet of royal paper.

Not found in Br. Museum.

No. 6. Historical and Philosophical collections, by Dr. Tearne.

MS. Sloan. 1916, 21.   No 1884 is also one of the Tearne *MSS.* but is in 4to.

No. 7. Notes taken out of the General History of the Turks before the rising of the Othoman Family, with all the Notable expeditions of the Christian Princes against them, by Richard Knolles, once Fellow of Lincoln College in Oxford, 1603.

MS. Sloan. 1910, 77-89.

No. 8. A Journey from Genoa to Bordeaux.

Not found in Br. Museum.

No. 9. A catalogue of medals.

Possibly this may be *MS. Sloan.* 1923.

No. 10. Papers of Dr. Edwd. Browne, designed as a Supplement to his Travels.

MS. Sloan. 1922.

No. 11. Collection of Plants.

General Index.

GENERAL INDEX.

A.

A. B. Strictures on Digby's Observations on *R. M.* ii, xxx.

Abgarus, king of Edessa, his picture of our Saviour, iii, 111.

Abraham, picture of, sacrificing Isaac, *P. E.* v, ch. 8, iii, 113, 114. How incorrect; Isaac not then a little boy, 113. A type of Christ bearing his cross, *ib.* More absurd pictures of this incident, *ib.* n. His grave at Beersheba, 392.

Absalom, whether hanged by his hair? iii, 328.

Academia naturæ curiosorum, i, 309.

Aconitum hyemale, in flower in Jan. i, 48.

Acta eruditorum, i, lxv, n. Remarks on *R. M.* and on the author, ii, xv, n.

Actæon, fable of explained, ii, 221.

Adam, whether an hermaphrodite, ii, 30. Thought by some to have been thirty years old at his creation, 57. Augustine hereon, *ib.* n. Whether a negro? iii, 272. His apple, what, 296.

Adam and Eve drawn with navels, *P. E.* v, ch. 5, iii, 99-102. By whom so drawn, 99 and 99, n. incorrectly—and why, 99-102. This opinion examined and controverted, 99, n. Adopted by Dr. J. Bulwer, 100, n. Still more absurd pictures of, 99, n.

Adam, Dr. Walter, on the osteological symmetry of the camel, &c. iii, 424, n.

Adams, description of England, with maps, i, 338.

Adipo-cire, iii, 479.

Adolphus Cyprus, i, lxxiii.

Ælian Claudius, his *Hist. Animalium* and *Varia Historia* contain some false, some impossible things, ii, 238.

Æneas Sylvius, his epp. quoted, i, 188.

Æschylus, said to have been brained by a tortoise dropped by an eagle on his pate in mistake for a rock, iii, 365. An argument drawn from this against the motion of the earth, *ib.*

Æsop, his *Fables*, done into Eng. by L'Estrange, i, 370, n.

Ætites, or eaglestone, fabled to promote delivery, ii, 356. What it is, 355, n.

Ætius, mention of the basilisk, ii, 414.

Agat, his collection, i, 103.

Agen, E. B. at, i, 105.

Agricola, Geo. *De Mineral. et Metall.* i, 183, 185, 188.

Agriculture, Jewish, iv, 152. Ancient, 155.

Agues, a powder against, i, 47. Quartan, many cases, 228. Seldom twice, 227. At what seasons, 266. A charm against, iii, 182.

Ahasuerus, iii, 160.

Ahaz, sundial of, iii, 142, 297, n.

Aikin, John, M. D. his life of B.; particulars respecting, i, *Pref.* 11, n. Reprobates the asperity of German criticism on Br. lxviii. Remarks on B. lxxxiii.

Air, Boyle's Experiments on, i, 169. Curious particulars respecting its nature, ii, 485-489. Safety lamps, 489, n. Change of, sometimes too late to try, iv, 38.

Aix, see Aken.

Aken, [or Aix-la-chapelle,] i, lxxix, 243. E. B's. account of, 102.

Albertus, Magnus, his works on natural science to be received with caution, ii, 241. His error concerning crystal, 267. Says that garlick hinders the attraction of loadstone, 306. Says the diamond is broke by goat's blood, 334.

Alboin, tragical history of alluded to, iii, 370. More correctly stated, *ib.* n.

Alboran, a desolate island, T. B's. account of, i, 123.

D'Albret, family of, kings of Navarre, lords of Pons, i, 18.

Alchymy, B's. opinions respecting, i, xcvi.

Alciat, J. *Emblemata*, ii, xxv.

Alcoran, see Koran.

Published by Payne, *ib.* Editor's preface, 55. Corrected at iv, xi. Dedicated to the Earl of Buchan, 57. Archdeacon Jeffery's preface, 58. Exhortations to practice virtue on right grounds; and from virtuous motives, 59. To overcome anger, 60. To practise chastity, honesty, charity, 61-62. Acquire habits of virtue, 63. To carry honesty beyond mere law, and judge thereof by gospel rules, 64. To avoid envy, and cultivate humility, 65. To forgive injuries, 66. To controul propensities towards evil, 67. To be deaf to tale bearers, 68. To be grateful for the mercies of God, 69. Not to extenuate our faults, nor praise our own deeds, 70. To govern ourselves, 71. To observe and acknowledge Providence, not to neglect or refuse the blessings placed within reach, 72. But to be content with our station; to extenuate the errors of others, 73. Not to be impatient of apparent misfortunes, 74. Not to persevere rashly in error, 75. Nor to waste our moments in indolence, 76. Not to sound our own praises, 77. Rather to value honest and virtuous than exalted parentage, 78. The true English gentleman has no peer, 79.

Part II. Exhortations to avoid luxury, 79. Detraction, 80. Dogmatism, 81. To value solidity of judgment rather than imagination, 82. To avoid censoriousness, 83-85. Self-estimation, 85. To observe physiognomical indications, 86. To observe the providences befalling others, 89. Good dispositions of great value in this life, 90. Remarks on various contrivances to soften death, 90-92.

Part III. Good examples hard to select, 92. It were good to imitate God, 93. In doubtful cases, to enquire which is the more virtuous alternative, 94. To wait for Providence, 95. Not to indulge propensities to evil, 96. To act upon principle, not fate or omens, 97. To act consistently with our age, *ib.* To be choice in our companions, 98. To be moderate in our hopes, 100. To study to be meek and patient, 101. Not to speculate as to futurity, 102. Not to degrade the dignity of our nature, 103. Nor be blind to our true character, 104. In prosperity to remember the uncertainty of all things here, 105. To abhor ingratitude, 106. To be sometimes silent, and ever to keep our vows, 106. To endeavour

singleheartedness; to aim at Christian, not Heathen ethics, 107. Remarks on long life: whose close may be its brightest portion, 109. Exhortations to be happy in virtue, 109. And content with our sphere, 110. General reflexions on life,—God's merciful providence,—the number who will be saved, 111-113. And concluding exhortations not to complain of our life as too short; not to reckon upon length of days, but spend them in a near apprehension of eternity, 114.

Chrysostom, on John Baptist's food, iii, 320. Asserts the death and burial of St. John, 322.

Church of England, B. a sworn subject to her faith, i, 6.

Churchman, Sir John, of Thetford, his family and character, i, 273.

Churchman's, epistle, *(Rel. Clerici,)* ii, xx. Second character of, xxi. Answer to, *ib.*

Clagenfurt, E. B. at, i, 186.

Clark, Richard, Chamberlain of London, presented to Trin. Coll. Camb. in 1824 a drawing, formerly B's. i, lxxv, n.

Classical passages for mottoes, iv, 454-456.

Claudian, error concerning crystal, ii, 267.

Clavell, set out a catalogue of books, i, 308.

Clavicles, monkeys have, i, 46.

Clay, used for coffins as well as urns, iii, 470.

Clayton, Dr. C. L. Principal of Broadgate Hall, i, 470.

Clayton, Sir Robt. Lord Mayor, &c. i, 260 and n.

Cleopatra, picture of her death, *P. E.* v, ch. 12, iii, 124-126. As to the manner of her death; whether by asps, 125. As to the number of asps, 126. Why the breast was the place chosen for the wound, 126. Long and very curious account of an ancient encaustic picture of this event, by R. R. Reinagle, Esq. 124, 125, n.

Clepsydræ, iii, 141.

Clergymen, of old, left little behind them, i, 203.

Cleves, Duke of, i, lvii, n.

Climacterical year, *P. E.* iv, ch. 12, iii, 47-68. Introductory reflexions respecting numbers, 47. Bp. Hall's reflexions, *ib.* n. Enumeration of special numbers, 48, 49. Many examples respecting the numbers seven and nine, 49-56. Number of mouths of the Nile, 50, n. Decretory days,

brough thence, 240, n. No spiders in the roof of King's Coll. Chap. Cambridge, because it is built of Irish timber, *ib.* B. had seen spiders in Ireland, and in Irish timber, 344.

Iron and steel have polarity though not excited by the loadstone, ii, 287. How far this assertion is true, *ib.* n. Heated in the fire contracts a verticity in cooling, ii, 288-291. Prof. Barlow's remarks on this point, *ib.* n. Contracts polarity from position, 291. Its alleged conversion into copper, 302. Explanatory remarks, *ib.* n.

Isaacs, Petrus, an engraver, i, 47.

Isidore, Bp. of Seville, *De originibus*, a compilation relying too much on former writers, ii, 241.

Isiodorus Pelusiota, error concerning crystal, ii, 267. Fable concerning a diamond, 334. Fable concerning coral, 350. Supposes the pigeon to have no gall, 399. Countenances the fables told of the viper, 458. Opinion respecting the food of John Baptist, iii, 320.

Israel, escutcheons of the tribes of, *P. E.* v, ch. 10, iii, 117-122. Whether rightly derived from Jacob's blessing, 117. Rabbinical authorities, 118. Ezekiel's cherubim, 119. Emblems of the four evangelists; reasons for them, by dean Wren and Victorinus, 119, n. Uncertainty as well as antiquity of heraldry, 120. Its origin traced to the bible, by Bp. Hall, and by Morgan and Favine, 120, 121, n. Cabalistical fancies, 121. Various opinions on this, *ib.* n. Protest against Sir Wm. Drummond's remarks on Gen. xlix, 122, n.

Israelites, not guilty of dishonesty against the Egyptians, ii, 197, n.

D'Israeli's Curiosities of Literature, ii, 39, n. Whitefoot's term *stochastic* quoted in it, i, xlvii, n.

Istria, remarkable for cripples, iv, 44.

Italy, E. B. travels there, i, lxxvii. Why compared to an oak, or to ivy, iv, 409.

Italian, who poniarded his enemy on his renouncing christianity to secure his life, iii, 371.

Ivy, that a cup made of it will separate wine from water found incorrect, ii, 381. Farraday's experiment, 381. Will only grow where it has support, 433. Incorrect, *ib.* n. Where it will grow, iii, 431. Different kinds of, *ib. Remarks on*, 448, 449.

J.

Jael and Sisera, picture of, questionable, iii, 159.

Jamaica, Chas. II, talked of giving up to Spain, upon his marriage, i, 10.

James I, iv, 30.

James II, when D. of York, accompanies Charles II into Norfolk, i, xci. Afterwards at Norwich on his return from Scotland, *ib.* n.

James, Capt. his travels mentioned, i, 132.

Jann Thomas, Bp. iv, 17.

Jansenius, supposes the pigeon to have no gall, ii, 399.

Janus and Noah the same person, iii, 231.

Jaundise, a magical cure for, i, 48. A country remedy for, 53.

Jay John, member for Norwich, i, 8. High Sheriff, 246.

Jeffery, Archd. editor of *Christian Morals*, in 1716, i, xvii, n.

Jegon, Jno. Bp. iv, 18.

Jenkins, Sir Leolyn, E. B. accompanies him to Cologne, i, xcvii. Eng. minister at Nimeguen, i, 213. Returned, 258, n.

Jephthah, the picture of, sacrificing his daughter, *P. E.* v, ch. 14, iii, 131, 134. Questioned, as to the accurate interpretation of the scriptural account, on various grounds, 131-134. Dr. Adam Clarke's proposed interpretation of the passage, 131, n. Fable of Iphigenia arose from this incident, 133. Doubtful meaning of the text, 134.

Jeremiah, of Constantinople, a Greek priest, well treated at Cambridge, &c. i, 170. Writes by E. B. from Vienna, i, 171.

Jericho, see Rose.

Jersey, passage to England from, most usual by Guernsey, i, 322.

Jesse, Mr. remarks on miseltoe, ii, 368, n.

Jesuits, round church at Rochelle, given to, i, 19. Town of la Flèche given to, 21. Expelled from Venice, ii, 7. Readmitted in 1657, and why, xxi. Their asserted miracles, 40. Various writers thereon, *ib.* n.

Jesus Christ, no salvation but to those who believe in, ii, 77. Hence the author's queries as to those who lived before or never heard of him, 77. Extract from J. J. Gurney, hereon, 78, n. List of heresies respecting, 257. Picture of, with long hair, *P. E.* v, ch. 7, iii, 111-112. According to Lentulus's description in a letter to the Senate, 111. This letter a forgery;

Lilly, William, B's. letter to, i, 462. His *Christian Astrology*, 463, n.

Lime, quick, increases the force of gunpowder, ii, 348, n.

Lincoln, city and cathedral, T. B. visits, i, 24.

Lindley, Professor, on the forbidden fruit, iii, 296, n. On quinary arrangement in plants, 441, n. On the growth of miseltoe, ii, 367, n.

Lingard, Dr. *Hist. of England*, quoted, ii, 6, n.

Linnæus, his sexual system, ii, 361, n.

Linschotten, his account of porcelain, ii, 353.

Lion afraid of a cock ? ii, 523. Prince of Bavaria's experiment, *ib.* Ross's solution, *ib.* n. Bp. Andrews tried the experiment, *ib.* n.

Lion's heads, why the common ornament of aqueducts, &c. iii, 168.

Lisbon, T. B. at, i, 121. His account of, 146.

Lister, Martin, M. D. of York, his table of spiders, i, 284. Account of a monster, 344.

Liturgy, see Prayer Common.

Lithotomy, case of, under E. B. i, 278. To his credit, 279.

Livius, his *Hist. Rom.* quoted, i, 383, 415.

Loadstone, rock on the coast of Finland, i, 130. Many opinions concerning it which are true, *P. E.* ii, ch. 2, ii, 284-303. Sagacity displayed in this chap. 284, n. Will not attract *crocus martis*, 301. This assertion explained, *ib.* n. Takes up the most of that steel which is the poorest, 302. How far true, *ib.* n. Rejection of sundry false opinions concerning it, *P. E.* ii, ch. 3, 303-325. Its alleged attraction and repulsion of iron is in fact mutual, 303-305. A species of, said to attract flesh, 305. Whether hindered by garlick, as delivered by many grave writers, 306. And believed by Ross, *ib.* n. Its attraction said to be prevented by the diamond, 306. Falsely, *ib.* n. Falsely said by Paracelsus to lose its attraction for ever if put into quicksilver, 307. Impaired by age, &c. *ib.* Said by Pliny to attract glass, 308. Attracts emery and other bodies, 309. Why, *ib.* n. Increases not its weight by the addition of iron, 311. Various other absurdities concerning, *ib.* Mines and rocks spoken of by Pliny, 313. Medical efficacy falsely ascribed to it, 317-320. Magical tales relating to its efficacy, 320. To detect incontinency and thievery,

ib. To divine thereby, 321. Sprinkled with water emits a voice like an infant, *ib.* By means of two needles touched with it communication is said to be held with absent friends, *ib.* Confuted by B's. own experiment, *ib.*

Lobster, has one claw sometimes longer than the other, ii, 409. Cause of this and its cure, *ib.* n.

Locust, an unusual kind of, i, 339. Distinct from *cicada*, iii, 93; iv, 185.

Locust-trees, many at Paris, i, 61.

Locke, John, Dunton's enlargement of *Rel. Bibliopolæ* dedicated to, ii, xix.

London, *R. M.* supposed by Dr. Johnson to have been written in, i, iii. B. born in, i, xvii. Bp. of, (H. Compton,) E. B. too slow to gain friendship of, i, 237.

Longevity of the deer, *P. E.* iii, ch. 8, ii, 424-437. That of various other creatures, 424. A very ancient opinion, *ib.*

Longitude and latitude, differences between ancient and modern compute, iii, 291.

Longomontanus on the seventy weeks of Daniel, iii, 199.

Lorenzini, a Florentine, on the torpedo, i, 270.

Loretto, M. le Gros's pilgrimage to, i, 49. E. B. at, 89.

Losel, de Podagra, i, 253.

Lot's daughters, question respecting, iii, 346. Similar matters, 348.

Lot's wife, was her transformation real or metaphorical, iii, 327. Dr. Clarke's commentary on, *ib.* n.

Louis XIII, rased Rochelle walls, i, 19. Xainctes castle, 18.

Louvre, not likely to be finished soon, i, 107. Fault found with, by Bernini, *ib.* By Wren, 112.

Love, Dr. of Cambridge, i, 280. Warden of Winchester College, 281.

Love, Morley, Charles, M. D. on the epidemic, i, 280, n. B. read, 281.

Lover's knot, iii, 165.

Lower, Rd. *M. D.* his treatise *de Corde*, dedicated to Dr. Millington, i, 243. With E. B. attends Dean Astley, 316.

Lozenge, see GARDEN OF CYRUS.

Lucan, T. B. read at sea, i, 142. His opinion of, 143. B. approves the verses, but not the example, 144.

Lucca, E. B's. account of, i, 75.

Lucian, ii, 31, n. Plagiarist from Lucius Prakensis, 217.

Lucretius, ii, 30, n. *De Rerum Naturæ*, B's. opinion of, i, 209.

Ludolf, Job, *Hist. Ethiop.* Englished, i, 340.

a stout believer of equivocal generation, *ib.*

Michael, Sundevogis, vegetable verticities asserted by him, ii, 311.

Micklethwayte, Sir John, Phys. to St. Bartholomew's, succeeded by E. B. i, cii.

Micrælius, J. attacks B. i, lxvii.

Middleburg, E. B. at, i, 156. Worth seeing, 158.

Middleton, Wm. Bp. account of, iv, 15.

Milan, rumors of plague at, i, 97, 99.

Mileham, Chas. of Yarmouth, B's. brother-in-law, i, 2.

Mileham, Edw. Esq. Burlingham, Co. Norf. father of Lady Dorothy Browne, i, xxvi.

Militia, well settled, i, 8.

Millington, M.D., E. B. well acquainted with, i, 243.

Milo, fable of his carrying a bull, iii, 365.

Milton, quotation from, applied to B. i, lvi, n.

Minerals, in Germany, what, i, 166. In Austria, Hungary, &c. for Soc. Reg. 172. Wernher, wrote of, 176. E. B's. collection of, 447-449.

Mines, queries from R. S. concerning; salt, how deep, asked, i, 172, answered, 173. Copper, at Herrn-grund, no quicksilver, 173. All other in Hungary, quicksilver and sulphur, *ib.* Silver, in Bohemia, 195. Tin, at Slackenwald, 196. Gold, silver and copper, lxxx. Quicksilver, lxxxi.

Mingay, of Norwich, sold some ground to H. Howard, Esq. i, 44.

Minotaur, whence the fable of, ii, 221.

Miracles, B. thankful that he lived not in the days of, ii, 14. Of brazen serpent, 27. Their cessation, 39. Of the Jesuits, 40. Of popish relics, 41. B's. life a miracle of 30 years, 110. Johnson's remarks on this passage. L'Estrange ascribes popish miracles to the devil, 174.

Misapprehension and fallacy, causes of error, (*P. E.* i, ch. 4,) ii, 202-208.

MISCELLANIES, &c. iv, 251-270. Containing speculations on the difference which a slight alteration in a given train of causes might have produced, 251, 252. *Upon reading Hudibras,* 253. *Account of Iceland,* in the year, 1662, 254-256. *Letters from Theodore Jonas,* 256-270.

MISCELLANY TRACTS, iv, 115 to 250. Evelyn's copy of, xii. True date of, *ib.* Additional collations to the 9th and 10th Tracts, *(mislaid during the*

printing of them) xv, xvi. Editor's Preface to, 117, 118. Abp. Tenison's Preface, 119-120. *(For the subjects of the Tracts, see contents to vol. IV.)* Several of these tracts addressed to Sir Nicholas Bacon, 121, n.

Miselthrush, *turdus viscivorus;* why so called, ii, 369.

Miseltoe of the oak, where found, and where not, i, 279. Supposed by the ancients to be produced from seeds dropt on trees by birds, especially thrushes, ii, 367. Opposed by B. for a reason which Wren deems triumphant, *ib.* n. Professor Lindley's and Mr. Jesse's remarks on it, 367, n. Deemed an excrescence, 358. Wren's curious mistake on this point, *ib.* n. Various species of, 369, n. Magical virtues ascribed to it; the relick of Druidism, *ib.* On what trees and in what countries to be found, iii, 432.

Mist, *account of the dark thick mist which happened Nov.* 27, 1674, iv, 341.

Mitford, Rev. J. of Benhall, Suffolk, ii, xviii, n.

Modestus, an Irishman, planted the gospel near Vienna, i, 175.

Mola, i, 47.

Moldavia, account of, i, 170.

Mole, at Tangier, a great work, i, 148.

Moles, that they are blind, *P. E.* iii, ch. 18, ii, 473-476. Various acceptations of the phrase, 473. Ross's absurd theory hereon, *ib.* Aristotle spoke of a different animal, which is blind, *ib.* n. Some have said the water rat and shrew are blind, 475. Whether correctly, *ib.* n.

Moltfarius, see Moltke.

Moltke, Levin Nicol Von, or L. N. M. E. N. wrongly named in Johnson's Life, i, xxv. Some account of him in Niceron, who ascribes to him *Conclave Alexandri* VII, &c. *ib.* n. Edited the Latin Version of *R. M.* with notes, at Strasburg, 1652, reprinted 1665 and 1677, xxv, lxiii; ii, xii. His opinion of *R. M.* ii, xxiv. Keck's opinion of him, xxv. Extract from his Preface and remarks on his edition of *R. M.* by Keck, xxiv, xxv. Extract from his Preface to his edition of *R. M.* 155, 156.

Moltkenius, see Moltke.

Moly, mentioned by Homer, ii, 364.

Monasteries, and religious houses of Norwich; Austin Friars, Black Friars, White Friars. Many persons of family buried in them, iv, 19.

tians derived the practice of embalming, 273. Joseph embalmed; Rabbinical stories about this, 274.
Musæum Clausum, &c. Tr. 13, iv, 239-250. In return for a catalogue sent for inspection. Mr. Crossley's remarks on Warburton's suggestion, as to the motive which led to the composition of the present Tract, *ib.* n. Various printed accounts of museums, 239. Rare and unknown books, 240-243. Rarities in pictures, 243-247. Antiquities and rarities of several sorts, 247-250.
Muscles, Aristotle did not understand, i, 322.
Music, Grecian instrument of, called *Tzibori*, like the Italian *mandolino*, i, 170. Of love, ii, 106. The spheres, *ib.* Philosophical theory of musical effect, *ib.* Remarks on the passage, *ib.* n. Tavern musick, *ib.*
Musicians at Cologne, i, 206.
Mussulmans forbid burning the dead, iii, 459.
Mustard seed, its size, iv, 137-139.
Mutiny at the Nore, i, 131. T. B's. opinion of, 132, 133. In the wilderness, ii, 197.
Myrtle, iv, 126. Crowns, 175.
Myrrh, fossil, B. asks for, i, 177, 183. E. B. cannot get, 185. What, iv, 128, and n.

N.

Nails, *ungues*, B's. hints for E. B's. lecture on, i, 231, 232. Superstitions about paring, iii, 167. Spots in, popular presages from, 174. Cardan applied them to himself, *ib.* How died red, 369.
Nantes, city, described by T. B. i, 20. E. B. at, 106.
Napkins of *Asbestos*, iii, 476.
Naples, E. B. at, i, lxxvii. Account of, and neighbourhood, 77. Cardinal d'Aragon, viceroy of, 81.
Naphtha, ii, 28, n. Creusa and Alexander's boy set on fire by, 489. Lamps, 488, and n.
Narbonne, E. B. at, i, 103.
Narborough, Capt. his voyage to the S. Sea, i, 450.
Nard, the ointment of the evangelists, iii, 314.
Natural arrangement, see Quinary.
Natural history, B's. collections in, i, 393-408.
Nature's Cabinet Unlocked, professing to be by B.; disclaimed, iii, 448.
Naumachiæ, Latin description of a sea-

fight, iv, 294-297. Probably written as an exercise in Latin naval terms, 294, n. Several authors referred to, *ib.* n.
Naval Fights, remarks and queries concerning, *P. E.* v, ch. 5, iii, 99-102. Several, iv, 287-289.
Navel, see Adam and Eve.
Navigation of the ancients, how performed, ii, 300.
Nazarite, iii, 112.
Nearchus, incident respecting, iv, 418.
Necks of birds and animals, iii, 339.
Necromancy, belief in, a delusion of Satan, ii, 252.
Needham, Jasper, M. D. his death, B. regrets, i, 264, 268, 273.
Needle, (see Magnetic), touched with a diamond said to be magnetized, ii, 311.
Negro Slavery, its termination prophecied, iv, 235.
Negroes, skin of, noticeable, i, 213. Of the blackness of, *P. E.* vi. ch. 10 and 11, iii, 263-275. Causes of colour the chemists reduce to three, 263. The heat of the sun, or the curse of God assigned as the causes of blackness, 264. The first generally asserted by the ancients but admitting many objections, 264. 1. A river sufficient to separate black from tawny races, 265. 2. If in man why not in animals? *ib.* 3. If sun alone were the cause why are transplanted negroes still black? 266. 4. Why not all, equally exposed to the sun, equally black? 266, 267. 5, 6. Why are not all, even in Africa, negroes? 267, 268. Nor can the aridity of Africa be urged in aid as a cause, for they are negroes, where the rivers are mighty; and not so in the drier parts, 268. Seeing the sun cannot be proved the cause, what might be so in the first instance? Whether some peculiarity of water, 269. Or the power of imagination as with Jacob's cattle? 269, 270. Or disease, *ib.* Or art? 271. After all, we cannot assign cause for many similar varieties in animals, 271, and n. Many curious and equally insoluble queries follow, 272-274. Physical cause of complexion; various opinions as to that of Adam, 272, n. Variety the striking feature throughout the works of God, iii, 273, n. The effects of colour on heat, *ib.* Dr. Stark's paper on odours, 273, n. Edible dogs and whitefooted hogs, how first obtained, their colour is clearly transmitted by

thens the fourth has been preferred, 8. What the practice of antiquity, 8, 9, n. What implied by wearing rings, 9, 10, and n. Discussion of the opinion, 10-13.

Rings, various particulars respecting their use, iii, 9, n.

Rio de la Plata, iii, 250.

Riolan, John, M. D. his *Enchiridion*, i, 232, 235, quoted, 255, 259.

Rivers, tropical, swell like the Nile, i, 440. A classed catalogue of, iv, 414, 415.

Rivière, Lazare, M. D. at Montpellier, to be read, on diseases, i, 357.

Rivington, and other merchants, seized at Rajapore, i, 429.

Robinson, John, *Endoxa*, &c. in reply to *Ps. Ep.* with Whitlock's remark on it, i, lxiv. Further account of him and his works, ii, 169, n. Supports the fables of the ancients respecting the elephant, 387, n.

Robinson, Reuben, M.D. of Maldon, letter from, i, 421.

Rochelle, worth seeing, ships pass to, from Yarmouth, for salt, i, 8. T. B. describes, 19. E. B. visits, lxxvii. Writes from, 106.

Rochester, E, B. through, i, 56.

Rochester, E. of, E. B. attended his last illness, i, cii, 202, 278, n.

Rocks of Iceland, described, iv, 255.

Rod, divining, its origin, and use in mining, iii, 178. Moses's, *ib.* Modern accounts of, *ib.* n.

Rodd, Thomas, bookseller, ii, xviii, n.

Rodolf II. Emperor, gold and silver ore first found and worked at Cranach by, i, 172. His magical glass, &c. 175-177.

Rogers, Dr. his two orations, i, 347.

Rohr. Phil. *Pictor Errans,* iii, 161, n.

Rolfinck, quoted, i, 234.

Rollo, D. of Normandy, converted by the V. Mary's shift, i, 22.

Rollrich stones, iii, 469. Some like them, i, 470.

Roman battalia quincuncially arranged, iii, 398.

Roman stations in Britain, iii, 462. At Brancaster, *ib.* Coins found in Britain, 463. Emperors in Britain, 465.

Roman highways, Watling-street, iv, 457-462.

Roman theatres in Gallia enumerated, iv, 405.

Romans used garlands, iv, 174.

Rome, not built in a day; contrasted with the assertion of Strabo, that Anchiali and Tarsus were built by Sarda-

napalus in a day, iii, 365, and n. E. B. at, i, lxxvii, 76. Again, 82. His account of, 77, 83, 85, 86, 93. The bishop of, entitled, as a temporal prince, to the duty of good language, ii, 7.

Rondelet, i, 399.

Ropalic, or Gradual Verses, Tr. 7, iv, 193, 194.

Ros Solis said to give the rot to sheep, ii, 381. Remarks thereon, *ib.* n.

Rose, "under the," import and origin of the phrase, iii, 165. Modern accounts of, *ib.* n. Five brethren of the, 413, n. Of Jericho flourishing at Christmas-eve, ii, 370. Its dry flowers, if moistened, will expand, *ib.* Very curious fact related by Dean Wren, *ib.* n. What it is, *ib.* and iv, 141. Sir R. K. Porter's description of, *ib.* n.

Roses brought brom Egypt to Rome, till cultivated there, iv, 176.

Rosenberg, Count, patron of Dee, the alchemist, i, 466.

Rosenmülleri Scholia, ii, 33, n.

Ross, Alexander, attacked *R. M.* and Digby's *Obss.* in *Medicus Medicatus,* or the *Physician's Religion Cured, &c.* 8vo. 1645, i, xxv, lxii; ii, viii. The only one who did, xxiv. H. Bates's wit upon, i, 354. *Arcana Microcosmi,* in answer to *Ps. Ep.* i, xxvii, lxiv; ii, 169. Johnson's remarks on him, contrasted with that of Sir Thomas Urquhart, i, lxii, n. Keck mentions, ii, xxiv. His speculations on apparitions and bleeding dead bodies, 132, n. Some account of, and Kippis's opinion of his *Arcana,* 169, n. Supports the ancient fable that an elephant has no joints, 387, n.

Rotterdam, E. B. at, i, lxxxiii, 154. His account of, 155.

Roy du, or Regius, commended, i, 362. His *Fundament. Phys.* quoted, 363.

Royal Society, i, 162, 166. Its transactions came out monthly, 169. Queries, 13, from the Sec. of, sent to E. B. at Wien, 172. B's. advice about, 176.

Rubicon, E. B. passes, i, 96.

Rueus says that garlick hinders the attraction of the loadstone, ii, 306. Concerning coral, 350.

Ruffinus, story of an iron chariot suspended by loadstones, ii, 316.

Rugge, W. Bp. iv, 15, and n.

Rump of sheep very large in Judea, iv, 168.

Running much exercised about Stafford, i, 38. At the ring, at Bologna, 97.

Scythians, subject to *Sciatica*, iii, 130. Their languages supposed the fountain of the languages of Europe, iv, 196.

Sea, course of, how altered, i, 390-392. Its ebb and flow, iii, 334.

Seasons, their division, *P. E.* vi. ch. 3, iii, 204-209. Various rules for determining by sun and stars, 204-206. Diversity of climes to be regarded, 206-209. As marked by the different length of the days, *P. E.* vi. ch. 4, 210-213. Compared to the progress of man's life, 210. Prognostics as to temperature, 211.

Sebets, or Zebets, little known of, i, 244. Probable account of, 246, n.

Sebund, Raymund, a physician, wrote on Natural Theology, ii, 228.

Seed, consideration of its increase, iv, 145-148. The seven years of plenty in Egypt, 146.

Sedgwick, Professor, supplied copy of E. B's. admission at Trin. Coll. Camb. i, lxxv, n. And account of a crayon drawing formerly belonging to B. preserved in the College lodge, i, lxxv, n.

Selden, John, his comment on *Drayton's Polyolbion*, i, 315. Executors and library, 386.

Semiramis, her immense army, iii, 234.

Seneca, ii, xxiii, 10, n. Of books with odd titles, xxiii. Character, and translations of, i, 302. His *Morals*, L'Estrange translated, 370, n. Three lines of, ii, 29, n. Error concerning crystal, 267.

Senigaglia, E.B. at, i, 89. Its carnival, 96.

Sennert, Daniel, M. D. of Wittemberg, his *Institutions*, i, 357-360. On diseases, *ib. de Febribus*, 360. *Praxis, ib.* New edition of, expected, 362.

Sens, E. B. at, i, 69.

Septuagint, its antiquity, credit, and history, iii, 193.

Sepulture, observed by some animals, iii, 461. With what variety of rites, 483.

Seraglio, daily provision for the use of, iii, 352.

* This solution was suggested to the editor by Mr. Hawkins, of the coin department, in the British Museum.

logue with an African as to Adam's complexion, iii, 272, n.

Wave, the tenth, conceit respecting, iii, 355. Curious particulars in illustration of, *ib.* n. Similar conceits respecting the number ten, 356.

Weather, very severe in winter, 1664-5, i, 89. In 1666-7, 132, 134. In June, 1676, very hot, 212. Boisterous, 217.

Wecker, his *Antidotarium Speciale*, i, 357.

Weight, of the human body, *P. E.* iv, ch. 7, iii, 28-31. That men are heavier dead than alive. Not probable, 28. Ross's absurd argument, *ib.* n. Dalton's theory, *ib.* n. Whether before meat than after, 29. Several parallel notions, 30, 31.

Welsh, language, iv, 197.

Werner, (Geo.) *de Aquis Hung.* i, 182.

Wernher, *de Rebus Pannoniæ*, i, 176.

Wetherley, M.D. observations of, on the sickness, i, 373.

Westminster, abbey church, House of Commons had communion at, i, 10.

Whale, B's. queries about one, i, 368. Answered, 369, 70. L'Estrange's account of one, ii, 173. On the spermaceti, *P. E.* iii, ch. 26, ii, 515-517. Modern name of this whale, 515, n. Account of one on shore at Overstrand 1822, iv, 326, n. Another at Runton, *ib.* A steak of it cooked at Northrepps Hall, *ib.* B. objects to the picture of, with two spouts, instead of one, iii, 146. The picture correct, *ib.* n.

Wharton, Rev. preached at Norwich, i, 48.

Wheat, dear at 45 shillings the coomb, i, 14. Later than barley, 152.

Whelps, whether blind for nine days, ii, 523, 524. They are so for a longer time, *ib.* Aristotle's opinion on, *ib.*

Whitaker, Rev. J. D. *Loidis and Elmete*, i, lix. *History of Craven*, quoted ii, xx.

Whitchurch, T. B. visits a friend in, i, 38.

White, Francis, Bp. iv, 18.

White, H. K. remarks on the magicians of Pharaoh, ii, 251, n.

White, Thomas, ii, 125. Some account of him and his works, *ib.* n.

White Powder, and noiseless, inquiry respecting, ii, 343. Notice respecting the fulminating powder, *ib.* n.

Whitefoot, Rev. J. M. A. some account of him, i. *Preface*, 11, n. Letter to Lady Browne, *ib.* His *Minutes for the Life of B.* Lent by Mrs. Lyttleton to Bp. Kennet, cx. Quoted, cx, 366. Printed at length, xlii-xlvii.

His description of B's. person, dress, acquirements, memory, feelings and deportment, his activity, his extensive acquaintance with languages, his religious feelings, his calmness in the hour of death, his liberality and kindness, his great sagacity; he excelled in the *stochastick* faculty. This term quoted by D'Israeli, xlvii, n. His sermon for B. never printed, cx, n. A MS. discourse of his in Brit. Mus. *ib.* He is supposed to have superintended the second edition of *Ps. Ep.* ii, 166, n.

Whitefriars, see Monasteries.

Whiter, Rev. Walter, his work on the *Disorder of Death*, extract from, ii, 252.

Whiting, Mr. a surgeon, i, 219.

Whitlock, Richard, remark in his *Zootomia*, on Robinson's *Endoxa*, i, lxiv.

Wien, see Vienna.

Wight, Isle of, T. B's. account of, i. 137.

Wilkins, Bp. *Mechanical Powers*, i, 87.

William the Conqueror, iv, 30.

Williamson, Sir Joseph, E. B. accompanies him to Cologne, i, xcvii. Account of, 262, n. A benefactor of Qu. Coll. Oxon. 264. Member for Thetford, 305. A patient of E. B's. i, cii.

Willis, Thomas, M. D. his way of dissecting the brain, i, 217. Imitating chalybeate waters, 227. In his *Pharmaceut. Rationalis*, speaks of Matthew's pill, 248.

Willoughby, Francis, his *Ornithologia, Eng. by Ray*, i, 327.

Windet, a medical pedant at Yarmouth, his letters to B. omitted, i, 351.

Windham, Sir Thomas, account of, iv, 10.

Windows, glass, not then usual, i, 101.

Wine, of Cognac, drunk in England, in summer, i, 19. Of Orleans, &c. exported at Nantes, 21. French, not to be had in war, 243. Spirit of, cheap sort of, 413.

Winter, in 1664-5, very severe, i, 89. In 1668-9, open, 161, 168.

Wisbich, T. B. saw, i, 41.

Witchcraft and Satanic influence, B's. opinions respecting, i, lxxxii-lxxxvi; ii, 43-45, 56, 256, n; iv, 389. Accordant with those of Bacon, Bp. Hall, Baxter, Hale, Lavater, &c. i, lxxxv, n. ii, 43. Illustrated by extracts from *Ellis's Polynesian Researches*, *ib.* n. List of writers on, 43, n.

Witches, trial of, in 1664, at Bury St. Edmund's, iv, 389. Author's evidence on, i, lxxxii. Omitted by Whitefoot, Johnson, and Kippis, *ib.* Related by Dr. Hutchinson in his *Essay on Witch-*

THE END.